American Icon

American Icon

The Fall of Roger Clemens
and the Rise of Steroids in
America's Pastime

Teri Thompson,
Nathaniel Vinton,
Michael O'Keeffe,
and Christian Red

ALFRED A. KNOPF　　New York　2009

For Mom and Dad—and, of course, Jim
—TT

For Mom and Dad and all my teachers
—NV

For Mom and Dad, Tim and Terry,
and especially Lorna and Aidan
—MO

For Beth, Mom and Dad, all the Reds and O'Neils
—CR

THIS IS A BORZOI BOOK
PUBLISHED BY ALFRED A. KNOPF

Copyright © 2009 by Teri Thompson, Nathaniel Vinton,
Michael O'Keeffe, and Christian Red

All rights reserved. Published in the United States by Alfred A. Knopf,
a division of Random House, Inc., New York, and in Canada by
Random House of Canada Limited, Toronto.

www.aaknopf.com

Knopf, Borzoi Books, and the colophon are registered trademarks of
Random House, Inc.

Library of Congress Control Number: 2009924885
ISBN 978-0-307-27180-8

All Rights Reserved

Manufactured in the United States of America
First Edition

Contents

Authors' Note

This is not just a book about Roger Clemens and his fall from grace. He is at the book's core, of course, but there are others who also play crucial parts: Brian McNamee, Andy Pettitte, Tom Pettitte, Rusty Hardin, Richard Emery, Earl Ward, Kelly Blair, along with other ballplayers, lawyers, and politicians. But this book isn't really about them, either. They are basically role players in a drama about cheating and lying and fame — all the elements that seem to have taken over and dominated what once was America's purest and favorite sport.

At the time of this writing, Roger Clemens has not lost his legal war with his former trainer Brian McNamee, who told former senator George Mitchell and the Mitchell Report investigators that he injected one of the greatest pitchers in the history of baseball with steroids and human growth hormone. But there is little question that the seven-time Cy Young Award–winning pitcher and his high-powered legal team lost the public relations battle a long time ago. Their aggressive challenge of McNamee's claims has done far more to hurt Clemens than McNamee.

In a survey conducted by the Gallup Poll about a week after the February 13, 2008, congressional committee grilling of Clemens and McNamee at a hearing on Mitchell's blockbuster report on steroid use in Major League Baseball, only 31 percent of those surveyed believed Clemens was telling the truth when he said he never used performance-enhancing drugs. And the overwhelming majority of the 80,000 respondents to an unscientific ESPN poll also agreed that Clemens had lied and McNamee had told the truth (McNamee would later tell friends with great glee that he'd "won all 50 states"). Even more devastating for Clemens, the two men who presided over that five-hour hearing had their doubts too. In a February 27, 2008, letter to Attorney General Michael Mukasey, Representative Henry Waxman (D-Calif.), the chairman of the House Committee on Oversight and Government Reform, and Representative Tom

Davis (R-Va.), the panel's ranking Republican, asked the Justice Department to investigate whether Clemens had lied during the hearing and in his February 5 prehearing deposition. FBI and IRS agents fanned out across the country to conduct a long investigation. That investigation is still under way as this book goes to press in early spring 2009.

"We are writing to ask the Justice Department to investigate whether former professional baseball player Roger Clemens committed perjury and made knowingly false statements during the Oversight and Government Reform Committee's investigation of the use of steroids and performance-enhancing drugs in professional baseball," the letter from Congress said. "We believe that his testimony in a sworn deposition on February 5, 2008, and at a hearing on February 13, 2008, that he never used anabolic steroids or human growth hormone, warrants further investigation."

The letter pointed out that "significant questions have been raised about Mr. Clemens' truthfulness." After a year of extensive reporting, the New York *Daily News* Sports Investigative Team reached the same conclusion.

Since the release of the Mitchell Report in December 2007, Clemens has vehemently denied using steroids in several forums, including on television in a *60 Minutes* report, in a courtroom in a defamation action against McNamee, on the Internet in videos posted on YouTube and on his charitable foundation's Web site, and in an angry press conference in Houston. He toured Capitol Hill before the hearing to convince lawmakers of his innocence, and has told friends he is the victim of a great injustice.

Despite his fervent denials and challenges to his accuser, in the winter of 2009, a grand jury in Washington, D.C., began reviewing evidence to determine whether Clemens should be indicted for perjury. That evidence presumably included much of the material our investigative team reviewed, including the Mitchell Report, mountains of court documents, congressional depositions, police reports, medical files, candid e-mails, transcripts of secretly recorded phone calls, photographs, and shipping receipts. We interviewed scores of sources—baseball players, steroid suppliers, trainers, doctors, gym rats, and anti-aging-clinic employees, as well as Major League Baseball executives, Players Association officials, congressional leaders, law enforcement agents, attorneys, and doping experts. We traveled across the United States in the course of our investigation to Washington; Houston; San Francisco; Nashville; Myrtle Beach, South Carolina; Lexington, Kentucky; Fort Myers and Kissimmee, Florida; as well as the Bronx; Breezy Point (Queens); Midtown Manhattan; and Manhattan's Upper East Side.

It was challenging and difficult work. We were threatened with lawsuits and physical violence, not to mention regular doses of verbal abuse from many corners.

McNamee was not a perfect witness: As a memo from the committee's Democratic staff says, he had a history of misleading investigators. He told the committee he lied to police during a 2001 sexual assault investigation in Florida. He also admitted during the recent investigation that he withheld evidence from prosecutors in a loyal attempt to mitigate the damage to Clemens. But the federal investigators who first interviewed McNamee in the summer of 2007 gave him a very powerful motive to tell the truth: the threat of criminal prosecution and likely jail time if he lied to them or to George Mitchell.

McNamee's claims in the Mitchell Report—an investigation into steroid use on behalf of Major League Baseball—that he injected Clemens's longtime friend and teammate Andy Pettitte with human growth hormone were verified by Pettitte, who also told the congressional committee that Clemens had admitted to him that he had used human growth hormone. Pettitte's wife, Laura, gave the committee an affidavit that said her husband had told her about Clemens's admissions. Testimony from Chuck Knoblauch, the former Yankee who, like Pettitte, has acknowledged receiving HGH from McNamee, supports the trainer's account. Jim Murray, an employee of the sports agency that represents Clemens, corroborated parts of McNamee's statements. So did Kirk Radomski, the admitted steroid supplier who says he provided illegal drugs to McNamee to deliver to ballplayers.

Clemens's own statements damaged his credibility. He told the committee's investigators that he never discussed human growth hormone with McNamee, but as the Democratic staff memo points out, he admitted having two specific conversations about HGH with the trainer later in the deposition.

The committee's Democratic staff memo also noted that there was an abundance of medical evidence that indicates Clemens lied to Congress. An MRI expert told the committee that an abscess on Clemens's buttocks was consistent with an injury from a Winstrol injection. Medical records and interviews with doctors and experts also contradict Clemens's claims that he had received lidocaine and B_{12} injections from McNamee and pain injections from team trainers, but no steroid or HGH injections.

There may also be physical evidence that ties Clemens to steroids. In

January 2008, McNamee and his attorneys gave prosecutors used needles, bloody gauze, and steroid vials the trainer claimed he had saved from an injection session and that he believed contained Clemens's DNA mixed with the contents. The results of the lab analysis were not available at the time this book was published.

We hoped to meet with Clemens to hear his side of the story. We sent numerous interview requests through his spokesman, Patrick Dorton; Clemens's lawyer, Rusty Hardin; and his agent, Randy Hendricks. Our requests were either ignored or declined. Hardin and Lanny Breuer, the Beltway attorney who advised Clemens on his congressional appearance and was nominated by President Barack Obama to lead the Justice Department's Criminal Division, also declined to be interviewed for the book, although they were all interviewed many times for the newspaper articles our investigative team wrote.

After more than a year of reporting, we believe the evidence strongly suggests that Brian McNamee told the truth when he said he injected his longtime friend and employer with steroids and human growth hormone. That evidence also leads us to believe that Clemens lied when he testified under oath that he had never used performance-enhancing drugs. This book tells the story of that drug use and of the damage it would ultimately inflict on one of the greatest pitchers in baseball history, and an obscure trainer from Breezy Point. It also tells the story of how steroids and HGH became so prevalent in and out of the clubhouses of America's pastime. We've tried to explain the causes of such widespread drug use in the game as well as the culture that didn't just allow but also encouraged that use.

We stand by the sources, both on and off the record, we've chosen to believe. And we feel strongly that anyone who reads this book carefully and objectively will come to the same conclusion.

American Icon

Prologue

On the night of October 22, 2003, in Miami, 41-year-old Roger Clemens was struggling through a wretched first inning against the Florida Marlins at Pro Player Stadium. Not only was it Game 4 of the World Series, but this was also expected to be Clemens's final major league start. Throughout that baseball season, the hulking right-hander had been on a mission, a legendary pitcher who had dominated his sport for two decades, trying to leave the game as a champion. He had pitched powerfully and successfully all year long, notching his 300th career win on a rainy June night at Yankee Stadium, and he was intent on helping the Yankees snatch one more World Series title during his reign and adding another line to his Hall of Fame legacy. But even Clemens was mortal, and even his Texas swagger could no longer hide the enormous strain that 20-plus years of throwing 90 miles per hour had put on him. And now, Clemens was struggling in the 78-degree heat, fighting off the humidity and his exhaustion and Ivan "Pudge" Rodriguez's deadly patience at the plate. With two outs in the bottom of the first, Rodriguez fouled off four pitches, including two with a full count. Clemens was probably the greatest pitcher any Marlin would ever face, but Rodriguez and the rest of the team knew they could possibly expose some weaknesses in later innings if they could tire him out early. So when Rodriguez ended an eight-pitch at-bat with a single to right, his real reward was the sweat dripping down Clemens's reddening face.

Clemens greeted the next batter, Miguel Cabrera, with an inside fastball that backed the 20-year-old rookie off the plate. This was quintessential Clemens, the same intimidator who, in a spring training exhibition several years later, would even aim a fastball high and inside to his own son Koby, a minor league prospect. But Cabrera was not bedazzled. Dipping into his own store of machismo, he shot Clemens an icy stare and then hammered a 2-2 pitch over the right field wall for a quick 2–0 Marlins lead.

Clemens needed 42 pitches to get through that inning alone, as the Marlins tacked on another run with Derrek Lee's RBI single. The Yankees eventually lost 4–3 in 12 innings, the fatal blow an Alex Gonzalez homer off Jeff Weaver. The Yankees would never recover, losing the Series in six games to the underdog Marlins. Florida won the clinching Game 6 in the Bronx, an added insult for a city of sports fans with little tolerance for losers. But what happened in the later innings of Game 4 was quintessential Clemens.

The Rocket pitched six scoreless innings after his eventful first. After surrendering five hits in the first, Clemens allowed only three hits the rest of the way. He put on a demonstration of tenacity and grit that had rarely been seen on a baseball diamond. While the few pitchers still practicing their craft at his age had come to rely on finesse, guile, and opposition research, Clemens repeatedly hurled bolts of lightning. His last four fastballs of Game 4 hit 94 miles per hour on the radar gun. He did not—would not—give in to the pressure, the heat, or to age. After freezing Luis Castillo, one of the Marlins' best hitters that season, to end the seventh, Clemens walked off the mound. What followed was one of the most memorable scenes in World Series history.

As Clemens departed, fans at Pro Player took to their feet and cheered. So did the entire Marlins team. While the national television broadcast was on a commercial break, the cheers began to grow and grow, finally becoming so loud that Clemens had to come out of the visitors' dugout to acknowledge the ovation. He waved his cap at the crowd, and the noise built, even as the home team was coming out on the field for the top of the eighth. The people—65,934 of them—were still standing and clapping, as were the Marlins. The opposing players pointed at Clemens in acknowledgment of his performance and he pointed back. Pudge Rodriguez walked slowly from the dugout to his catcher's position, clapping his hands as he moved, and Clemens looked at him and put a fist to his heart. He waved again at the Marlins fans, waving goodbye this time, then disappeared into the Yankee dugout.

Baseball fans were still clinging desperately to their innocence in 2003, and superhuman performances were viewed in the traditional way: as a sign not just of ability but also of extraordinary character. Even as those performances had grown more and more superhuman and the stats had become gaudier and more and more suspect, fans looked upon the heroics on the field and saw only virtues.

"Roger Clemens is Roger Clemens. He is a great pitcher," Rodriguez said later that day in 2003. "He deserves a standing ovation like that anywhere he goes."

Four years later, as he sat on the patio of a casita in Cabo San Lucas, Roger Clemens received the phone call that would fundamentally alter his life.

The pitcher's personal trainer, a former NYPD cop named Brian McNamee, had told federal law enforcement agents that he had helped Clemens use steroids and human growth hormone over a period of several years, beginning in 1998. McNamee had also been cooperating with former United States senator George Mitchell, who was due to deliver a report on performance-enhancing drug use in baseball.

Clemens tried to absorb the news. It was one of the most pivotal points in his life, but to friends who were with him in Cabo—ballplayers and businessmen—he didn't seem panicked. Clemens had spent a lifetime cultivating an ability to control his world. His childhood had been defined by an absent father, a tight family budget, and exceptional physical gifts; Clemens harnessed the latter to earn a fortune and build a palace for his own family, giving his four sons every advantage he'd been deprived of. In the late 1990s, as Major League Baseball became distorted beyond recognition by pharmaceutically enhanced home run hitters and Clemens's dominance seemed threatened, he had found a way to reshape his own destiny once again.

Clemens had become friends with men who were powerful and well connected, and some of them were with him that night in Cabo, helping him get a read on the Mitchell Report situation. Clemens's agents were already turning to the bulldog Houston lawyer Rusty Hardin, who shared with Clemens the competitive refusal to accommodate losing. Clemens could have taken a different route—hired a lawyer who could quietly pull some strings, cast doubt on McNamee, do the talking.

Most important, his friends said, Mitchell was occupying a legal terra incognita. Baseball was ultimately a private enterprise with a long tradition of enforcing its own rules: Nobody told baseball what to do. Steroids had never been a priority in the government's war on drugs, not remotely in the same league as cocaine or crack. But Congress still had some power over baseball (giving it an antitrust exemption that almost no other American business enjoyed) and steroids had become a concern for some prosecutors. The gaudy home run quests of Mark McGwire and Barry Bonds had inspired the government to start cracking the whip, putting pressure on baseball to clean up its house. The media had begun to ask questions: What did baseball know and when did it know it? Bud Selig had brought the game to new financial heights, and he was determined not to let this drug issue cloud his legacy. Mitchell had stepped in on baseball's behalf, but for all his accomplishments he was still a private citizen. He was walking a hazy moral-legal line. There wasn't a person at Clemens's table that night in Cabo who didn't believe that Mitchell couldn't be swayed to one side of that line with a well-placed phone call from a Hall of Fame player. They were sure he wasn't looking to name names and ruin lives, but rather to lay everything out and let the game move on. Clemens could simply say nothing and let the story play out. The pitcher heard all this advice, but on some level he didn't hear anything at all, so deafened was he by the audacious challenge to his sense of control.

Throughout Clemens's entire career he'd shouldered enormous psychological pressure, risked public failure, and ruthlessly crushed opponents, and he knew how to handle the unexpected. At some point in the life of a revered athlete, the thrills end. So do the surprises. There is really nothing more to do than just maintain it all for as long as you can, pretend it's all business as usual. Clemens was the best at doing that, and he wasn't going to let news like this change anything.

In the course of three dramatic months, from December 2007 through February 2008, everything did change for Clemens. He went from a shoo-in for Cooperstown to the target of a Justice Department investigation. A man who had spent much of his life embracing the perks of stardom—celebrity golf, philanthropy, goofy cameos in movies—virtually disappeared from the public landscape. A man who loved the history and strategy of Major League Baseball was reduced to furtively dropping into a few minor league towns to watch his son play, arriving at the tiny ballparks quietly but with security guards at hand, moving from box to box, as if—as one reporter described him—he were traveling from safe house to safe house. There was no swagger anymore, no Texas-sized ego on display. As spring began to bloom across the Southwest, Clemens summoned his agents and his sisters and other family members to a secret meeting at a hideaway in the Texas hill country. The seven-time Cy Young Award winner was faced with a decision that would shape the rest of his life: He could drop the defamation suit he had filed against McNamee, even though he knew doing so would encourage the government's investigation, or he could fight. He consulted with his lawyers and his wife, Debbie. He knew that the code professional athletes live by—the protection of a shadow life at all costs—had broken down, that the walls were beginning to crumble: The women, the drugs, the excuses, the hypocrisy, all of that was being exposed. Reporters and government agents were scouring the suburbs of Houston, digging through records and talking to gym rats. They knew about the women and the private plane trips and the diamond earrings and even that Deb had used HGH. They knew about the Viagra and the bloody gauze and the needles McNamee had kept in a FedEx box in his basement all those years as insurance.

Dropping the lawsuit would stem the tide of headlines that had already begun to engulf him—CLEMENS HAD 10-YEAR AFFAIR WITH COUNTRY SINGER . . . MCCREADY WEEPS AS SHE CONFIRMS AFFAIR . . . JETSETTING CLEMENS AND HIS BEVY OF BEAUTIES. He could stop giving late-night talk show hosts punch lines for their monologues . . . *Clemens isn't retired, he's just been playing in the minors* . . . *Clemens is the winner of the Cy Really Young Award* . . . He could end the battle that had turned him into a national laughingstock. His own mother-in-law would describe him as a beaten man.

"All this has been a tremendous impact on the family and on the business and everything concerned," Jan Wilde told Bloomberg News, describing her son-in-law as "really mixed up. It's like he died, like he never played baseball, like nobody acknowledged him, like he's nonexistent."

No player in baseball's long and rich history has fallen from grace as fast and as far as Roger Clemens. Comparing him to Pete Rose or Denny McClain or Barry Bonds or other tainted stars seems inadequate. Clemens's fall is straight out of Greek mythology: The very traits that made him dominant on the pitcher's mound, his tenacity and mercilessness, contributed to and possibly even caused his downfall. The barely harnessed anger that served him so well on the field sabotaged him in the legal arena, on Capitol Hill, and in the court of public opinion. His destruction was inflicted by the same forces that made him a superstar.

It all happened with astonishing speed and public scrutiny, but in some ways the man's fate was sealed in an interlude of quiet meditation in Cabo San Lucas in early December of 2007, when Clemens decided that in the face of defeat he had to do what he'd always done. He would wipe the sweat off his face, zone in on the enemies, and summon up the courage to knock all of them right on their asses. He would not lose. Could not lose. Certainly not to someone like Brian McNamee.

Despite what was at risk—the Hall of Fame legacy, the adulation, his own family, millions of dollars in legal fees and future endorsements, and even his very freedom to walk the streets—Clemens would fight on. The man whom many consider the greatest pitcher who ever lived would continue the fall into disgrace, a fall arguably deeper than that of any other player in baseball history.

But in Clemens's mind, it was the first inning on a sweltering October night in Miami.

He could win this thing. He could gut his way through it. He just needed to throw his opponents a little chin music.

CHAPTER ONE

June 1998

Even to a former New York City cop, the question was jarring.

"Can you help me?" Roger Clemens asked. "I can't inject in my bootie."

This is how Brian McNamee, the Toronto Blue Jays' new strength and conditioning coach who'd come to baseball after his days on the NYPD, remembers it all starting. He glanced up at Clemens, the pitcher's broad frame blocking most of McNamee's view of the rest of the SkyDome clubhouse. There were a few other Blue Jays players milling about the room, preparing for the upcoming series with Baltimore. Toronto designated hitter and occasional outfielder Jose Canseco was picking through his stall nearby, his back to Clemens and McNamee.

McNamee was slumped in his own stall. Why, he wondered, was arguably the greatest pitcher of his era suddenly asking for help in sticking a hypodermic needle in his ass?

Clemens handed McNamee a small, white opaque container resembling an aspirin bottle, but with no label.

"What do you think of these?" Clemens asked, the pills rattling inside.

McNamee took the container, still mulling the question about needle injections, his mind spinning with images from a couple of days earlier, when the Blue Jays were in Miami to play an interleague series with the Florida Marlins: There had been a barbecue at Canseco's palatial Miami home. A nanny chasing after a young boy. Clemens talking in secret with Canseco and another man. Debbie Clemens and Canseco's wife incongruously comparing their boob jobs. The three men adjourning to a room inside Canseco's home. What had they discussed? There had been a transaction of some kind, and McNamee was certain that Clemens and Canseco had gotten steroids at Canseco's home.

McNamee poured the white pills into his hand. They looked like oral testosterone, a substance he had only recently researched and studied.

McNamee remembered talking with Clemens about this kind of thing during spring training. Clemens had said something about not wanting to play football for the University of Texas because he was queasy about having to get needle injections in his thigh.

"That looks like Anadrol-50," said Canseco, suddenly barging his way into the conversation. Before McNamee or Clemens could interject, the burly Canseco was shoving a couple of pills into his mouth. McNamee wheeled around to face Clemens.

"Don't take that," McNamee told Clemens. "That's really bad for you."

The pitcher then gave McNamee a bag filled with 50 to 100 glassine bottles of what the trainer later suspected was cypionate or ethanate—straight testosterone—and told him to get rid of them. He figured Clemens was tired of the nasty side effects of hard-core testosterone and ready to use the somewhat less toxic Winstrol he'd picked up in Miami.

Clemens was Toronto's staff ace and highest-paid player in 1998, pulling in a cool $8.55 million. Two and a half months into the season, however, the pitcher was a pedestrian 6-6. He was 35 and less than a year removed from posting a 21-7 record, blitzing through the American League en route to winning his fourth Cy Young Award. But in 1998, something was off, and his club was suffering as a result. Toronto was already fading fast in the AL East standings, and the trip to Miami had done nothing to pull the Jays closer to the front-running Yankees.

During spring training, McNamee had taken stock of Clemens's flabby physique. He didn't think Clemens's success would continue without a change in the pitcher's conditioning routine, even if Clemens still maintained that his workout regimen and ethic were unequaled in professional sports. He'd no doubt noticed that McNamee had been in the gym himself and was looking pretty cut.

Now the Rocket wanted somebody to help him with needle injections? Clemens had obviously caught wind of McNamee's personal strife in recent weeks. At the end of spring training, McNamee was just starting to develop a decent rapport with the players when a family emergency called him home to Queens. His one-year-old son, Brian Jr., was diabetic, the condition serious enough that the boy would require close monitoring for his entire life.

McNamee had spent the better part of that week home in the hospital, getting educated on how to manage the potentially deadly disease. He and his wife, Eileen, learned how to prick their infant's finger for a drop of blood, test it for hyperglycemia, and then inject the baby with the appropriate dosages of short-acting and long-acting insulin. McNamee had learned to mix the insulin and draw it into needles for subcutaneous injections. It was a delicate process, getting the exact amount of the hormone into a pinch of fat so that it would be released gradually into the bloodstream.

The Jays players and staff had been sympathetic toward McNamee's situation and had become a kind of family away from home. Clemens was among the group who had expressed concern for Brian Jr. But now, his motives seemed decidedly personal.

McNamee looked back at Clemens.

"Yeah," McNamee said. "I think I can handle that."

"All right," Clemens said. "I'll let you know."

And according to McNamee, that is how it began.

One of the perks of playing for the Toronto Blue Jays (and there weren't that many of them in the late 1990s) was staying in the luxury hotel attached to the stadium. After a hard game you could leave the jock-strewn locker room exhausted, stumble through the beery tunnels of Sky-Dome, and five minutes later crash in one of the 70 rooms hanging over the outfield.

No matter how beaten down you were at the end of the night, you could always count on renewing your love for the game the next morning, because the rooms had floor-to-ceiling windows overlooking the diamond. Throw back the curtains and there it was beneath you, the breathtaking field and all the infinite possibilities it presented.

It was enough to make a 35-year-old pitcher feel like a kid again: the bright green AstroTurf, shining in the early-morning sunshine; the deep blue tiers of stadium seats; maybe a few groundskeepers sprinkling water on the freshly groomed clay of the basepaths; maybe the scoreboard was already welcoming fans to that night's game. Even if you were one of the league's elders, well beyond the age when power pitchers normally begin their decline, this sight could make you feel like a Little Leaguer.

Roger Clemens's SkyDome apartment was a living space befitting the Blue Jays star: The rooms that spanned the length of the outfield looked out onto the diamond. The hotel rooms had become famous over the years, especially after an amorous couple was caught having sex with the drapes open, their images flashed up on the JumboTron screen. By the middle of the 1998 season, McNamee was occasionally staying in the room connected to Clemens's apartment; that is, when the pitcher's family or girlfriends weren't occupying the room. One of those girls was a beautiful blond country western singer named Mindy McCready. She sang of girls behaving badly in her hit song "Guys Do It All the Time" and Clemens often talked about her and brought her along on the road. One morning when McNamee knocked on the door of the SkyDome apartment to wake the pitcher for a workout, he found a half-naked McCready stumbling in the background.

But McNamee's visit to Clemens's apartment this time was purely business. Clemens had summoned him shortly after their conversation in the SkyDome clubhouse, and McNamee had agreed to help. When McNamee arrived, Clemens had already laid out some clear glass vials containing cloudy white liquid. The labels identified the substance as Winstrol, an anabolic steroid. There were some large needles there too, and a little bit of sterilizing alcohol.

Now McNamee was getting a good look at the real thing.

There was one problem. McNamee had experience only with the small-bore, subcutaneous needles he used to inject Brian Jr. Those needles were designed to get a very small amount of waterlike fluid into a pinch of fat. McNamee was now looking at wide-bore, intramuscular needles, meant for puncturing dense muscle and delivering a thicker fluid deep into tissue.

His mind was racing. He had no authority to give injections to players, let alone the face of the franchise, but Clemens had asked, and McNamee had answered. His research had been scant, but he wasn't naive about the changes in players' physiques or the mind-boggling statistics they were accumulating.

Canseco had long been dogged by rumors of steroid use, and his brazen pill-popping act in front of Clemens and McNamee, not to mention his jacked physique, offered further proof. Now there was no turning back. And what could be the harm? McNamee figured Clemens was more prone to hurt himself by sticking who-knows-what into his ass, anyway. McNamee was relieved they were doing this in a clandestine manner, much better that way. Keep it furtive, they both knew that. Clemens bent over. McNamee dabbed Clemens's skin with alcohol so as not to drag a contaminant into the flesh, which could cause an infection. Then he stuck the needle into the pitcher's buttocks and depressed the plunger on the syringe.

Now they were accomplices.

From that moment McNamee and Clemens were codependents. It

was the kind of relationship that can create the tightest bonds of loyalty—
And pave the way for the most painful of divorces.

They met each other when both men were on the rebound. Clemens and
McNamee, their fates intersecting just as each went looking for a second
chance. Each of them was adjusting to life in a new uniform.

It was spring training 1998, and pitchers and catchers were reporting
to the Jays' facility in Dunedin, Florida. Clemens was the aging ace, and
McNamee, the former cop, was the team's new strength and conditioning
coach.

When he first met the famous pitcher, Mac thought the Rocket looked
soft. Clemens still had remnants of the bitterness he'd felt over his dismissal from the Boston Red Sox after the 1996 season. He'd poured 13
years of guts and sweat into that team, only to be sent off with an insult,
Boston general manager Dan Duquette insinuating that he was washed
up. Clemens had reached "the twilight of his career," Duquette had said.
By the time Clemens reported to spring training with Toronto in 1997, he
was trashing Duquette.

"I must have had 20 to 30 guys tell me Dan Duquette was all business
and not a people person," Clemens said after signing a three-year, $24.75
million contract to play for the Blue Jays. "But I had to find out for myself.
Their first offer $4 million, $3 million, then two option years for $2 mil-
lion and $1 million—the way I saw it was 'four-three-two-one, blast off,
Rocket!' And later Duquette said he didn't care if I left because he'd get
two draft choices for me. Well, I hope he's happy with those two draft
choices. As for me, I could pitch till I'm 45 because of the conditioning I
do, especially with my legs."

Clemens was one of the best pitchers of all time, and he wasn't ready
to leave the grand stage, certainly not ready to give up the money. Not by
a long shot.

At 31, McNamee was new to the Blue Jays' staff. After a three-year
career with the NYPD, he worked briefly with the Yankees as a bullpen
catcher before accepting a job with Toronto. Police work was the family
business, but McNamee had an itch for something different, and this gig
was his foothold into the glamorous world of professional sports. He
wasn't paid much, but he was closer to fame and glory. He'd played baseball for Archbishop Molloy High School in Queens and had been a good
enough catcher to play for St. John's University, helping his team upset

defending national champion Stanford in 1988 in the NCAA tournament. Pitcher Mike Mussina had been on that Stanford team. McNamee had even played a little semipro in the New York area after college.

The swaggering jock from Texas and the sardonic wise guy from working-class Queens—it sounded like some kind of Hollywood pairing, two archetypal American males washed up on Canadian shores. For all the contrast of accent and income, both men had a passion for baseball. Clemens was determined to prove he wasn't fading, and McNamee was just arriving at the Big Show, and wanted to stay there.

Clemens had been unprepared for Duquette's sudden disloyalty, and if there was one value McNamee understood, it was loyalty. McNamee came from Breezy Point, the oceanside neighborhood where the Irish stuck together more than any other place in the country (60 percent of residents identified themselves as having Irish ancestry in the 2000 census, which was said to be the highest concentration of any ZIP code in the country). After St. John's, McNamee had entered the police department, following other men in the family into the institution that was famous for its codes of fidelity. McNamee's father had been a copper—as McNamee called them—before joining the FBI, and his brother had a good career in the Midtown North precinct. McNamee himself did all right in his three years with the force.

"He's probably the best police officer I've ever been around," McNamee's former partner Tim Lyon told SI.com's Jon Heyman. Lyon believed McNamee could have become a captain or even an inspector. Working undercover, McNamee had patrolled Manhattan in a Yellow Cab. He locked up 77 people and won numerous commendations.

But like any virtue, an excess of loyalty could be self-destructive, and both before and after he commenced his career as Clemens's drug link, McNamee would suffer for putting someone else's interests before his own. Despite all that promise, McNamee mysteriously left the police department after just three and a half years. During his tenure as a cop, McNamee took the fall for another officer; it would not be the last time McNamee took a hit for a friend. McNamee handcuffed a female prisoner outside a holding cell and asked the other cop to watch the woman while he completed the paperwork. When he returned minutes later, the handcuffs were still there but the prisoner was gone. The other cop was a sergeant on probation who would have probably been demoted if McNamee hadn't stepped up. "It's my prisoner, I'll take responsibility," Lyon recalled McNamee's saying. McNamee was slapped with a 30-day suspension.

And so within months of their first meeting, McNamee would give Clemens that first dose of anabolic steroids one afternoon at SkyDome. There would be other injections, but with the first one they crossed a stark line into territory they would never escape.

For all the gray areas of performance enhancement, that first shot changed them forever; Clemens became a cheater, and McNamee became a drug dealer. That was reality. And the harder you fight reality, the more real it becomes.

After more than five hours of baseball in sticky Miami humidity, the opener of a three-game interleague series against the defending World Series champion Marlins came to a thudding halt just after midnight on June 9, the Jays on the wrong end of a 17-inning marathon.

It was only the second year of interleague play, and a midseason trip to Miami was a welcome novelty for the American League Jays, and especially nice for the team's high-living, hot-swinging Canseco. But Blue Jays manager Tim Johnson and his club could not have envisioned a more frustrating start to this quick trip south, especially with Roger Clemens on the mound for the first game. The staff ace had given Johnson seven quality innings, surrendering three runs, but the Toronto bats had come up woefully short — 2-for-10 with runners in scoring position, while leaving 13 men on base. The Marlins finally scratched a run across home in the bottom of the 17th for a 4–3 win.

"Well, we haven't been doing very well," said Florida manager Jim Leyland. "So we gave [the fans] two for the price of one."

It was a long night, but there was a good reason for the Toronto players to shake off the drowsiness that Tuesday. Like numerous wealthy pro athletes, Canseco had a home in the posh Miami suburb of Weston. He and his wife, Jessica, had decided to invite the entire Blue Jays team over for a midday barbecue. And when the 30–40 Blue Jays players and staff arrived by bus at the mansion at the end of a cul-de-sac, they discovered a scene that was mind-boggling even to athletes accustomed to VIP treatment and luxury.

There were plenty of distractions to put the Monday night loss in the back of everyone's mind: a choice of three pools where, hopefully, some of the players' wives and female guests would prance around in bikinis, a full-size basketball court, a guesthouse, a tanning salon, movie screen, a lake, and Canseco's pride and joy, a 5,000-square-foot gymnasium that one party attendee said "looked like a house."

Brian McNamee, who was used to the cramped apartments of New York City and the crowded beaches of Long Island, grabbed a sandwich, sat down by the pool, and admired the beautiful people mingling around the four-acre spread. So this was Scarface territory. Not bad.

In the years since his 1986 Rookie of the Year and 1988 AL Most Valuable Player awards, Canseco had become one of the best—and highest-paid—players in the game. He had left behind a string of records, including becoming the first player in baseball history to hit 40 home runs and steal 40 bases in one season (1988), but also controversies big and small: an arrest for having an unlicensed handgun, domestic abuse charges, and unapologetic philandering. Over and above all that, Canseco was thought to be—and was—an ardent steroid enthusiast. In the 1988 playoffs, just after *The Washington Post* called him out as a steroid user, Canseco and the Oakland Athletics faced the Red Sox at Fenway. The Boston faithful took up the chant of "ster-oids, ster-oids" when Canseco came to bat, and he responded with a home run and some flexing. "I thought it was kind of fun," he said afterward.

A decade later, Canseco and Clemens were good buddies. They had been teammates in Boston in 1995 and 1996, and in the spring of 1998, Clemens had urged the Blue Jays to sign Canseco as a free agent for just over $2.1 million—a bargain, because a string of injuries and scandals had made Canseco burdensome in the eyes of team owners. When Canseco bashed 17 homers in April and May that year, it looked like a wise deal for the Blue Jays.

Congress classified steroids as a controlled substance in 1990 and Major League Baseball commissioner Fay Vincent issued a memo to each team and the Players Association the following year that stated "the possession, sale or use of any illegal drug or controlled substance by Major League players or personnel is strictly prohibited. . . . This prohibition applies to all illegal drugs . . . including steroids."

Nobody—especially not Jose Canseco—took Vincent's edict seriously.

That is why it was all the more curious to McNamee when he spotted Clemens and Canseco adjourning inside Canseco's home with another man McNamee did not immediately recognize. Years later, that furtive meeting between the men was one of three distinct images that McNamee would remember from the party. Another was of a young child, maybe two years old, running toward the water and being scooped up by a thin woman, probably in her mid to late 30s, wearing board shorts and a peach bikini top with green in it. When McNamee asked who the woman was, one of the players told him that she was Lily Strain, the nanny Clemens and his wife, Debbie, had hired to look after their young boys. McNamee had never seen a nanny chasing kids around in a bikini before. Strain and the "kiddos"—as she called them—had stayed at the Canseco place the night before.

The third image was Debbie Clemens and Jose's wife, Jessica, comparing their breast augmentation jobs. The two women, blond Barbie Doll–like stunners, had each had enhancement surgery, and they playfully compared their profiles while the men looked on. Hard to forget that.

But it was that first image that was most puzzling to McNamee. Clemens meeting with a rumored juicer and another man. Bizarre. There had to be some kind of drug transaction taking place. When the team prepared to head back to Canada, Canseco handed McNamee a bag and told him to store it along with his equipment gear for the plane ride back to Toronto.

Steroid users were on strict schedules. Bodybuilders had identified "cycles" (pauses in the drug taking to allow the body to recover its hormonal balance) and "stacks" (combining several substances) as two essential components of a muscle-building program. Clemens already had his drugs and was on a strict regimen when he approached McNamee; the trainer was just the needle guy.

McNamee repeated the injection process every five days for the next several months, injecting Clemens no fewer than eight and no more than 14 times, mostly in the privacy of Clemens's SkyDome apartment. After that first Winstrol injection, the Rocket went on to win his next start against Baltimore. After that, he didn't lose a single game the rest of the 1998 season, and finished the year 20-6. He was 9-6 before the All-Star break, with a 3.55 ERA. In the second half, he was 11-0, with a 1.71 ERA. It wasn't just the drugs. McNamee noticed Clemens was also sticking to the diet he had drawn up for the pitcher, and he was training harder than ever.

There was at least one away game shot that McNamee would long remember. In mid-June, around the time when McNamee was still getting used to the fact that he was helping one of baseball's biggest stars use steroids, the Blue Jays traveled to Tampa for a three-game series. The Devil Rays swept them, giving the Jays a 34-37 record. One of the games had just ended and McNamee was in the locker room when Clemens said it was time for his shot. McNamee looked around and found a pantry off to the side of the clubhouse, the kind of place where the clubhouse attendant would store nonperishable items. When no one was looking, Clemens and McNamee ducked into the pantry and McNamee gave Clemens a hurried shot.

Right away, McNamee had a bad feeling about the injection. In his haste, he had pressed down on the plunger faster than he wanted. There was a danger, he knew, of sending a sudden surge of liquid into the gluteus muscle; the steroids were entering a contained space, expanding an area that didn't want to expand. And, sure enough, there were problems. A little later that summer, prior to a game in SkyDome, McNamee happened to walk into the trainer's area to find Clemens facedown on one of the three training tables while the team's trainer, Tommy Craig, ran an ultrasound wand over the pitcher's ass.

It was a surprise. Every night McNamee would get a list of who on the team was injured as well as the nature of the injury, so that he could custom-tailor each player's conditioning in a way that didn't aggravate the injury. He didn't think Clemens was on his injury list.

"What's wrong?" McNamee asked.

"He developed an abscess," Craig told him.

"Is he all right?"

"Yeah, he'll be fine."

McNamee turned around and walked out. Abscesses, he would learn, were infections commonly associated with steroid injections; so were cysts, which were uninfected pockets of fluid.

The Blue Jays medical staff decided there was no infection, but just to be safe they put their star pitcher on the antibiotic cloxacillin, applied heat packs, and ordered up an MRI. They thought the injury might have been the result of a B_{12} shot that the team's doctor, Ron Taylor, had given Clemens. Earlier that month, the pitcher had come to Taylor for the shot, which supposedly raised energy levels, although most doctors viewed B_{12} as a harmless psychological boost. Mostly harmless, that is. Over the years Taylor had given thousands of B_{12} shots to his patients (but only a few to players) and had never seen such a reaction.

McNamee was convinced it was his fault. Injecting into Clemens's muscle, he had opened a pocket inside the tissue and a pool of fluid had formed there. In McNamee's mind, it was clear that Clemens too thought it was the steroids. He immediately stopped the Winstrol injections, walked right up to McNamee's locker, tossed a brown plastic bag with the remaining vials of Winstrol at the trainer, and said he was done. "Get rid of it," Clemens told him.

McNamee gave the drugs to Canseco. He was no longer a police officer, but he still had the instincts. Now McNamee started keeping an eye
on Canseco and sure enough, he began noticing things, like a refrigerator
in the Toronto clubhouse with beer and soda in it. The guys on the team
used it like a Coke machine, storing drinks and their tobacco in the back
right-hand corner of the machine. One day—not long after the Miami
trip—Canseco left a small Ziploc bag in the clubhouse refrigerator. Later,
after a game, McNamee saw Canseco remove the package and take it to
his locker. There he opened it up and McNamee saw several—he
believed there were four—loaded syringes with tinfoil wrapped around
where the caps should have been. Canseco slipped the package into his
travel bag and left the locker room for the night.

Both Clemens and Canseco deny this incident ever took place.
McNamee swears that it is exactly what happened.

For Major League Baseball, 1998 was the year when the stars lined up
perfectly.

It was the year when Mark McGwire and Sammy Sosa thrilled baseball by chasing the ghosts of Babe Ruth and Roger Maris and the single-
season home run record. But it was so much more than tape-measure
dingers and Bunyanesque sluggers. It was a season of jaw-dropping individual accomplishments and inspiring team triumphs. It was a feel-good
season, a summer right up there with the magic of 1941, 1951, and 1969.

It was a year in which the hitters seemed to have all the advantages—
"Pity the pitchers," Roger Angell opened one of his celebrated medita-
tions in *The New Yorker*—but pitchers had some sterling moments too.
The first hint that 1998 would be special came in May, when Chicago
Cubs rookie Kerry Wood fanned 20 Houston Astros in a 2–0, one-hit win
that tied the record for strikeouts in a nine-inning game. Wood shared the
record with fellow Texan Roger Clemens, who struck out 20 batters over
nine innings not once, but on two separate occasions. Less than two weeks
after Wood dominated Houston, Yankee pitcher David Wells threw the
15th perfect game in modern history on May 17, 1998, a 4–0 gem over the
Minnesota Twins. Not to be outdone by Wells and Wood, Clemens
notched his 3,000th career strikeout that season, en route to his fifth Cy
Young Award.

After appearing in a record 2,632 consecutive games, Baltimore Orioles Ironman Cal Ripken Jr. finally sat one out, a 5–4 loss on September
20, 1998. Two new clubs—the Tampa Bay Devil Rays and the Arizona

Diamondbacks—joined the big league fraternity that year. The Yankees, the most venerable franchise in sports, fielded one of the best teams in baseball history in 1998, winning an astounding 114 regular season games and the 24th World Series title in the club's 95-year history.

By 1998, the national pastime was ready to embrace the magic. The owners had called the shots for more than a century, but they had lost a series of battles with the Major League Baseball Players Association in the decades since Marvin Miller created the union in the 1960s, looking impotent and foolish with every defeat. Free agency had cost the owners the power to decide who played for which team, and for how much. The NFL and its union had agreed to a salary cap in 1993 and the NBA instituted its salary cap way back in 1984, but for MLB brass, a salary cap was the impossible dream. By the early 1990s, the Lords of Baseball believed they had lost control of their game.

The greatest setback came in 1990, when a federal arbitrator ruled that the owners had colluded to suppress salaries and crush free agency by not offering contracts to eligible players. The arbitrator ordered the owners to pay the players $280 million to make up for lost wages.

"We have the only legal monopoly in the country," Atlanta Braves owner Ted Turner told his fellow owners, "and we're fucking it up."

Even more aggravating, the commissioner they hired to manage the game, Fay Vincent, seemed soft on labor issues and utterly uninterested in expanding the bottom line. Vincent saw himself as a beneficent overlord who used his office as a bully pulpit, but to many owners, he was nothing more than a windbag drunk on the power and fame that came with the job. In 1992, a coalition of owners led by Milwaukee Brewers president Bud Selig and Chicago White Sox chairman Jerry Reinsdorf staged a coup, engineering an 18–9 no-confidence vote that prompted Vincent to resign. Selig took over as interim commissioner, a title he would hold until the middle of the 1998 season, when the owners voted to give him the job on a permanent basis.

With Vincent gone, the owners were ready to settle decades-old scores with the Players Association, but it was a fight that was doomed before it even started. The growing role of cable television exaggerated the already significant differences between big-market teams like the New York Mets and Los Angeles Dodgers and small-market teams such as the Kansas City Royals and Pittsburgh Pirates. For instance, the Cleveland Indians pulled in $7 million a year in cable revenue, while the Yankees annually brought in $80 million from local TV. Revenue sharing was seen as one way to bridge the gap between the haves and have-nots, but Yankee owner

George Steinbrenner and other big-market executives resisted—why should they write a check for a small-market owner without any guarantees that he would not simply pocket the money instead of improving his team?

Despite those ugly internal divisions, most of the owners agreed on one thing: The time had come to take on the union. In January 1994, the owners agreed to a revenue-sharing plan that would be implemented only if the players agreed to a salary cap. A day later, the owners voted to give acting commissioner Selig total control of labor negotiations. The players, still seething over the collusion of the 1980s and years of hawkish rhetoric, believed a salary cap was management's first step in ultimately breaking their union. When the owners decided in June 1994 to withhold $7.8 million from the union pension and benefit plans, any hopes of avoiding the eighth work stoppage in baseball history were dashed. On August 12, 1994, the Players Association went on strike, bolstered by a $175 million strike fund that had been fattened by the late 1980s trading card boom. The strike cost San Francisco Giant Matt Williams, who had hit 43 home runs and was on pace to hit 61, the opportunity to beat Roger Maris's record four years before McGwire and Sosa.

The strike was settled in time for the 1995 season, but by then many fans were fed up with baseball. Attendance dropped to 50,469,236 in 1995, just a blip more than during the strike-shortened 1994 season and well below the 70,257,938 recorded in 1993, when the Colorado Rockies and Florida Marlins joined the National League. On Opening Day at Shea Stadium, three fans wearing T-shirts that said "GREED" ran onto the field and threw 150 $1 bills at Mets and Cardinals players before being escorted off the field. Another fan hired a plane to fly over Cincinnati's Riverfront Stadium with a sign that said "Owners and Players, to Hell with All of You."

The hard feelings dissipated with time; new, taxpayer-subsidized stadiums in Cleveland, Baltimore, and Denver, ballparks that merged retro baseball design with the downtown shopping mall, diverted the attention of the fans and the press. By the end of 1996, it was also clear that baseball was enjoying a power surge, and fans dug the long ball. Brady Anderson of the Baltimore Orioles, who had hit just 72 homers in 945 games before the 1996 season, wound up with 50 that year, and the power numbers for scores of other players soared as well. Some attributed the spike to the new ballparks, which were smaller and more intimate. Others said the ball was tighter or that expansion had diluted the pool of pitching talent or that the strike zone had become smaller.

And some blamed the dietary supplements that had become standard fare in big league lockers, and the illicit performance-enhancing drugs that Canseco and his disciples believed helped them work out harder and recover faster. The myth surrounding steroid use in baseball, driven as much by simply watching Jose Canseco as by anything else, was that the primary benefit of using them was in packing on muscle to generate a more powerful swing. What users knew, including Canseco, was that the real benefit of steroids was their ability to aid in recovery, and in that respect they were particularly helpful to pitchers. The baseball season was long, and pitchers in particular put a lot of wear and tear on their joints and muscles. As pitchers aged, they learned to rely on strategies and skills rather than just strength and ability, but their arms fell apart. Steroids could postpone the inevitable decline and deterioration.

Even with the Cy Young he'd won in the 1998 season, Clemens wasn't happy. He was 36 and still hadn't won a World Series ring. He was ranked first among active pitchers with 233 victories and 3,153 strikeouts and third-best in earned run average (2.95), but what was the point when your team finished the season third in the American League East? The Blue Jays finished 26 games behind the New York Yankees, who won the first of what would be three straight Fall classics. Clemens must have felt a pang of envy.

CHAPTER TWO

1999

"With all the things he's done, how can you not like Roger Clemens?" Yankee owner George Steinbrenner asked. "It's like saying you don't like chocolate ice cream."

It was February 18, 1999, spring training had just begun, and Toronto had traded Clemens to the reigning World Series champions for utility infielder Homer Bush and pitchers Graeme Lloyd and David Wells. The city of New York was sad to see the lovably blunt and pudgy Wells leave for Canada, but the acquisition of the iconic Clemens was cause for celebration. Finally, Clemens would get a chance at the World Series ring that had eluded him in the tragic 1986 Series, when the infamous ground ball hit by Mookie Wilson slipped between Bill Buckner's legs. Steinbrenner, who had wanted Clemens so badly back in 1996 that he had flown to Houston to make a personal plea—even reportedly dropping into Clemens's gym and doing some bench presses—agreed to pay Clemens $16.1 million for 1999 and 2000.

Following the 1998 season, New York suddenly looked pretty good to Clemens. The Yankees were a mature, highly motivated, no-drama club that played fundamentally excellent baseball. Like the Beatles, the team was more than the sum of its parts. The Yankees led the American League in runs scored, but only batting champion Bernie Williams and Derek Jeter, who led the league in runs, finished in the top five in any major offensive categories. It may have been the year of the long ball, but the Yankees were not Bombers; the team's most prodigious slugger—first baseman Tino Martinez—hit just 28 homers that year. These Yankees were different in one way: Unlike other great Yankee clubs, pitching was not an afterthought. Wells was 18-4 that year, while David Cone went 20-7. Andy Pettitte was 16-11, and won Game 4 of the World Series, completing the sweep against the San Diego Padres.

McNamee wasn't part of the Yankees' party. He spent 1999 in Toronto, living in SkyDome while supporting his family back in Breezy Point, Queens. When he'd go on the road with the team, they'd put his stuff in storage, and when he got back he'd take the cheapest room available. He still had to pay for the room, but the Blue Jays would give him $600 a month to offset living expenses. McNamee finished his PhD dissertation—entitled "Body of Work"—in May 1999. He had begun work toward the degree in Behavioral Sciences after the Blue Jays suggested continuing education 'might help them justify keeping a non-Canadian resident on their staff. He took nearly a dozen courses, covering subjects like weight training and nutritional supplementation. The dissertation dealt with techniques for increasing fastball velocity, and McNamee even asked Clemens for permission to use his name. He had also bought a book on how to write a thesis after failing his first course in the program.

During the first part of that season, Clemens ran into McNamee a few times and signaled that he wanted his trainer to come back to New York. McNamee had worked for the Yankees as a bullpen catcher in 1993, getting the job through a friend, former assistant general manager Tim McCleary, and had traveled with the team for three years, but such a change was harder now for someone in his position. He couldn't just make the switch; his contract said that if he jumped ship with the Blue Jays he would be barred from working for another team for seven years. Clemens had a guy for that. No problem was insurmountable when your agents were Randy and Alan Hendricks, who knew the ins and outs of baseball contracts as well as anyone. McNamee faxed his contract over to them, and they agreed: McNamee was stuck in Toronto for the time being. But in the fall they could work something out.

There was a reason Clemens was anxious to get McNamee back to New York.

His first season in pinstripes had been anything but smooth. The intimidating power pitcher Yankee fans had seen the previous two seasons when Clemens wore the Blue Jays uniform seemed lost in the Bronx. He struggled with command. Maybe it was the glare of the media. Maybe the expectations in the Bronx were too much for Clemens, even after he had weathered Boston's intense scrutiny all those years.

"I'm not concerned about the numbers. I've had success," said Clemens, following a shaky August 5 start against Seattle, during the same week he turned 37. "There are seasons I've won 20 [games] and could've won 25 and still at the end of the season you get a handshake and you go home. . . . I definitely want to pick up the pace, but I can't overdo it. I just want to give the guys chances to win."

In his next start, August 10 in Oakland, Clemens was lit up for five runs on nine hits over six and a third innings, causing manager Joe Torre to ponder whether Clemens was trying too hard.

"It's going to be a lot tougher if we don't have Roger pitching the way Roger can pitch, and we need him very desperately," Torre said. "I just think sometimes he's a little too analytical and puts a little bit too much on himself, instead of just letting it happen. Roger just hasn't been Roger this year. . . . But he's had a pretty good bank account. He's got a lot in the bank that he's accomplished. Even if [the struggle] goes the whole year, it's not going to diminish that."

But Clemens obviously felt diminished. For several months, he had been laying the groundwork to get McNamee to New York, floating the trainer's name to newspaper writers where the Yankee management could read it. "Roger Clemens thinks he knows what ails him," read an August 15 report in *Newsday*. "He misses his Blue Jays fitness trainer Brian McNamee."

It turned out, however, there was still something in the bank when it mattered most. Clemens sputtered to a 14-10 record that 1999 season, but delivered a vintage Clemens performance in the Game 4 World Series clincher over the Braves to complete the four-game sweep. Clemens pitched seven and two-thirds innings and gave up a lone run on four hits.

"I think I finally became a Yankee tonight," said Clemens, who was joined on the field after the 4–1 win by sons Koby and Kory.

That autumn McNamee's contract with the Blue Jays expired, and he called Roger, who now had the Series ring that had eluded him all those years. McNamee hoped for a better situation for himself and his family, but a lot depended on Clemens: He had a superstar's influence over the Yankees' front office, where a former intern named Brian Cashman had taken over as general manager the year before.

"Roger, am I going back to the Toronto Blue Jays?" McNamee asked.

"No, you're not going back," Clemens said in the clipped, matter-of-fact way he announced many of his decisions that affected other people's lives.

McNamee called Cashman and listed the reasons why the Yankees should put him on staff. He was a former Yankee employee, a friend of Clemens's, and a native New Yorker forced to live in Toronto while maintaining a family back home in Queens. It was a perfect fit. Clemens contacted Cashman too, recommending McNamee for the job. Cashman got in touch with the Hendricks brothers, and together they worked out a solution whereby McNamee would work with Clemens on a semipersonal basis and the money the Yankees paid him would come out of Clemens's salary. McNamee would get health insurance and meal money from the team and be allowed to travel with the players. This was the side of Roger Clemens that endeared him to so many of the people who were closest to him. This was the Roger Clemens who was always quick to lend a hand, to share his influence and wealth with others. This was the Roger Clemens who on one occasion, surprised his nieces and nephews by buying each of them a car. According to a friend, "They had a Tex-Mex get-together and all of a sudden they brought the cars in — for all the kids over 17. The kids were crying. Everyone was crying."

The 2000 season would begin with McNamee in a Yankees uniform, but charged with the special task of helping keep the 37-year-old Clemens holding up into the postseason so the dynasty could continue. It was a strange arrangement, one that risked creating a perception of favoritism on the part of the Yankees. Some members of the front office, particularly Torre, weren't thrilled about the setup. But then again, Clemens was a living legend, entitled to special treatment.

The more dangerous problem was the increasing codependency of the two men. Clemens received injections from McNamee — his numbers had slipped, in their separation, to something that closer resembled those of a 37-year-old power pitcher — but McNamee needed Clemens just as much. His income and status were linked to Clemens's benevolence and power. He was a Yankee employee, but Clemens was his benefactor, the one to whom he felt loyalty. The Yankees didn't pay McNamee much, but there were enormous intangible benefits of being the trainer for a player like Clemens. The press loved the story of the fitness guru who made athletes great, and if McNamee could make a name for himself as Clemens's hard-driving conditioning coach, there was no telling what kind of business he could get down the road. In a culture as driven by physical appearance as New York at the start of the new century, McNamee could earn big bucks marketing himself as the guy who postponed the physical breakdown of a power pitcher nearing 40, and made him, in fact, better than ever.

Everything's bigger in Texas, so it stood to reason that the Clemens family occupied one of the grandest homes in Houston, on the scale of Chez Canseco. The 16,000-square-foot Clemens palace just off Blalock Road in the Piney Point neighborhood of Houston sat on three acres, with a giant heated pool and a guesthouse out back. There was a giant treehouse too, and video games everywhere, as if Clemens—remembering his own financially strapped and fatherless childhood—was compensating by spoiling his four boys, Koby, Kory, Kacy, and Kody. (Their names all began with K, the letter that represents a strikeout on a baseball scorecard.)

The most striking feature of the place was an addition the pitcher built for himself: a 7,000-square-foot gymnasium with a basketball court, a batting cage, a pitcher's mound, and even bleachers. The gymnasium—and the beck-and-call power over McNamee—was the primary reason the Clemens manse became, as the winter of 1999 ticked over into the new century, a sort of Yankee outpost in the Lone Star State. Clemens flew McNamee in for private workouts, and then invited fellow Houstonians Andy Pettitte, C. J. Nitkowski, and Justin Thompson to come over and train with them. Pettitte and Clemens each paid McNamee a little bit on the side for his help. The trainer stayed in Clemens's poolside guest-house—he would call it his Kato Kaelin place—and helped out with projects for the kids. He helped them build a birdhouse for a school project and designed a gym for Koby too, once the oldest boy headed to Memorial High School.

McNamee and Pettitte had met back in 1995, when Pettitte was a rookie with the Yankees and McNamee was the bullpen catcher. But now they really hit it off and were developing a solid relationship, with McNamee advising Pettitte on his chronic elbow problems. McNamee also came to like and respect Pettitte's dad, a former cop from Louisiana. When McNamee came to Texas for the workouts, Pettitte would lend him his wife's SUV.

So everyone was already buddy-buddy when spring training started in 2000, and McNamee showed up in Tampa as the team's new assistant strength coach. On a daily basis he ran through a quick set of meetings with minor league coordinator Cash Ventori and trainer Gene Monahan, then went out on the field. Throughout that spring, McNamee trained Pettitte and Clemens independently, even though they were also doing the regular team workouts every day.

For the first time, writers began to take note of Brian McNamee, the mysterious guru behind Clemens's remarkable longevity. Jon Heyman, writing for *The Sporting News*, was among the first to write about the Clemens-McNamee relationship.

"Some scouts are predicting major improvement for RHP Roger Clemens in his second season in the Bronx, and it has nothing to do with any adjustment to New York," Heyman wrote in a brief spring training notes package on March 22. "Some believe Clemens wasn't completely healthy last year. That might explain why Clemens had the Yankees import Brian McNamee, his personal trainer with the Blue Jays, from Toronto."

It was notices like that—many more would follow—that began earning Brian McNamee a reputation as something of a miracle worker. He started getting more gigs as a personal trainer, from Wall Street guys hoping to stave off middle-age bloat to young baseball prospects wanting to get in shape. McNamee might not be getting a ton of money from Clemens, but he was making very good money because of his association with Clemens.

CHAPTER THREE

2000

By the summer of 2000, McNamee was feeling flush, and he decided to buy a luxury automobile.

Clemens was going in on a share of a private jet so he could make it to his boys' baseball games as well as his own. He used it to fly home the night before every Yankee off day, no matter where the club was playing. His family used the plane too, and so did the women Clemens squired around the country. McNamee didn't have anywhere near that kind of money, but he did have status as the personal trainer to the Rocket. He felt that he couldn't show up for his freelance gigs, especially with those titans of finance, in an old beat-up car. It was Yankee pitcher Jason Grimsley who helped him settle on a Lexus.

Grimsley had pitched all over the league, and he knew everybody. He had a friend out on Long Island who could get McNamee a deal on a car. The friend's name was Kirk Radomski, and Radomski had connections with a Lexus dealer. McNamee had heard of Radomski, a former clubhouse attendant for the Mets, from journeyman major-leaguer David Segui earlier that year. Radomski was just 15 when his neighbor Charlie Samuels, the Mets' longtime equipment manager, helped him get a job at Shea Stadium as a batboy, and he was there for the 1986 season when the raucous Mets, assisted by the ground ball that slipped through Bill Buckner's creaky legs, snatched the World Series from Roger Clemens and his Boston Red Sox. Radomski was a streetwise kid from the Bronx, and from his perch in the Shea clubhouse he learned at a tender age all about cocaine, booze, and bimbos, about serving ballplayers—the dark side of baseball that never gets written about on the back of baseball cards and only rarely in the media.

Radomski was a man who had connections—he could get a deal on a Rolex, a car, whatever a player might want. It didn't take long for McNamee to realize that Radomski also had steroid connections, but you didn't have to be an undercover cop to figure that one out. The guy was big, six feet–plus of chiseled muscle. With his severe crew cut, angular face, massive arms, and huge torso, Radomski looked like a human cinder block.

By 2000, Radomski was one of the worst-kept secrets in baseball; he had been providing steroids, human growth hormone, and amphetamines to dozens of major-leaguers since he left the Mets after the 1994 season to become a personal trainer. In the early 1990s, he had become a competitive bodybuilder and started using Deca-Durabolin and Winstrol, reading everything he could about the pros and cons of various steroids, their side effects, whether they could be detected in urine tests. When he arrived at spring training in 1993 looking bigger and buffer than ever, players flocked to him for advice and assistance.

Radomski liked the idea that he was helping world-class athletes get the most out of their talent. He was hardly a baseball groupie. He wasn't even much of a fan of the game—the bloated egos and self-important blowhards he saw roll through Shea all those years destroyed most of his interest in the sport. But while he was sour on baseball, he still had a lot of friends in the major leagues, and it gave him a sense of accomplishment to help them play their best. He wasn't involved in steroids for a quick buck. He didn't want his clients using veterinary drugs or products that had outlived their expiration date. He bought high-quality steroids from guys he met at a gym; he approached AIDS patients as they left pharmacies, offering to buy portions of their freshly filled prescriptions of human growth hormone.

Segui was one of Radomski's earliest and best customers. He met Radomski in 1994, when the Baltimore Orioles traded him to the Mets. Radomski first advised Segui on nutrition and weightlifting, but he soon started providing him with legal supplements, anabolic steroids and clenbuterol, an asthma drug that supposedly burns fat. Segui liked Deca-Durabolin because it did not expire for three to four years, and because it alleviated joint pain. Deca lingers in the body for a long time and is easily detectable in urine tests, but it didn't matter. Baseball didn't test for steroids for most of Segui's career.

Segui, a first baseman who hit .291 and 139 home runs over 15 seasons—performance-enhancing drugs obviously didn't help his power numbers—was just an occasional steroid user, but he played an important role in baseball's juicing scandal. He was a player who took teammates under his wing, organizing impromptu dinners when his club was on the road, counseling rookies, supporting teammates when they struggled through slumps. When other players asked Segui about his fitness regimen or about supplements and steroids, Segui introduced them to Radomski. "He was someone you trusted," Segui would one day tell the Baltimore *Sun*.

Radomski's business grew because he got results, and because players trusted him to deliver quality products. "I always had a feeling—I knew when more and more guys were going through him—that there is probably going to come the day when he is going to get caught," Segui told the *Sun*.

Selling drugs to ballplayers wasn't a full-time business for Radomski, it was just one of many services he provided clients. He had learned by trial and error how to design a drug program that was tailored to a player's position and needs. "Tell me your position and I'll outline a program for you," he would tell players. They would defer to him completely, but usually they were coming to him for the same thing: a boost of energy. The baseball season was long and arduous and painful, and players wanted drugs to get through the dog days of summer, to help them pile up the numbers fans had come to expect.

By 2000, Radomski was shipping drugs to players across the country. After purchasing Deca and testosterone in 1996, Mets catcher Todd Hundley, who had never hit more than 16 home runs in a season, hit 41. Lenny Dykstra, the outfielder who helped both the Mets and the Phillies reach the World Series, was a customer. Several members of the 2000 Yankees—Grimsley, starting pitcher Denny Neagle, designated hitter Glenallen Hill, and outfielder David Justice—were also named as Radomski's clients. (A claim Justice would deny.)

McNamee and Radomski had a lot in common—they were interested in fitness, they were blue-collar New Yorkers who worked with wealthy clients and were beholden to their demands—and they quickly became friends. McNamee was soon plugged in to the broadest, deepest steroid network in professional baseball.

Clemens needed a boost during the first two months of the 2000 season. By the end of June, he was 4-6 with a 4.76 ERA, hardly All-Star numbers. Despite the offseason workout regimen that baseball writers were extolling as the most hard-core in sports, "the SEAL Deal," catcher Darrin Fletcher called it in Toronto, an allusion to the brutal workout regimes of the Navy SEALs, Clemens looked more and more like any other 37-year-old power pitcher: mortal.

So McNamee wasn't totally surprised when the midpoint of the 2000 season rolled around and Clemens approached him about getting back onto the drug program. McNamee didn't hesitate; Clemens was virtually his boss. The pitcher didn't want to use Winstrol again—the abscess had made him nervous about the drug. McNamee asked Radomski which drugs would be good for pitchers, and Radomski put a bag together for him—Deca-Durabolin, Sustanon, Parabolan. McNamee also suggested Clemens try human growth hormone; McNamee had heard that other pitchers were using it with good results. It was the first McNamee had heard about human growth hormone, and it sounded good. He didn't know about his boss, though; he wasn't sure what Clemens had used in the past.

Congress had amended the Food, Drug, and Cosmetic Act 10 years earlier, making it illegal to use human growth hormone for off-label purposes—the drug could be legally used to treat only a handful of very specific ailments, including AIDS-related muscle deterioration and pituitary gland disorders. The restriction was widely ignored, and by 2000, anti-aging clinics and pharmacies across the nation were hyping HGH as a miracle drug that boosted energy and libido even as it removed wrinkles and reduced middle-age flab. HGH quickly turned the anti-aging industry into a $2 billion-a-year business that openly advertised and sold its products on TV and magazines—even though the drug was highly regulated and much of what was marketed was little more than a placebo.

For athletes, the benefits came in the form of accelerated recovery from injury and from workouts, allowing them to exercise harder and more frequently. For pitchers—especially aging pitchers—HGH helped them bounce back between games. It was effective, Radomski said, especially when used in conjunction with the kind of steroids Clemens was already taking. Better yet, it was delivered the same way insulin was, subcutaneously, into a small pinch of fat in the abdomen. It even required the same type of needle that diabetics used. The only drawback was that it required a greater frequency of injection. It often came as a powder that you mixed, and only after it was mixed did you need to refrigerate it.

McNamee would later claim he injected Clemens with steroids and human growth hormone 15 to 20 times in 2000, as the Yankees turned in another strong season, winning 87 regular season games. Clemens was astonishing; after his crummy 4-6 start, his won-loss record finished up at 13-8. He pitched 204 innings and finished sixth in the Cy Young voting.

It was true that Clemens worked as hard as anybody in the gym, but if the sportswriters asked if an illicit rocket fuel was powering those sessions, the answers didn't appear in their stories. Reporters were in a difficult position—short of extensive government involvement and court documents, or a testing program in baseball, or firsthand accounts of drug use, it was difficult to publish the reasons for the physical changes in players and the statistical anomalies. So the baseball press accepted whatever explanations Clemens and McNamee offered. Clemens had rebounded from the lackluster 1999 season to collect 188 strikeouts in 204.3 innings in 2000, when he turned 38 on August 4. Writers made much ado of Clemens's tight bond with McNamee and his military-style workouts.

In early April, Jon Heyman of *Newsday* said of Clemens, "It's remarkable that he still throws close to 95 mph" and reported that catcher Jorge Posada saw new power in Clemens's pitches. It was noted that McNamee had come down from Toronto at Clemens's request.

Later that month, Dan Graziano of Newark's *Star-Ledger* observed that Clemens was staving off the injuries that normally afflict aging power pitchers, forcing them out of the sport unless they learn to rely on guile and accuracy. The story marveled at the rigor of the workouts McNamee had put Clemens through when he flew to Houston repeatedly over the winter:

> They are serious. So serious, in fact, that Clemens and McNamee both balked at the idea of discussing the specifics of his workouts. They worry that someone else, either a minor-league pitcher or a younger pitcher or player, would apply Clemens's techniques to his own workout.
>
> "Some things I do in the weight room, I don't even like younger kids to see," Clemens said. "In the off-season, there's certain public places where we'll go and work out and there'll be some minor-league kids there working, and there's certain things we'll stay away from doing just because it might not be good for them. Might make them sore, might hurt them. To each individual their own."

Writers loved this idea of the secret guru. It gave readers a sense of solving the mystery behind heroic performances and cut against the conventional wisdom that baseball players were the least fit of all athletes. Now, Clemens was discovering revolutionary conditioning possibilities. Buster Olney of *The New York Times* discovered a plyometric technique that would raise fastball speed: "McNamee developed an exercise that the pitchers refer to as a power ab: while Pettitte or Clemens is doing a crunch, McNamee places added pressure on the movement to further isolate and develop abdominal strength."

In August, a story in *Newsday* quoted Jose Canseco explaining

Clemens's resilience as the by-product of "great condition, dedication to the game, a lot of work." The story described a nexus of Clemens, Canseco, and McNamee: "When they were teammates in Boston and Toronto, Canseco witnessed those workouts firsthand. The muscle-bound mammoth shared with Clemens a love of physical conditioning as well as a favorite strength and conditioning coach in Toronto, Brian McNamee, whom the Yankees hired this year at Clemens's behest."

The Yankees picked up Canseco off the waiver wire from the Tampa Bay Devil Rays in August. They didn't need another designated hitter/left-fielder—that slot was already filled by Justice, Hill, Luis Polonia, and Ryan Thompson—and because of back injuries, Canseco was no longer the threat he once was, but he was still a dangerous hitter, and the Yankee front office was afraid the Red Sox would grab him if they didn't.

The Yankees marched all the way to the World Series in October, where they faced the crosstown Mets—the first Subway Series for New Yorkers in 44 years. There was plenty of hype going into the showdown on just about every angle possible, but most fans and certainly the New York media were anxiously awaiting Game 2 on October 22 at Yankee Stadium. A sold-out crowd would witness Clemens facing Mike Piazza for the first time since July, when a Clemens fastball had drilled Piazza in the head during an interleague game.

Piazza had owned Clemens at the plate (he would finish his career with a .421 regular season average—8-for-19—against Clemens, with four homers) leading up to that July game, and Clemens might have been sending a message with the inside fastball. After being hit, the catcher lay prostrate on the ground that summer day, until he was helped off the field. Piazza later ignored Clemens's attempts to apologize.

In Game 2 of the Fall Classic, it took only three batters into the top of the first inning before the two combatants stood 60 feet and six inches apart, the fans in a frenzy. Clemens pumped two fastballs in for strikes. The third pitch to Piazza was outside. Then Clemens dug in and tried to jam Piazza inside. Piazza swung and fouled off the pitch, shattering his bat as if it were made of balsa wood. As the crowd roared, the bat barrel twisted toward Clemens. Rushing off the mound, Clemens picked up the shard and inexplicably fired it sidearm straight at the Mets catcher, who, not realizing the ball had gone foul, was running down the first base line with the bat handle still in his hand.

"What's your problem?" Piazza screamed, as he walked toward

Clemens on the infield grass. Home plate umpire Charlie Reliford rushed to get between Piazza and Clemens as both benches emptied onto the field. After order was restored, Piazza meekly grounded out to second and shuffled back to the dugout. Clemens and Yankee manager Joe Torre downplayed the incident after the game, a Yankee 6–5 win, suggesting that Clemens was caught up in the heat of the moment on baseball's grand stage. But to many Clemens critics, the two Piazza confrontations were nothing more than bouts of "roid rage." People close to Clemens and McNamee insisted those theories were bullshit, plain and simple. Mets reliever John Franco was said to even call Piazza out after the July beaning, allegedly saying, "Fuck Piazza, he's in the training room being a little bitch." Another person said that Clemens "was just so hyped up. [The World Series incident] was blown out of proportion. There was nothing intentional there."

In watching the replays of the bizarre bat incident—broadcast on news shows across the country the next day—it was easy to see that the man on the mound had the hair-trigger temperament of a testosterone-poisoned 15-year-old boy. But it didn't matter to the 38-year-old Roger Clemens, because after the season and another World Series triumph, the Yankees signed him to a two-year, $30.9 million contract. It was an extraordinary vote of confidence for a pitcher of his age.

CHAPTER FOUR

2001

The medical term was gynecomastia, but around the clubhouse they called them "bitch tits" or "man boobs"—and heaven help the player who sprouted them in the middle of his career and then took his shirt off in the locker room.

Taking anabolic steroids threw your whole hormonal system out of whack; your body noticed the surge of testosterone-related chemicals coursing through your system, so it suppressed natural production—a good reason for cycling off the drugs periodically. Meanwhile, to compensate for the testosterone levels, your body increased the amount of female hormones it produced.

In the end, the horror stories dispensed by anti-drug lecturers the league sent around during spring training—which in 2001 was about the extent of baseball's steroid policy—would be borne out: Your nuts might shrink and your breasts might grow.

Roger Clemens had man boobs, and he must have been embarrassed because he was often the first Yankee out of the shower and the first to get dressed after the game. In 2000, and again toward the end of the 2001 season, Clemens would approach McNamee after toweling off.

"Do you have time tonight?"

That was all McNamee needed to hear to know that he would be seeing Carlos the doorman again. McNamee would finish up his work with the other Yankees, then head out to the parking lot and make his way across the Third Avenue Bridge and on down to Clemens's place on East 90th Street. There Carlos would park his car by a fire hydrant and watch over it to make sure he didn't get a ticket. McNamee had become a drug delivery man on the same streets he'd once policed as an undercover cop.

In 2001, Clemens took human growth hormone out of the mix. McNamee said Clemens didn't like the shot in the abdomen. But he stayed on the steroids—with McNamee visiting him as many as 13 times at the Upper East Side apartment. It was there that McNamee injected his client in the buttocks with Sustanon 250, Deca-Durabolin, or Parabolan, gathered up the gauze, the cotton, the syringes, and needles and the broken ampule and stuffed them into a water bottle or a beer can, whatever was in the garbage. He'd either throw the stuff in the trash on the 23rd floor or take it home to dispose of there, along with the material from his son's insulin injections that he and his wife kept in an old Tide bottle that served as a HAZMAT container. Clemens always had the stuff out when McNamee got to the apartment, usually in the kitchen or his bedroom. Sometimes Clemens was on the phone, chatting with one of his sons in Houston about a game the kid had played, while he received the shot. The whole injection process took maybe five minutes. Break the ampule. Draw out the steroids. Flick the bubbles out. Boom. Out of there. "Take care, have a nice day. See you later, Carlos."

There had even been one injection in the Yankee clubhouse, near the Jacuzzi. Clemens had needed it because he was coming up on a getaway day for a road trip and didn't want to travel with the drugs. McNamee remembered the incident because another pitcher, Mike Stanton, noticed on the plane ride that Clemens had bled through the seat of his designer trousers. There wasn't usually a lot of blood with the injections, but this time a spot materialized right on his pants.

McNamee wasn't happy about Clemens's response. The trainer felt that Stanton, who always sat behind Clemens on the plane and who McNamee believed had also begun to use human growth hormone, had baited Clemens into admitting something about drug use, implying that McNamee had told Stanton about it.

"Hey, whatever I can do to get an edge," Clemens told Stanton.

Nothing much came of the incident, but McNamee noticed that Clemens carried Band-Aids with him after that.

Clemens turned 39 that season, and despite the man boobs, he turned in one of the greatest performances of his entire career. He couldn't help but notice that another superstar was tearing up the record book too: On the West Coast, Barry Bonds was jacking home runs into the San Francisco Bay with a ferocity that startled even his fiercest critics. He was having the greatest season in the history of the game, finally ending with 73 home runs and the single-season record. Mark McGwire had hit 70 in the famous 1998 season and Bonds was said to be obsessed with obliterating McGwire's record. Bonds believed the sportswriters and fans were biased toward McGwire and against him because of race, and he only had to look at the press accounts of McGwire's 1998 season to find proof. Despite his own reputation for rudeness and arrogance, McGwire was presented by the media as the antithesis of Bonds, a magnificent hero who saved the game from the ravages of the 1994 strike and lockout and dwindling fan interest.

The coverage of McGwire was worshipful. *Sports Illustrated* set the tone in October of 1998, with a 3,500-word profile by Tom Verducci called "Larger than Life." Under the headline came this teaser: "From his 20-inch biceps to his 500-foot blasts, everything about Mark McGwire is Bunyanesque—including his heart."

There were whispers that something funny was going on with Bonds—he grew to 225 pounds from 210 before the 1999 season, his hat size appeared to expand along with his power, and when he showed up at spring training that year with his new physique he was called "The Incredible Hulk." By 2001, Bonds's chase for the home run record was awash in mendacity, the nation suspicious of the man and his quest. Bonds himself summed up the mood when he told *The New York Times*, "When you come to the ballpark," he said, "you're walking into a place that is all deception and lies."

The skepticism didn't apply to Roger Clemens. The breathless stream of newspaper and magazine profiles expressing flabbergasted admiration for the rigorous McNamee-designed conditioning programs continued in 2001. McNamee suspected that Clemens was beginning to refer to him in hyperbolic terms, embellishing his credentials. On one occasion in Houston, when the trainer sat next to Clemens's brother-in-law on a small bus the pitcher had rented to take family and friends to a barbecue, the man asked McNamee what it was like to be "a Navy SEAL." McNamee told him he'd never been in the service—his father was a veteran and he didn't take claims of military service lightly. He'd also seen what Toronto manager Tim Johnson had gone through when he falsely claimed he had done combat in Vietnam—eventually he lost his job. The next morning McNamee asked Clemens where his brother-in-law had gotten such an idea. Clemens denied having said anything about the SEALs, but McNamee had a feeling the pitcher was doing what he'd noticed Clemens doing a lot of—rearranging the truth to suit the situation. He'd done that with Debbie, assuring his wife of his fidelity even as he cavorted around North America with Mindy McCready and a host of other women, flying them around in the private plane, and buying them expensive gifts.

By the summer of 2001, writers were noting that Pettitte was also in on the McNamee program. One article shared an anecdote about the day

Clemens and Pettitte showed up 40 minutes late for a workout at the Houstonian, an upscale spa and athletic club near Clemens's home. McNamee told the reporter the two pitchers were avoiding the workout "like kids on a Monday morning who don't want to go to school."

The stories were all very cute—here were these high-paid New York ballplayers being pushed around by a nondescript trainer—but they were also gold for McNamee, who was getting on a plane and leaving his family in Queens to travel to Houston every other week. His reputation as a taskmaster would serve him in good stead—as would the pitchers' endorsements. In the New York *Daily News*, Clemens was quoted touting the McNamee plan: "At the 110- or 120-pitch mark, you can reach back and get a little bit more. I enjoy seeing the payoff for Andy. It helped him mentally and now he can challenge hitters and have the stuff to back it up."

Reporters pushed stories on the cultish following McNamee was developing. "The accepted correlation between the workouts and the results have made McNamee a busy man, as nearly all of the Yankees' pitchers have begun working with him," one 2001 story related.

The same story had Ted Lilly, a young pitcher, tell what an inspiration it was to see Clemens turning 38 and still throwing heat. "He's inspiring to know that you never have to get old," Lilly said. "What's that saying? 'Age is nothing but a number.' I think that's the way he sees it. He's got a lot of energy and everything."

A profile of Clemens included an anecdote in which Lilly and another young teammate, Randy Keisler, tried to join one of Clemens's notorious workouts and couldn't keep up. An hour into the session, the story recounted, one of the kids got sick and the other nearly collapsed. "It made me ashamed of myself," Keisler was quoted saying. "I'm 25 years old, and I couldn't keep up with him."

That story credited Clemens's stamina and strength to the weightlifting, running, and endless stomach crunches McNamee was demanding. Digging aggressively into sports science, the writer noted that Clemens "closely monitors his nutrition."

Another story noted Keisler's inability to keep up with Clemens, quoting the young pitcher saying, "I have absolutely no idea how he does it every day," just before Keisler was demoted. But how Clemens had done it was "no secret," the writer claimed:

> At 6 feet 4, Clemens is 238 pounds thick. Some have pointed out that for someone who trains as hard as Clemens does, he is lacking

in muscle definition—perhaps this is because, aside from muscle, there is not much else to define. Clemens works up to five hours a day during the winters, and while he lightens that to about an hour-and-a-half during the season, it is one of the most grueling 90 minutes in sport.

At the end of August, Clemens took his 17-1 record and 96 mph fastball to Boston, where *Boston Globe* baseball columnist Dan Shaughnessy pointed out that Clemens was "fuzzy-faced and considerably leaner" than when he had similar performances in a Red Sox uniform. The writer mentioned that Clemens had turned Pettitte on to McNamee's workouts:

"Obviously, it's a great pleasure for me to watch a guy like Andy work," said Clemens. "Now if he wants to pitch till he's 40, or chase down Whitey Ford's records, he can do that. He was throwing 89 miles an hour, now he's up to 94."

In the same story, Yankee general manager Brian Cashman said it was Clemens's work ethic that explained the freakish late-career surge:

"It's no secret he's probably the hardest-working player in the game today," gushed Yankees GM Brian Cashman. "One impact of his work ethic is the effect it has on younger players. They've jumped on board and become better pitchers. He's a tremendous teammate. I tell our young players, 'Look at that guy.' I want them to live and sleep with Roger Clemens, see what he goes through. We're glad he's a Yankee. He's like Secretariat. You don't see something like that come along very often."

In 2001, the Yankees and Arizona played one of the more riveting World Series in history, only weeks after the country's soul was punctured in the wake of the 9/11 terrorist attacks. Clemens had been deeply affected by the events of September 11. He was to have pitched that Tuesday night against the White Sox, and was attempting to become the first pitcher in baseball to go 20-1 in a season. Instead, the nightmarish events that morning scuttled baseball's and all professional sports' schedules. The games that had been scheduled for September 11–17 were rescheduled to the first week of October, and the playoffs and World Series began one week later than their originally planned dates, which meant that the Fall Classic continued into early November.

Debbie Clemens was in Manhattan for her husband's possible pitching milestone on September 11, but in the aftermath of the twin towers' collapse, and with flights canceled across the country, Clemens drove Debbie all the way back to Texas. He remained there, comforting the kids, and worked out in preparation for when baseball resumed play on September 18. Clemens did secure win number 20 in Chicago on September 19, but the honor was hardly at the forefront of his thoughts.

"Right now, it doesn't have the same feeling it would've had a couple of weeks ago," Clemens told *The New York Times*. "You just know your purpose. After this past week, you realize: this is what I do, and what we do. But it's not who I am."

Back in New York for the playoffs, Clemens helped take the Yankees into the November World Series. Game 3 was the first game played in New York and President Bush threw the opening pitch (wearing a bulletproof vest under New York Fire Department fleece), and then Clemens came to the mound and allowed only three hits in seven innings, winning the game. At Yankee Stadium, the subdued crowd of 55,820 braced against the cold and wind and the devastation downtown, and there was a palpable sense that a baseball game could mean something to a wounded city. Clemens was a little late taking the mound, prompting some to wonder whether he was talking to the president, but from the moment he let his fastball fly, he was in control. When Diamondbacks third baseman Craig Counsell reached on an error to start the game, Clemens picked him off. He pumped his fists after key outs and was a one-man cheerleading squad. He shouted encouragement to teammates and ran over to congratulate them on crucial plays. The Yankees crawled back from a two-games-to-zero deficit behind his performance and would take a 3-2 series lead back to Arizona. In the pivotal Game 7, the 39-year-old Clemens started against 34-year-old Curt Schilling.

Clemens and Schilling, who was working on just three days' rest, matched each other for seven full innings, both finally leaving with the game tied at 1–1. With the Yankees ahead 2–1 in the bottom of the eighth, Joe Torre turned the game over to his ace closer, Mariano Rivera, and all of New York felt a ray of hope that something rejuvenating might occur on the baseball diamond. Rivera struck out the side in the bottom of the eighth, but a cruel twist of fate sank the Yankees an inning later. Rivera's cut fastball did its job breaking Luis Gonzalez's bat, but the Arizona outfielder was able to bloop a one-out, broken-bat flair over Derek Jeter's head, scoring Jay Bell for the winning run.

The Yankees lost the World Series, their magic disappearing in the desert, and the city returned to its grim cleanup job. Clemens ended the season with a record of 20-3, threw 220 innings, and won yet another Cy Young Award, one of the most dominant performances of his career. With the help of Brian McNamee, he had managed to reel in the years, all the way back to 1986, the year he'd gone 24-4 with Boston. But the fall of 2001 was significant in far less spectacular ways than 9/11 or an award-winning season: a sketchy incident in Florida damaged the relationship between Clemens, McNamee, and the Yankee brass, and reminded McNamee that when trouble came calling in the world of Major League Baseball, he was on his own.

The Yankees' September series against the Tampa Bay Devil Rays had been rescheduled for October 4–7 and McNamee was staying with the team at the Renaissance Vinoy Hotel in St. Petersburg. On the balmy night of October 6, following a game with the Devil Rays, McNamee returned to the historic Mediterranean-style hotel after midnight and joined a party in progress in room 364, second baseman Chuck Knoblauch's room. A few players were there, including utilityman Clay Bellinger and catcher Todd Greene, along with McNamee and a Yankee video technician named Charlie Wonsowicz, who'd been McNamee's college roommate at St. John's. There was a woman there too. McNamee and Wonsowicz had run into her in the lobby and McNamee had invited her to join them.

The woman had flirted a little bit with McNamee down in the lobby and she would say later that he had asked her if she wanted to come up to Knoblauch's room and watch some TV. He threw her over his shoulder and carried her a few steps into the elevator, all in a joking manner. She said she hadn't felt threatened because Knoblauch—a famous player—was there and she thought they were all just having fun. She neglected to tell police that she'd just come from the room of another Yankee employee, first base coach Lee Mazzilli, and that she knew Wonsowicz through Mazzilli.

The accounts of what happened next vary wildly between what appear in police records and McNamee's own descriptions, but one thing is undisputed: The incident cost McNamee his job with the Yankees and has followed him all the way to the present. The incident also revealed another side of McNamee: how far the trainer was willing to go to cover for ballplayers.

According to police reports by the St. Petersburg Police Department and interviews with investigators, McNamee was found in the hotel pool having sex with a woman who was virtually comatose while another man—Wonsowicz—looked on from a few feet away. A security guard approached the three, all of whom were naked, and ordered them out of the pool. Wonsowicz got out and left the area but McNamee stayed in the pool with the woman. The security guard ordered him out again and he obliged, leaving behind the woman, who, according to the security guard, looked "out of it." The woman asked for help and the guard called 911 as McNamee lifted her out of the water and tried to put her red bra and red thong back on her. Police opened an investigation into sexual assault. Records show that McNamee lied repeatedly during his initial interview, even denying that he knew Wonsowicz, or that he worked for the Yankees.

The woman, McNamee, and Wonsowicz told police that once they had gotten to Knoblauch's room, McNamee asked her if she wanted a drink. When she said "sure," a gin-and-tonic would be good, he offered to mix her a vodka and orange juice, since there was no gin in the minibar. According to her account, he left the room to make the drink, came back with it, along with what she thought was a water bottle with a yellowish green substance in it. She told one investigator she didn't think the water bottle had been there when he left, but it was there when he sat back down next to her. She remembered he then asked her if she wanted some GHB. She asked him what it was and he told her "it will relax you. It's no big deal."

By 2001, GHB–gamma hydroxybutyrate—was a Schedule I controlled substance in the United States, meaning it had a high potential for abuse and no approved medical use. If it was sold as Xyrem, a narcolepsy drug, it was a Schedule III substance—a high potential for abuse, and some medically approved uses. But it was still being used by bodybuilders and clubgoers. Athletes used the clear liquid too, as a sleep aid or just to party, often carrying it in water or Gatorade bottles. They loved how it made them feel—intoxicated, happy, talkative, sociable, affectionate, uninhibited, sensual. Except when it didn't. If you took too much of it, you would lose muscle tone, become nauseated, lose consciousness, lose your gag reflex, maybe die.

The woman said she didn't want any and drank her drink. She said Knoblauch then went to bed, and she decided to go to her car and head home. She didn't feel intoxicated, although she'd had five or six drinks throughout the night. She said the last thing she remembered was walking down the hotel hallway. A water bottle containing a greenish liquid that tested positive for GHB was later found by the pool.

There were problems with the woman's story. She failed to say that she had come to the Renaissance Vinoy to meet Mazzilli, that they had had a relationship for about a year, and that a pair of panties she'd had in a Saks Fifth Avenue bag found poolside had been the ones she was wearing when she'd had sex with Mazzilli earlier in the evening. The woman had told police she'd just purchased the panties at Saks Fifth Avenue that day. She also refused a rape kit and, after her initial statements, declined to cooperate with the investigation and admitted lying about why she had been at the hotel. She later said she remembered being at the pool but nothing after that. The state's attorney declined to charge McNamee, based on lack of evidence and the witness's materially inconsistent statements under oath to the state's attorney and the St. Petersburg police.

McNamee told friends a very different story about the night at the pool, one that was pretty well backed up by Wonsowicz's original account. This version was that they had all been trying to get out of the water when the woman, who had been looking for an earring she had dropped, suddenly went under. McNamee tried to pull her out but had trouble lifting her. They had all been shivering in the freezing water. "I hear her moan because it's cold," he told police. "Sound like she's freezing."

He wasn't having sex with her but trying to boost her onto the deck after Wonsowicz got out and ran back to the hotel. McNamee told friends he'd lied to the security guard and the cops to protect the Yankees and the players, including Knoblauch, and that he was guilty of nothing more than bad judgment. He'd had only a couple of Miller Lites that night and was sober; he'd ingested no GHB, even though it had been openly passed around like shots of vodka in Knoblauch's room. According to McNamee, Knoblauch himself had mixed the woman's drink and said it tasted great. The story seemed plausible to McNamee's friends—skinny dipping was not a big deal; he'd grown up swimming naked in the Atlantic waters off Breezy Point, "free balling," they'd called it. He claimed he didn't like GHB's effects—he'd had it slipped to him twice and it had messed him up. And the details made some sense—Wonsowicz had been with the girl in the center of the small section of the pool while McNamee had his elbows up on the ledge. When the security guard told them to get out, both Wonsowicz and McNamee began to walk out of the pool. The girl was looking for an earring she'd dropped and then she started yelling for help. As McNamee was getting out of the pool, she went under. He went back to grab her, asked her what was wrong, and saw that her eyes had rolled to the back of her head. He walked her to the ledge in what was probably three or four feet of water. She was heavy, about 160 pounds, and he put his arms under her armpits and tried to lift her onto the ledge. As they were thrashing around in the water her legs had locked around his waist, making it look to the security guard as though they might have been having sex. He lifted her onto his shoulder and got her out of the water. The security guard just stood there through the whole ordeal, even as McNamee put the woman's clothes back on her and the police and an ambulance arrived. By the time the cops got there, he had her fully dressed, and was claiming that he was just a New Yorker down in Florida to watch the game. He said he didn't know the man who'd been with him in the pool, much less the woman. He'd met her at the bar at closing time.

Wonsowicz's account, at least until detectives arrived in New York and pressured him into finally saying that "in his opinion" McNamee and the woman might have been having sex, described a woman who remained coherent as far as he knew throughout their time in the pool, which he estimated was only eight or nine minutes. He wasn't sure what had happened after he got out but he hadn't seen anyone actually having sex, perhaps just "frolicking around."

The cops investigated for more than a month in 2001, piecing together accounts of the incident from the security guard and another backup guard, the police, hospital personnel, Yankee security, Knoblauch, the woman, Wonsowicz, and McNamee himself. During one interrogation, McNamee admitted that they had kissed a little, but he never wavered from his claim that he did not have sex with her.

One of the St. Petersburg police investigators, Detective Don Crotty, flew to New York to reinterview Wonsowicz and tried to get to the various Yankees who'd been in the room. Because of the lack of cooperation from the alleged victim, and difficulty in getting to the players without subpoenas or cooperation from the Yankees and the Players Association, Crotty gave up. "I was planning on interviewing some of the ballplayers, even though I didn't think they had a whole lot of information," he said. "This was during the playoffs and I couldn't even get close to the players. Several of those interviews, specifically the ones who were actually in the room, I had to coordinate at some point in time with their attorneys. The way the case played out, we didn't need to do that, because the case pretty much died in the water there." It had become apparent that McNamee and the woman acted in concert in one area: They both lied to protect players.

After the season ended and the year wound down, with news of the investigation hitting the papers, the Yankees quietly let McNamee go. Risky business by players could be tolerated to a large extent, but there was no reason to keep a lowly strength coach whose presence had made a few people nervous anyway. None of that stopped Clemens and Pettitte from working with McNamee. When their trainer told them his side of the story, the pitchers kept using him as their personal trainer, Clemens even summoning McNamee to the New York apartment to help him pack up after the season ended. But McNamee knew there were no guarantees with these players, especially Clemens, and that he needed to protect himself from whatever might lie ahead, especially anything to do with this steroid business.

There were bits and pieces about steroids showing up in the newspapers, especially in the wake of the Mark McGwire andro scandal in 1998. (After a reporter for the Associated Press had spotted a bottle of androstenedione in McGwire's locker, McGwire admitted to taking the steroid precursor, which later became illegal to acquire without a prescription.) During the 2000 season the Yankees' team rep, David Cone, had approached McNamee on the team plane and told him that the owners and players were looking for an excuse to give to the media about why they didn't need to add a testing program to their next collective bargaining agreement. They wanted to tell the media that steroids couldn't help hand-eye coordination and wouldn't enhance a baseball player's performance. "Good luck with that," McNamee thought.

Maybe that was why he tossed a few of the needles and syringes and bottles of liquid he'd shot into Clemens's stomach and butt into a Ziploc bag, took it home from the apartment, and secreted it in a closet in his house for safekeeping.

"A gut feeling," the ex-cop called it.

CHAPTER FIVE

2002

On April 15, 2002, in the third inning of a game against the Red Sox at Fenway Park, Yankee starting pitcher Andy Pettitte fired a fastball to Boston's Tony Clark and felt a strange twinge in his left elbow. The joint had been a problem for him since 1996, but this felt different. This was serious. He left the game.

A tall and pious Texan with a Toucan Sam nose and a famous cut fastball, Pettitte had done well in the majors despite frayed ligaments in his elbow. His career had been interspersed with MRIs, joint specialists, and oral cortisone treatments. Technically these were steroids, but not the anabolic kind. They could reduce inflammation, but couldn't repair tissue.

Between the care of the Yankees' medical staff and Joe Torre's perceptive management, Pettitte had gotten through seven strong seasons in pinstripes despite the pain. But in spring training in 2002, the elbow problems had forced Pettitte to cut short his preseason preparations. Then, after leaving the mound early that day at Fenway, Pettitte found himself on the disabled list. The Yankees put him on a flight to Tampa to rehab the injury at their spring training facility.

Pettitte was 29, an age when big league pitchers historically started to feel the strain of hurling a baseball 90 miles per hour over and over again. The team was paying him nearly $10 million that year, and Pettitte felt awful not being able to do his job.

And so it was that Pettitte called Brian McNamee, his trainer and friend.

"Dude, I am hurt," Pettitte said. "You know my elbow is hurt. What can I do? Is there anything I can do?"

Human growth hormone is not a steroid. It properly belongs to a category of organic chemicals known as "peptide hormones," and it occurs naturally in the body, particularly in young people, since it is instrumental in the development of the musculoskeletal system. HGH is produced in the pituitary gland, and like most hormones it seems to work in a mysterious and delicate balance with the rest of the endocrine system.

In 1979, researchers developed ways in which to mass-produce artificial HGH, which could be useful to the very small percentage of the population that needed it for hormone deficiencies. To this day, the situations in which the federal government approves of human growth hormone prescriptions are syndromes like dwarfism and muscle wasting associated with AIDS. A huge market for HGH has grown up in symbiosis with the alternative medicine movement and the United States is full of naturopathic doctors and straight-up hucksters who have little trouble finding loopholes in the regulatory regimes established by the DEA, the Drug Enforcement Administration, and the FDA, the Food and Drug Administration, agencies that have bigger fish to fry.

"Growth," to use the most common slang, is massively popular on the black market for bodybuilders and athletes, not least because it is almost impossible to detect in even the most sophisticated anti-doping programs. Given its popularity with the touchy-feely alternative medicine industry and the anti-aging industry, the drug lacks the stigma associated with steroids. Baseball didn't even bother to ban HGH until January 2005, and it didn't make much of a difference, because baseball conducts only urine tests and most scientists believed that laboratories were years away from developing a urine test for it.

These were some of the considerations that Andy Pettitte made that spring in 2002 when he called Brian McNamee looking for a solution to his elbow problem. Pettitte had already spoken with McNamee previously, and learned that the drug could help aid in tissue repair. But this time, Pettitte specifically asked for HGH. The two men had discussed the drug before, but now Pettitte was ready to use it. McNamee told him HGH was supposed to be a wonder drug, as far as recovery went. McNamee told him HGH would help repair tissue and wasn't banned by baseball. Pettitte decided to go for it.

Pettitte flew McNamee down to Tampa, where the Yankees liked to have their injured players rehabbing at the team facility. As with their usual training agreements, it was understood that Pettitte would pay for McNamee's airfare and food, and write him a check for $1,500 at the end of the week. McNamee was there for about 10 days, and he and Pettitte talked about the course they were about to take for several days before Pettitte finally decided he was ready. McNamee had brought the drugs to Tampa, and had gotten them from Kirk Radomski—although he didn't tell Pettitte that.

Pettitte went to McNamee's room to get the injections on four different occasions—morning and night, on two different days. The method of injection was similar to the insulin therapy that any diabetic person would be familiar with, small needles in a pinch of fat in the abdomen. There, the drug would be slowly absorbed into the bloodstream and, hopefully, do its magical work to repair the frayed tissue in the arm that was worth eight figures to the Yankees.

Pettitte didn't feel comfortable with the drug. While there was actually little scientific consensus about whether HGH could repair damaged tissue, most experts agreed that you'd need a lot more than four shots to get that kind of benefit from it. What line had Pettitte crossed really? Sure, he'd used a drug for which he didn't have a prescription, and therefore had broken federal law, but people did that every day. He had not taken a banned substance. It wasn't like he'd taken steroids. Baseball probably couldn't suspend him even if he admitted to it.

He returned to baseball on June 14. He closed out the injury-marred 2002 season with a 13-5 record and a career-low 134 innings pitched.

Andy Pettitte was born in 1972 in Baton Rouge, Louisiana, the child of Tom and Joann Pettitte. His family had some Cajun roots, and his father was a police officer in the Baton Rouge Police Department. In 1981, the family moved to Deer Park, Texas, a leafy suburb east of Houston. Andy and his older sister, Robin, attended public schools. Tom worked a graveyard shift at a chemical plant. He taught his son baseball.

Deer Park was a suburban oasis adjacent to vast oil refineries on one side and, on the other, the unregulated suburban sprawl that would come to define Houston. From Deer Park, it was a short drive to the brackish water of Galveston Bay. Also nearby was the NASA facility that the Apollo 13 astronauts had reached out to when they reported "Houston, we have a problem."

Growing up, Andy immersed himself in sports, particularly football and baseball. But two years after the move, he found another passion when his 14-year-old sister, Robin, introduced him to the Baptist Church. The Pettitte parents weren't particularly religious; Robin was the first member of the family to strike up what Southern Baptists call a personal relationship with Jesus.

Pettitte would write about this conversion years later, when he collaborated on a 2005 book called *Strike Zone: Targeting a Life of Integrity and Purity*, coauthored by Bob Reccord, a leader in the Southern Baptist Convention. "She went to a revival at a Baptist church in our town and came home talking about getting saved," Pettitte wrote.

"I listened to what she said and decided to check it out for myself. Not long after, I asked Jesus to forgive me of my sin and to become my Lord and Savior. I was eleven at the time. Pretty soon my mom and dad started going to church with my sister and me, and they were saved as well."

It was through church that Pettitte met Laura Dunn. Their love blossomed when Andy was a sophomore at Deer Park High, already a standout athlete, and Laura was in eighth grade. Laura's parents disapproved—not of Pettitte, but of two people dating at such a young age; the Dunns were conservative people. Charles and Shirley Dunn stood at the head of one of the most well-known families in town. They had founded the Central Baptist Church in 1966, and Charles had given his first sermon there on Easter Sunday that year, with only 21 people in attendance. The church had grown tremendously, as had the Dunn family. Laura had three older brothers, whom Andy Pettitte came to know and admire. As time went by, Andy was allowed to take Laura to the movies for dates.

During his senior year, Andy Pettitte pitched the Deer Park team to within a game of the state 5A championship, and caught the attention of major league scouts. The Yankees drafted him in the 22nd round of the June 1990 draft, but Pettitte chose not to sign with them. In the neighboring town of Pasadena was a school called San Jacinto College. It was close to home (and close to Laura, who was still in high school), and it also happened to have a respected baseball team; Roger Clemens had pitched there before moving on to the University of Texas and then the Red Sox.

After a year at San Jacinto, Pettitte signed with the Yankees. By 1992 he was pitching for their minor league affiliate, the Greensboro Hornets in the South Atlantic League. After going 10-4 with a 2.20 ERA, Pettitte came home to marry Laura. They were on a church ski trip, snowmobiling in the mountains of New Mexico, when the 21-year-old Pettitte popped the question. Laura was a senior in high school. They married in January 1993, with Pastor Charles Dunn walking his 18-year-old daughter down the aisle and then conducting the ceremony himself.

Over the next two years, as Major League Baseball's labor battles culminated with the strike, Pettitte climbed through the minor leagues, playing for teams on the strength of a changeup, curve, and fastball—and avoiding late-night barhopping in the name of Christian purity.

On April 29, 1995, he had his major league debut, as a Yankee. He went 12-9 with a 4.17 ERA and finished third in the Rookie of the Year voting. The next year, he became the ace of the Yankees rotation, finishing the 1996 season 21-8 with a 3.87 ERA, and helping the team to its 23rd World Series title and its first since 1978. Pettitte was second that year in the Cy Young Award voting, close behind the Blue Jays' Pat Hentgen.

It was also that year that Pettitte first met his childhood idol Roger Clemens, who in 1996 was the anchor of the rotation for the Red Sox, the Yankees' division rivals. They crossed paths in the outfield, a fateful meeting that was later recorded for posterity in *Sports Illustrated* by Tom Verducci.

"We probably shouldn't talk too long here," Clemens said, "but I wanted to tell you everybody's proud you're holding up the tradition of Houston. Way to go, man."

At the end of the season, Clemens was on his way to Toronto for the rebirth of his career. It wasn't until 1999, when Clemens came to New York with two fresh Cy Young Awards, that Pettitte really got to see him up close. And they became fast friends. On the occasions Pettitte did venture into Manhattan from his second home in Westchester County, he might shoot pool with Roger at a bar not far from Roger's apartment on 90th Street and First Avenue. But mainly, they worked out, with McNamee leading them through grueling workouts, often at Clemens's home near Houston. Soon baseball writers noticed the change in Pettitte's body, even as they marveled at Clemens's longevity.

"Clemens would help remake Pettitte's body and his pitching style," wrote Verducci in an *SI* piece about the duo in early 2004.

> Once a crafty, slightly lumpy lefthander who relied on cutting and running the ball, Pettitte grew into a powerhouse of a pitcher with hair on his four-seam fastball, blowing it by hitters at the letters when he wanted. "He's 6′5″, 235," Clemens says. "Nobody should be surprised. He is a power pitcher. He took the program and ran with it."
>
> Says Yankees general manager Brian Cashman, "Andy became more streamlined. He was always a terrific pitcher. But if there was a small percentage of Andy's ability that wasn't being maximized, Roger found it and got the most out of it."

It had been during one of his workouts with Clemens and McNamee when Pettitte first discovered that Brian McNamee was getting drugs for Roger Clemens. They had all been in the gym at Clemens's house in Houston, and several younger players were there, including C. J. Nitkowski. As McNamee recalled it, the workout was winding down, and he had been cleaning up the area before he approached the corner where Pettitte was standing. Pettitte had been playing long-toss with Nitkowski while chatting with Clemens, who was seated, tying his shoes.

"Why didn't you tell me about that stuff?" Pettitte asked McNamee as Pettitte backed away from Clemens.

"What stuff are you talking about?" McNamee asked Pettitte.

"Growth hormone," Pettitte said.

"Why?" McNamee asked.

"Well, Roger is telling me that he's taking it, and, you know, you get me all this protein and this recovery stuff and why don't I take it?"

McNamee was angry that Clemens had violated the trust.

"Well, Andy, it's illegal, and I know how you are," McNamee said.

As McNamee remembered it years later, Pettitte just stared at him.

"Well, if it's illegal never mind, never mind."

McNamee's reluctance to put Pettitte on growth hormone was warranted—thanks to the burgeoning concern about steroids in professional sports, Major League Baseball and the Players Association agreed to their first-ever drug-testing policy in August 2002, a late addition to a collective bargaining agreement that focused more on economic issues than baseball's steroid scandal. The new policy called for survey testing to begin in 2003 to gauge the extent of steroid use; there would be no penalties levied, but if more than 5 percent of the tests came back positive, a random drug-testing program that mandated suspensions would be implemented the following year. The union agreed, convinced there was no real steroid problem in the game and certain the positives would never approach 5 percent.

The negotiations over the 2002 agreement started more than a year before the contract expired with a series of getting-to-know-you sessions intended to build trust between the negotiators. Images of the hard feelings and the fan backlash from the 1994 strike were imprinted on the memories of the union and management leaders, and they were eager to avoid a repeat of that dismal chapter in baseball history. Another strike might bankrupt several teams, taint the anniversary of the September 11, 2001, terror attacks, and cost the game its status as the national pastime.

But as the 3 P.M., August 30, 2002, strike deadline set by the union loomed, the talks became more and more contentious, and fans feared baseball was hurtling toward another work stoppage. With just hours to spare, nearly a decade after the 1994 strike canceled the World Series for the first time in 90 years, the union and the clubs struck a deal.

"All streaks come to an end, and this is one that was overdue to come to an end," said union chief Donald Fehr, referring to the eight walkouts and lockouts of the past.

While much of the celebration the next day centered on the league's new policy of revenue sharing, the union had made an extraordinary concession by agreeing to mandatory, although random, testing for steroids, a clause added at the last minute early that morning. Bud Selig, who had unilaterally implemented a testing program in the minor leagues in 2001, insisted on some kind of testing program for major league teams, perhaps remembering his June appearance before the Senate Commerce Committee hearing in which Senators Byron Dorgan (D-N.D.) and John McCain (R-Ariz.) told Selig and Fehr that a strict drug-testing program at the major league level had to be negotiated during the collective bargaining for a new Basic Agreement. Baseball had never before tested players without cause.

But that looming, intrusive change in a player's life was barely a blip in August 2002. Players were just grateful that the games—and their paychecks—would go on.

"I got up this morning assuming we weren't going to play, so I'm just glad I had a chance to come to work," said Mike Mussina, a Yankee teammate of Pettitte's and Clemens's, before a game in Toronto. "It would have been tragic if we weren't here today."

For about nine months in 2002, Roger Clemens had been turning down a request by *Sports Illustrated* to shoot him and his wife for the 2003 swimsuit issue. The magazine had taken to including players and their beautiful wives in the issue and SI's swimsuit issue project coordinator, Jennifer Kaplan, had been after Clemens's agents to line up Mr. and Mrs. Clemens. Clemens was reluctant to make the commitment, but Kaplan was friendly with Jimmy Murray, the Hendricks brothers' employee, and she kept pestering him about getting Clemens to agree.

The breakthrough finally came when Debbie heard about the shoot. She was over the moon with the possibilities. She was in great shape— McNamee had worked her out on occasion and she was thinking about some kind of a modeling career, maybe with a fitness magazine. At 39, the mother of four looked amazing. An appearance in *Sports Illustrated* would surely open doors to appearances in other magazines and Web sites.

"She really wanted to do it," Kaplan remembered. "He'd said no but she said yes. He did it because she wanted to do it. She was into all the girlie stuff—'I want to wear this kind of bikini and I want my makeup to look this way.' She was a doll. Her body was insane and she wanted to show it off. She was in great shape, and so nice."

Debbie looked like a million bucks as the photographers and makeup artists and editors entered Central Park at the West 72nd Street entrance sometime in September 2002. She posed standing over her husband, who was wearing his Yankee uniform unbuttoned down the front as he reclined on a patch of grass overlooking the park. Debbie Clemens's Norma Kamali–designed black-and-white string bikini with a Yankee logo on it barely covered her ripped body. She held a bat behind her shoulders, mimicking a barbell, and it was clear that she had spent a lot of time in the gym.

Kaplan remembered the shoot as being a fun, relaxed session that lasted from nine in the morning until about four in the afternoon. Clemens signed baseballs for everybody. Debbie sent flowers to the crew after the shoot was completed and even came to the launch party for the debut of the February 18, 2003, issue.

On her own Web site, Debbie described the shoot as one of the most empowering events of her life. After the issue hit the stands, she established DebbieClemens.com, a site devoted to dispensing advice to women on "family, health, life and relationships." She discussed the "laws of life and fitness" and described a rigorous exercise program that included running the stairs at Rice Stadium, abdominal work, stretching, "hot" yoga, lower body work with weights, sessions at the tony Houstonian Club, golf with friends, and salads with dressing on the side. McNamee noticed that she was touting the merits of green tea and he reminded Clemens that she could get in trouble for dispensing nutritional advice without the proper credentials.

As the baseball season began to wind down, Debbie returned to Houston thrilled with the possibilities, happy that Roger had cooperated with the shoot, ready to continue her career plans, and maybe ready to get a little help with her workout program. In New York, McNamee was helping her husband pack up the apartment again. Because he hadn't been with the Yankees in 2002, McNamee wasn't with Clemens as much as he had been the previous years, but he'd still trained him. Something had changed between them. Clemens was no longer freely talking about drugs; McNamee figured the pool incident in St. Petersburg had scared him off.

They had just come back to the apartment from a workout session at a nearby gym when Clemens handed him another Ziploc bag of Anadrol-50 and clenbuterol, drugs the pitcher didn't want to take on an airplane. McNamee recognized some of the stuff as having come from Radomski but not all of it. When he got back to his house in Breezy Point, he placed the Ziploc bag, along with some more unbroken ampules of testosterone and 22-gauge needle heads sealed in plastic, into the FedEx box in the closet.

After Clemens got back to Houston, McNamee returned there for the first of several offseason training sessions. His routine was usually the same: He would stay in Clemens's pool house for five days, head home for a few days, and then fly back for another five days of work. He and Roger sometimes hung out after the workout, swinging by one of Clemens's kids' baseball practices or basketball games. Sometimes they watched TV. And sometimes McNamee saw Debbie too. He worked her out occasionally or chatted with her in the family kitchen early in the morning as he waited for Clemens to come down, Debbie in her teddy and robe sipping a big cup of green tea at the kitchen's island before getting the kids ready for school.

On one of those early mornings, Debbie had asked McNamee about human growth hormone. She'd learned that it was a popular drug in Hollywood, where actresses were taking it to reduce body fat and keep a youthful appearance. Baseball wasn't the only venue where HGH was trendy, and Roger wasn't the only member of the Clemens family obsessed with doing whatever it took to stave off aging.

A couple of trips after McNamee's conversation with Debbie in the kitchen, Clemens was asking for a favor. Debbie wanted to try human growth hormone, and Roger wanted McNamee to inject it. Not long after that, McNamee was chilling in the pool house when the intercom rang. It was Clemens, asking the trainer to come over to the main house.

McNamee went in the back door of the house and made his way up to the master bedroom suite. He had been there once or twice before, to help Clemens move some stuff out of the closet. One summer he'd watched Clemens shave his kids' heads up there. There was a bathroom off to the side of Debbie's bedroom, and Roger and Debbie were in there, a mixture of growth hormone (water and powder) and a syringe laid out before them. In Clemens's shaving kit, McNamee noticed more growth hormone, the distinctive kind that Kirk Radomski sold.

"He had it and he wanted me to teach her how to do it," McNamee said.

For all of the time that McNamee had been injecting Clemens with banned performance enhancers, they hadn't talked about it much. But now Debbie was asking questions, and her husband was answering them. McNamee showed her how to clean both heads with an alcohol swab. He showed her how to draw the water, then put it into the bottle, then turn the bottle upside down to draw the mixture for the injection. Then the three of them just stood there, according to McNamee, who would never forget the surreal dialogue that followed.

"I can't believe you're going to let him do this," Debbie said to her husband. She seemed embarrassed.

"He injects me," Roger Clemens answered. "Why can't he inject you?"

Debbie Clemens was shorter than McNamee, tiny really, and McNamee was uncomfortable bending down in front of her so he kneeled down behind her, reached around with his left hand and took a pinch of fat from the right side of her belly button—just above a scar— and injected her diagonally with two ampules of human growth hormone, about half the recommended dose for men. She didn't complain; she didn't say anything. McNamee went home for five days and when he returned to Houston, he asked Clemens if Debbie was continuing to take the drug. Clemens said she had lowered her doses because she got a tingling sensation in her fingers, a side effect of an excessive dose.

"I never dealt with dosages for a woman," McNamee said. He was mostly just guessing on the dose.

McNamee never injected Debbie Clemens again with human growth hormone. He wasn't sure if he'd been the first to do so—or the last.

CHAPTER SIX

2003

The only milestone left after the World Series rings and the six Cy Young Awards was for Clemens to cross the magical 300-win plateau, a pitching stat that would make him a virtual lock to enter Cooperstown. But first, Clemens had to find an employer.

The 2002 season had fizzled badly for the Yankees, as they were unceremoniously booted from the first round of the playoffs by the eventual champion Anaheim Angels, and George Steinbrenner made no secret of what he thought was the cure for putting his club back at the top of the American League East: pitching. Clemens was one of eight possible starters going into spring training, but The Boss also was keenly aware of the attention and exposure Clemens's pursuit of 300 wins would give the Yankee brand.

"I don't want the fanfare to distract what we're doing," Clemens said during an appearance at St. Ephrem School in Brooklyn on January 13, 2003, only weeks after signing a one-year deal for $10.1 million, deferred over 12 years. "We're going to have it, with 300 being crazy enough. But in a way, that's good. That's good to take a little bit of the focus off some of the other guys. But [2002] was another year we did not win and got knocked out early, so we're going to be accountable for that. Our boss is not happy, and we can't be happy or satisfied with that."

He had 299 wins going into a chilly, rainy Memorial Day at the Stadium with the rival Red Sox in town. Clemens had made plans to have family, friends, and former teammates on hand, including his ailing mother, Bess. As drizzle pelted the Bronx, the Clemens contingent pulled up in several black Chevrolet SUVs, with Bess Clemens-Booher helped into a wheelchair by Clemens's sisters. Emphysema had weakened Bess considerably, and Clemens knew that she might not be able to travel around the country if his chase dragged on for weeks.

Before the first pitch that Monday, Clemens's stepsister Bonnie Owens slipped outside the Stadium for a cigarette.

"We're jacked to be here," said Owens. "Against Boston, with my mom feeling good. We're thrilled to be here."

There was no thrill in the outcome. Clemens was pummeled for eight runs on 10 hits in five and a third innings, as the Yankees lost their fifth straight. "Everyone had a great time," Clemens said, referring to his entourage. "It couldn't have worked out better, except for a win."

Clemens's traveling caravan—without Bess—continued across the country as he made a second, then third attempt at notching 300. First stop: Detroit, where a bullpen collapse did in Clemens, even though the Yankees won the game. Then it was on to Wrigley Field, where the Yankees and Cubs met for the first time since the 1938 World Series. Again, a key bullpen mistake torpedoed Clemens, Yankee reliever Juan Acevedo serving up a three-run homer in the 5–2 loss. Clemens had been battling a respiratory infection for a week, but still fought Torre when the manager came out to pull the plug at six and a third innings. After the game, Clemens ducked reporters and issued his remarks in a statement.

"Everything considered, I felt good," Clemens said. "I went long and hard the whole way. It just didn't work out. With the game being close, they just needed one big hit and they got it."

The fourth try came back at the Stadium, with Clemens facing the Cardinals in interleague play. Again, rain fell in the Bronx, as it had on Memorial Day. Debbie Clemens and the four "K" boys were on hand, along with Clemens's sisters and several in-laws, when Clemens finally got his 300th victory. Bess Clemens-Booher was back home in Texas, cheering on her son from more than a thousand miles away.

The 40-year-old Clemens became the 21st pitcher in history to reach the 300-win mark and, as a bonus, recorded his 4,000th strikeout on the same night. His fastball was sizzling and diving, and he lasted six and two-thirds innings before three relievers helped shut the door on the 5–2 Yankee win. Afterward, as Debbie Clemens rushed from her field-level seat to the mound, making her way through the raucous sold-out crowd, the Stadium speakers blared Elton John's "Rocket Man." The four "K" boys crowded into the clubhouse, all of them clutching plastic bags of dirt from the mound.

"It's been a lot of hard work, and it's paid off," he continued at the postgame press conference. "I've been fortunate that I still have my fastball, and I've never wavered from that. I'm a power pitcher, and I enjoy that."

Asked what else he could accomplish by coming back another year, Clemens shot back, "Well, I'm not coming back," breaking up the packed media room. Debbie Clemens, sitting to Clemens's right at the postgame press conference, mouthed, "No, he's not."

The celebration lasted into the early hours of Saturday, June 14, with 20 or so relatives and friends toasting the Rocket over and over again at his Manhattan apartment. The party finally broke up around 3:30 A.M. when Clemens kicked everyone out. Six and a half hours later, Brian McNamee was rapping on Clemens's door. Workout time. The only consolation for Clemens was that Mac took it a little easier that Saturday morning, putting the pitcher through half the normal grind.

As Clemens sat in front of his locker later that day, a horde of reporters scribbled furiously as the newest 300-game pitcher reflected on his future. Clemens said that if he got into Cooperstown, he'd be wearing a Yankee cap. He'd won his two World Series with the Yankees and they were the team he'd gotten to 300 with. How could he go in with a Red Sox cap? Clemens was asked what he would do if the Hall of Fame people tried to tell him otherwise, a question he had been waiting years to answer.

"I've played 20 years," Clemens said. "They're not going to tell me what hat I'm wearing when I get there. There will be a vacant seat. I'll take my mom to Palm Springs, invite y'all, and we'll have our own celebration.

"I love what I did in Boston. But to me, once the decision was made that my services weren't wanted in Boston anymore, I got the opportunity to go to Toronto and had a great two years there. But I became a Hall of Famer here. If I had listened to the people there [Boston] I'd have been done."

Bess Clemens-Booher had talked to her son by phone following the Friday night victory, too ill to attend the event in person.

"I told her I loved her on TV; I knew she'd be watching," Clemens said. "She sounded great. She was pitching every pitch with me."

As Clemens and his entourage toured major league cities in search of his 300th win, baseball was quietly beginning its first season of drug testing, a "survey" program in which players would be tested beginning in spring training and continuing throughout the season. The players were promised the results would trigger no penalties, and would remain confidential and anonymous, with the urine samples destroyed. The new collective bargaining agreement had gone into effect on September 30, 2002, and it was assumed that any player who was using would stop in plenty of time for the tests.

For those who knew what was going on in the game, however, that was a dangerous assumption. Brian McNamee was worried about his famous client, and concerned for himself too. He had kept the vials of steroids and the needles for a reason: He knew that if Clemens went down for drugs, he would take his trainer with him.

McNamee was no longer routinely injecting Clemens with steroids as the season got under way, but he figured the guy had to be using drugs. There was the Ziploc bag Clemens had given him to dispose of at the end of the previous season and, of course, the simple fact that Clemens was still pitching—dominating, in fact. McNamee was concerned that Clemens was going to get busted.

McNamee didn't want to go straight to Clemens, because he didn't want to mess up the pitcher's concentration in the middle of what was supposed to be his final season. Besides, for all of the injecting that went on, McNamee and Clemens never really talked about steroids all that much. But this testing thing was real, so after giving it about a week of thought, McNamee decided to reach out to one of Clemens's representatives with the Hendricks agency.

And so one rainy day early in the season while Clemens was on a road trip, McNamee called Jimmy Murray.

That year—supposedly the last for Clemens—the Hendricks brothers had dispatched a young agent named Jimmy Murray to be Clemens's right-hand man. There was a big media push to document the close of Clemens's historic career, and there would be endless appearances and interviews. Clemens needed a personal secretary. It might seem extravagant for a ballplayer, but it was just another one of those perks of seniority and success.

Murray stayed home while Clemens was on the road trip, so he agreed to slip McNamee into his schedule. Murray lived in Hoboken, New Jersey, and McNamee was in Queens, working with a host of clients around the city. They decided to meet in between, at a location that was easy and familiar enough for each of them: the Starbucks in the lobby of Clemens's building on the Upper East Side, near the corner of 90th Street and First Avenue.

The neighborhood was perfect for someone like Clemens, who could afford to have a base in the city but whose true home was elsewhere. The area might not have had the prestige of some parts of the Upper East Side, but there was easy access to the FDR Drive, an excellent gym at the Asphalt Green sports complex a block away, and some no-fuss restaurants and sports bars. Clemens had even picked up a pretty girl there in the neighborhood—a bartender at a nearby watering hole. Her name was Angela Moyer, and soon she was one of Clemens's regular away-from-home girlfriends.

McNamee got to Starbucks early, took his usual seat, and read the newspapers. He was in sweatpants, and a shirt and hat from Cardillo, a weight-training equipment and apparel company his friend owned. Soon Murray came in, wearing black pants, a blue shirt, and a coat. Murray took out a notepad and McNamee told him everything there was to know about Clemens's steroid use. He told him there was a guy named Kirk on Long Island who got the drugs from doctors. Murray took notes on a yellow legal pad, writing down everything McNamee told him in his tiny handwriting.

Murray didn't seem at all shocked to hear that the greatest pitcher of his generation had been fueled by banned substances during a period in which that pitcher won two Cy Young Awards, two World Series rings, made millions of dollars, and secured a place in the Hall of Fame. "You know, it doesn't surprise me," Murray said. "[Jason] Giambi takes a lot of shit." McNamee asked Murray not to tell the Hendrickses what he'd just heard; McNamee wanted to tell Clemens himself about his concerns. But when Clemens got back from the road trip, McNamee sensed that Clemens was acting a little strange toward him. He started to wonder if Murray had told Clemens about the conversation and confronted Murray.

"You went to the Hendrickses with that stuff," McNamee said to Murray.

"Yeah," Murray answered.

"Did you tell Roger?"

"No," Murray said.

"Did they tell Roger? I bet my last dollar they told him," McNamee said.

"I bet my last dollar they didn't," Murray replied. "Mac, I'm telling you 100 percent that there's no way the Hendrickses told Roger about that conversation we had."

Years later, Murray would be called upon to remember this conversation, and others. He would recall that McNamee brought up drug tests at the Starbucks meeting, and relaying that to his boss, but Murray would struggle to recall the other details.

. . .

As the 2003 season wound down, Roger Clemens was pitching every game as if it were his last—which, in a way, was the case. In August and September, he started making what were billed as his final appearances in the various American League stadiums. Camden Yards, Fenway Park: On every road trip, fans around the country turned out for one more chance to see the legendary Rocket pitch. Clemens received standing ovations from the opposing team's fans—even in Boston.

But because nobody quite knew when the season would end for the Yankees—or where—there was a series of false alarms. His last start at Fenway Park, for instance, turned out to be the second-to-last since the Yankees wound up facing the Red Sox in the playoffs.

His final start came that unforgettable October 22 night in Miami, when the Yankees lost Game 4 to the Florida Marlins. But Yankee manager Joe Torre said that if the series went to seven games, he might see a possibility that Clemens would come out of the bullpen for relief—and yet another final appearance at Yankee Stadium.

But it didn't happen; the Marlins, behind the strong arm of young Texas fastballer Josh Beckett, eliminated the Yankees in Game 6. It was officially over. Clemens walked away from the sport he loved, 41 years old, with 310 wins and a spot all but waiting for him in the Hall of Fame.

Clemens said he was looking forward to playing golf. He said he wanted to try his hand at teaching young people about baseball. He said he was eager to represent his country in the 2004 Olympic Summer Games in Athens. Doing so would mean running a gauntlet of drug tests.

In 2002, an Internal Revenue Service criminal investigator from San Jose, California, heard a rumor about a nearby nutritional supplements company named the Bay Area Laboratory Co-Operative, or BALCO.

The agent, a 6-7 former collegiate basketball player named Jeff Novitzky, was playing pickup basketball with some friends when one of them started talking about BALCO. In addition to providing vitamins and supplements, the lab was also dispensing anabolic steroids to professional athletes. The story was almost too good to be true; the business's founder was the charismatic Victor Conte, a former bassist for the funk band Tower of Power.

Novitzky happened to know that BALCO had a history of tax-related legal problems, and he saw an opening to investigate the company. So began a year of surveillance that included not just e-mail snooping and phone taps but weekly harvests from the lab's Dumpster. Donning thick gloves to protect himself from dirty hypodermics, Novitzky painstakingly figured out what was making BALCO tick.

With the help of a "rogue chemist" in Illinois named Patrick Arnold, Conte had been selling a designer steroid called "the clear," which later became known as tetrahydrogestrinone, or THG. Working secretly with the country's top anti-doping scientist, Don Catlin, Novitzky soon unlocked the most powerful attribute of this powerful steroid: It was undetectable.

By September of 2003, Novitzky had found enough evidence to win authorization from a federal judge to serve a search warrant on BALCO's offices in Burlingame, California. The massive raid took place on September 3, and the rest was sports history.

BALCO blew the lid on the widespread doping that had corrupted American sports. Dozens of athletes were BALCO clients, including Barry Bonds, Marion Jones, Tim Montgomery, Jason Giambi, Dana Stubblefield, and Gary Sheffield. Drawing on the rich trove of evidence Novitzky gathered from the raid—doping calendars, drugs, financial records, and witness statements—federal prosecutors set out to get criminal indictments for Conte and his co-conspirators.

The prosecutors needed a grand jury to approve the indictment, so in the fall of 2003, the feds sent out letters summoning professional athletes to appear before the grand jury and discuss, under oath, what they knew about the clear. If they lied, they could be prosecuted for perjury, which is the roundabout way the crackdown on doping in American sports really began in earnest. Not because the commissioners of the leagues recognized that their sports were losing credibility. Not because athletes were dropping dead from liver damage or overdoses. And not because weak steroid laws were infecting a billion-dollar industry—sports—which sat right at the heart of the nation's culture.

The crackdown began because an IRS agent who happened to love sports found a way to make athletes tell the truth—or face serious consequences if they didn't.

Even at the high point of America's war on drugs, before Islamic terrorism became law enforcement's highest priority, the United States dumped billions of dollars into fighting cocaine and marijuana but still went pretty easy on illegal distributors of steroids and human growth hormone. Throughout the late 1990s, the Drug Enforcement Administration barely seemed to worry about the issue. The obvious explanation for this was that HGH had many more legitimate medical applications than heroin, and steroids didn't seem to be propping up any of the world's hostile regimes—unless you counted the Oakland A's as such.

To this day, the Drug Enforcement Administration categorizes steroids as Schedule III drugs, which means relatively soft penalties for dealing them, relatively few resources for investigating steroid distribution networks, and relatively little glory for the prosecutors who put the kingpins behind bars. All of this was perplexing to the European law enforcement agents, who were the first to see the incentives for cracking down on doping in professional sports; there was plenty of acclaim to be had if the end users of the steroid rings happened to be involved with professional sports.

In 2002, it emerged that a team doctor for the top Italian soccer team Juventus had provided a sophisticated doping regimen to the players. A prosecutor in Turin named Raffaele Guariniello successfully charged the doctor with "sporting fraud." After all, ticket buyers, television broadcasters, and sponsors had all been sold a poor product under false pretenses. In 2006, when Spain's Civil Guard caught the boss of a Tour de France cycling team bringing a cash-filled suitcase to a doctor whose Madrid clinic was stocked with refrigerated bags of blood, the authorities charged that doctor with "offenses against public health." In France, the criminalization of doping led to the common practice of border searches during the major sporting events, revealing that cycling team masseuses and riders' girlfriends were importing drugs in thermoses and wheel wells.

All of this police action spurred European sports and the International Olympic Committee to establish rigid independent anti-doping programs, with frequent, unannounced testing, stiff penalties, and a codified appeals system. It wasn't pretty, but at least the Europeans were facing the problem. One of the easiest reforms was the limits placed on an athlete's entourage; long before Bud Selig banned personal trainers and hangers-on from clubhouses, Olympic sports began restricting access to venues and events.

But until 2003, the United States government showed a relative lack of interest in enforcing laws about performance-enhancing drugs. As the steroid problem grew out of control in professional sports in the late 1990s, the government remained happy to treat doping as an in-house discipline problem best left to the leagues, which were all too happy to watch it fester. Everyone in Major League Baseball who had the power to confront the epidemic that was distorting the game beyond recognition—including team owners, league officials, union bosses, and players—struggled with an inherent conflict of interest; the same people creating and enforcing the anti-doping policies also wanted to minimize bad press for their game. Even the media were in on the scam; soon the home run got its very own nightly celebration on ESPN, each edition of *Baseball Tonight* dedicating a segment to huge home run blasts.

Soon enough, the illegality was so glaring that law enforcement had little choice but to crack down. Even though the Justice Department devoted relatively few resources to breaking up steroid rings, American prosecutors discovered what their European counterparts had found: There was a certain glory available to investigators and prosecutors when the end users of those steroid rings happened to be world-famous, record-setting athletes.

BALCO roiled the sports world for years. While Novitzky chased down leads, assistant U.S. attorneys Matt Parrella and Jeff Nedrow started racking up indictments and guilty pleas of BALCO's primary co-conspirators. Meanwhile suspicion fell on the dozens of prominent athletes and coaches who had been summoned to the U.S. District Court in San Francisco to testify to the grand jury about BALCO.

As more and more of this testimony was leaked to the media—particularly Mark Fainaru-Wada and Lance Williams of the *San Francisco Chronicle*—two things became clear: 1) A lot of prominent sports figures who had denied knowledge of doping in public had been forced to confess under oath, and 2) Some of those sports figures may have made false statements, either before the grand jury or in their interviews with Novitzky and other federal agents.

Under Title 18, United States Code, Section 1001, it is illegal to lie to a federal agent. More specifically, it is illegal to knowingly and willfully make a materially false, fictitious, or fraudulent statement or representation to a federal agent. In effect since 1934, the rule was most famously used to prosecute Martha Stewart.

Following the BALCO raid, Novitzky set off on a mission to tie up the loose ends of his investigation. He was armed, in his interviews, with Section 1001. The law gave him extraordinary powers to ferret out the truth; people who lied to him could face up to five years in prison, and if they refused to talk, their lawyers warned them, they risked receiving a subpoena to appear before a grand jury. Among the sports figures that lied to Novitzky were track star Marion Jones and her coach, Trevor Graham. Both would ultimately be convicted and go to prison. Through Graham, Novitzky found out about a steroid dealer in Texas named Angel Heredia, who was shipping drugs to top sprinters. In putting the screws to Jones and her boyfriend Tim Montgomery, Novitzky stumbled across a check fraud conspiracy.

There were some who criticized Novitzky's methods. Some said he was on a "witch hunt," and others said that it was inappropriate for a tax man to be busting dopers (Novitzky's answer: Drug dealing almost always went hand in hand with money laundering). But in the end the criticism did nothing to deter the agent. The high-profile BALCO bust had made him one of the stars of federal law enforcement, and even President George W. Bush signaled his approval in January of 2004, when he referred to steroids in the State of the Union speech:

> To help children make right choices, they'll need good examples.
>
> Athletics play such an important role in our society, but, unfortunately, some in professional sports are not setting much of an example. The use of performance-enhancing drugs like steroids in baseball, football, and other sports is dangerous, and it sends the wrong message—that there are shortcuts to accomplishment, and that performance is more important than character. So tonight I call on team owners, union representatives, coaches, and players to take the lead, to send the right signal, to get tough, and to get rid of steroids now.

With that kind of implicit endorsement, and with the public outcry over the corruption in American sports reaching its fever pitch, Novitzky had all the license he needed to pursue new targets. It wasn't long before he'd set his sights on the black market feeding steroids into the clubhouses of Major League Baseball.

Had Roger Clemens known about this, he might have rethought his decision, late in 2003, to return to baseball after a brief retirement.

CHAPTER SEVEN

2004

In the winter of 2003, the billionaire owner of the Houston Astros, Drayton McLane, decided he wanted his team to have a World Series championship to go with its beautiful and ultramodern three-year-old stadium, Minute Maid Park (formerly named Enron Field).

In late November, just a month after Clemens had made his emotional farewell from baseball at the World Series in Tampa, a Houston television station broke the news that Andy Pettitte and his agents were in conversations with McLane. The Astros probably couldn't match the $11.5 million the Yankees paid Pettitte in 2003, but McLane could dangle a carrot that George Steinbrenner couldn't: a 20-minute commute from the clubhouse to Deer Park, the town where Andy and Laura Pettitte had grown up and were raising their family.

The Pettitte deal became official on December 16. He would earn $31 million over a three-year period, at the end of which he would be 34 years old. The signing set off a tremendous celebration in Deer Park—particularly at Central Baptist Church. Businesses in town saluted the homecoming with homemade signs—"Congratulations, Andy," "Fire It Up, Andy," "Welcome Home, Andy." People around the area delighted in seeing the big league hero filling his tank at the gas station or sitting in the bleachers watching a Little League game.

But that was only a prelude to the big wet kiss McLane was about to plant on Astros fans. Roger Clemens, it turned out, was too restless for retirement. Despite all the pomp and circumstance surrounding his farewell in 2003—or who knows, perhaps because of it—Clemens couldn't pull himself away from the Big Show. And so the Rocket reentered, one month after Pettitte's signing, his retirement having lasted 78 days. After a tedious dance with the Hendricks brothers, the Astros announced that they had signed Clemens to a one-year contract for $5 million.

It was a unique deal, with perks that perhaps only a player of Clemens's age and stature could demand. He would be allowed to skip road series in which he wasn't scheduled to pitch, so he could stay home with his family or jet away on a quick fishing trip. (His eldest son, Koby, was now a junior at Memorial High School in Houston, a standout in football and baseball, and only a year from being drafted by the Astros.) McLane sought the approval of the team's clubhouse leaders before moving forward with the deal. Craig Biggio and Jeff Bagwell assented.

Bagwell was quoted later in a *Newsday* article agreeing with McLane's reasoning: "The bottom line was: 'Are we a better team with Roger Clemens?' You can answer that yourself. It would have been different if he was a free agent [looking to make the best deal]. But he had already retired. This was a special situation for a special player."

The contract also contained incentives. Part of Clemens's salary would be based on attendance—and plenty of fair-weather Astros fans were sure to show up for the games. For the last decade, Clemens and Pettitte had been two of the most successful pitchers in the game, but they had been stuck in the American League, and rarely made in-season trips to the area where they had grown up.

Now there was talk of the Astros finally winning a World Series. The team was stacked. Even before the acquisition of Pettitte and Clemens, the starting rotation featured young guns Roy Oswalt and Wade Miller. The offense was anchored by rising star Lance Berkman and future Hall of Fame candidates Bagwell, Biggio, and Jeff Kent.

But it was Clemens who was the center of attention. Right from the very first day of spring training, he asserted himself as the alpha male on his new team, and an observant one at that. Walking onto one of the practice fields, he informed the team's groundskeeper that home plate was "off center."

The groundskeeper scoffed at the claim. "No it's not," he said. "We just did it. We [aligned it] with a laser."

Clemens persisted. "You need to fix it," he said.

The groundskeeper double-checked, and sure enough, home plate was off to one side by a quarter of an inch. That was how *Sports Illustrated* writer Tom Verducci retold the story in 2005, using the anecdote to demonstrate Clemens's "jeweler's eye for detail" and how "his body works in concert with the baseball." Verducci heard the tale from the Astros manager, but a few who read about the scene would notice that it was a baseball variation on a similar legend put forward by John McPhee in the classic 1965 essay about basketball star and future senator Bill Bradley.

In that tale, Bradley notices that a hoop is one and one-eighth inches too low.

The mythmaking had resumed in high style, and while everyone wondered how a 41-year-old man was able to throw a baseball faster than most 30-year-olds, few would spoil the fun with talk of steroids.

Andy Pettitte's return to Houston was about more than just the hero's welcome. His father was ill, and part of what drew Pettitte home was the desire to spend more time with Tom Pettitte. Throughout Andy's childhood, Tom Pettitte made a lot of sacrifices as he raised a boy who wanted to be a great pitcher like his idol, Roger Clemens. The father had seen Andy through Little League and high school ball, all the way to the New York Yankees. But just as Andy began making his mark on the game, his father had become seriously ill. In October of 1998, Tom Pettitte had open heart surgery in Houston, while his son was pitching in the World Series. Andy had rushed home to be with his dad for the surgery, just days before he would help the Yankees to a sweep of the Padres. "When I left, he was still in ICU," Andy told reporters covering the Series. "And he had tubes in him and stuff like that, so he could barely talk to me. He always talked about baseball. He told me not to worry about him; he's going to be fine."

The surgery worked, but the elder Pettitte remained in bad health, and as Andy's star continued to rise, his father's health worsened. The open heart surgery had left him with nine stents in his heart. Once a month, it seemed to Andy, the ambulance came to pick Tom Pettitte up at his home in Deer Park. From the age of 48, he'd been on disability. Being out of work made him depressed, even suicidal. It didn't help that he had to get shoulder surgery as well—twice, in 2001 and 2003.

Like millions of other people suffering from chronic aches and illnesses, Tom Pettitte was fed up with the doctors and specialists who couldn't make him whole again. Snake-oil salesmen have taken advantage of those who suffer for centuries, offering "natural" products that the medical establishment eschews, and Tom Pettitte was one of the Americans who had grown suspicious of traditional medicine. He didn't need the government to tell him how to take care of himself, and he felt so bad he was willing to consider just about anything, including a controversial alternative medicine treatment called chelation therapy, in which patients are led to believe that they are alleviating heart disease by removing heavy metals from their bloodstream. Patients are injected with the organic compound ethylenediaminetetraacetic acid, or EDTA, which was first synthesized in Germany in the 1930s. The EDTA has a special "clawlike" structure ("chele" is Greek for claw) that binds divalent and trivalent metallic ions. For this reason, legitimate doctors sometimes administered chelation therapy for lead poisoning. But using chelation on patients as a remedy for heart disease had been widely discredited. The American Heart Association and the FDA cautioned that its benefits were scientifically unproven, and the American College of Physicians warned that it could lead to severe kidney problems.

Chelation therapy was expensive. Medicare and most insurance companies would not pay for the treatment so when Tom Pettitte received the therapy for about eight months, his son paid for it.

Although Clemens had been born in Dayton, Ohio, there was no question that the Lone Star State was his home—the place where he learned the game that gave him everything he had. Nearly 30 years earlier, a teen-aged Clemens enrolled at Spring Woods High School, which had one of the best baseball programs in the Houston area. His brother Randy had taken charge of Roger's burgeoning baseball career, making sure his kid brother got the right coaching and faced challenging competition. At Spring Woods, Clemens also played center on the basketball team and defensive end for the football team. Spring Woods baseball coach Charlie Maiorana had no idea he had a budding star in his ranks—he would later confess that, to him, Clemens was an oversize kid with fat cheeks. But Maiorana does remember Clemens as an extraordinarily intense competitor.

"A lot of kids, you have to stay on top of to keep them focused; not Roger," Maiorana, who coached at Spring Woods for 33 years, was quoted as saying in a 2000 article about Clemens in *Texas Monthly*. "He didn't say much, but you could tell he was deeply motivated to accomplish things. He did his work every day without fail, wore his uniform proudly, and on the mound, never gave in to a single hitter. Not a single one while I had him."

It was during those years that Clemens developed his deep commitment to fitness and conditioning, thanks to a daily ritual he called "draining himself." Perhaps it was a response to his status as a have-not—while other kids drove slick new cars, Clemens couldn't afford even a used vehicle, so he ran to and from school every day with a knapsack full of books on his back. When other kids were partying on the weekends, Clemens was running laps. By his senior year, he had established himself as the best pitcher on Spring Woods's staff.

Nolan Ryan, then 35, joined the Houston Astros, and Clemens tried to go to the Astrodome every time he pitched, sneaking down to watch him warm up. He started adopting some of Ryan's signature moves. "That's why Roger yells at hitters," Maiorana told *Texas Monthly*. "He got that from Nolan."

Clemens wasn't impressed with the college scholarship offers he received—he was 13-5 in his senior year and he struck out 18 batters in one game. His mother, Bess, and Randy urged him to get some seasoning close to home, at San Jacinto College. Clemens blossomed under coach Wayne Graham. He grew two inches, going from 6-2 to 6-4, and his body hardened and filled out. Clemens always had great control, and for the first time in his life, he was blowing the ball past opponents. "Graham calls that period in my baseball life a crossroads," Clemens wrote in his autobiography, "and I was clearly on the right road."

Pettitte had pitched for San Jac too. A decade after Clemens, it was Pettitte who, under the tutelage of Wayne Graham, had developed into major league material. At nearby Deer Park High School, Pettitte had been good, but under Graham he became great, reportedly increasing the velocity of his throws from about 78 to 80 miles per hour to the low 90s.

"He's the one who made me realize how important fitness is," Pettitte said in a 2001 *New York Times* article about the day that Graham visited his former protégés in New York, took a tour of Yankee Stadium, and marveled at how much their physiques had changed. Clemens and Pettitte had gotten big.

Everyone in Houston knew that Pettitte and Clemens were going to be liabilities on offense for the Astros. They had spent their careers in the American League, where designated hitters replace pitchers in the lineup. Until that spring, Pettitte had been to the plate only 28 times in his nine-year career—during interleague games and the World Series. Clemens was expected to have bigger problems at the plate than Pettitte; he was a decade further removed from his college days, and as baseball's most famous headhunter, he was now coming to a league where he would be held accountable. The opposing team could retaliate against him if he threw hard at the skulls of their teammates.

But just when the season got under way, it was Pettitte who flinched the second he picked up a bat. Stepping into the box on April 6, 2004, Pettitte had second thoughts about a pitch and checked his swing. As he did so, he felt something release in his chronically painful left elbow. An MRI two days later showed inflammation in the joint, and a strain of the flexor tendon. Pettitte got a cortisone shot on April 11, and went on the disabled list. He managed to come back to the mound, but the pain was so bad that Clemens, watching from the dugout, could barely stand to watch his friend on the field. The pain was apparent on Pettitte's face. He would return to the disabled list again in May and once more in August.

The Astros had started the season strong, but despite all that talent, they fell apart, eventually trailing the St. Louis Cardinals by 11 games in the National League Central. Wade Miller suffered a rotator cuff injury and was out for the season after 15 starts. Jeff Bagwell struggled through the worst slump of his life. General manager Gerry Hunsicker fired laid-back manager Jimmy Williams, replacing him with hotheaded Phil Garner.

By late July, in his intermittent starts, Pettitte had cobbled together a 6-4 record and 3.90 ERA, but his fastball had dropped from 93 mph to the mid-80s, and the word had gotten out that he was vulnerable. Still he pushed on. Even as his teammates and team officials recommended he shut it down, Pettitte refused; he was making way too much money, he felt, to just ride the bench.

But Pettitte wasn't along for the ride. By mid-August he had pushed his elbow just as far as it would go, and in a bullpen session on August 16 things started to feel really weird. Tests revealed that the tendon was torn, and Pettitte would need surgery. "I'm in unfamiliar territory," he told reporters in a conference call, announcing that the famed baseball surgeon Dr. James Andrews would operate on him August 24.

Pettitte traveled to Birmingham, Alabama, for the surgery. The Astros' medical director, Dr. David Lintner, accompanied him in order to help Andrews take a knife to the team's treasured hired gun. Tom Pettitte was along for the trip too. Andy was nervous—he'd never been under a general anesthetic before, never been put to sleep. He wanted his dad to tell him it would be okay.

"Everyone gets scared," Tom Pettitte told his son. That was all Andy needed to hear. Just a simple reassurance from the man who had been through so much more than a simple anesthetic, the man whose heart had been stopped and a ventilator tube shoved down his throat while doctors reconfigured his arteries, the man Andy couldn't imagine losing.

Andrews and Lintner found that scar tissue had built up around the injured area near the tear, and cleaned that out before repairing the rip in the flexor tendon.

. . .

Given the level of desperation Tom Pettitte felt about his health, and his willingness to experiment with alternative medicine, perhaps it wasn't much of a leap for him to dip into the black market and try the drug that was being described from Hollywood to the major leagues as a miracle cure: human growth hormone.

In 2004, as his son was struggling with elbow pain, Tom Pettitte was using HGH. He picked it up in a gym not far from his home. Conventional medicine wasn't helping him, and neither was the chelation therapy, and he was willing to try just about anything to feel good again. The gym was 1-on-1 Elite Personal Fitness, its owner a former high school football player named Kelly Blair. For years, Blair had bragged to associates about supplying athletes with muscle-building drugs. He bought steroids and human growth hormone, used a little for himself and sold the rest.

Everyone in this area loved to say they knew Andy Pettitte, but Blair had a real connection: He was related to Pettitte through marriage. Blair's older sister, Michelle, had married Jason Dunn, part of the Dunn clan that ran Deer Park's Central Baptist Church. Jason's baby sister was Laura Dunn, Pettitte's wife.

Blair and Pettitte had known each other since they were kids growing up in Deer Park—Pettitte the unassuming alto in the Central Baptist choir, and Blair the hulking party boy with the strong, slightly nasal Texas twang and, in time, tribal tattoos stretching across his broad upper back. However different in style they might be, they were family. In the gym, Kelly kept a prized photo that showed him standing next to Pettitte inside 1-on-1 Elite, a little kid sitting in between them.

When he learned his father was using HGH, Andy Pettitte found himself in a difficult position. He had used the drug himself, and it was not yet banned by baseball. He knew what Brian McNamee had told him years before—that it could repair tissue. But he also knew the Astros trainer had told him it might accelerate disease, especially cancer, and he worried about his father's fragile state. But by July of that year, Andy Pettitte was facing other types of pressure. With his elbow falling apart and the possibility of season-ending surgery looming on the horizon, the pitcher was getting desperate. An entire city—his hometown—was counting on him to help bring the Astros to the postseason, and here he was with a deteriorating elbow.

So Andy Pettitte did what he often did when he ran into trouble: He turned to his dad, asked him if he still had any of the HGH he'd had before. Tom Pettitte said he did and brought two syringes over to his son's house. Andy did something McNamee had done for him in 2002—he injected himself with the drug, once in the morning and once at night. It didn't make a whole lot of sense—Pettitte knew the drug probably wasn't going to help him. His flexor tendon was already ripped. He knew he needed surgery. It was just that this time the drug wasn't coming from the Radomski-McNamee pipeline, it was coming from his dad, and 1-on-1 Elite Fitness in Pasadena, Texas.

Pasadena is the largest incorporated suburb of Houston, the nation's fourth-largest city as well as one of its fastest-growing, adding nearly a million people to its census rolls in the 1990s alone. The boom was reflected in the layout of Pasadena, where unbridled consumerism combined with the population explosion had created a city with no discernible center, an endless string of box stores, subdivisions, and concrete highway extensions lined by strip malls. Churches and strip clubs rub elbows along service roads and boulevards. Every fast food chain that has ever existed seems to have at least one franchise in Pasadena. Its first claim to fame is that the city was home to Gilley's, the enormous honky-tonk opened by country singer Mickey Gilley and featured in *Urban Cowboy*, the John Travolta–Debra Winger fucking-and-fighting flick that was a box office hit in 1980.

Pasadena and neighboring Deer Park call themselves the birthplace of Texas because the final battle of the Texas Revolution, which created the independent Lone Star State from a chunk of Mexico, occurred in the area in 1836. Nearly 200 years later, Pasadena was still making news because of gunplay: In 2007, a 61-year-old retiree named Joe Horn shot two men as they were breaking into a neighbor's home, sparking a national debate about self-defense and gun control (the shots were recorded on a 911 call). Pasadena was also part of the congressional district represented by onetime exterminator Tom DeLay, the born-again Christian whose hammer-swinging political tactics as House majority leader kept his fellow Republicans in line and Democrats at bay until he was indicted on conspiracy charges in 2005. DeLay resigned from his leadership post shortly after the indictment, and stepped down from his congressional seat the following year.

There are plenty of gyms in Pasadena too, a logical complement to the fast food joints and strip clubs. There are dozens of choices—karate gyms, yoga gyms, round-the-clock gyms, and gyms for stay-at-home moms. But for hard-core meatheads—guys who weren't afraid of injecting the juice to get big and ripped—there was only one logical choice: 1-on-1 Elite Personal Fitness, owned by Kelly Blair.

From the moment it opened in 2003, Blair's shop was the scene of power-lifting competitions. Heavy metal music blared from the speakers, and customers came by in jacked-up pickup trucks and long-forked choppers to do dead lifts and bench presses. Housewives and high school kids alike signed up for his military-style "boot camp" workouts on the weekends. Among Blair's trainers was Melody Manlove, a fitness model whose father, John Manlove, resigned from the mayorship of Pasadena to run for the Republican nomination for the congressional seat vacated by DeLay. (Manlove lost.)

From the beginning, Blair had somehow been able to draw professional athletes from around the country. A lot of them. When this happened, Blair never missed the opportunity to get a picture taken with them. Blair's office at the gym was wallpapered with pictures showing him standing next to the pros. Blair loved to brag about his connections to professional jocks, and he loved to brag about his role in their success. Mainly, he just loved to brag, even though many of the athletes he knew were on the pro sports B-list. One of the guys Blair posed with was former NFL quarterback Chuck Clements, who had played for the Jets and Eagles. Clements's entire career experience on the field had taken place in a single regular season game in 1997, a blowout in which Clements came on the field in the final two minutes and earned a career total of three negative yards. Professional golfer Mike Standly was on Blair's wall, along with Javier Bracamonte, who wasn't even a player: He was the bullpen catcher for the Astros. Donnie Elliott—perhaps the best baseball player to come out of Deer Park not named Pettitte—had played 35 innings of major league ball. He was on the wall. Richard Hidalgo, a baseball player for the Astros who had jumped from 15 home runs in 1999 to 44 in 2000, was there too.

Nearby Deer Park was an upgrade over Pasadena, an oasis of community pride on the edge of the vast network of gleaming, steaming oil refineries that line the Houston Ship Channel. Refineries, shipping-related firms, and petrochemical companies are the town's main employers, along with NASA's nearby Lyndon B. Johnson Space Center. On summer evenings the workers return to their tight-knit community and watch Astros baseball games on television, or attend Little League games in the town's manicured parks.

Both Pettitte and Blair were into sports during their overlapping years at Deer Park High School in the 1980s, and then each moved on to chase his personal athletic dream. The two men took vastly different paths, but their fates remained intertwined—in part because of the family connection. This tenuous family tie between the two men—the pitcher and the pusher—proved to be a critical one, linking a highly paid member of the Yankees' starting rotation to an underground steroid network.

Around the time that Andy Pettitte married Laura Dunn, Kelly Blair found love with Chelsi Smith, one of the most beautiful girls at Deer Park High School. "Guys wouldn't ask her out because she was black," Blair told *People* in 1995. "We lived in a major redneck town." Smith was biracial, born to a black man and a white woman—both 19 years old—in Redwood City, California. Her parents divorced before she was two years old, and her mother, struggling with alcoholism, signed over custody of Chelsi to her grandparents. When Smith was seven, her grandparents moved to Texas and then they divorced as well.

After graduating from Deer Park, Chelsi entered the Miss Houston pageant and finished as the runner-up. She began taking elementary education classes at San Jacinto College—the community college where Andy Pettitte was taking the mound—and then won the Miss Texas title. With her boyfriend, Blair, supporting her along the way, she entered Miss USA and won, bringing in more than $200,000 in cash and prizes. Soon she was engaged to Blair, who at the time was majoring in kinesiology at the University of Houston and coaching weightlifting there on the side, under the tutelage of John Lott, who would go on to serve as a strength and conditioning coach for the New York Jets, Cleveland Browns, and Arizona Cardinals. Kelly and Chelsi moved together to California, where Chelsi pursued acting and singing gigs and Blair trained a professional athlete for the first time: overweight NBA center Kevin Duckworth.

In 1995, Chelsi joined 80 other young women in traveling to Windhoek, Namibia, to compete for the Miss Universe title, where she came away as the first American winner of the pageant in 15 years (Kelly was there in the audience, looking enormous in his tuxedo). On December 28, 1996, the couple got married. Blair was 26, and Chelsi—who took his name—was 23. They came back from Africa to live in Hollywood, where Chelsi pursued acting gigs.

By that point, Pettitte was meeting his destiny with the Yankees, emerging as a reliable ace beloved by fans for his steely resolve on the mound and his mellow affability in the clubhouse. But the good times didn't last long for the Blairs. After living together in Los Angeles, their marriage fell apart acrimoniously—Smith finally left the courthouse, her fortunes depleted but her divorce officially complete, on September 11, 2001. By then, Blair had moved back to the Deer Park area, where he worked in gyms as a personal trainer and bought and sold steroids.

Blair felt limited working for others. There was not a lot he could teach his clients in someone else's gym. So in 2003, he opened his place a few miles away at a strip mall at 6005 Fairmont Parkway in Pasadena. Most of the customers were previous clients and referrals. The gym would specialize in customized weight training programs. Blair's father, who was backing the business, cut a lot of the checks for the trainers. It was a place for hard-core weightlifters. Cops and strippers made up a large part of the clientele.

When the gym launched a Web site, Blair's collection of client photos moved online. There was Kelly Blair, standing alongside Major League Baseball players like Pedro Borbon, Eric DuBose, Danny Bautista, J. C. Romero, Hector Carrasco, and Kelvim Escobar. There was also a picture of Blair with the ferocious Chuck Liddell, the star of the ultraviolent Ultimate Fighting Championships. Mixed martial arts, or MMA, was a new sport and a new scene, and Blair liked it. If you went to Vegas to watch a fight and you knew the right people, you might get into the after-parties where it wasn't uncommon to see the fighters themselves show up, just hours after leaving the cage fight bloodied and dizzy.

One of the primary sources for the performance-enhancing drugs that moved through 1-on-1 Elite was an old bodybuilding associate of Kelly Blair's named Craig Titus. The hulking Titus moved from Michigan to the Houston area in the late 1980s, working out in gyms and using massive amounts of steroids as he tried to get his bodybuilding career off the ground. Soon he found success in competitions, flexing his increasingly freakish muscles for judges and magazine photographers. It was in those years that he first met Kelly Blair; they'd met at the World Gym, where Titus worked for a while when he was still an amateur bodybuilder.

In order to finance his career, Titus had begun selling MDMA, the designer party drug most commonly known as ecstasy. And so it was that in September of 1994, Titus was 29 years old and an established star in the bodybuilding world when he got nabbed for drug distribution. Federal authorities intercepted an express mail package Titus had sent from his home in Houston to a Louisiana man named Walter Pellerin. The package included hundreds of ecstasy tablets in a plastic bag that had Titus's fingerprints on it.

Titus later testified that he had met Pellerin at a bodybuilding show and expected Pellerin to send him the anabolic steroid Winstrol as a trade for the ecstasy. Titus cooperated with the feds, ratting out some of his drug-dealing associates and reportedly setting up a buy that sent one of his old friends to prison. Indicted on December 13, 1994, Titus pleaded guilty to a count of conspiracy to possess with intent to distribute. He received an eight-month prison sentence to be followed by eight months of home confinement and three years of probation. A condition of Titus's probation was drug testing.

In professional sports, anti-doping labs detect testosterone abuse by measuring the ratio of testosterone to epitestosterone, which is normally a level one to one. To accommodate anomalies, the legal T/E ratio for Olympic sports is four to one, a gap that when violated is a pretty sure sign of testosterone use. In 2006, Floyd Landis lost his Tour de France title when his T/E ratio suddenly spiked to an unseemly 11/1. "You'd think he'd be violating every virgin within 100 miles," cracked World Anti-Doping Agency president Dick Pound after the test came back. "How does he even get on his bicycle?"

In the fall of 1996, a court-mandated urine test showed that Titus had a T/E ratio of 50/1, and subsequent tests showed traces of the steroids boldenone, Winstrol, and methandienone had been in Titus's system over a period of months. Titus was summoned to court for violating his parole, and there he and his attorney claimed that the positive tests had been triggered by deep-tissue massage. Titus testified that years of repeated steroid injections—six to eight cc's of steroids a day—had caused scar tissue to grow at injection sites all over his 270-pound body. Cysts formed at the sites, Titus said, and they were bursting open during massages, releasing the stored-up chemicals into his system.

The judge listened to the testimony, but ruled against Titus and sent him to Lompoc Penitentiary, a prison full of gangs 175 miles north of Los Angeles. Craig Titus was released from Lompoc in 1998.

Nearly eight years would pass after his release before Titus was arrested for the murder of Melissa James, his live-in assistant. During that time, Titus would make a comeback in professional bodybuilding, and resume dealing drugs through the mail. Some of the steroids he shipped around the country would find their way into 1-on-1 Elite Personal Fitness— where Tom Pettitte went to get the HGH that he eventually shared with his son Andy.

And so the violent criminal underworld of muscle-building drug distribution would find its intersection (in Pasadena, Texas, of all places) with the glamorous, public world of professional sportsmen. Craig Titus and Roger Clemens, two vastly different men who had taken bold and even reckless shortcuts to achieve their vastly different athletic dreams, would be separated by just a few degrees—by a secret handshake between a washed-up high school jock and an ailing father who would do just about anything to help his son.

But the secrecy wouldn't last forever. Given the brazenness of doping in baseball, the relative leniency that the federal government showed in enforcing steroid laws, and the insecurity that drove Kelly Blair to brag about his connections to pro sports, perhaps it's unsurprising that the Titus-Blair-Pettitte connection didn't stay entirely secret in Pasadena.

One day, in the years following Clemens's return to the Astros, Sammy Woodrow,* an associate of Kelly Blair's, dropped by 1-on-1 Elite and found Blair in the back office preparing a huge CARE package of drugs. Blair was placing the drugs in a milk carton. The box was divided into three compartments, each compartment containing a different collection of drugs. Blair was moving back and forth between the refrigerator and another box, putting the collection together. Sammy's eyes nearly popped out of his head. He knew that Blair himself was a steroid user, and that Kelly and his friends dealt the drugs a lot too—gathering them from Mexico, Canada, and AIDS patients around Texas. But he was amazed at the sheer amount of stuff being handled.

"Hey, is this stuff for sale?" Sammy asked.

"No," said Blair. Then he mentioned the names of three famous baseball players to whom he was shipping them. Two of them were Roger Clemens and Andy Pettitte.

Many years later, Blair would deny providing performance-enhancing drugs to athletes, but would admit he did deal them. Perhaps he knew that too many people knew. For instance, even today there is a man who lives in Houston who quietly goes about the business of selling used cars, tries to stay out of trouble, and nurses a severe grudge. The man did six years in federal prisons because Craig Titus pinned a steroid distribution rap on him to curry favor with federal prosecutors. The man was arrested and charged with distributing Deca-Durabolin, testosterone, and Anadrol, as well as fluoxymesterone, a relatively rare and extremely potent oral steroid that bodybuilders use to look more cut before shows. After lengthy negoti-

* The real name of this source has been changed.

ations through a third party, the man met with a reporter in early 2008 and talked about Houston's steroid underworld while driving around the same Houston neighborhoods where he and Titus used to sell their wares.

"I didn't talk then," says the man, who was offered an opportunity by prosecutors to rat on his associates in exchange for leniency. "I haven't talked at all, except for this."

The man described the network of gyms and trainers where he and Titus bought and sold anabolic steroids and human growth hormone. The drugs came from Canada and Mexico, but also from doctors whom the trainers knew to be liberal with prescriptions—including some who are still practicing medicine in Houston.

"They all traded back and forth," he says. "If you need some GH, I've got some Deca-Durabolin, that kind of thing." The Drug Enforcement Administration soon caught wind of the little industry, and undercover agents infiltrated the social circles Titus and the man moved in. An agent got cozy with Titus and the man, joining them in the gyms while they worked out and at the strip clubs where they hung out. After his release from jail, the steroid dealer worked as a private security contractor in Iraq and Afghanistan before settling into legitimate business in Houston. He often sees many of the trainers and dealers he knew before his sentence. Others, he says, have died.

One of the names he recalls being a contact of Titus's in Pasadena, Texas, was Kelly Blair.

On his visits to Houston, McNamee had come to know and respect Tom Pettitte, who was, like McNamee's own father, a former cop. McNamee respected Tom Pettitte tremendously and was concerned for his health. McNamee also knew that Tom Pettitte would do anything to get better, maybe even take some risks with medical treatment.

But McNamee was thrown for a loop when Tom Pettitte told him that he was using HGH for his heart, and had gotten it from a trainer friend at the gym near his house. McNamee was shocked, and worried that Tom Pettitte might even be getting it from back-alley channels in Mexico. He warned Tom that he could get himself in trouble, and he was the one who told Andy that his father was using the drug.

By 2004, McNamee was still working with Pettitte and Clemens, even though he wasn't injecting either one of them. On his trips to Houston, he would often lead them through workouts at Clemens's house, and stay in their homes. And although he felt he could still confide in Pettitte on personal matters, McNamee felt a wedge being driven between him and his clients, mostly courtesy of the two pitchers' agents, Randy and Alan Hendricks.

McNamee recalled a party in that period where Randy Hendricks approached McNamee in a hallway. McNamee was sitting on a chair against the wall, removed from the din of the guests, his typical behavior in social situations. McNamee thought it was odd that the powerful agent was carrying around a can of soda. A fancy party and Hendricks was drinking out of a Coke can? McNamee was nervous enough being in such close proximity to Hendricks, and was still leery about the fallout from the meeting with Murray in 2003. That exchange, McNamee was sure, was the reason that any semblance of a relationship with the Hendrickses was fast going down the toilet.

"We don't have enemies, because we bury them all," Hendricks told McNamee in that hallway. "We never lose."

McNamee had already had a nasty exchange with Clemens and the Hendricks brothers over photos showing McNamee with his two famous clients in an ad for a vitamin company called InVite, a humiliating incident that he couldn't get out of his head. McNamee was working for InVite as a consultant—he'd intended the InVite project to be only a means for new work opportunities outside baseball—and the company had run the ad in a promotional magazine, identifying him as a member of its Scientific Advisory Board. "Dr. Brian McNamee's dynamic physical performance program has been profiled nationally," the advertisement read. Identifying McNamee as a former strength and conditioning coach for the Yankees, the text said he was widely recognized for his work with Clemens, Pettitte, Jorge Posada, Mike Stanton, and many other star athletes. "These major league players rely heavily on Dr. McNamee's program to keep them injury free while performing at the highest level."

Debbie Clemens had spotted the ad and thrown a fit: She felt Roger should be paid for the use of his photograph and the Hendricks brothers agreed, demanding $300,000. On a plane trip back to Houston, where Pettitte and Clemens were with the Hendrickses, Clemens had continued to gripe about being compensated. "They gotta pay us," Clemens fumed. Pettitte sat in the back of the plane and tried to ignore the commotion. He didn't want any money from McNamee or InVite. He liked using their vitamins. But the matter didn't end there. To further exacerbate matters, McNamee had referred to himself as "Dr. Brian McNamee, Ph.D." in the InVite ads. It would later be revealed that the correspondence college from which McNamee had gotten his "doctorate" would be discredited as a diploma mill that now operates out of Mississippi after being shut down in Louisiana, but McNamee had completed all the course work and believed he had a legitimate degree. Clemens wasn't buying the Ph.D., though, and lashed out at McNamee, demanding to see proof that he'd earned his doctorate.

"So what—you're a doctor now?" Clemens derisively asked McNamee in a text message before demanding that he fax all his transcripts—undergrad and graduate—to Clemens, so the Rocket could pass them on to the Hendrickses. McNamee had faxed him the transcripts, including the one reflecting the Ph.D. from Columbus University in Louisiana, the diploma mill.

"Right," Clemens responded. "Got it. Good."

McNamee never heard much about it again but he'd seen firsthand how Clemens reacted when he, or those around him, thought his livelihood might be threatened.

And after the 2004 season, the value of Roger Clemens was higher than ever. In his first season in the National League, Clemens had been able to compile an 18-4 record with a 2.98 ERA and 218 strikeouts. When it was over, he had a record seventh Cy Young Award.

With those kinds of numbers, Clemens had energized the Astros' fan base, and the Hendricks brothers were able to demand a lot. If Drayton McLane declined to meet their terms, Clemens could just walk away from the game.

The Astros had turned their 2004 season around at the end, ultimately squeaking past Barry Bonds and the San Francisco Giants for the National League wild card. But Carlos Beltran had departed for the New York Mets after the season, and Houston was in need of another big name on the roster, or else they might revert to their small-time status. Attendance at Minute Maid Park had exploded from 2.4 million in 2003 to 3.08 million in 2004, and season ticket sales climbed from 15,000 to 20,000. Attendance spiked on the days Clemens pitched.

And so after weeks of negotiations, during which Clemens visited Japan and vacationed with his family in Hawaii, the Hendricks brothers landed a whopper of a contract. In January of 2005, Clemens signed with the Astros for $18 million, the highest salary ever paid to a pitcher in the history of baseball. He was 42 years old.

CHAPTER EIGHT

2005

By January of 2005, reporters all over the country were starting to hear rumblings about a Jose Canseco steroid book. Canseco was promising to lay it all out, names and places included. The publisher should have known these were stories too juicy to remain secret until the book was ready for bookstores. But HarperCollins and its lawyers were surprised and angry when, weeks before the book was due for release, the New York *Daily News* published a story telling readers what was coming in *Juiced: Wild Times, Rampant 'Roids, Smash Hits, and How Baseball Got Big.*

On February 5, the paper ran a front-page story entitled "Steroid Firestorm, Explosive Book Rocks Baseball." Sources had verified the contents of the book and those named were given the chance to respond. One of the most explosive claims in *Juiced* involved Mark McGwire.

"You've never seen Jose Canseco like this: huddled in a bathroom stall at the Oakland Coliseum, jabbing a hypodermic needle into Mark McGwire's bare behind," the *Daily News* story began. "Or McGwire and a young Jason Giambi heading into the men's room to inject each other with the anabolic steroids that would turn them from lanky lads into musclebound behemoths."

The book described both scenes and much more: Canseco claimed to have injected some of the most prominent names in baseball, including All-Stars Rafael Palmeiro, Juan Gonzalez, and Ivan "Pudge" Rodriguez, with performance-enhancing drugs. He told of a Wild West culture in which steroid use ran rampant through baseball. Canseco claimed he was almost solely responsible for spreading steroids through the sport during the 1990s, but he expressed no regrets in the book. He predicted that steroids and human growth hormone would eventually be decriminalized and help people lead longer, healthier, and sexier lives.

"If the book is a confessional, Canseco isn't seeking redemption," the story said. " 'Juiced' is a love letter to the clear liquids that turned him from a struggling skinny prospect to one of the biggest names in the game."

The story shook up the sports world, and prompted HarperCollins to speed up the book's release date by a week, to Monday, February 21. The CBS program *60 Minutes* rushed Mike Wallace's interview with Canseco onto the air the day before the book came out.

There were few factual challenges to the doping allegations Canseco laid out in *Juiced*, and the only assertion that eventually withered under further scrutiny was his strange claim that Roger Clemens was one of the very few baseball players who never cheated on his wife. But in the weeks that followed the release of *Juiced* the denials from the various characters in the book fell like fat raindrops.

First came McGwire. "Once and for all . . . I did not use steroids or any other illegal substance," he said in a statement.

Then came Rafael Palmeiro.

I categorically deny any assertion made by Jose Canseco that I used steroids. At no point in my career have I ever used steroids, let alone any substance banned by Major League Baseball. . . . As I have never had a personal relationship with Canseco, any suggestion that he taught me anything, about steroid use or otherwise, is ludicrous. We were teammates, and that was the extent of our relationship. I am saddened that he felt it necessary to attempt to tarnish my image and that of the game that I love.

He was joined by his current team's owner, the Baltimore Orioles' Peter Angelos, who issued a statement on behalf of the club:

The Orioles are solidly behind Rafael Palmeiro and have absolute confidence in him and in his denial of the Canseco story. The Orioles will do everything we can to be of assistance to Raffy in meeting these allegations that have no foundation. We know him well and the kind of athlete he has been and the vigorous manner in which he has trained. He is a highly professional athlete.

Giambi's agent, Arn Tellem, added his two cents, even though it had already been reported that Giambi had admitted to the grand jury investigating the BALCO steroid scandal that he had used steroids and was days away from holding a press conference to apologize, without saying what for. "This book, which attacks baseball and many of its players, was written to make a quick buck by a guy desperate for attention, who has appeared on more police blotters than line-up cards in recent years, has no runs, no hits, and is all errors," said Tellem.

Even the White House chimed in. Canseco wrote that President Bush must have known about his players' steroid use when he was managing partner of the Texas Rangers in the early 1990s, an allegation Bush's press secretary, Scott McClellan, hastily denied.

"He has recognized, for some time now, that steroids is a growing problem in professional sports, particularly Major League Baseball," McClellan said. "That's why the president has made addressing the issue a priority in his administration."

But the biggest outcry came from Major League Baseball itself. A week after reporting on the contents of Canseco's book, the *Daily News* also reported that an FBI agent who had investigated steroid use in the early 1990s had warned MLB's security chief Kevin Hallinan that Canseco and many other players were using illegal anabolic steroids. Special Agent Greg Stejskal's warning was based on evidence gathered during a far-reaching steroid investigation dubbed "Operation Equine," but Stejskal said Hallinan and baseball did not act on the information.

"I alerted Major League Baseball back in the time when we had the case, that Canseco was a heavy user and that they should be aware of it. . . . I spoke to the people in their security office. Hallinan was one of the people I spoke to," said Stejskal, who headed the FBI's Ann Arbor, Michigan, office.

Hallinan "seemed interested," Stejskal said, adding that while the FBI's investigation was centered in Michigan and primarily involved weightlifters and bodybuilders, it reached as far as Canada, Mexico, Florida, and California and revealed widespread steroid use in baseball too.

"There's little question the use of steroids was very widespread in baseball," Stejskal said. "And Major League Baseball in effect, they didn't sanction it, but they certainly looked the other way."

Stejskal said he first contacted baseball security in the mid-1990s to inform officials about steroid use by Canseco and other players. He contacted MLB again after Canseco claimed in 1998 that up to 80 percent of ballplayers were using steroids and again in 2002 and 2004 when he put Hallinan's office in touch with a convicted steroid dealer who had connections with several players, including Canseco.

"The first time I talked with Kevin about it was in the mid- to late

1990s," Stejskal said. "I wouldn't have talked to him about it when our case was going on."

Baseball officials immediately denied that they had been informed of steroid use, and angrily denounced Stejskal's charges, putting out a press release that said the *Daily News* story "was not accurate."

"It did not happen," Hallinan said. "Not with this guy, not with anybody else."

For a couple of days, MLB stuck to its denials, insisting that it had no knowledge of steroid use and had not ever been contacted by Stejskal, before finally admitting that it had been contacted by the agent in 2002. Their story now became that Hallinan could have been told by Stejskal at an FBI conference in Quantico, Virginia, in 1994 that baseball had a steroid problem. But even with this vague confession, MLB still continued its attacks on Stejskal. Several defenders quickly stepped forward on his behalf, including the late Hall of Fame college football coach Bo Schembechler.

The University of Michigan legend, who had known Stejskal for 20 years, called Hallinan's response "bullshit." He said Stejskal had told him about meeting Hallinan at the FBI conference and that "they had beers together." Schembechler had helped spark Operation Equine when he asked Stejskal in 1989 if he knew how college players were acquiring the drugs (especially those at Michigan rival Michigan State). The investigation, which centered on dealers, netted more than 70 convictions.

"If Greg Stejskal said it, that's the way it is," said Schembechler, who was president of the Detroit Tigers from 1990 to 1992.

The headlines were calling attention to the steroid issue all over the country, no place more so than Washington, D.C. By mid-February, Congress was on the case. Stejskal had been contacted by the office of Senator Joe Biden (D-Del.), who had long railed against steroids and other illegal drugs.

"I wouldn't be surprised if we had hearings," one Senate staffer said.

In early March, the invitations went out, not from Biden or the Senate but from the House Government Reform Committee. Henry Waxman (D-Calif.) had urged the chairman, Tom Davis (R-Va.), to hold the hearing.

"Steroid use in America is a significant problem," wrote Waxman in a letter to Davis. "The steroid scandal that has unfolded over the last several years calls into question the fundamental integrity of the game."

The committee invited seven players—Canseco, McGwire, Giambi, Palmeiro, Sammy Sosa, Curt Schilling, and Frank Thomas—to testify about steroids in a hearing that would be held on March 17. Commissioner Bud Selig was called, along with MLB executive vice president and former Oakland A's general manager Sandy Alderson, who had challenged Stejskal's claims. Players Association chief Donald Fehr and San Diego Padres general manager Kevin Towers, who had admitted that he was aware that the late Ken Caminiti, who had died of a drug overdose the year before, used steroids while playing for the Padres, were also asked to appear. Notably absent was Barry Bonds, who had been named in Canseco's book but was under investigation in the BALCO probe and wouldn't be expected to incriminate himself at a congressional hearing.

"There's clearly a cloud over baseball, and perhaps a public discussion of the issues can offer baseball and baseball fans a glimpse of sunlight," said David Marin, a spokesman for Representative Tom Davis. "Second, there's a public health rationale. Davis is very concerned about the message being sent to children around the country. Young people look up to baseball players as their heroes."

The committee let it be known that it expected all to attend voluntarily, but after the Players Association and MLB issued a joint letter to Davis and Waxman saying they doubted the committee had the jurisdiction to issue subpoenas to the players, the congressmen responded with a terse reply. "Your legal analysis is flawed, and any failure to comply with the committee's subpoenas would be unwise and irresponsible," Davis and Waxman wrote back.

Davis and Waxman weren't bluffing; the committee they led had some teeth. When Republicans won control of the House in 1994, the committee had become a launching pad for attacks on the Clinton White House. The committee's rules had been changed so the chairman could issue subpoenas unilaterally, without objections from the minority party; Rep. Dan Burton, the Indiana Republican who was the committee's chairman from 1997 to 2002, issued hundreds of subpoenas to investigate alleged misconduct by the Clinton administration. Burton was obsessed with President Clinton, whom he portrayed as a sleazy politician willing to commit any sort of crime to further his agenda and ambitions. In 1993, Burton brought a homicide expert to his backyard and put on a demonstration that included shooting a pumpkin with a rifle. The demonstration, he said, proved that Clinton adviser Vince Foster had not committed suicide, but had been murdered. In 1995, he demanded to know if taxpayers were paying for the stationery and postage for the Socks Fan Club. The White House assured him that taxpayers weren't picking up the tab for the Clintons' cat.

"If I could prove 10 percent of what I believe happened, he [Clinton] would be gone," Burton told *The Indianapolis Star* in 1998. "This guy's a scumbag. That's why I'm after him."

Davis had taken over as chairman in 2003, and unlike the hyperpartisan, ultraconservative Burton, the Virginia Republican was known as a business-oriented moderate skilled at building consensus. And steroids in sports seemed like something both parties could get behind.

All eventually agreed to appear, although Giambi, Palmeiro, and Frank Thomas asked to be excused. The committee agreed that Giambi had a legitimate out—he too was still in the middle of the BALCO investigation. But it didn't accept Palmeiro's reasoning that he should be excused because he had already denied using steroids and had done extensive charity work for foster children and the Make-A-Wish Foundation: Palmeiro would have to appear. Thomas had recently undergone major ankle surgery and was still undergoing rehabilitation so the committee told him he could answer questions by video hookup.

For most of the players, including McGwire, the hearings seemed like a necessary evil, but one that could probably be managed by MLB and the Players Association, in the same manner that they handled most of the unpleasant issues players faced. Everybody was now talking about toughening the drug-testing program and the feeling was that would probably mollify the committee. Besides, who could take Jose Canseco seriously?

Four days before the hearing, things would change drastically. The *Daily News* reported on Sunday, March 13, that Mark McGwire, contrary to his adamant denials, had indeed been a hard-core steroid user, mixing a potent cocktail that called for one-half cc of testosterone cypionate every three days; one cc of testosterone enanthate per week; the veterinary steroids Eqipoise and Winstrol V, one-quarter cc every three days, injected into the buttocks, one in one cheek, one in the other.

Two dealers caught in Stejskal's Operation Equine told the newspaper that a California man named Curtis Wenzlaff provided Canseco and McGwire, among others, with illegal anabolic steroids. One informant in the case said Wenzlaff injected McGwire at a gym in Southern California on several occasions, and established "arrays" of steroid cocktails. The paper's lengthy investigation of court documents, FBI records, and interviews with sources on both sides of the law found that Operation Equine was indeed a massive warning sign of what was to come in the American sports landscape. Dealers like Wenzlaff were befriending ballplayers like Canseco all over the country, and those players were passing on their newfound expertise to friends in the game.

On the same day the *Daily News* story broke, a retired FBI agent named Bill Randall told the newspaper that the FBI had records of Stejskal's meeting with Kevin Hallinan at Quantico in September 1994. Randall, who worked undercover during Operation Equine, confirmed the information from the informants and exposed MLB's denials as false. It was, in essence, the last time that MLB would be allowed to keep its collective head buried in the sand.

At the behest of Stejskal, Wenzlaff had testified before the Senate in the summer of 2004, telling Joe Biden's committee why athletes use steroids. But that hearing had garnered little press attention, especially compared with the House of Representatives' 2005 hearing, which began at 10 A.M. on March 17 in room 2154 of the Rayburn Building, in an austere wood-paneled, blue-carpeted room with several rows of seats occupied by the press horde. The combination of baseball stars, steroids, and D.C. politics had drawn more media requests than President Clinton's impeachment hearings. Before the hearing began, reporters roamed the halls with cameras and notebooks, looking for lawyers to answer questions about what players were going to say to the committee. The reporters were especially looking for someone to talk about McGwire. He had denied using steroids earlier that week, and another denial, maybe even a public threat of a defamation suit, wouldn't have been surprising.

The players filed in wearing dark suits, their attorneys at their sides, somber looks on their faces as they took their seats at the tables at the front of the room. The committee members looked over them from a dais. Sammy Sosa, who had joined forces with McGwire in 1998 in the most famous single-season home run record chase since Yankees teammates Roger Maris and Mickey Mantle in 1961, brought an interpreter with him, although he is known to speak decent English.

It didn't take long for the drama to begin. McGwire choked up during his opening statement.

My name is Mark McGwire. I have played the game of baseball since I was 9 years old. I was privileged to be able to play 15 years in the Major Leagues. I even had the honor of representing my country on the 1984 Olympic Baseball Team. I love and respect our national pastime, and I will do everything in my power to help the game, its players and fans. . . . First and foremost, my heart goes out to every parent whose son or daughter were victims of steroid use. I hope that these hearings can prevent other families from suffering. I admire the parents who had the courage to appear before this committee and warn of the dangers of steroid use. My heart goes out to them.

McGwire went on to say that he would not participate in naming names and implicating friends and teammates.

> I retired from baseball four years ago. I live a quiet life with my wife and children. I have always been a team player. I have never been a person who has spread rumors or said things about my teammates that could hurt them. I do not sit in judgment of other players—whether it deals with their sexual preference, their marital problems or their personal habits—including whether or not they used chemical substances. That has never been my style, and I do not intend to change just because the cameras are turned on.

He attacked Canseco's book and then said that he had been advised that his testimony could be used to harm friends and teammates and that

> Some ambitious prosecutor might use the words of convicted criminals who would do and say anything to solve their own problems, and create jeopardy for my friends. Asking me, or any other player, to answer questions about who took steroids in front of television cameras will not solve this problem. If a player answers no, he simply will not be believed. If he answers yes, he risks public scorn and endless government investigations. My lawyers have advised me that I cannot answer these questions without jeopardizing my friends, my family or myself.

The committee members peppered McGwire with questions about drug use, and while he never formally invoked the Fifth Amendment, he refused to answer their questions directly, repeating a phrase that would come to define his baseball legacy: "I'm not here to talk about the past."

When Elijah Cummings, Democrat of Maryland, asked McGwire if he was taking the Fifth, his answer was the same: "I'm not here to talk about the past."

William Lacy Clay, Jr., Democrat of Missouri, got a similar answer: "Mr. McGwire, we are both fathers of young children. Both my son and daughter love sports and they look up to stars like you. Can we look at those children with a straight face and tell them that great players like you play the game with honesty and integrity?"

"Like I said earlier," McGwire responded, "I'm not going to go into the past and talk about my past."

He then offered to be a spokesman against steroids. "An excellent one," McGwire said.

Two families whose sons committed suicide after they stopped using steroids sat in the row behind McGwire. He listened to their testimony as they described the ordeal their boys, Taylor Hooton and Rob Garibaldi, had gone through. The parents blamed their deaths on drug-induced depression and speculated that their sons would be alive if players such as McGwire had spoken out earlier about the dangers of steroids.

"Players that are guilty of taking steroids are not only cheaters but you are also cowards," Don Hooton said. "You hide behind the skirts of your union and now, with the help of management and your lawyers, you have made every effort to resist facing the public today."

Sosa flatly denied using steroids. "To be clear, I have never taken illegal performance-enhancing drugs," he said in a carefully crafted sworn statement that didn't address the question of whether he might have taken steroids in a country where they are not illegal, such as his native Dominican Republic. Sosa had been the subject of much speculation over the years about whether he used steroids, famously refusing to accept an offer from *Sports Illustrated* columnist Rick Reilly to settle the issue by taking a drug test in front of Reilly.

Palmeiro jabbed his finger in the air and told the committee unequivocally that he too was drug-free. "I have never used steroids. Period," he said.

Two months later, he tested positive for the anabolic steroid stanozolol. (Following Palmeiro's positive test and suspension from baseball, Tom Davis announced that he would open an investigation into whether Palmeiro had perjured himself before Congress. But by November, citing a lack of sufficient evidence, the committee concluded it would not recommend perjury charges against Palmeiro. Since the drug test was conducted in May 2005, there was no proof that Palmeiro lied when he said two months earlier that he had never used steroids. Davis stopped short of exonerating the player, saying the committee had received evidence that was "confusing and contradictory in many respects" and that they couldn't prove he'd taken steroids before the hearing.)

Canseco sat at the end of the tables, ostracized from the other players, and told the committee that steroids are dangerous and should be banned, exactly the opposite of what he said in his book.

The players' testimony blared from television sets on the evening news and was splashed across newspapers and computer screens. It was all very public. But behind the headlines and the sound bites was a dramatic attack on those who run the sport. The committee was livid when, earlier in the week, the members had received a version of baseball's revised drug policy. The revision included a passage on the penalty phase allowing a first-time offender to be suspended 10 days *or* fined up to $10,000. When baseball had announced its new policy in January, it said that first-time offenders would be suspended, identified publicly, *and* fined. The committee was outraged at the softening of the language and by the possibility that a steroid cheat could get off with a fine. And not much of a fine at that.

When their turn came to appear before the committee, Selig, Fehr, and Selig's lieutenant, MLB senior vice president Rob Manfred, looked like schoolboys in front of an angry principal. At one point, Waxman even questioned whether Selig should keep his job.

"I think whoever makes the decisions for baseball ought to look at whether it's time for new leadership," Waxman said to the game's commissioner.

Manfred claimed that the committee had mischaracterized the drug-testing policy and that the language at issue was unintentional. Fehr agreed. "I've heard about these holes in the program," Fehr said of the committee's comments. "I'm not sure they're there or that any real analysis has been done of the program."

The committee members continued to hammer at Selig, complaining that baseball's policy did not include four substances banned by the World Anti-Doping Agency. It also did not ban masking drugs that might make steroids difficult to detect. By late in the day, when Manfred and Fehr spoke in detail on the issue of the penalties, Davis seemed to accept their argument that the language describing suspensions and fines was simply a mistake.

"The language should have been altered," Manfred said. "But there is no dispute between the bargaining parties."

Representative Christopher Shays, a Republican from Connecticut, got the last word. "You're asking us to accept something that boggles the mind, that you sent us something that you say is not accurate," Shays said. "It's sloppy. You're the best lawyers in the country. All you make me want to do by your answers is know more what the hell you do. You haven't been responsible."

A weary Selig left the Rayburn Building around 9:30 P.M., flanked by

Capitol Police and his own aides. As he headed to his private plane at Dulles International Airport, the commissioner was already beginning to think about his drug policy and what it was doing to his legacy as one of the most successful commissioners in the history of sports. Within a few months, Selig would be on the phone to his longtime friend, former Senate Majority Leader George Mitchell.

While the sports media and baseball fans were focused on Canseco's book and the congressional hearing in early 2005, authorities in upstate New York were quietly preparing to raid the home of a small-town physician who had been signing a shocking number of prescriptions for steroids. Investigators found a massive stash of drugs and paraphernalia during their March 2005 raid on the home of Dr. David Stephenson, including the steroid DHEA, ketamine, testosterone, Zoloft, hypodermic needles, and a bong stored in a tequila box.

To Mark Haskins, an investigator with the New York State Bureau of Narcotic Enforcement, the case was much bigger than a rogue doctor. It didn't take Haskins and his colleagues long to figure out that doctors, anti-aging clinics, rejuvenation centers, and pharmacies were making a fortune by illegally offering controlled substances over the Internet. The raid marked the beginnings of "Operation Which Doctor," the multistate, multiagency steroid investigation initiated by Albany County District Attorney David Soares that would offer further proof that Major League Baseball and other sports had been corrupted by illicit drugs.

In 1994, David Stephenson moved from his native Texas to Lee, New York, a town of 6,900 approximately 120 miles northwest of Albany, to work as an emergency room physician at a nearby hospital. In Lee, Stephenson became known as a pharmaceutical prophet who promoted a new world of drugs he claimed countered aging and genetics. Although Stephenson wasn't tech-savvy when he moved to New York—he had to hire a local kid to show him how to turn on his computer—he got the hang of the Internet quickly. He established a Web site called docstat.com to share his pharmaceutical enthusiasm and knowledge, and to offer antidepressants, steroids, and other prescription drugs to customers across the United States and as far away as New Zealand and Germany.

Stephenson was earning $300,000 a year repackaging drugs he bought in bulk from a Mobile, Alabama, company called Applied Pharmacy Services and then jacking up the prices, sometimes by as much as 1,000 percent. But while his side business was thriving, his relationship with his girlfriend, Kimberly Zammiello, had turned ugly. Zammiello, the mother of Stephenson's two sons, told Oneida County authorities that Stephenson had assaulted and threatened her during what she called steroid-induced rages. The couple split, and Zammiello hired an attorney to help resolve child custody issues. But when her lawyer was arrested on drug charges in August 2003—authorities said he was part of a Hells Angels methamphetamine ring—Stephenson went to Zammiello's home and warned her that with her lawyer in jail, she'd never be free of him. Then, according to police reports, he punched her in the face, breaking her teeth.

Stephenson was arrested on domestic violence charges, and, as a result, Oneida County District Attorney Scott McNamara started looking at Stephenson's drug business. He backed off when he got a call from Soares's office. They had kicked off their own investigation after Haskins and the state regulators began suspecting that Stephenson was signing prescriptions for patients he hadn't met or examined in person. (Signing a prescription without a face-to-face meeting is illegal in New York, according to Soares, although defense attorneys representing Operation Which Doctor defendants argue that the law is not as black-and-white as Soares claims.)

Haskins had initiated the investigation by placing an order for testosterone, methadone, and other drugs on Stephenson's Web site. Haskins claimed to be an overweight, alcoholic pilot who was also addicted to heroin. Haskins wrote that he needed the drugs because "I want to get high to fly."

The drugs arrived by express mail a few days later.

"Basically you have an anti-aging clinic with an Internet presence," Haskins told *Sports Illustrated*:

[Clinic operators] put the product on the Internet. The customer finds them online, fills out a brief questionnaire and requests steroids, hormone therapy, whatever. Someone from the clinic contacts the customer and then develops a prescription for the steroid treatment or hormone treatment. Then the clinic sends or e-mails the prescription to a doctor, who is often not even in the same state. He'll sign it because he's being paid by the clinic, usually $20 to $50 for every signature. The signed prescriptions get faxed to the compounding pharmacies, which know from the very beginning that there is no doctor-patient relationship. The pharmacy then sends the product to the customer.

Albany's aggressive investigation marked a turning point in the war on drugs. Law-enforcement agencies had historically ignored steroids and human growth hormone, preferring to expend their resources on street drugs. As a result, the sale of drugs to combat aging and enhance performance became a huge business. Worldwide sales of growth hormone were estimated to be $1.5 billion to $2 billion in 2005; anti-aging industry officials estimated as many as 30,000 people in the United States used HGH to reverse the ravages of time, spending $400 to $500 a month to use the drug in an illegal manner. In the United States, HGH's limited legal uses—the legitimate reason for which it can be prescribed by doctors—do not include eliminating wrinkles, improving libido, increasing fastball velocity, or repairing elbow tendons.

Soares had come into office on a platform that included reforming New York's harsh Rockefeller Drug Laws that target the poor and minorities. He was the perfect law enforcement official to attack the Internet drug rings because he didn't seem to care if the perps were cops, stockbrokers, or elite athletes, or what their explanations and excuses were for getting the drugs.

"It makes total sense for athletes to do it this way," Alex Wright, an agent with the Florida Metropolitan Bureau of Investigation who participated in Operation Which Doctor, told *Sports Illustrated*. "If they get caught, they can say, 'I send my blood work to the clinic like it asked me and the doctor said my levels are low.' This is the best way they can get stuff. They have the comfort of anonymity because there is no face-to-face. They are just a name and a credit card."

Since the 2003 testing survey revealed more extensive steroid use in the game than baseball's leaders had bargained for, it had become obvious that players were willing to use whatever performance enhancers they thought they could get away with, including a virtually undetectable substance that had once been drawn from the pituitary glands of cadavers. By 2005, drug manufacturers were producing synthetic growth hormone and rogue doctors all over the country were prescribing it to just about anyone who could fill out a simple online medical form, including baseball players. There were side effects, of course, including the one that hit Yankee first baseman Jason Giambi in the summer of 2004. By that summer, Giambi, who had already admitted his steroid and HGH use to the BALCO grand jury, was lethargic and losing weight in what was portrayed as a mystery ailment. Finally, on September 3, it was reported that he was suffering from a pituitary tumor, a possible side effect of HGH use, and would be treated with corticosteroids, a nonanabolic and legal substance that millions of people use for a variety of ailments. Not even the Yankees had been aware of the July 30 diagnosis and while the tumor was not life-threatening and easily treated, it surely sent a message to Major League Baseball: HGH had infiltrated the game in as big a way as steroids. In January of 2005, baseball added human growth hormone to its list of banned substances.

For Andy Pettitte, all the talk about HGH and the news coming out of the congressional hearing were disconcerting. He'd used growth himself and he knew how secrets that seemed like they would forever stay in the dark could somehow find their way into the sunlight. The government was poking its nose into the whole affair and reporters were asking questions. Pettitte was certain they would ask him what he knew about steroids and HGH. He didn't want to have to lie about what he'd done or clam up like McGwire. Besides, he'd used growth to help recover from an injury—McNamee had said it would help repair tissue. Plus, it hadn't even been against baseball's rules—so that wasn't cheating. He decided he'd just admit to having used the stuff and he wondered if Clemens might do the same.

So as spring training began to wind down in Kissimmee, Pettitte approached Clemens. "Dude, what are you going to say if anyone—if any of the reporters ask you if you had ever used HGH?" Pettitte asked.

"What are you taking about?" Clemens responded.

"Well, you told me you had used HGH," Pettitte said.

"I never told you that," Clemens said.

"You didn't?"

"No," Clemens said. "I told you Debbie used it."

As far as Pettitte was concerned, the matter was closed. Like anyone who'd been around Clemens very much, Pettitte knew the drill. In Clemens's mind, it had already been decided—no matter the truth, the official line was that he hadn't used human growth hormone. He hadn't ever told anyone that he had, and he wasn't ever going to tell anyone that he had.

And the case was closed, at least temporarily. Pettitte was spared the embarrassing questions—reporters didn't press him about drug use.

. . .

The exchange between the two pitchers was all but forgotten as the season began and the Astros bumbled to a 15-30 start by late May, quickly dousing preseason predictions that they would at least qualify for the wild card in the postseason. In a May 24 tilt at Wrigley Field, they were hit with a double dose of bad news—Clemens's start had to be aborted after five scoreless innings of work when he suffered a strained right groin muscle. Although the Astros built an early 2–0 lead, they wound up losing 4–2, their seventh straight defeat.

"We'll start treating it tomorrow and go from there," said Clemens after the game. "I had a little problem in the third. We just didn't have time to wrap it in the fourth. I continued to push it. In the fifth inning, again location became the most important thing. Pitch selection and my location became very important. I'm not concerned right now. I'll know more [tomorrow]."

Clemens made his next start and lost 9–0 to the Cincinnati Reds at Minute Maid Park. A few days earlier, manager Phil Garner took stock in the team's precipitous fall in the standings, alluding to the toll each loss was taking on the players. "You don't want to say things that are going to put negative thoughts into their heads," Garner told the *Houston Chronicle*. "But at the same time, this thing is becoming a 900-pound gorilla sitting in the room, and nobody wants to look at it. What it is right now when you go through this type of a slump, it's in your head."

Clemens took a more military-style approach, saying it was incumbent upon the veterans to take charge, and shoulder the responsibility of leading the team back to .500. "The veterans have to try and do a little more so you don't put that kind of stress on our younger players," Clemens said. "You don't want them to feel that side, especially because they have not been in that situation that much. We have and I have, so I take that challenge head-on."

Whether it was Clemens's pep talk or the fact that Roy Oswalt, the team's ace, and Pettitte, and an underrated bullpen started to flourish, the Astros seized upon the challenge and began to right the ship. After the dreadful start, the club pulled off one of the game's historic comebacks, going 74-43 the rest of the way to earn the wild card slot, just edging the Phillies on the last day of the regular season. Hamstring and groin issues had dogged Clemens through the summer; as a result, he was anxious to make a mark in the postseason.

By the time the Astros got to their first-ever World Series, Clemens had accomplished just that. He was the winning pitcher in the divisional round Game 4 clincher against the Braves, pitching the final three innings in relief during a nearly six-hour, 18-inning epic that the Astros won 7–6. The game featured a combined 14 pitchers, and Clemens was pitching on three days' rest after getting strafed in his Game 2 start. He then won Game 3 of the National League Championship Series against the pesky St. Louis Cardinals. By the time Oswalt pitched the Astros to a 5–1 victory over the Cardinals in Game 6 for the pennant and the trip to the Series, Clemens was downright giddy. He led the celebration at Busch Stadium, climbing atop the mound and grabbing Pettitte around the neck in a bear hug. Clemens whispered something in Pettitte's ear, then gave him a push, much like an older brother would to a younger sibling.

Astros owner Drayton McLane had dreamed of this moment when he'd lured Pettitte and Clemens back home with a mountain of cash. And while the 43-year-old Clemens had shown signs of his age late in the season with the nagging left leg problems, Pettitte had been superlative, finishing 17-9, a redemptive season in many ways after his injury-plagued 2004. As the Astros basked in their World Series berth, both pitchers seemed relieved.

"This is exactly why I came off my couch," Clemens said after the Game 6 win.

"The main thing is that it's all happened so fast," added Pettitte. "When I signed here, it was to try to help the organization win a playoff series. I know when Roger signed, it was like: 'O.K. We might have a chance to get to the World Series with this staff.' "

Clemens was awarded the Game 1 World Series start against the White Sox for his gutsy effort through the first two playoff rounds. On the eve of the game against Jose Contreras, he glared down one reporter who dared to ask about his left hamstring, which had started barking at the most inopportune time. "It doesn't matter," Clemens said. "I don't care how my body feels at this time of year. If you need aspirin, if you need more heat, if you need more ice, this is the time you get it, and you don't ask questions."

He might not have asked questions, but he got the answers anyway. As the Series got under way in blustery Chicago, Clemens lasted just two innings before his hamstring betrayed him. Garner gave his pitcher the hook after Clemens gave up three runs on four hits. The Astros could not solve Contreras, the Cuban defector who had fizzled in the Bronx when he played for the Yankees. The White Sox won Game 1, 5–3, and never looked back, sweeping the Astros in four games for the club's first Series title since 1917. Clemens's dismal outing would turn out to be his last World Series start, and was no comparison to the Game 4 start two years earlier in Miami with the Yankees, except perhaps for the explosion of flashbulbs once again from appreciative fans of the opposing team.

After the Series, the annual "Rocket Watch" went into immediate effect, the speculation rampant about whether Clemens would return for a 23rd season in the majors. "Certainly we would love to have him back," said McLane. "He's just been so important to this franchise. He helped lift it to the next level."

The feds arrived at Kirk Radomski's door before dawn on December 14, 2005, dozens of armed agents entering the two-story house in a sleepy Long Island suburb and searching for evidence that linked the personal trainer to Major League Baseball's steroid supply line. Radomski's wife was shocked; she had no idea her husband had been providing performance-enhancing drugs to athletes. Neighbors on Radomski's block were also surprised. They knew Radomski as the nice guy who owned a car-detailing business and plowed the street after snowstorms, not the go-to guy for Deca-Durabolin or testosterone.

Radomski's neighborhood, with its manicured lawns and broad drive-ways, couldn't have been more different from the nondescript office that housed Victor Conte's BALCO headquarters in Burlingame, California. But like the raid on BALCO's West Coast offices two years earlier, the search of Radomski's home was led by IRS agent Jeff Novitzky—and both generated evidence that would ensnare some of baseball's biggest stars.

Radomski knew why the agents were there, and he knew that the anonymous life he had been living was irrevocably changed. He insisted he hadn't made much money providing the drugs to his clients; he was simply known as a procurer—a guy who could get you just about anything you needed—and he did it because he wanted them to excel at the high-est levels of their sport. "I could have charged these guys a lot more," he said after the raid. "If I made so much money, where is it? Where did it go? I wasn't peddling this stuff. I wasn't a drug dealer. I didn't ruin anyone's life. I made guys millions of dollars."

Radomski couldn't bullshit or bluster his way out of this mess. He fig-ured the best thing to do was cooperate with the 50 agents with firearms and flak jackets standing outside his front door.

According to court documents, the agents seized thousands of doses of anabolic steroids during the raid, as well as vials of human growth hormone and syringes. Novitzky described Radomski in the documents as "a major drug source in professional baseball who took over after BALCO laboratories were taken down."

That wasn't entirely accurate. Radomski had been providing drugs to ballplayers long before he'd ever heard of BALCO. But Novitzky was correct in one regard: Radomski was a major drug source in professional baseball. According to a search warrant affidavit prepared by Novitzky before the raid, the feds learned about Radomski's role as a baseball steroid supplier from an informant who was awaiting sentencing in a felony real estate case. The informant told the FBI he had heard about a New Yorker who was supplying steroids to ballplayers. The informant contacted a baseball source, who put him in contact with Radomski. Beginning in April 2005, the informant ordered steroids at least five times from Radomski. The last shipment was sent to a San Jose address provided by Jeff Novitzky.

It took Radomski a while to figure out who had fingered him and he was certain the FBI informant wasn't the only person talking to the feds.

The players who had reached out to Radomski for the drugs that helped them through so many grueling seasons suddenly vanished. The only player who called after Radomski's arrest was David Segui, his long-time friend from the Mets who had retired a few years earlier. Radomski had helped athletes make hundreds of millions of dollars, but only Segui stepped up when Radomski needed support.

Radomski wasn't certain if the players he had helped make rich had informed on him, but he was sure of one thing: He had a wife and child to support, and he couldn't support them from prison. Novitzky had canceled checks, phone records, and tapes of wiretapped phone calls. So Radomski also knew he would have to cooperate with the feds, not fight them. "What was I going to do," he said. "Spend millions of dollars on lawyers and wind up in prison anyway?"

By the time Radomski stopped talking, he'd provided information that would ultimately implicate scores of big-leaguers—stars and scrubs alike—as steroid users. The trail would lead to some of the biggest names in baseball, including the man many considered the greatest pitcher of his generation. "I'm just a guy from the Bronx," Radomski said. "Did I help baseball set attendance records? Will they still be talking about this 100 years from now like we're still talking about the Black Sox?"

CHAPTER NINE

2006

On March 25, 2006, Roger Clemens tried to sneak into the conference room unnoticed, just another spectator at Jeff Bagwell's presser in Kissimmee, Florida. The veteran slugger was announcing he would begin the season on the disabled list and would consider surgery on his ailing right shoulder. Bagwell even hinted that his illustrious 15-year career—all with the Astros—could be over.

"I may never play again," said Bagwell.

But a gaggle of New York reporters—in Kissimmee for a game between the Mets and Astros—were barely interested in Bagwell's remarks. A Clemens sighting was big. There was speculation about whether the Rocket would come out of retirement yet again, maybe join the Yankees for a second stint in pinstripes.

Clemens, who had just come back from playing in the World Baseball Classic, brushed off the New York media as he signed autographs near an exit, saying he was undecided about his 2006 baseball plans. He did share some thoughts with Astros beat writer Brian McTaggart, though. "I'm going to look at all my options," Clemens said. "If I get an itch and somebody goes down, I know I'm going to get phone calls. It was the same thing in the [World Baseball Classic]. I was wearing a red batting practice top for the United States, and [Cincinnati Reds outfielder Ken] Griffey looked at me and said, 'You look great in red.' I want to win. But I'm not going to torture myself to go out there and have another OK season. You want to get to the dance and you have to play well and you want to win."

Clemens had come straight to Kissimmee from the WBC and spent several days working with the Astros' minor-leaguers, trying to keep in shape.

It was an unusual spring for Clemens. He'd missed his first spring training in 22 years, and he was trying to decide if, once and for all, he was definitely through with baseball. In past seasons, when Clemens had some free time on his hands, he would occasionally make the trip across the state to see his longtime girlfriend Mindy McCready. They'd met 15 years earlier during spring training when Clemens and some Red Sox teammates were partying at a Fort Myers karaoke bar called the Hired Hand. Clemens was already a married father of two young boys, but that didn't stop him from setting his sights on the slender teenager belting out songs on the stage. The players hooted and hollered and tossed a signed T-shirt at McCready. Later, Clemens took her to his hotel, where they watched a movie and she fell asleep on Clemens's chest. They would connect again over the years as McCready blossomed into a bona fide country music star and Clemens continued his dramatic career rebirth in Toronto and New York. They met in cities all over North America, from Clemens's Sky-Dome apartment in Toronto (where McNamee spotted a half-dressed McCready), to Las Vegas, to New York and beyond, McCready often arriving on Clemens's private jet. One getaway found McCready and Clemens holed up in the swank SoHo Grand in Manhattan. The couple partied in the hotel lobby with Michael Jordan and Monica Lewinsky. McCready scored a cigar from Jordan to give to Clemens and came to Lewinsky's defense when a patron taunted the ex–White House intern about her dealings with Bill Clinton.

McCready and Clemens traveled together to Vegas and Cabo and McCready's favorite getaway, Palm Springs, rubbing elbows with the famous and hangers-on of the famous. On one boozy evening in Sin City, McCready and Clemens went out with Phil Maloof—one of the sons of the powerful entertainment and sports family whose assets include the Palms hotel and casino and the Sacramento Kings basketball team— actress Tara Reid, and a Playboy Bunny who was Maloof's date. By night's end, Reid was passed out on McCready's lap while the Bunny was whispering in McCready's ear that she had "the hair, but I've got the bod." Clemens, ever the competitor, told Maloof that McCready had a much higher "morning after" quotient than the Bunny—loosely translated, Maloof wouldn't exactly be thrilled to wake up next to the Bunny when the booze wore off. Clemens touted his girlfriend's clear, beautiful skin, using his white button-down shirt to rub against McCready's face to prove that she was wearing no caked-on makeup. The Rocket then marched over to the Bunny, who had taken to dancing in a circle by herself, and scraped off a thick paste of foundation from one cheek as the woman continued to teeter around in high heels.

Clemens lavished McCready with gifts and sent her money when she ran into financial or legal trouble, a not infrequent occurrence. McCready fell on hard times in the years following her 1996 platinum-selling album, *Ten Thousand Angels*, her life at times playing out like a bad country song. She pleaded guilty to prescription fraud in 2004 (she had tried to obtain the highly addictive painkiller OxyContin), was nearly killed by her drug-addicted boyfriend Billy McKnight, and attempted suicide while she was pregnant with their son in 2005. There were probation violations and jail sentences and a rich string of headlines. There was also a brief engagement to actor Dean Cain of *Lois & Clark* fame and a romance with former NHL player Drake Berehowsky.

Clemens and McCready's odd affair had survived all those obstacles and during one spring training, Clemens found himself in the McCready household, striking up a friendship with her father. Clemens hadn't been favorably received by McCready's mother, Gayle Inge, when he had paid his one and only visit to the modest North Fort Myers home. Inge had divorced McCready's father, Tim, when Mindy was 12, after Inge believed her husband was cheating with another woman. It was no surprise that Inge frowned on her daughter's relationship with a married man, let alone a famous one. "A conversation about his sons came up. Of course, I didn't say anything to him," Inge recalled, remembering the visit. "I said plenty to Mindy about, 'Is there a wife?' I think Mindy was afraid to bring him over here because she was afraid I would say something."

Clemens knew he was better off visiting Tim McCready, Mindy's father, who was an unabashed Clemens fan. Sure enough, soon after Clemens's arrival, they were driving golf balls into an open field in front of McCready's Cape Coral home, or fishing on Tim McCready's boat.

"Roger hit the ball pretty well," Tim McCready would say years later. Clemens reciprocated by giving his host a set of high-end clubs that were identical to the set Clemens owned. But the visit was less than idyllic, and the relationship soon began its descent toward a merciful end.

By the spring of 2006, McCready was a new mother and Clemens was thinking about playing again. It would be on his terms, of course, and it would include the "family plan" perk that would surely appease his wife. Debbie Clemens put up with a lot from her husband but she made it clear where she drew the line. "If you cheat on me, she better be good-looking because you're going to spend the rest of your life with her," she would tell Clemens. Canseco had made the claim in his book that Clemens was one of the very few players in the game who didn't cheat on his wife, writing that he was "amazed" by Clemens's fidelity. "His wife should be very proud of him," Canseco wrote in his book *Juiced.* "You see all these other guys—oh, my god, every chance they got, they would be hitting the strip clubs. They would have extra girls staying in the team hotel, one room over from their wives, so they could go back and forth from room to room if they wanted. . . . Roger was the exception to that. I went out with him a bunch of times when there were beautiful women around, and he had a lot of opportunities and never took them. I was with him enough times to realize: This man never cheated on his wife."

It was an endorsement that those who spent much time around Clemens, especially Brian McNamee, found odd. McCready wasn't Clemens's only girlfriend, and when a fax of the page arrived at the Clemens house from the Hendricks brothers around the time the book was released, McNamee, who was waiting to begin a training session with Clemens, was incredulous. He wondered how Clemens had gotten Canseco to put that in the book. They all gathered in the kitchen, ESPN blaring in the background, and Debbie cried as she read Canseco's testimonial. She said it was the greatest thing in the world.

Before Clemens would finally take the field that summer, his "family plan" clause in place, MLB commissioner Bud Selig held a news conference in baseball's Park Avenue offices to introduce the most exciting new face in the game that season, a man whose presence would forever change Roger Clemens's already complicated life.

It was March 30, and Selig was in New York City that day sitting next to George Mitchell, the former majority leader of the United States Senate. In a move that surprised nobody—except perhaps the Players' Union—Selig had hired Mitchell to prepare an authoritative report on performance-enhancing drug use in baseball. More precisely, Selig had hired DLA Piper, the prestigious international law firm where Mitchell was a partner. The lawyers at the firm would assist Mitchell in conducting a deep investigation and produce a report with findings and recommendations. Mitchell had been promised complete independence and authority.

The report would be the "final word" on the issue, and it might just get the House of Representatives off Selig's back. There was no question that Congress would be pleased that Mitchell was the man chosen for the task. Prior to representing the state of Maine, Mitchell had been a U.S. attorney and federal judge, so he could be both aggressive and fair. After leaving office he had become a successful diplomat, helping to bring peace to Northern Ireland. Mitchell had a reputation for getting results. As a bonus, he was a passionate baseball fan, and was on the board of directors of the Boston Red Sox.

Selig seemed genuinely happy and proud. After years of benign neglect, his tolerance for baseball's culture of chemical cheating had run out. Rather than be known as the man who let the problem become a can of worms, Selig would forever be known as the commissioner who found the can opener. "Senator Mitchell's leadership of this investigation ensures that it will be both thorough and fair," Selig said. "Indeed, should Senator Mitchell uncover material suggesting that the scope of this investigation needs to be broader, he has my permission to expand the investigation and to follow the evidence wherever it may lead."

Selig had actually wanted the investigation for more than a year, but had met stiff opposition from the Major League Baseball Players Association, one of the most powerful unions in the country. For years, Selig had struggled to even introduce drug testing and penalties that Olympic athletes would have found laughably weak.

But one event changed all that in March of 2006, and that was the publication of *Game of Shadows: Barry Bonds, BALCO, and the Steroids Scandal That Rocked Professional Sports*, the dramatic investigative book by Mark Fainaru-Wada and Lance Williams of the *San Francisco Chronicle*. Over the previous two years, they had published verbatim quotations of the testimony witnesses had given to the BALCO grand jury—risking prison, since grand jury testimony is confidential. Under oath and behind closed doors, dozens of athletes and coaches had admitted involvement with doping, but none of those admissions were as momentous as the equivocating, possibly felonious denials of Barry Bonds. It came as no surprise when, in early March, *Sports Illustrated* published a long excerpt from the book. The cover of the magazine showed a portrait of Bonds with the words "The Truth" under his giant head. That, along with rave reviews from high-minded book critics (Michiko Kakutani called it "necessary reading"), made *Game of Shadows* a best-seller. With the full scope of the BALCO scandal laid out in long form, even the apologists for dopers—including the very large share of baseball fans who preferred to tolerate it—were forced to see that a corrosive culture of lying and cheating had taken root in the game.

The day Selig spoke on Park Avenue, Bonds was entering the new season with his eyes on the all-time home run record. He had 708 home runs to Babe Ruth's 714 and Hank Aaron's 755. With fans, congressmen, and Michiko Kakutani all calling it a disgrace, Selig had all the political cover he needed to give Mitchell the green light.

. . .

From the very beginning, Mitchell made it clear he expected baseball players to cooperate with his investigation. Mitchell hoped to interview players such as Jason Giambi, whose BALCO grand jury testimony and pituitary tumor pointed to the use of performance enhancers, but who had been publicly silent on the issue. "I invite those who believe they have information related to the use of steroids and other illegal performance-enhancing drugs by Major League Baseball players to come forward with that information, so it might be considered in the context of all the evidence," Mitchell said.

Some guessed that Mitchell had been selected because he had a working relationship with Fehr, the executive director of the Players Association; both men had served on the Special Commission that investigated the 2002 Salt Lake City Olympics bribery scandal. Fehr, however, refused to comment publicly about Mitchell's role, and union officials privately expressed a great deal of trepidation about the probe. It was easy to see why the union would be leery of Mitchell and why it feared his investigation would lay the blame for baseball's steroid scandal on players and ignore the role of MLB officials, team executives, managers, and coaches. Mitchell had been the director (without an equity interest) of the Florida Marlins and the Boston Red Sox, so he already had significant ties to the owners. Mitchell had also taken over as the chairman of the Disney Company's board during a period of upheaval after the ouster of Michael Eisner in 2004, and while he never ran the day-to-day operations of the company, he remained as chairman. (He would resign on January 1, 2007; it was noted too that Disney was the parent of ESPN, one of baseball's national broadcast partners.) He had also served on Selig's blue ribbon panel that produced a report on baseball's finances before the 2002 labor agreement. Despite the participation of Mitchell, former Fed chairman Paul Volcker, conservative political columnist and baseball fanatic George Will, and Yale president Richard C. Levin, many economists mocked the 2002 report for its owner-friendly findings.

Union officials were unhappy that Selig hadn't consulted with them before appointing Mitchell. In the decades after Marvin Miller created the Players Association in a dusty office in New York's Biltmore Hotel in 1966, union officials and club executives engaged in a full-scale labor war that resulted in several costly work stoppages. But since the 2002 collective bargaining agreement, both sides were proud to have established a cordial working relationship. The union felt that by hiring Mitchell to head a steroid investigation, Selig and his lieutenants were undermining that relationship.

Fehr and other union officials believed they had made significant concessions on baseball's drug policy, despite their deep opposition to testing. Fehr believed urine tests were a violation of a player's privacy, but he had put those reservations aside and agreed to survey testing in the 2003 season and eventually to a testing program. He thought it was important to give the drug program a chance to work. Instead, it would now be eclipsed by an investigation led by a politician with significant ties to owners and Congress. There was another reason for the union's nervousness about the Mitchell investigation. The union had failed to deal with the issue of steroid use for years, ignoring the interests of players who hoped to play without the help of performance-enhancing drugs, those who believed that the cost of doing business shouldn't have to be putting dangerous substances into your body. A 2002 *USA Today* poll of more than 500 players conducted anonymously revealed that four-fifths, or 79 percent of those polled, would embrace some form of a drug-testing program. Of that same number, 44 percent said there was intense pressure to use performance-enhancing drugs to maintain the same level of competition on the field. (And always remember: In professional sports, "level of competition" translates to "bigger paycheck"; if someone on steroids can hit more home runs than a non–steroid taker, the drug user will have a better-paying contract. The non–drug user could easily be out of a job altogether.) But this cry for action failed to resonate with the union, which stuck with a fading ideology that drug testing was not the best way to deal with the issue of performance-enhancing drug use in baseball.

Whether they liked it or not, Mitchell's inquiry got under way. And while Mitchell might not have subpoena power, the authority to issue search warrants, and the other tools of a federal agent, others did — including the federal agents who nailed Kirk Radomski.

On April 19, three weeks after Selig announced the launch of Mitchell's investigation, tubby 38-year-old Arizona Diamondbacks pitcher Jason Grimsley came to the door of his home at 10792 East Fanfol Lane in Scottsdale, Arizona, and accepted a package that contained two kits of human growth hormone for which he had no prescription. Each kit included seven vials of powder and seven vials of sterile water. Patients with dwarfism or AIDS-related muscle wasting were expected to mix the two substances and inject themselves in a pinch of fat. Grimsley didn't have either of those syndromes. He was just an aging pitcher, struggling to be effective against gigantic sluggers in the National League.

Grimsley had ordered the kits through the mail from Kirk Radomski, the Long Island contact he had discussed with Brian McNamee five years earlier, when McNamee was searching for a Lexus. Grimsley had sent checks to Radomski for drugs 10 or 12 times over the years. This time, he'd sent Radomski $3,200 for the two kits, the standard rate Radomski charged players all across the game. It was enough to last a season. And it was enough to get a jail sentence.

Grimsley accepted the package and went back into his home, where he was entertaining guests. But soon someone else was at the door. This time Grimsley's wife went to answer, and she came back to tell her husband that visitors had arrived. When Grimsley went back, a tall, bald man was waiting for him at the entrance. The man identified himself as Jeff Novitzky, a criminal investigator from the Internal Revenue Service.

Despite his very central role in the BALCO case that had been agitating the baseball world for the previous two seasons, Novitzky was still a shadowy figure. As an undercover agent, he had scrupulously avoided appearing in photos, and he never gave interviews. He had been looking for other drug cheats, and here in Scottsdale he had found one. After 15 years in the major leagues, Grimsley was a rickety reliever barely holding on. In the five years since he left the Yankees, he had earned more than $7 million. He could not make anything like that kind of money anywhere else. Steroids and human growth hormone had helped him defend his spot in the big leagues from hungry youngsters. Who could tell if one of those players might have had a chance to bloom into a baseball hero if Grimsley hadn't been blatantly flouting the rules?

Novitzky was a commanding presence, tall and serious and backed by the full weight of the Treasury Department. He was accompanied at Grimsley's home by two other federal agents with whom he'd worked closely over the years: Erwin Rogers of the IRS Criminal Investigation Division and Heather Young of the FBI. Several other agents waited near Grimsley's home in Scottsdale's vast suburban sprawl. On this day, Novitzky had worked in conjunction with the FBI, the FDA, and the U.S. Postal Inspection Service to monitor the illegal drug shipment. Novitzky gave Grimsley a look at an "anticipatory search warrant" that had been signed the day before by U.S. magistrate Judge Edward C. Voss. It allowed the agents to search the premises for drugs and seize what they deemed relevant to a drug distribution crime.

But Novitzky also dangled the carrot of discretion. He promised Grimsley that if the pitcher would agree to cooperate with the investigation, Novitzky would keep the existence of the search warrant hidden from the houseguests and neighbors. All Grimsley had to do was hand over the HGH he had just received and come downtown for an interview. Grimsley accepted the offer. The three federal agents waited at the entryway to his home while he got dressed, quietly got in his truck with Novitzky and Young, and drove to an alternate location. Grimsley was not under arrest, and he was free to leave at any time. In the two-hour interview that followed, Grimsley told Novitzky he bought and used steroids, clenbuterol, amphetamines, and HGH to enhance his pitching performance. He said he used Deca-Durabolin after shoulder surgery in 2000. He said he failed a drug test in baseball's first year of testing (2003, the "survey" testing year in which results of tests were to be kept confidential and used to determine whether a testing program would be implemented the following season), and started on human growth hormone after that.

Grimsley's story fit with a counterintuitive pattern; he was a pitcher, and half of the players who had failed drug tests since 2005 weren't home run sluggers but pitchers, using the drugs for their healing properties, as their arms grew tired from the strain of throwing. At 38, Grimsley pitched only a few innings a game, but he apparently needed drugs to do even that. Grimsley told Novitzky and the others that performance-enhancing drug use in Major League Baseball was rampant. He named names too, telling Novitzky about players who went to "wellness centers" for HGH or had back acne from steroid use. At the end of the debriefing, he even made a phone call to Radomski, corroborating the information, while the feds recorded the conversation.

Until that moment, Grimsley's most famous contribution to baseball history had perhaps been his covert leading role in the madcap "corked bat incident" of 1994. In July of that year, the Chicago White Sox were hosting the hot-hitting Albert Belle and the rest of the Cleveland Indians in Chicago when the White Sox learned that Belle was using a cork-filled bat—a violation of baseball rules. The White Sox manager notified the umpire, who confiscated the bat and stored it in his locker so he could examine it later on.

Grimsley was a pitcher for the Indians. Knowing that Belle's suspension would damage the team's standings, he volunteered to climb through Comiskey Park's ventilation system, drop down into the umpires' locked room, and replace the corked bat with a legal one. The caper worked, at least for Grimsley. The umpires realized the replacement bat wasn't Belle's, and they suspended the slugger, but they couldn't figure out who made the switch. It wasn't until 1999 that Grimsley confessed to baseball writer Buster Olney that he had been the one climbing through the air vents with a flashlight in his teeth.

"That was one of the biggest adrenaline rushes I've ever experienced," Grimsley said upon confessing to Olney. "I went skydiving once, and I can compare it to that."

Grimsley wasn't punished for his confession. It was just the sort of misbehavior that was part of baseball's roguish fun. The line between cheating and mischief was often hard to locate. Spitballs, stealing signs, somehow those were part of the game. Whether people would be as forgiving about regular injections of a drug that was banned by baseball was another question. And what would they think of Grimsley's ratting out of his fellow players?

These were apparently questions that occurred to Grimsley himself; in the days following his conversation with the feds, he had second thoughts about all this cooperation, and did what he probably should have done the second Novitzky appeared on his doorstep: He called an attorney. About a week after Grimsley's "low-key" interview, a lawyer representing the pitcher contacted the United States Attorney's Office and informed them that Grimsley no longer felt like cooperating.

The carrot had been spit back, and now Novitzky used the stick. The report that Novitzky sat down and wrote, an application for a search warrant on Grimsley's home, would soon become the most famous 20-page document in the sports world. In it, Novitzky summarized for Judge Voss his April interview with the pitcher. Novitzky said the information gave him probable cause—the standard Novitzky needed for the warrant, according to the Fourth Amendment of the Constitution. Grimsley was involved with drug dealing, Novitzky told Voss, and the agent wanted to find "any and all records showing contact or relationship with any and all amateur or professional athletes, athletic coaches or athletic trainers."

On June 6, 2006, two and a half years after the BALCO raid, Novitzky served the warrant on Grimsley's home in Scottsdale. Thirteen agents spent six hours searching his place. Novitzky got the items he wanted out of Grimsley's home, but he had blown his cover. The affidavit was a public record, and it didn't take long before it was very public indeed. The sensational news broke that the BALCO investigators were moving deeper into baseball's drug culture.

Grimsley pitched his last game on May 31, the day Novitzky signed the affidavit. That day he was the Diamondbacks' losing pitcher against the Mets in New York. Shea Stadium was the building where Radomski had once been a clubhouse attendant, and so it was an appropriate place for Grimsley to end his career. If cheating at the game, breaking the law, and giving the federal government a way to wedge itself into intimate clubhouse business didn't make him a pariah to his baseball peers, the fact that he named names certainly would.

The Grimsley affidavit bounced around the Internet, a strange new artifact of baseball's drug culture. In it, readers could see that Grimsley had fingered six players and a trainer in his interview. The fact that their names were blacked out seemed to underscore that baseball was still a game of shadows.

The night before the raid on Jason Grimsley's house in Arizona, the San Francisco Giants were playing host to the Florida Marlins. In the fifth inning of the game, right-hander Brian Moehler became the 422nd pitcher to give up a home run to Barry Bonds, who launched Moehler's 0-1 fastball into center field for the 716th home run of his career. The legendary Babe Ruth had hit only 714, and according to a banner that Philadelphia Phillies fans had raised earlier in the season to taunt Bonds, "Ruth did it on hot dogs and beer."

Outside of San Francisco, baseball fans hated Bonds, particularly after *Game of Shadows* came out. He had already set the record for home runs in a single season. Now Bonds was on his way to breaking Hank Aaron's all-time career mark. Pitchers couldn't stop him. Injuries only slowed him a little bit. The BALCO grand jury hadn't yet issued an indictment, but here was an intriguing thought: Could it be possible that Jason Grimsley would be the one to step up to the plate and stop Bonds's inexorable march to the top of the record books? When the news broke about the Grimsley affidavit, and people started guessing about the blacked-out names, that seemed like a distinct possibility. Why else was BALCO-buster Novitzky involved? Had Grimsley fingered Bonds?

This was a burning question for Mitchell, Bonds, and any baseball writer hoping to catch up to the BALCO story (by now there was greater glory in covering the steroids beat). Everyone had questions about this new front in the baseball drug war, but the truth remained buried underneath the black ink of the redactions; the Grimsley matter, despite the public document, was still an active federal investigation.

And almost nobody was sweating as hard as Brian McNamee. Living in New York, his personal training business starting to mature, McNamee watched the Grimsley affair play out in the newspapers with a queasy anxiety. Grimsley, after all, had introduced him to Radomski back in 2000. McNamee didn't need his police training to understand that he was close to getting caught up in the BALCO investigator's web, if he wasn't caught already. The affidavit was available online, and it read:

> Grimsley stated that ██████████████, a former employee of the ██████████████ and personal fitness trainer to several Major League Baseball players, once referred him to an amphetamine source. Grimsley stated that after this referral he secured amphetamines, anabolic steroids, and human growth hormone from ██████████████ referred source. . . . Although Grimsley has never referred anyone to the source he got from ██████████████, Grimsley stated that he is sure that 'boatloads' of players in baseball use this same source.

On June 22, 2006, Clemens returned to the mound for the Astros. Throughout the spring and early summer, the Hendricks brothers had been trying to jack the price up for Clemens's services by leveraging Houston with a pocketful of other clubs, including the Yankees, the Red Sox, and the Rangers. He would be pitching only a portion of the season, so they needed to wring as much out of a team as they could. Clemens had been a hit in Houston in 2004, a season in which he went 18-4, won another Cy Young Award, and turned in a phenomenal 214 innings pitched. The 2005 season had gone well too, with the Astros reaching their first World Series in team history before being swept by the White Sox. Clemens wound up with a record of 13-8 and an ERA of 1.87. But in 2006 Clemens scaled back. He didn't even start pitching until late June, a move billed as a way to save his arm for the postseason. What wasn't mentioned was that the late entry had the added benefit of keeping him out of the way when baseball's drug-testing agents came around.

There were other concessions to age and success beyond the late arrival. Astros owner Drayton McLane again extended to Clemens the "family plan" perk that Clemens had enjoyed. His Astros teammates largely supported the deal, as long as he delivered on the mound.

By this time, all those injections at 90th and First Avenue in New York City seemed like a distant memory. Brian McNamee was still Clemens's personal trainer, but the Rocket had left New York City behind. McNamee didn't know where Clemens was getting juice but assumed the guy had to be getting it somewhere. He thought maybe Houston.

For all the fanfare in Houston and the outpouring of goodwill as another return from retirement got under way, Clemens, who would soon turn 44, showed his age in his 2006 debut at Minute Maid Park. Clemens opposed the Twins' 22-year-old rising phenom Francisco Liriano in an interleague game that drew a crowd of 43,769 — the largest in Minute Maid's short history — and included Hall of Famer Nolan Ryan and former First Lady Barbara Bush. The Dominican rookie left-hander, who was only seven months old when Clemens made his major league debut, was the hero of the game. Liriano nearly went the distance in the 4–2 Twins victory, pitching eight innings and surrendering two runs on four hits. Liriano whiffed seven while Clemens struggled through five innings, striking out four. He was charged with two runs on six hits.

Houston manager Phil Garner had promised to keep his aging right-hander on a strict pitch count — in the area of 100 — but Clemens needed 38 pitches to get out of the third inning alone. He had had only three minor league tune-ups leading to the June 22 debut, but Clemens chose to focus on what went right following the game. "It was positive. My body felt better than expected and I hope and expect to get stronger each time I get out there. I'm excited about it, but I know the work that's involved," Clemens said. "I've got a lot of work in front of me. It's going to be a huge challenge."

Clemens lost his next start at Detroit, as his teammates gave him no support on offense. On June 28, during the same series, Pettitte posted a 5–0 loss to the Tigers, completing Detroit's three-game sweep and dropping Pettitte's record to 6-9 on the season. It was a long way from the previous October, and the World Series appearance. "Obviously, we didn't swing the bats well," Pettitte said after the loss. "We're not playing well right now. This is not a good game. There's nothing positive you can take away from it."

The good times for the Astros would never materialize, despite a late-season surge when they won 10 of their final 12 games. There were no playoff appearances and little return for McLane on the $12.25 million investment he'd made in Clemens. The Rocket finished a mediocre 7-6 in 19 starts and lost his final start in Atlanta on September 29. Pettitte finished 14-13.

. . .

For years Kelly Blair had bragged to people about the steroids and athletes that moved through 1-on-1 Elite, but by the fall of 2006 he didn't want to be known for his links to performance-enhancing drugs anymore. With Barry Bonds becoming a pariah and Craig Titus extradited to Nevada to answer for Melissa James's murder, Blair reached out to his local newspaper to distance himself from the taint of steroids. He spoke to *Pasadena Citizen* reporter Jennifer Branch, who earlier that year had written a story about his gym.

"What I want to do," Blair told Branch, "is get this message out to as many kids as possible. They don't know what they're getting themselves into, and I want them to understand what a dangerous decision taking steroids can be."

On September 4, 2006, the *Citizen* ran a story by Branch alongside a photo of Blair standing in 1-on-1 Elite with his massive arms crossed across his thick chest and a "soul patch" below his lower lip. Blair spoke about having personally witnessed the side effects of steroid use. The headline read: "Trainer Stresses Need to Bulk Up Naturally."

"People that use steroids suffer near-constant joint pain later on down the line," Blair said in the article. "I've seen 30-year-old men that have the joints, tendons and organs of a 70-year-old." Blair explained how rapid muscle growth could put unnatural strain on unprepared joints, not to mention psyches. "I've seen so many [athletes] suffer from depression when they have to cycle off of the stuff, and it's not something that's really talked about," he said. "From what I've seen, it's one of the worst."

Blair authoritatively described how steroids give a person an incredible appetite that lingered when he or she cycled off the drugs, sending them into a vicious cycle of weight gain and depression. "Aggression, broken relationships, increased sensitivity—the problems [run the gamut]," he said. "Using steroids is [essentially] shooting synthetic testosterone into your body, and that causes all kinds of problems."

Blair, the man with photos of all those professional athletes and fighters on his wall, added a word for any professional athlete considering steroids. "You're not going to get away with it," he said. "You're going to get busted and your career will be over." He recommended that athletes build muscles like his the natural way, with good nutrition and proper strength training. Echoing the party-line excuses for baseball's steroid epidemic, Blair claimed that "nutrition technology" had come a long way in the previous decade.

"I've seen the effects steroids have on a body, and it's not worth it," Blair said. "It's just not worth it. Go to someone who can help you train.

Go to someone who can get you on a correct [regimen], who can help you do it the right way, otherwise, your career could be over before it even starts. If you want the fame, you'll have to put in the time, and that will be worth it in the end."

When Sammy Woodrow saw the story, he laughed. It was the world's worst-kept secret among the regulars at 1-on-1 Elite Personal Fitness that Blair was a dealer. His source was the AIDS patient who provided him with the human growth hormone his doctor prescribed to combat wasting. Then there was Titus, who got stuff on his trips to Mexico.

"They all knew about it," said a gym regular. "Every single one of those guys. You gotta understand, they don't try to hide shit from anybody."

In the wake of the BALCO scandal, as the 2003 grand jury testimony of so many players found its way into newspapers, the feds had cracked down hard to plug the leaks. The FBI began an investigation into the leaks, and the judges in the federal court in California expressed outrage.

The secrecy of grand jury testimony is one of the most sacrosanct principles of criminal law; witnesses appearing before such a body could be vulnerable to violent retribution. Furthermore, they aren't allowed to have a lawyer in the room while the prosecutor drills into them, so they are exposed. Prosecutors in the U.S. Attorney's Office with access to the leaked BALCO materials were forced to sign statements promising they hadn't shared the testimony. U.S. District Court judge Jeffrey White also ordered *Game of Shadows* authors Mark Fainaru-Wada and Lance Williams to tell the court who their sources were. When they refused to comply, White charged them with contempt, and toward the end of 2006 it looked as if the two writers might end up in prison. Their situation became a cause célèbre for First Amendment activists, journalists, and others.

Ultimately, the pressure from White led Troy Ellerman, the attorney who had represented BALCO founder Victor Conte's partner, Jim Valente, to come forward and declare that he was the leak. It made Ellerman look incredibly duplicitous; he was on record telling the court, back in 2004, that the leaks were "outrageous" and that "someone in law enforcement" was trying to undermine his client's right to a fair trial. Ellerman would ultimately go to prison. One consequence of the episode was to create ever-greater secrecy on the part of Matt Parrella, his colleagues in the U.S. Attorney's Office in California, and of course Jeff Novitzky, the Dumpster-diving IRS agent who had expanded his probe to include Grimsley.

Still, as the 2006 season drew to a close, there was one more major leak to come as one newspaper advanced the tantalizing story of the Grimsley affidavit, outing McNamee as a supplier, and linking Clemens, for the first time, to the expanding federal investigation that had started three years earlier with BALCO. On October 1, 2006, eight and a half years after Roger Clemens first approached Brian McNamee in the Toronto clubhouse to ask for McNamee's help injecting steroids into his "bootie," the *Los Angeles Times* became the first news outlet to link Clemens and McNamee to a steroid relationship. The front-page story's headline read "Clemens Is Named in Drug Affidavit" and proceeded to implicate Clemens and Pettitte in the Grimsley affair: "Roger Clemens, one of professional baseball's most durable and successful pitchers, is among six players allegedly linked to performance-enhancing drugs by a former teammate, The Times has learned. The names had been blacked out in an affidavit filed in federal court."

It was not the kind of punch a publication would throw without knowing that it would land. The report's author, Lance Pugmire, based his reporting on two sources and claimed to have seen the affidavit. The story continued:

> Others whose identities had been concealed include Clemens's fellow Houston Astros pitcher Andy Pettitte and former American League most valuable player Miguel Tejada of the Baltimore Orioles.
>
> Grimsley told investigators he obtained amphetamines, anabolic steroids and human growth hormone from someone recommended to him by, a source said, former Yankees trainer Brian McNamee. McNamee is a personal strength coach for Clemens and Pettitte.

Pugmire's victory lap was very short. Almost immediately after the story broke, the U.S. attorney for the Northern District of California, Kevin Ryan, made the rare gesture of commenting on it for the media, saying that it contained "significant inaccuracies."

On the Sunday that the story landed, Clemens and Pettitte were in Atlanta, helping the Astros finish up the 2006 season. On the night before the story hit, Pettitte had lost to the Braves. On Sunday morning, as the story was rocking the baseball world, both players denounced it.

"Like I told you guys before, I've been tested plenty of times,"

Clemens said. "My physicals that I've taken, they've taken my blood work. I've passed every test anybody wants. Again, I find it just amazing that you can just throw anybody out there. Like I was telling Andy and some of the guys here today, I guess tomorrow they're going to accuse us of robbing a bank."

Clemens suggested lawsuits would follow if his endorsement deals had been compromised, and he came out with his guns blazing in defense of Brian McNamee. "As far as the training part of it and Mac, I've probably over my career probably had 15–20 trainers," Clemens said. "He's at the top of the list as being one of the best, the most intense."

Pettitte was much more careful in his denials. "I've never used any drugs to enhance my performance on the baseball field before," he told the *Houston Chronicle*. In his own mind, this might not have been a lie; he had been using HGH only to recover from injury. "I haven't used any drugs to enhance my performance on the baseball field," Pettitte said to *USA Today*, repeating his Clintonian hairsplitting.

Pettitte said he wasn't working with McNamee at the time, but still talked to him once a week, and said in the future he would continue to use McNamee, whom he called "one of a kind."

"Mac is the greatest trainer that I've ever been involved with or around," Pettitte said. "Mac's been awesome. He's been awesome for my career."

Clemens and Pettitte did most of their venting to *Houston Chronicle* writer Jose de Jesus Ortiz, who had celebrated their stint with the Astros in a book called *Houston Astros: Armed and Dangerous.*

"I'm angry about it. It shouldn't happen," Clemens told Ortiz. "The assumptions that are out there, I just don't understand it. I don't understand how people can do that and get away with it. I really don't. I don't know how you can just on assumption or hearsay just throw it out there and it's fact."

Randy Hendricks spoke to the Associated Press, defending his guys. "I've grown weary of having to defend Clemens from innuendo and conjecture about every six months for the last several years, when he's complied with all of the rules and the regulations," Hendricks told the AP. "Andy is just surprised and stunned and has no knowledge of any such activity."

All of this was to be expected, of course. Adamant denials, particularly with threats of legal action, were a routine in such cases. The *Times* stood by its story, but there was something fishy about this case. Soon other law-enforcement personnel claimed to have seen what they believed to be the affidavit, raising speculation that someone had produced a phony document or that the document had been altered. The New York *Daily News* reported that a reliable FBI source believed the names were in the document.

The reporters and editors at the *Los Angeles Times* weren't the only ones who believed they had seen a legitimate affidavit with Clemens's name in it. Dan Patrick, then with ESPN, claimed to have received from a previously reliable source a fax of the affidavit months before the *Times's* report, with Clemens's name written in over the redacted portion. Patrick said he couldn't confirm the information.

McNamee, of course, didn't have to sit in a clubhouse and answer questions like Clemens and Pettitte did, so he didn't have to speak about the *L.A. Times* report. Suspicious reporters had been calling his cell phone all summer, ever since the redacted version of the Grimsley affidavit had turned up, but he'd been able to dodge them and keep his name out of the media. Now he was back in the newspapers again, for a mess that was arguably bigger than the sexual assault scandal. It was gratifying for him to see that at least Clemens and Pettitte were backing him up. In the *Houston Chronicle*, Clemens described McNamee in the most glowing terms the trainer could imagine, just after the Grimsley affair broke open.

"He's very good at what he does. I'll train with him any time. He gets the most out of you," Clemens told the *Chronicle*. "And he's not one of those guys that want to hang around with you or be around you. He wants to get your work done and get you where you need to be and be done with you."

On the same day he was answering questions about McNamee to reporters, Clemens sent an e-mail to McNamee with the words "ABOUT TODAY" in the subject line and his jersey number signing the message off.*

> Don't know if you are getting this. . . . Pet and I talk about the BS coming out. What a crock of shit! Anyway, both of us said you were, and are, great to work with and train us one on one now and when

---

* All of the misspellings and grammatical errors in the e-mails that follow have been transcribed exactly as they originally appeared.

you were working with the team. My sister are pissed about this dumb ass article, as is everyone else. Stay strong and take the high road. Who knows next week they will be saying we robbed a bank or something. Stay hot. 22

Within an hour, McNamee replied to his friend, letting Clemens know exactly how painful the situation was for him. He had lost his job with St. John's University:

Rock, Thanks for the email, my family is screwed, they brought up the florida accusations agin with you and pet, my boys cant go to school or practice they are going to get abused I don't know what to do, reporters keep calling, I lost the SJU gig, I can't work in this town anymore, I can handle anything an I will be strong but my kids and Eileen will not be able to deal with the sex thing in Florida all over again . . . please stay in touch . . . Mac

Clemens replied, showing the empathy and loyalty he was known for. Interestingly, he brought up an incident from back in 2001, when he and McNamee had been working out in Houston and came upon a man who appeared to be having a heart attack. Clemens had been impressed watching McNamee perform first aid, and now he commended McNamee again, as if to raise the trainer's self-esteem.

Thats weak for anyone to bring up the Fla shit. From what I remember there . . . it was good that you happened to be there to save someone from drowning. AND you get a oh by the way thanks on the deal at Mem. Park when you tried to save that older man who was jogging. I will never forget how you went in to action that day.
      Same on this end as far as family goes. All the boys are crying and upset.
      Nice comments from people you've always tried to help.
      Anyway, from what I've been told MLB is giving all off us there full support. Hopefully this will blow over in the next couple of days.
      Just remember when these jerks keep asking . . .
      I told them what my mom always told me to remember . . .
      "Don't GET IN A PISSING CONTEST WITH A SKUNK"

The real problem will be if any of the people I represent pull out. Then I will be going after someone with many law suites.
"TOUGH ALL DAY"

McNamee replied with a message suggesting that he meet with Clemens or Jimmy Murray from the Hendricks agency. He also seemed to misinterpret Clemens's threat of lawsuits as a threat against himself.

Thanks for the positive side that no cares about except the people who were there, I still have to talk to Murry or you about some information that I believe is important in a good way for all mentioned today, I would only speak to him as not to bother you so what ever you think, I would also like to sit with you and visit on somethings I would like to get going on, can I shoot out for a couple of days on my dime? Lastly, I am not sure what that last statement meant but if it has anything to do with me in regards to being a rat or flipping on you or anyone of my clients I will hop on a plane, find you, and slap you very hard, if not then I still not sure what it means, Thanks for staying in touch and please continue. Mac.

Later that afternoon Clemens did reply to McNamee, assuring him that the threat of legal action had been directed only at Lance Pugmire, the writer of the *Los Angeles Times* report. With his challenged spelling and grammar, Clemens tried to reassure McNamee of that, and he never reacted to the idea that McNamee might "flip" on Clemens.

Not an anyway is that directed your way. It directed at the dushbag writing the story, and they are hunting down the the person that gave him the paper work so he could on this witch hunt! And that is exactly what this is. 22

Apparently reassured, McNamee apologized to Clemens for getting defensive. The trust was back.

No, I apologize for that, I got it when I read the chronicle which was great I had to get a copy over to my Dad (82 years old and he wont go to church now because of this crap) which made him happy. . . . What should I do about the reporters that show up at my door, avoid them??

The media were on to McNamee by now, and the freelance personal trainer didn't have the vast resources that Clemens and Pettitte had to protect them in such a situation. With the Astros season over, the pitchers could head off for their vacation spots, but McNamee was exposed. Clemens didn't seem to get it.

No comment from here out is the way to go. All they will do now is take stuff we say and spin it how they want. Randy Hendricks will handle it from here out. I will shoot you my schedule next week.

And that was that. As the *L.A. Times* controversy passed, the baseball media got back to writing about free agency, but a Google search on McNamee's name brought up nothing but scandal. There was an overwhelming temptation for McNamee to answer one of the reporters hounding him and try to clear his name, but Clemens had advised against it. McNamee obeyed this directive for a little more than a month.

When McNamee finally broke his silence, he spoke with Jon Heyman of *Sports Illustrated*, the writer who first identified him in print back in 1999, when Heyman was with *Newsday* and McNamee was with the Blue Jays. Heyman's story, based on a pair of interviews with McNamee, hit SI.com on November 10, characterizing McNamee as "one of those old-school people who believes to his core the sign on the clubhouse door that says, 'What happens in here, stays in here.' "

"I don't have any dealings with steroids or amphetamines," McNamee told Heyman. "I didn't buy it, sell it, condone it or recommend it. I don't make money from it, it's not part of my livelihood and not part of my business."

McNamee told Heyman that he still hadn't heard from the U.S. Attorney's Office, and that was the truth. Privately, he was seriously considering just telling the government to fuck off; if the feds ever called.

In December of 2006, nine weeks after the *Los Angeles Times* story and one year before the release of the Mitchell Report on the use of steroids in Major League Baseball, Andy Pettitte decided to return to the Yankees once again, for $16 million and a chance to redeem the dynasty. The split with Houston was unpleasant, but arrival in New York was pretty ugly too.

His implication in the Grimsley affair—however contested—made him suspicious in the eyes of skeptical reporters like Pulitzer Prize–winning William Sherman of the *Daily News*, who teamed with T. J. Quinn, one of the paper's investigative sportswriters, to produce a December 10 article entitled, "Andy Totes Baggage to the Bronx."

"As Andy Pettitte returns to the Yankees, reminding fans of the team's best days, he will also bring a reminder of one of its ugliest episodes," the story read:

> Pettitte remains a devotee of trainer Brian McNamee, reportedly the "amphetamines" source listed in the infamous Jason Grimsley affidavit earlier this year, and a former suspect in a sexual assault investigation at a team hotel in 2001.
>
> McNamee, who has also worked extensively with Roger Clemens, was employed by the Yankees as an assistant strength and conditioning coach at the time of the incident, but his contract was not renewed the following season.
>
> Contacted by the Daily News last month, McNamee said he never provided drugs for anyone, and denied assaulting the woman. McNamee said he wanted to "clear [his] name" after hearing he might have been among the names Grimsley gave investigators following a raid on the former Yankee pitcher's home earlier this year.
>
> "I never, ever gave Clemens or Pettitte steroids," said McNamee, 39, a native of Springfield Gardens in Queens and a former New York City police officer. "They never asked me for steroids. The only thing they asked me for were vitamins."

The story went on to revisit the disturbing details of the sexual assault investigation, and ended with a quote from McNamee saying, "I just want to put all this behind me and clear my name."

Instead, it caused a furor—particularly with the Hendricks brothers, who handled the paychecks McNamee received from Clemens and Pettitte, and were already nervous about the trainer's proximity to their moneymaking athletes. By this point, every agent in the game was worried that George Mitchell was going to target his guys. McNamee sensed the Hendrickses' discomfort, and sent an e-mail to Jim Murray on January 3, 2007, trying to ease Murray's mind.

Hey Jim,

Hope your New year went well, long story longer, final confirmation from Jeff Novitki [Novitzky], the FBI/IRS agent that interviewed Grimsley said" I am Not the trainer in the report and was main reason for there statement of Gross inaccuracies regarding the names, they actually feel sorry for me and that I have nothing to worry about regarding anything.

That article that came out a couple of Sundays ago basically recked any chance of being hired by St John's and or any other job, I never went to the news, my attorney spoke to Sherman and said I was not in the report and wanted to clear me name and that is it

When the e-mail became public a year later, the middle section of McNamee's notes was redacted, but the final words open a window on the paranoia that was filtering through Clemens's world as the government cracked down on steroids.

My point is to fill you in because the players you represent and like last night with andy [Pettitte] you did not know about the [T.J.] quinn [Pettitte] thin, also I WAS NOT OFFICIALLY TALKED TO AND WILL NEVER BE, I WILL NEVER BETRAY MY CLIENTS AND I WANT THEM NOT TO WORRY ABOUT BEING AROUND ME.

If you know any lawyers that would take this case let me know, they can have all the money, I do not care and also sorry to bother you with this but being informed is good no matter how trivial it may be.

Hope all is good, regards,
Mac

By the end of 2006, it had been more than a year since Radomski's house had been raided, and still nobody knew what the ramifications were ultimately going to be. McNamee had his suspicions—given Radomski's ties to Grimsley—but despite the fact that Jeff Novitzky and Matt Parrella had recovered what appeared to be baseball's biggest network, still, somehow, no players had been brought down yet or even seriously threatened.

Radomski was cooperating with Novitzky and Parrella. He basically had no choice; with reams of shipping receipts and personal checks proving that he was a source to dozens of players, the feds, as he would later characterize it, had him by the balls. Specifically it was Parrella, the assistant U. S. Attorney who had led the BALCO prosecutions, who had let him know the trouble he faced.

Parrella came all the way from the Bay Area to Long Island to let Radomski know what the score was (a former assistant district attorney in Suffolk County, Parrella had prosecuted some of Long Island's nastiest murderers in the mid-1990s). He gave Radomski a choice: go to jail for up to 25 years or cooperate and possibly get off easy. It was a squeeze play the Justice Department had put on thousands of dealers over the decades, only this time there was something a little bit different: Rather than asking Radomski to give up someone higher up the distribution chain, the feds wanted to know the identities of the end users.

CHAPTER TEN

April 25–May 8, 2007

Kirk Radomski was overwhelmed with dread as he boarded a flight at New York's John F. Kennedy Airport for San Francisco on April 25, 2007. Radomski had agreed to plead guilty to steroid distribution and money laundering. In exchange, prosecutor Matt Parrella had promised to ask for leniency when the time came for sentencing, as long as Radomski told the truth and cooperated fully with federal investigators. But there were no guarantees that he wouldn't go to prison, separated from his wife and young daughter.

Radomski knew that no matter what happened in the courtroom, his life was about to change immeasurably. He didn't trust the media—he'd seen the good, the bad, and the tabloids during his years in the Mets clubhouse—and he knew there would soon be an army of reporters at his front door, upsetting his family, bothering his neighbors, interrupting his business at Pro Touch, the auto detailing shop he owned in the Long Island town of St. James. The guilty plea would cost him the right to vote and it would cost him business opportunities. He would go down in history as the heavy of the steroid era, the snitch who put the sizzle in Mitchell's report, the no-name clubbie who compromised the national pastime. But if he could just avoid jail, he could be there to see his daughter grow up.

On April 26, Radomski entered the federal courthouse on Golden Gate Avenue through the same doors Barry Bonds, Marion Jones, Gary Sheffield, and Jason Giambi had passed through during the BALCO grand jury proceedings. Like those elite athletes, he too testified in front of grand jurors, his appearance lasting about two hours while his Long Island attorney, John Reilly, waited outside the grand jury room.

Radomski returned to the San Francisco courthouse the following day to enter his guilty plea. "During my past employment in Major League Baseball," Radomski said before U.S. District Court Judge Susan Illston, "I developed contacts with Major League Baseball players throughout the country to whom I subsequently distributed anabolic steroids and other performance-enhancing drugs. I had personal contact with some of my baseball drug clients, but consulted and conducted drug transactions with others over the telephone and the mail."

He went on to say that he'd begun dealing drugs in 1995 and continued through December 14, 2005, when Novitzky executed the search warrant at his house. "I distributed anabolic steroids and other performance-enhancing drugs, including Human Growth Hormone and clenbuterol, as well as amphetamines, to dozens of current and former Major League Baseball players (on teams spread throughout Major League Baseball) and associates," he said. "I deposited the payments for those anabolic steroids into my personal bank account and I then used the proceeds to finance my residence, which was the base of operation, warehouse, and communication center for my anabolic steroid-dealing business."

The plea agreement also spelled out the details of Radomski's service as a cooperating witness for the government, including as an undercover informant and an ongoing grand jury witness, standard terms for a drug-related plea bargain. One condition, however, was far from ordinary, and it immediately raised eyebrows in the legal community: Radomski would have to "cooperate with non-governmental anti-doping agencies at the direction of the government," according to the plea agreement. In other words, Radomski would become a star witness for George Mitchell.

By the time the Radomski plea agreement was entered into the publicly accessible filing system of the U.S. District Court, the news had already broken on the Web sites of three publications—the New York Daily News, the Washington Post, and Sports Illustrated—and the strong whiff of scandal was spreading across the country. Kirk Radomski, former Mets clubhouse attendant and proprietor of Pro Touch Detail Center, was front-page news.

McNamee suspected it was only a matter of time before those blacked-out names would become public. Paranoia struck deep. McNamee had written checks to Radomski for a couple of thousand dollars.

McNamee had a lawyer at the time, a New York attorney named Tom Harvey, who'd seen him through the Tampa sexual assault ordeal and the attendant media attention. Harvey had been introduced to McNamee through Clemens and a mutual friend named Kenny Jowdy when the trainer had needed legal help after the St. Petersburg police started their investigation into the pool incident. Harvey had been reluctant to take on this eccentric trainer, but Clemens and Jowdy persuaded him to help the guy.

Harvey had been involved in a variety of high-profile cases over the years with a roster of A-list clients that read like something out of a Dan Brown novel: Wall Street financiers, Robert De Niro, Hollywood producers, alleged high-ranking mafia members, billionaires, former operatives for the Central Intelligence Agency, law enforcement officials, and even the Catholic Church.

Six years after the sexual assault incident, when McNamee told Harvey that he'd been talking to Radomski off and on for months, Harvey was concerned that the government had put Radomski up to making the calls.

McNamee's dealings with Clemens and Pettitte were ancient history. Whatever Radomski was telling the feds, McNamee was pretty sure they couldn't connect him to getting stuff for ballplayers. He could say the rest of the buys were on behalf of the Wall Street clients he trained. Maybe the feds weren't too interested in them.

Radomski's guilty plea blindsided the Players Association. Just a few hours before the story broke, Don Fehr told a meeting of the Associated Press sports editors that drug testing was working. "The incidence of use is down," Fehr told the editors gathered in New York. "Ten to 15 years from now, people will say, 'with the war, global warming and 9/11, why did we spend so much time on things like Anna Nicole Smith and steroids?' " As the Radomski story began to gain traction, union officials began calling current and former players, warning them to prepare themselves in case Radomski named names. Radomski's clients weren't identified in any of the court documents and press statements available that day—player identities had been redacted from Jeff Novitzky's search warrant affidavit.

Commissioner Bud Selig had ordered league and club employees to cooperate with Mitchell and his investigators, but the Players Association was far less helpful—Radomski was the breakthrough he'd been waiting for.

During the course of Mitchell's investigation, the union repeatedly rejected the senator's requests for documents. Fehr agreed to just one interview; the union's chief operating officer, Gene Orza, refused to meet with the Mitchell Commission at all. The union even barred Mitchell from interviewing the director of the Montreal lab that analyzed baseball's drug tests, although it did permit her to send Mitchell a letter addressing a limited number of issues. In an e-mail to certified agents, Michael Weiner, the union's general counsel, complained that Mitchell had ignored protocol and common courtesy by failing to tell the union about former players he was contacting during the course of his investigation— even though the Players Association no longer represented retirees such as Jose Canseco, Mark McGwire, and Sammy Sosa.

Weiner asked agents to inform union officials when Mitchell's investigators contacted their clients. "The scope of the investigative efforts is plainly inconsistent with the provisions of the basic agreement, related agreements and other statutory rights of all players," Weiner wrote. Before Radomski walked into the San Francisco courthouse on April 27 and entered his plea, the union clearly had the upper hand; the players could stifle Mitchell's investigation by relying on the union's advice to cling to the statutory force of the country's labor laws and, of course, the clubhouse code of silence.

While the plea agreement kept Radomski out of jail and gave Mitchell's investigation credibility, it also left a lingering question: Was it proper for the government to pressure a criminal defendant to cooperate with a private investigation conducted at the behest of a professional sports league? Why should the government share the names of Radomski's clients with Mitchell, but not the *Albany Times-Union*, the New York *Daily News*, *USA Today*, the *New York Times*, or the average citizen?

During a sleepy Sunday home game for the Yankees on May 6, 2007, about 52,000 fans were watching the Yankees trample Seattle when, in the middle of the seventh inning, legendary Yankee public address announcer Bob Sheppard—"the voice of God" as Reggie Jackson had called him—directed the audience's attention toward the private box of Yankee owner George Steinbrenner.

By this point, it was an open secret that the famously micromanaging Steinbrenner was fading into senescence and was disengaged from the Yankees, having handed the day-to-day operations to his sons, Hank and Hal. But it wasn't Steinbrenner the cameras showed in The Boss's box—it was Roger Clemens. There he stood like a papal figure, larger than life and relishing his stardom. Microphone in hand, smartly dressed and wearing a tie, Clemens announced his return to New York after a three-and-a-half year absence.

Soon Clemens was receiving one of the most ecstatic ovations he had heard since that World Series night in Miami in 2003. On the radio broadcast, Suzyn Waldman, a normally sensible voice, seemed to lose all perspective when she spotted Clemens in the owner's box, gushing through an over-the-top description that would become the subject of parodies and viral YouTube clips.

"Roger Clemens is in George's box and Roger Clemens is comin' back!" Waldman shouted on the radio. "Oh, my good—goodness gracious! Of all the dramatic things—of all the dramatic things I've ever seen, Roger Clemens standing right in George Steinbrenner's box announcing he is back! Roger Clemens is a New York Yankee!"

Passing the broadcast to her colleague, John Sterling, Waldman continued: "Roger Clemens is a New York Yankee. You don't have to worry about who's going to take that spot in the rotation. You should see what's going on in the Yankee dugout! Big grin on Jorge Posada's face! Andy Pettitte knew. Big-size Roger Clemens is now a Yankee! Attention, fans! He is here. And now we don't have to discuss who takes that spot in the rotation."

Desperate for pitching, the Yankees had persuaded Clemens to rejoin the Yankee roster, but it was going to cost them. The team had agreed to a pro-rated one-year deal worth $28,000,022, the final $22 corresponding to Clemens's jersey number. That came out to about $4.5 million per month, depending on when exactly Clemens rejoined the squad. The crowd went nuts as Clemens made a brief statement. "Thank y'all," he said. "Well, they came and got me out of Texas, and uhh, I can tell you it's a privilege to be back. I'll be talkin' to y'all soon."

It was the second season in a row that Clemens was making a late arrival to the game. The explanation that was given and dutifully repeated was that teams needed to think strategically about their budgets, and not commit if it didn't look like they'd make a playoff run. But to people who paid attention to the doping issue, it seemed possible that Clemens might be retiring and unretiring to avoid the drug-testing program. The testing that was done was mostly in-season, so there was no reason to get on the testers' radar until it was necessary. But even in a city full of cynics, such calculations rarely occurred to Yankee watchers, who focused on the discovery that Superman would not be available to help the team for a month. For the Yankees, their pitching in tatters, that day couldn't come soon enough. But there was a little problem of getting into playing shape before Clemens could take the ball from Joe Torre for real. Steinbrenner, even in his diminished state, stole the thunder of the signing with a thinly veiled shot at the team's current standings under Torre and general manager Brian Cashman. "As I pledged a few days ago, I will do everything within my power to support Brian Cashman, Joe Torre and this team as we fight to bring a 27th championship back to New York," Steinbrenner said in a statement issued by longtime publicist Howard Rubenstein. "Roger Clemens is a winner and a champion and he is someone who can be counted on to help make this season one that all Yankee fans can be proud of. The sole mission of this organization is to win a world championship."

In the giddy clubhouse after the 5–0 win over Seattle, Steinbrenner's All-Stars looked like awestruck rookies as reporters peppered them with questions about their newest teammate, whom many had played with in his previous stint in New York. "Any team in baseball would love to have him," said Derek Jeter. "Rocket's stuff is still good. The last two years he's been just as good as ever. He's one of those rare players that gets better with age." Johnny Damon had faced Clemens when he was with the Red Sox, and had helped bring a World Series championship to Boston for the first time in 86 years, but he still ranked Clemens's seventh-inning announcement earlier that day as "one of the big highlights of my career. The guy's in such great shape, I'm sure he could run rings around us younger guys. Just knowing he's going to be here real soon is definitely a big lift for us. It's awesome. I can't wait until he pitches for us."

Clemens attributed his choice of the Yankees over Boston and Houston to the private meeting he'd had with Steinbrenner during spring training, a tête-à-tête that he said he would "keep close to my heart for now." As always with Clemens and so many athletes, what was rarely discussed as a matter to the heart was money. Steinbrenner's offer had blown the competition away. Although there was definitely another factor in the decision too: Andy Pettitte had decided to turn down the Astros' one-year, $12 million offer to return to the team in 2006 and he'd accepted the Yankees' one-year, $16 million deal with an option for a second year (the dollars for Pettitte were also a bigger factor than all the self-proclaimed desire to stay near home and family). But there's no question that Clemens was anxious to be reunited with his close friend and training partner.

By the time the excitement over the announcement died down, Clemens was off to Lexington, Kentucky, where he had the luxury of having the state university's baseball facilities at his disposal. He also could watch over son Koby's progress firsthand as a third baseman/designated hitter with the Single-A Lexington Legends. Plus, Clemens had made arrangements for Mac to be there, inflicting punishment on Clemens's body and helping to mold the power pitcher into the Rocket of old. Things had settled down since the Radomski plea, and McNamee was feeling good about himself.

On Tuesday at 10 A.M., two days after his announcement, Clemens arrived at the University of Kentucky's Cliff Hagan Stadium in a Ford Explorer, with McNamee in the passenger seat. Clemens held court talking life lessons to the university's baseball team players in the dugout before jogging to the outfield to stretch and have a long-toss session with McNamee. The Kentucky players were unaware that Clemens would be visiting and they were awestruck by the pitching tips he gave them during a bullpen session on the mound. A couple of players stood in the batter's box while Clemens pitched, but they didn't swing at the pitches, per NCAA rules. Clemens was straddling a fine line as it was by even setting foot on the university field, putting the Kentucky players' collegiate eligibility in jeopardy. The newest Yankee didn't seem particularly worried that his presence might cause the young players problems, and in a 12-minute session with reporters he explained that his real passion was passing on the secrets of his success. "There's a difference between coaching and teaching, and I like teaching," Clemens said. "I enjoy it probably a lot more than what I'm getting myself into again."

Clemens then had the reporters thrown out of the stadium, claiming he didn't want to put the spotlight on Koby, who had come to take batting hacks with his famous father. Later that evening, at nearby Applebee's Park, where Koby's minor league team was playing, Clemens retired to a private suite with McNamee and declined media requests for interviews. It was a rough night for the younger Clemens, who finished 0-for-3 at the plate, as the Legends fell 10–7 to Lake County. After the game, Koby Clemens hacked away in the batting cages behind the home clubhouse, working out his frustrations while his teammates' parents and a few fans milled about. The following morning, the Legends had a rare ten o'clock start, but Koby Clemens's late-night work didn't improve his stats. He went 0-for-2 in another Legends loss. "Just trying to figure stuff out. Real frustrating," Koby said after the game. No sooner had he showered and cleaned up than he was driving the short commute to Cliff Hagan Stadium for an extra workout.

Under a cloudless azure sky the next day, Wednesday afternoon, Roger Clemens dug into his grueling workout with McNamee: sprints, agility drills, and loosening up the $28 million right arm. Dressed in blue shorts with white stripes, a blue T-shirt, and a Yankee cap, Clemens huffed around the basepaths and later fired a bullpen session at Koby, who was able to crack a few line drives off the old man. Media requests to interview Clemens were being filtered through Scott Stricklin, Kentucky's associate athletic director, and Clemens made it clear that he didn't want to talk to New York reporters. Clemens had private use of the stadium courtesy of Kentucky's baseball coach John Cohen, after a friend of Cohen's who worked in the office of the Hendricks brothers had reached out to secure the favor. That special request for privacy did not extend to the area surrounding the stadium, so reporters could observe Clemens from a center field wooden deck as he switched from drills to pitch off the mound, while McNamee acted as a baserunner so Clemens could practice throwing to first. "Pinch-running for the Yankees, Brian McNamee," Clemens said from the mound, mimicking a public address announcer.

Stricklin joined the reporters briefly, and the only sounds echoing off the outfield wall were the occasional cracks of Koby's bat, Clemens's fastballs popping into the catcher's mitt, or Clemens's voice as he occasionally tweaked Koby's stance at the plate. McNamee, in light gray shorts, a gray shirt, and a Kentucky cap, shagged fly balls while Clemens made a few jokes. Late in the workout, several of the Kentucky players took to the outfield to once again watch the legend at work. Stricklin, sensing Clemens was nearing the end of his regimen, slipped from the center field deck around to the front of the stadium to confer with Clemens about interviews as Koby clacked across the pavement toward his Hummer, snickering that he could envision the next day's headlines: "Roger Clemens Beats Up New York Photographer."

Clemens soon followed, barking, "Where's your cohort?" as a photographer and Stricklin followed, looking like punished students headed to the principal's office for detention. Stricklin said little, as Clemens quickly confronted a reporter.

"Weren't you here yesterday?" Clemens asked.

"No," the reporter answered.

"I'm tired of doing the photos of snot coming out and sweat dripping down my face. We've done all that before," Clemens shouted. He had marched out to center field immediately following the workout to curse a photographer and had threatened to "take some film" from him, apparently unaware that most professionals used digital cameras instead of film. The pitcher's patience was running painfully thin outside the stadium. He spotted Koby walking across the parking lot and yelled out, "You, where you headed?" pointing his index finger at his son.

"Going home," Koby replied, still amused by the exchange.

Clemens wheeled back around to face the reporter. "Well, what do you want to talk about?" he said. By that time, an ESPN crew had arrived. They quickly followed Clemens into the weight room to discuss an upcoming interview. Later, it emerged that Clemens didn't want reporters around because he had indeed been made aware that his presence actually could jeopardize the Kentucky players' eligibility. Whether the media crews recording McNamee's presence had made Clemens nervous was unclear, but one thing was certain: McNamee had far bigger things to worry about.

Around four or five o'clock that afternoon, as he was shopping for some sweatpants in a Dick's Sporting Goods store in Lexington while Clemens waited in the car outside, McNamee's cell phone rang. The polite, professional voice on the other end belonged to IRS special agent Jeff Novitzky. The timing could not have been worse. As McNamee stood there, cell phone pasted to his ear and his stomach churning, he could see Clemens. He too was chatting away on a cell phone, oblivious to the drama unfolding inside the air-conditioned store.

CHAPTER ELEVEN

May 15–December 12, 2007

The following Tuesday, May 15, Roger Clemens was exactly where he felt most at home, atop a pitcher's mound, whipping split-finger fastballs while a gaggle of adoring future pitching stars watched his every move. Clemens was officially on the clock for his return to the Yankees and threw 71 pitches while a couple of dozen reporters watched from behind the backstop at the club's Himes minor league complex in Tampa. Decked out in pinstriped pants, a blue long-sleeved Adidas shirt, and a Yankee cap, Clemens began the throwing session as he chatted with the team's vice president of player personnel, Billy Connors, the portly pitching guru who had tended to concentrate on reclamation projects over the years. Word spread through the complex that the Rocket was pitching, and soon Clemens had an audience, the young guns gathered in a semi-circle around the mound. There was Phil Hughes, the can't-miss Yankee right-hander who had injured his hamstring just two weeks earlier during a bid for a no-hitter against Texas, Dominican reliever Jose Veras, right-hander Jeff Karstens, who had suffered a broken right leg in a game against Boston April 28, and Joba Chamberlain, the Nebraska native and first-round draft pick who would star for the Yankees later that season after a rapid rise through the minors.

"Fastball, down the middle?" Clemens asked switch-hitting prospect Hector Gonzalez, who warily took his place in the batter's box. Clemens's pitches made a loud thwap in the mitt of catching prospect James DeSala, who later called the experience "one of the greatest days of my life."

Clemens took a break every so often, demonstrating the proper grips for the different pitches that had defined his lengthy career. Clemens finished up the workout, while the reporters made the short commute to a small press room beneath the field-level seats at Legends Field. About an hour later, Clemens finally took his seat at a table in front of the room, his hair spiked and still wet from a shower. He wore a blaring red polo shirt with the words "Roger Clemens Institute" printed on the front. The institute was part of the Memorial Hermann Medical Center in Houston, and the center had named its sports rehabilitation wing for the pitcher. Here in the spotlight, Clemens looked the picture of happiness, proclaiming "I think I'm right where I need to be to get this under way on Friday." He was alluding to the first of what he anticipated to be two minor league starts before joining the Bombers' rotation, perhaps as early as the end of May. His next assignment was in three days with the Yankees' Single-A squad at Legends Field against the Fort Myers Miracle. Clemens was surprisingly loose and chatty, periodically sipping water and talking about everything from his enjoyment in passing along tools of the trade to young pitchers to the Yankees' place in the American League East standings to getting his 44-year-old body in shape.

"I have the same questions y'all do: Is my body going to hold up?"

Clemens was asked how he would prepare for the grind of the regular season and who, outside the Yankee staff, would be helping him with conditioning and training. "Nothing right now," Clemens said. "To me, what we would consider the little people mean a lot to me. I know the ones that are passionate about their work and that are very good at their work make a difference behind the scenes. I have some old numbers, searching for some people. Therapists that I've had around the country, they know who they are and they've helped me greatly, helped my body recover faster. I can't get soreness out as easy as I used to."

There was no mention of Brian McNamee, a curious omission that led to speculation about his status. A story appeared in the New York *Daily News* that indicated Clemens may have started a search for a new trainer. In adherence to baseball's new rule preventing private trainers from appearing in club facilities, McNamee had returned to New York.

It had been years since McNamee last helped Clemens with an injection. All of that had begun to tail off after the sexual assault investigation in 2001. What trust remained after that point seemed to have been further damaged by the 2003 meeting at Starbucks where McNamee told Jimmy Murray about Clemens's use. But even if Clemens no longer confided in McNamee on the drug front, he had kept McNamee on as his private trainer. McNamee still worked Clemens out, advised him on conditioning, stayed at his home, and traveled all over the country, wherever Clemens wanted him to go.

McNamee assumed Clemens had simply found another source for his performance-enhancing drugs—someone in Texas, perhaps. These drugs were everywhere, after all, and the loopholes in MLB's testing program were so big you'd think the union had negotiated them on purpose. But the pitcher still worked with McNamee for regular workouts. And he was still something of a friend.

So when McNamee read the *Daily News* story, which also mentioned the Tampa pool incident, he fired off an e-mail: "Roc—I saw Redds article and nothing was mentioned, I was looking for something to vindicate myself in the eye of the public and nothing was mentioned," McNamee wrote. "If it's true than please let me know, I do not look very good right now in anyones eyes and to be hones am very upset about it."

Clemens was also asked at the Tampa press conference about the ongoing Mitchell investigation and if he had been contacted by Mitchell. As he would often do when confronted with an uncomfortable topic, Clemens acted as if the question were presented in a foreign language. "I don't know anything about that. I wish I could help you on that one. I can't comment on that because I know nothing about it. I guess that kind of answers your question," he said. The press briefing ended but Clemens stayed seated at the table as a few of the reporters approached him to chat and shake hands. There were no further questions about George Mitchell.

In his first minor league tune-up, Clemens threw 58 pitches—42 for strikes—as George Steinbrenner watched from his luxury box along with a capacity crowd of 10,257. He lasted four innings and his fastball topped out at 91 mph. Then it was on to Trenton, to pitch for the Double-A Thunder five days later. Again, crowds flocked to see the pitching legend, who spent most of the evening before the first pitch in the comfort of a luxury bus parked next to the Delaware River just beyond the park's right field wall. In the style of a rock star, he was later driven in a black SUV to the clubhouse, which was only about 300 yards away. This start, however, did not go as smoothly. Clemens needed 30 pitches to get out of the first inning and struggled to find his command, lasting into the sixth inning.

Finally, it was a trip to Moosic, Pennsylvania, for a start with the Triple-A Scranton/Wilkes-Barre Yankees on a picturesque Memorial Day. With Debbie in the stands, Clemens finally showed what the Yankees were looking for, dishing his splitter and curve, whiffing six Toledo Mud Hens in six scoreless innings. Clemens's controlled performance was undercut by his tantrum after the game. Toward the end of a mostly civil press conference, Clemens's anger flashed when reporters asked whether he considered himself a mercenary and what he thought about the stories written in the last two weeks that had suggested that's what he was. "If you want to be negative, be negative—I'm not a negative person," he said.

"You be negative as much as you want. When I stink and I don't pitch well out there, I know I stink. I don't need you to tell me that. I have pride in what I do. I'm going to pull my heart out and set it right there for you to see it when I perform. I've done that since I was 20. Everything has to be negative these days. There always has to be a negative. If it makes you feel good to write negative stuff, then go ahead. I'll answer [questions] as honestly as I can so that 10-year-old out there, when he reads about it, won't assume things. You can tell how passionate I am about it. Okay?" Clemens pounded the table with his right fist, nearly knocking the tape recorders off the table, then lurched out of his chair toward the exit, Debbie right behind him.

McNamee hadn't told Clemens about Novitzky's phone call in early May, or that the net was closing around him. Instead, he'd traded e-mails with Novitzky, confirming the agent's identity, as Novitzky had suggested he do. Having studied the Grimsley affidavit the year before, McNamee knew exactly what he was up against; the same people who had nailed Victor Conte four years earlier were coming after him.

While Clemens was moving through the Yankee farm system in May, McNamee had reached out to Tom Harvey, the lawyer who had seen him through the 2001 sexual assault investigation. Harvey got in touch with Novitzky and Parrella, and confirmed what McNamee had predicted long before—that they had learned about McNamee through Radomski, and that they were investigating McNamee for drug distribution.

On June 7, just days before Clemens was to take the mound to throw the first pitch of his 24th season in the majors, the federal officers who had busted Barry Bonds came to New York to meet McNamee and Harvey face-to-face. They chose an out-of-the-way office because McNamee was nervous about being seen with the government's de facto steroid regulators.

The federal agents filed into the office with all the businesslike confidence of an old Yankees lineup strolling onto the field at Yankee Stadium. Joining Novitzky and Parrella were Erwin Rogers of the IRS and Heather Young of the FBI—two of the agents who had accompanied Novitzky a year earlier for the trip to Jason Grimsley's house in Scottsdale. Parrella and Novitzky were very matter-of-fact, almost gentle with their prospective witness, laying out the parameters of what they were looking for. There was one thing they wanted him to understand: If he agreed to talk to them, they wanted the truth. If he was going to lie, they preferred that he not give them an interview at all. Talk to your lawyer here, they encouraged him, about the consequences of lying to federal agents.

Once McNamee signed the proffer, a simple, one-page contract in which the government would promise not to use any evidence obtained in its interview in any case-in-chief against McNamee, Novitzky did most of the talking. In the jargon of criminal law, proffers such as the one McNamee signed that day and in days to come were often called "queen for a day" agreements. It was not an immunity deal. They weren't looking for a lot of factual information. That would come later. For now they told him to think about it, talk it over with Harvey.

What was in it for him? McNamee wondered. The government was basically willing to play poker with McNamee, Harvey explained—a behind-closed-doors game where the stakes were McNamee's freedom and the cards were the pieces of information McNamee held about what he'd done with the steroids and HGH he'd obtained from Radomski. There would be no bluffing; McNamee wouldn't know when Novitzky and Parrella were fishing for information, or when they were just quizzing him to verify what they already knew from snitches, phone taps, or even hidden clubhouse cameras. That was why being on the wrong end of a federal probe could induce paranoia—unless you were absolutely honest. McNamee had to be totally candid with the feds. He would never know if they were talking to other people like Radomski—or, for all he knew, Pettitte or Clemens.

McNamee wondered what would happen if he just refused to cooperate. That was an option, Harvey said. But if he did that, and Parrella and Novitzky had something big on him, they could just hit him with an indictment. McNamee would need to be prepared to go to jail in that case, because well over 90 percent of people indicted by the Justice Department ended up convicted—by dint of either pleading guilty or losing their trials—and that would make him a felon. Harvey explained the options: talk to the feds or refuse their request. If you talk, you must tell the truth. If you refuse, you'd better be willing to risk an indictment. Harvey told McNamee he didn't think they'd flown 3,000 miles to try to bluff him. To some extent, it was a lose-lose situation. Even if McNamee staved off the indictment, he would be on the hook. Be prepared to spend a couple hundred thousand dollars defending yourself, Harvey told him. Know that your life will be different for three or four years, that you will go to bed each night knowing you might go to jail.

When it was over, McNamee felt sick, a 180-degree turnaround from when they had walked into the office. Then, he'd felt fairly confident, signing the proffer and moving ahead with the interview. Even though the call from Novitzky the month before had been terrifying, he had given it some thought: He was pretty sure the only checks they would have that he'd sent to Radomski were for the stuff he'd procured for his Wall Street clients. What he'd done for Clemens and Pettitte was ancient history. But by the end of the meeting, it was clear to McNamee that these guys were for real; he'd gotten the sense that Novitzky and Parrella had plenty on him, and he was devastated.

As they walked down the streets of Manhattan, Harvey told McNamee that it was obvious to him that there was more to this whole thing than McNamee had told him, and that if it involved baseball players, especially someone like Clemens, whom Harvey was friendly with, he would need to find someone else to help him out.

Harvey knew just the man.

If there was one constant theme in Earl Ward's legal career, it was that he fought for the underdog. Homeless men brutalized by cops, elderly women protesting the Iraq War: These were Ward's clients. An African-American civil liberties lawyer from New York, Ward was an idealist, willing to take a stand against abuses of power. That meant he was accustomed to suing policemen, not saving them, but when a miserable-looking former cop named Brian McNamee walked into his office in June of 2007, Ward knew right away he was looking at an underdog.

"He looked like he had the weight of the world on his shoulders," said Ward.

A day after signing the proffer agreement, McNamee felt wretched about the position he'd put himself in. With a few strokes of the pen, his fate had been decided. Like that very first Winstrol injection he'd given Clemens way back in Toronto, it was amazing how much a modest little act could change a man's life forever.

Now Harvey had referred McNamee to his friend Ward. Ward was busy with some other cases but he reluctantly agreed to meet with McNamee as a favor to Harvey. The feds wanted another meeting with McNamee that afternoon, and Ward said he would accompany McNamee. This meeting was supposed to be a little more substantial. Rather than reviewing the meaning of cooperation and truthfulness, Parrella and Novitzky were going to be digging for real information.

Harvey had given Ward only a rough outline of what was going on, and said it was simple: just keep the guy out of jail. But Ward took one look at McNamee and knew it wasn't simple at all; the trainer was being asked to rat out his friend and employer. As McNamee sat down in Ward's office in Rockefeller Center and started telling the lawyer the whole story, Ward became aware of the full extent of McNamee's troubles.

In the course of the morning, Ward learned about another side of Roger Clemens, baseball titan and New York hero. McNamee described his role in supplying and injecting Clemens with drugs—most important, the steroids and human growth hormone that McNamee had gotten from Kirk Radomski, whose cooperation with the feds had been public knowledge for several months now. Ward was floored, but empathetic. McNamee was in an almost unbearable position, trapped between two powerful forces, the celebrity of his co-conspirator and the ruthlessness of the war on drugs. Clemens and Novitzky were headed for a collision, and both of them had vastly more resources to draw upon than the man caught in the middle. Ward was thinking of Greg Anderson. Barry Bonds's trainer had done three months in prison after pleading guilty to the BALCO drug distribution charges. No sooner was he out than Parrella ordered him back to the stand to testify against Bonds. Anderson refused, and he went back in the clink again, this time for contempt.

By June of 2007, Anderson was still in the Federal Correction Institution in Dublin, California, and Parrella was pushing forward to secure an indictment against Bonds for perjury. Parrella needed to break Anderson. To put pressure on him, he looked into some irregularities in the tax returns of Anderson's family, and found what he was looking for. In time, Parrella leaned directly on Anderson's family in his attempt to choke information out of Anderson. It was brutal stuff, but the criminal justice system wasn't known for its gentility.

These were the federal agents who were coming to visit the office that afternoon. Never lie to these guys, Ward warned his new client. They will nail you to the cross.

"Parrella was not a stuffy Ivy League guy who couldn't relate to someone like Brian," Ward later recalled. Parrella was, in fact, from Long Island, and had been a Suffolk County prosecutor. He wasn't particularly impressed by the big-name baseball players who were showing up in the investigation. He and McNamee could relate to each other. Ward was comfortable around him too, but not so comfortable that he'd forget the lengths Parrella had gone to to break Anderson and his family.

They all did their best not to show the others their cards. Novitzky and

Parrella weren't explicit about what they had from Radomski, but McNamee had to assume there were shipping receipts, telephone transcripts, and, of course, Radomski's testimony. Ward and McNamee weren't sure what McNamee's exposure was. "Part of him wanted to shut his mouth," said Ward. "But he was a father, had kids. Do you risk being prosecuted?"

For his own part, McNamee held back, downplaying his involvement with Clemens and Pettitte, a tactic he'd refined in his dealings with baseball players over the years. He was cordial but nervous, Ward thought. And while Ward admired McNamee's loyalty, it was his lawyerly duty to make certain that McNamee understood what a losing position that would be; anything less than full cooperation could put McNamee in prison for drug distribution. Besides, there were other people to be loyal to, Ward reminded his client.

"I told him he had to think about his family," said Ward.

There was something else, however, that gave Ward confidence coming out of the meeting. Toward the end of the session, Parrella made a strange suggestion; as part of the cooperation agreement, he might ask McNamee to speak to George Mitchell about the report he was compiling and tell the former senator everything he knew about drug use.

Ward had never come across a demand like that before. As far as he could tell, Mitchell was a private citizen, his ongoing investigation bankrolled by Major League Baseball. It was a hard development to read, Ward thought. It might suggest that Parrella wasn't planning to hit McNamee with an indictment (why would a prosecutor compromise an active investigation that way?). Such an unusual move by a prosecutor might also suggest that Parrella and Novitzky were bluffing—that they didn't really have the goods on McNamee. It was possible, Ward thought, that McNamee's drug-related activities fell outside the statute of limitations. But unless McNamee could come up with another explanation for his dealings with Radomski, he really had no choice. Ward had one job at this point: saving his client from an indictment. It wasn't his place to go questioning the Justice Department about its tactics. He and McNamee agreed to meet with Mitchell later that summer.

Exactly one day after McNamee and Ward had met with the feds in Manhattan and talked about where all of the steroids and human growth hormone had gone, Roger Clemens was just a few miles uptown in the Bronx, finally returning to the mound for the Yankees to start earning that record-setting pile of cash. Joe Torre's club was listing by that point. The Yankees were 28-31 entering Clemens's first game, and were light-years behind the division-leading Red Sox.

The road back had been bumpy for Clemens. After working out at Yankee Stadium on May 30, an appearance in which he had Debbie in tow, Clemens spoke with reporters at Bryant Park for the annual "Pinstripes in the Park" event later that evening, with Debbie accompanying him there as well. The Yankees were playing in Toronto, but the game was broadcast live on a jumbo screen for the audience to see.

"They're all important now," Clemens said over the din of fans outside the tent behind the Public Library, when asked whether he minded missing the upcoming weekend series in Boston. "There's going to be drama wherever I go. It doesn't make a difference."

Instead of starting on the road in Chicago that following Monday, however, Clemens was scratched due to a strained groin. He flew to Tampa for an MRI, which showed scar tissue from an old injury. Yankee fans and management were getting antsy at that point, since Clemens would now be on track to make only roughly 18 to 20 starts if he remained healthy.

Clemens earned the victory that June 9 at Yankee Stadium against a weak Pirates team, the Yankees' fifth straight win. Debbie was in attendance, but spent part of the middle innings visiting the memorabilia store on the field level, with her youngest son, Kody, holding her hand. Clemens was not overpowering, but gutted out six innings of work, giving up three runs on five hits and striking out seven in a 108-pitch outing. But he could not save the Yankees single-handedly—after all, he could be expected to climb the hill only every fifth day and was nearing 45 in a couple months.

"There was good energy here, as expected, and the guys played well, so it was a good day all around," Clemens said after the 9–3 win. "Obviously, I was excited to be back. Each start now I expect to grow stronger."

Clemens took the field four more times in June. He was on the mound for various stretches while the Yankees lost to the Mets, Rockies, Giants, and Orioles. The June 24 loss to the Giants was notable in that Clemens came in as a reliever and faced Barry Bonds—walking him.

Clemens didn't know about the vastly more serious loss he endured that month. June of 2007 was when Kirk Radomski sat down with George

Mitchell at DLA Piper's offices on Sixth Avenue—not far from Major League Baseball's headquarters—and spilled the juice. Radomski arrived at the big conference room on the 29th floor, accompanied by John Reilly, his Hauppauge, Long Island–based attorney. Radomski spoke at length with Mitchell and his staff on three other occasions that year, twice in person and once by telephone. Parrella had promised to push for a lenient sentence after the April guilty plea, but only if Radomski remained truthful and candid with investigators and Mitchell's staff. Radomski delivered, and not just during his interviews. He also provided Mitchell with a massive trove of documents to back up his story—copies of checks, money orders, telephone records, and shipping receipts. There were checks from stars such as Mo Vaughn, Eric Gagne, and Paul Lo Duca, and from scrubs such as Adam Riggs, Bart Miadich, and Mike Bell. There was a shipping record from Kevin Brown, the six-time All-Star pitcher who had played for the Yankees, the Dodgers, and several other teams. In the interviews Radomski did with Mitchell in the summer of 2007, Radomski told Mitchell that when he returned home after being away one day, he found an express delivery package on his doorstep. The package, drenched from the rain, contained $8,000 in cash sent by Brown. And there were checks—for $3,275, $2,400, $1,000, and $825— from Brian McNamee.

Did Radomski know where the drugs he sent to McNamee had gone? Radomski told Mitchell that he knew that McNamee was a personal trainer for Clemens, Pettitte, and Chuck Knoblauch. He suspected that the drugs were going to them. Occasionally, Radomski said, McNamee would acknowledge good performances by Knoblauch or Clemens by "dropping hints" like "he's on the program now." And McNamee would ask Radomski questions, such as what types of substances were best for pitchers.

Earl Ward had arrived with his mother at Kennedy Airport in January 1970, a nine-year-old boy entering the United States for the first time from Kingston, Jamaica, a big bandage on his left eye. On the losing end of a slingshot fight in the backyard of their house in August Town, he'd been struck in the left eye with a rock and the hospital in Kingston hadn't treated the wound properly. His mother, Iris, was taking him out to the house in Great Neck where she had arranged for them to live with a family while she worked for them as a housekeeper. Her son needed an operation on his eye and New York was the best place for him to have it. It was snowing, Ward remembered, and he'd never seen snow before. Ward had the operation in Great Neck, near the house where he lived, but it was too late to save the eye.

Iris Ward eventually brought all five of her children to Long Island, where Ward's father joined the family. During Ward's recuperation from the surgery, and for the next three years, he stayed with the family whose house his mother tended. Ward was reluctant to talk about his accomplishments and the success he forged in a new home with people he had never before met, but he was quick to acknowledge the role that family played in his life—and it wasn't just any family. Earl and his mother lived with the Schwartzes. Fred Schwartz was well known to New York television and radio audiences in the 1970s and 1980s as "Fred the Furrier," described by the *New York Times* as an urbane, avuncular, silver-tongued spokesman for the pelt-purveying shops he operated. In commercials and advertisements, he urged women to step into his "fur vaults" for coats priced far less than fur had traditionally cost. Fred Schwartz was a pioneer in marketing furs—he had locations far from the haughty, high-priced, old-line fur salons—and he had a huge influence on Earl Ward.

The Ward family moved to Parsippany, New Jersey, where Ward made it into Rutgers, graduated in 1982, and entered New York University's prestigious law school, graduating in 1985. By the time he took on Brian McNamee, Ward already had a career straight out of the Atticus Finch handbook. From 1985 to 1989 Ward worked for the Legal Aid Society, and in 1989 he went to work for Norman Siegel at the New York Civil Liberties Union, which in the mid-1990s went head-to-head with Mayor Rudy Giuliani. From 1992 to 1996 Ward served as both a staff attorney and a supervising attorney for the Neighborhood Defender Service of Harlem, for which he represented indigent defendants in criminal matters. He was appointed to the New York City Civilian Complaint Review Board in 1997, his appointment somehow getting past Giuliani. "He didn't know much about me," Ward would say.

In 2006 Ward and Siegel teamed up again to represent the Granny Peace Brigade, the group of elderly women who protested the Iraq War, standing their ground on Fifth Avenue in front of Rockefeller Center just about every day until they were arrested in 2005 for blocking a door to a recruitment center during a sit-in. Ward and Siegel won them not-guilty verdicts. That made for a sweet little story, but most of Ward's cases were much grittier, fought on behalf of the city's truly oppressed, where life-and-death justice hung in the balance every day. One of those cases involved Ronald Davis, a 23-year-old Harlem numbers runner who had fatally shot a neighborhood bully named Eddie Ray Leonard, also known as Bubblegum, in the spring of 1992. Ward helped Davis beat the murder rap but the jury convicted him of manslaughter and sent him to prison.

But the jury had not been instructed to take into account Davis's shocking testimony that he killed Leonard in self-defense, and it was on that basis that the Second Circuit Court of Appeals reversed the manslaughter conviction. Bubblegum, who was six feet tall, weighed 435 pounds and was 20 years older than Davis, had previously robbed Davis three times at gunpoint, raped him, and recently threatened to kill him when he next saw him. The account of one of the rapes was especially chilling. Davis told the trial court:

I was on 146th Street, 518, where I usually take the numbers. I was hanging out there, drinking coffee and I had a danish. It was early in the morning . . . A tall guy comes up to me and he is asking me about drugs. Did I know where to get them? I was telling him, No, I don't know . . . I didn't know that person . . . He kept talking to me. I was trying to walk away from him and ignore him because once I told him no, he still kept talking to me. Then he pulled out the gun and pushed me into the hallway. When I got to the back of the hallway that is when Bubblegum came in . . . [Bubblegum] said, ["T]ake him upstairs.["] [Bubblegum had a gun, and] [t]he other guy had the gun to my back. They both led me upstairs . . . [t]o the top landing of the building. . . . They went into my pocket . . . [Bubblegum] said[,] "I know you got more money." I didn't have any more money. He made me strip . . . [Bubblegum] kicked [Davis's clothes] into the corner . . . Then he sent the guy downstairs, told him to go watch out . . . When he left, Bubblegum hit me in my head with the gun . . . After he hit me in my head I bent down. He took my head and slammed it into the wall . . . That is when he did what he did to me . . . That is when he raped me . . . He stuck his penis in me . . . I was bent down. I told you he held me against the wall . . . I kept screaming, telling him "stop." I was in pain . . . He said, "Shut the fuck up." He said he would treat me like one of the bitches. [Davis said he did not know how long the attack lasted, but it stopped] because somebody had opened the door downstairs and they had closed it . . . I heard the door open and I heard it close. I started screaming even more, figuring somebody would come out . . . I was saying "please stop." [Bubblegum was saying] ["]Shut the fuck up before I kill you.["] . . .

After he stopped he hit me again. I was on the floor. Then he was zipping up his pants. Then he tells me, next time he sees me he is going to kill me.

There had also been the case of Kenneth Banks, a sometimes homeless man selling bootleg videotapes on 125th Street in Harlem. Banks was killed when a police officer hurled a radio at his head as he tried to flee after cops said they saw him in a drug transaction. Ward brought a civil action against the city, winning a large settlement for Banks's family and a judgment that Banks's civil rights had been violated.

On July 9, Ward and McNamee walked together to DLA Piper for McNamee's first of what would be three interviews with Mitchell and his men. The offices, across from Radio City Music Hall, bustled with the activity of millionaire lawyers wearing crisp tailored suits despite the withering heat wave afflicting the city that month.

McNamee came in to the meeting with a wad of chewing tobacco in his cheek and a small plastic cup to use as a spittoon. Tom Harvey would later joke that he was certain Ward had made straight for the buffet of food laid out at the side of the room (the field of law that he had chosen didn't often serve up perks like this, so he took advantage of it).

McNamee sat across the long table from Mitchell and four or five other men. Laptops were open. The trainer wasn't sure which one was Mitchell, but he began to talk. He went back to 1998, and the party at Jose Canseco's house. He told Mitchell about the injections at SkyDome, and the abscess. He talked about how Clemens had arranged for him to come down to the Yankees from the Blue Jays, and he told him about the injections that commenced in 2000, leading to Clemens's surging performance late that season. McNamee told Mitchell about all the injections on the 23rd floor at Clemens's apartment at 90th and First.

Novitzky and Parrella participated in the meeting, as they would in subsequent meetings later that year. In each case, McNamee and Ward were reminded that anything McNamee said that was false would be a violation of Section 1001—the false statement law that Novitzky and Parrella had wielded like a club over Marion Jones and others.

McNamee knew the score; he had to be strictly honest, sharing every detail in order to be covered if the feds or Mitchell unearthed the truth elsewhere. He'd lied to the media plenty of times, and even to the St. Petersburg cops, but he knew this was different: There were no games to be played. But there was one secret that he kept to himself, one thing he didn't tell Mitchell. He hadn't told it to Novitzky and Parrella, and he hadn't even told it to Ward. McNamee didn't tell anyone that back in 2001, growing suspicious that Clemens might not stand by his side forever, he had put some bloody gauze, used needles, and steroids Clemens had given him in a box and kept the box in his closet for the past six years. McNamee never told that story, in part because he knew it would blow Clemens out of the water, and he still was trying to protect the guy to the small extent that he could.

When the meeting was over, and Ward and McNamee had left, Mitchell's people brought Kirk Radomski back into the conference room. He'd been waiting downstairs and he confirmed everything he could about what McNamee had told them.

A little later that month, Pettitte wasn't pitching well, and he'd summoned McNamee to his home in Westchester for a workout. But it hadn't taken long for the weightlifting to devolve into a nervous conversation about federal agents and Mitchell's investigation. According to testimony that would later emerge, Pettitte had no idea—neither during nor immediately after the conversation—that McNamee was familiar with the subject.

They were in the gym at Pettitte's house when Kirk Radomski's name came up. Pettitte was sitting on the weight bench and McNamee was sitting on an inflatable physio ball they used for various exercises.

Like everyone in baseball, Pettitte knew that Radomski had pleaded guilty to steroid distribution in April, and in the weeks that followed, details had trickled out that this former clubhouse attendant for the Mets had links to people all over the sport, and that the feds had seized personal checks for drug purchases. The same agents who had busted BALCO open now had this Radomski character cooperating for a reduced sentence.

Radomski and McNamee were friends. They were both New Yorkers. Pettitte wanted to know, was McNamee going to be next? Would the feds find McNamee's phone number, for instance, in Radomski's contact list?

"I'm not concerned about me," Pettitte told McNamee that day. "I have enough money. I'm loaded. What I'm doing is I'm concerned about you."

Pettitte had seen up close the damage that a bad news story could have on the career of someone like McNamee, who was much more replaceable in the eyes of the baseball establishment than a pitcher with a strong postseason record. The Yankees had cut McNamee loose the first chance they had after the sexual assault allegations surfaced in 2001, and after the *Los Angeles Times* story came along in 2006, Pettitte had seen McNamee struggle for clients.

It was hard for McNamee, in the face of such apparent goodwill from Pettitte, not to tell the pitcher that he had in fact been sucked into the Radomski affair—had met with the prosecutors and with Mitchell.

"I can't help what Radomski said, and I got stuff from Radomski," McNamee told Pettitte. "I dealt with him. I got stuff from him."

Pettitte promised McNamee some level of protection if Mitchell came around. If the senator asked about human growth hormone and Brian McNamee, Pettitte would tell him about the first conversation he had with McNamee.

"I would immediately tell him that, you know, you told me not to do it and that I heard about it from Roger," Pettitte had told McNamee.

Prior to the breakthrough disclosures that resulted from the Radomski plea and the McNamee proffer agreement, Mitchell's investigation had been stymied by the lack of cooperation it was receiving from players and their union. One chink in the wall of silence had been Jason Giambi, who in May of 2007 had let fly with a random burst of candor about steroids during an interview with *USA Today*—after which Commissioner Bud Selig forced him to talk with Mitchell. "I was wrong for doing that stuff," Giambi told the newspaper. "What we should have done a long time ago was stand up—players, ownership, everybody—and said: 'We made a mistake.' . . . We should have apologized back then and made sure we had a rule in place and gone forward. . . . Steroids and all of that was a part of history. But it was a topic that everybody wanted to avoid. Nobody wanted to talk about it."

Mitchell certainly did, and Selig saw an opening. In the commissioner's eyes, Giambi's words constituted an admission of having violated the league's drug policies, providing Selig with cause to punish the player. Selig threatened that he would suspend Giambi if he didn't talk to Mitchell. Giambi briefly considered fighting Selig's decision (an arbitrator might decide that it wasn't much of an admission). But after his involvement in the legal battles around the BALCO affair and his pituitary illness, Giambi was tired of fighting. It would distract him from baseball, he declared, and would put too much stress on his family. "I will address my own personal history regarding steroids," he said in a statement announcing that he would talk to Mitchell. "I will not discuss in any fashion any other individual."

And so Giambi became the first active player known publicly to speak with Mitchell. The wall of silence was cracking.

While Mitchell and Parrella went about their work chasing down Clemens in the summer of 2007, and while McNamee and Radomski secretly spilled some of the juiciest secrets in baseball, the public feasted on a new doping scandal that emerged from upstate New York. Back in February, a new front had opened in the war on steroids in sports. The city of Albany might not have been a major league city, but an investigation led by its district attorney, David Soares, would be felt in big league towns from New England to Southern California: Operation Which Doctor.

Soares's investigation, like Mitchell's arrangement with the Northern California prosecutors, represented a new public-private approach in the battle to eradicate doping from sports. Sports leagues that had relied for decades on urine tests and educational programs to combat steroids were joining forces with law enforcement officials and adding subpoenas, seizures, and arrests to their arsenals. Authorities would share evidence gathered through the course of criminal investigations with sports officials, including shipping receipts from drug suppliers, canceled checks, phone records, and court testimony. This "nonanalytical evidence" could be used by leagues and sport federations to issue suspension.

The World Anti-Doping Agency had already teamed up with law enforcement officials in Spain just a few weeks before the 2006 Tour de France to investigate doping in cycling. The BALCO investigation gave the U.S. Olympic Committee and the United States Anti-Doping Agency, WADA's domestic counterpart, information that was used to crack down on drug cheats in track and field. John Clarke, a New York lawyer from Mitchell's law firm, DLA Piper, met with Soares in Albany on September 13, 2007, just a few days after two attorneys representing Major League Baseball also met with the Albany district attorney.

"The next generation of breakthroughs in the fight against doping in sport will be sport authorities working with public authorities who have the power to investigate and seize evidence the sport authorities don't have," World Anti-Doping Agency chairman Dick Pound had said in May 2007 at a WADA conference in Montreal. "They have the power to regulate trafficking in substances we don't have the power to do."

Mark Haskins, the New York Bureau of Narcotic Enforcement investigator who had posed as the fat, drunk, smack-addicted pilot to buy drugs from Dr. David Stephenson, had since gone undercover online to learn more about the network of doctors, clinics, and pharmacies that provided steroids to athletes and regular Joes alike. Armed with a fake medical license and drug-prescribing number furnished by the Florida Department of Health, Haskins created a bogus medical résumé that he advertised on a Web site, using a government office in downtown Albany as his business address. It didn't take long for anti-aging clinics to contact him, offering him up to $50 every time he signed a prescription.

The investigation became international news shortly after pitchers and catchers reported to spring training camps in 2007, when officials from Albany—joined by officers from Florida's Metropolitan Bureau of Investigation, New York's Bureau of Narcotic Enforcement, the DEA, the Internal Revenue Service, and other agencies—raided Signature Compounding Pharmacy, an Orlando, Florida, business that Soares and other officials claimed was at the heart of the Internet steroid network. In 2002, the company reported revenue of about $500,000, but thanks to its booming Internet business, its revenue topped $35 million in 2006.

Four Signature officers—chief executive officer Naomi Loomis; her husband, Robert "Stan" Loomis, the chief operating officer; Stan's brother Kenneth "Mike" Loomis, the head compounding pharmacist; and marketing director Kirk Calvert were arrested and charged with 20 felony counts, including insurance fraud and criminal diversion of prescription medications.

Albany officials told reporters that seized records indicated that the steroid ring's customers included athletes and celebrities, but Soares insisted that he was after dealers, not users. Ballplayers were not targets of the investigation. "The involvement of athletes and celebrities makes this a very sexy story, but I assure you at this point that it is not our focus," Soares said.

Still, names on those records began leaking out almost immediately, and one of the first athletes identified as a Signature customer was Jason Grimsley.

The biggest name linked to the Albany probe was Rick Ankiel, baseball's feel-good story of the 2007 season. Ankiel had begun his major league career as a pitcher for the St. Louis Cardinals in 2000, posting an impressive 11-7 record and 3.50 earned run average in his rookie season. But in the third inning of Game 1 of the National League Division Series against the Atlanta Braves, Ankiel lost control of his arm, walking four batters and throwing five wild pitches before he was removed. A week later, in the National League Championship Series against the New York Mets, his control problems returned. He was demoted to the Cardinals' Triple-A club in 2001 and was playing in the Rookie League by season's end, labeled a head case whose difficult family life might have accounted for his troubles. Ankiel's father, Rick Sr., was a demanding man who micromanaged every element of his son's athletic development, frequently clashing with the boy's coaches. In Fort Pierce, Florida, Ankiel's hometown, Rick Sr. was known for drinking too much, and he had a long rap sheet dating back to the 1970s that included arrests for offenses such as burglary, carrying a concealed weapon, and aggravated assault. In 2000, Ankiel stood beside his father in court as Rick Sr. was sentenced to six years in a federal prison on drug charges.

Ankiel retired as a pitcher, eventually deciding he'd try to make it back to Major League Baseball as an outfielder. A knee injury sidelined him for 2006, but he hit 32 home runs in Triple-A in 2007 before the Cardinals called him up on August 10 of that year. He hit three home runs in his first three games back in the big leagues. Ankiel was back—and his was an unbelievably inspirational story: Ankiel's arm had let him down on the mound but it was serving him well in the outfield—and he could hit.

The euphoria didn't last long. A month after his return, it was reported that Ankiel had received eight shipments of human growth hormone from Signature Pharmacy between January 2004 and December 2004. Ankiel's prescriptions were signed by Florida physician William Gogan, who provided them through a clinic called the Health and Rejuvenation Center. Seeing Ankiel exposed as a doper was a shock to many baseball fans, even though he had acquired the drugs back when his throwing problems were mounting. It was becoming clear that there weren't a lot of happy endings in these tales of heroism. Fans of track and field and cycling had suffered through these hollow stories for more than a decade, but in baseball the climate of vigilance was still something of a new development, and fans weren't conditioned for such letdowns.

Ankiel wasn't the only ballplayer outed by the Albany probe. In October 2007, with his team battling the Boston Red Sox for the American League pennant, the *San Francisco Chronicle* reported that Cleveland Indians pitcher Paul Byrd bought nearly $25,000 worth of human growth hormone and syringes from the Palm Beach Rejuvenation Center, one of the anti-aging clinics targeted by Albany. Byrd claimed he had a prescription for HGH to treat a pituitary gland tumor, but Commissioner Bud Selig's office denied that Byrd—or any other player—had been given a therapeutic use exemption for growth hormone. The names of other ballplayers with links to the pharmacies and clinics continued to emerge, including journeyman outfielder David Bell, Jay Gibbons of the Baltimore Orioles, Toronto Blue Jays infielder Troy Glaus, and New York Mets pitcher Scott Schoeneweis. A few celebrities—R&B star Mary J. Blige, rappers 50 Cent, Timbaland, and Wyclef Jean—were linked in the press to the pharmacies and clinics. Even police officers were identified as steroid users. When Haskins and his colleagues raided a mom-and-pop Brooklyn shop called Lowen's Compounding Pharmacy in May 2007, they found a woman wearing a surgical gown mixing a witch's brew of stanozolol, the powerful, popular anabolic steroid, in a bowl. Against a wall, a fax machine churned out requests from all over the country for steroids and human growth hormone. Stacks of 50 to 60 FedEx packages filled with steroids for athletes, from high school kids to pros, leaned against another wall, waiting to be shipped out. Authorities said Lowen's may have done as much as $30 million worth of business in illegal drugs in the previous year alone. A second raid at the Bay Ridge business in October 2007 was even more fruitful. Investigators seized $8 million worth of drugs from the pharmacy and found records that indicated that more than two dozen New York Police Department officers bought steroids and human growth hormone from Lowen's.

The building that housed Lowen's was owned by Julius Nasso, a pharmacist–turned–film producer who spent nearly a year in prison after conspiring with Gambino associates to shake down action star Steven Seagal for $3 million in 2001. The pharmacy's owner, John Rossi, shot himself in the head in January 2008 while sitting at a desk in the building, before ever meeting with authorities.

Seventeen doctors and wellness center executives pleaded guilty to charges from Operation Which Doctor, and many of them agreed to testify against Signature's operators. But Albany County Judge Stephen W. Herrick threw out the indictment against Naomi Loomis, Stan Loomis, Mike Loomis, and Kirk Calvert and barred prosecutors from bringing the case to a new grand jury. Herrick ripped prosecutors for the way they had handled the case, saying the indictment and the instructions to the grand jury considering the case were confusing.

"The court finds that the amorphous quality of the evolving indictments, coupled with the cursory and inadequate instructions in the fourth presentment, have impaired the integrity of the grand jury proceedings to such a degree that dismissal is warranted," Herrick wrote in his decision.

A few weeks later, Signature's operators filed a lawsuit in Florida's

Orange County Circuit Court alleging that Soares and other law enforcement officials violated their civil rights during their investigation.

Clemens finished 2007 with a 6-6 record and a 4.18 ERA after having battled everything from foot blisters to elbow inflammation to a nagging left hamstring that limited him to two starts down the stretch in September. While Clemens showed flashes of his youthful self as the season unfolded, the results didn't follow. His teammate Andy Pettitte finished 15-9. After the tumult that Joe Torre endured in the first half of the season, it was all the more remarkable that the manager was able to guide his team into the postseason for the twelfth straight year. The Yankees finished two games behind Boston in the standings. When the Yankees arrived at Jacobs Field in Cleveland to work out on the eve of their series opener, Clemens defied any talk that he would miss his postseason start in Game 3 at the Stadium.

"It's very gratifying to have this opportunity. Now that you're here, all bets are off," said Clemens. "You've got to make the most of it."

The Bombers limped back to the Bronx down 0–2 in the best-of-five series, including the bizarre Game 2 at the Jake. That night a swarm of Lake Erie midges—gnatlike insects—basically took over the stadium, covering the field, flying into players' hair and mouths. It totally unhinged Yankee reliever Joba Chamberlain, leading to a Yankee loss. When Clemens finally did take the mound October 7, the results were terrible. He trudged off the mound after just two and a third innings, his left hamstring having "locked up" while he faced Kenny Lofton, who was leading off the second inning.

The Yankees prevailed 8–4 after three Yankee relievers picked up the slack—"We fight another day," Clemens said after the game—but the Rocket's final stat line in the majors was hardly something to save for the scrapbook: three runs on four hits over two and a third, with two walks and a strikeout. Clemens threw just 59 pitches.

"There was no reason to expect anything," Clemens said. "I felt great. It happened out of nowhere."

As a safeguard, the Yankees took Clemens off the divisional roster the following day, making him ineligible for the championship series if the Yankees were lucky enough to win two games in a row. The normally stubborn Clemens did not even put up a fight against Torre and general manager Brian Cashman. "Normally, he'd fight, but he knows his body and he knows he did enough damage in there that he wouldn't be ready," Cashman said. "There was no fight. There was disappointment, but an understanding that he wouldn't be ready for the next series."

As it turned out, there would be no next series. The Yankees bowed humbly to the Indians in Game 4, their third straight first-round playoff boot. Clemens was not around to speak with reporters after the elimination. But as journalists speculated on whether this was really the true end to Clemens's career, the pitcher was a mere two months away from his Hall of Fame résumé going up in smoke.

Clemens's 2007 record was hardly the payoff that Yankee management and fans were expecting for the amount of money Clemens received and the fanfare that accompanied his arrival. After all, this was the power pitcher who was still whipping 98 mile-per-hour fastballs at the age of 39 during his 2002 season with the Yankees. He'd earned his seventh Cy Young Award in 2004, the year he turned 42. Typically, a pitcher's numbers begin to fade at around 30, but Clemens's career improved after he turned 35 in 1998, his second season in Toronto and his first with McNamee, an anomaly that was difficult for even his apologists to explain. Several months later, when all of Clemens's accomplishments were under scrutiny, an analysis from the Wharton School of Business, published by the New York Times in 2008, showed that Clemens's performance declined as he entered his late 20s and improved into his mid-30s and 40s. The writers of the story didn't speculate on what caused the upside-down performance, but they did write that it appeared that "some unusual factors may have been at play in producing his excellent late-career statistics." Clemens was 26-20 from 2005 to 2007 in 68 starts for Houston and the Yankees, but the 2005 and 2007 seasons were marred by injuries. Had he stopped pitching after 2004, Clemens would have left the diamond exactly as he arrived in 1984—a dominant power pitcher. Instead, he resembled a broken-down warrior, unable to muster one more flash of heat.

George Mitchell, former federal judge and international peacemaker, did not come by his reputation for fairness by accident, and throughout the late summer and autumn of 2007 he sought an opportunity to speak with Roger Clemens directly about Brian McNamee's allegations. Mitchell wanted to give Clemens an opportunity to respond, but the pitcher was steadfastly hidden behind the skirts of the players union and the Hendricks brothers, and was inaccessible to Mitchell. His first attempt to speak with the pitcher had come on July 13, when he'd sent a letter to the union requesting an interview with Clemens. "We have received information that this player allegedly used performance enhancing substances sometime between 1998 and 2001 while a member of the Toronto Blue Jays and New York Yankees," Mitchell wrote. The union notified Randy Hendricks, who more or less ignored it. Hendricks and Mitchell had exact opposite goals when it came to Clemens. One man wanted to find out the truth; the other wanted to protect his client at all costs.

On September 6, as the season was still unfolding, Mitchell sent a letter to all major league players, practically begging them to speak with him. He stressed that the "integrity of the game" was at stake, and he promised confidentiality. He pointed out that while 221 professional baseball players had tested positive for steroids, none had been prosecuted or convicted for possession. And he acknowledged what was now an open secret—that Radomski had been cooperating with his investigation at the direction of the U.S. Attorney's Office, the USAO.

"Under our agreement with the USAO, neither I nor my staff are required to supply any information to that Office," Mitchell told the players. "The USAO has not made any request that we supply them with information nor do we anticipate receiving any such request. I previously served as a United States Attorney and can confirm from direct personal experience that the USAO has at its disposal a vast array of investigative tools—subpoena power, search warrants, the use of agents from several federal agencies, to name just a few—which eliminate any need on their part for my assistance."

Upon reviewing Mitchell's letter, the players union's two top executives—Donald Fehr and Michael Weiner—sent out their own memo to every player. It didn't explicitly advise major-leaguers against speaking to Mitchell, but the memo did say that they should speak to the union or a private attorney before doing so.

"Remember also that there are a number of ongoing federal and state criminal investigations in this area, and any information gathered by Senator Mitchell in player interviews is not legally privileged," the memo stated. "What this means is that while Senator Mitchell pledges in his memo that he will honor any player request for confidentiality *in his report*, he does not pledge, because he cannot pledge, that any information you provide will actually remain confidential and not be disclosed without your consent. For example, Senator Mitchell cannot promise that information you disclose will not be given to a federal or state prosecutor, a Congressional committee, or even turned over in a private lawsuit in response to a request or a subpoena (a legally enforceable order)."

The letters reached the Hendricks brothers, as they did every baseball agent of record. They may or may not have briefed Clemens on the matter, but it probably wouldn't have made much difference. It was in their interest to stick to the company line: Nobody was talking, so why should their client?

Six months later, Clemens told a skeptical audience that if he had known Mitchell wanted to talk to him about steroid use he "would have been down there in a heartbeat." But at the same time, Clemens explained, the assumption was that Mitchell's request had something to do with the discredited Grimsley affidavit, which the Clemens camp considered a closed case. In October, Mitchell and his associates met with union officials and repeated the offer to meet with players whose names had come up in the investigation and present the evidence to them. They sent a letter on October 22, promising players could "examine and answer questions" about relevant information. Five weeks later, the union replied. The union letter said the players had been recontacted. Some had already met with Mitchell; the rest declined to meet with him. By that point, the Mitchell investigation was winding down, and the fuse was lit.

By November of 2007, the 30-year-old Hendricks Agency gofer Jimmy Murray was finally fed up with Brian McNamee. There was no question that Murray had built his career on access and proximity to Roger Clemens, just as much as McNamee had, if not more so. But in Murray's book, only McNamee was the parasite. That's why Murray called him a "gravy-trainer," the word Murray used to describe the hangers-on who got a piece of a ballplayer's action and were always angling for more. It was like the HBO show *Entourage*, which a lot of sports agents followed religiously; any modern-day celebrity attracted a cohort. In *Entourage*, Jeremy Piven played a very thinly veiled version of super-agent Ari Emanuel, who knew how to put the gravy-trainers in their place when they got in the way of financial interests. For some reason, it seemed to Murray, the gravy-trainer phenomenon was the worst with the Yankees. Maybe it was because the perks of being a ballplayer in the city were so great. Like seeing Bruce Springsteen play at Madison Square Garden. That fall, Springsteen had come to play at the Garden, and Roger had called Murray about obtaining hard-to-find tickets for the show. When

Murray told Clemens that tickets might cost as much as $5,000 apiece, Roger was appalled. Murray had asked who the tickets were for, and at first, Roger wouldn't answer. Maybe they were for one of Roger's girl-friends—Mindy or the bartender Angela or the beautiful girl Jennifer. Or maybe they were for Roger himself, or one of his fellow ballplayers. That would be helpful, Murray knew; since celebrities like to be around other celebrities, Murray might be able to work out some kind of deal with Springsteen's management firm. Maybe Bruce would want to chill with Roger. This was the kind of thing Murray set up. But as it turned out, when Murray pressed Roger about who the tickets were for, Roger said they were for McNamee. It pissed Murray off, the idea that he'd help McNamee catch another ride on the gravy train.

By the autumn of 2007, people had begun referring to the forthcoming report on performance-enhancing drugs in baseball as the Mitchell Report, even though a document with that name already existed. Seven years earlier, President Bill Clinton's request had sent Mitchell to the Middle East to investigate the causes of and possible solutions for the vio-lent Arab-Israeli conflict. After the investigation, Mitchell delivered to the State Department a paper called "Sharm El-Sheikh Fact-Finding Com-mittee Report," which was soon universally known as the Mitchell Report.

By November of 2007, word began creeping out that the second Mitchell Report would be published before the end of the year. The offi-cial word was that the senator would share the report with Bud Selig shortly before releasing it to the public, but to honor the promise that the report would be independent, the commissioner would not be allowed to edit the final document. All of this would take place sometime before Christmas, right in the thick of the flurry of free agent contract negotiations.

The biggest remaining mystery, then, was whether Mitchell would name names. At the New York *Daily News*, the reporters who were fol-lowing the steroid story closely were told by a reliable source that McNamee, Clemens, and Pettitte were in the report. "Go with your best instincts," the source had told the newspaper as the Thanksgiving holidays wound down. As it had been in the late 1990s and early 2000s, it was diffi-cult to verify the information of steroid use by certain players without con-firmation from baseball officials or the government, and neither was talking. It was known that Mitchell had spoken to Kirk Radomski, Jason Giambi, and the Albany investigators, but to many reporters, the Radomski cooperation in particular seemed especially unfair. Radomski had yet to be sentenced, but already he was talking to Mitchell, a private citizen with no more right to Radomski's secrets than a journalist had. That was why the Hearst Corporation, which owned the *San Francisco Chronicle*, had sued in June to get access to some of the Radomski information. On December 4, 2007, seven media companies came to Hearst's side, filing briefs with a federal appeals court. The Associated Press, Bloomberg News, CNN, the New York *Daily News*, the *New York Times*, Advance Publications, and the Tribune Company all wanted access to unredacted information related to the raid on Radomski's home. (Radomski's conviction was now eight months old, and his sentencing had been delayed until the following February.)

McNamee was still clinging to the hope the Radomski business would stay secret as long as possible, and that his debriefings before Mitchell would remain private forever. For six months, McNamee had been choking out information to Novitzky, Parrella, and Mitchell, all the while feeling like a rat for selling out his clients. Throughout the summer and fall of 2007, McNamee had suffered under the knowledge that his disclosures might bring Clemens and Pettitte down the way BALCO had brought down Barry Bonds, and that the feds might squeeze him the way they had Greg Anderson. He agonized over the idea that two guys who worked so hard—it wasn't like drugs were the only reason they won games—would have their achievements questioned. And he knew that his own accomplishments would be questioned—maybe it was the steroids, not the trainer, that'd added speed to Clemens's fastball and years to his career. McNamee was still able to enjoy a somewhat normal interaction with Clemens, even using some of the pitcher's fishing equipment when he visited the pitcher's friend Kenny Jowdy in Cabo that autumn. They were alike in that way: each able to compartmentalize the people and the events in their lives. McNamee had had no trouble lying to newspaper reporters over the past year (what was he going to do, admit injecting Clemens, give the drugs a bigger role than they really deserved, expose him as a hypocrite?), but it was much harder to be untruthful to Roger and Andy. He wanted to warn them about the trouble they were in, but Ward had advised against it, reminding him that the feds could lock him up if he did so.

All hope vanished for McNamee on December 3, when he got a phone call from Charlie Scheeler, a former prosecutor who was a partner at DLA Piper. For the past 20 months, Scheeler had been assisting

Mitchell's investigation and McNamee had dealt with him several times. On the other end of the line, Scheeler was holding a final draft of the most explosive piece of Mitchell's report, the nine pages that dealt with Roger Clemens.

Now he wanted to read them to McNamee. It was not a courtesy call; this was McNamee's last chance to correct any information. Scheeler began reading, and McNamee was stunned by what he heard. There were the stories of the injections at SkyDome and the injections at Clemens's apartment. There was mention of the party at Canseco's house in 1998, and the drugs McNamee ordered from Radomski up to 2004; there were graphic descriptions—words like "buttock" and "bellybutton shot."

For McNamee, the phone call was the final straw. Six months as a secret informant had been psychic torture for him. It had damaged his marriage, perhaps irretrievably. It brought total chaos to his bank accounts, and destroyed any image he had of himself as a loyal friend. The stress had ultimately put him in the hospital. He'd lost 25 pounds due to worry. But the worst part of it all was not being able to tell anyone about it.

After the call from Scheeler, McNamee cracked. Early on the morning of December 5, he got in touch with Earl Ward, asking if Ward thought it would be okay for him to call Clemens and Pettitte and warn them about what was in the report. "I don't recommend it," Ward said, but told him he was free to make the calls if he wanted to. Ward knew that McNamee wanted to minimize the public relations hit to Clemens and Pettitte. McNamee had told his lawyers he was prepared to take a beating publicly, as long as he didn't jeopardize his agreement with the government. He picked up the phone and started warning people about the massive betrayal he had been forced to perpetrate. It was a fateful decision. The phone calls McNamee made sent the entire hurricane toward landfall.

The phone calls Brian McNamee made on the morning of December 5, 2007, were like hanging sliders—pitches that fail to break the way they're intended to break. Instead of slipping outside the strike zone, a hanging slider just stays straight, easy prey for even the clumsiest of batters. McNamee's calls had the same results. They were pivotal and irretrievable.

The first one went to Jimmy Murray, who woke up that Wednesday morning in Nashville to find a weird text message waiting for him on his BlackBerry Pearl. It was McNamee, asking Murray to call him from a hard line. Murray was annoyed. He never trusted Mac, and not just because of the Starbucks meeting several years earlier. McNamee always seemed unhappy to Murray. He always seemed to want something.

Murray was in Nashville for the winter baseball meetings, an annual affair where big league executives, team owners and general managers, and top baseball agents all convened to settle contracts, finalize deals, order expensive bottles of wine, and strategically leak news to the baseball writers who roamed the lobbies and hallways. For a 30-year-old aspiring agent like Murray, only a few years beyond living with his parents after college, being there was like being at the grown-ups' table.

Murray got up and went over to his cluttered desk in the hotel room. He walked on a knee that he had damaged while he was a student at Muhlenberg College, effectively ending his own football- and baseball-playing days. The desk was stacked high with a mess of papers—the detritus of the many deals he was working on with Adidas, Reebok, and Nike. The Hendricks firm managed close to 100 ballplayers, and Murray handled shoe contracts. It definitely wasn't big-time deal brokering—Murray certainly couldn't strut around like Ari Emanuel—but it proved Murray was a real sports agent, not some kind of gravy-trainer.

Murray picked up his digital recorder off the table. It was a slim little gadget—the reporters all had them—that allowed you to upload a conversation to your laptop. Murray had picked one up so he could dictate stuff related to deals. It was so much easier than using a tape recorder. He needed the gadget because business got so confusing during the busy times of the year. Here in Nashville, he was able to put a caller on his speakerphone and record the conversation, just to keep track of things.

Murray wondered if he should do that with McNamee. One concern was that McNamee and Pettitte were close, and the news about Pettitte's $16 million option still wasn't public. Murray couldn't prove it, but in the past he and his bosses had suspected McNamee was a news leak. Over the years, details about trades and injuries—details Murray didn't even know about—had somehow appeared in the media. In particular, the tips had gone to Newsday, where McNamee was known to have friends. Handling the media was simply a much easier situation for the Hendricks agency down in Texas, where the local writers at the Houston Chronicle lapped up anything you handed them and never rocked the boat. It was in New York City where you started to get paranoid about the papers. The media there were brutal, in Murray's opinion. They crucified everybody.

So Murray decided that yes, he would record McNamee's phone call. Murray turned on the recorder and set it on the table beside the papers. He put the hotel phone on the speakerphone setting and dialed McNamee's number.

"Jimmy?"

"Mac."

"What's up?"

"I got your text. What's going on?"

"Well, I just wanted to tell you that I'm sick to my stomach," McNamee said. "I'm just trying to alert Roger and Andy that they're going to be in the Mitchell Report."

They talked for a few more minutes. No sooner had McNamee hung up than Murray was running down the hallway of his Nashville hotel to deliver the tape to Randy Hendricks. For the first time, Hendricks heard McNamee's voice explaining how the federal government had linked McNamee to Kirk Radomski, and forced him to talk, and would have locked him up if he hadn't. "I feel like I've been violated," McNamee said on the tape. "So, all I'm doing is trying to give Roger and Andy a heads-up. And I don't know where this is going to go. I don't—I mean, it's terrible. It's—it's terrible. You know, they're going to make me out to be a rat. And I don't know what they're going to make Roger and Andy out to be because all I know is they're looking to hammer them."

Murray would never forget the stunned look on the face of Randy Hendricks. A contract lawyer originally from Kansas, Hendricks liked to feel in control, but now his whole empire was endangered. Randy and his brother had more or less built their careers on Clemens. They represented scores of athletes, but Clemens was their cash cow. When Randy wrote his book, *Inside the Strike Zone*—he sold it on his Web site for $24.95—it told the story of free agency and labor negotiations through the case study of his work on behalf of Clemens. Hendricks took the tape from Murray. The next day he left for Houston. And the day after that he planned to sit down with a very good and very expensive attorney to explore all of his and his clients' options. There was only one lawyer he could think of—Rusty Hardin—who seemed to have the price, the mouth, and the hairdo for a job this big.

McNamee's next call was to Andy Pettitte, who was navigating his green Chevy pickup through the snarl of concrete highways that define Houston, a city built on easy access to cheap petroleum. Pettitte was just setting out for a deer-hunting trip at his 5,000-acre ranch on the other side of the Lone Star State, close to the Mexican border, when he saw Mac's number flash up on the cell phone screen. Ahead of him was a long drive on a more or less straight trajectory toward the beautifully spare uplands of South Texas. He would be on the road for most of the day, going southwest on a highway that ran toward San Antonio and Laredo and the Mexican state of Tamaulipas. Just that week Pettitte had decided to pitch for another season, picking up a $16 million option from the Yankees for his services. From one perspective, it was a huge payday for a couple of quick swipes of the pen. From another point of view, he would earn that money over the course of maybe 30 nights of painful stress on his chronically sore left elbow. Now, all the final details were in the able hands of his agents, the Hendricks brothers, and Pettitte himself was headed out for a week in the South Texas desert, enjoying some solitude and relaxation before he had to start earning all that money by stressing his ligaments again. Cell phone coverage was blissfully unreliable out there. But he wasn't there yet.

When the phone beeped, Pettitte picked up to hear the familiar voice of Brian McNamee, the man who had done so much—even broken the law—to help Pettitte stay healthy enough to pitch. His urgent tone and Long Island accent were a jarring invasion of New York impatience into what Pettitte had hoped would be a relaxing week in the Texas chaparral.

"Hey, man, I need you to call me from a landline as soon as possible," the trainer said, sounding frantic.

Two months earlier, Pettitte had finished his 13th season in the major leagues with a 15-9 record. He had nine weeks before he needed to report to the team's spring training complex in Tampa. But now here came Mac. Pettitte had a reputation for unfailing politeness. He was known to speak softly and patiently even when a bunch of stressed-out reporters crushed in upon his locker with their harsh questions and midnight deadlines after a big loss. What could be so important that Pettitte couldn't talk to him next week, after the signing of the new contract was announced?

"I'm heading to my ranch," Pettitte told McNamee. "I won't be able to get to a landline. I mean, it'll be five or six hours. You know, I'll try to call you when I get back from there."

McNamee's request was as inconvenient as it was strange. Pettitte was still at least five hours from the ranch outside San Antonio, and even then he was hoping to minimize business dealings and focus on chasing whitetails. In the previous year's hunt he had taken down a 183-pound buck—winning his archery category in the Cola Blanca Big Buck Contest organized by the Laredo Chamber of Commerce. And besides, Pettitte tried to save the offseason for family time as much as possible.

Mac said, "I could get in a lot of trouble if anybody knows I'm talking to you."

McNamee hung up, and Pettitte was left with a terrible feeling. He knew this had something to do with the Mitchell Report. He knew that for more than a year the former senator had been compiling a report on performance-enhancing drugs in baseball. Pettitte hadn't spoken with him, but he had heard the chatter and read a few stories. The papers had been saying that Mitchell was prepared to name names. Pettitte had even talked to McNamee earlier that year about what was going on. He hesitated, then picked up his cell phone and called Randy Hendricks. The agent's office was north of Houston, but this week Randy was on the road in Nashville, finalizing contracts. Pettitte wasn't able to reach him.

But Hendricks didn't need to learn anything from Pettitte. He was finding out about the Mitchell Report soon enough, through Jimmy Murray.

Roger Clemens sat on the patio of a casita in Cabo San Lucas and tried to make sense of the news that his agent had given him over the phone. He, Roger Clemens, was going to be named as a drug cheat in George Mitchell's long-awaited report on performance-enhancing drug use in baseball; his longtime trainer, Brian McNamee, had fingered him.

His phone had been beeping with calls from the Hendricks brothers all day, and now Clemens knew why. The words echoed through his mind as he looked out upon the stunning beauty of Cabo, but they didn't knock him out cold. He had been through this kind of thing before with the *Los Angeles Times* story 14 months earlier. That dark cloud had passed, and his reputation had remained mostly untarnished. Besides, the Hendricks brothers could deal with whatever was on the horizon.

For months, any player even remotely under suspicion should have been taking this independent drug investigation seriously. Mitchell had a reputation for getting results, and even if the *Los Angeles Times* had whiffed on Clemens and Pettitte, there was still some suspicion out there about the unnatural longevity of Clemens's pitching arm. No one could figure out how a pitcher could gain speed on his fastball after he turned 35. But as he sat on the patio in Cabo, the sun beginning to set, Clemens had other things on his mind. That day in December, Clemens still had paradise within his reach. He was staying at an exclusive resort and spending his days on a magnificent seaside golf course stretching across the sand dunes to the Pacific. One of his closest friends, golf course developer

Kenny Jowdy, worked and lived in a house down the road. He and Kenny had known each other for 20 years, had neighboring apartments on East 90th Street in Manhattan, worked out together all over the United States, and played golf together. They'd hung out in the regular-guy restaurants and bars Clemens preferred to the bright lights of Vegas and New York. Jowdy had been there for many of the wonderful moments on the field too. He was as good a friend as anyone could ask for.

Clemens had been coming and going from Cabo the last few days, playing golf and hanging out with Jowdy, a few other ballplayers who were also in Cabo, and the winners of a charity auction who had paid close to six figures for the privilege of teeing off with the best pitcher of his time in one of the most glorious pieces of real estate in the hemisphere. To Jowdy, Clemens's reaction upon hearing the news suggested innocence. "I saw how Roger reacted to the L.A. *Times* article, and it was the same way he reacted to this," Jowdy would later say. "He knew it was something he had to deal with, but he had done nothing wrong, so he didn't have anything to worry about." Jowdy would wait for exoneration for his friend. "It is just a shame that such a good man who has done so much for so many has had to endure this."

Clemens was proud of his work with the charity—they called the event "The Day of Golf for Kids," and the proceeds went toward YMCA and youth programs in Houston. Clemens was one of the sponsors of the event, along with another Houston celebrity, former Oiler quarterback Giff Nielsen. Clemens never made a big deal about his charity work. People inside and outside baseball who thought they knew his every move never really knew about all that or about Cabo, where he could relax with friends or rendezvous with a beautiful girl.

What surprised Clemens the most in the phone call from his agent was the growing realization that McNamee might have linked him to this Mitchell business.

That night, Clemens and Jowdy joined a group of friends for dinner at an old Mexican restaurant in the historic district of Cabo San Lucas. At one point, the conversation turned to the phone call Clemens had gotten from his agents. He wasn't sure what McNamee had told them, but he knew it had to do with the Mitchell investigation into performance-enhancing drugs, and the conversation moved to a question that no one would quite answer.

"What is a performance-enhancing drug?" one of the baseball players at the table asked.

"Everything you do could be a performance-enhancing drug," another player answered. "What is cortisone? Is sticking a needle in my ass so I can pitch that day, is that a performance-enhancing drug?"

Nobody at the table was sure, least of all the 45-year-old Hall of Fame–bound pitcher.

Even if they lacked the sophistication to say it, Clemens and his friends were right about one thing that night in Cabo: The lines between what was accepted and what wasn't could be maddeningly hazy. Sports fans and officials had tolerated all kinds of performance-enhancing measures over the years, like amphetamines and oxygen chambers and Lasik eye surgery. Even weight training and the use of personal trainers were relatively new developments that certainly changed players' bodies as well as their stats. Perhaps injections were where people drew the line. Maybe it was as simple as needles. But even that category vanished upon closer inspection; teams shot up players with every kind of painkiller or anti-inflammatory you could think of and there were never any repercussions or cries of outrage. In fact, it was just the opposite: Players were applauded for their machismo and their willingness to ignore or deal with pain. The men at the table knew what it took to stay on the field. They didn't view Clemens as a cheater. As one of the men at the dinner table said later: "Anyone who knows him and everything he's done wouldn't believe he used steroids."

Jowdy was one of the believers. He had seen how Clemens had reacted to the phone call that afternoon.

"Looking back," Jowdy said, "it's hard for me to believe that Roger is guilty. Especially since we were discussing what could be considered a performance-enhancing drug. Why would Roger be searching for the definition, scratching his head trying to figure that out if he really took steroids like Mac had said? It just didn't make any sense."

What went unsaid that night was that they didn't believe he had cheated. If a player, even one like Clemens, took performance-enhancing drugs, it was for an unbelievably good reason: He was injured and was trying to recover, or his contract was ending and he was hoping to sign a new one for the biggest possible bucks, or his legacy was at stake. Team loyalty, money, and pure competitiveness. That's why athletes took drugs. And to athletes those reasons were totally legit.

What the players and their friends at the table hadn't really figured out was that by 2007, Americans were getting sick of all the lying. They had seen it in baseball since at least the 1980s. A long line of lies: *No one was using, no one knew, no one asked, trainers didn't see signs, the commissioner wasn't worried, the union wasn't worried.* And then, even if players *were* using: *It doesn't help. Steroids don't help you see the ball. Baseball is about hand-eye coordination. Bulking up slows bat speed. HGH doesn't work. Fans don't care.* But fans did care. They had seen Floyd Landis lie about the Tour de France, explaining how drinking whiskey had caused a radical spike in his testosterone levels (no explanation, however, for why the testosterone was synthetic). They had seen Marion Jones deny doping in big red letters, pointing her finger at others and suing her accuser even as she used a wide array of drugs to win Olympic gold medals and millions in endorsements, and ultimately go to prison. They had listened to Mark McGwire refuse to discuss the past and heard Barry Bonds and others swear that they were using flaxseed oil rather than steroids as their home run totals doubled and tripled.

This was to say nothing of the corruption infusing the United States on every other level. In a country founded on democratic principles, the notion of fairness was quite basic for people, but they were seeing the social contract breaking down in the economic crisis and its impact on the political landscape. Who owed what to whom was a subject much larger than money. Clemens and his friends could make any justifications they wanted. Steroids were medicine. Fans expected it. Batters were doping, so pitchers were simply leveling the playing field. But the fact remained: Injecting banned drugs was cheating. It was in the rule book, whether they liked it or not.

The first thing children yell out on the playground is "No fair!" and those words are the basis for every moral standard and human interaction they will eventually have. Kids struggle to learn fairness and to accommodate the absence of it. It's no coincidence that a lot of those struggles take place on a ball field or a basketball court or in the streets with a stick and a Spaldeen. The game of baseball, to some extent, exists as a sort of laboratory of fair play, a closed system of finite and specific rules often learned before you can even ride a bike.

That night in Cabo, Clemens and his friends discussed the Mitchell Report and what it might mean. They were not concerned with fairness: They were concerned with winning. They were not going to ponder the gray area, they were going to take action. And so of course a man like Rusty Hardin appealed to them.

Back in Houston, Clemens's agents settled on Hardin, one of the most famous and flamboyant lawyers in Texas. Like Clemens, Rusty Hardin didn't paint corners. He challenged his opponents. He called press conferences. He filed lawsuits. For Clemens, there was no turning back.

"It's what you do when you're innocent," he told his friends. "I didn't do what they said."

With his killer one-liners, round helmet of silver hair, and smooth-as-honey Southern accent, Rusty Hardin seemed to have leapt off the pages of a John Grisham novel. Long before Randy Hendricks called him with the news of a big-time scandal brewing around a big-time baseball player, he had made a name for himself as a celebrity lawyer. A Vietnam veteran and then a bulldog prosecutor in Harris County, Texas, Hardin went into private practice in 1991 and quickly became one of the most prominent defense attorneys in Texas.

Hardin's persuasiveness with juries was legendary. In all of his dealings, he could nimbly adjust his attitude—from honey to venom—to suit his purpose. Around Houston, he was frequently in the news, representing Fortune 500 corporations and quite a few professional Houston athletes.

On December 7, 2007, in Houston, Hardin sat with a stricken Randy Hendricks and listened to the bizarre and shocking phone call that some guy named Brian McNamee had made to Hendricks's employee, Jimmy Murray. The tape was astonishing. In a very short amount of time, McNamee shared an enormous amount of detail about what he had been telling the government over the previous six months about Roger Clemens and Andy Pettitte, two of the city's favorite baseball players.

Under normal circumstances, two prosperous Houstonians like Hendricks and Hardin might have been spending this Friday at a country club. But these were not normal circumstances. In fact, to Hardin, this sounded like a genuine Category 5 hurricane of legal trouble. "I feel like the federal government came in and raped my whole family," McNamee's agitated voice said on the tape:

I can't even tell you what I've been through, Jimmy. I lost 25 pounds and I didn't have 25 pounds to lose. I shouldn't be calling you right now. They told me if I told somebody I'd get locked up. I can't—this is the least I can do. Word for word, if I tell anybody, both deals are off and they're going to come to my house and get me. That's word for word from my attorney and to me.

No lawyer is as successful as Hardin had become without the ability to absorb a lot of information quickly, and there was a lot for Hardin to catch up on: Prior to calling Murray, this guy McNamee had apparently tried to reach Clemens directly, but the pitcher was in Cabo San Lucas at that time; McNamee had gotten through to Pettitte that same morning, and Pettitte had called Hendricks. When they'd connected, the agent told Pettitte not to call McNamee back; Murray had taped the conversation they were now listening to:

> They kept telling me that they wanted to make sure I was telling the truth, that they already knew everything already. They wanted to see if—first of all, they were going to lock me up if I lied. They would lock me up for distribution. And they said that they wanted to see if I'd be a strong witness for them. Those are the things they kept saying.

This was a blockbuster all right, and it could burnish an already high-profile reputation. But Hardin was extraordinarily busy. At that moment, he was representing a Department of Justice employee accusing a federal judge of sexual harassment. That case was heating up: The FBI had initiated an investigation, and the judge, Samuel Kent, had hired Hardin's longtime rival, Dick DeGuerin, to represent him.

Hardin and his firm had other high-profile cases on the horizon too; in the coming year, Hardin would convince a Houston jury that his client Victoria Osteen, the wife of megachurch preacher Joel Osteen, did not attack a Continental Airlines flight attendant who filed a lawsuit claiming she had assaulted her. Hardin would be less successful in defending the Las Vegas Sands Corp.; a Clark County, Nevada, jury awarded Hong Kong businessman Richard Suen $43.8 million after Suen filed a lawsuit claiming the company and its chief executive officer, Sheldon Adelson, stiffed him after he helped them win a lucrative gaming license in Macao.

When a lot of money or prestige was on the line, Hardin was often right there with his dynamite team at Rusty Hardin & Associates, fighting for justice and the status quo. So Hardin agreed to work with Hendricks, Clemens, and Pettitte.

McNamee was in trouble for drug distribution. He was suggesting on the tape that he'd distributed drugs to Clemens and Pettitte. But it was sketchy stuff. Any reasonable trial lawyer had to consider the possibility of a shakedown. Hardin represented a lot of celebrities—the Houston kind, and the real deal too—and he had seen that kind of action up close. It wasn't rare for someone in an athlete's entourage to try to get rich by brewing up a little scandal. "I told them that, you know, between—you know, the first time that Roger's involvement, he used steroids a couple of times," McNamee said, almost seeming to choke on the words. "I just told them—I mean, word for word, from what I remembered—from what I think they would know that I would remember. And the only thing I would remember is when I helped Roger do stuff."

Hendricks and Hardin could then hear Murray, trying to keep his cool, asking McNamee, What kind of stuff was that?

"Steroids," McNamee said.

Okay, what about Pettitte, they heard Murray ask.

"It was one time in the 2001 season—or 2002 season, I believe," McNamee answered, almost stumbling over the words. "When he was on the DL, down in Florida, he—uh—he used growth hormone for two days."

Murray sounded shocked—even though McNamee had told him most of this at their Starbucks meeting—as he asked if that's what McNamee had revealed to Mitchell.

"Yeah," said McNamee. "This is a disaster. For me to have to say this was unbelievable."

On the tape, McNamee told Murray that he had been cooperating with what sounded like a massive government investigation. But to Hardin and Hendricks, it was confusing because McNamee, in his panic, spoke of meetings with FBI agents and an assistant district attorney named "Adam Peralta." McNamee talked about George Mitchell's investigation, and even said that someone in authority had claimed to have some sort of incriminating videotapes from a stadium clubhouse.

> I was assuming they had all the information anyway, other than the fact that they had me to confirm it. They had me to confirm it with Roger and Andy. They really harped on Roger. They wanted to bury—they wanted to bury Roger.

Hardin was a big sports fan (he sat courtside at Rockets games) so he hardly could have missed the news that for nearly two years Mitchell had been working on an internal investigation commissioned by Major League Baseball. Everyone who followed sports—particularly lawyers—wondered what kind of cooperation Mitchell was getting from the government, and how that could work legally. Now McNamee was explaining it.

"And Adam Peralta looked me in the eye and said, 'If you don't speak to Senator Mitchell, you're going to get locked up,' " McNamee said.

Who was Adam Peralta? On the tape, McNamee called him a district attorney, and later, "the one who just locked up Marion Jones." Jones, of course, was the gold medal sprinter who had indeed pleaded guilty to lying to federal agents just a few months earlier. But that was Section 1001, the false statements law; it was a federal case, not something for some local district attorney to handle. And elsewhere on the tape, McNamee talked about the feds. Hardin and Hendricks could only conclude that Peralta was with a U.S. Attorney's Office.

> The federal government gave Mitchell my bank records. They knew Roger—how much Roger and Andy were paying me for the year. They knew how much money I had in my bank account. They knew that I had an apartment. They knew that I had credit cards.

To any lawyer, it sounded downright weird. A private citizen like Mitchell having access to a witness in an ongoing federal investigation? Hardin didn't believe that would fly in a court of law, deputizing some citizen and letting him see bank records.

> They knew—Mitchell knew this—this private investigation firm— the law firm had all like security-type stuff you would need a warrant for. They had my phone records. They had everything. Everything.

Just that day, there had been an item in the *Houston Chronicle* saying that the Mitchell Report was due to be issued the following Thursday, December 13. But nobody knew what was in it, except for a small group of people that now included Hardin. He was one of the few who knew that 354-game winner Roger Clemens was less than a week away from being named as a drug cheat.

> I didn't interview with Mitchell. All I did was sit there and Novitzky had—Mitchell had this whole team of people there, right? . . . His lawyers and Senator Mitchell and then all the FBI people. And all of—Novitzky sat next to me and all he did was read two pages of statements that I made. And he would say "Did you say that?" And I'd just say "Yeah."

At this point, Murray didn't jump in and ask McNamee who Novitzky was. That was probably a good thing. The kid hadn't said much during the call beyond encouraging McNamee to go on spilling his guts. Now they heard McNamee talking up Radomski, sounding somewhat unhinged. "He would get legitimate, good stuff, and guys were taking crack," McNamee said. "Like garbage, like horse shit and cow shit and whatever."

It was an amazing phone call, short but revealing. In just a few minutes, McNamee had sketched out a broad and complicated government investigation into baseball's drug culture. McNamee said that the feds had spoken with "every trainer, coach and strength coach, athlete that was involved with Radomski."

> Jim, I feel right now that I've been violated. I feel like a victim of a crime. As minuscule—it's about—as much as is going in baseball, Jim, I'm about maybe an eighth of it, not even a tenth of a tenth of what they have. Because I did some people some favors.

Toward the end of the call, McNamee had asked Murray if he would let the Hendricks brothers know about what was going on. Murray hadn't promised any such thing. McNamee promised to wait by the phone, and said he hoped Clemens and Pettitte would call him. As far as Hendricks knew, McNamee was still waiting.

Hendricks and Hardin quickly got to work on a plan. The two millionaire lawyers were now in possession of extremely volatile information. Because of the tape, they had a better opportunity than practically anyone of controlling the damage before it occurred, redirecting the hurricane to avoid a direct hit.

Clearly Hendricks was exposed. His firm not only employed a team of accountants to handle finances for Clemens, they managed a nonprofit foundation for the man. On top of that, the massive contracts that the Hendricks brothers firm had landed for Clemens had set the brothers up for life. What if it was all built on a foundation of steroid use? The first logical question that would certainly be asked: Did they know about it?

For Hardin, this was the opportunity for something really big, something that crossed the line from B-list celebrity or titan of finance to superstar athlete. He had represented Houston sports figures before, including Warren Moon (the former NFL quarterback was cleared by a jury of assaulting his wife). But this was much bigger in scope. Pettitte and Clemens were not just a pair of local sports legends, they were national figures.

What was amazing was that McNamee had even made the call. His lawyer would be upset about that, but on the tape McNamee spoke disparagingly of his counsel, who he said was working pro bono. McNamee also hinted that he was looking for new representation. He said he had called John Keker in San Francisco, one of the most successful trial lawyers in the country, but that Keker hadn't called McNamee back. That was as of December 5, the date the tape was recorded.

There were a lot of questions to be answered. Hendricks and Hardin would have to act fast. Should they contact McNamee directly to learn more? On the tape, he sounded ready to talk. He seemed ambivalent about his cooperation with the authorities. Maybe he could give them something to undercut his own credibility. It would be unethical for Hardin to contact McNamee when he knew perfectly well that McNamee had representation. But McNamee had never named his lawyer.

Hendricks and Hardin made a plan to meet with the two pitchers on Sunday night, two days later. Clemens was on his way back from Mexico. Pettitte was cutting his own vacation short too. They would meet with Hardin at Hendricks's house, and decide on a plan. Actually, Hardin was already working out a plan, and it involved two private investigators from his law firm and a hidden recording device.

On December 12, 2007, Brian McNamee opened the front door of his new home in Long Beach, a seaside community just east of New York City, and found two former Houston cops, Billy Belk and Jim Yarbrough, standing on his front stoop. One of them held a letter identifying them as representatives of Clemens and Pettitte. One of them wore a concealed device that would secretly record everything McNamee would say.

McNamee knew this meeting could blow up in his face. God only knew what Ward or Novitzky would say. Parrella might decide it violated the proffer agreement he'd made with them and file criminal charges after all. But McNamee felt it was a risk he had to take.

Jim Yarbrough had spent two decades in the Houston Police Department's homicide and internal affairs divisions before becoming the director of investigations for Rusty Hardin & Associates. Yarbrough and Hardin had been buddies for decades, their friendship going back to the 1980s, when Yarbrough was a police detective and Hardin a state prosecutor. Billy Belk had put in 30 years with the Houston police, mostly as a homicide detective, before leaving the job two months earlier to join his friend Yarbrough on Hardin's staff.

Belk and Yarbrough had flown from Texas to New York that day, driving directly from the airport to McNamee's one-story brick bungalow in this Long Island beach town. It was the day before the Mitchell Report's release. Their job was to find out exactly what McNamee had told the former senator about his most famous clients.

"Hey, Brian, how are you doing?" Yarbrough asked as McNamee opened the door.

"Fine," McNamee lied as he led his visitors into his bungalow-in-exile.

The truth was, things were anything but fine. Things were pretty damn bad. McNamee had been living with his gnawing secret for months. Since reaching out a week earlier to Pettitte and Murray, he had mostly been left to twist in the wind. Not until the day before, December 11, did Murray call and tell him that Belk and Yarbrough would stop by. Now all those months of worry, fear, and anxiety attacks were about to boil over in his new living room.

McNamee wanted to talk directly to Roger and Andy about the information he'd given to Mitchell, information he knew would be all over the newspapers, TV, radio, and Internet in 24 hours. He wanted to give Roger and Andy a heads-up and beg their forgiveness. He wanted a chance to explain why he'd done it. The feds had threatened prosecution, and McNamee couldn't risk a prison sentence. He would do just about anything for his friends, but he wouldn't go to jail for them. He couldn't do that to his kids. Surely Roger and Andy, each the father of four children, could understand that.

McNamee knew his life was headed for the sewer. His connections to the superstars—and the fame and opportunities those connections provided him—would be severed. The introductions to other pro athletes who might want to use his services would be gone. So would the big bucks he'd made training Wall Street traders impressed by his link to Clemens. He'd prayed that the Mitchell Report would not name names. He'd prayed that he would not go down as the biggest rat in baseball history. But he knew, deep down, that his prayers were not going to be answered. He had heard Charlie Scheeler's voice on the other end of the line—and had sensed the presence of the usual complement of law enforcement types, including Novitzky and Parrella—reading to him a selection of the report itself. Soon the whole world would know about everything, all the way back to the injections in SkyDome.

"Tomorrow," McNamee said, "it's going to be a disaster."

Andy might understand, McNamee believed. He'd be angry but he'd get over it. Roger was different. Roger never backed down once something became a test of wills. That was what had made him a great pitcher. That tenacity.

For McNamee, Roger was something of a friend, too, a confidant, even a hero. The fact that the bonds they had forged over fitness and the pursuit of excellence would likely be shattered forever—that was devastating to him. Even McNamee's friends and relatives would wonder why he turned rat. McNamee came from a family of cops, in a neighborhood of cops. The blue wall of silence was practically one of the Ten Commandments in Breezy Point, the tight-knit, blue-collar beach community where McNamee grew up. Cops, like mobsters, didn't snitch on their friends.

McNamee had sent his wife, Eileen, and their three children to Disney World, hoping to shield them from the news that would soon uproot their lives like the late-summer storms that ripped up trees and fences on the barrier island that now served as home. His marriage to Eileen, a schoolteacher, was already strained, and his starring role in the Mitchell Report was going to inflict further damage to their relationship. She'd asked McNamee to move out of their house in Breezy Point, to protect the kids from the media horde that would soon be looking for him. He'd been exiled to Long Beach, a onetime resort town 15 miles to the east that had slid into decay for decades before rebounding as a New York City bedroom community.

McNamee was no stranger to hard times. There had been Brian Jr.'s illnesses, and the Florida sexual assault investigation that had cost him a job he loved with the greatest franchise in American sports. Criminal charges were never filed—McNamee had long claimed his only offense that night was lying to the cops to protect the Yankees—but the damage was done. The *Los Angeles Times* story, although debunked, had irretrievably linked him to drugs, and that had done damage too. Each of those episodes was nightmarish in its own way. But nothing had prepared McNamee for what was happening now. And what he knew was about to happen. He was definitely not "doing fine," as he told Belk and Yarbrough.

"Hey, Brian," Yarbrough asked as McNamee led the men into the house. "Can I use your restroom real quick?"

"Sure," said McNamee, pointing to the bathroom door. "Do you want water, soda—the restroom is—"

"I'll have some water," Yarbrough said.

"I've got water, juice, milk, soda, beer, uh, Red Bull," McNamee continued.

"I'll take some water—some bottled water," Belk said. "Jim was telling me that you were a former New York police officer."

Belk was wearing the concealed recording device that would capture their two-and-a-half-hour conversation. Belk would have to stick to McNamee the whole time, while Yarbrough was free to take a leak. Maybe he shouldn't take that bottle of water after all. He and McNamee fell into small talk.

"Yeah, I was a New York City cop," McNamee said.

"I was just retired from the Houston Police Department," Belk said, trying to find common ground with the man who held the secrets. "October 6th."

"In Houston we had some of the most sensational murder cases in all the country," Belk added. "It seems like we always had them."

Belk had been particularly close to a grim double murder known as the Lover's Lane case. In 1990, the bodies of Cheryl Henry, 22, and her boyfriend Andy Atkinson, 21, were found in a wooded section of Harris County, a remote location where kids parked and made out. Both had been tied up with rope; both had their throats slashed. Henry, an exotic dancer, had been raped. It was a national story and remained unsolved for nearly two decades. The case had haunted Belk. For 18 years, he had gone all over the country chasing leads into dead ends. A week after he retired to join up with Yarbrough at Hardin's outfit, he got a call saying that DNA evidence from semen found on Henry had matched another unsolved rape from 1990. The victim in that case, another stripper, had provided a sketch. The murders could finally be solved. But instead of working on the case of a lifetime, he was on Long Island, wearing a wire for Rusty Hardin.

McNamee tired of the chitchat. "What are you guys doing?" he blurted out. "What are you guys trying to accomplish?" McNamee was ready to talk. The pressure that had been building inside him since early summer needed to be vented. "This can't help me and it can only hurt me. I mean, obviously, I told you guys to come here because I want to help them."

Yarbrough tried to calm the strong, athletic man. "I'll try to be just as straight with you and up-front with you as I can, Brian," he said. "Our goal is simply on behalf of Roger and Andy to talk to you about the knowledge that you have concerning what may or may not come out in the Mitchell Report."

"I know exactly what's going to come out," McNamee replied.

"Well, we don't."

McNamee was surprised to learn that Yarbrough and Belk didn't work for the Hendricks brothers; the agents had outsourced the job to a lawyer. Yarbrough said that Hardin had represented Pierce Marshall, the son of oil billionaire J. Howard Marshall, in the Anna Nicole Smith case. That was supposed to impress him. But McNamee thought he'd be talking to somebody from the agents' office, not a couple of private dicks sent by a Texas lawyer. Despite his reservations, the story poured out of him. Once he got going, he couldn't stop talking.

McNamee began by telling Belk and Yarbrough about his summer meetings with Novitzky and the prosecutor, Matt Parrella, whom he had mistakenly called Adam Peralta, while on the phone with Jimmy Murray. Matt Parrella was an assistant U.S. attorney (not an assistant DA, as McNamee had also told Murray). For six months, McNamee said, he had been talking to them about Clemens and Pettitte. It wasn't just George Mitchell, private citizen operating under the auspices of Major League Baseball, who was sitting on McNamee. It was the feds.

McNamee told Yarbrough and Belk that Novitzky must have heard about him from Radomski. On his way home from the Bronx, McNamee sometimes met Radomski just off the Belt Parkway in Howard Beach, to pick up the high-quality steroids and human growth hormone wrapped in FedEx packages that he would deliver to Yankee players.

"They said, 'We know you picked up stuff. We know you dropped stuff off,' " McNamee told the Texas investigators. " 'We don't see you as a target, but we want to make sure that if you talk to us—we know the truth already, but if you tell us the truth, we want to make sure you're a reliable witness. Also, if you lie to us, we will lock you up.' "

McNamee explained that he'd tried to bullshit his way through his first meeting with Novitzky and Parrella. He told the feds that he didn't know anything about Clemens and Pettitte using performance-enhancing drugs. McNamee said his lawyer had dragged him into a hallway and warned him that the feds knew he was lying. But McNamee wasn't ready to snitch on his friends just yet. He told Yarbrough and Belk that he'd thrown the feds a bone, hoping that would get them off his back, by telling them that a former client, Yankee pitcher Mike Stanton, used human growth hormone and had asked him to pick up a shipment from Radomski.

The bluff hadn't worked, McNamee told Belk and Yarbrough. Parrella confronted McNamee in the follow-up meeting with Ward present. "You have three strikes to go to jail," McNamee said Parrella told him. "You know, you're a cop. You picked up steroids and delivered steroids. That's a federal crime. And if you lie to a federal agent, you go to jail. You have two strikes against you to go to jail. You have one more strike."

The government, McNamee told Belk and Yarbrough, had done its homework. They had examined his bank records. They had reviewed clubhouse videotape, McNamee said. They had interviewed locker room attendants, possibly even players. McNamee had no choice but to tell them about how he had helped Clemens and Pettitte join baseball's steroid fraternity.

A lot of what McNamee was telling Belk and Yarbrough was slightly embellished. In his heart, he feared looking like a rat, so he wanted to impress upon Clemens and Pettitte that he had had no choice but to cooperate. McNamee put a little extra emphasis on how rough Parrella had been, and how much evidence they had against him.

About the injections and transactions, McNamee was brutally honest, having gotten quite used to telling and retelling the stories so many times. Now he told Yarbrough and Belk about the time in 1998 when Clemens handed him the vials of testosterone and a bottle of steroid pills—right there in the SkyDome locker room!—and asked him to get rid of them. He told them about shooting steroids into Clemens's ass in the visitors' clubhouse in Tampa. He told them about the abscess Roger developed on his butt because of a sloppy Winstrol injection. He told them about how Andy had approached him for human growth hormone to help heal his elbow injury.

Even worse, McNamee said, Peralta, Parrella—whatever his name is—told McNamee that it would be in his best interests if he talked to Senator Mitchell for the steroid report he was preparing on behalf of Major League Baseball. McNamee told Belk and Yarbrough he'd refused, but the prosecutor threatened to charge him with conspiracy to distribute if he didn't cooperate.

"That's interesting to us that they would use the arm of the federal government to fund a private investigation for Major League Baseball," Belk said.

"That's what I'm raising hell [about]," McNamee replied. "But no one gives a shit and they just want me to shut up."

Throughout the interview, Belk and Yarbrough were happy to let McNamee ramble, his story fueled by a desire to help Clemens and Pettitte. He was so willing to do this that he would take whatever punishment might come as the result of his cooperation with Novitzky, Parrella, and Mitchell. The Houston cops rarely interrupted, except when they wanted further explanation about a point McNamee had made or to steer him in a direction they thought might be important.

For Belk and Yarbrough, the conversation was as much an education in steroids as an assessment of McNamee. At times, McNamee spelled out the names of the drugs involved. "As your body wears, especially at a certain age, I think the testosterone will aid in healing and recovering on a seven-to-10-day protocol," McNamee said.

McNamee went into great detail, almost as if he was showing off his knowledge of the drugs and his intimate connections to the players and their secrets.

"Roger had an injection once and it bled through his pants," McNamee said. "I know Roger started buying little Band-Aids with the injections, if they bled."

"When was that," Belk asked, "the blood on the uniform pants?"

McNamee corrected him—they were Clemens's dress pants, and it took place on the airplane, where Mike Stanton noticed.

"I think he said something to Roger, and Roger like—something around the lines of 'So Mac's got you?' . . . he made it sound like I told Stanton that Roger was taking something, a growth hormone. And Stanton—and I know Roger's reply was—to Stanton, 'Hey, man, I'll take anything for an edge' or 'I'll do anything for an edge.' And I caught that. And then I grabbed Roger, I think, either that night or the next day; and I said, 'Listen, I never said anything to Stanton.' "

Yarbrough had a lot of questions about how McNamee got paid. Did the IRS guy ever put the squeeze on McNamee about that? About not reporting his earnings or anything like that? McNamee said it never came up, although he told Belk and Yarbrough about the strange arrangement with the Yankees in 2000, when Clemens underwrote the bulk of McNamee's salary even though McNamee was paid through the Yankees. Randy Hendricks set that up, McNamee said.

The meeting was long and arduous, and after several hours of spilling his guts, McNamee was exhausted. He suggested they break for lunch, head down the street and get sandwiches and then bring them back.

"Brian, is there anything else?" Yarbrough asked. "I mean, I know we've—we've asked you a ton of questions and you've been very forthcoming talking to us. Is there anything that you can think of, maybe, that we hadn't touched on or that you think would be important for us to know with regards to these two guys?"

McNamee said he had to make some phone calls, but he'd talk to them more after a break. He complained about the New York *Daily News* hounding him.

"I'm not allowed to tell the media that the government put a gun to my head," McNamee said. "I'm not allowed to say that. So the people that are reading this are going to say, 'Well, McNamee went to Mitchell and told them everything,' which is not what I did. As soon as I felt comfortable enough about going to jail, because my life can't get any worse, that's when I called Murray. Because, right now, I'm pretty comfortable going to jail."

"Let me ask you this," said Belk. "Are you comfortable with us saying — and I'm saying that 'collectively' — saying 'Look, the government put a gun to his head.' "

McNamee didn't like the idea. It could activate the wrath of Parrella and Novitzky. They could come after his taxes. "Roger and Andy will be fine without baseball. Roger and Andy don't have to give back any money. Andy's going to play next year for [16] million dollars. I'm done. I'm done right now. I'm done working. No one's going to hire me."

Yarbrough cut in. "Let me ask you something along the lines of the truth," Yarbrough asked. "I want you to shoot absolutely straight with me. Hypothetically, if Roger Clemens said, 'That is absolute bullshit. None of that ever happened,' is there any doubt in your mind that what you told us today is the absolute truth?"

This was an incredible question. These guys had traveled all the way to New York to look him in the eye and were now suggesting he was lying?

"You first said that Roger and Andy would love to talk to me, but they can't and you know why," McNamee said. "They know I would only tell the truth."

Yarbrough tried to speak, but McNamee's words took on a new edge. He had stuck his neck out at this most desperate hour of his life to tell them what was coming their way and now these guys dared to imply that he might not be telling the "absolute truth"? It was galling.

"Jim Murray would only know that I'm telling the truth," McNamee said. "You know what my biggest problem is? Telling the truth. That's my biggest problem."

"Hey," Yarbrough tried to interject. "Brian."

"And you know what," McNamee said. "I told you more truth than I told the federal government, who wants to lock me up."

Then Yarbrough made a major mistake: At this emotional moment, at the end of the long debriefing, he showed his hand as someone whose interests weren't in sync with McNamee's, not at all. At this moment, Yarbrough brought up the sexual assault allegations in Florida.

"I mean, I know this incident in Florida," Yarbrough said. "I know that's been talked about in the media, the sexual assault allegation. Is there anything in your background from a credibility standpoint that they're going to use against you?"

"Who?" McNamee asked, stopping in his tracks.

"Anybody," Yarbrough said. "If anybody looks at your credibility, is there anything in your background that if someone picked you apart—and I'm assuming the government did, because they told you they knew more about you than you did. Do you think there's anything out there that's going to hurt your credibility? I mean, you sound to me like a very credible person."

A minute earlier, McNamee had been eagerly helping Belk and Yarbrough anticipate the next day's big event, but now he saw that the people in Texas had sent these two cowboys to New York for another reason: to dig up dirt that could be used against him.

"The only people that are going to hurt my credibility are you guys," McNamee said. "I mean, as far as I'm concerned, the only people that were going to—and I'm prepared for this—that are going to hurt my credibility are Roger and Andy, which is what any attorney or agent would say to do."

If Hardin or the Hendricks brothers were going to fight this thing, McNamee knew, a good start would be to attack McNamee himself. That was obvious. The sexual assault question was the biggest red flag anybody had ever waved in his face, and it pissed him off; instead of thanking him for risking the wrath of Parrella by meeting with them, Yarbrough had come right out and asked for his own lynching rope.

Belk tried to defuse the situation. The wire under his clothing still recording every word, Belk began talking about newspaper articles where McNamee had been quoted. McNamee, now suspicious of his fellow cops, wouldn't have any of it.

"Are you asking me to help you or to help your clients?" McNamee asked. "Jim, is that what you're asking me? Is that what you're asking me, to help you to help your clients? I mean, what—why would you want to know my credibility as far as—there's no one else here that—I mean, if there were other people that I told you about, what do you care about them?"

Belk and Yarbrough were on the defensive, trying to counteract McNamee's rising sense of suspicion. They explained that the people bringing up the credibility question might be in the media, as if the Houston team were just preparing to plan to defend him.

McNamee listened, but he had heard enough.

"I think that Mitchell has the smoking gun," McNamee said. "I told them I injected them. You can call me a liar. You can do whatever you've got to do. I mean, what do you want? If you want me to say—I mean, you're telling me–"

"We're not telling you we want you to say anything, first of all," Yarbrough said (doing so could appear like witness tampering, and Yarbrough didn't want to do that, least of all on Belk's tape). "The only thing we want to hear from you, Brian, is the truth. That's—that's all. I just want to make sure that we've got the truth and that we've not got embellishments or anything like that."

"Well, that's up to you to decide," McNamee said. "You're here. That's why you—that's why we didn't do this over the phone."

"Right," Yarbrough said. "Exactly."

"So I'm saying that's up to you," McNamee said. "I'm not going to help you with that. As far as my credibility, I'm looking at it right now. You guys are taking these notes just like the feds did and you're looking at any way—first of all, obviously, you know that's the truth. You don't have to ask me that. You know it is."

It was laughable to McNamee that anyone could have listened to the previous two hours of storytelling and think he'd made it up. The details were too specific, the knowledge too deep. Belk and Yarbrough were cops; they knew how to tell when an interviewee was lying. McNamee hadn't really hesitated or contradicted himself. He had spelled out words like Anadrol, and told them about the day he saw Canseco pop that pill in his mouth. He had described the abscess in Toronto, and the trainer who worked on it, Tommy Craig, "C-R-A-I-G"—all without any pausing, even though his phone kept ringing with reporters' calls.

"I can't see Andy telling you anything different than what I told you and Roger probably, because he doesn't remember any of it," McNamee said. "I don't know. I can't see Roger remembering all that, but this—he's got a lot of stuff going on. But, you know what, if they told you any different, it would only be vaguer; but I'd be surprised if they told you anything different, but I don't know."

McNamee sent Belk and Yarbrough on their way, with directions to a few delicatessens and diners in the area. He didn't know what would happen. He was pretty sure Pettitte would admit to the HGH use, but he didn't know what to expect from Clemens.

"I hope it salvages whatever relationship I had with Andy and Roger," he said as Yarbrough and Belk were leaving.

The most important thing to McNamee was that the two pitchers understood that he given them up to Mitchell only because Novitzky had given him no choice. Novitzky had trapped him between two laws punishable by prison—conspiracy to distribute and false statements to a federal officer—and McNamee had done what he had to do.

"They're going to do whatever their professional lawyers tell them to do and that's best for them in their best interest and I'm going to take whatever—a back seat to that. But in hindsight, no matter what they do, I would prefer that they—at least they know the truth."

Yarbrough promised that Pettitte and Clemens would know everything.

"They will know everything that we know," Yarbrough said. "I can assure you of that."

So would a lot of other people, because by the end of the next month, the investigative staff of a committee of the United States House of Representatives would have a notary's transcript of the tape.

CHAPTER TWELVE

December 13, 2007–
January 7, 2008

If the staff of the Grand Hyatt New York in Midtown Manhattan had its hands full on December 13, 2007, then the doormen had it particularly bad. A freezing rain pounded the shimmering streets of New York City, and unoccupied taxis were scarce. A growing cluster of the hotel's guests waited impatiently for cabs, disrupting the flow of foot traffic along 42nd Street and Lexington—a mix of commuters rushing to their trains at Grand Central Terminal and out-of-town Christmas shoppers bravely striking out for Madison Avenue.

That was not unusual, but on this day the doormen had to work around an army of anxious photographers and cameramen who were also staking out positions under the portico, edging forward each time a limo pulled to the curb. Britney Spears herself could have climbed out of one of these vehicles, but the only "get" these lensmen sought was 74-year-old George Mitchell, heretofore a man of no particular interest to paparazzi. He was due to arrive for a news conference at 2 P.M., rain or shine.

For several hours, the Grand Hyatt's spacious atrium lobby had been a wilderness of media members who had tracked in slushy water and occupied every seat, making an obstacle course for the hotel's regular guests. Dozens of camera crews speaking baseball's three primary languages—English, Spanish, and Japanese—trooped through the opulent lobby. Scores of print journalists were there too, many hunched over their laptops on the leather couches.

Emerging from one of the town cars, holding a big black umbrella, was Jose Canseco. But even though Canseco was an author and an authority on the topic of steroids and baseball, he was not a credentialed member of the media, and despite his vehement protests, he was denied entrance to the Manhattan Ballroom and Mitchell's news conference.

Inside the ballroom was the stage where the senator was due to describe his findings. Facing that were rows upon rows of chairs, many of them already reserved by the coats and the bags journalists had deposited there to claim their seats. On a platform in the back of the room was a forest of tripods, trained on the podium. Technicians in headsets bustled around them, tending to cables that would link these cameras to vans parked outside, with satellite dishes ready to transmit live images for television broadcasts from Toronto to Santo Domingo.

Off to one side of the ballroom stood a mountain of brown cardboard boxes, guarded by a phalanx of attendants. Inside each box were freshly bound copies of one of the season's most anticipated publications—one that was going straight to paperback. Each copy was bound in a pale baby blue cover, emblazoned with the official title in black, capitalized letters:

REPORT TO THE COMMISSIONER OF BASEBALL OF AN INDEPENDENT INVESTIGATION INTO THE ILLEGAL USE OF STEROIDS AND OTHER PERFORMANCE ENHANCING SUBSTANCES BY PLAYERS IN MAJOR LEAGUE BASEBALL

The conclusions had been a zealously guarded secret, printed less than a week before the New York press conference. Bud Selig, the commissioner of baseball who had funded the multimillion-dollar project, had learned the contents of the report just two days earlier, when his vice president for labor relations, Rob Manfred, reported back to him after poring over the report in Mitchell's DLA Piper offices in Midtown.

Selig hadn't held the actual report in his hands until that morning, while union chief Don Fehr, who had done almost everything he could to stifle Mitchell's investigation, had received a copy only that afternoon, an hour before Mitchell's appearance.

Shortly before 2 P.M., one of the Grand Hyatt's doormen scampered to the curb, opened the door of another black town car, and held out an umbrella for the man of the hour: The Honorable George J. Mitchell, former United States senator from the state of Maine, lifelong Red Sox fan and Democrat, had arrived.

The young men and women who had been guarding the boxes started handing out copies of the Mitchell Report to reporters at the exact moment a digital version was posted on Major League Baseball's Web site for anyone to download. Inside those bound covers was a bombshell disguised in lawyerly prose, simultaneously a history textbook and a corporate strategy sheet.

Mitchell had been diagnosed with prostate cancer a few months before he stepped behind the podium at the Grand Hyatt. But his voice was strong and unwavering as he described how players and owners alike had allowed and propelled the steroid epidemic to sweep through the national pastime. His team had interviewed more than 700 "witnesses" in the United States, Canada, and the Dominican Republic, and reviewed more than 115,000 pages of documents from the commissioner's office and the 30 major league clubs. More than 550 of those interviewed were current or former club officials, including managers, coaches, physicians, trainers, or security agents. Selig himself and 16 people in his office had met with Mitchell, as had 68 former players.

"Everyone involved in baseball over the past two decades—commissioners, club officials, the players' association and players—shares to some extent the responsibility for the steroids era," Mitchell said. "There was a collective failure to recognize the problem as it emerged, and to deal with it early on."

The report, the product of 21 months of investigation, was 409 pages with summary and appendices attached, and there were 585 footnotes. The meat of the document contained a history of baseball's herky-jerky efforts to police its drug problems, and a detailed accounting of the investigation's findings, but the most important part, in Mitchell's eyes, was a list of specific recommendations for moving beyond what the senator called the "steroids era."

The recommendations were compelling, but the news of the day was the names of 89 players the senator identified as drug cheats, especially the biggest name—Roger Clemens. By the time Mitchell had stopped speaking, reporters had skimmed through the report, posted stories from their laptops and BlackBerrys, and begun the process of analyzing what had just transpired.

And the the media's work was far from over. Selig conducted his own press conference a few blocks away at the Waldorf-Astoria. He vowed not to let the steroid problem fester any longer.

"If there are problems, I wanted them revealed," Selig said. "His report is a call to action, and I will act."

Selig also promised to address the prickly growth hormone issue, one that had given MLB a major black eye since there was still no testing for HGH in the league's drug-testing program, even though it was banned before the 2005 season. "So long as there might be potential cheaters in the game, we have to constantly update what we do to catch them," Selig said. "And that's exactly what I intend to do. We will not rest. Anybody who knows me well has to know that this is not something I wish had happened, but it has. And I have to do something about it. I cannot say it any more plainly. I have to do something."

The Players Association held its own press conference, at the Inter-Continental Hotel, and union chief Fehr went on the offensive, arguing that players' rights had been compromised and that their reputations were sullied "probably forever."

"Many players are named. Their reputations have been adversely affected, probably forever—even if it turns out down the road that they should not have been," Fehr said. "The program in place today is a strong and effective one and has been improved even in the last two years. The report does not suggest that the program is failing to pick up steroid use, which it is possible to detect."

With Mitchell, Selig, and Fehr each taking a turn at their separate podiums in Midtown Manhattan, there wasn't a lot of space for anyone else in baseball to grab the cameras' attention that day. But Jose Canseco did his best.

Canseco was waiting when journalists came spilling out of the Manhattan Ballroom with their copies of the Mitchell Report, and he wasted no time in belittling the report and pitching a sequel to his best-selling book *Juiced*. During an interview in the Waldorf's frumpy Bull & Bear bar with the Fox Business Network, Canseco, dressed in sequined leather pants and a lavender jacket, said Mitchell's report was incomplete because it didn't name Alex Rodriguez—who had officially signed a 10-year, $275 million contract with the Yankees earlier that day—as a steroid user.

"All I can say is the Mitchell Report is incomplete," Canseco said. "I could not believe that [Rodriguez's] name was not in the report."

Then Clemens's name was mentioned by Fox *Happy Hour* host Rebecca Gomez, and Canseco, who had been one of the first to publicly air suspicions about Clemens's longevity, now wavered.

"As you say in your book [*Juiced*], you introduced Roger Clemens to steroids," said Gomez before a commercial break.

"That's an absolute lie," Canseco said, cutting her off.

"That's a lie?" asked Gomez.

"I have no reason to lie. I never, ever introduced or gave—or any way, shape, or form—any type of steroids to Roger Clemens. I'll polygraph right now and prove it," Canseco said. "We spoke about it. I couldn't put 100 percent certainty that Roger had ever used any type of steroid. I never injected him. I never put him in contact with anybody that could get him the substance. Never."

Canseco and his opinions, however, were secondary in the days after Mitchell released his report. Mitchell and his investigation had exposed a side of Major League Baseball that fans had never seen before, and nobody was left more exposed than Roger Clemens.

On the day the Mitchell Report was released, the Democratic chairman and ranking Republican leader of the House Committee on Oversight and Government Reform issued a joint statement calling December 13 a "sad day for Major League Baseball but a good day for integrity in sports."

"The Mitchell Report is sobering," Henry Waxman and Tom Davis wrote. "It shows the use of steroids and human growth hormone has been and is a significant problem in Major League Baseball. And it shows that everyone involved in Major League Baseball bears some responsibility for this scandal."

Waxman and Davis announced that they would ask Mitchell, Selig, and Fehr to testify before the committee in a public hearing on January 15, 2008. They would ask questions about the report's recommendations and whether "additional measures" were necessary.

"We want to commend Commissioner Selig for authorizing this investigation and thank Senator Mitchell for his dedication to this effort," Waxman and Davis wrote. These words were a building block in Selig's effort to amend his legacy in the sport, to go down in history as the man who finally took a swing at the steroids issue after letting it fly by him until he was down in the count. At no point in the oversight committee's statement did the congressmen say anything about calling players to a hearing.

From his office down in Houston, Rusty Hardin issued a statement too that set the exact tone Clemens was looking for. It was angry, combative, and self-righteous: "Roger Clemens vehemently denies allegations in the Mitchell Report that he used performance-enhancing steroids, and is outraged that his name is included in the report based on the uncorroborated allegations of a troubled man threatened with federal criminal prosecution."

Hardin wasn't the only one sticking up for Clemens. The reporters who knew him, and had covered him for years, were more than willing to take up his cause over the wild claims of a nobody trainer whose reputation had already been sullied in the news for an unseemly incident in St. Petersburg. While Hardin was speaking for Clemens, Brian McNamee was watching ESPN, and in particular the musings of Peter Gammons, who had reported on baseball for nearly four decades. Gammons was known as one of the sport's ultimate insiders, but was also Clemens's biographer, having ghostwritten Clemens's 1987 biography, called *Rocket Man: The Roger Clemens Story*. On the day of the report's release, Gammons stood before the camera and praised the Mitchell Report for its "portrait of the era." Then he called Radomski and McNamee "sewer rats." Also on air at the time was the network's new investigative reporter T. J. Quinn, who calmly refuted that characterization. Later, Quinn got a phone call. It was Brian McNamee, thanking Quinn for sticking up for him.

The next day, Gammons repeated the "sewer rat" line on his blog. "When I awoke this morning, I felt as if I had spent a fortnight sleeping underneath the Gandy Bridge," Gammons wrote, calling the report "a sordid tale of associations, hearsay and the witness cooperation of sewer rats." Gammons was in something of a difficult spot. His conflict symbolized that of ESPN itself, trying to appear as a legitimate news-gathering operation without harming its role as baseball's broadcast partner and head cheerleader. There were other conflicts at ESPN. One of the network's baseball analysts, Fernando Vina, was named in the report as a user, and another, former Mets general manager Steve Phillips, had given contracts to some of the players who had apparently used some of that salary to buy drugs from Radomski. And of course Mitchell himself had been the chairman of the board for ESPN's corporate parent, Disney. John Kruk, an ex-Phillie turned *Baseball Tonight* commentator, struggled with his role too. Mitchell had outed his old teammate Lenny Dykstra, and Kruk took sides. "Why do you gotta name the names?" he asked. "Why drag them all through the mud? Let them go. You don't have to get out in the public with this."

On the morning of December 14, as newspapers around the country carried the news of the report on their front pages, a wide swath of the public started to get to know Hardin, the tenacious lawyer behind a tenacious client. By this point, Hardin had been on the case for a week. Because his private dicks, Belk and Yarbrough, had been to McNamee's house, Hardin knew a lot more than the public did about McNamee's allegations. The Mitchell Report hadn't included anything about an abscess, for instance.

"It is very unfair to include Roger's name in this report," said Hardin on that first day. "He is left with no meaningful way to combat what he strongly contends are totally false allegations. He has not been charged with anything, he will not be charged with anything and yet he is being tried in the court of public opinion with no recourse. That is totally wrong. There has never been one shred of tangible evidence that he ever used these substances and yet he is being slandered today."

One noteworthy element of Hardin's statement was what it lacked: namely, anything about Andy Pettitte. Something had changed during the December 9 meeting between Hardin, Clemens, Pettitte, and the Hendrickses: Pettitte had told them all that what McNamee had said about him was true. This presented a potential conflict, maybe even turning Hardin himself into a witness, if anyone raised the issue of whether he'd questioned Pettitte about McNamee's claim that Pettitte had discussed human growth hormone with Clemens. Hardin had been representing Pettitte just the day before, but now he was speaking only on behalf of Roger Clemens. In the hours between December 12, when Belk and Yarbrough had brought letters to McNamee's house identifying themselves as part of the law firm that represented Clemens and Pettitte, and December 13, when Mitchell released his report, Hardin was no longer the lawyer of record for Andy Pettitte. And Pettitte wasn't talking for himself. The day after the Mitchell Report came out, the reporters and photographers who were staking out his home and following him on outings chased him to the gates of the exclusive Shadow Hawk Golf Club, a favorite of Houston Astros players. There, he refused to comment. "Sorry, buddy," he told Adam Nichols from the New York *Daily News*. "Can't talk."

In his statement, Hardin called McNamee "troubled," indicating that a serious character attack was on its way. It wasn't the first time Hardin came out with guns blazing even though authorities had his house surrounded. There were other instances when Hardin seemed to win even when his client lost. He had represented accounting giant Arthur Andersen LLP when the now defunct firm was charged with destroying evidence in the Enron affair. The government, observers agreed, had a strong case, and the jury pool was especially hostile to anyone accused of trying to protect Enron, the huge Houston-based energy company that became a symbol of corporate fraud and corruption. Almost half of the 106 prospective jurors who came to the federal courthouse in Houston were disqualified because of prejudice.

"The antipathy toward anyone who had anything to do with Enron, whether it was Arthur Andersen or anybody else, was just palpable," Hardin told *FDCC Quarterly*, a legal journal. "In the 27 years I've been trying cases, I've never seen those types of numbers."

To even the odds against his client, Hardin took a cue from *Miracle on 34th Street*, re-creating the famous scene when postal workers haul bags of mail into a court hearing on the competency of a man who claims he is Santa Claus. Hardin's staff hauled 21 boxes into court to demonstrate that a witness actually kept more documents than he destroyed. The prosecutor decried it as a stunt and the judge accused Hardin of running a circus and catering to the media. But the move got the jury's attention. After seven days of deliberation in what was supposed to be a slam dunk for the feds, the jury announced it was deadlocked. The judge ordered them to deliberate more, and three days later the jury returned a guilty verdict. Hardin had lost the fight but got kudos for how well he'd fought it.

Hardin's showmanship and corn-fed persona masked toughness—some would say ruthlessness—and made him a formidable foe. Hardin liked to boast that he helped send 15 men to death row as a prosecutor for the Harris County District Attorney's Office, and the Vietnam veteran approached even civil cases as if he was engaged in a righteous battle on behalf of truth, justice, and the American way. He wasn't afraid to attack conventional wisdom, and he wasn't afraid to challenge the way people looked at evidence. He knew how to simplify a murky, complicated argument and lead people to see things in black and white.

The best portrait of Rusty in action came in a 2002 profile by Pamela Colloff in *Texas Monthly*. Colloff wrote of Hardin's defense of Houston Rockets guard Steve Francis, for example, when he was charged with drunk driving in 2002. According to police, Francis, arrested in his white Mercedes after running a red light at 4:48 A.M., slurred his words as he admitted he had been drinking and taking painkillers for an injured ankle. Wobbly on his feet, the basketball player refused to take a Breathalyzer test and failed the sobriety screen. But then came Francis's bench trial—the verdict would come from the judge, not a jury. Hardin only needed to plant a seed of doubt in one mind, not an entire jury's.

During cross-examination of the arresting officer, Sergeant Charles Allen, Hardin walked a fine line, polite and deferential even as he pointed out inconsistencies in Allen's testimony, portraying Allen as an overzealous cop who saw evidence of a crime when none existed. Francis didn't run a red light because he was loaded, Hardin concluded. He simply grew impatient with a long light in the dead of night and became yet another African-American man pulled over by a Southern cop. Even Allen seemed swayed: After their exchange in court, the sergeant called to Hardin outside the courthouse, and according to Colloff said, "Rusty! Can I get Steve's autograph for my son?"

The next day, Hardin told the court that allergies had caused Francis's bloodshot eyes and that his gimpy ankle had been caused by injury. It was true Francis had four drinks that evening, but he had consumed four massive meals that offset the effects of the alcohol. The judge retired to his chambers for all of 10 minutes, then returned with a terse verdict: "I've got reasonable doubt, so the defendant is not guilty."

Hardin's country charisma wasn't just a manufactured courtroom tactic. He was born in 1941 in Durham, North Carolina, and raised in Monroe, a small town southeast of Charlotte, where his father operated a cotton warehouse. Hardin attended a military high school and then moved north in 1960, to Connecticut, to attend Wesleyan University. Hardin was the first member of his family to go to college, and he dragged the experience out (his leisurely approach to deadlines would become a campus legend). When he finally graduated, Hardin moved on to Montgomery, Alabama, where he met his future wife, Tissy Ely, and taught American history at a private high school. But he soon figured he'd rather make history than teach it.

He decided to join the army and fight in Vietnam. At a time when many young men of his generation were taking drastic steps—fleeing the country, feigning disability, tapping into family connections—to avoid the war, Hardin was voluntarily signing up, despite not one but two legitimate reasons to avoid the draft. As a teacher, he had an education deferment. His vision problem—Hardin is legally blind in one eye—also made him ineligible for the service.

"I felt guilty that I had an education deferment while others were going to Vietnam," Hardin recalled in 2008, so he refused to use that as an escape valve. He got around the vision problem by memorizing the eye chart and wearing a contact lens—a rarity in the 1960s—that went undetected by the recruiters. In the winter of 1966, in Fort Dix, New Jersey, Hardin's unit was on the firing range when a tough African-American drill sergeant asked Hardin why he was firing his weapon left-handed. Hardin told the sergeant that he couldn't see out of his right eye and admitted cheating on the eye exam. Hardin recounted the story nearly 40 years later for the *Texas Monthly* profile, claiming the story demonstrated his talent in winning people over.

"You mean we got guys fleeing to Canada and you cheated to get in?" Hardin said, quoting the sergeant, who had done two tours in Vietnam. "You've got to be the dumbest son of a bitch I've ever met."

But later that night, that same sergeant invited Hardin to hang out with him, watch some TV, and drink beer. "From then on," Hardin said, "that guy protected my ass."

Hardin moved to Washington, D.C., after his 15-month tour in Vietnam and worked for a North Carolina congressman. He applied for law school but, thanks to poor test scores, had a hard time finding one that would admit him. According to the joke at the Harris County District Attorney's Office, only one of the 22 law schools Hardin applied to—Southern Methodist University—accepted him. He was 31 years old when he enrolled there.

Hardin went to work for Harris County District Attorney Johnny Holmes in 1975. He graduated from DWIs and misdemeanors to some of Houston's most notorious cases, prosecuting more than 100 cases without a loss. Hardin didn't just deliver closing arguments; he delivered a show. In the trial of James Means, charged with slaying an armored truck driver with a shotgun, Hardin grabbed the murder weapon and shouted "barroom," as he pretended to fire it indiscriminately. At the end of one rape case, Hardin had the lights turned off and asked the jury to consider the victim's fear.

One of his most famous closing arguments was a condemnation of Cynthia Campbell Ray, who allegedly manipulated her boyfriend into shooting her parents as she looked on. Hardin described the terror felt by Ray's two young boys, who also witnessed the shootings, and reminded the jury what Ray had said after the slayings: "They're young. They'll get over it." Hardin repeated the words, contempt dripping off his tongue, according to Texas Monthly.

After fifteen years as a prosecutor, by the late 1980s it became clear that Hardin had gone as far as he could go in the District Attorney's Office. Holmes wasn't due to retire until 2001, and Hardin had outgrown the second-fiddle role. Intra-office politics and rivalries had taken their toll. In September 1990, Hardin handed in his resignation and set up shop as a trial attorney. He would still get to exercise his legendary prowess before juries, he would just make a lot more money doing it. Within a few years, he was widely acknowledged as the best trial lawyer in Houston.

One of the many sports celebrities Hardin represented was Wade Boggs, a teammate of Clemens's for eight years with the Red Sox. Hardin successfully defended Boggs from a salacious sexual harassment case, and

Boggs would be just one of many professional athletes who would long revere the man who'd saved them from trouble.

"Once his name was linked to the report, he had to defend himself," Boggs said of his former teammate. "And then once he defended himself, that's when McNamee came into the picture, and McNamee had to defend himself. Now they're in the ring together. Once your name gets linked on a piece of paper with using [drugs], you've got to defend yourself and say that you didn't."

Boggs didn't refer Clemens to Hardin, the Hendricks brothers did, but in the fallout of the Mitchell Report, Boggs said Clemens had picked the right man for the job—someone who had shared Clemens's tendency to bet more aggressively just as the chips were stacked against him.

"Rusty's one of the best, believe me," Boggs said. "He's good for Roger. He's a fighter, Rusty's a fighter. You back him into a corner and he comes out swinging. And that's the way both of them are together. He's really smart. He crosses his T's and dots his I's."

Hardin's greatest fame, however, didn't come from representing an athlete, but from his cross-examination of Anna Nicole Smith, the former stripper and *Playboy* centerfold who married billionaire oil tycoon J. Howard Marshall when he was 89 years old and she was 26. Marshall died fourteen months after the odd couple's eyebrow-raising wedding, setting off a full-scale war for his riches. In the legendary probate battle that followed, Hardin, representing Marshall's son Pierce, clearly got under Smith's alabaster skin. According to *Texas Monthly*, at one point during the six-day cross-examination that became known in Houston legal circles as "The Anna and Rusty Show," Smith expressed her love for Marshall and tearfully clutched a photograph of the deceased husband to her famous ample bosom.

"Mrs. Marshall, have you been taking new acting lessons?" Hardin asked sharply.

"Screw you, Rusty," Smith spat back.

After Smith declared that she had been the light of her late husband's life, Hardin took a page out of his Cynthia Campbell Ray handbook and during closing arguments played Debby Boone's "You Light Up My Life" on a boom box. The jury found that Smith shouldn't get even a dime of Marshall's money, then, in what had to be one of the strangest scenes to ever come out of a Houston courtroom, began serenading Hardin with the sappy 1970s ballad.

. . .

George Mitchell also gave a round of interviews the day after his report was released. He wouldn't give up the biggest mystery of his 21-month investigation—how he got access to key witnesses in active government investigations. Who in the Justice Department had given approval for such an unconventional arrangement? Matt Parrella, or the attorney general? Mitchell wouldn't say. Did Selig ask President Bush to green-light it? Did Waxman grease the rails? Mitchell guarded that secret. He also declined to share the names of players he had spared. Mitchell said he had left out the names of several players about whom he had received allegations, and indicated that cooperation might have spared others whose names did appear.

It was clear that Mitchell's investigation had hit its stride when Mitchell scored the cooperation of the United States Attorney's Office for the Northern District of California. Kevin Ryan had been in charge of that office throughout the early stages of the BALCO case. He was Parrella's boss from the initial raid on BALCO right up through early 2007, and he had met with Mitchell right after Selig had appointed the former senator (and federal prosecutor) in March of 2006, and pledged to help to the extent that he could.

"His investigation is historical," Ryan said a week before the report was released. "Everyone can agree that there is a problem in sport—Olympic cycling, the Tour de France—[the report] will confirm what we already know. We were responsible for [starting to clean up sports]. We took the lead."

Mitchell said some players had avoided being named in the report. "One player came in and admitted that he bought the drugs from Radomski and said that he had not used them, told a story that was credible and which was supported by other credible evidence. And I believed him, so we didn't put his name in the report. I asked every player about whom we received allegations to come in and meet with me. I was open to hearing what anybody had to say and if anyone had come in and denied it and provided credible support for their position I certainly would've taken that into account."

Although most players identified in the Mitchell Report as steroid users acknowledged the allegations or said nothing at all, Clemens wasn't the only one to protest loudly. David Justice, Clemens's Yankee teammate in 2000 and 2001, complained in the days after the Mitchell Report's release that he had been unfairly accused. Radomski told Mitchell's investigators that he sold two or three kits of human growth hormone after the 2000 World Series to Justice, who paid by check. The check was not published in the Mitchell Report. McNamee also told the Mitchell Commission that Justice had asked him about human growth hormone in 2000 or 2001. "According to McNamee," the report says, "Justice admitted in this conversation that he had obtained human growth hormone from Radomski." "Mac is lying, and he knows he's lying," Justice told *The New York Times*. "He was going to go to jail, and they told him: 'Look, you get a free pass, but we need names. Tell us about everything you know.' That's what he did. I'm not saying everything's a lie about everybody, because some of the stuff he said was pretty convincing because he offered details. But with me, he's lying."

That same morning, December 14, Jose Canseco was up early, wearing the same leather pants he had worn to the Hyatt the day before, making an appearance on the Fox News Channel. Canseco told Fox's Gretchen Carlson that "Alex Rodriguez is not who he appears to be. And we'll just leave it at that."

Juiced had already made a pariah of Canseco, but many of the bestseller's claims had been borne out—particularly with regard to his former teammates Mark McGwire and Rafael Palmeiro. Now, Canseco was hinting that his forthcoming book, *Vindicated*, would expose even bigger names. During his two-day media blitz in New York, Canseco and his attorney, Rob Saunooke, combed the Manhattan publishing industry for a taker, securing a deal with Penguin by the end of the month. Unlike the former senator Mitchell, Canseco hadn't negotiated any peace accords—far from it—but he felt like an authority on the subject of steroids, and wasn't quite ready to fully concede the spotlight. Within a matter of weeks, he would find a way to inject himself back into the thick of the headlines.

On December 15, the Saturday following the release of Mitchell's report, ten days after receiving that heart-stopping phone call from Brian McNamee, Andy Pettitte issued a statement through Randy Hendricks that was entirely different from the one Hardin had dispensed for Pettitte's longtime ally Roger Clemens. In 285 carefully chosen words, Pettitte said that for two days in 2002 he had tried human growth hormone—admitting to the specific allegations in the Mitchell Report, and exactly nothing more.

First, I would like to say that contrary to media reports, I have never used steroids. I have no idea why the media would say that I have used steroids, but they have done so repeatedly. This is hurtful to me and my family.

In 2002 I was injured. I had heard that human growth hormone could promote faster healing for my elbow. I felt an obligation to get back to my team as soon as possible. For this reason, and only this reason, for two days I tried human growth hormone. Though it was not against baseball rules, I was not comfortable with what I was doing, so I stopped. This is it—two days out of my life; two days out of my entire career, when I was injured and on the disabled list.

If what I did was an error in judgment on my part, I apologize. I accept responsibility for those two days. Everything else written or said about me knowingly using illegal drugs is nonsense, wrong and hurtful. I have the utmost respect for baseball and have always tried to live my life in a way that would be honorable. I wasn't looking for an edge; I was looking to heal.

If I have let down people that care about me, I am sorry, but I hope that you will listen to me carefully and understand that two days of perhaps bad judgment should not ruin a lifetime of hard work and dedication. I have tried to do things the right way my entire life, and, again, ask that you put those two days in the proper context. People that know me will know that what I say is true.

The statement didn't come close to closing the book on Pettitte, but it certainly bolstered the credibility of Brian McNamee. Mitchell's report said that McNamee had traveled to Tampa in 2002 and "injected Pettitte with human growth hormone that McNamee obtained from Radomski on two to four occasions."

It was a courageous admission for a pitcher planning to return to the mound in Yankee pinstripes the following spring. It separated him from Clemens and exposed him to punishment from both the league and his team. The careful wording—Hendricks was an attorney, after all—avoided outright apology in the legalistic sense. But among the self-justifications and denials, the tone of contrition was unmistakable. Whether fans would accept it was still something worth praying for.

Issuing his statement and confessing had been an enormous step into the unknown. Although Mitchell had recommended leniency for the players he named, it wasn't yet clear whether Bud Selig would suspend the players, or if the government would step in, looking for crimes. In the unlikely event that Pettitte's confession would get him banned from baseball for life, at least the lanky left-hander would be able to look back proudly on an impressive big league career. In 13 seasons he had won four World Series rings, amassed a 201-113 record, and earned nearly $100 million.

In crafting his statement, Pettitte chose to appeal directly to the fans' sense of loyalty. He had used HGH, he explained, because he was injured and wanted to rejoin the team. He had felt an "obligation" to return. He wasn't trying to gain an unnatural advantage over batters, and he wasn't using something specifically banned by baseball. Pettitte had also been careful to admit to only the bare minimum of what McNamee had alleged. McNamee had said "two to four occasions" and Pettitte had admitted to only two.

But the memory of the shots in early 2002 in Tampa were too vivid for Pettitte to run away from, and he recalled the circumstances all too clearly: going over to Mac's room, seeing the syringe lying there ready to go, watching as the trainer injected the liquid into a pinch of fat near his belly button. He had gotten the injections over two days—one in the morning and one at night for a total of four.

There were things he kept to himself. Pettitte didn't disclose that he was related to someone named Kelly Blair, the owner of 1-on-1 Elite Personal Fitness, and that Blair was a steroid dealer; he didn't admit that his ailing father, Tom, had turned desperately to human growth hormone; Andy didn't admit that as he was facing surgery in 2004 he'd decided to use his dad's HGH stash; he did not admit that he had walked across their conjoined backyards, collected some of the HGH, and then injected himself with it. None of that had anything to do with Brian McNamee and it wasn't in the Mitchell Report, so Pettitte couldn't see how those actions were related to the use of performance-enhancing drugs in baseball. In light of what Kirk Radomski and Victor Conte had done, it didn't seem like dealing in drugs. Pettitte had practically buried the memory, and hadn't even been thinking of it when he issued his statement.

If what happened the next morning on the lawn outside Central Baptist was any indication, Pettitte's statement was more than good enough for the members of Pettitte's church, despite their hard-line stance against illegal drug use. That morning, as the worshippers arrived for services, they found reporters and photographers waiting in the parking lot. As the Pettitte family arrived at Central Baptist on Sunday, the churchgoers swarmed the interlopers, blocking their cameras and warning them to stay off church property. When *Daily News* photographer Andrew Theodorakis pulled into the church parking lot and stepped out from his rental car, a woman caught sight of his camera and yelled "Media!" the way beachgoers might yell "Shark!" The woman pounded on Theodorakis's vehicle with her fist and stationed herself in front of it, telling him she had called the police and would not move until they arrived.

Within minutes, officers from the Deer Park Police Department were there and a calm negotiation ensued (the Pettittes and other church members had entered an adjacent building that Central Baptist used for prayer meetings, Sunday school, and social gatherings). After speaking with the church leadership, the police officers told the out-of-towners that Central Baptist would welcome print reporters to observe the services, but that the photographers would need to stay away. Theodorakis, a veteran of countless New York crime scenes, positioned himself on the public sidewalk to take his photos when Pettitte emerged. The reporters attended Bible study and were treated warmly. When one churchgoer asked for a "blessing on Andy and Laura" the reporters scribbled that on their notepads, recording it for Yankee fans back home.

The Pettittes were regulars at Central Baptist. In fact, Pastor Tim Dunn was the brother of Laura Dunn Pettitte, the pitcher's wife. "Pastor Tim" had taken over from his and Laura's father, Charles Dunn, who had established the church more than 40 years earlier. Andy and Laura Pettitte sang in the choir and occasionally led Bible study. Normally, it was something that interested baseball writers very little.

Sitting through his brother-in-law's sermon, Pettitte might not have known that his statement was winning him nationwide praise. A central argument in the statement had been his claim that he had used HGH for only two days—"two days of perhaps bad judgment" as he put it—in 2002. Well, he'd used the same bad judgment two years later. His 2002 decision was coming back to haunt him. He didn't know what the result of his 2004 transgression would be. Andy sat in the pew with Laura at Central Baptist and listened as Tim Dunn delivered a sermon that seemed to contain a message for his brother-in-law. "It doesn't matter what you have done, what's in your past or what decisions you have made," Dunn said from the pulpit, the baptismal font to his back. "It is all God's design, and it is all for good." Pettitte hoped that was true.

A week after the release of the Mitchell Report, on December 20, United States Magistrate Judge Edward Voss finally unsealed an unredacted version of the notorious Grimsley affidavit—the 20-page search warrant application that had started Brian McNamee's nightmare way back in June of 2006.

Conspicuously absent from the document were the names of Roger Clemens and Andy Pettitte, and in case the *Los Angeles Times* didn't know it had egg on its face for reporting that those names lurked underneath the black ink, Voss let the paper know, issuing a letter accusing the paper of "abusive reporting."

In seeking authorization to raid Grimsley's home in Scottsdale, Jeff Novitzky wrote that Grimsley had identified Jose Canseco, Lenny Dykstra, Glenallen Hill, and Geronimo Berroa as steroid users, and named Rafael Palmeiro and Pete Incaviglia as amphetamine fans. Novitzky said Grimsley told him in their first interview that Chuck Knoblauch had used human growth hormone; he also claimed David Segui and Allen Watson used performance-enhancing drugs. Nothing about Clemens or Pettitte.

"At best, the article is an example of irresponsible reporting," Voss wrote. "At worst, the 'facts' reported were simply manufactured."

Hardin, seizing a rare opportunity, cited the unredacted affidavit as proof that people couldn't believe what they were reading about Clemens and steroids. Hardin acted as if it was just a matter of time before someone proved the Mitchell Report was flawed too, and that there would be hell to pay for those responsible.

"We acknowledge the inaccuracies of the report and deeply regret the mistake," *Los Angeles Times* spokesman Stephan Pechdimaldji said. The paper put a correction on its front page.

"When this grossly inaccurate story broke in October 2006, Roger said it was untrue and the *Los Angeles Times* chose not to believe him," Hardin said in a statement. "As the record now clearly proves, Roger was telling the truth then, just as he continues to tell the truth today. Roger Clemens did not take steroids, and anybody who says he did had better start looking for a hell of a good lawyer."

There was no Christmas tree in the background and no holiday cheer in his voice. Two days before Christmas Day 2007, and 10 days after his name appeared in the Mitchell Report, Clemens was finally speaking — by way of a video clip that was released on his Web site. Dressed in a crisp button-down shirt, his hair spiked up, Clemens thanked the people who had supported him during this "difficult" stretch and made the first of what would be numerous public denials of performance-enhancing drug use. On the wall behind him hung a drawing of Clemens in a Yankee uniform with the logo "Rocket 300 Wins" visible over his right shoulder.

> Over the last 15 days or so, this has been extremely difficult for my family, my children, my extended family. I'm holding up better than they are. I'm almost numb to some of these suggestions that I would even use steroids. And again, it's amazing to me that I have to—that I'm going to go to the lengths that I'm going to have to defend myself to do this.
>
> I faced this last year when the L.A. *Times* reported that I used steroids. I said it was not true then. And now the whole world knows it's not true, now that that's come out. It's surfaced again later now with this Mitchell Report. And let me be clear, the answer is no. I did not use steroids, human growth hormone, and I've never done so.

In a minor burst of fury that telegraphed what was ahead, Clemens made a point to address his accuser in the one minute and 47 second clip.

> I did not provide Brian McNamee with any drugs to inject into my body. Brian McNamee did not inject steroids or human growth hormones into my body either when I played in Toronto for the Blue Jays or the New York Yankees. This report is simply not true. I'm, I'm angry about it, to be honest with you.

Clemens announced that he would talk about all the issues with Mike Wallace of *60 Minutes* after Christmas, "and he'll ask me a ton of questions on this subject, and I'll answer them right there in front of him. And we'll do all of this again," Clemens said.

The clip concluded with Clemens reflecting upon the holiday season and being thankful "for those blessings," referring to his career. The video clip was posted on YouTube, and almost instantly spawned a comical parody in which Clemens's speech was jumbled and spliced so that in every other sentence he admitted to some type of steroid use by him, his whole family, or the rest of the country.

"I want to say thanks to steroids," Clemens said at one point in the parody version, which soon had more viewers than the original.

But this was hardly any laughing matter for Clemens or McNamee. The die was cast. Clemens was getting out in front, planning a major public relations offensive against McNamee that would unfold over the next few weeks. First, Clemens would be taking off with the family to the sunny climes of the Bahamas, where they hoped to forget about the dark clouds of the Mitchell Report in the Caribbean sun.

Richard Emery was on a skiing vacation in Aspen, Colorado, when he got a phone call from his old friend Earl Ward, offering Emery an official part in the ongoing Brian McNamee drama. Emery signed on, finished skiing, and a few days later returned to New York to get to work on a high-profile case in a career that included many of them.

For months, Emery had been assisting Ward's defense of McNamee in an unofficial capacity. The two lawyers were fellow travelers in civil rights law, with neighboring offices on the 20th floor of a Rockefeller Center building with a handsome view of St. Patrick's Cathedral.

In the days after Clemens put his video denials up on the Internet, Ward saw an opening for a First Amendment specialist like Emery. Clemens was apparently headed for *60 Minutes,* and if he denied using steroids it would be tantamount to calling McNamee a liar. "When the issue of *60 Minutes* came up and there was the potential for a national audience to hear Brian being called a liar, knowing that Richard specializes in libel issues, I knew it would be good to have someone with his experience as part of Brian's representation," said Ward.

McNamee had no money, of course, but both Ward and Emery were energized by the idea of helping out the little guy—keeping an underdog like McNamee from seeing his rights trampled upon by vastly more powerful men like Clemens and Hardin.

With his sharp mind and urbane demeanor, Emery had the confidence of a man who knows how to think on his feet and reduce abstract ideas to precise language. He had taught law at New York University and George Washington University. He was also a die-hard liberal, so there was a certain joy for him in taking on a case that would pit him against an overconfident Texan who happened to be a close friend of the Bush family. From the moment he stepped onto the stage, Emery brought a panache and swagger to McNamee's legal team. He was a tough-talking quote machine, easily able to go toe-to-toe with the silver-tongued Rusty Hardin.

Emery came from a family of mathematicians and scientists. His grandfather was Richard Courant, the world-renowned German mathematician who fled Germany in 1933 and later founded the prestigious Courant Institute of Mathematical Sciences at NYU. Emery himself was a child of the 1960s, a history major at Brown University who graduated with good grades and a deep feeling of alienation about the Vietnam War. "It felt like the people who were right had no power," said Emery, who set out to become the kind of lawyer who represented the powerless: whistle-blowers, disabled people, juveniles, and prisoners.

After graduating from Columbia Law School, Emery's affection for Ken Kesey novels drew him to the Pacific Northwest, where he clerked for U.S. District Court Judge Gus Solomon, and then got a job in a legal ser-vices group in Washington State. For several years he worked for the rights of the institutionalized—mental patients and prisoners. In the late 1970s, he returned to New York to work for the New York Civil Liberties Union, doing police abuse cases and rights of students work. He represented Harold Brown, a supervisor who had helped lead a walkout of air-traffic controllers in 1981. Emery was a fixture of Manhattan and Hamptons social circles. In 1981, he married the actress Lori Singer, who starred in the 1984 hit *Footloose*. (They divorced in 1998.)

Emery began to make a name for himself when he fundamentally changed New York City government and politics with the 1981 federal lawsuit he brought on behalf of three Brooklyn residents that challenged the Board of Estimate, a powerful municipal panel consisting of the mayor, the city council president, the city comptroller, and the five bor-ough presidents. The Board of Estimate played a significant role in shap-ing New York's budget, and it also ruled over municipal contracts, land use issues, and water rates. Emery's lawsuit argued that the board was fun-damentally undemocratic, since the borough president of Staten Island— New York's least populous and racially diverse county—carried the same weight as the borough president of Brooklyn, the city's most populous bor-ough. Emery believed in the case and pushed it all the way to the United States Supreme Court in 1989.

Emery came out of the hearing with a good story. At one point in his argument, Justice Thurgood Marshall stopped Emery to ask him a ques-tion. "Mr. Emery, I have a question," Marshall asked with some theatri-cality. "Do you know of another jurisdiction in the United States other than New York City that has boroughs?" The question came from far out in left field, but when he racked his brain, Emery was somehow able to summon a piece of trivia he'd happened across in his research. He wasn't certain, Emery said, but he thought Virginia Beach, Virginia, might have boroughs. Marshall considered this, and Emery was just about to resume his argument when Marshall interrupted him again and, with the same gravity, said he had another question. Emery waited. "Can you name one more?" Marshall asked, and everyone in the courtroom cracked up. Later, Marshall and his colleagues on the court ruled that the Board of Estimate was unconstitutional. The court, in essence, told New York City that it had to figure out a new way to govern itself.

"It's nerve-racking and wonderful," Emery said years later. "It's the fun of doing what I do. That's why I love it. It's a performance, and not rehearsed."

By the time Brian McNamee came along, Emery's firm—he helped found Emery, Celli, Brinckerhoff & Abady in 1992—was one of the most respected civil liberties and First Amendment firms in the country. Emery was a crusader for good government, a bulwark against overzealous and abusive law enforcement officials, and a protector of whistleblowers. He had dedicated his career to progressive causes and social justice. And just two months before he joined Ward in representing McNamee, Emery prevailed in a lawsuit he had filed against the New York City Department of Corrections on behalf of tens of thousands of nonviolent inmates who had been wrongly strip-searched.

Emery also represented Reade Seligmann when the former Duke lacrosse player and his teammates Collin Finnerty and Dave Evans filed a federal lawsuit, in October 2007, against bumbling prosecutor Mike Nifong, the city of Durham, and the detectives who investigated a stripper's discredited rape allegations. That work would provide a dash of unintentional irony to Rusty Hardin's attempt to portray the Mitchell Report as the "second edition" of the Duke lacrosse case. ("I warn you, in five, six or seven months, any of you who got on the bandwagon about Roger taking steroids is going to be embarrassed," Hardin would say. "It's a fabricated story.")

As 2007 came to a close, Emery and Ward got to work on the McNamee case. While Ward worked the back channels, Emery took to the airwaves and the newspapers, dealing with his media friends and the reporters covering the fallout from the Mitchell Report with equal zeal. The war brewing between Clemens and McNamee drew massive interest, and the Clemens legal team was besieged with phone calls from all over the country—not just from the media, but also from lawyers offering to help them out with the high-exposure case.

McNamee had more than enough legal firepower, though. Behind the scenes, McNamee and Ward confided in and relied on Tom Harvey, which led to at least one spat within the legal team when Harvey got word that Emery had told McNamee not to listen to Harvey's advice to concentrate on protecting McNamee rather than responding to Clemens's attacks in the media. Harvey called Ward to ask him about what Emery had said, then told Ward to keep Emery in the office because Harvey was coming over to "kick Richard's ass."

"I'm on my way," he told Ward. "Keep him there."

Just in case, Emery hastily put on his coat and fled the office. It was left to McNamee to make peace.

Emery and Harvey had opposite styles in dealing with the media. While Emery's office had framed clippings of newspaper articles in which he'd been photographed and quoted, Harvey worked obsessively to keep his name out of the press even as he developed close relationships with reporters. In lieu of press clippings, he cultivated an air of mystery—as *Sports Illustrated* writers discovered one day when Harvey joined them for a round of golf with Donald Trump. Harvey appeared to enjoy the Donald's ribbing and trash talking. One of the reporters found it odd that Harvey hadn't said a word about his profession or how he had come to play in the foursome. Curiosity got the better of the reporter, and he asked Harvey what he did for a living. "Lawyer" was the one-word response, as Harvey changed the subject to how great a golfer the Donald was. After a few more holes, the reporter couldn't resist and asked Harvey, "What kind of lawyer are you?" With an air of frustration, Harvey said matter-of-factly, "Look, if you ever wake up in Vegas with a dead hooker in your bed, give me a call, and I'll take care of it." Something in the way he said it suggested he wasn't kidding.

By the time Brian McNamee picked up the phone on Friday, January 4, to call the landline in Roger Clemens's office—something he'd never done before—he was already sensing that things weren't going to go the way he'd been hoping they would, the way they always had in the past. He and Clemens had overcome so much together. No matter what the problem had been—McNamee's involvement in the pool incident, the nastiness over the ads for the vitamin company, the money disputes, and the *Los Angeles Times*—Roger had always picked up the phone and called him back. For 10 years they'd been playing this game, but for a month McNamee hadn't been able to reach Clemens at all.

Finally, after he'd sent Clemens a message about his son, Brian Jr.'s, worsening medical condition, he'd gotten a response. "I'll be back in town

Friday," Clemens text-messaged back. "If you still want to talk, call me then."

Clemens and his family had just returned to Houston from a vacation in the Bahamas—"A little time we had together, and it wasn't good," Clemens said. The getaway had been soured not only by the events of the past month but by another urgent message from McNamee. The events of the last three weeks of December had weighed on Clemens, although not enough for him to cancel a long-planned, five-day hunting trip with the "K" boys in South Texas, or the family trip to Paradise Island to celebrate the New Year. His eyes shaded by an orange Texas Longhorns visor, he and Deb had tried to relax on the beaches of the beautiful resort, but the moments were tense. Deb was a mess and so were the boys, especially the next-to-youngest, Kacy. Things weren't good for his eldest, either: Koby was in baseball now and the steroid issue was crushing him. They had played golf and hit the casino a couple of times and tried to forget the Mitchell Report, but they all knew that the eyes of the other guests were on them, wondering how they were handling the accusations.

McNamee had interrupted what little serenity the Clemens family had found on Paradise Island, texting Clemens about Brian Jr.'s medical condition. The boy, already a diabetic, was suffering a setback. Could Clemens help? Maybe call Brian Jr.? Here was McNamee, again, reaching out for a favor (amazingly enough, just days before McNamee's December 5 phone calls to Pettitte and Jim Murray and his attempt to reach Clemens, McNamee had been in Cabo, and had asked to use Clemens's fishing equipment that the pitcher kept there). When Clemens realized that McNamee had asked about the fishing equipment—and, of course, Clemens had willingly lent it to him—knowing that his Mitchell testimony would soon be released, Clemens couldn't believe it. Until he saw Brian Jr.'s name in the text, he hadn't even considered talking to McNamee ever again.

Clemens got in touch with the Hendricks brothers and Hardin, and they came up with a plan: Clemens was to tell McNamee to call him on a landline; Clemens could hear about Brian Jr., maybe even find a way to help, and they would tape the call. At the very least, it would be good PR. And, with luck, McNamee would reveal something damaging.

McNamee, surrounded by old barbells and his broken-down car outside the door of his shabby bungalow in Long Island, placed the call to Clemens's palatial Piney Point mansion. Hardin, two associates from his law firm, and an investigator surrounded Clemens, a tape recorder rolling close by.

"Rocket," said McNamee.

"Mac," Clemens replied.

"'Sup, buddy?"

"What's happening?" asked Clemens.

"Nothing," McNamee replied. "It's a disaster, man."

"Uh, I got your e-mail about Brian."

"No, I know. He's not doing good," said McNamee.

"I don't like hearing that," said Clemens.

"No, it's real, man. This is real. Everything else is a joke. But uh, he had his blood work done. His A1C. Now he's got celiac disease. He's got, like, all this shit going on," said McNamee. "You gotta take heart. Now he's getting ragged on by the kids. I know, man, your kids are gettin' hit too, man."

Clemens knew he had to be careful on the call. Hardin had drilled him on how far he could go with McNamee, reminding his client that the trainer was now a federal witness against him. "You've got to be very careful so nobody can ever suggest you were trying to persuade a federal witness," Hardin told him. So Clemens waded in.

"Yeah they're gettin' . . . It's not good," he said. "Deb's not doing well. We're doing everything that we can. We got a couple buddies that aren't doing well, but . . ."

"I'm out East in a one-fucking bedroom bullshit, fucking place," McNamee interrrupted.

"What's that?" asked Clemens.

"I'm out East fucking in a one-bedroom place I'm paying for, because I got 30 reporters showing up at my house," said McNamee. "Same shit you got going on. I had to pay the security, my attorneys, I mean, this is bullshit."

When the conversation took a turn from Brian Jr.'s condition to the situation the two men were in and McNamee's attempts to reach Clemens to explain things, Hardin listened carefully, ever sensitive to creating the impression that they were witness tampering. "You have to be triple, double careful that you don't say anything that has somebody else later contending that you were trying to either bribe or influence," Hardin explained to the pitcher.

"It is what it is and it's not good," McNamee said. "I want it to go away and I'm with ya. I'm in your corner. I don't want this to happen. But I'd also like not to go to jail too, but it has nothing to do with you. I would like to sit down with you in person and talk to ya. . . ."

"I just . . . Like I said, you know, I get home from vacation here and I find out now that, uh—I'm just hearing a ton of other things," said Clemens. "Just the stuff that I'm reading or hearing, so much of it's untrue, that it's just tearing everybody apart."

"I know, man. I reached out to you because, I tried to help as much as I could, as late as I could," said McNamee, his voice becoming a whisper. "It was too late, I guess, to help, but, what it comes down to, the way it affects our kids. They got nothing to do with this. They have nothing to do with any of this. As much bullshit as it is, nothing to do with anything. Brian, I don't know. Whatever you can do to help would be great. Whatever you want me to do. Obviously, I'm on a cell phone. And I understand that, I don't expect . . . I can't open up the way I want to. And I know you can't. You know how I feel about you."

"I don't know who's on our lines or whatever," said Clemens.

"I got nobody on my line," said McNamee. He would later say he knew the conversation was being recorded, "because, as long as I've known him, I never called him on his office line. Ever. He never spoke to me like that, either. He was cagey, like reading a script."

The conversation continued, Clemens's voice becoming alternately frustrated and wounded, his lengthy sighs coming across the line. He began to say he "just wanted the truth . . . I just want the truth out there," as though he knew others would soon be hearing his pleas. "Like I said, I just can't believe what's being said. We're getting it from all angles. I haven't talked to anybody other than my representatives and• Randy. Everybody's just so upset."

"This to me is nonsense," McNamee said. "It's bullshit. The pain this is causing you and me and everybody, is nonsense. Brian, your kids, my kids, they have nothing to do with this. The truth is the truth and it is what it is."

"Like I said, I just don't know why you did it," said Clemens. "I just can't . . . Like I said, everybody asks me about you and I tell them, I treat you like I treat anybody else in the world. I think you know that. Treated you just like anybody else."

"No, you treated me better. You treated me like family," said McNamee. "From day one, I was family to you. You treated me like that. You know, I'm glad to hear your voice. I just . . . I don't believe that . . . Whatever. I just, bottom line is, I'm glad to hear your voice. I'm sorry that your family's going through this and I'll do whatever I can do to help. And, you know . . ."

"You just need to come out and tell the truth," Clemens said.

In some way, both men were telling their version of the truth. In Houston, Hardin was hearing his client proclaim his absolute innocence and possibly hearing a plea for money from McNamee; in Long Beach, McNamee felt he was begging Clemens to understand why he had told the federal government and George Mitchell about the drug use, and how hard it had been to have to tell them anything at all.

"I don't have any money," McNamee told Clemens. "I have nothing. I'm not doing the book deal. I got offered seven figures to go on TV. I didn't do it. I didn't take it. I didn't do anything. All I did was what I thought was right. And, I never thought it was right, but I thought that I had no other choice, put it that way. I think that when I spoke to your guys, that I laid it out there. I was sick. I was in the hospital. Talk to Kenny [Jowdy], I was throwing up. That was me. I could deal with that. You know, I could deal with that. Whatever you want to do. Just let me know what you want me to do. Brian has nothing to do with this."

Clemens continued to talk about the effect all this was having on the kids, on Deb, on Clemens's business relationships—"The calls from the people that we worked with. They're just going crazy. They just can't believe what's being said"—and McNamee offered again to meet in person.

"I'll fly down tomorrow to talk to you face-to-face. Whatever you want me to do. What do you want me to do? Tell me what you want me to do."

"I don't know," answered Clemens, but McNamee was starting to understand that Clemens did know what he was going to do, knew exactly what he was going to say. At Hardin's suggestion, Clemens had already denied everything in his online video clips, and there was no sign that he would now change course and admit to anything. McNamee knew how Clemens dealt with controversy: He would shut down, let somebody else handle the unpleasant details, the Hendrickses or McNamee himself, and now, Hardin.

"I didn't do it, all this stuff," said Clemens.

"Roger, what do you want me to do? What do you want me to do? What do you want me to do?" McNamee repeated.

"Mac, I'm doing a press conference on Monday, and . . ."

"You want me to go? You want me to show up?"

"I'm gonna just tell the truth, flat out tell the truth, but it never seems to get behind me. I had to deal with the bullshit from uh, the *L.A. Times* story and all's I got was an apology when they found out that wasn't true. I had to deal with that. Like I said, I asked you about . . ."

"That was the greatest thing in the world," said McNamee, referring to the statement from Judge Edward Voss, but Clemens was already moving on, establishing a record of denial about a lot of what McNamee had told Mitchell, especially about Kirk Radomski.

"The other thing is, I don't know how many months ago it was, I asked you . . . I didn't know who this cat was in the New York Mets, this guy," said Clemens, but McNamee was ready for that.

"I spoke to . . . I told your guys, man. I told [Jim] Murray. I told him his name. I told him already," said McNamee.

"I asked you point-blank, 'Do you know who this cat is?' when we were working," Clemens said. "There's some rumblings about some guy with the Mets. I said, 'Do you know who this guy is?' You told me 'no.' "

"You know what, I would have told you 'yes.' If I remember that, if you told me that, I would have told you 'yes,' " McNamee said.

"I asked you point-blank," Clemens said. "Randy and them all called me to ask."

"I told Jim Murray, I told Jim Murray. I told him. I told him. I sat down with him in Starbucks on the corner where you used to live. And I told him the guy's name. And I told him, 'Please don't tell Roger yet' but to be careful. Rog, if you asked me, I would have told you that. If you remember, if you remember, I was trying to get with you to talk to you. I was reaching out to you. I told you, I didn't want Kenny around."

"Brother, you were a foot in front of me doing ab work," said Clemens. McNamee had seen this kind of response from Clemens for years. If Clemens said he remembered something a certain way, despite reality, then that was the way it was. There was no point in arguing. Clemens had the power; he was the boss.

"All right, well then, you know what, then I messed up," McNamee said. "You know what, if I remember that, I would have told you. I would have told you. Like I told Jim Murray. I got Jim Murray's name. I told him, 'Be careful.' "

"I don't know anything about . . . Again, Jimmy's never told me," said Clemens.

McNamee described the yellow legal pad, said Murray took notes and said he believed Murray had relayed the information to Randy Hendricks. McNamee told Clemens that Murray had even assured McNamee that he wouldn't go directly to Roger.

"Nobody said a word to me, just like everything else," said Clemens.

"Well, I'm telling you the truth. I met with Jimmy in '04. And I told him, I said, 'Jimmy, I just wanted to give you guys a heads-up because you better have some information that, I'd rather you be prepared than not prepared.' And he took all these notes."

"I just need somebody . . . I got a press . . . I need somebody to come tell the truth," Clemens persisted. "I got this press conference on Monday that I've got to deal with next. And, like I said, everybody's got ulcers here. It's a . . . It's ridiculous. Like I tell everybody, I enjoy training with ya. I treat you like you were, like I treat anybody else."

As the call began to wind down, McNamee was back to thanking Clemens for treating him "better than everybody else. Like I said, you treated me like family. You brought me into your house. I ate with your family. I helped you with your school projects. I can't deny that. And I've used how you were as a dad to your kids, I tried to be like you. I told people that. That's one thing. This is another."

"Where you at right now?"

"Where am I at?"

"You're still in the East, you're sayin'?"

"I'm out East in a fucking bullshit . . . I've got a . . . fucking barbell with weights on it, training college kids," McNamee said. "Trying to. I've got a car that doesn't work and I've got fucking attorneys saying shit they shouldn't be saying, and trying to make a name for themselves, where I lose control. Roger, look at me. What the fuck do I have? I have nothing. Everything I have to this day, I have because of you."

On his end, Clemens continued on with claims of innocence, his pleas for the truth, and it might have sounded like he too was asking for something: for McNamee to change his story.

"Like I said, Mac . . . I can't . . . For the life of me, I'm trying to find out why you would tell guys that I used steroids from . . ."

"I understand that. I understand that. Like I told the guys that tape-recorded me . . ."

"Who's the guys that tape-recorded you?" Clemens asked.

"Yarburl and . . ."

"Oh, you're talking about . . . The two investigators that came down and talked to you."

"Right. Why in the world . . . If I was lawyered up, if I had any idea what the fuck was going on, why would I do that?" asked McNamee.

"I just don't know why," Clemens said, "and like I said, I got the press conference Monday. I need, somebody's got to come tell the truth."

For McNamee, there was no changing the story to suit Roger's version. The feds had made it clear that it was the truth or nothing. Why didn't Clemens understand that he'd already gone as far as he could go in trying to protect Clemens? What was Clemens asking him to do?

"Roger, tell me what the fuck you want me to do? What do you want me to do? My son is dying. He's 10!"

"I understand that. Listen to me. That's why I answered your e-mail immediately. For me there's more important things. Those things are important to me. I just had my college coach's son pass away. I got to go to his funeral. It's on Monday, the same time I'm supposed to have this press conference."

"Right."

"And, so . . . I just need . . . Like I said, I'm telling the truth and I want it out there. And . . ."

"Tell me what you want me to do. I told you . . ."

"I understand that. I understand that."

"What do you want me to do? I'll go to jail. I'll do whatever you want."

"I just need somebody to tell the truth, Mac."

"What do you want me to do right now?"

"It's ridiculous."

"What do you want me to do right now, Roger?"

"You're just being ridiculous."

"I'm . . . Who, me?"

"No, no, I said everything."

"Roger I'm in a one-fucking bedroom bullshit thing with . . . weights from 1945. Tell me what you want me to do. I'm firing my lawyers. I'm getting rid of everybody. I have nothing. What do you want me to do? My wife is gone. My kids are gone. What do you want me to do?"

"I didn't do this, Mac. Let me just uh . . ."

"Fine."

"I didn't do it and just . . . just . . . I need some, like I said, I'm trying to get a direction and trying to comfort everybody. And, like I said, you know what I think about your wife and your boys. You know that. I don't think I've left that uncovered one bit. Like I said, I'd do anything for 'em. And that's just what's eating at my gut in this whole thing. And uh . . . so . . . I mean . . . Just give me a little time here tonight. Just give me a little time. And I'm glad at least you told me that, you know, about your boys. Because I don't want . . . they can't . . . I know over the years the up and downs that the little man's had. And all of our boys. And it's killing 'em. Right now, Kacy's just like . . . They're all in just a state. Like I said, it's unbelievable. I just need somebody to tell the truth. Let me just, I've got to visit with some people. Like I said, I'm just devastated by this. That's just where I'm at. I'm just so . . . I'm hurt. I'm upset. I'm shocked by some of the other things that have been said. And I just know that I didn't do it. And we need to, uh, you know, move on from there."

"Just tell me what you want me to do. Just tell me what you want me to do."

"I'll, uh, lemme just get back with you, bro. I just can't . . . I'm about ready . . . Like I said . . . I'm . . . I just wanted . . . Again, like I said, I'm with you with your boy and everything that's being said there. And I hear ya. That's why I got back with you so quick, because that bothers me."

"I knew you would. I knew you would."

"Let me just visit with some people and we'll go from there."

"All right."

"All right."

By the time the phone call ended, Henry Waxman had announced that the House Committee on Oversight and Government Reform had sent letters to Clemens, Pettitte, Chuck Knoblauch, Kirk Radomski, and Brian McNamee inviting them to testify at a January 16 hearing on the Mitchell Report, which meant that they would all have to go under oath or take the Fifth Amendment. Bud Selig, Mitchell, and union president Don Fehr would still appear before the committee for the previously scheduled hearing on January 15. Congressional sources told the *Daily News* that Clemens's vociferous denials of steroid use in the weeks since the report's release had persuaded lawmakers that they needed to question him under oath.

Congress hadn't commissioned the Mitchell Report: Baseball had. But Congress had made it clear to Major League Baseball that if the sport didn't want the Oversight Committee breathing down its monopolized neck, Selig had better authorize something along the lines of what was recommended in the report. They were pleased that a respected former senator had taken charge. In an indirect sense, the report had congressional endorsement.

So when Mitchell delivered the goods, and Clemens challenged the report's integrity, Waxman and ranking minority member Tom Davis felt they were being called to the mat. Clemens was disputing the very document that Waxman and Davis had hoped to call the final word on the matter. As Waxman and Davis saw it, they had no choice but to get to the bottom of the conflict. If the report was flawed, Waxman and Davis needed to know why.

The committee had also seen the YouTube video and had read reports of the contents of a *60 Minutes* interview with Mike Wallace that would be broadcast on Sunday, January 6, in which Clemens said McNamee injected him with B_{12} and the painkiller lidocaine but not with steroids or human growth hormone.

Hardin quickly put out a statement that said Clemens welcomed the committee's interest in steroids and baseball. "Roger is willing to answer questions, including those posed to him while under oath," Hardin said. "We hope to determine shortly if schedules and other commitments can accommodate the committee on that date."

Right away, McNamee's lawyers made it clear that if Clemens did invoke the Fifth Amendment against self-incrimination, they would inter-pet it as an admission that McNamee had told the truth about Clemens. Ward and Emery had tossed around the idea of a defamation suit based on the YouTube video and they were waiting to see the full interview on *60 Minutes* before moving forward. "If Roger takes the Fifth, in my view, he's pretty much admitting to the public at large that Brian is telling the truth," Emery said. "And if he acknowledges that, there's probably no real reason for a defamation claim."

Asked what he thought Clemens should do in the time before the hearing, Emery said: "He could certainly reverse course in the sense that he could tell the truth. Either that or take the Fifth and disappear."

By the time the ticking stopwatch and the *60 Minutes* logo appeared on televisions across the country that Sunday night, January 6, Clemens's defamation suit against McNamee was already on the court's electronic recording system, the first of a two-pronged salvo aimed at McNamee.

Dressed in a light gray suit and dark tie, 89-year-old Mike Wallace sat in front of a huge Big Brother photo visage of Clemens to introduce the segment, the pitcher's face partially obscured by a blown-up front cover of the Mitchell Report. Here was Clemens in the national spotlight again, only not in uniform atop a baseball mound, but at his home, dressed casu-ally in a lavender button-down shirt and slacks, berating McNamee and spilling his thoughts.

Wallace had developed a friendship with Clemens that dated back to the spring of 2001, when Clemens had just started his third year in Yan-kee pinstripes. The veteran newsman traveled to Clemens's Piney Point home to conduct the interview. McNamee had very much been a part of that interview, with video footage showing both men during a workout at Clemens's private gym and training facility. "When we went down there to profile him, we went to his home, I watched him exercise, I watched him work out and he became my friend," Wallace said of Clemens in a *New York Times* article published on Christmas Day 2007.

During the 2001 *60 Minutes* piece, Wallace questioned Clemens on everything from the pitcher's two controversial incidents with Mike Piazza during the 2000 season, to Clemens's childhood without a father figure, to the time the Rocket brushed back wife Debbie—while she was pregnant, no less—during a throwing session. Debbie had stood in the batter's box in their personal gymnasium, leaning over too much of the plate. Clemens explained to Wallace that there was a very simple reason for backing Debbie off—she had just lined a ball off his leg in a prior at-bat. "Hit a bullet," joked Clemens. "I wound up, threw the next one where?"

"He hit me with the pitch," Debbie giggled, sitting next to her husband.

Wallace was also a frequent visitor to Yankee Stadium, often sitting in owner George Steinbrenner's private suite. During Clemens's march to his 300th career win during the 2003 season, Wallace attended Clemens's first attempt on May 26 against the rival Red Sox. Wallace was there again four years later for the 2007 Yankee home opener. It seemed only natural that when Clemens sought to squash the swell of negative press swirling around him in December 2007 that he would seek out a reporter he trusted. "He trusts me and is going to talk to me and I hope he can answer all the questions on my mind," Wallace said in the same December 25, 2007, *Times* article.

Clemens had announced on his December 23 YouTube video that he would sit down with Wallace. His camp had already reached out to request an interview, and on December 28, a *60 Minutes* crew and Wallace were roaming the grounds of the Clemens home. It aired on January 6, 2008. As the segment opened, Wallace began the introduction in a conciliatory tone—"With 354 wins, Roger Clemens is one of the best pitchers in the history of baseball, no question about it." Wallace explained how "we found [Clemens] to be frustrated, even furious" about McNamee's accusations in the Mitchell Report and how much of the public and media had already labeled Clemens a cheat.

Then it was vintage Clemens, guns ablaze, camera zoomed in tight on his clean-shaven face, the pitcher expressing disgust about this annoyance named McNamee and by whoever was buying the suggestion that Roger Clemens was anything other than natural sweat, hard work, and pure grit. "I'm angry that what I've done for the game of baseball, and as a person, in my private life what I've done, that I don't get the benefit of the doubt. The stuff that's being said, it's ridiculous. It's hogwash for people to even assume this. Twenty-four, 25 years, Mike, you think I'd get an inch of respect. An inch," Clemens barked, holding his left thumb and index finger an inch apart before him, for emphasis. "How can you prove your innocence?"

"Apparently you haven't done it yet," answered Wallace. "People I talk to say, 'Oh, c'mon, 45 years old? How does he still throw a ball and compete and so forth? It's impossible.' "

Clemens cut Wallace off. "Not impossible. You do it with hard work. Ask any of my teammates. Ask anybody that's come here and done the work with me."

Wallace alluded to the 2001 interview, how when he last interviewed Clemens in Texas, the pitcher was throwing to McNamee during a workout. Wallace's voice-over then played—"He's been called the hardest-working man in 'throw business' "—and the segment cut back to the 2001 video footage of McNamee standing over or by a sweating Clemens, while the pitcher ground through different weight repetitions. The camera cut back to Wallace and Clemens, and Wallace began to read portions of the Mitchell Report, describing how McNamee injected Clemens with steroids and human growth hormone. The camera switched to Clemens, his eyes darting up and down, up and down, his head bobbing.

"Never happened. Never happened," Clemens said.

Clemens continued to deny the Mitchell Report claims as Wallace sifted through the pages on his lap. "Never. I've trained hard my entire career. It just didn't happen," Clemens said.

"Why would Brian McNamee want to betray you?" asked Wallace, jabbing his left index finger at Clemens.

"You know, I don't know. I'm so upset about it, how I treated this man and took care of him," Clemens answered, his voice rising in anger. Wallace speculated that McNamee might be watching the segment. "I hope he is," spat Clemens.

"Okay. Anything you want to tell him?" asked Wallace.

"Yeah, I treated him fairly, I treated him great as anybody else. I helped him out."

Not satisfied with just repeating his denials of drug use, Clemens later ratcheted up the emotion, trying to paint McNamee's claims as outlandish. According to Wallace, McNamee had declined to be interviewed for the segment.

"My body never changed. If he's puttin' that stuff in my body, if what he's saying, which is totally false, if he's doing that to me, I should have a third ear coming out of my forehead," said Clemens. "I should be pulling tractors with my teeth. Why didn't I keep doing it if it was so good for me? Why didn't I break down? Why didn't my tendons turn to dust? That's all it's good for. It's a quick fix. I don't believe in it. I don't do it."

Tucked away in his cramped Long Island bungalow, McNamee watched his former longtime employer and friend continue to contradict and humiliate him on the TV screen. McNamee couldn't contain his own anger and vented to *Sports Illustrated* senior writer Jon Heyman, who had scored an interview with McNamee and sat nearby. Wallace pecked away on the screen, revisiting the fact that McNamee had talked with federal investigators and the Mitchell investigators, and would go to jail if he failed to tell the truth.

"What did McNamee gain by lying?" asked Wallace.

"Uh, evidently not going to jail," said Clemens.

"Jail time for *what*?"

"Well, I think he's been buying and movin' steroids," said Clemens.

"I'd rather be called a liar than a drug pusher," McNamee said to Heyman. "The feds look at bank accounts, and there's no money unaccounted for. I don't launder money. I don't have anything in my mattress. If I was pushing drugs, what did I do with the money?"

Further west from McNamee, Richard Emery was equally disgusted as he watched *60 Minutes* at his plush Manhattan apartment with *Daily News* columnist Mike Lupica.

"Clemens is accusing the government of pressuring McNamee to pin the tail on the Clemens donkey," Emery said. "And that did not happen. Earl Ward was in the room with the government and the opposite of what Clemens is saying is what happened. They didn't have Clemens as a target. They had steroid use as a target. It came as a surprise to them. McNamee reluctantly gave them Clemens because he had to tell the truth to stay out of jail, not lie."

Wallace broached the subject of Andy Pettitte and how the Yankee left-hander had corroborated McNamee's Mitchell Report claims of injecting Pettitte with human growth hormone. Again, video clips from the 2001 *60 Minutes* interview flashed on the screen, this time showing Pettitte, Clemens, McNamee, and another man playing catch with a football on Clemens's indoor basketball court. Back to the present. Clemens shook his head, his lips pressed together while Wallace uttered Pettitte's name.

"I had no knowledge of what Andy was doing," said Clemens. "Andy's case is totally separate. I was shocked to learn about Andy's situation. Had no idea about it."

Clemens did admit to Wallace that there were two substances McNamee had injected into his body: lidocaine and B_{12}. Lidocaine, he said, was for "joints" while B_{12} was something Clemens said he'd used throughout his career and still used. There were other shots, administered by trainers or doctors, that Clemens said he received "many" times during a season, often to alleviate swelling, inflammation, and aches from the rigors of pitching. He also confessed to Wallace that he consumed the painkiller Vioxx "like it was Skittles," the colored candy pellets.

"Pain shots, to go out and perform," Clemens told Wallace, before recounting the moments before a crucial World Series game in which he had defied Yankee manager Joe Torre's attempts to yank Clemens from his start because of a hamstring tear and a "golf ball" in his pitching elbow.

"I told Joe Torre that I'll be damned if 15 minutes before I'm going to start a World Series game, I'm going to go out there and look my teammates in the eye and tell them I can't go. I'm going to take this Toradol shot and hope it works and mask some of this pain so I can get out there and do my job. That's the things I've put my body through," Clemens told Wallace.

When asked a final time if any of those shots Clemens took over his career were ever growth hormone, testosterone, or anabolic steroids, Clemens was adamant: The answer was no.

"Swear?" asked Wallace.

"Swear," said Clemens, looking Wallace straight in the eye.

Clemens ended the interview with a defiant twist, saying he would probably never pitch again because of the frustration and pain he was enduring in the fallout of the Mitchell Report. Of course, this was the same Clemens who had already come out of retirement four times since the end of the 2003 baseball season. "I understand that as a public person, you're going to take some shots. The higher you get up on the flagpole, the more your butt shows. I understand all that. But I'm tired of answering to 'em," said Clemens. "That's probably why I will not ever play again. I want to slide off and be just a citizen."

"You're retiring? Period?" asked Wallace.

"Probably," said Clemens, sounding unconvinced of his own plans.

"Oh, not for sure?" asked Wallace.

"I would say, 'Yes.' If I had to sit here and tell you right now, I would say, 'Yes.' "

"You're not gonna pitch again?" asked Wallace a final time.

"You'll never see me pitch again," concluded Clemens.

Did Clemens, asked Wallace, think that people would believe his side of the story after all was said and done? After the video on his Web site, after 60 Minutes, the upcoming press conference, and testifying before Congress?

"I think the people that know me, believe me," said Clemens.

"McNamee also intentionally made defamatory statements regarding Clemens to the Mitchell Commission, knowing that the Mitchell Report would be widely circulated and cause its greatest harm to Clemens in Texas where Clemens lives and works."

Earl Ward read those words in astonishment. No one who saw McNamee's face in the summer of 2007, when McNamee was coming to the realization that he would have to sell out his primary employer, would dream of thinking that McNamee had intended to harm Clemens anywhere, let alone in Texas. The defamation lawsuit, signed by Rusty Hardin and four other attorneys in his firm, was filed against Brian McNamee on January 6, the same day Clemens's 60 Minutes episode aired. Of all the countless audacious aspects of the 14-page suit, the greatest might have been that it was filed in Harris County, Texas.

The lawsuit singled out 13 "absolutely false and defamatory statements" from the Mitchell Report, all of which McNamee had made in New York City. It pointed out that Clemens had disputed McNamee's allegations, including in the 60 Minutes episode that hadn't even aired when the language was drafted. In addition to damages, Clemens was asking the court for a declaration that Clemens had not defamed McNamee.

The words "intentionally" and "maliciously" popped up—key principles in American defamation law, where First Amendment protections of free speech made those necessary standards. But to a large extent, the suit was more of a press release than a legal document. On page five, the lawsuit launched into a glowing biography of Clemens, detailing his rise from high school sports star to the majors, celebrating all of his accomplishments along the way. Some of it was a downright ridiculous departure from legal writing. Paragraph 12, for instance, concluded "After the game, Clemens' manager reportedly commented that 'I watched perfect games by Catfish Hunter and Mike Witt, but this was the most awesome pitching performance I've ever seen.' "

Next, as if on the cue of sinister music, McNamee entered the narrative. Hardin described the trainer's arrival in Toronto, and his relationship with Clemens before Clemens left for New York. "In 2000, McNamee began to aggressively lobby Clemens for a job with the Yankees," Hardin wrote. Then Hardin got to the tricky part. He was walking a tightrope, needing to smear McNamee with the Florida incident without simply ignoring the fact that Clemens, informed of the sexual assault allegations, had stuck with McNamee for six years. The solution, Hardin found, was to paint McNamee as a devious trickster and Clemens as the unsuspecting naïf.

"The rape investigation and McNamee's termination from the Yankees left McNamee embittered, and he pleaded with Clemens for work," the lawsuit claimed. "McNamee's explanation for the Florida incident was totally at odds with the conclusions of the police officers conducting the official investigation, but that Clemens rehired McNamee because he gave McNamee the benefit of the doubt."

The lawsuit then returned to language befitting an introduction at the Hall of Fame induction ceremony that was becoming less likely to happen every day. Outlining Clemens's success with the Astros, Hardin sounded like a contrarian baseball fan armed with sabermetrics, pointing out that Clemens was again dominating as a pitcher, but won only seven games "because of low run support by the offense" and an abbreviated season. Then, in paragraph 26, Hardin showed the cards he was holding. Ward and Harvey had picked up on the possibility that their client had been taped. Now, reading the lawsuit, Ward realized it was true, and that Hardin had a tape, and was going to quote it in the suit.

According to what McNamee has "told others," Hardin wrote, he was confronted by the feds in 2007 and told that they had evidence to send him to prison. "Throughout a lengthy interrogation the first day, McNamee told others that he repeatedly denied that Clemens had used steroids or HGH." Ward found this puzzling. That's not how he remembered the first interview with Novitzky and Parrella. He remembered the two men quite calmly informing McNamee that he was part of an investigation and that he could choose to cooperate. There hadn't been threats. They hadn't even ever told McNamee they were ready to indict him.

Who were these "others" that Hardin referred to?

The next paragraph started with Hardin calling Ward out, suggesting that Ward had misrepresented the interviews. "Contrary to his lawyer's statement that he was not pressured or bullied in any way"—and here Hardin footnoted an interview Ward had given to the New York *Daily News*—"the second day of interrogation proceeded as follows."

And then Hardin cited a chunk of the Belk and Yarbrough interview, the part where McNamee imitated Matt Parrella playing a tough-guy prosecutor. "You have three strikes to go to jail," McNamee said. "He goes, he goes, 'You know, you're a cop.' He goes, 'You picked up steroids and you delivered steroids. That's a federal crime.' He goes, 'And if you lie to a federal agent, you go to jail.'"

Hardin continued to quote McNamee imitating Parrella during his interview with Belk and Yarbrough. "You have two strikes against you to go to jail. You have one more strike."

Hardin also noted in the lawsuit that McNamee said Novitzky was outraged when the trainer told him that he didn't know anything about Clemens and steroids. "Novitzky went on this big tirade because it was the biggest embarrassing thing I've ever heard from anybody. He's trying to tell me that I, that how can I tell him that I don't know anything about steroids and Clemens with, first of all, what they know and then I must not be good at what I do because I stretch him and I train him; so if I put my hands on his body, how can I not know that his body's changing by taking steroids. And then he threw a piece of paper at me and he goes, 'Do you know how many people we've talked to?' He goes, 'You're going to jail.' My attorney just sat there."

It was the first time Ward had ever seen anything from the Belk and Yarbrough interview. He didn't know what was more shocking: that his client had been talking to someone apparently working for Hardin, or that Hardin had made these laughably exaggerated accounts the basis of a lawsuit. Ward picked up the phone and called Tom Harvey.

"What the hell did you get me into here?" Ward asked his friend. It had become clear that this was not the simple defense case Ward had signed up for, that things had changed dramatically since the release of the Mitchell Report and Harvey's prediction that Clemens would make a short statement, lie low, wait a few months, and then go after McNamee. If they know what they're doing, Harvey had told Ward, you'll be getting a call very soon from Hardin and his people. That call had never come, and now Ward was frantic.

"Is this guy McNamee out of his mind?" he asked Harvey.

"Relax," Harvey told him. "You're misreading the story. This guy Hardin is the dope."

"Yeah, okay, Tom, relax, whatever you say, it's not your ass on the line," Ward shot back.

"Earl, read the fucking story again! If you had a tape with the main witness contradicting himself, wouldn't you be playing it every news cycle? The guy [Hardin] is a fucking dope."

"You're right. Why wouldn't he play it?" Ward replied.

"Because the tape hurts them," the attorneys stated in unison.

Harvey reminded Ward that McNamee was a former cop, a member of the anti-crime unit, and that he'd known right away that the investigators weren't really prepared. It seemed to McNamee that they hadn't bothered to debrief their own client, and now Hardin was going to base an entire defamation suit on the truth of this one distorted anecdote?

Later that day when Ward and McNamee spoke, Ward said, "you know, for a cop you're pretty smart."

"Yeah, and for an attorney, you're pretty dumb," McNamee said.

The civil libertarian who had served on the Civilian Complaint Review Board, the commission charged with overseeing charges of police brutality, and the former NYPD anti-crime unit cop were starting to bond.

From a Texas point of view, it was perhaps unsurprising that Hardin and Clemens thought suing McNamee for defamation would amount to good communications strategy. After all, such tactics seemed to work wonders for another Texas sports legend accused of cheating with drugs—Lance Armstrong. The seven-time Tour de France winner faced doping allegations throughout his career, and he frequently fought back with attorneys, retaining expensive legal counsel in Texas, Paris, London, and beyond. Doping accusations had led Armstrong into bruising legal battles with adversaries large and small, from an international event insurance company to his former bike mechanic. And several defamation suits Armstrong initiated went a long way toward muzzling his accusers while creating a public perception that the evidence those accusers relied upon was baseless.

By the time George Mitchell started investigating baseball, Armstrong had left the doping-riddled sport of cycling as something of a saint in the American public's eye. While his nonprofit foundation raised millions for cancer awareness, Armstrong dated Sheryl Crow and Kate Hudson, and went mountain biking with President George Bush. He bent the ears of Bill Clinton and Michael Bloomberg, and many observers believed Armstrong was headed for a career in politics, speculation that he did nothing to refute. And yet Armstrong had lived through his own Mitchell Report moments—accusations that threatened to destroy his legacy—and he fought them off with a brilliant mix of legal artillery and strategic spin.

In 2004, Armstrong's world was rocked by L.A. *Confidential: Les Secrets de Lance Armstrong,* a meticulous exposé by two respected cycling journalists, David Walsh of the *Sunday Times* of London and Pierre Ballester of the French sports daily *L'Équipe.* The book was first published in French, and cast a wide net over circumstantial evidence that Armstrong used erythropoietin, or EPO, an anemia drug that boosted a body's red blood cell count and thereby helped deliver more oxygen to the muscles. The writers dug deep into the disturbing relationship that Armstrong had with a notorious Italian doctor named Michele Ferrari, who had a reputation as a proponent of EPO and who later was convicted of sporting fraud and abusive prescription practices.

Just as the book hit the shelves in France, Armstrong went on the attack, unleashing a barrage of litigation at virtually everyone involved with the book, including the authors, the publisher, the sources, a magazine that ran an excerpt, and a British newspaper that ran a preview of the book. In a Maryland press conference on June 15, 2004, Armstrong indignantly attacked the book, which probably eased the minds of the executives at Discovery Channel, who had just signed on to sponsor Armstrong's team for more than $30 million. The world understood that Armstrong would fight the book with the same relentless drive that helped him overcome cancer, Jan Ullrich, and the Alpe d'Huez.

Days after his press conference, Armstrong also initiated a special emergency hearing with a French court in Paris. There, he tried to get a disclaimer inserted into the book, calling the book's allegations defamatory. But Walsh and Ballester were prepared to defend their work. They had hired Paris attorney Thibault de Montbrial, who presented documents proving that the authors had made a good-faith effort to get Armstrong's reaction to the charges (just as Mitchell would later write to the Hendricks brothers). De Montbrial argued that ordering such an insertion would be the death of investigative journalism. "It would have been very convenient for all the rogues of the world to ignore uncomfortable questions and then just silence their accusers afterwards," Walsh said.

The judge in the emergency hearing sided with the authors, and even hit Armstrong with a small fine for abusing the French legal system. But Armstrong pushed forward with the regular lawsuits, asking for two million euros in punitive damages. This was 10 times the record for punitive damages awarded in a French defamation case, a 1994 lawsuit against two journalists who accused a member of parliament of arranging an assassination.

As the defamation suits wound their way through the courts, Armstrong raced and won the Tour de France twice more, and retired. The shotgun blast of lawsuits and the inspiring tale of Armstrong's recovery from cancer had apparently frightened English-language publishers from translating the book that painted such a sleazy portrait of him. Then in the fall of 2005, months after Armstrong retired and just before a defamation trial was about to begin, Armstrong quietly withdrew his claims.

"In France, we say it had *l'effet d'annonce*," said de Montbrial. "He makes the announcement, but when the emotion goes away, no one realizes that he didn't go to court."

Armstrong did, however, persist with the litigation over the book review in Britain. Libel laws there were much more favorable to claimants. Prior to the release of *L.A. Confidential*, a colleague of Walsh's at the *Sunday Times* of London had run a story about the book. Armstrong argued that that story, by Alex English, had created the perception that the allegations in the book were true. After two years of expensive legal fighting, the *Sunday Times* finally relented in the summer of 2006 and settled with Armstrong, publishing a statement that the paper hadn't meant to create the impression Armstrong cheated.

Armstrong immediately issued a triumphant statement of his own, claiming "the article was based on untrue allegations which are without substance contained in a book published only in France." It was brilliant PR; Armstrong interpreted a small legal victory over a British book review as a refutation of the explosive claims in *L.A. Confidential*, which were never tested in court. He declared victory and walked away. "In a sense, it was an effective play," Walsh later recalled. "The American publishers were frightened. Why would you take on a book that you knew was being sued in France?"

In 2007, Walsh was finally able to publish the claims from *L.A. Confidential* in the United States under the title *From Lance to Landis*, but by then Armstrong was retired and apparently much less inclined to unleash the dogs of law. Rather than sue the book's publisher—Ballantine Books, a division of Random House—Armstrong simply issued another statement, putting a little topspin on the facts when he claimed to have "won every court case."

Armstrong was a master of doping damage control, deploying a PR strategy not unlike the foreign policy that Senator George D. Aiken of Vermont advocated during the Vietnam War: Declare Victory and Leave.

But it was a costly, risky legal tactic, and for all the scrutiny Armstrong faced, he was never on the hot seat quite the way that Clemens had been in the final month of 2007.

The biggest difference between Roger Clemens and Lance Armstrong, when it came to their respective defamation suits, was timing. Armstrong was quicker on the draw, preparing his lawsuits in the months ahead of the book and firing them off as soon as the book came out, on his own terms. For Clemens, three whole weeks passed after the Mitchell Report came out before he got around to suing McNamee (and a month had passed since the Hendricks brothers first learned about McNamee's cooperation agreements). The delay allowed for the perception that Clemens wasn't sure he'd been defamed.

Then there was the question of aim; Clemens sued McNamee alone, avoiding a fight with the actual author of the claims, George Mitchell, or the sponsor of the investigation, Major League Baseball. And while this looked smart on the surface—McNamee, after all, didn't have the kind of money or legal muscle that protected Mitchell and Selig—he did seem to have the U.S. Attorney's Office in his corner, implicitly vouching for his credibility. Without seeing the proffer agreement, how was Hardin to be sure what kind of immunity McNamee had or didn't have?

There was another worry that Hardin faced that Armstrong's lawyers never had to consider: Andy Pettitte. In the weeks since Clemens had supposedly been defamed, Pettitte had emerged to validate McNamee's claims—at least regarding Pettitte's own use. That would seem to make Pettitte a likely witness for McNamee's side in any defamation proceedings, swearing to his former trainer's credibility.

Add to that the awkward fact that Hardin had represented Pettitte from at least December 9 right up through the day he dispatched Belk and Yarbrough to interview McNamee on December 12. If during that period Pettitte ever said anything in defense of McNamee's truthfulness, Hardin would have one client calling the trainer a stand-up guy while another client branded him as the worst kind of liar.

At the moment that Hardin was filing the defamation suit, disgraced track and field star Marion Jones was exactly one week away from being sentenced to six months in prison for check fraud and for lying to Jeff Novitzky about her steroid use. She had tripped up for violating Section

1001, the same law that McNamee ran up against. When Novitzky questioned her about BALCO, she lied about using drugs, and in trying to save her gold medals she was headed to a correctional facility.

Long before Marion Jones lost her freedom to walk the streets, she launched an attack on freedom of speech. Although Jones was a poster child for fraudulent sporting success, she laid an interesting blueprint for Clemens, having effectively used a defamation lawsuit to silence the very person who claimed to have helped her cheat her sport: Victor Conte.

On December 15, 2004, Jones sued the BALCO founder for $25 million, claiming Conte lied and defamed her when he went on the ABC program *20/20* and said he had helped Jones use performance-enhancing drugs on her way to five medals at the 2000 Olympics. Her lawyers sprinted to the courthouse with their complaint.

"Jones has never taken banned performance-enhancing drugs," her lawyers wrote in the suit. "Driven by his long-standing vendetta with Jones, Conte seems willing to do and say whatever it takes to destroy her career and reputation." The suit relied in part on the claim that Jones had passed a lie-detector test the lawyers arranged, administered by a former FBI agent.

Jones's lawyers hammered Conte in the press as well as in the courtroom, where they kept his legal team busy with paperwork to the tune of $150,000 before the case was finally settled in 2006. In October of 2007, after Jones confessed her sins, none of her lawyers (Rich Nichols, Craig Budner, Beth Bivans, and Joseph Burton) would return phone calls from reporters. Ronald Homer, the FBI agent who had administered the polygraph test, declined to explain how Jones had passed his test. (She had passed more than 150 drug tests too, for what that was worth.)

"They force you to respond and drain you financially until you shut up," Conte said after his jail and probation period ended. "It's about who has the deepest pockets. If you know full well that you have used drugs, and there's all kinds of witnesses and evidence, and you've lied to the grand jury, you still get to sue somebody to silence them," he said ruefully.

After Jones entered a Texas correctional facility in 2008, Conte thought of suing her for the money he'd spent defending himself from her suit. But by that point Conte was facing another suit from another one of his clients. Conte had written a tell-all book—*BALCO: The Straight Dope on Steroids, Barry Bonds, Marion Jones, and What We Can Do to Save Sports*—and he mentioned to reporters that one of its revelations would be how champion boxer Shane Mosley used BALCO's drugs to beat Oscar De La Hoya in 2003. After reading the comments, Mosley sued Conte for defamation, claiming Mosley thought BALCO's products were legal and safe. Conte spent $75,654 defending himself from the suit over four months. "Once they engage you, you have no choice but to do what they want, or start bleeding money," Conte said.

When it looked like there was a good chance a judge would dismiss it in California federal court, Mosley's attorney Judd Burstein dropped the complaint and filed a nearly identical one in New York, forcing Conte to begin again. Such tactics weren't unusual for Burstein, who was famous for his "Rambo lawyering," one judge had called it. In 1999, Burstein had narrowly escaped a sanction for a letter in which Burstein promised a rival lawyer he would conduct the "legal equivalent of a proctology exam" on the lawyer's finances.

Now, in addition to the new complaint, Burstein threatened to sue Conte's publisher, Skyhorse, which promptly cut Conte and his book loose rather than face a wealthy boxer's legal team. Mosley, meanwhile, continued to fight and win, even after the New York *Daily News* published transcripts of his 2003 grand jury testimony from the BALCO investigation, where he admitted to injecting the EPO Conte had given him in preparation for his fight. The testimony, along with doping calendars that showed him to be on a steady and expensive drug regimen in the months leading up to his De La Hoya fight, became public as the judge lifted a protective order in preparation for the Barry Bonds trial.

Seven seconds into the tape-recorded conversation, Brian McNamee already sounded defeated.

"It's a disaster," the tape had McNamee saying, his voice barely a crackle on the other end of the phone line.

The horde of media listened intently as the conversation between McNamee and Clemens was broadcast publicly for the first time that Monday, January 7. Right at that seven-second mark, when McNamee's weary enunciation of "disaster" echoed throughout the drab third-floor, windowless conference room at the rear of the sprawling George R. Brown Convention Center, Roger Clemens was smiling at his attorney, Rusty Hardin, who was sitting to Clemens's left.

Hardin was decked out in a cream-colored suit, white shirt, and orange and yellow tie. He grinned back as Clemens reached under the table to snag a plastic bottle of water for his lawyer. Cameras clicked furiously, the flashbulbs dancing off Clemens's royal blue button-down shirt, gel-spiked hair, and freshly shaven face. Two dozen TV cameras hummed at the back of the room where two Houston police officers guarded one entrance. Reporters hastily scribbled in their notebooks. Clemens stared down at the pile of papers on the table or out at the audience, his left index finger occasionally curling under his nose during the opening minutes of the tape.

Clemens arrived at the conference room with great fanfare just after four o'clock, his bulky frame following Hardin in step, like a military recruit performing morning drills to the exact orders of his commanding officer. The two men ascended the steps of the raised dais as flashbulbs exploded. The only man getting more attention that afternoon was Joe Householder, a Houston-based PR executive who, with his beard and mustache, looked like an Ivy League English professor. Householder had fielded the deluge of media calls leading up to the press conference, and he would become a ubiquitous presence in Washington the next few weeks.

Outside the gun-metal-gray convention center, it was warm for an early January afternoon. A construction crew was at work just up the street on a new building. Hardin's law firm offices were a short walk away, at 5 Houston Center, a glass and concrete rectangular slab at the corner of McKinney and La Branch. It was another humdrum business day in downtown Houston, with people still settling into the work routine after the holidays. There were scores of other activities going on throughout the convention center's cavernous floors, but Clemens's press conference was surely the only one attended by armed police officers.

As dawn broke in Houston that Monday morning, news outlets began to scramble to post the latest developments in a weekend of jockeying. The *Houston Chronicle* detailed the 14-page defamation suit Hardin filed electronically on his client's behalf late Sunday, and other media outlets followed with their own accounts. By the time reporters crowded into the George R. Brown seminar room to see and hear Clemens's performance, dozens of copies of the suit were available in cardboard boxes near the podium.

The press conference was another public relations strategy aimed at image repair by burying McNamee. The *60 Minutes* appearance less than 24 hours earlier had featured plenty of Clemens's sniping at McNamee before a national audience—from denying the drug use, calling McNamee a drug pusher, even carping on the fact that McNamee had asked for one more favor only days before the Mitchell Report was about to detonate and change both men's lives forever.

"[McNamee] e-mails me and asks me where all the good fishing equipment is down at Cabo, that I bought, so he can go fishing. Thank you very much. I said, 'Have a good time. Go fishing.' Doesn't say a word that, you know, 'I'm fixin' to bury you, all these accusations, what do we do about it?' Didn't say a word about it. That's what pisses me off," Clemens had told Mike Wallace.

Now Clemens and Hardin sat alongside each other, intent on exposing a vulnerable man. Many reporters would later characterize McNamee as "desperate." The taped call was their proof positive. Sitting on the dais next to Hardin, a dark curtain serving as the backdrop, the bellowing, animated Clemens who had appeared across from Wallace was replaced by a detached, emotionless man who stared straight ahead or looked down as the tape played. Hardin too showed little expression, saving his trademark charm and unctuousness for the end of the press conference.

"No, it's real, man. This is real. Everything else is a joke," said McNamee, who added that his son also had celiac disease. "He's got, like, all this shit going on."

The pleas from McNamee intensified and an uneasiness settled over the conference room as McNamee's voice became more and more plaintive, his repetitive "What do you want me to do?" cries amplified by the speakers. Clemens conferred briefly with Hardin at times, other times occasionally scribbling notes on the papers before him. Clemens's live reactions before the media and McNamee's raw, recorded emotions made for a weird contrast in the news reports that followed on the Internet and in the next day's print headlines. Clemens was roundly vilified for having brought McNamee's son's illness and personal woes into a public forum.

"This is war," Emery fumed. McNamee went a step further, telling friends that the playing of the tape was a critical turning point in the case. "That was the biggest mistake you could possibly make," McNamee said after the Houston press conference. "If you go after my family, I will bury you." He had been holding back until that point, still trying to save Clemens from the worst of it.

Clemens and Hardin had been convinced that playing the tape would give them the ammunition and momentum to level McNamee and his claims. Hardin breezed up to the podium after the 17-minute taped conversation ended and spoke in his easy Texas drawl. He proclaimed Clemens's innocence again and said, yes, a lawsuit was necessary since he believed it was McNamee's side who had leaked news of the Friday night call to Newsday.

"You'll notice all during this tape when Roger says he didn't do [steroids], McNamee never says, 'Yes, you did.' When Roger says, 'I just want the truth to come out,' McNamee never corrects that," said Hardin. "McNamee never says to him on this tape, 'Yes, you did, Roger, you did.' Is that definitive? No. Is it something we hope everybody will consider in making up their minds? Yes."

Hardin's soothing tone gave way to his client's bullying stance, as Clemens strode to the microphone, body tense, a murderous glare fixed on the reporters in the audience. This was the real Rocket, the pitcher who'd ruled the mound with intimidation for 24 seasons, the competitor who had drilled Piazza in the head in that July 2000 interleague game, and who whipped a bat shard at the Mets' catcher three months later in the Subway Series.

Clemens had every intention of taking on the media that day in Houston. The Q&A began innocently enough, with Clemens sending condolences to his University of Texas baseball coach Cliff Gustafson, whose son Deron had died the previous week. Clemens said that, regrettably, he was missing Deron Gustafson's funeral because of the press conference — as if he had no control over the timing of the event. The truth was that Clemens, at Hardin's suggestion, was the one who had arranged the appearance and summoned the assembled media.

"I'll answer your questions even though there are some in the audience that, I'm really not, I'm very uncomfortable even looking at right now, for things that I've . . . Again, I'm just gonna try and rise above it — some of the things that have been said in my hometown especially, without giving me the benefit of the doubt or really looking into the details of what's going on here," said Clemens.

He paused for a few seconds, his eyes wide, lips pursed, palms pasted to the podium.

"Go ahead," Clemens said, inadvertently tossing a pen in his right hand that skidded across the podium surface and echoed throughout the room.

Reporters mostly volleyed softball questions over the next 12 minutes: Who advised him not to talk to Mitchell? What are B_{12} and lidocaine injections? Why not respond more angrily to McNamee during the phone call? As a response to the latter question, Clemens offered a tight smile, relishing the opportunity to answer in the same way he enjoyed whiffing an opposing batter. "Oh boy, I was angry. I would love for him to come down here. I would be afraid for him, because my family's very upset. Like I said, I'm trying to keep my composure through all this," he said. "But he initiated the phone call and I wanted to see where he was going with it."

Clemens mockingly asked the press halfway through his Q&A if he could quench his thirst. "Can I drink water? Is that, like, is that good or bad?" It was a jab at all the media stories analyzing Clemens's 60 *Minutes* performance, many saying that Clemens drank too much water. But toward the end of the press conference, the anger in Clemens's voice began to rise. Throughout his baseball career, he had admonished any reporter who'd questioned his heart or desire to win. It was happening here, in Houston, and the veins on his neck started to bulge. In mid-question from a reporter, Clemens looked down and read a note Hardin had scribbled on a piece of paper. "Lighten up," the missive read.

"You want me to lighten up?" Clemens responded, handing the paper back to Hardin. "It's hard. Thank you."

"I sent him a note saying 'Lighten up,' " Hardin interjected, looking into the cameras, as several reporters laughed.

Moments later came a final question: How was Clemens dealing with the fact that many already viewed him as guilty? It was all the Rocket needed. Out spilled a diatribe that somehow ended up on the topic of Cooperstown. The previous night on 60 *Minutes*, Clemens had told Wallace in a firm tone that, "I didn't play my career to get fame or go to the Hall of Fame or worry about all that. That's nice. Again, it's not who I am. I've worked my tail off to get where I'm at." But in front of a group of reporters for which he had much disdain, Clemens expressed the same reverence for baseball's shrine that he would for a piece of gum stuck to his shoe.

"How do you prove a negative? How do I do it? I'm gonna pay a lot of money to try and defend myself again from all the lies," said Clemens. "Do I just keep shelling out millions?"

Hardin tried a little comic relief, saying, "I think that's a good idea," but Clemens plowed ahead.

"Is that what I do? And at the end of the day, I'm still gonna probably get 'We're sorry.' And an apology. And I got another asinine question the other day about the Hall of Fame," Clemens spat out. "You think that I played my career because I'm worried about the damn Hall of Fame? I could give a rat's ass about that also. If you have a vote and it's because of this, you keep your vote. I don't need the Hall of Fame to justify that I put my butt on the line and I worked my tail off. And I defy anybody to say I did it by cheating or taking any shortcuts. Okay? I made a statement through [Hardin] when it first happened. I made a statement through my foundation, that wasn't good enough. And now I'm here doing this. I cannot wait to go into the private sector and hopefully never have to answer it again. I've said enough."

Clemens abruptly stormed off the stage, grabbing a water bottle from the table as Hardin's faint, "Thanks, y'all," was swallowed by the scrambling of reporters rushing to the front of the room to catch the retreating Clemens. "Roger, why won't you just say whether it's cheating or not?" one female reporter shouted.

Hardin was left behind to clean up the mess, and he gamely sparred with the media throng that intercepted him on the dais once Clemens was out of reach. Hardin fired away at everything from McNamee's failings as a "truth-teller" because of the 2001 Florida swimming pool incident to deconstructing Clemens's performance on *60 Minutes*—"I hear people say, 'He drank too much water. He swallowed several times,'" Hardin smirked. "The reason he's mad . . . most of you have judged him convicted"—to scoffing at any suggestion that Clemens had tried to bribe or coerce McNamee during the call they'd just played.

"If you're not careful, you're going to get into a situation—if [McNamee] starts asking for anything, if you start acting like you're willing to give it to him—you're going to potentially, going to be trying to bribe—not bribe—affect a federal witness," said Hardin of the situation Clemens was in when they taped the January 4 call. "He's got a federal deal. 'Whatever you do, Roger, don't say anything that tries to get this guy to do anything in return for anything. And don't threaten him. Don't get pissed off at him.'"

But mostly, Hardin gave a hint of the showmanship he would put on display in the coming months, as Clemens's saga spilled into the halls of Congress. Hardin told one reporter to be more "courteous" and chastised others for not doing the "Watergate deal," meaning they had not uncovered the facts, à la Woodward and Bernstein. He nearly begged reporters to revisit McNamee's 2001 pool rape incident, to dig deeper and interview the detectives and law enforcement who handled the case. But it was also a convenient opportunity for Hardin to take a backhanded swipe at Mitchell and his team of investigators.

"All I'm saying to you is, and all due respect, none of you folks are checking these things out," Hardin chirped. "I'll give you another example: in the incident that happens in St. Petersburg that involved [McNamee] with the rape case. No charges were filed. I'm not asking you to conclude whether he did or did not commit the offense. That's not what I'm after. That investigation was ultimately closed because charges weren't filed. But if you're trying to decide whether McNamee is a truth-teller, wouldn't you want to at least talk to those police officers down there and say, 'In your investigation, did you find him to be a truth-teller?' Because what they have told us, 'No, he lied to us.' Well, that's relevant.

"All I'm saying is, when you ask us whether it should go down to the Mitchell people, if you're going to make these kind of allegations in a public report, that blast somebody like that, don't you want to run things to the ground before you do it? All I'm saying is, we are finding they didn't. Did they do it maliciously? No. Did they mean to do something bad? No. And at the end of the day, what's the conclusion? What we're having to do, quite frankly, [is] y'all's work, because nobody is going to check things out."

In other words, the media majority was being too quick to judge Clemens. Hardin even took aim at local *Houston Chronicle* columnist Richard Justice, a longtime Clemens supporter who had only recently turned his pen against Clemens. When Hardin was asked if he was worried about Clemens's impending date with Congress, the lawyer dismissed the notion that Clemens would take the Fifth or avoid questions.

"You see what the allegations of McNamee's lawyers are. Their contention is that I'm leading [Clemens] down a primrose path into jail. And actually I think [Richard] Justice said the same thing here, locally. Obviously I don't want to do that. One of the things we wanted to be comfortable with, is that once [Clemens] started publicly, it is no secret that he would then be before Congress being asked about those same things," said Hardin. "So, no, I don't have reservations about it. I don't have reservations about him under oath. He will not plead the Fifth. And hopefully he won't be quite as angry as he was today."

CHAPTER THIRTEEN

January 8–February 4, 2008

On the morning of January 8, Brian McNamee was back at the house in Breezy Point. He was pissed off, to say the least. The newspapers were full of accounts of the previous day's press conference from Houston, and the television showed Clemens and his dapper attorney sitting on a dais while they played the tape of the phone call. McNamee knew he sounded pathetic on that tape. Worse, he had publicly exposed his family to the chaos that life had visited upon him. His son's illness had become part of the story. Now McNamee was looking for revenge. And he was starting that search in his basement. For years he had been saving his ace in the hole for just such a rainy day.

Five weeks had passed since Charlie Scheeler had called with the bad news about what would be in the Mitchell Report. Ever since then, McNamee had been trying his best to protect Clemens from further damage, although he realized this was like a batter unsuccessfully checking his swing. But now Clemens had turned around and slapped him across the face. And not once, three times: a defamation suit that would probably cost hundreds of thousands of dollars to defend; an appearance on *60 Minutes* spewing a bunch of nonsense about B_{12} and lidocaine; and finally playing a secret tape of their phone call on national television. It was beyond humiliating. Clemens had crossed the line by broadcasting McNamee's comments about his son's precarious medical condition. "My son is dying," McNamee had shouted, his voice cracking. "He's 10!"

The whole nation had heard McNamee say that. Brian Jr. would hear it too. How on earth could a 10-year-old handle hearing his dad saying something like that on national television? McNamee himself had dragged his son into this situation. He hadn't broadcast it to the public, of course, but he had sent that e-mail to Clemens, asking for help. The combination of celiac disease and type 1 diabetes was unlikely to kill Brian McNamee Jr., but it would compromise his quality of life forever. The boy would need to maintain a strict gluten-free diet—an immense challenge given that gluten, a wheat product, is used as a stabilizing additive in everything from ice cream to ketchup. McNamee was livid. At himself, at Clemens, at life itself.

And then he found what he was looking for.

It was a rigid FedEx box marked "CLEM" that had been bouncing around in closets and the basement for all these years, since 2001, a two-inch by eight-inch box about the size of a textbook stuffed with what McNamee called "hazardous material." Biologically hazardous, yes—but also hazardous to Clemens's denials that McNamee had ever shot him up with steroids.

In the box were needles. McNamee had used them to inject Clemens. He'd also saved the bloody gauze he'd used to wipe away the blood after each injection. There were some cotton balls and a piece of white toilet paper he'd used to wipe off a syringe. There was a wrapper from a used 22 gauge needle and a 1½-inch syringe.

All of the material had been stuffed inside a Ziploc bag and a Miller Lite can. Drop the used syringe and needle in a can and then crush it a little bit—that was the best method for disposing of the material. Raising a child with type 1 diabetes taught you such things.

He usually dumped waste like this in the trash on his way out of Clemens's East 90th Street apartment as he returned to his car parked right in front of the building, saying good night to Carlos the doorman, who watched the car for him. Sometimes McNamee would take the waste home and drop it in the same homemade HAZMAT container he kept for his son. But something told him to hold on to this stuff. Some voice in his head, a gut instinct, told him he needed to cover his ass in case Clemens ever tried to screw him over. Maybe it was the overwhelming wealth that Clemens had and the power it afforded him. Or that McNamee was so familiar with the alternate universe in which Clemens lived. He'd been in Clemens's house when the fax arrived from the pitcher's agents telling him that Canseco had made a rather amazing claim in his book *Juiced*— that Clemens was one of the few players in the game who never cheated on his wife. Debbie had broken down in tears of joy, or maybe it was relief. McNamee just sat on the couch watching ESPN, thinking "That's a load of shit." Maybe it was McNamee's self-protective instincts stemming from his background as a New York City cop: With the world slowly waking up to steroids in baseball, he knew he might go down, and he wasn't going to take the full rap, not alone, not when he didn't deserve it. Or maybe it was because deep down he knew the real Roger Clemens.

He'd heard all the half-truths Clemens came up with over the years, the way Clemens thought he could say anything—and make anyone believe anything—no matter the truth. It was even a joke around the Yankee clubhouse; David Wells called Clemens "Eli." ("Because every time he opens his mouth," Wells joked, "he lie.") Clemens got wind of the joke and turned it around on Wells, but McNamee knew where it began. The bottom line was he knew he needed to protect himself against Clemens. There was no honor among thieves, and he and Clemens had been thieves together—stealing a long series of late-career victories from the cold grip of advancing age.

Whatever it was, 2001 was the year of the pool incident in Florida—and it was after that when McNamee decided to tuck this stuff away. Clemens distanced himself from McNamee after that, at least on the drug front, even though no charges had been brought. The pool incident taught McNamee that when the heat came down, the players would be protected. But a trainer was expendable. McNamee and his whole family could be at risk. His wife felt the same way. She knew he'd kept the material. And she knew why.

Down the road, it might be hard to explain why he'd held on to it. He understood that, even at the time he'd done it. But what were the chances he'd ever have to really explain it? It was an extreme long shot. But still. So he'd just stuffed the waste into a FedEx box marked "CLEM" and stored it in the basement. He almost never thought about it. He hadn't really thought about it in years. Not until the day that he took the material out of his house and set out for Manhattan, to his lawyers' office in Rockefeller Center.

If McNamee was upset about the taping and airing of the phone call, so were his lawyers. Twice in two days, Ward and Emery learned the hard way that Hardin had used hidden surveillance to take advantage of their client's desire to reach out to Clemens, the man who had—as McNamee himself had said in the phone call—treated him like family. Emery and Ward had gotten to know their client fairly well in the previous weeks and months, and they watched the Houston press conference with dismay. But it also steeled them for no-holds-barred legal warfare. For Emery in particular, the tape was proof that Clemens was a bully, and sticking up for people who were being bullied—whistle-blowers, prisoners, children—had been at the heart of Emery's legal practice for 30 years.

"I've always represented people who felt that they were oppressed or less powerful than their adversaries," Emery later recalled. "This was very much a First Amendment case, like every defamation case is at some level, but it was much more a case about a bully and his victim. Brian had been made the victim of a bully. We were offended by that, and we decided to stand up for him, or with him."

Ward thought the taping and airing of the phone call was mean-spirited on Clemens's part, unethical on Hardin's, and somewhat point-less from a PR standpoint. But it wasn't illegal. Ward had to explain to an enraged McNamee that while many states had laws against taping a phone call without mutual consent, Texas wasn't one of those states and neither was New York. McNamee might feel wronged, but he didn't have the law on his side.

"I thought the tape didn't really add anything to the case," Ward told the Associated Press after the press conference. "It was really just a very emotional and tormented Brian McNamee, who clearly demonstrated that what he is doing is something that he's tormented by. At that point he still had tremendous reverence and adoration for Roger." That was no longer the case. McNamee was seeing the value in not holding back any-more, not protecting Clemens. He was going to have to let loose with the ammunition he had against Roger. There was no other choice.

The phone call Hardin had aired at the Houston press conference was the second time in a month that Hardin had arranged a secret communi-cation with McNamee while knowing perfectly well that McNamee had a lawyer. There had also been the interview that Billy Belk and Jim Yarbrough conducted on December 12, the day before the Mitchell Report came out. It was only after seeing the transcript of that interview quoted in the defamation suit filed on January 6 that Ward and Emery discovered what had actually transpired, that their guy had briefed Hardin's men. Ward confronted McNamee, and learned that the conver-sation must have been recorded on a hidden tape. McNamee handed over the letters the men had brought, attesting to the fact that they repre-sented Clemens and Pettitte.

Ward and Emery began to see an opportunity; they realized that McNamee had one thing and one thing only on his side—the truth. And the truth would be devastating to Clemens. So why not demand the release of these communications? With his remarkably vivid memory, McNamee was able to reconstruct almost everything he had told Belk and Yarbrough: the injections, the abscess, the federal investigation—the same old story. The fact was, Ward and Emery realized, this could be nothing but embarrassing and damaging for Clemens. McNamee had told his tale hoping to help Clemens, to prepare him for the truth that had been revealed to Mitchell and his committee. Why not call their bluff and demand the release of the tape? It was hilarious, actually; McNamee and his team could get his revenge for one ambush recording by insisting on the airing of another. So with a sort of morbid glee, they spent a few days publicizing the Belk and Yarbrough meeting and demanding that Hardin release the tape.

"Brian told these investigators the same thing he told the federal authorities and Senator Mitchell," Ward wrote in a statement to the news media on January 7. "We hereby demand the tape be released in its entirety immediately."

Instantly, the Clemens camp was on the defensive. Joe Householder, the spokesman hired by Hardin to manage the media onslaught, said that Hardin did not plan to release the tape in the near future. "It's an item in the discovery process," Householder said. "It'll probably become public during the discovery process."

In that statement, Ward and Emery saw the myopia of the Clemens legal team. Discovery? The discovery phase of the defamation suit could be months or even years away. It was as if Hardin had forgotten there was a congressional hearing coming up. The House Oversight Committee had subpoena power. Ward decided to tell the committee to collect the Belk and Yarbrough tape. Then, perhaps, Congress would learn about all the nasty details that Mitchell had left out of his report—such as the abscess Clemens had developed on his ass back in 1998 as a result of McNamee's injection. Ward didn't want to appear presumptuous or arrogant by directly telling Henry Waxman what to do, but he needed to get his message across. So he met with a group of reporters on January 8 and asked why Hardin had access to a tape that he didn't have access to: "They should ask for the entire tape of the interview back in December. That's the tape they should ask for." If Hardin didn't turn it over, Ward said, the committee should subpoena it.

Ward and Emery had the letters that Belk and Yarbrough had brought to McNamee's house, and they didn't see any reason not to make them public. Now all the world would see how manipulative the whole Hardin operation had been from the start. Ward had talked to McNamee and knew there was nothing to fear from the December 12 interview. It wasn't as if McNamee had asked for a bribe or admitted to lying to Novitzky. All he had done, McNamee told Ward, was repeat all the stuff he had said to

Novitzky, Parrella, and Mitchell. If Congress heard the tape, it would only underline how consistent McNamee had been and would continue to be as a witness to Clemens's doping.

The press conference in Houston demonstrated more about Clemens's dishonesty than McNamee's, Ward believed, because Clemens had repeated his claim that if he had only known what McNamee had told George Mitchell he would have addressed the issue "in a heartbeat." Ward now knew better. Clemens had known his name was going to be in the Mitchell Report well before Mitchell arrived at the podium at the Hyatt to announce his findings. Ward's client had been telling the Clemens camp about his cooperation with Mitchell as much as a week before the report came out, in his conversations with Jimmy Murray and Andy Pettitte.

By opening his mouth on *60 Minutes* and holding this bizarre press conference, Clemens was showing himself to be an unreliable custodian of the truth, and Hardin was allowing that to happen. In his remarks to the media, Ward seized on the "in a heartbeat" line Clemens seemed to like so much. "Mr. Clemens did in fact know that he was named in the report prior to its release and the only thing he did in a heartbeat was to hire a lawyer," Ward told the Associated Press. "Brian told the federal authorities the truth."

Representative Waxman heard the message. After seeing the internecine warfare that had erupted between Clemens and McNamee a week before the two of them were scheduled to appear before the committee, the chairman decided to push the hearing back a month. Waxman announced the postponement on Wednesday, January 9.

Waxman also announced that in the five-week interim before the February 13 hearing with Clemens, McNamee, Kirk Radomski, Andy Pettitte, and Chuck Knoblauch, the committee "asked" for each witness to provide a deposition to committee staff lawyers. Waxman didn't mention it, but the committee's investigation would also involve gathering documents, such as the transcript of the interviews McNamee gave Belk and Yarbrough, which of course was vastly more detailed than the Mitchell Report was.

It was time for all of these men to get Washington counsel.

The offices of Richard Emery's law firm, Emery, Celli, Brinckerhoff & Abady LLP, are usually a place where people gather for sober discussions of civil rights law and commercial litigation. But on January 9, 2008, the table in the corner of Emery's office was strewn with the bloody gauze, spent syringes, and the array of needles that had come out of McNamee's box in the basement. Emery's assistant was snapping pictures of the waste with a digital camera while McNamee and his lawyers looked on.

When McNamee came in with the medical waste that morning, Emery wasn't quite able to find the words to describe the sight; the term "smoking gun" had become a sick punch line during the administration of George W. Bush (whom Emery detested). But here it was. Emery had known about the existence of the waste for a couple of weeks at this point, but it hadn't really seemed real and personal until he'd seen it: the dark red stains on the wadded-up gauze, the syringes in their plastic wrappers, vials, and ampules. The future of not only the defamation case but the entire legal landscape of this case might lie inside that half-crushed Miller Lite can.

Emery's first instinct was to send the stuff to a lab for DNA testing, to see if the needles still contained Clemens's biological material. But Ward quickly pointed out that that wouldn't work; Hardin would claim that the laboratory had messed up something—anything could have happened to the contents of that box. There were already chain-of-custody issues here. This stuff had been in McNamee's basement for six or seven years. Hardin would be quick to discredit any evidence that had even been touched by the accuser, let alone kept secret for that long. With Clemens already claiming that McNamee injected him with B_{12} and lidocaine, it was only a small step further down the road to absurdity for the pitcher to claim that McNamee had somehow stolen his blood and smeared it onto some medical waste as part of a devious trap. They had already suggested in their Houston press conference that they thought McNamee wasn't above a little extortion.

Then again, what about the very real possibility that these syringes had Clemens's fingerprints on them? What if the needles contained traces of Clemens's DNA? What if there was blood or even flesh down in the bore of the needle, where it would have been extremely difficult for McNamee, or anyone else, to place it? There was only one thing to do, Emery and Ward had decided, and that was hand this stuff over to the government. Parrella and Novitzky were coming to New York City the next day anyway. In the meantime, they could take pictures.

Matthew Parrella and Jeff Novitzky were in town that week for a very special occasion: the sentencing of disgraced track star Marion Jones. A lot of people had lied in the BALCO investigation, many of them under oath. Grand juries had indicted Barry Bonds and cyclist Tammy Thomas for perjury, and track coach Trevor Graham for Section 1001, making false statements to a federal officer. But Jones had taken it to the next level, even beyond lying to Novitzky. She filed a $25 million defamation suit against Conte for outlining her drug program on television, talked trash about other sprinters she suspected of doping, and was outraged by even the merest suggestion that her performances were somehow unnatural.

It wasn't until the government got Jones on a check fraud scheme tied to her former boyfriend and father of one of her children, Tim Montgomery, that Jones finally came clean, at least in part. She admitted during her plea acceptance in U.S. District Court in White Plains, New York, in October 2007 that her coach, Trevor Graham, had given her a substance that turned out to be the designer drug THG. She said Graham had told her it was flaxseed oil but that after she stopped training with Graham she realized she'd been taking a steroid. She told Judge Kenneth Karas of the Southern District of New York that she knew the substance was a steroid by the time she was asked about it in an interview with Novitzky and Parrella in 2003. In that interview, she had denied recognizing or taking the drug.

Parrella had asked Judge Karas to give Jones a serious sentence but the prosecutors were somewhat surprised when the judge sent her to jail for as long as he did—six months. Karas told a packed courtroom that included many members of Jones's devastated family that he was troubled by Jones's statement during the October hearing that she thought she was using flaxseed oil and hadn't realized she was doping until she stopped taking it. "That's a very difficult thing to believe that a top-notch athlete, knowing that a razor-thin margin makes the difference, would not be keenly aware and very careful about what he or she put in her body, and the effects," Karas said.

The day before heading to White Plains for Jones's sentencing hearing, Parrella and Novitzky decided to check in on McNamee to see how he was doing. They knew he must be hurting after Clemens put on that show down in Houston. But they weren't expecting that he would be hitting back quite so hard. And with quite so much ammunition.

The same day, January 9, Congressmen Henry Waxman and Tom Davis decided to delay the committee's session involving Roger Clemens and other players in order to do a little investigating on their own. They had heard talk of abscesses and parties at Jose Canseco's house, as well as debates about lidocaine and B_{12}. They joined a curious media in asking whether a player's personal trainer would even attempt to inject a substance like lidocaine into a player without proper medical training. The process could take as much as five minutes to prep for and to find the landmark for the injection, the effects of which typically would last for one to two hours. Given that timeline, if McNamee had been giving Clemens lidocaine injections before a game, it most likely would have had to occur in the clubhouse, which meant other club personnel would have witnessed them.

Parrella and Novitzky arrived at Emery's office on Thursday, January 10, to find that their cooperating witness, who had been required to give them honest answers about his drug dealing, had held a few things back. All along, he'd possessed a box filled with medical waste left over from injecting Roger Clemens. Parrella was angry. It was Parrella who had extended the proffer agreement to McNamee, passing up on a drug distribution rap that would have added another scalp to his collection.

Parrella wanted to know why McNamee hadn't produced this evidence earlier, or at least shared word of it, as per the terms of the agreement. McNamee said he was trying to minimize the damage to Clemens, trying to give the guy a way out. Then he gave Parrella and Novitzky a tour of the exhibit, pointing out which needles were used for which purposes. Emery was nervous through the entire meeting. He knew that this was a clear violation of the proffer agreement, and that McNamee could now be charged with a crime. Even if that didn't happen, he knew they were handing over their trump card. They would probably never see the evidence again without seeking a subpoena for it in any civil suit down the road.

Any federal prosecutor will admit that cooperating witnesses don't always give them everything the first time around, and Parrella and Novitzky were accustomed to dealing with cooperators. Despite the initial tension, Emery and Ward could tell that the two men were pleased that McNamee had come clean. This would be very useful material for them. Perhaps even a smoking gun.

"Look, if he had decided never to produce this, he wouldn't have put himself in jeopardy," Emery would say later. "But he did come clean with it, potentially placed himself in jeopardy, and they were happy [the material] was turned over."

As nervous as Ward and Emery were about the feds, they were thrilled to think of what this might mean for Clemens. In the next few weeks,

Congress would be scheduling a deposition. Clemens might make some kind of bizarre immunity request, but Emery was certain it wouldn't fly. The pitcher would be under oath, and if he said he never used steroids and this evidence undercut that assertion, he would be locked in to his testimony. It was a perjury trap, and how often do two defense lawyers working pro bono get to set a perjury trap?

Hardin was working under the illusion, they could tell, that there was no corroboration for Brian's claims. Hardin thought it was just a he-said, he-said case. That was why he was mounting this PR campaign to discredit McNamee. That's why he was being so careful not to alienate Andy Pettitte. It was why he had advised Clemens to face Mike Wallace, make the YouTube video, hold the press conference. Hardin and Clemens had no idea there might be objective, scientific corroboration for what Brian was saying.

"We can hold this in our back pocket all the way through, march them right down the primrose path to perjury," Emery thought.

Of course, that all depended on a number of things. First and foremost, the existence of the evidence had to be kept secret until Clemens was under oath and a lot of people were digging for secrets.

On January 11, 2008, Sammy Woodrow was searching the Internet. Woodrow was the onetime associate of Kelly Blair's who had, several years before, seen the milk carton of drugs at 1-on-1 Elite Personal Fitness, the drugs Blair told him were earmarked for Roger Clemens and Andy Pettitte. Woodrow was on the Internet, trying to find a journalist who would slow down long enough to consider an outrageous but true story: that Tom Pettitte had been a drug connection for Major League Baseball. Sammy didn't want money for his information. That would be cool, of course, but it didn't have to be that way. The main thing Sammy wanted was for the truth to get out. After following the baseball steroids controversy for years, Sammy was frustrated by how little people seemed to understand about the drugs in question.

The previous Sunday, Sammy had been enjoying a few beers at a bar in Pasadena, Texas, when the television drew his eyes to the big, round, angry face of Roger Clemens. It was fleshy and determined. Sammy watched the pride of Houston tell Mike Wallace on *60 Minutes* how insulted he was that so many people believed this "hogwash" about his using performance-enhancing drugs.

To many who saw the interview, this comment betrayed Clemens as someone who didn't seem to understand the difference between respect and blind faith. You could respect a public figure and still ask him to remain accountable. Sammy was resentful, watching in gathering frustration as Wallace assured Clemens that yes indeed, people distrusted his performances now. The Mitchell Report was two and a half weeks old and most of the players it named—including Pettitte—had confirmed the truth of its contents.

Clemens told Wallace his success came from hard work, but Sammy also knew that hard work and steroids went great together. People who hadn't used them seemed to think that simply injecting the drugs would make you strong. You needed to lift weights while on steroids for them to have their anabolic effects.

Sammy had used all kinds of steroids. HGH too. He remembered how growth would make his skin "baby-ass-soft." On steroids, you would feel the pain from a heavy session, the microscopic tears in whatever muscle fibers you had taxed. But on a cycle of Deca or Winstrol—and especially if you combined them with twice-daily injections of "growth"—you could get back in the gym the next day for more dead lifts and bench presses. It was miraculous, even addictive. But you still needed to do the work.

Wallace, reading from the Mitchell Report, listed the drugs that Clemens was accused of using. It sounded like a pretty sensible regimen to Sammy and it seemed ridiculous that Clemens was trying to say it was all made up. But it wasn't until Sammy heard Clemens's next words that he realized the power he had in this situation.

"Never happened," Clemens told Wallace. "Never happened. And if I have these needles and these steroids and all these drugs, where did I get 'em? Where is the person out there gave 'em to me? Please, please come forward."

Sammy had an idea about that. He didn't think that Kelly Blair was going to do it himself. So he paid for his beers, went home, and started looking on the Internet for a number to call.

As the Mitchell Report saga unfolded in the first week of January, these two unforeseeable events—McNamee's retrieval of bloody medical waste and Sammy Woodrow's decision to blow the whistle on Kelly Blair and Tom Pettitte—were the wild cards in the high-stakes poker game that McNamee's old clients, Clemens and Pettitte, were playing with the House Oversight Committee. They remained ticking time bombs in the congressional investigation. As Congress began its investigation,

McNamee's lawyers were determined to keep the existence of the medical waste secret until Clemens had taken his denials to Washington and told them during sworn testimony. As for Sammy Woodrow, he did find a newspaper that listened and ultimately confirmed the outlandish tale he was so intent on telling—that Andy Pettitte had gotten HGH through his own father, and his father had gotten it at 1-on-1 Elite Personal Fitness. And because Andy Pettitte started receiving questions about Kelly Blair from the newspaper Sammy Woodrow had spoken to, he knew that before the end of the month, he was going to have to tell the whole truth about his HGH use, or else risk committing perjury before Congress.

In the years since Pettitte had first dipped into the stash of human growth hormone that Tom Pettitte had procured at Kelly Blair's gym, the primary source of a lot of the performance-enhancing drugs moving through 1-on-1 Elite Personal Fitness had dried up. The bodybuilder Craig Titus hadn't been caught for shipping steroids to Pasadena. That had continued unabated. But Titus had been unable to dodge a murder rap. And so just as Congress started investigating the mail order drug network Kirk Radomski had set up in baseball, Titus was sitting in a Nevada jail cell awaiting his trial on homicide charges.

Early on the morning of December 14, 2005, a trucker crossing the lonely desert southwest of Las Vegas around 4:30 A.M. noticed a fire burning about a quarter-mile off in the darkness. The trucker notified a dispatcher, and soon a volunteer firefighter was climbing out of bed and setting out from Mountain Springs, a tiny highway outpost that was home to the closest fire department.

A few hours later, as the sun came up over the cold desert, detectives from the homicide unit of the Las Vegas Metropolitan Police Department arrived at the scene. A car was still smoldering at the end of a sandy wash. It was a 2003 Jaguar that belonged to a well-known fitness model named Kelly Ryan, a former member of the United States gymnastics team who had trained under legendary coach Bela Karolyi. She lived in Las Vegas, and was married to Craig Titus, a former champion bodybuilder who had led a life of crime.

In the trunk of the Jaguar were charred remains of what police would later determine to be the corpse of 28-year-old Melissa James, a personal assistant to Titus and Ryan. As it happened, her murder had been committed on the exact same day that Novitzky had served his warrant to search Kirk Radomski's home in Long Island.

Titus was a star in his own right. He was hired as a personal trainer by Mötley Crüe lead singer Vince Neil to whip the heavy metal star into shape for *Remaking Vince Neil,* a special that aired on VH1. Neil's exercise regimen included steroids and human growth hormone. "He would shoot me with steroids and human growth hormone and you know, all that stuff," Neil said on *48 Hours,* the CBS newsmagazine. "So obviously, you know, he was really into that."

James had moved to Las Vegas to manage a clothing store Titus and Ryan were hoping to open. She moved in with the bodybuilder and his wife and soon got sucked into their hard-partying lifestyle. There were whispers that Titus and James were having an affair. Ryan, already insecure about her looks—she was a cosmetic surgery veteran—viewed the pretty, friendly James as a threat. Eventually, passions boiled over during an argument at the home the three of them shared.

The detectives had little trouble solving the crime over the next few weeks, even though Titus and Ryan told them outrageous lies and then tried to flee the country before they were apprehended. Prosecutors claimed James had been beaten, drugged, shocked with a stun gun, strangled, and bound with duct tape before Titus torched the Jaguar and fled the scene with the help of a friend. A coroner determined that James probably died of asphyxiation.

Titus and Ryan were nobody's idea of criminal masterminds. Among the evidence cops gathered were credit card records and surveillance videotapes showing that just an hour before the car was spotted, Ryan had gone to a local Wal-Mart to purchase three and a half gallons of charcoal starter fluid and a barbecue utensil set. The remains of the barbecue utensils were found in the burned car.

After years of delays, Titus and Ryan were finally due to face a trial in May of 2008 (at the last minute, Titus would plead guilty to second-degree murder, first-degree kidnapping, and arson, while Ryan would plead guilty to arson and battery with a deadly weapon). At his sentencing, Titus would say he accidentally killed James during a drug-fueled struggle.

Titus had used boatloads of steroids for nearly 20 years, and the abuse he inflicted upon his own hormonal system may have left him dangerously volatile. He was also a dealer at the dark headwaters of the black market for performance-enhancing drugs, only a few steps upstream in the river of drugs flowing into Major League Baseball.

. . .

For weeks now, Earl Ward had been hinting that going after his client in such a personal way might backfire: There were two sides to these attacks. "Brian knows a lot about Roger's moral character and knows a lot about his extracurricular activities," Ward said. "There's a lot that he could say to damage Roger's reputation, but we plan to take the high road."

The fact was, Ward and Emery were starting to amass information about Clemens in preparation for the defense of the defamation suit. Character is central to a defamation case, and when Ward and Emery got word that Hardin had dispatched investigators to Florida to locate the woman involved in the hotel pool incident seven years ago, they knew the fight was on. Hardin's investigators contacted Donald Crotty, the detective who had worked the case, and asked if Crotty could help them find the woman. "After the Mitchell Report came out, [investigators] came down and got a copy of the police report," Crotty said. "They asked me if she was still in Florida and I said, 'I have no idea. I haven't had any dealings with her.' But they felt that they were going to locate her and identify her." Because the case involved allegations of a sexual assault, Florida laws prevented her name from being disclosed and news organizations had not identified her. Hardin obtained the records and urged reporters to dig deeper.

Ward said that the attempt to raise questions about the 2001 incident, which the feds and Mitchell knew about, and attempts by Hardin to locate the woman amounted to a "smear campaign" to distract attention from the facts. "It's the information that Brian provided to Mitchell and to federal investigators that they should be focused on, and not trying to damage Brian's reputation," he said.

He then gently reminded everyone that McNamee had worked with and known Clemens for a significant period of time. "Brian knows a lot about Roger's moral character and if some of this stuff were to come out, Roger Clemens would look very, very, very bad," Ward said. "What does it all mean, in terms of our legal strategy? I think it's something that we'll look at in any defamation suit."

Emery was a little more direct. "My client has a lot of information on Clemens and he'll guide us," he said. "We will depose various people with knowledge of Roger's reputation."

McNamee had started to remember things, and not just the FedEx box in the basement. He recalled shooting up Debbie with HGH and asking Kirk Radomski to ship those drugs to Clemens's home. He remembered the Winstrol shot that he'd hurriedly given Clemens and the abscess it had caused. They had treated Clemens for that in Toronto, laid him out on a table and applied ultrasound to his butt, and the team might have kept a record of that treatment. He remembered Mindy McCready and the long relationship. And the Manhattan bartender named Angie Moyer and the beautiful girl Jennifer. He'd been on the plane with Jennifer and he'd seen the diamond earrings Clemens had presented her with. There were a lot of girls Clemens traveled with, meeting up with them in Palm Springs, Vegas, New York, and Cabo. He would run them in and out of spring training and set them up with box seats at Yankee Stadium. McNamee hadn't paid much attention to the girls—they were fixtures in ballplayers' lives, they were an accepted part of life on the road, especially for superstars—but he knew enough. More than enough.

It was almost as if the committee's chairman, Henry Waxman, often frustrated by his inability to summon members of the Bush administration before his committee, was using Roger Clemens as a stand-in for the Texas pitcher's friends in the Bush family.

Clemens may not have publicly identified himself as a Republican the way Red Sox pitcher Curt Schilling vociferously did, but to the extent that Clemens followed politics, the GOP was the team he rooted for. He had met Ronald Reagan and Norman Schwarzkopf, and kept photos at his home commemorating those visits. And of course he was friendly with his Houston neighbor, former first baseman George H. W. Bush. Alan Hendricks had arranged for him to take a USO tour of the troops in the Persian Gulf and Afghanistan in 2002 and he'd been moved by the reception he'd gotten from the 4,000 sailors and marines he spoke to in an aircraft carrier hangar.

"I was overwhelmed by that," he said after the visit, still visibly moved by the experience.

Not long after the release of the Mitchell Report, Clemens was sitting in a deer blind in South Texas when the elder Bush called him. It was during the period when the number of people Clemens thought were his friends was dwindling. (Curt Schilling, on his blog, 38pitches.com, had even called for Clemens to either clear his name or give back all four of his post-1997 Cy Young Awards.) But here was Bush 41, going out of his way to be supportive. As Clemens later told it, the former president "expressed his concerns" with the report by Mitchell (who, incidentally, happened to have clashed with Bush more than once while leading the Democratic majority in the Senate). According to Clemens, Bush told him, "Hold your head up high"—that the Mitchell Report was "unbelievable" and that Clemens should "stay strong." (It so happened that Clemens was on a form of legal steroids on one of the several visits he made to the White House. As a treatment for his swollen and painful shoulder, Clemens had taken prednisone, a corticosteroid. Prednisone didn't have anabolic properties—it didn't build muscle—but it was known to reduce swelling and it was a common legal treatment in professional sports. "My head looked like a stop sign because you retain so much water," Clemens later recalled.)

But Bush's faith in the pitcher and Clemens's politics notwithstanding, the committee hearing was going forward.

The plush lobby of the Hotel Monaco in Washington has marble floors, eager bellhops, stacks of influential newspapers, and large silver cisterns full of coffee for the movers and shakers who are the hotel's guests. Walking calmly into scene early on the morning of January 15, 2008, was the Honorable George J. Mitchell, who paid his room bill and greeted the several attorneys who had gone there to accompany him for his testimony about baseball and steroids before the House Committee on Oversight and Government Reform.

Their conversation was unexpectedly interrupted, however, when a fellow graduate of Mitchell's alma mater Bowdoin College, recognized the senator and came over to shake hands. Mitchell engaged in a brief but warm chat about various parts of Maine's rocky coast. Then, with a nod to his companions, returned to the day's careful script. He stepped out to the sidewalk and climbed into the back seat of the black town car that took him about a mile away, across Pennsylvania Avenue and the National Mall, to the Rayburn House Office Building.

About an hour later, this old lion of the Senate was speaking into the Congressional Record again. The person who asked him to raise his hand and give his oath was the committee's chairman, Henry Waxman, a liberal Democrat who had represented California's 30th Congressional District for 33 years and was known as one of the great watchdogs of Capitol Hill.

A tenacious investigator, Waxman was well known for locating the people with dark secrets, be they American security firms with contracts in Iraq or White House operatives with knowledge of press leaks, and dragging them before the committee to answer his questions under oath—or refuse to answer, looking guilty and petty in their refusal. Waxman's crusading had won him the nickname "The Mustache of Justice," a reference to the facial hair that appeared underneath his pug nose.

One of Waxman's legacies was taking on Big Tobacco; in 1994, he oversaw the famous "seven dwarves" hearing at which seven tobacco industry executives said, under oath, that nicotine was not addictive. Mitchell had been on the other side of the issue, defending the tobacco industry. Indeed, progressives considered it one of the biggest blemishes on his legislative career.

But when Mitchell and Waxman met this day, it was a historic interaction. From opposite sides of the country, the two lawyers had come to Washington in the post-Watergate power shuffle of the mid-1970s, as the legislature reclaimed the constitutional powers that Richard Nixon had grabbed. The backlash to Nixon's overreaching White House was a tide that lifted the Democratic Party, and Waxman and Mitchell had risen with that tide.

Mitchell left the Senate in 1994, but Waxman had stayed on in the House of Representatives through the Republican Revolution, during which his G.O.P. rivals once tweaked him by placing his photo underneath ashtrays in subcommittee meeting rooms, where smoking was still allowed. One of Waxman's top aides, Phil Schiliro, was angry enough about that to speak out in *Time* magazine. "That's what passes for wit among some Republicans," Schiliro said. "That epitomizes their philosophy: 'Those Democrats didn't know anything, and if they're against smoking, we'll be for it and blow smoke in their faces.' " In 2000, Waxman found himself back in the fight against White House incursions into legislative authority. Waxman had become one of the most energetic antagonists of the Bush Administration, and particularly Dick Cheney's belief of the "unitary executive."

Coming to power in 2007, as soon as the Democrats took majority control of both houses of Congress, Waxman restored the word "oversight" to the committee's name, a symbolic gesture that foreshadowed what was to come. All year, Waxman issued subpoenas and raised awareness of much of the waste, fraud, and abuse that had taken place during the previous six years. But Waxman had always been vigorous in his investigations. In 1989, a fellow representative from California joked to the *National Journal* that when he arrived at Congress he thought Waxman's first name was "sonuvabitch" because "everybody who had to deal with him kept saying, 'Do you know what that sonuvabitch Waxman wants now?' "

Waxman frequently cited House Rule X, which granted his committee broad oversight jurisdiction, including authority to "conduct investigations of any matter" within the jurisdiction of any standing committee of Congress, and to make available "the findings and recommendations" following that investigation.

He was also a fan of House Rule XI, under which his committee was authorized to "require, by subpoena or otherwise, the attendance and testimony of such witnesses and the production of such books, records, correspondence, memoranda, papers, and documents as it considers necessary."

People might have said baseball was a matter that didn't deserve the attention of Congress. Those people might have needed a reminder that Waxman's predecessor in the chairmanship of the committee, Tom Davis, had issued a subpoena to Terri Schiavo and her husband, interfering in Schiavo's very personal right to die. Baseball had a legitimate reason to be kept under scrutiny. The government had granted it the right to be a legal monopoly and so had a duty to make sure those rights were not abused. Drug taking was certainly an abuse—and not just of public trust. It could certainly affect the outcome of games and could even lead to potential gambling abuses. If owners wanted the rewards that came with the privileged status, there had to be some oversight.

Waxman had taken on the Bush administration over its e-mail retention policy, its evisceration of environmental safeguards, Iraq reconstruction, and the leaking of the identity of CIA officer Valerie Plame. By 2008, he was positioning himself to work in synchronicity with a possible new Democratic president. But one thing he wanted was to finish his stint as baseball's de facto steroid policy umpire. The public was ready to see Congress move on to more important issues. But before that could happen, the committee needed to see the Mitchell Report stand without challenges as an authoritative historical document. They needed to get to the bottom of the dispute. "A little government sunshine can go a long way," Waxman said.

It had taken more than three years to get to this point. The story of how it had come to this—how Congress got Selig to call Mitchell—began with the publication of a book. Not a sober, 409-page report by a team of lawyers, but a best-selling tell-all that was so juicy, in fact, that it had to be called *Juiced.* Jose Canseco's tell-all had been ridiculed and attacked but it also was, for the most part, true. And it opened a lot of eyes, including those of government officials. The first hearing—with McGwire et al.— had clearly not produced the desired results as far as cleaning up the game went. And so, over the next several hours, Waxman took testimony from Mitchell, baseball commissioner Bud Selig, and players union boss Donald Fehr. Mitchell spoke frankly about what he had found: widespread use and a cover-up by the entire game.

"Obviously, the players who illegally used performance-enhancing substances are responsible for their actions," he told the committee. "But they did not act in a vacuum. Everyone involved in baseball over the past two decades—Commissioners, club officials, the Players Association, and players—shares to some extent in the responsibility for the steroids era. There was a collective failure to recognize the problem as it emerged and to deal with it early on. As a result, an environment developed in which illegal use became widespread."

Mitchell went on to say that there was much he did not learn, certainly about other suppliers and users. "It is clear that a number of players have obtained these substances through so-called rejuvenation centers, using prescriptions of doubtful validity. Other investigations will no doubt turn up more names and fill in more details, but that is unlikely to significantly alter the description of baseball's steroids era, as set forth in my report," he said. "The Commissioner was right to ask for this investigation and report. It would have been impossible to get closure on this issue without it, or something like it. It's appropriate to acknowledge, Mr. Chairman, that it was you and this committee who originally suggested that such an inquiry be conducted."

Waxman surely appreciated those words. The public could complain about Congress wasting its time on sports issues but Mitchell himself was paying homage to the committee's work of the past three years.

"Now we have before us the Mitchell report," Davis said. "Its 409 pages paint a sordid picture of backroom drug deals involving clubhouse personnel; players injecting each other with illegal substances right in their locker rooms; and more efforts aimed at obfuscation and confiscation. The report names 89 players with varying degrees of involvement with steroids and HGH. But they are just part of a far wider culture in a sport that values home runs and victories over fair play. The report confirms that active participation or passive acquiescence and drugging cannot coexist with the responsibility to set a proper example for those stepping up the lower rungs of the ladder of athletic success. In other words, while two years ago we hoped otherwise, our work here is definitely not done. Stiffer penalties and stepped-up enforcement have caused some players to back off of steroid use. Unfortunately that progress has created a strong, perverse incentive to develop substances that can't be detected by current testing regimes. But as a panelist in our last baseball hearing famously said, We're not here to talk about the past. Our panel today will address in essence one question: Going forward, what will the leaders of baseball do to implement the recommendations outlined in this report?"

During the hearing, Waxman followed the established rules of congressional procedure, allowing different members of the committee allotments of time to ask questions or read statements. One of the most powerful came from a Democrat from Minnesota named Betty McCollum.

"In my opinion, what we have here is a criminal conspiracy to defraud millions of baseball fans of billions of dollars over the past years," McCollum began. If baseball were just a form of entertainment, where the audience weren't operating under the presumption of fair play, "then there would be no difference between Barry Bonds and Britney Spears," she said.

"But in fact Major League Baseball is sold as a legitimate athletic competition in which the outcome of the game is decided on the field in a transparent fashion for every fan to see," McCollum said. "The fact that league officials, owners, players, and the players union all knew this massive illegal drug abuse problem existed—and continues to exist with the use of human growth hormones—demonstrates a fraud to millions of baseball fans."

Where many people in authority who shook their fingers disapprovingly at baseball's steroid problem fell back on a familiar justification—concern for children—McCollum made a reasonable argument for the dollar. The committee's chief jurisdiction, after all, was monitoring waste, fraud, and abuse.

"Every fan who bought a ticket to see games for the past twenty years has been witness to a fraud—an industry promoted as honest that is in fact rooted in cheating for profit," McCollum said. "The more home runs hit, the more fans in the seats, the more money in owners' pockets, the bigger salaries for players—it is all a big lie when the industry is filled with lawbreakers and co-conspirators who ignore the problem or actively fuel the problem."

Anyone who thought the hearing might be dull had a nice surprise when Waxman made an announcement that the committee was referring shortstop Miguel Tejada to the Justice Department on suspicion of perjury. The reporters, who had come to cover the hearing in case Mitchell or Selig or Fehr said something outrageous, weren't expecting any real news to come out of the event. They were taken aback when Waxman announced that Tejada was under criminal investigation, and they couldn't help but note that it looked very much like a shot across the bow at Clemens.

First, however, Waxman would revisit the past. Miguel Tejada had appeared prominently in the Mitchell Report as a customer of a former major league player named Adam Piatt, who was the only player to voluntarily admit his use of performance-enhancing drugs to Mitchell and to accept responsibility for his actions. Piatt and Tejada had been teammates on the A's in 2003 and Piatt told Mitchell that during this period he discussed steroid use with Tejada and provided him with steroids and human growth hormone. Piatt recalled that he provided Tejada with testosterone or Deca-Durabolin, as well as HGH. As corroborating evidence, Mitchell produced copies of two checks written by Tejada to Piatt, both dated March 21, 2003, for the amounts of $3,100 and $3,200. Mitchell also noted that Kirk Radomski corroborated information provided by Piatt, specifically that he had received a call from Piatt saying he needed extra testosterone because "one of the guys wanted some." Later, Piatt told Radomski that the testosterone was for his teammate Miguel Tejada. The account in the Mitchell Report was in direct contradiction to what Tejada had told the committee.

Waxman took the occasion of the first day of the hearing to make his announcement of a criminal referral of Tejada, one that would run parallel with the investigation the committee would eventually open on Roger Clemens. Waxman pointed out that Tejada had knowingly made false material statements to the committee in connection with his investigation of Rafael Palmeiro, a violation of 18 U.S.C. 1001. Waxman and Davis asked Attorney General Michael Mukasey to open an investigation of Tejada. "We do not presume that Mr. Tejada lied to the Committee," Waxman and Davis wrote. "But we do believe that this is a serious enough issue to warrant further examination by the Justice Department. We are especially concerned about the veracity of Mr. Tejada's statements because they materially influenced the course of the Committee's investigation in 2005."

For Washington counsel, Hardin turned to, of all people, a Democrat. On January 18, Hardin announced that he had chosen Washington lawyer Lanny Breuer. "I'm honored to be joining Rusty Hardin in representing one of the greatest pitchers and athletes in history," Breuer said after he joined Team Rocket. Breuer was hardly a household name, but for Hardin it was like signing Mariano Rivera to a free-agent contract a month before the World Series. Now a partner at the white-shoe firm of Covington & Burling, Breuer reportedly charged clients $800 per hour for his services and was celebrated as one of Washington's top lawyers, a master at preparing clients for congressional investigations. *Washingtonian* called Breuer "one of the cleverest" lawyers in Washington. After graduating from Columbia Law School, Breuer worked as an assistant district attorney in Manhattan from 1985 to 1989. As a special White House counsel, he represented Bill Clinton from 1997 to 1999 during independent counsel and congressional hearings as well as the impeachment hearings. Breuer also represented the University of California in an investigation of Los Alamos National Laboratory, Moody's Investor Service in the wake of Enron's collapse, and Halliburton KBR in a hearing conducted by the House Committee on Oversight and Government Reform. Breuer also represented his friend Sandy Berger, Clinton's national security adviser, when Berger was accused of unauthorized removal of classified documents from a National Archives reading room in 2004. Berger eventually pleaded guilty to a misdemeanor. "Breuer's Berger defense was a case study in Washington lawyering," *Washingtonian* said. "He masterfully parried most of the charges and got Berger a favorable plea despite all the damaging evidence. Justice Department veterans say that when a lawyer comes in looking for a light sentence today, he is apt to say, 'I want a Berger.' "

In 2006, Breuer represented the Hewlett Packard board of directors during the scandal that ensued when HP's chairwoman hired private investigators to spy on the electronic communications of board members and journalists. The Energy and Commerce Committee investigated that blowup too, and Paoletta and Breuer had crossed paths then.

His role with Clemens's legal team presented a problem for Major League Baseball, though, which had commissioned the study that identified Clemens as a steroid user. Covington & Burling also represented MLB in Washington, and MLB officials privately griped that the law firm blundered when it failed to get the league's approval before it agreed to represent Clemens.

Despite Breuer's high profile on the Hill, he made it clear from the outset when he joined Clemens's team that he wanted to be the anti-Rusty. Reached by phone in the days after he was retained, Breuer told the *Daily News* he wanted to "calm things down." Hardin had been spouting sound bites full steam since the release of the Mitchell Report in

December, but Breuer was pitching a different strategy. That would change in due time.

In the weeks following the December 2007 release of the Mitchell Report, Kelly Blair had told people he couldn't afford the lease at the Pasadena, Texas, strip mall that housed his gym, and he moved it to a small, nondescript garage at 3118 Blue Bonnet Street, the former location of Morgan's Concrete Pumping Service. His colleagues were surprised when he suddenly left the country, traveling to Bulgaria for several months to train heavyweight boxer Sergei Liakhovich. He left the gym in the care of some young trainers, who were told that they should do something to bring in more clients for the struggling business.

On January 21, Kelly Blair logged on to his MySpace page to find a message waiting for him from a reporter. The reporter was from New York City, but he was apparently in Pasadena, and wanted to talk to Blair. "We are doing a story about performance-enhancing drugs in Deer Park and Pasadena and the name of your gym keeps coming up," the message read. "We have received what we believe is credible information about your gym and clients."

Later that day, Blair responded with a brief message of his own, mentioning his famous relative who played for the Yankees, even though the reporter had never asked about any specific baseball players, certainly not Pettitte or Clemens: "i have NEVER worked with Andy Pettitte; he is just a family friend, he has never even been in my gym. Sorry, I cant help you with your story!!!!"

This was demonstrably untrue, because at that very moment Blair's Web site had a picture of Pettitte at the gym, standing beside Blair. The reporter sent several more e-mails to Blair, who responded again on January 24, referring the reporters to the *Pasadena Citizen* article by Jenny Branch.

Feel free to get to know the real me and what i am really about!!!! i am very well respected in the fitness world and not you or anyone else can change that! i have worked very hard in my life to maintain a respectable business and i will not let jealous people try to change that either; its all about he said she said BULLSHIT!! just a reminder that deprivation of character and slander are very ugly things that my lawyer cant wait to see. do not contact me again or anyone in my family or even my trainers again! any thing that even insinuates me or my business in a negative manner will result in legal action.

There was no way for Blair to know about another bit of information linking him to Pettitte—that back in the summer of 2007, Brian McNamee had told federal agents Jeff Novitzky and Matthew Parrella that Tom Pettitte used human growth hormone he had collected from the parking lot of a gym near Pettitte's hometown.

Kevin Schexnider was a muscular man, a former bodybuilder who had done a little cage fighting in his day. Bench presses had made his chest thick, but his thumbs weren't especially powerful. Anabolic steroids, used in conjunction with a disciplined weight-lifting program, might make you strong—but it couldn't save your thumbs from text message fatigue. Schexnider was writing an extremely long text message to two reporters who'd somehow gotten the numbers of his cell phone and home phone in Arizona. "To the 2 douche bag, yankee 'reporter' lowlifes who have been harassing my family, employees, friends and clients at my gym," he began.

Schexnider had bought into the 1-on-1 Elite Personal Fitness business at the end of 2007, agreeing to help finance the gym. Now an engineer, Schexnider had been formerly employed as a security man at Babe's Cabaret, a strip club owned by Jenna Jameson, the porn star and entre-preneur. It helped that he was enormous, carrying around the kind of muscles that are normally seen only in bodybuilder magazines.

The previous week, the two reporters had visited 1-on-1 Elite Personal Fitness back in Pasadena, looking for Kelly Blair. The kid Kelly had hired to run the place when he wasn't around, Travis McIntyre, told them Kelly was in Bulgaria training a fighter, but that they might reach out to Schexnider. McIntyre didn't give them Schexnider's numbers, but they'd found them. "This message is the one and ONLY communication that will ever come from this end. My advice to you is go back home ASAP. My lawyer is in the process of filing harassment charges against the two men who have trespassed on my business and making my clients nervous."

At first Schexnider thought he could ignore the whole thing, but he soon got reports that the reporters had spoken to Blair's ex-wife, Chelsi, and that they had tried to reach Kelly through his parents. They even called Schexnider's parents' house looking for his phone number. That's what sparked the text message.

The reporters came back to the gym again, this time snapping pictures of the outside of the building. McIntyre had run out of the building's office with his own camera and snapped pictures of them, resulting in a silly digital showdown. "I have pictures of both of you, your rental car and license plate," Schexnider wrote. "Tomorrow morning there will be restraining orders issued, barring you both from within 1000 feet of my business and, shortly there after, harassment charges if there is one more phone call, text, letter, etc. to anyone you have contacted including the Schexniders, Blairs, Chelsi, my employees and everyone else you have harassed."

The reporters had been coy about their purpose for being down in Pasadena, looking into 1-on-1 Elite, but from talking to his friends, Schexnider thought he knew. "I know your so called agenda and 'proof' you say you have on the individual that you are seeking and that you will write some bullshit story that will be so inaccurate that not only will your newspaper be sued for slander, but you 2 nobodys will be homeless. You do not mess with another man's livelihood by pressuring people into something that isn't there."

Not that Schexnider had gotten a lot of livelihood out of 1-on-1 Elite. The place was struggling financially. Simply meeting the rent at the previous location was difficult, and now the gym was occupying a garage. It wouldn't help to have these prying Northerners showing up and exposing its dirty laundry. "You have been pushing for trouble and I gave you the benefit of the doubt, but you have outworn your welcome. It has gone on too long. And if everyone from NY is as stupid as you, then 'you all' are in for a big surprise! You are wasting your time, barking up the wrong tree . . . and it will only end up making you look like the idiots that you are."

Schexnider was annoyed by the Yankee interlopers, but he was especially angry that the reporters had called his parents. His mother was sick. "My mother has cancer and you call her house after my father told you to get lost? What kind of lowlifes are you? If you really had dirt on a clean as a whistle man, you still wouldn't be in my town. So, like I said, if anyone is harassed again tomorrow (here, California, or wherever) you will both regret it . . . as well as your editor and newspaper. People in Texas are smarter than you 2 yankee boys think."

Schexnider let the reporters know that he had records of the phone calls, to go along with the photographs, in case they ever challenged the harassment claim. "you have both been recorded on almost every conversation since you first harassed Chelsi (who does not speak to her ex husband). So, if you want to make a name for yourselves, go chase a story that has meat . . . some REAL PROOF. The worst thing Mr. Blair has done is get a speeding ticket. I've known him for over 20 years and absolutely everything he has done."

That wasn't quite true. Blair had been in plenty of trouble over the years, but Schexnider was on a roll. The text message was now more than 400 words, and the writer's thumbs were getting tired. It was time to wrap things up with a legal threat. "And, by the way, my lawyer is begging you to write something slanderous. Do not attempt anymore contact because it will be used against you. A copy of this text will be filed along with all other recordings going to a detective friend (who is a client) as well as my lawyer who is one of the most well known former judges in our state. You have been warned."

Schexnider hit send. It was late evening on January 23. Somewhere out there the Yankee reporter would get a message so long that it would come into his cell phone in pieces that would have to be pasted together. It would take 15 minutes for the whole thing to be reassembled on the phone. That would show them. It was amazing that in this day and age people still hadn't learned you don't mess with Texas.

Eight miles from Schexnider's home in Arizona was a strip mall medical clinic named Revolution Medical Centers, owned and operated by Dr. Jeremy Bula, a former chiropractor who drove an oversized red pickup. He called himself the CEO of the clinic, which he said had about 4,000 patients at two locations. Bula wasn't a typical doctor. When he wasn't running his clinic, he shaved his chest, donned skimpy bikini briefs, and joined in bodybuilding competitions where he showed off his unnaturally large muscles. The pastime reflected the kind of medicine he practiced.

Revolution Medical Centers readily dispensed powerful anabolic steroids and human growth hormone to a wide range of patients. For a small fee, patients could walk in, consult with any of several naturopathic doctors, and have their blood drawn and tested—a formality that was often followed up by hormone therapy. There was a pharmacy on the premises. Within days they could return to the clinic, receive instructions about intramuscular injections, and walk out with a small black bag full of syringes, needles, and drugs. Kevin Schexnider was a patient at Revolution and a friend of the people who operated it. His doctor at the clinic was Jesse Haggard, a naturopathic physician with a soft, mellow voice and a calm way of explaining away the prescription infractions that had landed him in trouble in the past.

Haggard was typical of many doctors in the hormone therapy game.

He regularly prescribed steroids or human growth hormone for a variety of causes, handing out prescriptions to everyone from menopausal women to people who came in complaining of low energy or mood swings. In 2006, Haggard gave Schexnider prescriptions for two steroids, testosterone cypionate and oxymetholone—the latter also known as Anadrol, the potent oral testosterone that Brian McNamee saw Jose Canseco nonchalantly pop into his mouth back in 1998. Packages containing both of these controlled substances were shipped in Schexnider's name to Revolution Medical Centers.

Records of the shipments were later seized by authorities in a nationwide investigation of corrupt pharmacies and anti-aging clinics. Haggard was one of 12 people indicted by a federal grand jury on January 22, 2009, for their role in what court documents described as a $4 million steroid ring that operated in at least 10 states. The indictment also named the owners of Applied Pharmacy Services, the Alabama company that allegedly sold performance-enhancing drugs to John Rocker, Jose Canseco, and other athletes.

For years, Applied and Florida's Signature Compounding Pharmacy distributed potent anabolic steroids right under the noses of federal law enforcement agencies that had de-prioritized steroids while fighting the war on drugs on other fronts. That left it to Albany County district attorney David Soares to do exactly what Schexnider's text message would later urge reporters to do. "If you want to make a name for yourselves, go chase a story that has meat."

Nearly eight years after they were teammates for the third and final time—during the 2000 season when one was still in the peak of his second coming as a power pitcher, the other nearly finished in baseball, barely hanging on to his fame as one half of the "Bash Brothers"—Jose Canseco was with Roger Clemens again. There were no clubhouse high jinks this time. No banter about the moon shot over the wall or how well the fastball was humming. Neither Roger Clemens nor Jose Canseco was playing in late January 2008, but three alleged incidents that took place during their Toronto baseball days had brought Canseco to Houston to meet with Clemens and his attorneys on January 22.

Canseco hadn't swung a bat in the majors since 2001 with the White Sox—seven long years without the million-dollar paycheck or the roar from the crowd as No. 33 launched another pitch into a stadium upper deck. Canseco had instead supplemented his baseball riches by taking his pen to paper and ratting out all of his teammates who had been steroid users. *Juiced: Wild Times, Rampant 'Roids, Smash Hits, and How Baseball Got Big,* written in 2005, torpedoed Bud Selig and forever changed the course of Major League Baseball and its drug culture, paving the way to congressional hearings, stricter testing, and making the asterisk a necessary accessory to a generation of baseball stats.

And Canseco wasn't through. The day he flew from California to Houston first-class—courtesy of Clemens—he was finally closing an agreement to write his sequel to *Juiced,* after the original publisher, Penguin, had backed out. *Vindicated* was scheduled for release Opening Day 2008. Canseco was promising more names. Big names.

Clemens had appeared in *Juiced,* but Canseco had written about the pitcher in mostly laudatory terms, including the claim that had made Debbie so happy—that her husband was one of the few players who were faithful to their wives. Canseco hinted in *Juiced* that Clemens had used performance enhancers, noting that Clemens had talked around teammates about the virtues of "vitamin B_{12}"—clubhouse code for steroids— but said he'd never actually seen Clemens inject himself.

"I can't give chapter and verse on Roger's training regimen. But I'll tell you what I was thinking at the time: One of the classic signs of steroid use is when a player's basic performance actually improves later in his career," Canseco wrote in *Juiced.* "One of the benefits of steroids is that they're especially helpful in countering the effects of aging. So in Roger's case, around the time he was leaving the Boston Red Sox, Roger decided to make some changes. He started working out harder. And whatever else he may have been doing to get stronger, he saw results."

Clemens would turn up in *Vindicated* as well—again, with Canseco's veiled remarks linking Clemens to steroids. But by January 22, 2008, Canseco had become more of a Clemens ally, unequivocally backing the pitcher in his war against Brian McNamee. Clemens's team had sent a couple of attorneys to talk with Canseco weeks before in preparation for an affidavit they would ask him to sign and submit to the House Committee on Oversight and Government Reform.

"His attorneys wanted to verify that what was said in the Mitchell Report was true," Canseco recalled. "They flew and rented an office in the Sherman Oaks [California] area—the Galleria. We talked. They showed me the Mitchell Report, the parts where Roger and myself and McNamee were involved.

"I scanned through it. I noticed that McNamee mentioned something about a party. I said 'Wait a minute. Roger wasn't there.' I remember that like it was yesterday because I had this barbeque party for the players. And I invited family over, friends and all the players. I was extremely disappointed because Roger didn't show up. He was probably the only one that did not show up. I think he had some type of golfing engagement. I remember the next day even mentioning it to the media, mentioning, 'I had a pool party at my house, a barbeque pool party and Roger Clemens was the only individual that didn't show up.' There were also several other individuals who testified that Roger was not there."

McNamee had testified in the Mitchell Report that Clemens was not only at the party, but had conferred with Canseco and another man inside Canseco's home, possibly about steroid use. That was the furthest thing from the truth, according to Canseco. And once Clemens's attorneys got wind of Canseco's take on the matter, they weren't going to waste a golden opportunity.

After the California meeting, Clemens's team arranged for Canseco to come to Houston to etch his recollections in stone. Canseco went without his attorney, Robert Saunooke, instead opting to carry out this sensitive transaction with Glenn Dunn, Canseco's high school baseball coach at Coral Park, in Miami. Dunn had remained close to Canseco throughout his major league career, and Dunn had been in Canseco's home the day of the 1998 party.

"They asked me, 'Jose, would you validate this, would you fly down to Houston and sign an affidavit?' I said, 'Sure, definitely.' They got me a first-class ticket and I flew down there," Canseco said. "Got in about 10, 11 o'clock at night. Went to his attorney's office. Roger picked me and my friend up from the airport, Glenn. Signed the affidavit and then they took us to a local hotel."

Canseco said he was never pressured by Clemens's attorneys while reviewing the affidavit, although he found that the document needed "restructuring." "Some of it was a little improper, meaning, of the events that happened that day [at the 1998 party]. So I restructured it slightly, and then I signed it. Basically just reiterated the truth, what actually happened. He was not there," Canseco said.

The affidavit also included Canseco's refutation of two other claims that McNamee had made in the Mitchell Report. First, that Canseco had received the bottle of Anadrol-50 from McNamee during the 1998 season, and second, that Canseco had been present when Clemens told him and McNamee at a Florida bar that he'd won two Cy Young Awards due to steroid use.

"I have been told that McNamee has stated that Clemens made a statement in my and McNamee's presence about winning two Cy Young Awards while using steroids or human growth hormone," he said in the affidavit.

"McNamee's allegation is completely false. Clemens has never said anything like that to me or in my presence."

It was an odd thing for Canseco to address. McNamee had made the statement about the bar incident to Belk and Yarbrough back in December when they were taping their interview with him. McNamee's recollection of the bar incident hadn't been included in the Mitchell Report and no one had really been inquiring about it. Then Jim Yarbrough asked McNamee if there was anything else that might come out, and McNamee said yes. McNamee told Hardin's investigators about a conversation he had with Clemens after the two had spent an evening at a Miami bar with Canseco and a few other people.

"And I said, 'I know Canseco mentioned something about steroids.' And Clemens's response was, 'I know. I got—I won two Cy Young awards on that shit,' which I didn't appreciate him saying. I never talked to him about it. But I know that's what he was talking about," McNamee said during the interview.

Canseco scoffed at both claims. Backing away from his insinuations in *Juiced,* he shied away from any Clemens controversy whatsoever. "I have no doubt that I spoke to Clemens about steroids just like I did with other people. However, I have never had a conversation with Clemens in which he expressed any interest in using steroids or human growth hormone," he said in the affidavit. "Clemens has never asked me to give him steroids or human growth hormone, and I have never seen Clemens use, possess, or ask for steroids or human growth hormone. I have played on three teams with Roger Clemens and I have no reason to believe that he has ever used steroids, human growth hormone, or any other performance enhancing drugs."

Canseco and Dunn retired to a nearby hotel (also paid for by Clemens) and prepared for a golf outing with Clemens the following morning. Inclement weather intervened, however, and Canseco and Dunn instead spent several hours at the Clemens compound before returning to the airport. Canseco was hurting financially by January, despite signing the six-figure deal for his second book, but when asked several weeks after the hearing if he'd gotten anything in return from Clemens for signing the affidavit, he called the idea far-fetched.

"Absolutely not. Not even close," said Canseco. "He didn't ask me to lie. He didn't offer me money. It was just about, 'Jose, look at this Mitchell

Report and tell me what you find truthful.' I said, 'That didn't happen and that didn't happen.' It just didn't. I barely knew Brian McNamee, by the way. When we were in the locker room—now see if this makes sense—he said he handed me a bottle of steroids. I ask you this question: I've got my own supply. Why would I take a bottle of steroids from a complete stranger? Does that make any sense to you?"

The public wouldn't learn just how desperate Canseco's financial situation was until later in the year, during Canseco's appearance in a celebrity boxing match against former NFL player Vai Sikahema.

There had been some real confusion and drama in the weeks since Chuck Knoblauch had first been "invited" to a hearing before the committee. The hearing had been announced, and every news outlet from local papers to ESPN had covered the fact that Henry Waxman wanted to see Knoblauch and the others named in the Mitchell Report in Washington. But Knoblauch had been slow to respond. In fact, he hadn't responded at all. When the committee went looking for him, they were surprised to find that nobody in baseball knew where he was. The Yankees didn't know. The White Pages didn't carry a listing. Knoblauch, it appeared, hadn't kept in touch with anyone from baseball since his final game, September 27, 2002.

Phil Schiliro, Waxman's chief of staff, had finally located a phone number for the former second baseman for the Twins, Yankees, and Royals, and left several messages, getting no reply. Finally, it fell to Thayer Evans, a Texas-based reporter for *The New York Times*, to track down Knoblauch in a suburb of Houston and talk to the enigmatic former player, who stood in front of his home in a U.S. Open tennis T-shirt, blue jeans, and sneakers. In Evans's story, published January 11, Knoblauch appeared almost comically aloof about the Mitchell Report controversy.

Describing the report as "crazy" and "interesting," Knoblauch explained to Evans that he had nothing to do with baseball anymore. He also claimed that no one from the committee had contacted him, raising the remote possibility that Schiliro had used the wrong phone number, and that some random Texan was going to show up at Congress on February 13. It didn't seem, from Evans's telling, that Knoblauch was trying to be evasive. He even said he'd show up if someone just told him where to go. "I have nothing to defend," Knoblauch said. "I have nothing to hide at the same time."

The committee members and their staffs were embarrassed when they opened the *Times* that Friday morning and saw one of their witnesses basically accepting the committee's invitation through a college sports reporter. "I read my name in the paper and see it on the news, but I haven't heard a word," Knoblauch was quoted as saying. "I'm supposed to be somewhere, but I haven't been told where to be."

Throughout the next week, even as columnists and sports radio hosts teased the committee as a bunch of Keystone Cops, Knoblauch remained silent and inaccessible. Finally, on January 22, the committee flexed its muscles and issued a subpoena for him to appear for a deposition and the hearing on February 13. They were not fooling around. If Phil Schiliro couldn't get a response from Knoblauch, maybe a U.S. marshal could. Suddenly, it looked to many observers that this would be the tenor of the committee's inquest. Congress, it appeared, would get the same kind of stonewalling from lawyered-up ballplayers that George Mitchell had gotten, and the public would find plenty of reason to complain about the waste of government dollars.

On the night that the subpoena was issued, Keith Olbermann, host of the MSNBC program *Countdown*, held forth on the Knoblauch situation. It was Olbermann's practice to compile a nightly list of the "Worst People in the World," and that night he included Knoblauch in it. This was a bit of an inside joke, because in June of 2000—when Knoblauch's famous throwing problem was at its very worst—one of his many errant throws to first base had sailed seven rows deep into the crowd and hit Olbermann's mother in the face, breaking a lens out of her glasses and sending her to the first-aid room at Yankee Stadium.

"Old friend of the family," Olbermann said wryly as he named Knoblauch the third-worst person in the world, and described Knoblauch's resistance to the congressional inquiry. Olbermann wrongly claimed that Mitchell had named Knoblauch as a steroid user (in fact, the Mitchell Report said Knoblauch had used human growth hormone seven to nine times).

"My theory is that Mr. Knoblauch got their invitation, wrote a letter back and then tried to throw it into a nearby mailbox and instead hit my mother," said Olbermann.

Not long after the Mitchell Report was released and it became well known that Earl Ward was representing Brian McNamee, Ward started getting letters from lawyers all over the country offering to help out with the financially unremunerative job of representing McNamee. One attorney had written to Ward from Chicago, signing off his letter with the words "this is a wonderful opportunity for you." Ward had to laugh at that. "Where's the fucking wonderful opportunity?" he wondered. He was breaking his back on the work, under siege from Hardin and his henchmen, getting all the help he could from Emery, and fielding calls from reporters in the middle of the night.

But Ward got a different feeling on the sidelines of his kid's soccer game on Sunday, January 27, when Mark Paoletta called, offering to help out as Washington-based counsel. Best of all, he'd expressed a willingness to do it pro bono. Paoletta was one of the most connected lawyers in Washington, a partner at Dickstein Shapiro LLP, specializing in the high-stakes practice of counseling those who had been summoned to Capitol Hill for congressional hearings. Up until 2007, Paoletta hadn't needed to search out clients; his clients were the American taxpayers. Paoletta had spent 10 years leading investigations for the House Committee on Energy and Commerce, one of the most powerful committees on the Hill. During that time he managed 200 congressional investigations, several of which became high profile hearings, including Enron, HealthSouth, and ImClone. As chief investigative counsel for the committee, he stage-managed some blockbuster hearings that led to serious legislative changes. More than most attorneys, he was used to seeing justice move quickly. Paoletta had four kids, and he loved spending time with them, happily running a parent's domestic errands so that his wife, Patricia, whom he'd met when they were both at Georgetown Law, could represent her own clients in the telecom industry. If it weren't for his BlackBerry, Paoletta didn't know what he would do.

And so it happened Paoletta was rushing around the capital doing some Christmas shopping with his kids when the Mitchell stuff began to blow up. He was keeping a keen eye on all the amusing back-and-forth between Roger Clemens, Brian McNamee, and their respective attorneys. When the hearings were announced, his ears perked up. Suddenly it looked like the whole traveling shit show of baseball's steroid scandal was coming to D.C., and Paoletta wanted a role in the cast. Paoletta first approached Clemens's team, thinking that Clemens had the most to lose and it would be an exciting opportunity to represent the greatest pitcher in the game's history, but when he didn't hear back from Hardin, he reached out to Ward and Emery.

The McNamee case was generating huge publicity, and it would only get bigger now that Congress was officially involved. That meant exposure for lawyers building their practices. That had been the furthest thing from Ward's mind six months earlier, when McNamee had first come his way with his problems. Who could have known then it would have headed for C-SPAN?

Emery and Paoletta had actually crossed paths before, when Emery represented a client wrapped up in the ImClone cancer drug affair. The Energy and Commerce Committee had tackled that scandal as well, and when all the dust had settled, ImClone investor Martha Stewart was behind bars for perjury. It was clear to Ward and Emery that Paoletta, who would later serve on the Republican "truth squad" that fended off criticism of vice presidential candidate Sarah Palin, was a true Washington insider. While he was still in his twenties, the guy had served in the White House as assistant counsel to President George H. W. Bush, and had apparently played an elbows-out game in the brutal fight to win confirmation for Clarence Thomas as U.S. Supreme Court justice. Ward and Emery agreed that they needed to bring Paoletta on board.

As the Clemens-McNamee clash moved to the battlefield of Washington, the legal lines were drawn: On one side were two card-carrying civil rights lawyers from New York and a GOP operative from Washington; on the other side some old Clinton hands defending a friend of Poppy Bush's.

It made for an interesting opening-day lineup.

Jay Reisinger and Tom Farrell signed on to become Andy Pettitte's lawyers on January 6, promising to see Pettitte through the escalating congressional probe. Pettitte and Hardin had split up back on the eve of the Mitchell Report's release when it became apparent that Pettitte's memory of McNamee and steroids wasn't the same as Clemens's. Following a statement after the report came out, Pettitte had gone silent amid the noisy crossfire between Clemens and McNamee. And that was just fine with Reisinger and Farrell.

Unlike Rusty Hardin or Richard Emery, Reisinger and Farrell didn't court reporters and they didn't talk in sound bites. They preferred to fly under the radar and take care of business as quietly as possible. When a lawyer started swapping gossip and tidbits of information with journalists, they believed, the lawyer lost control of the case. This philosophy had served them well in the previous congressional baseball-and-steroids probe; in 2005, Reisinger and Farrell had represented Sammy Sosa. Compared with Mark McGwire and Rafael Palmeiro, Sosa had emerged from that go-round virtually unscathed, thanks in large part to simply keeping quiet. At the hearing, the Dominican-born Sosa had suddenly shown himself to have a problem understanding English. Many sportswriters who had known him to be quite loquacious were surprised, but at the end of the day, Sosa didn't look half as bad as McGwire.

Reisinger broke with his disregard for media attention on the afternoon of January 25, when he decided he had to return a phone call from the New York *Daily News*. The newspaper had alerted him to some very serious allegations about his client—allegations that came out of Pasadena, Texas, and revolved around a gym there called 1-on-1 Elite Personal Fitness.

Late that Friday afternoon, Reisinger listened patiently as the reporters laid out the story that Sammy Woodrow had told them: Tom Pettitte had procured human growth hormone at 1-on-1 Elite. The gym was owned by Kelly Blair, who was related to the Pettitte family by marriage. A lot of drugs moved through the gym, and Blair had been seen loading that milk carton full of steroids intended for the Astros.

"This is something I will address with my client," Reisinger replied, sounding more than a little surprised at the account. The reporters agreed to delay publication of the story to give Pettitte a chance to respond.

Reisinger and Farrell were experienced litigators. Reisinger was certified as an agent by the Players Association and he focused on salary arbitration, contract analysis, and civil litigation. Farrell had been a federal prosecutor in Pittsburgh and a federal public defender in New York's Eastern District, and he specialized in criminal defense and white-collar crime.

Just a few days earlier, Reisinger and Farrell had joined Dreier LLP, the boutique Park Avenue law firm that negotiated athletes' contracts and managed their careers. The firm's managing partner and founder, Marc S. Dreier, was an ambitious and driven lawyer who represented stars like Jay Leno and Jon Bon Jovi and hosted a summer charity bash with New York Giants star Michael Strahan that had become a hot ticket on the jock party circuit.

The reporters who had heard Sammy Woodrow's story had gotten it confirmed in other ways. McNamee had recently told federal investigators about a conversation he had with Pettitte's father: Tom Pettitte had told McNamee that he had obtained human growth hormone in Kelly Blair's parking lot and in Mexico. McNamee told Tom Pettitte that he could get his son in trouble, and warned him to be careful.

After the weekend of January 26–27, Reisinger wasn't in a mood to confirm anything about Sammy Woodrow's account. "There is no truth to the allegations," Reisinger said on Monday the 28th. "I'm telling you, if the story runs, it is going to be a big issue. I suggest you double-check your sources."

Pettitte's deposition was scheduled for the following Wednesday, January 30. Reisinger was preparing his client to go under oath and discuss the Mitchell Report. The lawyers for the House Oversight Committee would surely ask Pettitte about his statement six weeks earlier, confessing to the HGH injections McNamee had outlined for Mitchell and the feds. There was a lot to prepare for, and Reisinger was in no mood to discuss it further. "I am warning you," Reisinger added, "if you run the story as outlined to me you do so at your own peril."

Beyond that, Reisinger had no comment. He was bound by attorney-client priviliege, he said, and the House committee had asked for him to be quiet. Reisinger was parsing words: The reporters' questions had been broad enough for a denial like the one he issued, but that didn't mean there wasn't any truth to the allegations. The very next day came an announcement that seemed to say plenty about the legitimacy of the Pasadena story and Tom Pettitte's involvement with HGH. On Tuesday, January 29, a day before Pettitte was scheduled to give his deposition, the chairman and ranking member of the House Committee on Oversight and Government Reform announced that it had pushed Pettitte's deposition back five days. There was no reason given for why Reisinger was getting a little more time to prepare Pettitte to go under oath.

"Mr. Pettitte is cooperating voluntarily with the committee and we look forward to his testimony on Monday," the statement said.

"When you're up on the Hill, at least when I was chief counsel, I could literally open up the newspaper, read about something, and say, 'Let's look at that,' " Paoletta said. "I would go to my chairman. I did it for 10 years. I went through three chairmen and four subcommittee chairmen. I was sort of an institutional rock there. New chairman comes in. How do we do oversight? They're looking to you. You didn't need a client, a paying client. You looked at it, the chairman wants to look at it, and boom, you're off."

Almost anything, it seemed, fell within the broad jurisdiction of the Energy and Commerce Committee. Often, Paoletta would simply turn to one of the junior lawyers on the committee's staff and tell them to write a letter to the principals of the story, summoning them to Capitol Hill for accountability.

But at the end of 2006, when the Democrats won majority status in the House of Representatives, that meant a shake-up with every committee. Paoletta left for private practice. And now he needed to find clients, so he reached out to Earl Ward and Richard Emery, the two lawyers he'd been reading about. It was curious that Paoletta, a Republican to his core, turned to these two liberal civil rights lawyers from New York City. In Clemens, he might have found more of an ideological peer.

But even though Mark Paoletta was a Republican to his bones, there wasn't much chance he would end up helping Clemens navigate his way through the upcoming congressional investigation. Not with Rusty Hardin in charge. The two lawyers had clashed, back in 2002, over the little matter of Enron, accountancy, and document shredding.

In those days Hardin was serving as the lead counsel for the sinking ship called Arthur Andersen, the giant auditing firm that had been signing off on Enron's fraudulent finances for years. In October of 2001, as the Securities and Exchange Commission began an investigation into Enron's wacky accounting, an Andersen partner named David Duncan ordered an expedited document-shredding campaign that didn't stop until Andersen received a Securities and Exchange Commission subpoena two weeks later.

It was one of those injustices that Mark Paoletta read about in the newspaper and, being exempt from the powerlessness other readers might feel, took the story to his committee chairman, Billy Tauzin, a charismatic Republican from Louisiana, who agreed that something was fishy at Andersen. By the end of January of 2002 he summoned four top Andersen executives to the Hill: CEO Joseph Berardino, partner Michael Odom, in-house lawyer Nancy Temple, and Duncan himself, who had been fired.

Paoletta was an enthusiastic believer in the "art of the congressional hearing." This was how the elected representatives of the American people delivered change, even when it wasn't in the form of laws. Hearings were a type of theater, and you needed a script. For Paoletta and the other behind-the-scenes players at the Energy and Commerce Committee, it was essential that the congressmen and congresswomen—who, after all, had other matters to worry about—knew what were the smart questions to ask when the cameras were rolling.

"You want to build that testimony," Paoletta said.

And so it came to pass that in the days leading up to the hearing, Paoletta interviewed Duncan for four hours, getting the inside word on how the Enron debacle had gone down at Andersen. The company already seemed to be positioning Duncan as a scapegoat. Paoletta found the guy to be pretty forthcoming.

The hearing itself was a public flogging. With Paoletta feeding the committee members the results of the investigation, Andersen's strategy of isolating Duncan as a rogue employee couldn't be effective. Duncan himself, appearing at the hearing under subpoena, invoked his Fifth Amendment rights and didn't talk. By then he had decided to become a cooperating witness for the government in a Justice Department probe.

Andersen was screwed. As hundreds of the firm's big-time clients fled for the doors, the feds built a strong case against the accounting giant in a federal court in Houston. On March 14, Andersen was indicted, with U.S. District Court Judge Melinda Harmon promising a swift trial.

Hardin applied for a postponement in the proceedings, telling the judge that the public's fury over the scandal had created a "hanging atmosphere" that would prevent a fair trial. He pointed out that potential jurors had been asked to fill out questionnaires, and a third of them thought Andersen was guilty. The judge was not sympathetic. Even as the company fought the charges, its value declined and its workers were laid off in droves.

Next, Hardin tried to get the notes that Paoletta had taken during his interview with Duncan. Clearly, Hardin wanted to try to draw out inconsistencies in Duncan's statements. The Energy and Commerce Committee refused to hand over Paoletta's notes, and Judge Harmon wouldn't compel them to do so. As the trial began, Hardin lowered expectations.

"When I told the judge we wanted a speedy trial, we wanted it so badly to save the company," Hardin told a reporter on the eve of the trial. "That's almost become irrelevant now. We're almost trying Arthur Andersen's legacy, not its future."

It was a losing battle for Hardin from the very beginning. In court he bickered with prosecutors and even Judge Harmon. As with the defamation suit he brought against McNamee years later, a large measure of Hardin's legal strategy was public relations. In fact, the company's overseers could have accepted a government deal or pleaded guilty, but they wanted to use the courthouse as a stage.

"We do not regret going through this trial," said Andersen partner C. E. Andrews at the end of the trial. "The indictment itself crippled our organization. The trial was a way to get our story out there, and we did a good job of that."

On June 15, 2002, Andersen was convicted of obstruction. The company more or less died on the spot, agreeing to cease appearing before the

SEC. A month after the jurors returned their verdict, a *USA Today* article appeared, recognizing that Tauzin's committee hearings had become a can't-miss spectacle.

"No one has turned humdrum legislative process into made-for-TV melodrama like Energy and Commerce Chairman W. J. 'Billy' Tauzin," the story went. "His strategy: Demand and then dribble out damaging documents, orchestrate hearings down to camera angles and put the panel's 57 members to work pummeling even silent witnesses."

There were detractors, of course. In the same article, Hardin was quoted blaming Tauzin (and, by implication, his investigative attack dog Paoletta) for using the powerful stage of a congressional hearing to convict his client in the court of public opinion.

"I think that committee's use of documents is outrageously unfair," Hardin said. "They have a bunch of documents, which they get by subpoena. And without investigating, they're giving press conferences from which no one will recover."

When the writer of the article went back to Tauzin with Hardin's comments, Tauzin dismissed Hardin with an offhand remark.

"If I lost the case, I'd be looking for an excuse, too," Tauzin said in the same article.

Paoletta thought it was such a killer line he had framed the story and put it on the wall in his office. The outcome of the Arthur Anderson case made it seem unlikely that Paoletta and Hardin would ever be legal partners. But prior to the January 27 call he made to Ward, Paoletta sent an e-mail to Hardin to see if the Texas attorney would be interested in Paoletta's Capitol Hill expertise.

"I figured he would want someone on his team who knew what they were doing in a congressional investigation," said Paoletta. "I reached out, but never heard from Hardin. Once I read that Hardin had selected Lanny Breuer from Covington, I paused only a few moments before deciding to approach McNamee."

For Hardin, there were striking parallels between his work for Andersen and what he was doing in the Clemens case. In both cases, Hardin found himself representing a rich and powerful client confronted by allegations of criminality made by an isolated individual who had been thrown overboard. Both Duncan and McNamee were protected, somewhat, by the government agents they squealed to. Trying to discredit such an individual could get ugly, but that was why Clemens hired Hardin: It was Hardin's duty as an advocate to get in the trenches and fight for his client.

Six years after the Enron and Arthur Andersen debacle, Hardin needed to assemble a team for another high-profile case. He soon added another veteran of the Clinton wars to join the Clemens team: a "disaster management" specialist named Patrick Dorton. Like Hardin, Dorton had gone down with the ship with Andersen. Dorton was the accounting giant's public relations man during the tumult of 2002. Before that, he had been a communications assistant to President Clinton.

After the Andersen fiasco, Dorton had become the designated spin-meister for AIPAC, the pro-Israel lobbying group where two senior executives had been indicted for espionage-related crimes. He had built his own public relations firm, Rational PR.

"Even in the most certain times, in the healthiest businesses and organizations, and in the most prepared offices, crisis can come out of nowhere," read the firm's Web site. "Rational PR is experienced in the art of 'disaster management.' We work by one rule: 'control your crisis before it controls you.' "

On January 30, Mark Paoletta stood in the shadow of 30 Rockefeller Center, the post-holiday crowd still thick. Tourists busily snapped digital photos of the famous ice rink and Midtown workers shuffled past the Washington attorney, who was chatting on his cell phone. It was 10:15 in the morning and Paoletta had just hung up from a call with his wife, Patricia. He was eagerly awaiting his meeting 20 floors above at 75 Rockefeller Plaza.

Paoletta was about to meet his new client, Brian McNamee, for the first time—the meeting with McNamee and Richard Emery was scheduled for 11 A.M.—and Paoletta had made sure that he was early for the appointment. Emery and Ward had asked Paoletta to join McNamee's own crisis management team, a trio of lawyers who were being paid nothing. Then his cell phone rang again, the digital screen showing a 212 number.

"Hey, Mark, it's Richard. Can you come up a little early?" Emery asked.

"Sure," said Paoletta.

"I want to show you something," Emery said.

Paoletta hung up, entered the building, checked in with security at the front desk, and took the elevator to the 20th floor. They went into Emery's office and closed the door. Emery pulled out an envelope.

"Now that you're retained," Emery started, but Paoletta didn't really hear the rest of the sentence. He was mesmerized by the photograph Emery was holding, the one of a crushed Miller Lite beer can, bloody gauze, and a needle.

"This is new," Paoletta remembers thinking as he stared at the images. This was McNamee's evidence against Clemens and Emery could hardly contain himself.

"He realized the significance of the evidence," Paoletta recalled. "I knew this could be a game changer, perhaps not legally given the chain of custody issues, but in the court of opinion. I also did not doubt that Brian had really kept this material. It was not something you would fabricate. Now that would be crazy. These investigations move really fast, and sometimes you feel like you are on some roller coaster and you just pray you don't fall out."

A few minutes later, McNamee joined the meeting, and Paoletta got a sense of what it would be like to deal with the man Roger Clemens was painting as a troubled liar. His first impression of the trainer was that he was direct, even a little blunt. "The classic sort of, what you would think of as a guy who used to work on the police force," said Paoletta. "He has a way of looking you right in the eye when he's talking to you." He didn't seem like a troubled liar at all.

Paoletta would make the trip up to New York several more times in the following weeks, "trying to get up to speed on everything," as McNamee's deposition and the hearing loomed. He would be struck by a request McNamee made of him: Even with all the cramming and preparation ahead, McNamee wanted to set aside some time to talk with his new lawyer one-on-one, to find out what this white-collar attorney was doing linking up with a blue-collar fellow like him.

"When I flew in for one trip, Brian was like, 'Why don't you come by?' I thought, 'You know what? I think that's important,' " said Paoletta. "I thought it would be good to go out and meet Brian on his own turf."

After a taxi ride from hell—"I don't know what the guy was doing," said Paoletta, who had to ask someone in an auto repair shop for directions— the D.C. lawyer arrived at McNamee's Breezy Point home. McNamee's wife and father were there. McNamee soon discovered that the white-collar lawyer had some blue-collar roots. Paoletta may have worked for one of the most prestigious firms in the capital, but he never forgot his Bridgeport, Connecticut, background, where his father had owned a pharmacy. The elder McNamee—"a salt-of-the-earth guy," Paoletta recalled—had a connection to Paoletta's birthplace too. The three men got along just fine.

Paoletta and McNamee bonded over baseball as well, since Paoletta had grown up an ardent Yankee fan, storming the field at the Stadium as a teenager after Chris Chambliss's game-winning homer clinched the 1976 American League pennant for the Bombers. The teenage Paoletta had even stuffed a piece of turf in his down jacket as a memento.

As Paoletta talked, outlining the parameters of the deposition and the hearing, he could sense the tight family bond, and most of all, Brian's overriding sense of loyalty. "I believed him," Paoletta recalled. "I thought he was telling the truth. And every time you went over a fact or detail with him, he always said the exact same thing. With Brian, he went back over things, and it rang true. I'm very visual in my memory and I related to Brian. I'm replaying something in my mind, that's how Brian seemed to be. He was unshakable."

On January 30, just six days before he was due in Washington for his deposition, Roger Clemens climbed up out of the dugout at Minute Maid Park, the home of the Houston Astros, and jogged onto the field as he had done so many times before. There was an unusually large crowd of observers at the stadium that Wednesday, the third day of the annual event known as the Nolan Ryan and Jeff Bagwell Elite Pitchers and Hitters Camp. The four-day event was designed to showcase the rising stars of the Astros minor league system, bringing them together in Houston to take tips from some of the franchise's greatest alumni. Among the hopefuls on the field was 21-year-old Koby Clemens, who was working with the catchers. On the day the camp opened, Koby had predicted that his embattled father would be a no-show because of all the controversy.

"We're a real close family, and we're just staying away from the TV and all the nasty things that people have to say," Koby told reporters that Monday.

But on Wednesday here came the elder Clemens, defying anyone to alter his course through life. He wore a gray hoodie, a black baseball cap, and black track suit pants. He threw batting practice, coached some young players on throwing mechanics. Astros owner Drayton McLane had invited Clemens to the camp, and spoke to reporters in sentimental tones about seeing the veteran pitcher interacting with the club's future stars. "Baseball is made out of memories," McLane said. "These are memories. Everybody's said nobody's asked him anything. We need to move on."

The pastoral interlude didn't last long. As soon as the session ended, Clemens walked up to a cluster of journalists who had come to see him, and immediately began fouling off questions about the congressional probe. "I won't even discuss that," Clemens said. "We're handling that the right way. I've already done everything I've wanted to say, media-wise, on that . . . I'm getting ready to go through the process . . . I get a chance to say my piece again. That's really all I can say. Everybody is doing well. We're grinding away and doing what we have to do."

Since the unfortunate January 7 press conference across town, Clemens had been mostly hiding out, working with his attorneys to prepare for the firestorm to come. His only public appearance since then had been on January 12 at a convention center in Waco, where he fulfilled a long-standing obligation to speak before some 2,000 members of the Texas High School Baseball Coaches Association. For 90 minutes, he gave a speech and answered questions about baseball. Reporters were locked out, and Clemens came and went through a private entrance without acknowledging them.

But now he was at the Astros camp, trying to restake a claim to the professional baseball life that he had been living for 24 years. McLane had signed Clemens to a 10-year personal services contract with the Astros in 2004, but it wasn't designed to formally kick in until the pitcher's retirement became official—and of course, he'd kept unretiring. The previous November, just before the release of the Mitchell Report, Randy Hendricks had informed McLane that Clemens was ready to go to work for the team as a consultant. McLane danced around whether that would actually happen.

Jeff Bagwell was one of the other retired Astros reveling in his elder statesman status that day in Houston. As if to cement his old-school persona, Bagwell expressed exactly the kind of avoidance psychology that had gotten baseball to this juncture. "I'm tired of hearing about it, and I'm sure you're tired of asking questions about it," Bagwell told the *Houston Chronicle*. "I think the American public is tired of hearing about it. . . . We've got a lot of things to worry about right now, and we just need to move on."

The scene that day at Minute Maid Park was both similar to and vastly different from the one that Clemens had encountered almost 24 years earlier, during spring training in 1984 when he was a 21-year-old prospect. Clemens had arrived at the Red Sox spring training facility that year in Winter Haven carrying the weight of big expectations. The retired Boston players who showed up to observe his stuff were no less legends than Ted Williams and Carl Yastrzemski.

"Everyone has been taken with No. 21," wrote Tom Callahan in *Time* magazine, quoting Detroit Tigers manager Sparky Anderson, who called the young right-hander from the University of Texas "the best, most poised young pitcher I've seen since Tom Seaver."

Even one of baseball's greatest pitchers, Sandy Koufax, had been on hand to marvel at the young hotshot the Red Sox had plucked from the Texas backwater. Then 48, and nearly two decades past his retirement, Koufax was still affiliated with the Dodgers, and watched Clemens pitch in an exhibition game against his old team. Koufax talked that day about the challenges he had faced as a young pitcher in the major leagues. Koufax was enjoying the deference that comes with a Hall of Fame career. It was exactly the kind of moment Clemens was searching for on January 30 at Minute Maid Park, as he hurled batting practice and reveled in the optimism of the young players, including his own 21-year-old son.

In the course of a two-and-a-half-hour Capitol Hill interview with congressional investigators on January 31, Jimmy Murray of Hendricks Sports Management managed to say the words "I don't remember" 117 times. He also said "I don't recall" 15 times, and "I can't remember" 10 times.

The House Committee on Oversight and Government Reform had by now learned about McNamee's fateful December 5 phone calls to warn the Clemens camp about the Mitchell Report. That first call had gone to Murray, and now Murray was the first person in the whole affair to be summoned to Capitol Hill for a debriefing. Rusty Hardin had the tape of that phone call transcribed by a Texas notary; Congress had collected that transcript and now had some questions. But the committee quickly learned that Murray wouldn't be very helpful: He had come down with a bad case of the syndrome known as CRS—Can't Remember Shit.

In addition to the 142 things Murray didn't and couldn't remember, there were a lot of things he didn't know. "I don't know" was a phrase he repeated 75 times in the interview, where he faced questions from seven investigators for the committee, four of them Democrats and three Republicans. Among the things Murray didn't remember was if he'd ever talked with Clemens or Pettitte about any concern they might have had about being mixed up with steroid accusations in the 2006 Los Angeles Times story about the Grimsley affidavit. He didn't remember if he read that story, or if it had caused a crisis atmosphere at the company, where those two pitchers were by far the biggest clients. Another thing Murray didn't remember was whether he himself felt much concern in the spring of 2007 when the news first broke about Kirk Radomski getting busted, pleading guilty, and cooperating with the feds. "They show the picture of him, and he had his 80s hairdo, and you know I was kind of like, 'Oh, the Mets can't be happy,' " Murray said.

Murray had already forgotten some things about the phone call McNamee made to him two months earlier in Nashville. Murray knew he had taken notes during that call, but he didn't know where they were. Likewise, there were lots of things he neither knew nor remembered about the December 11 phone call he made to McNamee, the one where he brokered McNamee's meeting with Belk and Yarbrough. He didn't know that Belk and Yarbrough had taped an interview with McNamee.

Murray's memory seemed to suddenly improve, however, whenever the subject reflected poorly on McNamee. For instance, Murray remembered having suspicions that McNamee was a media leak, and he remembered the very specific details of different newspaper reports that he thought showed signs of McNamee's participation. Murray remembered how McNamee had wanted Springsteen tickets. He remembered ugly disputes with McNamee over endorsement issues with InVite and Under Armour. He remembered learning that McNamee was somewhat disingenuously attaching the title Ph.D. to his name.

But for most of the interview, Murray's memory deserted him, and the main area where Murray's CRS syndrome got the better of him was when he was asked about his meeting with Brian McNamee at the Starbucks on 90th Street and First Avenue. Murray said he had recently read about that meeting in the New York *Daily News* (which had started reporting on that meeting two weeks earlier), but his memory was very hazy. The lawyers on the committee's staff spent a considerable amount of the interview trying to help him recollect.

At Starbucks, Murray recalled, McNamee had said something about drug test results. But Murray didn't remember anything being said about Roger Clemens or Kirk Radomski. He didn't remember feeling alarmed by the conversation, or if he took notes on a yellow pad, or where he put the notes that he didn't remember taking. "My recollection of the meeting is he was asking for a job," Murray said. "And I remember him talking about making a percentage of players that he would train. He also brought up something about having knowledge of drug test results." Murray explained that during the meeting McNamee had told him he wanted to be part of the agency the Hendricks brothers were operating. When a player signed an endorsement contract, McNamee thought he should get a percentage of the money, Murray said. Murray remembered relaying the subject of the meeting to his boss, Randy Hendricks, and he remembered Hendricks saying "He's crazy."

Michael Gordon, the senior investigative counsel for the Democratic staff of the committee, asked why McNamee would have raised the question of failed drug tests with Murray.

"I have no idea," Murray said.

"Did he ask you to do anything?" Gordon asked.

"Not that I remember."

The investigators' questions conveyed how unlikely they thought it was that Murray wouldn't remember more from a conversation about failed drug tests—that it wouldn't have set off alarm bells, or caused him to be concerned, or made him curious to learn more. Waxman's chief of staff, Phil Schiliro, asked if a failed drug test wouldn't have an impact on marketing, Murray's specialty at the firm.

"You had someone come to you and say something that you recall about a drug test," Schiliro said. "You've told us you can't remember specifically what. But it had to do with a failed drug test. And according to your testimony, it doesn't sound as if you did any follow up except mention it to Mr. Hendricks?"

"Right," Murray said.

"You didn't pursue any other questions, you didn't do any other due diligence to try to find out more about the matter?"

"No," Murray said. "Not that I remember."

The committee's lawyers seemed skeptical about this. After all, Murray didn't trust McNamee; he made that clear. Under questioning, Murray said he recorded the December 5 phone call because of the trust issue. He thought McNamee was "shaky." Schiliro asked why, if Hendricks thought McNamee was "crazy" and Murray thought McNamee was "shaky," Murray hadn't expressed those concerns to Clemens.

"Because there's shaky people around a lot of our clients," Murray said. "We call them gravy trainers, people that want to be associated with an athlete. You never know what they want. You have to deal with family members or friends. There's a lot of shaky people. Especially in New York. I see it all the time with the Yankees' players."

"Who is the highest-profile client for your firm?" Schiliro asked.

"Roger Clemens," Murray said.

"And were there other shaky people around him?"

"Oh, yeah," Murray said.

"Do you want to tell us about that?" Schiliro asked.

"The specific people?" Murray said.

Murray hemmed and hawed for a while, and when Schiliro sounded unimpressed, Murray finally rushed in with an explanation.

"I'm still not—I'm—I do my job, like I do the marketing deals, I do some sort of client interaction with a lot of the Minor League players," Murray said. "But that's not something that I would—I wouldn't tell Roger Clemens, this guy's shaky, you shouldn't be hanging around with him. Because I'm 30 years old and Roger is what, 45 or so. I just wouldn't do that. I wouldn't—our clients hang out with—with whoever they feel they hang out with. It's not part of my job. I don't feel like that's part of my responsibility."

As the interview dragged on, the committee's lawyers appeared to notice the pattern of improved memory when the subject reflected poorly on McNamee. Two hours into the interview, when Republican staff lawyer Steve Castor seemed to get tired of prodding, he said: "What other sort of pain-in-the-neck vignettes can you share with us." Suddenly it all came back to Murray. He remembered how McNamee had persuaded Clemens to attend a banquet at St. John's University in New York— McNamee's alma mater, where he was trying to get a job. McNamee "played on Roger's heartstrings" to get Clemens to fly to New York for the event. "Roger could do a thousand banquets if he wanted to," Murray said.

Murray didn't remember having a conversation with Clemens about B_{12}, or whether he had ever met Jose Canseco or not. He remembered receiving Major League Baseball's drug-testing policy in his e-mail inbox, but he didn't remember talking about it within Hendricks Sports Management. And it wasn't just long-ago events that Murray had trouble calling up. When committee staff members discovered through their questions that Murray had met with Rusty Hardin just a few weeks before his trip to Washington, they were curious. It turned out Murray had spent nearly an hour with Hardin and several of the other lawyers at Hardin's offices in Houston. During that time Murray handed over to Hardin a stack of e-mails dealing with McNamee that Murray had found by searching for all messages with McNamee's name in them. But, the committee learned, Murray didn't remember reading through any of those e-mails. He only remembered printing them and handing them over, but not what they contained.

Did Murray talk about the Starbucks meeting with Hardin during that meeting? Murray didn't remember. Maybe, but he didn't remember the specifics of what was discussed. When the committee asked about different e-mail correspondences Murray had with McNamee, Murray was able to remember a mention of the St. Petersburg incident at the pool, but couldn't really remember whether steroids had been mentioned.

"These past few weeks have definitely been a whirlwind for me," Murray said. "So if it didn't have to do with me personally, I wasn't really paying attention to what they were discussing. With regards to me personally, I believe we talked a little bit about the Starbucks meeting. I don't remember specifics about the conversation."

The chime of the elevator announced Chuck Knoblauch's arrival—extremely punctual at 10 A.M. sharp—for his February 1 congressional interview in the Rayburn House Office Building. A passel of cameramen, reporters, and photographers rushed forward to greet them. For the sports reporters, it was baseball history; here, at long last, was the first professional ballplayer to come to Capitol Hill to explain his inclusion in the Mitchell Report. Others had been cited for HGH use, but Knoblauch had links to McNamee, and he was collateral damage in the Clemens-McNamee war.

At 39, Knobby had grown pudgy. Eternally boyish in his playing days, age seemed to have finally caught up with him in the five and a half years since his retirement. Almost nobody in baseball had heard from the man since his 11-year career in the big leagues had ended with a whimper in September of 2002, after he had proven himself unable to conquer a much derided throwing problem—he suddenly was unable to make the simple throw a second baseman needed to make over to first base (one tabloid headline ridiculing him for his string of errors: "Blauch-head!").

But it wasn't his changed appearance that stood out that day. Rather, what everyone noticed was the surprise that the witness had brought with him: his three-year-old son, Jake. The boy had shaggy blond hair and little sneakers, and Knoblauch carried him right into the media maelstrom rather than handing him off to an attractive young woman. It wasn't Lisa, the player's wife. Was she the new Mrs. Knoblauch? the reporters wondered. A nanny? She had arrived on the elevator and followed the scrum at a safe distance.

In addition to the media, a crowd of random onlookers had clustered around the door to the committee's offices that morning—secretaries and young congressional staffers from around the building. Lobbyists had lingered to see what all the fuss was about, while others came specifically to see this ballplayer, a four-time All-Star and the 1991 American League

Rookie of the Year. What they got was a man who might easily have been confused with an accountant or a high school principal. Knoblauch was dressed in a beige sweater and charcoal slacks, hair neatly combed; he smiled placidly without saying a word. Two Texas attorneys—Shaun Clarke and Diana Marshall—followed closely behind, eyeing the cameras suspiciously.

Jake clung to his father's neck and looked around in bewilderment at the pack of camera lenses that instantly surrounded him. Questions burst out from every direction: "What will you tell them about Roger? . . . Is it true what Mitchell said in the report? . . . What's the boy's name?"

Photos of the father and son would be hitting newspaper Web sites in a matter of minutes. He was only three, but Jake Knoblauch's Google fate was already sealed; for decades, in all likelihood, anyone typing his name into their search engine would get photos of him in his father's arms on Capitol Hill. It also might take decades before Jake would piece together what it all meant. He might remember playing with toys on the floor of the Oversight Committee's offices. But how old would he be when he learned that during that time, his father was in the next room, facing seven investigators from the House Committee on Oversight and Government Reform? How old would Jake be when he learned that those lawyers asked his dad a series of probing questions about his illicit use of human growth hormone seven years earlier?

As the group reached the warrenlike offices of the Oversight Committee, a young staffer held the door open. Here there were a few implacable Capitol policemen standing guard, making sure the media and onlookers went no further. Up until that moment, Knoblauch had made no comment.

The interview began at 10:09 A.M.

First there were formalities. The investigators, most of them lawyers, introduced themselves and their party affiliations; their master of ceremonies, Phil Schiliro, explained how the questioning would proceed: Democrats first, then Republicans, with each side getting an hour.

Things then got off to a slow start. Knoblauch was asked to assess his entry in the Mitchell Report, which came in at a mere 213 words. After quibbling with a few things in the one-page entry—he never played infield for Kansas City, for instance—Knoblauch admitted right away that the report, as it pertained to him, was "generally accurate."

"The next sentence, 'beginning during spring training and continuing through the early portion of the season, McNamee injected Knoblauch at least seven to nine times with human growth hormone,' " Schiliro read. "That's absolutely accurate?"

"That's accurate," Knoblauch said. "At least seven to nine times, yes."

So much for stonewalling. The lawyers could now get down to real business. Not only did Knoblauch want to be helpful and open, he even praised the lawyers for the work the government was doing.

"It is important to me because I love baseball," Knoblauch said. "You know, I want it to be fair. I want the players to be healthy. You know, if my son plays one day, I certainly don't want him to have to, you know, be involved in this."

With the factual matters out of the way, Knoblauch's interview could be short. Knoblauch said he never discussed HGH or steroid use with Roger Clemens or Andy Pettitte. The only other player he even spoke to about it was Jason Grimsley, who helped him get some HGH in 2002. It came from Kirk Radomski, Knoblauch now realized, but he never knew Radomski at all. "If he was here I wouldn't be able to point him out," Knoblauch said.

Did Knoblauch ever get a B_{12} shot with the Yankees? It was possible, he said, especially in New York, where the pressure was greatest. But he didn't know.

"With the game of baseball, you get sick because you get run-down, because you are playing three nights in a row," Knoblauch said. "With the Yankees, because you play prime-time games. So instead of a normal—I shouldn't say a normal team—a smaller-market team playing a day game on a getaway day to go to the next city, the Yankees always played at night. So you are finding yourself getting up or getting to the next town at 4:00, 5:00 in the morning. So people get—guys get sick."

Waxman's chief of staff since the early Reagan years, Phil Schiliro, had used subpoenas and interviews to explore far weightier issues than baseball's steroids problem. High-ranked government officials and powerful corporate players had gone to much greater lengths than Knoblauch had to avoid or delay Schiliro's questioning. Now that Schiliro had finally gotten Knoblauch in the hot seat, he was going to dig into the murk. As the House committee with the most unrestricted subpoena power, Oversight had tried to penetrate some of the Bush administration's shadiest secrets, like the Valerie Plame leak and the politically motivated firing of U.S. attorneys. Baseball players were not a big challenge.

"How did you meet Mr. McNamee?" Schiliro asked.

"I first met McNamee in spring training of 2000," Knoblauch said. "I believe it was 2000. Clemens, I think—I am not exact, because I don't remember everything about my career—but I think he was traded to the Yankees in '99, and I think—"

There Schiliro cut him off. This investigation would triangulate on the truth. The transcript would merely be a piece of a big legal puzzle, and Schiliro knew Knoblauch's guessing would only undermine the document's legal value. What Knoblauch *thought* was hollow; the committee was only interested, Schiliro now told Knoblauch, in what Knoblauch *knew* about performance-enhancing drug use in baseball.

"A good way to say it is just to the best of your recollection," said Schiliro. "That will always cover you."

About twenty minutes into the conversation, Knoblauch found himself talking about the same thing he'd discussed in so many interviews that came before: his throwing problem. He was "the second baseman who had forgotten how to throw to first," as Evans said, and he could offer the committee's lawyers no better explanation for his problem than he had been able to offer the reporters that had clustered around his locker as the strange case of the yips helped wind down his career. But the problem was inextricably linked to his decision to use human growth hormone, and that was the story he would tell that day in Washington.

"Can I give you a little bit of a personal aside?" Knoblauch asked. Schiliro said sure, and Knoblauch laid out the tale.

"I had a throwing problem," he began.

The affliction, Knoblauch said, had set upon him mysteriously in 1999, when he had 26 errors at second base for the Yankees. It intensified in 2000, as fans took notice and started giving him a standing ovation anytime he made a routine throw without dragging first baseman Tino Martinez off the bag.

"I still do not know to this day if it was physical or—I mean, my arm physically I think was okay," Knoblauch said. "And mentally—I really—it's a mystery to me to this day. I don't think about it that much anymore because I'm not playing baseball, and it's great. But I really have no answer for that. I still don't. I don't think anybody does. It's unfortunate."

New York fans were brutal to Knoblauch in 2000. They taunted him from the stands. Every night, it seemed, the highlight reel on television would show another Knoblauch goof, with Martinez or the pitcher scrambling after the errant ball as a runner advanced past Knoblauch. Soon the camera would find his face, wound into a look of tight regret. No one could tolerate a bad fielder for long; a pitcher's job was hard enough without having to worry about his infield.

Knoblauch committed 15 errors at second base in 2000 before Torre slotted him in as a designated hitter. The Yankees still won the World Series, and Knoblauch was determined to fix his problem in the offseason.

He had, after all, won a Golden Glove award, signifying the league's best-fielding second baseman, with Minnesota in 1997. He set out to conquer the yips.

"I went to spring training early in 2001," Knoblauch explained. "I went a month early, went probably around January—in the middle of January. And I worked Monday through Friday, worked my tail off to correct this problem."

In Tampa, Knoblauch worked like a demon (the Yankees, at that point, had the backup option of the promising infielder Alfonso Soriano). But Knoblauch, whose father had been a coach and had schooled his son in the fundamentals of the game, couldn't fix his throws.

"I got to my wits' end with that," he told the lawyers. "I wanted to try to work it out, and I went early, and I couldn't do it. Monday through Friday, three, four hours a day, a month before spring training, and I couldn't do it."

Soon pitchers and catchers reported to Tampa in mid-February. Then came the other position players a few weeks later, including Soriano, who was hot at the plate and respectable in the field. Soon enough, spring training was under way, and Knoblauch was exhausted.

It was then, Knoblauch said, that he talked to Brian McNamee, the team's assistant strength coach. McNamee was a vitamin and supplement guru. He was a fitness fanatic too. Knoblauch recalled seeing McNamee push Clemens and Pettitte so hard that they would vomit on the field.

Knoblauch described how McNamee came up to him and described how human growth hormone—at that point still years away from being banned by baseball—could replenish a person's youthful vigor.

"He approached me and talked about human growth hormone and said it was a natural substance occurring in your body, and that this could be of some help to you, could make you feel better," Knoblauch said. "I mean, he described to me that you lose growth hormone in your body as you get older."

McNamee wasn't lying. By 2001, HGH had become a huge part of the booming anti-aging industry, and everyone from housewives to Hollywood actors were using it, often with a prescription from a doctor who specialized in hormone replacement. And for professional athletes, perhaps scared away by the stigma of the steroid scandals involving Olympic sprinter Ben Johnson and the NFL's Oakland Raiders, there was one especially big incentive: HGH was a protein, not a steroid.

"I was trying to hold on to my career, you know, I made the unfortunate decision to try it," Knoblauch said. "I felt myself weak, vulnerable, you know, grabbing for—trying to get something—you know, just weak and vulnerable. And McNamee happened to approach me in spring training. And that's the first time I ever heard the three letters HGH or human growth hormone or anything."

Knoblauch hadn't heard of HGH, but Knoblauch had heard about three other letters—GHB. He was believed to have taken the powerful drug the night in 2001 when McNamee was investigated for sexual assault after the incident in the swimming pool in St. Petersburg. McNamee was never charged in the incident but it had become clear through police reports and interviews that Knoblauch figured prominently in the investigation of the possible sexual assault that McNamee was suspected of. It had been Knoblauch's room they were partying in and there was some suspicion that it had been Knoblauch who had mixed the GHB-laced drink for her. HGH wasn't the only drug Knoblauch was experimenting with and the questioners wanted to know more.

One of the lawyers present was Brian Cohen, the senior investigative counsel for the committee. He still had questions about B_{12}. It was clear that he wanted to explore (or perhaps rule out) the possibility that McNamee had in fact been giving B_{12} shots to all these players and calling it HGH. Clemens had emphatically told *60 Minutes* that McNamee had given him only B_{12} and lidocaine. From Miguel Tejada, the committee had learned that B_{12} vitamin shots seemed to be particularly popular among Latino players. Finally, from Jose Canseco's book *Juiced*, the world had learned that B_{12} often stood as a clubhouse code word for steroids. But B_{12} never looked like HGH. In a vial or syringe, it was often bright red.

"The preparation," Cohen asked. "Let's start from the beginning. What it looked like, how it was prepared."

"In spring training, I would go to his apartment, to McNamee's apartment," Knoblauch said. "And I had never seen this stuff before in my life." Knoblauch described the box that the HGH would come in, with vials of powder and vials of sterile water that McNamee would mix.

"What color is the powdery substance?" Cohen asked. "Do you know?"

"To the best of my knowledge, like just a white, powdery substance," Knoblauch said. "And then the clear water. You mix the two, shook it up, and then—and then made the injection."

Cohen wanted to know what it looked like after it was mixed up, and Knoblauch thought it was a "little cloudy." Without leading him to it, Cohen wanted to know if Knoblauch would describe the bright red B_{12}, rather than HGH. Was what he was taking brightly colored or anything?

"No, no, no," Knoblauch answered. "Just cloudy. And then he would inject me in my stomach area . . . It wasn't a fun thing."

Nor was it useful. For Knoblauch, it turned out that HGH didn't help him throw to first. Just before the 2001 regular season began, Yankee manager Joe Torre bumped Knoblauch out of the second base slot and into left field. Less useful to the Yankees there—and certainly less popular with fans—he was sent to Kansas City for the 2002 season. At the Royals' spring training facility, Knoblauch said, he procured more HGH from Jason Grimsley. Without McNamee around to help him, he did the injections himself.

"I injected myself, which is—I cringe about it to this day," Knoblauch said. "It was not a fun thing, and I don't know what I was doing. I was waiting for something to work, you know, I still had the problem."

It was in the spring training of 2002 that Knoblauch's father, who had been battling Alzheimer's for several years, died, and the grief, Knoblauch said, ruined what was left of his career.

"To be honest, without any disrespect to the Kansas City Royals, I probably should have just retired because I pretty much gave up, you know," Knoblauch said. "That was the last blow for me. I was—I was in bad shape. So—but I unfortunately made the mistake of still trying to do this stuff, and having not much knowledge about it. So that's the mistake that I made."

Beat reporters had never gotten such a personal description of the throwing problem, but the committee now certainly had. In part, he said, it was his own fatherhood that had changed his perspective on his HGH use.

"Hopefully, as I sit today, a father, hopefully I am not affected," Knoblauch said, inadvertently addressing one of the most salient questions in the argument against the use of performance-enhancing drugs: Does the cost of doing business in sports mean using substances whose side effects are largely unknown? "I just don't think there is enough long-term information out about it. And then at the end of the day, it didn't do anything. You know. And that's the point that people need to know, this stuff is not doing anything for anybody. So that's why I appreciate what you guys are doing again."

Knoblauch said that he hoped the committee's investigation would do for steroids what the Pete Rose gambling fiasco had done to minimize gambling in baseball. Rose had been banished from the sport—including the Hall of Fame—and players had been forced to attend seminars where reformed mobsters would tell them horror stories about the life of crime that awaited those who gave in to temptation. Now, Knoblauch said, it might be the same with steroids.

"You know, this generation of players, this is what will be drilled in their head," Knoblauch said. "And the gambling thing is gone, you know, from baseball. So I just wanted to add that."

Only those as ignorant of the doping epidemic as baseball people were could deceive themselves into thinking that the Mitchell Report, the congressional investigation, and increased testing were going to turn back something as rampant and pervasive as the entrenched doping culture in sports—both amateur and professional. For decades, Olympic sports had been tightening the testing procedures and strengthening the competition bans, and the doping problem showed no signs of abating for those sports. Whenever there was incentive to win, there was chemical cheating—and baseball, with its ballooning salaries, gave athletes vastly bigger incentives to win than, say, track and field, a sport that was struggling to maintain a modicum of credibility after serial doping scandals had made every record suspect. The Tour de France had staggered through three years of enormous doping busts, and only then were the people closest to it—the die-hard fans, the sport administrators—facing up to the depth of the problem. Time and again, in cycling and track, athletes had risked massive public humiliation to shave a few hundredths of a second off their times.

The unacknowledged fact in Congress on February 1, 2008—visible in the lawyers' easy ignorance and incuriosity about Knoblauch's well-documented history with GHB—was that George Mitchell was never more right than when he cautioned that his report only scratched the surface. The former senator's claims only reflected what he and his staff had been able to document, and nail down with evidence and testimony that satisfied their lawyerly minds.

No matter how candid Knoblauch felt he was or appeared to be, he was holding back a little bit—just as Pettitte had held back, in his "confession," on admitting to the HGH use following the release of the Mitchell Report. GHB was a drug on the Olympics' banned substance list. It was also a dieter's miracle drug, and it's unclear if the writer of Knoblauch's 1998 profile in *Sports Illustrated* knew that. "Knoblauch is not just a disciplined hitter, he's also a disciplined eater," wrote Franz Lidz.

To stay trim during the 1994 baseball strike, he hired a personal trainer who prescribed weight training and a diet that limited his daily fat intake to 21 grams. "I could drink anything I wanted," he says, "as long as it was water." When he showed up at spring training the following year, the formerly chunky Knoblauch was 20 pounds lighter and so brawny that his muscles seemed ready to tear through his uniform. "Even Chuck's facial features looked different," recalls first base coach Ron Gardenhire. "He used to be this chubby-cheeked kid, and now his face was chiseled rock."

It would have been hard for any writer to know in 1998 that human growth hormone had the ability to alter the structure of one's skull, and that users sometimes required braces to pull their teeth back into position. GHB was trendy in that 1990s club scene too, and not just for date-rapists. GHB had a stimulant effect. It went straight to the central nervous system, which is why overuse of it could lead to convulsions or twitching. It might even cause the yips. It could certainly cause a good-fielding second baseman to suddenly be unable to make a simple throw to first base.

Would it have been fair for the lawyers on the committee's staff to question Knoblauch about his role in the 2001 date-rape case in Florida? Perhaps not. The committee was focused on one thing: who was telling the truth about the Mitchell Report. But Knoblauch himself knew the lawyers were now looking with suspicion upon the almost mythical stories of the rigorous workouts McNamee had put them all through. In his interview with the Oversight Committee's lawyers, Knoblauch openly wondered now if those stories were "concocted" for a purpose.

Chuck Knoblauch left the Rayburn Building the same way he arrived, carrying Jake on his hip while his entourage followed closely behind. It had taken 90 minutes. It was possible that he could have asserted his Fifth Amendment right to remain silent and then stared down the lawyers for that entire time. But Knoblauch's face betrayed an unmistakable sense of relief. He smiled happily as he walked through the hall, and whispered a few things in Jake's ear. "He answered all their questions," said Shaun Clarke, one of his lawyers.

A reporter ran up alongside Knoblauch and asked him why he had brought Jake. That was when Knoblauch gave his only quote to the media that day. "I have him here today to learn a very valuable lesson," Knoblauch said about his decision to bring Jake. "If you do something in life, be prepared to talk about it openly and honestly."

Jake Knoblauch was only three, and had never known his father as a sports celebrity. Years down the road he might be able to read and understand the transcript of the interview, and see where his father had talked about him. But for now, there was no way he could have understood the significance of the trip he and his father were on. They had interrupted their vacation in Miami for a trip to Washington. There had been an airplane ride and metal detectors, toys, and now Jake Knoblauch found himself at the center of a noisy escort of cameras once again.

Three years earlier, Mark McGwire had come before the same congressional committee and infamously declared he was "not here to talk about the past." Then he had stonewalled. Chuck Knoblauch had taken a different path.

From the moment Andy Pettitte stepped into the Rayburn House Office Building at 9:55 on the morning of Monday, February 4, it was clear that this witness would be treated with deference and respect by the steely lawyers and investigators who conduct depositions for Congress. Pettitte had already publicly confirmed just about everything Brian McNamee had said about him in the Mitchell Report, and with his straightforward, easygoing manner there was no reason to treat him with anything but kindness.

Yet Pettitte had every reason to be a hostile witness: His close friend and longtime teammate was engaging in a life-and-death battle for his reputation; his personal trainer was disgraced; he was being outed as a drug user himself; and worst of all, his father had been thrown right in the middle of it all the week before when Pettitte's lawyers informed him that reporters knew about Kelly Blair.

Pettitte's attorneys, Jay Reisinger and Thomas Farrell, were with him. His wife, Laura, waited outside the deposition room. After the introductions, Michael Gordon, majority senior investigative counsel, thanked Pettitte for joining the group, and especially for doing so voluntarily. "You should know that the committee very much appreciates your cooperation in this matter," Gordon told Pettitte. "I'm assuming this is the first time you've ever appeared for a deposition before Congress, is that right?"

Pettitte told him that it was, and Gordon warned him about the perils of knowingly providing false testimony and asked if he wanted to provide an opening statement. "I'm not prepared for that," Pettitte said softly.

And so began what majority chief of staff Phil Schiliro characterized at the end of the deposition as the most forthcoming testimony of any player in the three years the committee had been holding steroid hearings. Pettitte would embark on a sometimes heartbreaking description of how his own use of human growth hormone had become intertwined with his father's involvement with the drug. Pettitte's lawyers had bought him an extra five days to figure out how far he would need to go with his admissions, and he exceeded those limits, at least in the eyes of the committee.

The interview began fairly innocuously, Pettitte answering as best he could remember about events that had occurred almost a decade ago. He described how he met Brian McNamee in 1999 and became friendly with him after McNamee joined the Yankees as an assistant strength coach in 2000.

"And I built up a great relationship with him just, you know, I worked out with him and Roger. Obviously worked out at Yankee Stadium, on the road, in the off-season, just would work out with him," Pettitte said. "He very quickly became someone that I basically entrusted all of his knowledge into me, you know, and really that's the extent of our relationship, you know. I just spent a lot of time with him working out and training. And you know, and obviously I've spent a lot of time with him. He's become a friend of mine."

Pettitte described the tough workouts McNamee put him through and talked about the sporadic way he and Clemens paid their trainer—$1,000 here or $1,500 there—until Pettitte hired McNamee full-time in 2004 and paid him a salary of either $62,000 or $64,000 for the year, he wasn't sure what the exact figure was.

Fairly quickly, Gordon moved on to the more serious topic of the Mitchell Report. Pettitte confirmed again, this time under oath, the stories of the HGH injections in 2002, when he was in Tampa rehabbing his elbow. He described his fraying ligaments, and the medications and treatments he'd undergone since the problem developed in 1996. Pettitte wasn't sure if he brought up the subject of HGH or if McNamee did; he just knew he needed something.

"I'm like, dude, I am hurt. You know my elbow is hurt. What can I do? Is there anything I can do?" he'd asked the trainer.

Gordon pressed Pettitte on whose idea it had been, and finally Pettitte said he thought it had probably been McNamee's idea, that McNamee had probably told him that he'd heard the stuff was good.

"The excerpt we were just looking at here at the bottom of the page said that you initially talked to him and he discouraged you from using it," Gordon said. "And you were saying later, later he ultimately agreed to give it to you. Is that generally correct?"

"Yeah," answered Pettitte. "He discouraged me from doing it. . . . I mean, he told me that he knows what kind of person I am. He knows—I mean, I'm a Christian man. I try to live my life a certain way. And he told me that he did not think that I would feel comfortable doing it once I did it. And can I keep—I definitely listened to what he had to say."

Pettitte went on to say that he felt using the drug was the right thing to do, the honorable thing for someone being paid as well as he was. It wasn't against baseball's rules and there were lots of things teams expected players to do that most people would have found shocking, the kinds of things that remained locked in the closely guarded confines of the clubhouse. Pettitte knew that the team expected him to take whatever measures were necessary to get himself on the field. The 10 men and one woman in the room understood and they appreciated words like that coming from a superstar athlete.

"I was making an awful lot of money," Pettitte said. "I wanted to give back to the team. I had been on the DL [Disabled List] before. But I knew I had hurt my elbow pretty bad this time. I was on there for an extended period of time, where before with my elbow I'd only missed a couple of weeks. . . . And I just felt like that it was the honorable thing to do, if I could do whatever I could to try to get back on the field and try to earn my money. I just told him I think that I ought to do it. And so that's why he agreed to do it."

He told the investigators that McNamee had injected him on two to four occasions in 2002, morning and night, in McNamee's room, in the stomach, "right close to the belly button." They'd used a small needle, and McNamee had pulled a little fat up near the belly button and put the needle right there.

Pettitte said he thought McNamee had told him he'd gotten the HGH from his family doctor; he certainly hadn't said anything about a Mets clubhouse trainer. "Or a Red Sox trainer," said Farrell, interjecting a joke into an otherwise grim moment.

By the time Gordon got to Roger Clemens, Pettitte had assured them that everything McNamee had said in the report looked pretty accurate, at least as far as he could remember. Now the committee's investigators wanted to know what Pettitte knew about his friend's possible involvement with human growth hormone.

"What did you ever talk to Clemens about with respect to HGH?" Gordon asked.

"I remember a conversation in 1999 where Roger had told me that he had taken HGH," Pettitte answered.

"Where were you when that conversation happened?"

"I believe we were at his house."

"And what did he tell you?"

"That's really all I can really remember, you know, about it. I can't remember specifics about the conversation. That's just, you know—that's really all I can remember about the whole conversation."

"Were you surprised to hear that?" Gordon asked.

"No. Not really because I had never—you know, I've—you know, I don't think I'd ever heard of it before at that time," Pettitte said. "So I think it was just like—it kind of just maybe made me curious, you know."

Gordon pressed Pettitte to recount the context of the conversation—Was it serious? Joking?—and any details, but Pettitte claimed he didn't want to speculate or mischaracterize anything from such a long time ago. As he would throughout the deposition when asked about his own drug use, or Clemens's involvement, he said just enough.

"Well, that's fair," said Gordon. "I don't want you to make things up."

When Gordon asked if Pettitte had told anyone about the conversation, he said he had mentioned it to McNamee, who had become angry about it. McNamee didn't really like to talk about what his clients were doing—it didn't usually suit his purposes—and he didn't like them talking to each other about what they were doing, either.

"He was upset. You know he was—you know, I went to Mac and just had told him you know that Roger had told me that he had took it," Pettitte said. "And he was—he was—he was pretty upset. I remember him just kind of getting angry and said, you know, who told you that? And I—I'm like, well, Roger did. And you know he was like, man, he shouldn't have done that. I don't remember a whole lot more than that. But I just remember that he was upset that I had told him that Roger had told me that."

Gordon wanted to know if it had been Pettitte's impression that McNamee had provided the HGH for Clemens and if that had been the reason Pettitte had raised the issue of using it with McNamee. Gordon then asked Pettitte if he'd told anyone about using the HGH and said that he thought he'd told his wife, Laura. "I have to say that I tell her everything," he said.

After some back and forth involving the timeline—Pettitte thought the conversation with Clemens had happened in the offseason in 1999 but he wasn't definitive—Gordon asked Pettitte if he'd ever talked to Clemens again about human growth hormone.

Yes, answered Pettitte, there had been one other time.

"When was that?" asked Gordon.

"In 2005," said Pettitte.

"Do you remember what prompted that conversation?"

"Yeah, The congressional hearings. They were going on."

Pettitte was referring to the hearings Davis and Waxman had called after the release of the Canseco book, the hearing in which McGwire had refused to answer questions about steroids. They'd been in spring training in Florida and Pettitte had tried to approach Clemens about what they would say if they were asked about drug use by a reporter.

"Can you sort of tell me the story there of what happened there, what you guys talked about?" Gordon asked.

"Well, I knew that the congressional hearings were going on," said Pettitte. "And I thought for sure that someone was going to come up to me, a reporter, and start talking to me and asking me questions about it. And I was going to go ahead and just admit that, you know, I had used HGH when I had used it.

"And so we were, you know, in spring training in Tampa—I'm sorry. In Kissimmee, Florida, when I was with the Astros. And I got Roger and just asked him, I said, 'Dude, what are you going to say if anyone—if any of the reporters ask you if you had ever used HGH?'

"And he said, you know, he said 'Well, what are you talking about?'

"And I said, 'Well, you had told me you had used HGH.' And he said, 'I never told you that.'

"And I said, 'You didn't?' And he said, 'No. I told you that Debbie used HGH.' And that's—that was the end of the conversation right there."

Pettitte had written the incident off to Clemens being Clemens but now he was having to explain it all to people who weren't quite as easily intimidated by Clemens as some of the people close to him were, including Pettitte. He'd known there was no point in arguing—"it's already been decided," Clemens used to say when a dispute arose or when someone contradicted him—but it was hard to get the committee people to understand that. They were beyond the sphere of intimidation.

"That was really the end of the conversation," Pettitte continued. "Just when he said that, I was like, 'oh,' just kind of walked out. I wasn't going to argue with him over it."

Gordon asked him if he thought it was likely that he had misunderstood Clemens back in 1999. Or was it that he just didn't want to get into a dispute with the guy?

"I'm saying that I was under the impression that he told me that he had taken it," Pettitte said. "And then when Roger told me that he didn't take it, and I misunderstood him, I took it for that, that I misunderstood him."

Pettitte told Gordon he had mentioned the incident to McNamee, and that he was going to probably have to own up to having used HGH if anyone asked. McNamee told Pettitte to do what he had to do but that he hoped Pettitte would keep McNamee out of it. Pettitte remembered too that he'd told his wife, Laura, about what Clemens had said about Debbie using HGH.

Gordon then moved on to whether or not Pettitte had ever discussed Clemens's drug use with McNamee. Yes, Pettitte said, he had. Pettitte remembered the scene. They'd been in his gym at his house in Deer Park and the way he remembered it, McNamee had come up to him while they were training and told him that he had gotten steroids for Roger. That had been in '02, or '03, and maybe even '04, he wasn't sure. But he was certain that McNamee had been upset.

"I remember that Mac was upset," said Pettitte. "I just remember that Mac was upset and he was venting and he was—you know, he was telling me that that, you know, that Roger, you know, had done steroids."

It had all had something to do with the InVite vitamin deal that Mac was trying to get going; there was very little money involved and Pettitte was happy to help his trainer with a little publicity. And he liked taking the vitamins, which the company gave to him at no charge.

"Mac had asked me and Roger to do some sponsor promoting for it," said Pettitte. "And they were trying to work out deals—you know, we were trying to work out a deal, compensation, stuff like that. Well, our under-standing from—my understanding from Mac was the company wasn't able to pay us a lot of money, you know, to, you know, have us, you know, maybe in their little brochure that they send out and stuff like that. And I just told Mac that I said, I mean, I don't want any money. If they give me the vitamin, I think it's a great vitamin. I hadn't been sick since I had been on this vitamin. And just you know I'd love to keep taking it. And just give me the vitamin. I don't want any compensation for it. And I remember Mac just being extremely mad and saying, you know, that Roger wanted to get a lot of compensation for it as far as money-wise. So that's really all I remember about the conversation, that Mac was kind of venting, you know, just venting about, you know, that. That's really all I remember about the conversation."

Pettitte had been surprised by the steroid talk; it was the first time he'd ever heard McNamee say anything about steroids. "So I just kind of, you know, I just kind of let it be as a wash, you know, just kind of go in one ear and out the other ear basically," he said.

"Other than the HGH that McNamee provided you in 2002 that

you've already discussed, was there ever any other time that you used HGH?" Gordon asked.

"Yes." Pettitte answered.

"Can you tell me about that?"

The story that Pettitte told to the people in the room was one any son or daughter could relate to: about an ill parent who would do anything to try to feel better again. Tom Pettitte had been through so much it was hard for Andy to even process it all. The stents and the open heart surgery. The ambulances and the panic. The disability and the depression. Only a couple of years ago, the doctors told Tom Pettitte he'd had a heart attack on the operating table. He still had blockage on the back side of the heart. He was 58.

"In 2004. 2004 I used it again. I was on the DL," Pettitte began. "My dad had been using it. I knew that—I had found out I believe through McNamee that my dad was using it. My dad's had a world of health problems. In 1998 he had open heart surgery. He's now—at this day he has nine stents in his heart. He's been on disability since he was 48 years old. Since he's had open heart surgery, he's never been back. He's had all kinds of different treatments and stuff like that."

Pettitte described the chelation therapy his dad had tried for about eight months. And he talked about the shoulder surgeries and the ambulances that would routinely pull up to the house to get Tom Pettitte and take him to the emergency room.

"I found out he was taking it. I believe I found out through McNamee maybe first," Pettitte said. "I'm not sure. I know my mother came to me also and was extremely concerned and asked me to get him to stop. So you know I had a conversation with my dad. When my mom came to me and was showing so much concern, I didn't know much about it. All I knew was what McNamee told me that it could help repair tissue. So when my mom came to me concerned with it, I tried to find out a little bit about it."

Pettitte described going to the Astros' trainer for more information about HGH and finding out that there might be side effects, cancer maybe.

"So I went back to dad with that, and you know just told him that I didn't think, you know, that he should be doing it, didn't recommend that he should do it," said Pettitte.

But even as he told his father not to, Pettitte said, he was considering using HGH again. It was 2004, his first season in Houston when he popped a tendon in his left elbow on a checked swing in his very first at-bat. Pettitte got a few cortisone injections in his elbow and tried to rehab his arm after coming off the disabled list. That didn't work and he went back on the DL. The prospect of surgery beckoned. He was desperate.

"I just signed a $30 million contract with the Astros. My first start with the hometown team and I was like, there's no way I'm going out like this."

Throughout it all, Pettitte said, he was receiving injections of the potent painkiller Toradol from the team's doctors to get him through his starts. Pettitte didn't need to point out to his congressional inquisitors the moral ambiguity he had faced—taking one type of injection from team doctors and passing up on another simply because it was supposedly a performance enhancer (and not even officially banned by Major League Baseball at the time).

"And anyhow, just ended up going back to my dad," Pettitte said. "We were just having a conversation. I had asked my dad if he had had any of the HGH that he had had before. He ended up bringing me two syringes over to my house. And you know, I injected myself once in the morning and once at night. He had brought two syringes over. That's what he brought over to my house. You know, that's the best that he recalls also, that he had brought two syringes over. And that was it. I did it that time. I did it for that day. And to this day, I don't know why, it doesn't make a whole lot—heck of a lot—of sense. I knew—I think that's probably why I didn't continue to pursue it. I did it. I was desperate and you know I really knew that it wasn't going to help me."

Pettitte's flexor tendon was already torn and he knew he needed the surgery he would have about a month and a half later. He said he didn't tell McNamee or Clemens about using HGH in 2004, or anyone else, presumably not even Laura this time. Only his dad knew.

Gordon asked if he'd taken HGH any other time. Pettitte said no and pointed out that when he took HGH, it was not banned from baseball. Pettitte had been quick to deny any attempt to cheat; he took the drug to help heal an injury, pretty much like his dad had done.

There would be other questions for Pettitte—did he remember the training session at Clemens's house with C. J. Nitkoswki and Justin Thompson in 2001–2002 during which the subject of steroids and HGH was discussed? It was then that McNamee had said that Pettitte had approached him during a long-toss session and asked him why he hadn't told Pettitte about the performance enhancers Clemens was taking and how good they made him feel. Pettitte said he didn't remember talking about drugs, and he doubted they would talk about them in front of the young players who were there. He was asked if he had any knowledge about whether Clemens had gotten injections of B_{12} or lidocaine from McNamee. He said he did not.

Over the next year, Brian McNamee would rely on much of what Andy Pettitte said in his deposition that Monday morning. He would be portrayed as an honest teller of the truth by McNamee's lawyers, by the media, and even by the committee investigators. But before Pettitte headed back to Houston, there was one thing they needed to clear up. When Gordon turned the floor over to the Republican staff, minority counsel Steve Castor asked the question that had been hovering over the interview: Why hadn't Pettitte mentioned the 2004 HGH use when he issued his statement following the release of the Mitchell Report admitting to using the drugs in 2002?

"The main reason why was because of my dad," Pettitte answered. "And I mean I knew that my dad had brought it over to me. I didn't want to bring my dad—he's my dad. I didn't want to bring my dad into it. And, at that time, I was having a real hard time recollecting even if I'd—what I did. I imagine because it was my dad just—and it was me and my dad, no one else. Nobody else knows about this. But, you know, I thought that maybe—that—I mean, I was just trying to protect him, I'm sure, you know. And, again, it was for a day and, you know, was very insignificant, but, you know, that was—that's—that's not—that's not a true statement, and I released that statement."

Pettitte went on to say that he'd tried to do things the right way his entire life and that he hoped the committee would put those two days of HGH in the proper context. He said that over the two months since the statement was released he realized that it wasn't exactly accurate.

"You know, I could recall doing it again," he said. "Like I told you, it was my dad that gave it to me, so I would imagine, just out of protection and trying to protect him, I was worried about what people would think if I did say that or bring him up that it would—you know, that it would look—it would look terrible. But, you know, that's what it is. I'm under oath now, and, you know, I have to tell you guys the truth about it."

He called taking the HGH "about as boneheaded as a—you know, just as boneheaded a thing as I could have done," and was gently reminded by Castor that taking HGH wasn't illegal under baseball's rules. That might have made Pettitte feel a little better but the next question hit him hard.

"Do you have any idea where your father obtained the HGH?" Castor asked.

"Yeah, I do now. Yes," Pettitte answered.

"Where is that?"

"The gym that he works out in. A guy that's the trainer there," Pettitte said. He then said he wanted them to know why he was telling them these things, wanted them to believe that it wasn't just because he was under oath.

"Because I just—I live my life and the truth, you know, and I just—I have to tell you all the truth," he said. "I mean, I got—I told y'all the stuff about my dad because I have to live with myself. And one day I have to give an account to God and not to nobody else of what I've done in my life. And that's why I've said and shared the stuff with y'all that I've shared with y'all today that I wouldn't like to share with y'all."

They wanted to clear up one more thing that there had been some confusion about: In 2005, when he'd asked Clemens what they would say if they were asked about drug use, and he'd said "oh no, it was for my wife," had Pettitte misunderstood their first conversation about HGH back in 1999?

"I don't think I misunderstood him. Just to answer that question for you when it was brought up to me, I don't think I misunderstood him," Pettitte answered. "I went to Mac immediately after that. But then, 6 years later when he told me that I did misunderstand him, you know, since '05 to this day, you know, I kind of felt that I might have misunderstood him. I'm sure you can understand, you know, where I'm coming from with that conversation."

It was a perfect answer from Pettitte, candid, descriptive, a little vague. The committee had gotten what it needed from its homespun witness—a humble, respectful ballplayer who loved his dad.

He had one question of his own for the investigators.

"Can I say one thing?" Pettitte asked. "I mean, I just—and y'all can do what you may with it. But I just would ask, you know, y'all—I know we're going to have this hearing I guess on the 13th. Obviously, it's going to be on national TV, and it's going to be televised for the whole world to see. And I don't see where my dad has anything to do with steroids and steroids in baseball."

Pettitte knew that the Kelly Blair story was coming. Even if it didn't come that week, the transcript of the deposition Pettitte was giving would one day become public record, and the world would know the truth about his dad and the Texas gym.

"And I know it's a great story, and I know that from the way things look that it's going to end up coming out," Pettitte continued. "I'm pretty sure of that. I've known that some, you know, people know about this, about my dad, before the Mitchell Report, even before I released my statement of what I said the first time. So it wasn't like I didn't think this about my dad was going to come up at some point in some time. But just was wondering, and whatever, but it would be a very uncomfortable situation for me to try to talk about this in front of the whole world about my dad. If Congress members have to ask me questions about it, I understand. Okay. You know, I'll deal with it. But I just may be pleading to the court here, if we didn't have to bring up my dad in that and y'all just ask me questions and I don't have to go there, which it might be tough. Because if anyone asked me if I ever at other times used it, I would have to say, obviously, I did and bring him up. But I believe that questions can be brought up to me—and a lot of serious questions to be brought up to me maybe without embarrassing me on national TV where I have to talk about my dad in this. I know I've got to deal with it. But that was really all I wanted to ask y'all."

Schiliro told Pettitte they would talk to the committee chairman and members about excusing Pettitte from the hearing. Schiliro stated for the record that the committee always tried to balance its legitimate investigative needs with the legitimate privacy rights of individuals. Pettitte's lawyer Tom Farrell reminded the investigators once again of the seriousness of Tom Pettitte's illness, saying he had been so depressed over not being able to work that he'd become suicidal at one point.

The appeals worked. The following day, Schiliro and Waxman decided to spare Pettitte the indignity of appearing at the February 13 public hearing, which by this point looked like a guaranteed circus. Apparently swayed by the raw honesty of Pettitte's emotion during the deposition, Waxman's staff arranged with Pettitte's attorneys the very next day to produce affidavits from the pitcher and his wife, Laura, attesting to the conversations they'd had about Clemens's use of HGH. Andy and Laura Pettitte signed those affidavits on February 8, and overnighted them to the home of a member of Waxman's staff.

At age 70, Dr. Ron Taylor had white hair, a deeply furrowed face, and no shortage of professional accomplishments. He was the director of a clinic for athletic injuries at Mount Sinai Hospital in Toronto, ran a family practice, and had been the team doctor for the Toronto Blue Jays since 1979. Before becoming a doctor, Taylor had been a respectable pitcher, playing 11 years in Major League Baseball. He finished his career with 72 saves for Cleveland, St. Louis, Houston, the New York Mets, and San Diego.

The highlights on his baseball résumé included a victory in the 1964 World Series with the Cardinals, where he collected three saves, and a perfect ERA in six postseason appearances.

But on February 4, 2008, all those achievements were mere background to an event in his life that was so small and insignificant he might not have even remembered it without the help of documentation; in July of 1998, Taylor had given Roger Clemens a shot of vitamin B_{12}. Taylor's interview with four members of the House Oversight Committee took place over the telephone. He had no lawyer. He said he'd given a B_{12} injection only twice in his career as the Blue Jays doctor, but had given approximately 1,000 in his practice, mostly to elderly patients to supplement their diet.

"Have you ever seen the kind of reaction that Mr. Clemens had, have you ever seen that kind of reaction in anybody else from the B_{12} shot?" asked Brian Cohen, a senior investigator on the committee staff.

"No," said Taylor, who didn't recall actually administering the shot.

More than a month had passed since Clemens first started talking about Brian McNamee giving him B_{12} shots. In the weeks since that claim had been floated on *60 Minutes*, the investigative staff of the House Oversight Committee had also learned of the possibility that Clemens developed an injection site abscess in 1998. This information—like the tales of B_{12} and lidocaine—had not been in the Mitchell Report. Congress knew about the abscess in large part thanks to the fact that McNamee described it during his December 12 interview with Jim Yarbrough and Billy Belk. After learning that a tape of that interview existed (Hardin had quoted from it in the January 6 defamation suit) the committee had followed up on Earl Ward's very public recommendation that the committee request the transcript.

"I know for a fact that Roger got an abscess from the injection and that's what made him stop taking Winstrol," McNamee had told Belk and Yarbrough. "I don't know if the federal government talked to the head trainers, because they have it documented that he got—I mean, it's documented he got an abscess. The only way to get an abscess is, usually, by injecting steroids in your ass."

Since reading those words, the committee's lawyers had gone looking for evidence of an abscess, along with any information about the use of B_{12} and lidocaine in Major League Baseball's clubhouses. One of the first places the staff had turned was the medical departments of the four Major League Baseball teams Clemens had played for. Before doing so, they had asked Clemens to waive his medical confidentiality rights. Clemens complied. He really had no choice; his whole public relations campaign might have fallen apart if he were shown to be hiding something.

When the committee staff got Clemens's medical records, they found a report on an MRI that had been taken of his backside after the abscess developed. The report was five pages long. Atop each page was the Toronto Blue Jays logo, and at the bottom of each page were the words "highly confidential." Despite heavy redactions, it clearly stated that the Blue Jays' medical staff had requested an MRI on Clemens's backside. Worried that he was looking at an abscess, Dr. Alan Gross, a surgeon affiliated with the Blue Jays, ordered that Clemens be treated with heat, ice, and antibiotics:

> Roger received a B_{12} injection approximately 7–10 days ago into his right buttocks from Dr. Taylor at Skydome. Roger started complaining of right buttocks soreness on July 28, 1998. He was examined by Dr. Gross on July 28, 1998. Diagnosis was a small collection of blood below the surface of the skin. Ok for all activity. Therapy should consist of hydrocollator packs, and ice packs alternating, plus Dr. taylor prescribed Cloxacillin 500 mg BID for 10 days. Monitor.

As the hearing approached, the committee would interview Gross, as well as Blue Jays assistant trainer Scott Shannon; Astros assistant trainer Rex Jones; David Lintner, the Astros' medical director; Gene Monahan, the Yankee trainer; and Arthur Pappas, the Red Sox medical director. None of these people thought it was normal practice for a pitcher to be given lidocaine, an anesthetic, least of all by a trainer. None put much credit in the idea that McNamee ever would have had access to lidocaine or B_{12}. It was silly, dangerous, illegal, and against team policy. By the end, the committee understood what seemed like common sense; if McNamee had been giving B_{12} or lidocaine shots, it would not have been out in the open, the innocent injections Clemens had portrayed as routine.

Clemens was going to appear for his deposition on February 5, and would be asked about the B_{12} and lidocaine questions under oath. He would be asked about the abscess as well. So the day before Clemens arrived, the committee lawyers spent an hour and a half interviewing Dr. Taylor. Right after that, they spent nearly two hours interviewing Tommy Craig, the Blue Jays' head trainer. Assisting in the interviews was Dr.

Stephen Cha, a medical doctor on the committee staff whose expertise had in the past been useful in the committee's many investigations into the safety, pricing, and marketing of prescription drugs.

Both Taylor and Craig asserted without any hesitation that they had never heard of Brian McNamee giving B_{12} or lidocaine injections to Clemens or any other Blue Jay. Both men insisted McNamee would not have had the authority or expertise to do such a thing. And both men said it was particularly absurd to think that McNamee would have been in a position to inject lidocaine.

Lidocaine was a painkiller, but not the type that would relieve the aches and pains of a 35-year-old pitcher. Lidocaine had a numbing effect. It was a local anesthetic commonly used in dental surgery and possibly by orthopedic surgeons. Taylor told the committee that probably not even he himself was qualified to give a lidocaine shot.

"I don't do lidocaine injections. If they're done, they're usually done by the orthopedic surgeon," Taylor said. "It can be used—it's an anesthetic. And if you have an injured ligament or tendon, if you inject around the tendon and move it, there's no pain. With the lidocaine there's pain, so you can learn how to locate the actual position of the injury using lidocaine. Also it's used in conjunction with some steroid shots—not steroid, I'm sorry, cortisone shots to reduce the pain of the shot. And I mean cortisone, okay?"

Cortisone was a type of steroid, but it was an anti-inflammatory medication—not muscle-building. It was a "diagnostic tool," Taylor said, and the numbing effect wouldn't last long.

"I think you've reviewed the records, as I understand," Cha said. "And the lidocaine and cortisone shots that Mr. Clemens did receive appear to be done under an X-ray while he was sedated. Can you describe these epidural injections for us just in plain English?"

Taylor said it would be better explained by an orthopedic surgeon, because a lidocaine injection wasn't the type of thing a doctor like him would normally do.

"Okay. I think what they do, and I'm not an orthopedic surgeon, I think you anesthetize the local area, then give a shot of cortisone that would decrease the swelling," said Taylor. "It's a very common orthopedic procedure. What you're doing is providing a localized anti-inflammatory, sending it through the whole body with the side effects it could cause."

Cha asked if something like this would give relief to lower back pain at all if the injection area was somewhere in the buttocks.

"You could get relief in that area, you know, in the area of the buttocks," Taylor said. "The buttocks is not the lower back."

A few minutes after hanging up with Taylor—the interviews were done via conference call—the committee staff called Craig, who as head trainer had been McNamee's superior with the Blue Jays. Craig echoed Taylor's assertion that McNamee was not authorized to give B_{12} or lidocaine shots to any player, and that he had never heard of such a thing. Craig said that it sounded out of character for Clemens to allow someone to shoot him up, and noted that a local anesthetic like lidocaine would do nothing to help someone pitch a baseball.

"I don't know what the advantage of that would be, to numb an area," Craig said. "I was kind of baffled when I heard that one."

Both Taylor and Craig said another thing that interested the committee; Clemens's legal team had contacted each of them, asking Taylor and Craig whether they remembered anything about a palpable mass on Clemens's buttocks.

CHAPTER FOURTEEN

February 5–February 13, 2008

With the confident stride of a Yankee legend, Roger Clemens arrived on Capitol Hill for his deposition on the morning of February 5. He wore a gray pinstriped suit buttoned tightly across his wide chest. He carried a small vinyl briefcase in his left hand, and in his right hand—the hand that helped him collect 354 big league wins—he carried a large paper cup with a tea bag label hanging out.

Flanked by Rusty Hardin and Lanny Breuer, Clemens strode into room 2157 of the Rayburn Building, took the oath, and promptly denied having ever used steroids or human growth hormone. He repeated this denial, in various formulations, a total of six times in just the first 30 minutes of the meeting. Later, he denied attending Jose Canseco's party, and denied having family members who had used HGH (although he revised that answer before leaving).

"I have not used steroids or human growth hormone," he said twice in the first half-hour of the exceedingly awkward five-hour meeting.

These denials were probably the most important sentences Clemens had spoken in his entire life. The sworn statements were unequivocal and direct, and the testimony was recorded verbatim. The stakes were enormous; from that moment forward, if it were ever proven that Clemens had used steroids or HGH, he could be prosecuted for lying to Congress. For much of the five-hour deposition, Clemens sat silently while his lawyers spoke directly to the committee, clarifying his answers and bashing the Mitchell Report's methodology. "I don't have enough malpractice insurance to handle the number of lawyers in this country that think I, and now Lanny, are insane to let a man be coming in here when he's already been warned publicly there's probably going to be a public referral—a criminal referral," Hardin said.

But Clemens had insisted on taking the mound. He had eagerly looked forward to testifying. His interview with the committee's lawyers was a chance to demonstrate his resolve and, it seemed, to blow off steam.

"Brian McNamee did not make me as an athlete, despite his ongoing claims by he and his lawyer that they continue to throw stuff out there, that he made me," Clemens said. "I had a great workout ethic before I met him."

It was Clemens's pride that was at stake, his legacy, everything he'd worked for all these years. For nearly two months, people had been wondering what drove Clemens to deny Brian McNamee's stories, even after Andy Pettitte had confirmed them. Like Pettitte, Clemens didn't want anyone to think he had cheated—that he had taken the easy route to the unprecedented honors and ability present late in his career.

"I have never smoked a cigarette, I have never smoked dope, I have never done cocaine," Clemens said, continuing his pent-up speech. "I would not put anything—allow anybody to put anything in my body that's going to be harmful to me. That's who I am as a person."

"I love coming to Washington," Clemens continued. "I love doing the things that I do here. I enjoy being around—not in this situation. This is harder than bases loaded. I hate being in these situations. But I am here because I want to set the record straight. And like I said, it's difficult because I'm answering questions on certain times, and lies that people have said about me."

Clemens claimed that the stuff he had learned in recent weeks was "shocking." The fact that Andy Pettitte had used growth hormone, Clemens said, had stunned him.

"Andy Pettitte doing growth hormone," Clemens said. "I don't know; I would think that we were close enough to know that if he was thinking of doing it, or did it, that I would have known; that he would have told me. It's shocking."

One of the primary mysteries of the Mitchell Report was why McNamee would have told the truth about Pettitte's human growth hormone and then would have lied about Clemens. All Clemens knew was that he was angry. The notion that he procured drugs at Jose Canseco's party in 1998 was particularly galling.

"I don't know if McNamee ever told Pettitte that I was using it to get closer to him or to bring him down," Clemens said. "I don't know what that situation was. It was never talked about to me. This man has me being a drug dealer. Very upsetting about that, as I think—if you have seen my interviews. Very upsetting."

The committee's attorneys had, in fact, seen his interviews. They had watched the YouTube denials, the *60 Minutes* program, and the Houston press conference. In those settings, Clemens had boxed himself in with the bizarre claim that McNamee had injected him with B_{12} and lidocaine. Phil Barnett, an aide to chairman Waxman for nearly two decades, began the deposition by reading line by line through the section of the Mitchell Report (marked as Exhibit 1) that contained McNamee's allegations. Barnett asked Clemens to respond to each paragraph. This was where Clemens entered his sworn denials of doping.

Barnett read from the Mitchell Report. "McNamee injected Clemens in the buttocks four to six times with testosterone from a bottle labeled either Sustanon 250 or Deca-Durabolin that McNamee had obtained from Radomski."

"Is that accurate?" Barnett asked.

"That is not true," Clemens said. "I don't—again, I have no idea and know nothing about the steroids or what is being said here."

"Anabolic steroids, which are performance-enhancing steroids, you have never used those?" Barnett asked.

"That is correct."

"And human growth hormone, have you ever used human growth hormone?"

"Never."

Roger Clemens could never take these words back. If someone came forward—McNamee, the feds, Waxman, reporters, his mistresses, Sammy Woodrow—with evidence and a convincing story, Clemens could now be accused of a felony, and a notarized transcript of his deposition could become Exhibit 1 in a criminal prosecution.

In what was surely one of the less dignified moments in the recent history of Congress, the permanent archives of the U.S. House of Representatives were officially expanded on February 5 to include a decade-old physician's report about "buttocks soreness" and a "palpable mass" that had afflicted Roger Clemens in the summer of 1998.

Barnett produced the medical report in the first hour of the deposition, right after Clemens said he received as many as eight B_{12} shots a season, from team doctors, nurses, and trainers, including Brian McNamee. While Barnett had the document formally marked as Exhibit 2 in the day's proceedings—thereby making it a public document—Clemens and his attorneys reviewed an extra copy that Barnett had provided.

"On the last page here says there was also a palpable mass on your left buttocks," said Barnett. "And I think that is highlighted in this copy. And further in the earlier record we were talking about the right buttocks. Do you remember this, having a palpable mass on both?"

Clemens had been testy and curt at some points in the interview. He had also rambled off on tangents. But this question led him into some of the most far-fetched explanations of the day, suggesting that he may have strained his gluteus maximus while pushing off the mound for a pitch. Barnett cut Clemens off.

"Do you know what caused those injuries?" he asked.

Clemens looked down at the report, compiled by Dr. Alan Gross a decade earlier and given to the committee the previous month. It appeared to have come across a fax machine three weeks earlier, on January 14. The report mentioned that Dr. Taylor's B_{12} shot had been administered seven to 10 days earlier. It mentioned the soreness, and the small collection of blood below the surface of the skin.

"I don't know what caused those, other than it says right here Dr. Taylor had given me a B_{12} shot, so that surely could have happened," Clemens answered. "And I just—again, I am trying to think back, to pull it in for you, that I know I have strained my glute on a couple occasions. I wish I could tell you how many occasions it has happened. But I have had that too."

The injury report also showed Clemens had had an MRI exam at Mount Sinai Hospital in Toronto, and that "the results were negative for an abscess." The Clemens legal team had received those results the night before, but had not yet shared them with the committee's staff (the results said that the MRI revealed a "collection of fluid deep within the subcutaneous fat, likely related to the patient's prior attempted intramuscular injections").

Clemens had learned what an abscess was (he described it as "a huge, pussy, nasty-looking thing that would cause me to miss time on the disabled list"). He said he didn't believe any such thing existed. The report Clemens held suggested that while monitoring Clemens's butt for a week, doctors had discovered a similar problem on the left buttocks as well.

"If you strained your glute, would that lead to a palpable mass in an MRI and this kind of procedure and a prescription of—I think they prescribed antibiotics for this," Barnett said. "Would that lead to this treatment?"

"It sure could have, yeah," Clemens said.

"A strained—it could lead to—a strained muscle could lead to an MRI?" Barnett asked.

"I would think," Clemens said. "I am not a doctor, but I would—"

"Would it lead to prescription for antibiotics, a strained muscle?" Barnett asked.

"It could," Clemens said. "I don't—I don't know."

It had been a risky proposition to make public statements amidst potential litigation, but in the weeks following the Mitchell Report's release and Andy Pettitte's confirmation of its claims, Clemens had felt the need to speak out against McNamee. Now Clemens was reaping the dividends of this strategy; he was being held to the *60 Minutes* story that McNamee gave him shots of B_{12} and lidocaine. Throughout his deposition, Clemens told the committee lawyers B_{12} shots were "extremely common" in major league clubhouses. A whole lineup of guys might come out of a shower, Clemens said, to find a row of preloaded syringes ready. With each team he'd been on, it wasn't just doctors administering the shots, but also the trainers. "Trainers, all trainers, have given me shots," Clemens said. "Again, I considered McNamee a trainer."

At one point Clemens said he got between six to eight B_{12} shots in his 24 seasons, but later he revised this estimate to "at least 25, maybe 50." He couldn't remember many specifics about these injections, even the one from Dr. Taylor that supposedly caused the problems. "I'm sure that in looking at this, that I probably complained about a shot I got from Dr. Taylor to Brian McNamee, and he told me he could give me B_{12} and give it better," Clemens said.

Clemens said there was no pattern to the B_{12} shots he'd gotten over the years—beginning in the late 1980s, at the recommendation of his mother, Bess. Everyone knew the baseball season was long and arduous; if a player got sick, teammates might get some precautionary B_{12}.

"Do you know if other players on the Blue Jays also received B_{12} shots?" asked Jennifer Safavian, the leading Republican staffer at the deposition.

Safavian didn't mention that she had spoken with Dr. Taylor the day before, when he said he had given only two B_{12} shots to players in his whole career, and that no one else in the organization gave players shots.

"It was extremely common," Clemens said. "I think you just asked."

"Who would you ask?"

"Anybody in there," Clemens said. "Any of the—if a doctor or trainer was in there, you would just ask if they could give you—they had everything, I guess, on property."

Clemens said McNamee had given him four to six shots of B_{12}

and one shot of lidocaine—that the shots all looked normal and he never asked where McNamee had gotten the substances that were in the needles.

In a few days, Brian McNamee would sit before the same committee lawyers and deny ever having given B_{12} or lidocaine shots to anyone. A parade of medical and training staff members from various teams would cast doubt on the idea that McNamee would have given B_{12} shots. It defied common sense to think that normal team policy provided for a lowly weight trainer to administer injections on pitchers making at least 100 times as much in salary. Teams like the Yankees and Blue Jays employed distinguished medical doctors to care for the bodies of players, which were the game's greatest assets. Why would Clemens turn to a strength coach for B_{12} shots? This was the gist of the next series of questions Barnett had for Clemens.

"Did anyone witness you getting B_{12} shots from Mr. McNamee?" Barnett asked.

"I don't think so, but it was—it was, like I said, in an open area, you know, his office," Clemens answered. "I don't know if anybody was in there working out at the time or anybody surely could have walked in."

Clemens said that the "four to six" shots McNamee gave came in 1998 and 2001. He told Barnett that the Toronto injections took place in the Blue Jays' weight room, where McNamee kept a desk.

When Barnett asked what was the venue for the B_{12} shots McNamee supposedly gave Clemens in 2001, Clemens began speaking of Asphalt Green, a nonprofit athletic center on the Upper East Side in Manhattan where Clemens sometimes worked out.

"I believe in New York it was on the second floor of the building I lived in," Clemens said. "We trained at a place that was a block—a place called Asphalt Greens. That is about a block from my apartment there, and I trained and had therapeutic work done on the second floor. And that's where—that's where it happened."

This was new; the Mitchell Report had described injections in hotel rooms, apartment buildings, and locker rooms—but nothing about injections at a very public facility like Asphalt Green, with a clientele of well-to-do New Yorkers. It was the kind of place where little kids often took swimming and gymnastics lessons.

"If he gave you shots it was in this open area, or would he take you in a back office area where it was private?" Barnett asked.

"It was open, an open area," Clemens said.

"Was that usual for you to get shots in an open area?"

"Sure," Clemens said.

"And that would include both shots in the arm and in the glute?"

"Sure."

If there were moments in the deposition that strained credulity, this was certainly one of them; Clemens had just suggested that he thought nothing of dropping his pants in a public gym to get a shot from a trainer, at a time when Clemens was one of the most famous and successful baseball players on a championship team in a baseball-crazed city.

It was not the last time in the deposition that Clemens would be trapped by his own public statements. Barnett turned to Clemens with a series of questions about lidocaine, a substance that Clemens might never have needed to discuss had he not brought it up, a month earlier, with Mike Wallace.

"In your *60 Minutes* interview, you said that Mr. McNamee gave you lidocaine shots," Barnett said. "In your press conference, you said this happened when you were with the Blue Jays, and it was for lower back pain. Can you tell us about the times Mr. McNamee injected you with lidocaine?"

"It was a lidocaine shot," Clemens said. "He only gave me lidocaine once, and it did give me comfort in my lower back. I experienced back problems in Toronto. The mound there is a wet mound of clay, and I always experienced lower back problems, which I am sure I have told Mr. McNamee many times."

Barnett asked for more specifics; when and where did it happen? Clemens was quite certain that it was in 1998, around the time of the All-Star break (the palpable mass was discovered by the Blue Jays' medical staff two weeks after the All-Star Game). Clemens said McNamee gave him the shot in the training room, where he was working out.

But Clemens was vague on almost every other question that Barnett asked: Did the shot work? Did he ever get another lidocaine shot besides that one? Did he talk to the doctors before getting the shot? Did other trainers ever inject him? What medications did they inject? Was McNamee authorized to provide a lidocaine shot?

Clemens said that he had had another lidocaine injection, this time in 2005, at the end of the World Series. Barnett pointed out that the pitcher's medical records showed that a specialist had administered the shot, along with cortisone. (Lidocaine injections, the committee had learned the previous day, were difficult enough that not even Dr. Taylor felt confident describing them.)

"And why did you go to Mr. McNamee for a lidocaine injection instead of to a doctor or a specialist?" Barnett asked.

"I don't think I went to him," Clemens said. "I think I probably complained about my back to him and he suggested it."

It was one of Clemens's first specific recollections, and Barnett asked for elaboration.

"Where did that conversation happen?" Barnett asked.

"I'm sure during a workout or with—it could have been—I don't know if it was before or after a game when we were working out. I can't pull it in."

Jimmy Murray's deposition had followed a similar pattern; when a question allowed Clemens to portray McNamee in a negative light, Clemens, like Murray, was certain of his answers. Several times, Clemens could remember McNamee pushing drugs on him, but he was hazy on most other specifics.

The committee's investigators had questions about how Clemens's relationship with McNamee evolved between the Blue Jays' spring training in 1998 to the summer of 2007, when McNamee had worked out with Clemens in Kentucky and New York even as the feds were closing their net around McNamee.

"I'm always working out," Clemens said. "So I don't—I work out without Brian McNamee and I'm going to—like my mother said, moss is never going to grow underneath my feet. I am going to be active. I have four boys so I'm always going to be active."

Clemens wanted it to be known that he had designed his own training program. That long string of stories in 2000 and 2001 had often credited McNamee's heavy-duty regimen, but now Clemens said McNamee had simply modified Clemens's routine and claimed credit for it.

"For me it wasn't his workout," Clemens said. "The bulk of it is my workout. When I met Brian McNamee, he followed me around. He studied my workout. And he added about three or four exercises to this workout that now is his, or his Seal program, or whatever that he states is his workout, that he is going to sue, and it is not patented."

On one hand, Clemens told the familiar story of his arrangement—the weeklong trips to Houston, the payments of $5,000 a month that McNamee received via the Hendricks agency. But as Clemens retold the tale, he introduced a new theme: his own passivity.

"I would probably have trained with him anywhere from four days to a week, and then he would leave Houston," Clemens said. "I don't know if—again, I assumed that he left Houston. I don't know if he went to Andy's and trained for seven days and came to my—I wish I could tell you exactly."

That made it sound as if McNamee had just happened to be in Houston, and Clemens had worked out with him simply because it was convenient. Clemens didn't keep tabs on the guy—McNamee just breezed into his life. When Safavian asked about the previous year, 2007, Clemens again painted McNamee as the opportunist, something of a schemer who had latched on to Clemens once again, with Clemens agreeing to the arrangement only because of passive generosity.

"It was known that I was going to play in 2007," Clemens said, "and he had learned about it. And he asked, he said, 'Listen, you're going back to working, what can I do? Can I help you?' You know, he needed work. And I said, I'm not ready to train with you yet. I'm going to get my body really good and see where I'm at. And if it seems like I can play or I feel good about it, then you can come to—to Kentucky."

Here Clemens digressed for a minute, explaining that Kentucky was where his son was playing minor league ball for the Lexington Legends, and suggesting that working out at the Astros complex might have been a conflict now that he was signed with the Yankees, but then sensed that he was going too far afield.

"I worked out at the University of Kentucky," he said. "And McNamee—had McNamee come there for a period of a week."

There was something a little off in Clemens's interpretation of events. More than a dozen published articles in 2000 and 2001 had explored the pitcher's remarkable late-career surge and located Clemens's devotion to trainer Brian McNamee as the cornerstone of his program. Clemens was on record in those articles saying that he swore by McNamee's grueling workouts. And after the Radomski affidavit had put them both in hot water in October of 2006, Clemens had sworn by McNamee again, saying "I'll continue to use Mac to train me. He's one of a kind."

But now Clemens was distancing himself from McNamee, and when Safavian asked how McNamee was as a trainer, Clemens was less effusive.

"Oh, he was fine, he was great," he said. "Not much of a personality, but that's all right."

"Did you recommend his services to any other players?" Safavian asked.

"I don't think I recommended him to—to any other players," Clemens said.

But wasn't Clemens essential in bringing McNamee from Toronto to New York, Safavian asked.

"I made, I think, one phone call and/or e-mail to Brian Cashman, the general manager," Clemens said. "It was also stated in here that I paid a portion of his salary. I don't believe that to be true. . . . But I did call Brian Cashman on one—an e-mail or a call, and that was it."

In the second hour of Roger Clemens's deposition, he nearly had a breakdown. Clemens, the ferocious competitor whose grit had won him seven Cy Young Awards, had to ask the attorneys for a minute to collect himself. After that point, his lawyers did a lot of the talking. One of the people who witnessed the moment was Representative Darrell Issa (R-Calif.), the only actual congressman to visit any of the depositions. Issa had strolled into the deposition during its second hour, when it was the turn of the Republican staffers to question Clemens. (The turnover required a game of musical chairs.)

They had not been going easy on Clemens when Issa arrived. Safavian asked a series of questions about the January 4 phone call between McNamee and Clemens that most of the rest of the world had first learned about when the January 7 press conference took place. Why had Clemens called McNamee in the first place? Safavian asked.

"I was hoping he would come to the press conference that I was having on—in Houston that Monday or Tuesday, and come down and tell the truth about me instead of lies he's telling about me," Clemens explained.

"Did you ask him to attend the press conference?" Safavian asked. (The tape that Hardin played that day appeared to have been edited, so there were parts she may not have heard while watching the press conference on TV.)

"I don't know if—I think I said something about the press conference in the conversation that I had with him," Clemens said. "And I said, I need somebody to come down here and tell the truth."

"Did you ask him why he was telling these lies about you?" Safavian asked.

"You'd have to ask him," Clemens said. "I don't know why he's doing—"

Safavian cut Clemens off: "No. I'm sorry. Did you ask him?"

The true answer was no. Clemens had never asked McNamee "Why are you lying?" He had never even accused McNamee of lying—at least not directly. On the part of the tape that Clemens and Hardin had played, the closest thing to an accusation of dishonesty was "I just need somebody to tell the truth, Mac," followed a moment later by "I didn't do it."

Rather than answer Safavian's question about January 4, Clemens hit rewind and expressed, again, his rage about November and December, when McNamee had asked to borrow Clemens's fishing rods in Cabo even while the Mitchell Report was imminent.

"He called me for fishing equipment on an e-mail and didn't say one word about that—what he was doing to me and my family," Clemens said. "Very, very upset about that. I don't know what agenda he has. But I can't wait until we get out there in front of everybody to find out. I'm extremely upset about it. Let me get a deep breath here."

"Sure," Safavian said.

It was clear that the betrayal made Clemens upset, but he wanted the committee to understand that he wasn't angry at them.

"I know it has nothing to pertain to all of y'all here," Clemens said. "I think he has an agenda."

"What do you think that agenda is?" Safavian asked.

"You ask him," Clemens said. "I'll leave that—you guys can ask him."

Almost 24 years after his major league debut, Roger Clemens was used to controlling his environment, but Safavian was having none of that.

"Why do you think he has an agenda?" Safavian asked.

"You ask him on that," Clemens said. "I have my reasons. And I'll—I'll leave that to my counsel here."

"You'll leave it to your counsel to explain what you believe his reasons are?" Safavian asked, sounding incredulous.

"Well, I think there are reasons," Clemens said.

"I understand that this is difficult for you," Safavian said.

"Sure."

For the next 15 minutes or so, Roger Clemens was more or less silent. The relievers stepped in for him, with Breuer coming out of the bullpen first.

"Jennifer, one of the hard things here is the committee, particularly the majority, said the necessity of this hearing is because Roger Clemens attacked the Mitchell Report," Breuer said. "That is the rationale. What Roger Clemens has said from the beginning is that he applauds the Mitchell Report for what it wants to do with steroids, but that he has a very personal issue with Brian McNamee's accusations of him, which have destroyed him. And the world right now believes that Roger Clemens has abused steroids because of this man's accusations. And it's deeply personal."

In fact, it had been personal for McNamee too. For the entire second half of 2007, he had tried to minimize the damage he was doing to Clemens but also keep himself out of prison for drug distribution. Breuer made it sound more like a nice opportunity for McNamee.

"It's very hard for a congressional deposition or a hearing ultimately to deal with such a personal issue, the issue of what one man will say about a famous man like Roger Clemens. And to try to get into Brian McNamee's head, I think, is very hard for Roger Clemens to do. But it does appear that it's become very difficult for him and that Brian McNamee, of course, has become a famous person as a result of all this. So you're asking our client to speculate."

Clemens sat by, silently composing himself as Breuer sought to explain that the issue was celebrity, not B_{12}.

"But, of course, through Brian McNamee's accusations and through the work of this committee now, Brian McNamee has become a celebrated figure, and I think much of the world has drawn very negative conclusions about Roger Clemens. And I think you are just seeing that right now. And that's really, I think, in some sense what he's trying to articulate."

Here Congressman Issa stepped in.

"I appreciate what you're saying for the last questions," Issa said, "but we have another deposition coming up. You have two sets of public statements in which one must be false. What we're asking for, I think, here, majority and minority, is to give us anything that might lead to constructive questioning, that might lead to finding out who is not telling the truth."

The committee, Issa argued, was giving Clemens an opportunity; if McNamee had an agenda, Clemens should let Safavian know about it, because she would have McNamee in the hot seat two days later.

"If we assume your client to be completely innocent, then we must assume that our next deposition on, what, Thursday, is going to be with somebody who has lied and lied to the Mitchell Report," Issa continued. "So in a sense, we may not be successful in getting everything out, but it is the question of is the Mitchell Report flawed because of someone who lied, that is still within, very much within the purview of this committee, that I think Jennifer's trying to get to. So to the extent that it could lead to us asking better questions on Thursday, I think it would be helpful if your client could give us those kinds of answers."

Now Rusty Hardin jumped in—but not to say what McNamee's agenda was. Hardin suggested that Safavian's questions about that topic forced Clemens to "speculate" too much.

"None of us have rational explanations for McNamee's—what we contend is McNamee's lies," Hardin said. "And Roger has been thrown by this from the very beginning. He is being asked to guess. He has very strong feelings about McNamee. And if you want to ask him to guess as to why McNamee would do it, I think he would be willing to do that. But we don't have an answer for why he's lying. We only have evidence, we think, that shows he is lying. We'll be glad to provide things, for things that you might want to ask him about. I mean, his statements are just full of inaccuracies."

Keith Ausbrook, the Republican staff's general counsel, stepped forward for the first time in the interview. He pointed out that the line of questions that had hurt Clemens so much was in fact very straightforward.

"If I could say something on that. The question was, you know, why do you think he's doing this? And Mr. Clemens said, 'I think he had an agenda.' The following question was, 'Well, what do you think that agenda is?' And it may be that the answer is, 'I don't know, but I think he has some kind of agenda, but I don't know what it is.' Or maybe that he has a reason to think that there's a specific reason to think that Mr. McNamee is telling stories, and we'd like to understand more about the agenda that Mr. Clemens thinks Mr. McNamee has."

Breuer then changed the subject from McNamee's agenda to his concerns about the "nexus" between Jeff Novitzky and George Mitchell. Breuer pointed out that more pages of the report were spent on Clemens than on any other player. And then he raised what he said was a demonstrably erroneous passage in the Mitchell Report—the part about Clemens meeting with a steroids dealer at Jose Canseco's house party in 1998.

"We were able to establish and we will be able to establish categorically, without question, that our client wasn't there," Breuer said. "We are deeply concerned, frankly, that it wasn't that hard to establish that, and we think others could have established it as well."

For weeks, Breuer and Hardin had been working hard to prove that Clemens hadn't been at the party. In addition to the affidavit they had collected from Canseco, they had come up with proof they were sure would help exonerate their client. Demonstrating one flaw in the nine pages that dealt with Clemens would undercut the legitimacy of the whole report—make it look sloppy.

"So we found one example in the nine pages, which I think is a fair way of saying, if you looked at it, is filled with innuendo," Breuer said. "But there is one concrete example, which is this man says that our client was at a party. And we can establish that he wasn't at the party and, quite frankly, anyone could have. The TV footage will prove that he wasn't at the party. Records will prove that he wasn't at the party. And I think an impartial person looking at it will find that. So that's an example that we think undercuts Brian McNamee completely."

Hardin began the delicate task of attacking the work of a "congressional icon" in front of the committee's lawyers.

"It is no secret among any of us how highly Senator Mitchell is thought of, and yet we know that they did not do any due diligence on this man or his story," Hardin said. "And that is just one example of things that you or I would respectfully suggest this staff, if you were tasked with doing it, you would have looked into it before you went out—not you—but before people went out and ruined this man's name."

The rules of the committee's deposition provided for Democratic and Republican staffers to get equal time for questioning a witness, but now a congressman from San Diego and a defense lawyer from Houston had hijacked the proceedings. Safavian's question about McNamee's agenda hung in the air, the clock ticking. Clemens sat silently listening to Hardin discuss Jose Canseco's party.

"The problem with the Mitchell Report is," Hardin said, "is that they took, hook, line and sinker, the prosecutor's referral to him as the truth told, and they did nothing to check it out."

Safavian, apparently, had heard enough. She spoke up, telling Clemens directly that she was not asking him to speculate about McNamee's agenda, but rather to help her question McNamee.

But Hardin wasn't done talking for Clemens. He assured Safavian that Clemens wasn't holding back "some secret smoking gun" and that no one was going to "parachute in at the hearings" with any kind of dramatic explanation.

"As we have investigated this case, we have been shocked at things the Mitchell people haven't looked into," Hardin said. "And all Roger knows is what we're telling him, that we're finding something here, we're finding something there. And it blows his mind. It's not the man he thought he was."

The House Committee on Oversight and Government Reform, in the years leading up to Clemens's deposition, had investigated problems with food safety, nursing homes, the Postal Service, Abu Ghraib, elections, and the government's response to Hurricane Katrina. Among those issues, steroids in sports was a small though not totally inconsequential issue. But at several points on February 5, seven well-paid members of the committee's staff were asked to consider questions that in most contexts would seem so silly as to make the whole enterprise look trivial: The questions about Jose Canseco's summer barbecue might have been among them.

Early in the deposition, Clemens had said "I never was at that party." If that was true, then McNamee was a liar and the Mitchell Report was indeed flawed. If it wasn't true—if someone could prove that Clemens had been there, if there was a witness—then Clemens had committed perjury. So Jennifer Safavian asked more.

"How do you know that for a fact?" Safavian asked. "Can you explain to us how you know for a fact that you were not at Mr. Canseco's house, at a party that occurred in early June 1998?"

Clemens said he'd read about it in the Mitchell Report, and knew he wasn't at the party. He allowed his lawyers to look into it, and it was discovered that Clemens had records that he was not at the party—golf course receipts, to be exact.

"Do you know that there was a party while you all were away?" Safavian asked.

"I do," Clemens said. "I do. I do now."

"You don't recall Canseco having a party?"

Before Clemens could get confused about what he had recalled and when, Hardin jumped in again. There was no reason to "lay behind the log," he said.

"We did several things," Hardin said. "We go down and we send people out to talk to Canseco to find out. When he read that portion of the report, he goes, That's a lie. We think, Well, how do you know? He said, Roger wasn't at that party. We said, How do you know he wasn't at that party? Because that's the only party I ever gave at my home there for the team. Roger was supposed to come and he didn't come. And I heard later he was out playing golf."

"We then—and I say, Well, how can we show that?" Hardin said. "Because we know that Canseco in some corners, people have different views. Canseco's father says, I think that game the next day, I think it was talked about on TV."

Hardin explained that people from his firm had gone to Major League Baseball to examine the television broadcast archives of the game.

"And we find on the broadcast that two announcers are laughing about the fact that Canseco had this party for the team the day before at his pool, and Roger didn't come," Hardin said. "And the other announcer says, 'That's right, I saw him playing golf.'"

Hardin said that was when he went to Clemens's credit card records and saw that Clemens had played golf that day. Canseco's affidavit, which Hardin had collected two weeks earlier, said that he had been "disappointed" that Clemens did not attend the barbecue and that he, Canseco, "later learned that Clemens had a golfing commitment that day."

The way Hardin laid the story out, the golf alibi seemed independently verified. Hardin believed that this proved Clemens never attended the party and that Mitchell's team had not investigated the issue thoroughly.

"They never called Canseco when they have that information and say, 'Was Roger Clemens at your party?'" Hardin said. "If they had, they could have found out and started doing the same thing we did. So there's TV coverage, there's an audio, there's a video. Roger was never at that party. And the key thing to remember is that's where he's supposed to have begun to get stuff that he's later delivered. The whole house of cards falls."

Safavian wanted to know if Clemens ever spoke to Canseco about anabolic steroids. Clemens said there had been a few conversations, including one where he advised Canseco to "get off any of the hard stuff," and another where he claimed, "I think that stuff makes you just look good in the lobby."

Clemens said he would tease other players who were muscular, telling them it would make them "tight" and cause them to break down. He said he never talked to Canseco about "cycling" or "stacking" as Canseco had written in *Juiced*, and pointed out that Canseco had disavowed those comments too. Clemens said he had never heard these terms prior to the report, even though, he said, he shared a corner of the locker room with Jason Giambi. The only time there had been much conversation about steroids, Clemens said, was around the time of the previous congressional hearings, in 2005.

"I wanted to know whether or not Mr. McNamee ever injected you with anything else for the time period that you have known him besides the B_{12} and the lidocaine shot?" Safavian asked.

"Never," Clemens said.

In the second half of the deposition, Barnett asked another series of direct questions about Clemens and performance-enhancing drugs. The phrasing was unambiguous, giving Clemens little wiggle room in a perjury case if it was ever proven that he had used these drugs. In answering a series of questions, Clemens said he never took anabolic steroids, never possessed or saw them, never discussed them with any player nor with any person outside baseball, and didn't know any players who he knew were taking steroids.

"And did you know other persons, acquaintances, people you worked with, family members who you knew were taking anabolic steroids?" Barnett asked.

"I did not," Clemens said.

Barnett had a similar series of questions about human growth hormone. In answering him, Clemens said he had never used HGH, possessed or seen HGH, discussed taking it with another player, or discussed taking it with any person outside baseball. He had no personal knowledge, Clemens said, of players taking human growth hormone.

"And did you have personal knowledge of other persons, acquaintances, people you worked with, family members who were taking human growth hormone?" Barnett asked.

"I do not," Clemens said. (Although he would return to the story of Debbie's injections later in the deposition, he seemed to have forgotten about them here.)

"Amphetamines?" Barnett asked.

"I have not taken any amphetamines," Clemens said.

A minute and several questions later, Hardin jumped in: "Can I ask you, there is—he asked you about amphetamines," Hardin said. "There was one incident that you have mentioned that you never knew, wondered, that you might tell them about that."

Clemens launched into the first of several long stories he would tell in the course of the deposition that seemed designed to cast McNamee in the light of a nefarious predator, slipping unknown substances into Clemens's power shakes.

"Brian McNamee, when he trained me at my house, would get up and come into the main house. He stayed in a house there—again, Jennifer [Safavian] asked me earlier, McNamee, when that—when I didn't have family staying at that house he would, you know, I would allow him to stay there so he didn't have to pay hotel expenses, but I knew he would stay at a hotel also sometimes. When he would come into my house, he would—the daily routine of the five, six days, whatever it might be that he was there, he would make a protein shake for me. I didn't ever see—you know, he would bring the powder in and mix the powder. I would have the drink and it is ready for me to drink. Some were good, some were bad-tasting.

On one specific occasion, he—he had a vitamin package that had two or three vitamins in it. And it was what I know now and I will tell you that, but let me just stay on the subject here. The vitamins he would have open and put in a little like butter dish or something like that where I would come in and take it. He would be off maybe going to the gym to get the lights on to work, whatever. And on one specific occasion he gave me a white, it was a white small pill. And within an hour-and-a-half of taking that pill, I was—I don't know what it is like to drink 10 cups of coffee, but I was throwing my pen, and I could barely hang on to the ball. And I asked him what that was. And he told me it was similar to a Hydroxycut or a Thermacore. And I said from that point on—I said don't ever—you leave my vitamins in their packs. And I feel that it was some kind of—like amphetamine or something. It wasn't a vitamin, because it made me, my body feel like I have never felt before. I was edgy, I really couldn't—not that I couldn't hold the ball, but I was edgy."

Before anyone could react to this, Clemens launched into another story, this one centering on how McNamee had wanted a job at a rehabilitation institute at Memorial Hermann Hospital. The institute had been named in Clemens's honor, after he donated generously, and Clemens told the committee how proud he was of it. Clemens said that McNamee had grown embittered about not getting a job there. That could answer the question about McNamee's agenda, Clemens seemed to suggest—that, or writing a book. And there was always the possibility that all this was still about the vitamin company dispute.

"It is my belief that he is going to write a book about me, or whatever he has done to all these other players that I had no knowledge of before I have heard about the report, what is in it," Clemens said. "I can't state to it. It is my belief that he was the so-called mole. All this stuff is again coming back to me about this guy that again I shake my head at, that he was the mole inside the Yankees clubhouse, which again we are investigating ourselves."

Clemens went on to say that he suspected McNamee was in "cahoots" with a reporter and might have tax problems. When he was done talking, it was not the committee but his lawyers who responded.

"And I think a lot of this was going back to her question, what agenda," Hardin said.

After that, Barnett quickly picked up where his questions had left off.

"Prescription medications to enhance your performance, did you use prescription medications to enhance your performance?"

Clemens had promised in his *60 Minutes* interview to talk to the committee about having used the painkiller Vioxx. He said he threw 70 or 80 Vioxx pills into a trash can; McNamee, he added, had gone into his trash and retrieved them. (McNamee would later laugh at this accusation.)

"On Vioxx, who prescribed the Vioxx for you?" Barnett asked.

"I don't know," said Clemens. "You know, it came from the—I don't know. It came from the team."

The committee had a series of questions about Clemens's lack of cooperation with George Mitchell, and a related series of questions that drove at exactly when Clemens found out McNamee had fingered him as a user. Clemens had given varying accounts of when he heard the news, but the fact was he had received a call in Cabo on December 5 or 6 that had spurred memorable conversations with his friends there.

The committee knew that Mitchell had tried to reach Clemens through his agent in July 2007, just days after speaking to McNamee for the first time. But in his public statements, Clemens had said he was not aware of Mitchell's efforts to give him a chance to respond to the allegations. Now Clemens said he did not know he had been named as a user until early December, but he was confused about the precise dates.

Throughout this part of his deposition, Clemens appeared to contradict himself several times. Hardin, apparently sensing that there was a problem, interrupted repeatedly, only muddying the waters more. Barnett lost control of the deposition; if ever Clemens were prosecuted for perjury, he would probably have deniability on these issues; the confusion that reigned would forever give Clemens a plausible excuse that he didn't mean to lie.

"In the July time frame Mr. Hendricks never said to you, by the way, Senator Mitchell wants to talk with you, I don't know what it is about, but he wants to talk to you as part of his investigation?" Barnett asked.

"That is correct," Clemens said.

Mitchell had sent a letter to the Players Association requesting interviews with Clemens and others, and got a letter back from the union saying Clemens and others had respectfully declined the request for an interview.

"Did you know in October 2007 that Senator Mitchell had made another request?" Barnett asked.

"I did not," said Clemens.

Clemens had an explanation for his agents' dismissal of Mitchell; Clemens told the committee Hendricks had assumed it was about the discredited *Los Angeles Times* story, which claimed his name appeared in the Grimsley affidavit. Clemens said he had done enough to fight those allegations.

"We assumed, and I thought that the—it would have been September 2006, about the Grimsley or the *L.A. Times* report," Clemens said, rambling (the most telling word was probably the "we," suggesting Clemens might have known about Mitchell's request after all).

"They came out of nowhere and it brought grief, you know, for a year that I had to deny those, saying it wasn't true, and it wasn't true," Clemens said. "And I believe that's what Randy Hendricks assumed it was about also. If I would have known of what Brian McNamee was stating in the report, I would have been there in a heartbeat."

Instead, Clemens said, he first heard about McNamee's allegations when Randy Hendricks called him to tell him about McNamee's call to Jimmy Murray, after Hendricks had first heard the tape on December 5.

"And do you remember when you were told about that call?" Barnett asked.

"I think—I am going to say December—December—I would say December 6th or 7th," Clemens said. "I'm guessing on the dates."

"And who told you about the call and what were you told?" Barnett asked.

"Randy Hendricks told me about the call, and basically heard what McNamee had to say, and I was stunned," Clemens said. "And that was it."

For the next several minutes, Hardin and Clemens went back and forth about a series of dates—when Belk and Yarbrough visited McNamee (December 12), when Clemens first met Hardin at Randy Hendricks's house to hear the Murray tape (December 9). Shortly Barnett asked how Hendricks told Clemens: "Did he tell you in person? Did he tell you over the phone? Do you remember how that was communicated?"

"It may have been the same day," Clemens said. "It may have been Sunday, December 9th, the same day I met at his house. I heard the taped conversation with Jim Murray and Brian McNamee."

Suddenly Clemens's sense of the timeline had shifted drastically. Now Clemens was saying he had learned of the allegations only when he returned to the United States from Cabo.

"Mr. McNamee reaches out to Mr. Murray on the 5th," Barnett said. "And was it the 6th—the 5th, 6th, 7th, 8th, 9th, the best you can do when you heard about this?"

"That would have been a Wednesday," Hardin said (unhelpfully, if he were attempting to clarify the situation, and helpfully if he were trying to create confusion).

"Okay," Clemens said. "I don't know—McNamee—you are saying Brian McNamee reached out to Jim Murray when?"

"On the 5th, December 5th?" Barnett asked.

"Okay," Clemens said. "And that's when the—I heard—the first I heard of it, I heard a taped recording at Randy Hendricks' house; and I believe it was Sunday, December the 9th."

"And prior to that time you had no—you had no knowledge that you would be named in the Mitchell Report and that there would be—that Mr. McNamee was making allegations about steroid, human growth hormone use?" Barnett asked.

"That's correct," said Clemens.

Now Clemens had shifted the date of his first learning about McNamee's allegations forward several days. Barnett would come back to that, but first he would ask Clemens if he had ever been aware—prior to the Belk and Yarbrough interview—of the Starbucks conversation, years earlier, between Murray and McNamee.

"I wasn't," Clemens said.

Clemens said he was shocked to learn that McNamee had been co-operating with the government at the same time that he worked out with Clemens in Kentucky and when he'd borrowed his fishing equipment.

Barnett pointed out an apparent double standard that Clemens was applying; Clemens was angry that McNamee had not informed him of the trouble he was in, but he didn't seem to mind that the Hendricks agency had passed up numerous opportunities to warn him that the noose was tightening.

"You have expressed your anger in terms of Mr. McNamee not telling you," Barnett said. "With Mr. Hendricks not telling you about the July and the October calls, what is your reaction about that?"

"I think that he knew my feeling," Clemens said. "I think he knew my feeling on the—how upset I was about the L.A. Times report."

"In July 2007, Mr. Mitchell made a request to interview Mr. Clemens, and that was not communicated," Barnett said. "Mr. Hendricks knew about it, but he didn't communicate that to you. And in October 2007, Mr. Mitchell made a request to Mr. Hendricks; and it was not communicated to you. And I was asking for your reaction to the fact that that wasn't communicated to you. You have said, had it been communicated to you, you would have wanted to speak with Senator Mitchell."

"Without question," Clemens said. "Of course, I would have liked to have known. But, again, not knowing what they wanted to talk to us about, I am not associated with the steroids and everything that is going on. That is not part of my life or who I am."

Clemens was using plural pronouns now, suggesting that he might have known Mitchell was trying to reach him after all.

"And that is why I was upset about the *L.A. Times* report again," Clemens said. "That I knew that wasn't true, but everybody—again, I had to go through a year of hell with that. And I stated—I think you can look at my interviews on that matter. And from what Randy Hendricks tells me, that's what we thought the questioning was about, and we already knew that wasn't true, and I had already stated that I had nothing to do with that. I never worked out with Jason Grimsley or anything that—I had no idea about anything going on with him."

Hardin stepped in once again, and told Barnett that it was possible that not even Hendricks had heard about what Mitchell was looking for.

"Phil, in fairness to Mr. Hendricks, I am not sure—in fact, I know the record doesn't show one way or the other as to whether he got all of those letters from the union," Hardin said. "I think all we know is the union and the Mitchell group were having those communications. I don't know what letters were passed on by the union to Randy."

But Barnett wanted to get back to the discrepancy in Clemens's attitudes toward people who knew what McNamee was telling Mitchell and yet didn't tell him immediately.

"And the difference between December 5th—there is the call from Mr. McNamee to Mr. Murray," Barnett said. "You don't hear about it until December 9th. Were you concerned about that gap in time?"

"I think I was on—I think I came back from vacation is what happened, if I remember correctly," said Clemens. "I came back from vacation, and Randy said I need you at my house. I want you to listen to something."

"If I may," Hardin said. "He doesn't get back—he is remembering correctly. The reason that we did not meet with him until Sunday is he was on vacation until Saturday night."

On page 211 of Jose Canseco's book *Juiced*, the section where he talks about trainers assisting in steroid injections, he wrote that in major league clubhouses a B_{12} shot was a code word for steroids.

"It was so open, the trainers would jokingly call the steroid injections 'B_{12} shots,' and soon the players had picked up on that little code name, too," Canseco wrote. "You'd hear them saying it out loud in front of each other: 'I need to go in and get a B_{12} shot,' a player would say, and everyone would laugh."

Clemens used the occasion of his deposition to defend B_{12}. He said his mother had suggested he take it, and that he and his sisters were offended by the aspersions being cast on the vitamin. He said B_{12} was common in clubhouses, and that he would often take it after a game. He said that with the Yankees, three or four guys would get shots all at once.

"Create a visual scene for them, how shots are handled," Hardin said.

Clemens said that he would tell McNamee that he needed a B_{12} shot following a game, and that there were "four or five needles already lined up ready to go. And you get it in your shirt or you pull your jeans down, and they give you a B_{12} shot, and you are out the door."

Hardin asked Clemens if he had ever seen the injections loaded into their syringes.

"I have never seen them load a needle," Clemens said. "It was already predone or whatever you want to call it."

Barnett asked if McNamee had done the shots, since they had never quite determined that.

"Yeah," Clemens said.

"Did he use one of those needles that was lined up that was provided by the club to give you a B_{12} shot?" Barnett asked.

"I don't know where he got his needles from," Clemens said. "I have no idea."

When Safavian took over, she had even more B_{12} questions, and Clemens had even more vague answers. He said he'd learned sinister things about McNamee, like that his Ph.D. wasn't legitimate, or that he was a newspaper mole. But Clemens said he didn't know these things in the past. Safavian pointed out that Rafael Palmeiro believed he tested positive for steroids because of a tainted B_{12} shot. Did Clemens have concerns about tainted B_{12}? No, Clemens said.

"I had asked you during my first round whether or not you had had any discussions or conversations with Andy Pettitte about HGH," Safavian asked.

Clemens said he and Pettitte talked about how HGH worked generally, and what it could do for your quality of life, like helping you play golf into old age. But Clemens said he never told Pettitte that he used it.

"It never happened," Clemens said. "The conversation, again, in my gym would have been something to the effect, the story about the men playing golf, having quality of life, being able to play golf, the older men that I think I talked about earlier.

"Number one, I was shocked to find out that he used it," Clemens said. "Number two, Andy Pettitte and I were close enough that he would have come to me and stated that he was thinking about doing it, number one. Number two, when he did use it, now that I know he used it, he would have come to me and said that he is using it."

Clemens said that after the *L.A. Times* report surfaced, Pettitte came to him in the manager's office in Atlanta, and they sat on a couch. At the time, Clemens said, he had no idea Pettitte had used HGH. He couldn't remember if it was a TV show or an article they had been talking about but they had a meeting with the media coming up, to answer the allegations. Clemens remembered Pettitte saying, "What are you going to tell them?"

Clemens said, "I told him I was going out there to say the truth. And I—again, I think if you ask Andy, he will recall that story also."

Clemens said it all made sense to him, in light of Pettitte's confessions. "Andy looked like he had seen a ghost and was wringing his hands in front of me and says, 'What are you going to tell them?'" Clemens said. "And now it would make sense to me. And I went out there and told him, I told him exactly what the truth is, that I've never done any of this stuff, and I'm going to let them know."

Clemens said that when Randy Hendricks told him that Pettitte had admitted to using HGH, Clemens was shocked. "I said no freaking way that Andy Pettitte would have used HGH," Clemens recalled. "I've never told Andy Pettitte that I was using HGH. And if I did tell him that, he would have come to me again and asked me, because he would have thought that I was using it or that I had taken it after he had taken it, that he would have asked me about doing it. I'm convinced of it. It didn't happen. The conversation did not happen. There might have been something in general, again, about quality of life."

Clemens thought he might have discussed HGH only a few times, like around the 2005 hearings. He thought Pettitte wouldn't have used it for healing. "We don't know enough about it," Clemens said.

Safavian asked Clemens if he wanted to try again with his answer to the question about whether or not any member of his family, to his knowledge, had ever used HGH. Clemens indicated he hadn't fully understood the question, hadn't heard the part about "family."

"I thought we were asked about employees or something like that," he said. "I think it was asked to me in three or four—but I didn't catch 'family.' "

Safavian acknowledged that there had been a grouping, and asked Clemens again. Did he know of any family members using HGH. Clemens then embarked on a lengthy description of his wife's HGH use that implied McNamee had, once again, nefariously slipped something past Clemens.

"I do," Clemens said. "My wife received a shot of HGH from Brian McNamee at my house. I think it was in our master bedroom. The year, I'm going to say 2003 possibly. I believe there was an article, from what I understand, about HGH in the USA Today that came out a couple days earlier that week. I don't know if it was the only article my wife had read. And he gave her a shot of HGH. She tells me that it happened extremely quick. He was gone after it happened, literally gone. He went to the airport, I found out. I was not present at the time. I found out later that evening. And the reason I found out, because she was telling me that something was going on with her circulation, and this concerned me. The very next day, it wasn't as bad, but I don't know if it was her feeling bad about it, or, you know, I'm not discussing too deep of detail about it with her other than that at this point she's embarrassed, she feels part of a trap that McNamee has set. The same thing, I think, that night or the next— that night and the next day, I told McNamee—we had a pretty heated discussion about it, that I don't know enough about it, and that we don't know enough about it. I believe he described to Deb as he got on the back end conversation with my wife, and I don't know if there's other ladies present that were in my house, kitchen area, I don't know where. I'm just going by some of the details that my wife gave me. And that he heard it, and then within—I don't think it was that day, I think it was the next day that he was leaving that he had it."

"So—I'm sorry—he overheard a conversation?" interrupted Safavian.

"I think he heard the conversation and suggested it to—he had it there," continued Clemens. "Obviously he had it there. And if I can remember right, because he stayed there on—again, a few days in the off season, I went out to the—I have what they call a pool house out in the back where they would stay, different people would stay, including McNamee when he was in town. He left luggage. We would mail luggage. I am trying to find my FedEx receipts here. He would carry his luggage. And I went through his luggage, and the only thing that I found was workout gear that he'd left behind. I didn't find any drugs."

If the committee had questions about this speech, they didn't need to ask; Hardin was ready with the follow-up questions himself.

"I'm wondering, are you saying that you believe that McNamee heard your wife talking about the possible effects to other people and then suggested to her you would give her the shot?" Hardin asked.

"From what I understand from Deb, Debbie, my wife, is that there was some article, and they're all talking openly about youth or—about this article. And from what I understand, McNamee offered this up, the HGH that he had on the property."

Safavian: "So she did not speak—she did not go to him and ask him questions about HGH?"

"No," Clemens said.

"Let's make sure the record's clear," Hardin said. "Okay. You find out about it when, the night after she's taken the shot that day?"

"That night."

Hardin wanted to know when Clemens confronted McNamee about it. Clemens said the next day he called McNamee, who had flown home.

"She was still not feeling comfortable, and something about her circulation," Clemens said.

"And what was your reaction to what happened?" Hardin asked. "And what did you say to him?"

Clemens was contradicting himself already. Earlier in his deposition he had sworn not only that no family member had ever used HGH, but that he had never discussed HGH.

"I wasn't happy about it," said Clemens. "I said basically, you know, we don't know anything about this. He says it's legal. There's no laws against it. It's legal. And I remember, you know—I'm not going to talk for Deb, but I think that's what the conversation, the gist of it, was to make her feel okay about it."

"Did you ask him where he got it?" Safavian asked.

"I didn't," Clemens said. "I sure didn't. But my concern was that, you know, again, in looking at my FedEx bills and everything else, I wondered if he had something on my property. That's why I went through his luggage. And I mailed his luggage out two or three different occasions, which, again, I believe we have the bills on. We're pulling all that together too, right now."

Hardin asked his client why he had looked through McNamee's bags.

"I thought he had drugs on the property," Clemens said. "I told him that."

"Because you knew he had at least human growth hormone to give her a shot?" Hardin asked.

"Sure," Clemens said. "And to mail his luggage. But it was just workout gear. The other things I've told him is that he can't drink on my property. I didn't want him to drink on my property. The maids were—the two maids that work there on the property were upset about that. But that had nothing to do with the HGH, HGH and her situation. Deb would say that, you know, she's cried about it, and she's apologized to me about it, and she knew I had no knowledge of it. And—"

"So you were not home when this happened?" Safavian asked.

"I was not home," Clemens said.

Clemens was pretty certain that the HGH snafu with Debbie had taken place in the offseason between 2003 and 2004—before he came out of retirement and rejoined the Yankees. Hardin said that he had found a *USA Today* article from November of 2003, but didn't know if that was the article that Clemens said had inspired Debbie to try it. Hardin said Debbie had gotten concerned about that use only when the Mitchell Report came along.

"And then she's blaming herself for wondering why did he have it there?" Hardin said. "Why would he ever suggest that to her unless he had some other motive?"

Clemens said there might have been other women around the house when they had talked about this article, including, possibly, Debbie's mother, Jan Wilde. But Clemens believed that nobody else was present when the shot actually occurred—but he couldn't be sure. Clemens said Debbie said she got the shot in her side, in a love handle. He said he never mentioned it to Andy Pettitte. He said Debbie was embarrassed, distressed, and felt she had been "pulled into a trap." Clemens said he had talked to McNamee, concerned that Debbie was "having circulation problems."

At the end of his deposition, Clemens responded to the specific allegations about him in *Juiced*, the Canseco book that had gotten Congress involved in the steroids issue in the first place, three years earlier. Clemens addressed each of the allegations in the book (aside from his exceptional fidelity) and said that he had never talked to Canseco about steroids, or B_{12}, or stacking or cycling, or how hitters are so darn strong from steroids.

"My job got harder because I was getting older, and not from worrying about—I said that earlier. I mean, it's been my stance all along. I don't think they help you. I think steroids only hurts you. I think they make you tight. You wonder about the guys blowing out their tendons and so on and so forth.

"I'm on the same page as Senator Mitchell with all this," Clemens said, claiming he would like to do a national campaign, presumably against steroids, like the one he did for COPD, or Chronic Obstructive Pulmonary Disease, which had afflicted his mother. "If I was approached by Senator Mitchell to do a national campaign, I would be the first one in line."

Clemens seemed particularly troubled by the thought that anyone might question his accomplishments, or his talent, or especially his work ethic, that they might think it had all come out of a syringe.

"My workout routine, I didn't get my workout routine through a bottle or shortcuts. I took no shortcuts," he said. "I think if you ask anybody in my career, any players, you can ask any players about my work ethic and my determination, my will I got from my mother and my grandmother. Again, this is another reason why this is very upsetting to me.

"My workouts. In 1996, and a couple years before that when I was in the twilight of my career, I set the major league record, my own record, for 20 strikeouts in a game. If I were to come to you with a player that was washed up or in the twilight of his career or past his prime and said that I have a guy for you that has led the league in strikeouts, is in the top five in ERA, is in the top five or eight in innings pitched, I think every general manager would say, 'Bring him to me.' I also think that the Toronto Blue Jays wouldn't have made me the highest-paid pitcher in the game at that time, which is, again, the Boston media, the people that you will never swing, the people that I will never get my good name back from this situation. I don't know if this will ever change, because they look past the evidence. And another reason why I retained these two gentlemen to my left is because Brian McNamee is not going to write a book telling how he brought the best pitcher down and all his lies for $1 million so you can write off after he's sold his soul or name out. I am extremely disappointed, which I will once again tell publicly I am here, by that. I think me being here proves that. And I do want to say that I am more comfortable that I have people in the room here that I don't feel have already made up their minds, what I've been told this."

Clemens said he was for "any kind of testing," and reminded the committee investigators that he had put himself out there for the world to see when he participated in the World Baseball Classic and its jacked-up drug-testing program.

"I am totally for any kind of testing," he said. "I put myself out there for the world games, took pride in putting USA on my chest, who—another person I am disappointed in is our commissioner of baseball, who that, regardless, I understand I was asked by Senator Mitchell to come down and see him, but before you change somebody's life on statements that were made by a liar—I'm an easy person to find. I'm a public figure. I come to Washington a lot. I am not running off to hide."

"I think that I've—what I've done for baseball, that the commissioner would have found me so I could deny these allegations without ruining my good name."

Time was up.

Safavian: "That's all we have. Thank you very much."

Hardin: "I want to thank you all for you all's courtesy today. I think you have been very fair and very courteous."

Breuer: "Absolutely."

Safavian: "Thank you very much, Mr. Clemens. We really appreciate it."

On the evening of February 6, Penn Station's Amtrak and New Jersey Transit commuters were jostling for position, eyes trained on the massive black billboard in the center of the floor plan where train schedules are posted, the times, names, and numbers ascending and descending every few minutes on the flickering digital panels. The 6 P.M. Acela, Amtrak's speedy commuter, was moments from arriving in the station.

Off to the side of the concourse, Richard Emery, Earl Ward, and Debbie Greenberger—a young lawyer in Emery's firm—frantically collected their Acela tickets from an automated dispenser, ran down an escalator to track 14 East, and boarded a train bound for Washington, D.C. They were on their way to Washington for Brian McNamee's deposition before Congress. In just 15 hours their client would walk down the corridors of the Rayburn Building, the final witness to be deposed by the House Committee on Oversight and Government Reform.

An hour into the ride south, Emery suppressed a grin, and glanced down at his briefcase. Inside were copies of two photographs—one of a crumpled Miller Lite can on its side at the top of the frame, surrounded by bloodied gauze, a syringe wrapper, and the tip of a used needle, the other of five clear steroid ampules and three dark yellow ampules, sealed needles, and a plastic bag with a piece of tape that read "Bag #2." It was the smoking gun that McNamee's lawyers considered damning evidence against Clemens, and they had successfully kept the secret until now, with Clemens locked in to his denials.

By the time Ward, Emery, and Greenberger were settled into their train seats that Wednesday afternoon, the New York *Daily News* had already posted an explosive story on its Web site earlier that day that said that Emery and Ward would present the evidence to committee members in Washington during McNamee's deposition on Thursday. The secret was out, and throughout the train ride, the lawyers' cell phones were buzzing incessantly. Ward finally attached his adapter and plugged the phone into a nearby outlet.

"This will really change the course of things, I think," Emery said.

Emery and Ward were also carrying dozens of white envelopes in their briefcases, each envelope containing copies of the two color photographs. But as much as McNamee's team seemed poised to deliver a haymaker, Clemens and his attorneys were set to unload what they hoped would be a smashmouth strategy of their own.

As Brian McNamee turned the corner in the marble hallways of the Rayburn House Office Building amid a media mob, the Breezy Point native looked more like an associate for a law firm than a witness preparing for a congressional appearance. Dressed smartly in a dark suit, white shirt, and flowery tie, with professorial glasses perched on his nose, McNamee appeared nervous, though he managed one faint smile as reporters lobbed questions and flashes popped. There was sweat on his broad forehead, perhaps a result of angst and the weight of the bulky briefcase he had slung over his left shoulder. He entered Rayburn 2154 and was asked if he wanted to make any statements prior to the deposition, but the trainer kept it simple: "I'm just happy to be here and help with whatever you need." With him at the table were Emery, Ward, Greenberger, and McNamee's newest pro bono advocate, Mark Paoletta.

At that moment, one floor above, Clemens was strolling out of Rayburn 2238, the office of Massachusetts Democrat John Tierney, a member of the Oversight Committee. "I'm just getting a chance to visit. It's been great," Clemens said in the marble corridor. He wore a dark blue pullover and a sand-colored collarless shirt and clutched a white binder to his side. His hair was cut in a marine buzz, a far different look than his gel-spiked style at the Houston press conference.

Flanked by Hardin, Breuer, and PR man Joe Householder, Clemens visited nearly a dozen committee members, including Chairman Wax-man and the ranking Republican, Tom Davis. It was an extraordinary display of public relations muscle. On the surface, it certainly looked as if Clemens was receiving special treatment from the politicians who were supposed to be seeking the truth. Elijah Cummings, the Maryland Democrat who had hammered Mark McGwire during the 2005 hearing for McGwire's silence, spoke to reporters following his meet-and-greet with the Rocket.

"I wanted to make sure that when all the dust settles, that he fully understood that baseball players—whether they want to be or not—are role models and that children are looking at them," Cummings said. "I told him it's not about anybody showboating, it's about trying to make sure the kids don't have the impression that they have to cheat, that they have to violate baseball rules and violate the law to be successful. I think sometimes we lose sight of that."

It made for one of the more bizarre spectacles in the halls of Congress, the seven-time Cy Young winner emerging from the legislators' offices, mostly stone-faced and unreadable but still playing the role of the superstar baseball player. A few visitors touring the offices of their lawmakers were startled to see the famous pitcher among them, and Clemens was happy to stop and sign baseballs and other items before ducking behind another wooden door. He did the same for several congressional staffers.

As Clemens made his rounds, McNamee sweated through his interview, and his lawyers sweated through it with him.

"Is the information in the Mitchell Report that you just read regarding your providing steroids and HGH to certain players accurate?" Michael Gordon, the Democratic senior investigative counsel, asked McNamee near the outset of the deposition.

"It's accurate, but it's not as accurate as far as the amounts to a degree," said McNamee. "Like the amount of injections I believe were more, as far as my memory at the time, and then as this got—you know I remembered more. But I would say everything is accurate other than probably it was more times."

"So what's written is accurate, but it omits additional instances in which you provided these substances?" asked Gordon.

"Yes," said McNamee.

McNamee then spoke in detail about the elevated number of injections he had given Clemens, about how in 2000, for example, the number of injections of Sustanon-250 or Deca-Durabolin was "more like six to 10 times," not the four to six McNamee told Mitchell. McNamee also explained to the committee the intricacies of growth hormone injections, how they were administered in multiple treatments. Those numbers too were higher than the figures McNamee had given Mitchell.

The committee brought up the Canseco party, and McNamee dutifully told them what he remembered from the event nearly a decade earlier. Clemens, McNamee told the investigators, was definitely present at Canseco's house for that party.

"I don't know if he was golfing. He might have showed up a little bit later, but no, he was there the whole time for the most part," said McNamee. "He was in the house." McNamee talked about the nanny, Lily Strain, how she was definitely there too, looking after what McNamee remembered to be two of the K boys. That bit of information would spark a mad frenzy over the next few days, with the committee scrambling to find Strain and either interview or depose her.

He described the bizarre scene of Debbie Clemens and Jessica Canseco comparing their breast augmentation. "I mean, they talked—no disrespect," McNamee told the committee investigators, "but they talked about how great Jose's wife's augmentation job was to Debbie and showed her. And then Debbie showed her her augmentation job."

McNamee's conflicting loyalties were laid out in the open, how he had lied in the past about certain things only to protect the people he was close to or for whom he worked, including Clemens, and how that meshed with the "gut feeling" he'd had about keeping the waste from the injections all those years.

"I kept them—well, because throughout my time with Roger Clemens, it was—there was always somewhat in the back of my mind I distrusted him to a degree, and my gut feeling and my—the fact that I was an ex-cop, I just felt—and I think there were like bits and pieces coming out in the paper," McNamee said. "I just felt that if I was going down, I wasn't going to go down alone because I never felt good about this."

The hours dragged on, McNamee describing in excruciating detail the drug injections in Clemens's New York City apartment, Clemens's connection to Radomski through McNamee, McNamee's resolute certainty he never gave any injections to Clemens after 2001. McNamee described the abscess Clemens developed "on his left butt cheek" that occurred after Clemens received a hasty Winstrol shot. McNamee gave a blow-by-blow account of the growth hormone injection of Debbie Clemens, at which, he said, Roger was definitely present.

The committee staffers were civil in their questioning, though toward the end of the deposition Phil Schiliro asked point-blank: "So if you put yourself in our place, why should we think you're telling the truth?"

"You don't have to think I'm telling the truth, because I am," said McNamee, sounding weary. "I mean, that's all I got to do. I mean, it's up to your interpretation. And if you don't believe me, I can't do anything about it."

"But you can understand how difficult it is when we have such a different story from Mr. Clemens. He's saying absolutely none of this ever happened," said Schiliro.

"I think it's extremely difficult, but if you look at my past record, you look at the fact that I've only lied about things to protect other people, that's a track record," replied McNamee.

"I mean, I'm sure you can understand how confusing this is when we have two people saying things that are just so completely opposite?" said Schiliro.

"Sometimes you just got to go with your gut," said McNamee.

This back-and-forth between McNamee and Schiliro concerned Ward and Emery. Ward felt his client was rambling on throughout the deposition, while Emery was stressed about McNamee's vacillating over the number of injections he supposedly administered to Clemens and others. They were worried McNamee was showing himself to be a poor witness.

Schiliro asked McNamee what he thought his son, Brian Jr., would take out of the entire experience the elder McNamee was confronting. "I guess just to be a man and, you know, be a human being and try not to make mistakes. But if you do the wrong thing, tell the truth," said McNamee.

"At one point, we were like, 'Is there any way we can postpone this?' " Ward said later. "We just thought he wasn't going to make a good witness before a national audience." But there would be no postponement. McNamee would have to get ready somehow, some way.

McNamee's team was the first to hold a press conference that afternoon. As reporters got wind that the deposition was ending, the horde broke away from the Clemens Watch and crowded into 2154. As the deposition ended, the McNamee team moved out to face the crowds and share the photos. Schiliro told McNamee to "just keep walking" and Paoletta ushered McNamee out of the building to a cab on Independence Avenue, while the media mobbed Emery and Ward, who were carrying their little stack of photographs.

When Paoletta returned and rejoined Emery and Ward, the lawyers were gleefully handing out the photos to the media. Emery was quick to point out that there was a very rational reason why McNamee would have retained medical waste for nearly a decade.

"He is a New York City cop, who thinks in terms of evidence," Emery said. "He had a sense that Roger was not trustworthy and would betray him ultimately. He said about himself that if he was going to get thrown under the bus by Roger, he was going to take Roger with him." ·

Ward challenged Clemens to submit a DNA sample to the government if he and his lawyers were certain the evidence submitted by McNamee was not legitimate. Then he unleashed the sound bite of the day.

"Roger Clemens has put himself in a position where his legacy as the greatest pitcher in baseball will depend less on his ERA and more on his DNA," said Ward.

A half-hour after Emery and Ward ended their press conference, the media mob hustled out of 2154, rushed down the hall to the right, and set up around a cordoned-off area near one of the exits. A short distance down the corridor, leaning against a wall near the X-ray machines and metal detectors, was Paoletta. He was an inconspicuous listener, tuned in to Hardin and Breuer about to unleash their ire on McNamee. Paoletta would later say that he thought Clemens's team had made a mistake with its full-court press to meet with committee members before the hearing.

"I think the visits to the members blew up in their face," said Paoletta. "It became too much of a spectacle. It took on this whistle-stop tour that I thought was totally inappropriate for this setting. I thought our time was best spent getting ready, in this situation."

The Clemens press conference started innocently enough, with Texas Republican Ted Poe delivering opening remarks. Hardin and Breuer hoped Poe would put a positive light on their client, and Poe didn't disappoint, gushing about Clemens. The Rocket then took his spot in front of the microphone, calling it a "great day," but taking no questions. It was probably no coincidence that Clemens was not allowed to go head-to-head with reporters as he had done in Houston a month earlier.

"Got a lot of walking in and learned a lot about the bowels of the buildings I was in and out of," Clemens said. "We had a lot of great meetings and I look forward to Wednesday of next week."

And with that, Clemens stepped aside, letting Breuer and Hardin go on the attack. Breuer called McNamee's photographs "a cheap publicity stunt," and labeled McNamee a "sad, tragic, obsessed man."

It was now Hardin's moment. "I can tell you now that in my view, you're about to see the second edition of the Duke case," said Hardin, referring to the Duke University lacrosse scandal that had unfolded in 2006 and 2007. Oddly enough, Hardin must have forgotten or not known that Emery was an attorney for one of the Duke lacrosse players—Reade Seligmann—who had been originally charged with sexual assault. "I warn you all now—five, six, seven months from now, any of you who have jumped on this bandwagon about Roger taking steroids and assumed any-thing Brian McNamee has to say about Roger is true will be embarrassed. This is a fabricated story. This man has a total history of lying."

When pressed about whether Clemens would offer a DNA sample, Hardin took another chance to dismiss McNamee, whom Hardin called a "troubled, not well man."

"Any time federal authorities make a request, we'll be glad to provide them with whatever they want. But they're going to have to come to us," said Hardin. "It's not going to be McNamee and them, out here with a bunch of pictures of waste."

Reporters hadn't been too successful eliciting comments from Clemens the previous day, which may have been why the group that gathered out-side Representative William Lacy Clay Jr.'s office in the Cannon House Office Building the morning of February 8 was significantly smaller. Or maybe some reporters were simply too exhausted to take on another day of marathon cardio training—scurrying between the Rayburn and Cannon buildings—as Clemens forged ahead with his meet-and-greet sessions with members of the committee.

There was a poster with the current national debt—"$9,226,000,000,000, Your share: $30,000"—displayed across from Clay's entrance. The gaggle of reporters checked BlackBerry messages or phoned their editors or spouses, the minutes ticking away. At one point, Clemens, who was dressed in a burnt orange button-down shirt (the Uni-versity of Texas's color) and dark jacket, emerged from the Missouri Democrat's foyer with Householder, and reporters scrambled to follow him. Alas, the Rocket was only taking a bathroom break. Householder sti-fled a laugh when reporters, in unison, halted their frantic movements and settled back into a stupor. No one was desperate enough to try to sneak an exclusive quote while Clemens was stationed at the urinal.

A half-hour later, there was another stir, and this time congressional staffers started spilling out from adjacent offices clutching any memento that had space for an autograph. Clemens had already kick-started a maelstrom of negative press with the autograph sessions on Thursday, a gesture that would have come dangerously close to violating lobbying rules had committee members been the recipients of Clemens's valuable signature. Householder never confirmed that Clemens had signed for any of the nearly two dozen committee members he visited over the two-day blitz.

While Clemens signed for two female staffers near Clay's office, using a three-ring black binder he was carrying as his writing surface, Rusty Hardin beamed, satisfied that the handshakes and chitchat with powerful lawmakers were going to do nothing but bolster Clemens's position as he prepared for the upcoming face-off with McNamee the following week.

"It's been a tremendously positive experience, both for Roger and us," said Hardin. "I think all of us are impressed by how receptive they've been to listening to him. They've all been very gracious. They all come from such different backgrounds. I know Roger would say, 'Well, this has been a fun experience.' "

By Friday afternoon, Clemens was still trudging from one office to the next. He was shadowed by Hardin and Breuer, Householder always a step away, glued to his cell phone. When they reached the office of Edolphus Towns, the 13-term Democratic congressman who represented the 10th District of New York and who would succeed Waxman as chairman of the Oversight Committee in December of that year, Towns flicked a curve-ball at the end of his meeting with the pitcher: He invited the media into the inner sanctum. It was as if the reporters had won the congressional sweepstakes. No other committee member had even pretended to want to entertain the media posse, but now a cluster of reporters shoved its way into the spacious office around 2 P.M., where Clemens lingered long enough for a couple of photo opportunities with Towns's staffers. Denise Mixon, Towns's deputy chief of staff, could not contain her excitement, posing with Clemens as the big Texan wrapped his arm around her.

When the commotion finally cooled, Clemens leaving for his next appointment, Towns graciously agreed to talk with three reporters about his time spent with Clemens. The Brooklyn congressman made no secret of what he thought of McNamee and the trainer's storage of waste.

"I mean, think about this—this guy has been walking around with this stuff for seven years. Doesn't that seem a little strange? For seven years, you hold on to it? That's longer than Monica Lewinsky kept it," said Towns, cracking a joke about the former White House intern and Bill Clinton paramour who had retained her infamous blue Gap dress with President Clinton's semen stains.

Towns said he had asked Clemens and his attorneys about McNamee's credibility and that the Clemens camp had labeled McNamee "money hungry" and someone with a sordid past. Hardin and Breuer had also rehashed the 2001 pool incident, just for good measure. Towns clarified why Clemens had not responded to George Mitchell's request to meet.

"He didn't feel he needed to address it," Towns said of Clemens, because the pitcher had explained to Towns that he thought the Mitchell invitation was about the allegations that pertained to the 2006 *L.A. Times* story. Towns said Clemens told him he didn't know that McNamee was going to make claims about injecting Clemens with steroids and growth hormone in the Mitchell Report.

As the meeting drew to a close, Towns laughed off any such nonsense as himself or his fellow committee members accepting an autograph from Clemens.

"None of that. No autographs in here," Towns said. "And I think we have some big baseball fans among us."

But Towns struck a serious tone about the upcoming hearing, suggesting that February 13 was too soon to have these two men testify. With all the deluge of information that had become public in the last few days, Towns thought the committee needed more time to digest everything. And he speculated that there would be additional hearings after February 13. But if Towns and committee members thought the waste photos were the last McNamee bombshell to come before the hearing, they were in for a surprise.

Clemens's last meeting of the afternoon was with Paul Kanjorski, a Pennsylvania Democrat whose Rayburn office was on the opposite end of a hallway from Waxman's staff offices. As Clemens was safely tucked inside Kanjorski's office, a *Daily News* reporter was getting details of some explosive information from his colleagues in New York—that McNamee had revealed in his deposition that he had injected Debbie Clemens with HGH in 2003, the year she appeared in the *Sports Illustrated* swimsuit issue.

Within moments, the *Daily News* story hit the Internet. By the time Clemens emerged from Kanjorski's office, at about 5 P.M., the media presence had swelled considerably. Television cameras zeroed in on Clemens as Householder and security helped carve a path to the elevators. Hardin and Breuer inadvertently made a right turn out of Kanjorski's office, instead of heading straight down the hallway to Waxman's staff office, where they had a final appointment. Hardin was bombarded with questions about the *Daily News* story—did he have a comment?—but he and Breuer tried to shoo away the questions as best they could.

"We can talk after our meeting," said Breuer. The two attorneys were so busy absorbing the latest news and the din around them that they did not realize they were walking toward a dead end. In a small moment of comic relief, the two well-dressed men came to an abrupt halt at an exit door, reporters nearly toppling over them. Hardin and Breuer turned around and made their way back down the corridor, as questions continued to fly, and reporters jockeyed for position, a rugby scrum in full motion, arms extended, recording devices stuck in Hardin's and Breuer's faces in an attempt to catch any nugget of a quote.

Breuer did not disappoint. "Did Roger get the Cy Young because his wife took the HGH?" he asked. In one ill-timed comment, he had seemingly confirmed that Debbie Clemens had indeed been given HGH. Finally, the lawyers arrived at 2157. Hardin wheeled around, understanding he would have to say something to quiet the masses.

"First he throws out waste and then he wants to talk about this," Hardin said. "I tell you what, guys, this guy never ceases to amaze me."

Four reporters waited in the hallway outside 2157 while Hardin and Breuer finished their final appointment. The rest of the floor was eerily quiet, most everyone else having left for the weekend. A custodian appeared. Householder emerged first, followed by Patrick Dorton and then Hardin and Breuer. It was already past 6 P.M. Hardin looked like he'd been in the ring with Mike Tyson. His beaming smile from the morning was long gone. His shoulders drooped. Even his famous hair was mussed. Reluctantly, he stopped and addressed the small group.

Asked what he thought of the report, Hardin took a breath. Dorton broke in before Hardin's answer and clarified one point—"To be clear, the *Daily News* report said that McNamee did the injections at Roger's direction, right?"

Dorton was told that was accurate. Hardin's face turned purple. (Three days earlier, Clemens had testified that he wasn't present for Debbie's injections.)

"That it was at Roger's direction? Let me repeat one more time—this guy is a colossal liar. And he has absolutely no shame. And I'll tell you also, any kind of specifics about any of those types of things, we'll address with you Monday. But this man is a colossal liar," said Hardin. He asked where the information was coming from, who the source was. Told it was a confidential source, Hardin snapped.

"You give me a name of somebody who says it," said Hardin. "I'm not addressing what he said in his deposition, 'cause I don't know what he said in his deposition. So let's make sure we're clear. I'm not addressing one way or the other about what he said in his deposition."

Hardin wasn't through.

"What I am addressing is the fact that this man has chosen to put it out there. When you say your sources, is the *New York Times* or somebody saying the source is Ward, his lawyer? Are y'all saying it's a confidential source? Because the committee's gonna get upset about that, because that would lead to the implication that they had something to do with it. Are you calling it a confidential source?" barked Hardin. "I don't respond to unnamed sources. You want to talk to me about somebody that says something, I know who they are, so I can figure it out. But I am not going to have us start responding to unnamed sources."

He couldn't resist one more barb. After all the meetings and conversations, Hardin still had a little fuel in the tank for another verbal blast.

"But I will tell you—to say that Roger directed that kind of thing is a colossal lie. And that's all I will say about that," Hardin said. Had he talked to Clemens about the story, he was asked.

"About what? I don't need to talk to Roger about that. I'm gonna tell you—that's a colossal lie." He was done. With his entourage in step, Hardin turned and marched to the exit to his left.

Hardin had dismissed the photos of the waste from the medical injections. He had dismissed the story of Debbie's being given an HGH injection by McNamee. But Hardin could hardly flush the fact that on February 8, Andy Pettitte and his wife, Laura, signed notarized affidavits for the committee that would excuse them from hearings and would further expose Clemens's shaky defense. The afffadavits clarifed several points of Pettitte's deposition.

In Pettitte's two-page affidavit, he outlined a conversation that he had had with Clemens "in 1999 or 2000 . . . in which Roger told me that he had taken human growth hormone ('HGH')," Pettitte testified. "This conversation occurred at his gym in Memorial, Texas." Pettitte stated that he had told his wife about the conversation with Clemens "soon after it happened," and that he had also spoken to McNamee about the same conversation. McNamee, according to Pettitte's affidavit, "became angry."

When the Astros were nearing the end of spring training in 2005, Pettitte approached Clemens about the 1999 or 2000 conversation and inquired what Clemens would do if reporters asked him if he ever used performance-enhancing drugs. "When he asked what I meant, I reminded him that he had told me that he used HGH," Pettitte testified in the affidavit. "Roger responded by telling me that I must have misunderstood him; he claimed that he told me that it was his wife, Debbie, who used the HGH."

Pettitte told his wife about the 2005 conversation with Clemens as well. Laura Pettitte's affidavit said as much, the entire testimony filling one page only. In three bullet points, Laura Pettitte corroborated everything her husband had said about conversations with Clemens in 1999 or 2000 and again in 2005, right up to Clemens saying it was Debbie, not he, who had used HGH.

Both Andy and Laura Pettitte signed their documents "under the penalty of perjury that the foregoing is true and correct."

While Hardin's investigators were former Houston homicide detectives, Ward and Harvey had at their disposal William Callahan, a former federal prosecutor and New York state trooper who had put himself through law school working for Joseph McCarthy's infamous henchman Roy Cohn. Callahan now ran a Manhattan-based investigations firm called UNITEL, which was stacked with former feds.

Harvey and Ward had turned to Callahan years earlier, when they were representing the actor Harvey Keitel in a bitter child-custody dispute with his ex-girlfriend, the actress Lorraine Bracco. That feud had exploded when Keitel grew distressed that their child was in contact with Bracco's new boyfriend, the actor Edward James Olmos, who had been accused of abuse. Callahan had done crucial intelligence work on Keitel's behalf, and his efficiency had impressed Ward—who might otherwise have been turned off by the photo of Callahan with former president Richard Nixon that Callahan kept on the wall of his office.

In the days leading up to the congressional hearings Callahan again proved indispensable to Harvey and Ward, this time refereeing a squabble that broke out between the two lawyers on Saturday, February 9, just four days before their client was due to appear before Congress. In the previous week, the tension between the lawyers had escalated; Harvey accused

Ward of being a press whore and unnecessarily going after Clemens—the
DNA/ERA quote, for example—while Ward countered that Harvey was
conflicted by his previous social ties to Clemens. "You're worrying more
about your friend Roger than McNamee," Ward had said.

The two friends had disagreed about how to handle the congressional
probe too. Harvey, incensed by the mere fact of the committee's probe,
strongly urged McNamee to "go after" the politicians at the hearings,
while Ward was urging deference, telling McNamee to roll with the
punches. McNamee was caught in the middle—he considered Harvey
infallible but had grown close to Ward too.

"We need to make peace," McNamee told Ward. "I need both you
guys. Isn't there anyone who can get you guys on the same page?"

Ward, exhausted from working round the clock on McNamee's case
and others, smiled for the first time in a week. "I'll call my Irish priest,"
said Ward, using the humorous handle that Harvey had applied to Callahan during the Keitel-Bracco war. Now Ward called up Callahan and
asked the man to make some peace. Later that day, Harvey picked up the
phone to hear Callahan's voice on the other end of the line. "Tom, it's
Bill," Callahan said. "I have Earl on the phone with us. You're wrong. In
fact, not only are you wrong, you're dead wrong." Callahan went on to
explain to Harvey why he needed to chill out and let Ward lead the case
that Harvey had, after all, dumped on him. Ward was always amazed at
the deference Harvey showed Callahan and was waiting anxiously to see
what the effect of the call would have when Harvey blurted out, "Screw
this; I'm converting to Judaism and getting a rabbi." The group burst into
laughter, but the problem was solved.

Brian McNamee's memory was pretty good, and one of the things he
remembered was sitting by the pool eating a sandwich watching a woman
in a peach bikini (with green in it) and board shorts, chasing after one of
Roger Clemens's kids at the barbecue at Jose Canseco's house. He asked
around and found out she was the nanny for Clemens's kids. "You can get
her," McNamee told Congress during his deposition. "If you want to talk
to her, her name was Lily," McNamee said. "They left on bad terms. She
worked for him for 14 years." Congress couldn't resist. Whether or not
Clemens had attended the barbecue—where he supposedly met with a
guy about steroids—had become one of the most radical discrepancies
between McNamee's sworn statements and those of Clemens.

And so the committee investigators contacted Clemens's lawyers on

Friday, February 8, to ask for the nanny's name and contact information, and continued to make similar requests throughout the weekend. It seemed a simple and straightforward appeal. But one day passed, and then another, and Hardin still had failed to produce the requested information.

The woman who'd been the nanny for the Clemens children, Lily Strain, had grown close with the Clemens family during the years she worked for the pitcher and his wife. She had traveled with the clan and had been there when the boys had taken their first steps and learned to ride bikes. She loved them as if they were her own family. Strain had left the job in 2001—not on bad terms, she said, but to spend more time with her children and grandchildren. It wasn't easy to leave the job; it paid well and she found it difficult to be involved in the boys' lives on a part-time basis. Strain decided it would be best if she made a clean break. Debbie had sent flowers when Strain's mother died, and the occasional card or note. Strain appreciated the gestures, but it was easier to keep her distance.

Strain was surprised to get a phone call that Sunday from Roberto, a man she remembered from the years she'd worked for Roger and Debbie. Roberto was an employee of the Clemens family, and he told her that Clemens had an urgent matter to discuss with her. She came to the family's suburban Houston compound that afternoon. It was great to see Roger and Debbie, and to hug the kids she had helped raise. Debbie Clemens's mother, Jan Wilde, was at the house, and so was Debbie's brother, Craig Godfrey. She had missed these people, and it was great to catch up after all those years. Clemens seemed happy to see Strain too, but he had more pressing matters on his mind. He told her that Congress was looking into the allegations about him in the Mitchell Report and that investigators would contact her about a party at Jose Canseco's home. The party, he told her, was in June 1998, right before she went to a luxury resort called the Cheeca Lodge with Deb, Craig, and the boys. Did she remember the trip to the Cheeca Lodge? Strain remembered the trip. She also remembered spending time at the Cansecos' place. She remembered tagging along as Canseco gave Clemens and his family a tour of the home—who would forget a spread like that? She remembered staying at the home with Debbie, Craig, and the kids that evening, but she didn't remember a party.

"While I was there, I know that it wasn't a party, it was just the kids and I and Greg [Craig Godfrey], and we were all in the pool," Strain would later say. "I would have remembered the party." There were varying accounts of who was at the party from just about everyone who attended, including those of McNamee, Clemens, Jose and Jessica Canseco; Jose's old friend and former coach, Glenn Dunn; and several Blue Jays players. McNamee remembered that Roger showed up with Debbie after having played golf that morning, Debbie still in her golf clothes. She had been in a foursome at Weston Hills Country Club that included her husband, her brother Craig, and Clemens's friend, James Clodfelter, who was the member at the club and had hosted the group. They had teed off at 8:58 A.M. sharp. McNamee testified about Debbie and Jessica Canseco comparing their breast jobs. He remembered Clemens and Canseco huddled with a "short guy" who looked like a "muscle guy."

Clemens remembered one thing for sure: He wasn't at any party. He may have stopped by the house after he played golf but he didn't go to a party. "I wasn't at this party that he had. I could have gone by there after a golf outing. But I was not at this party," he had testified.

Jose Canseco said Clemens was not at the party. His wife, Jessica, couldn't remember. Dunn remembered the barbecue quite vividly and seemed to make the same distinction as Clemens about Clemens's having stopped by the house but not during the party, which lasted about two hours, he said, beginning at about noon. Dunn said the Blue Jays arrived in the team bus and specifically recalled that Clemens was not there. He said, "Roger was not at the barbecue." He remembered Canseco complained during the function that "Roger was playing golf" and that Clemens came to Canseco's house after golf, but was there only briefly. According to Dunn, by the time Clemens arrived at Canseco's, the team function had ended and the bus carrying the Blue Jays players had already departed for the stadium. Dunn said he spoke with Clemens before Clemens left with Canseco for the stadium. He remembered that Clemens arranged to "have me take his two boys to the game . . . Jose drove Roger to the ballpark . . . I followed in a separate car with my son and Roger's two boys." Given all these conflicting stories, the committee hoped Strain would be an independent, impartial witness. But they were disappointed.

During her visit at Clemens's house, her former employer reminded Strain that the reason she didn't remember the party was because Clemens was not there—he had been playing golf. That may have been true; she knew Clemens played golf whenever he got the chance. But that was none of her business. She was paid to watch the kids, not monitor his schedule. Clemens again told Strain that the congressional investigators would contact her soon. "Tell the truth," he urged her. "Don't be afraid."

By late afternoon that Sunday, the Oversight and Government Reform

Committee investigators had become frustrated and more than a little suspicious. Hardin and Breuer continued to drag their feet in providing the nanny's contact information, and at 5 P.M., a staff member made yet another request for the name and phone number. This time, he asked the lawyers to refrain from speaking to the nanny until the committee had interviewed her. By then, Jim Yarbrough, the investigator from Hardin's office, had already called Strain, not long after she met with Clemens. He also asked Strain about the 1998 visit to the Canseco house, and he urged her to tell the truth when Congress called. Strain was happy to help. "I'm willing to do whatever I can to help, because he treated everybody—he treats everybody like family," Strain said about Clemens. "and that's why if there's anything that I can do to help, I will."

Hardin and Breuer finally provided Strain's name to the committee on Monday, February 11, three infuriating days after the investigators requested the contact information. The committee conducted a telephone interview with Strain the next day in which she said, among other things, that she doubted she would be wearing a bikini—that wasn't her style. Waxman was not happy when he learned that Clemens and Yarbrough had gotten to her first.

Hardin was already on Waxman's bad side. On Sunday, *The New York Times* had quoted Hardin taking shots at BALCO investigator Jeff Novitzky in a story that predicted Novitzky would attend the looming hearing. To Hardin, that was proof that the agent was involved in some kind of conspiracy to railroad Clemens.

"You know what? He does not have a sacred mission from God to mess up everybody's life," Hardin said of Novitzky, and then added: "I can tell you this. If he ever messes with Roger, Roger will eat his lunch."

Waxman immediately fired off a letter that called out Hardin for his tough-guy talk. "Under one interpretation it can be seen as an attempt to intimidate a federal law-enforcement official in the performance of his official duties," Waxman wrote, asking Hardin to clarify the statement. "Given your long service as both a prosecutor and a private attorney, I trust you did not intend your comments to be a signal that there could be adverse repercussions to a federal official."

Waxman's rebuke left the usually blustery Hardin chastened. "I lost my cool," he admitted. "It's not a very judicious statement. This is the frustration of what these guys are doing."

With the hearing just days away, Hardin knew his team was losing this battle on several fronts. He predicted that Clemens would wind up as the target of a federal investigation, just as Miguel Tejada had.

The phone number of the nanny wasn't the only piece of information that the committee had trouble extracting from the Clemens legal team. As of Sunday, February 10, the committee had been unable to persuade Hardin and Breuer to share the MRI results, and was considering using a subpoena to get them.

The MRI report had been referenced in Clemens's 1998 medical records from the Blue Jays (the same records that dealt with the palpable mass on Clemens's ass). But at the time of Clemens's deposition on February 5, the committee hadn't seen it. "There is one outstanding medical record regarding the abscess, which is the MRI report, which we would like to get," Barnett said during the deposition.

"We got that presented yesterday," Breuer had answered. "Yesterday evening."

Now nearly a week had passed, and the Clemens team was still hoarding the document, just as they had withheld the nanny's name and number. The hearing was approaching fast, and the committee was getting angry.

This was exactly the kind of lollygagging that Mark Paoletta would never have permitted the McNamee team to engage in. From his years with the House Energy and Commerce Committee, he knew that congressional investigators had little patience for such tactics.

Countless white-collar defense lawyers had been dismissive of his document requests, their instincts telling them to fight and resist because that's what they did in federal courts. That's why Paoletta had a Power-Point presentation that he showed to clients who might not be used to congressional probes. One of the slides showed a street sign: "one way" it said.

"There ain't a judge around here, guys, and this is going to play out a lot more publicly," Paoletta would tell his clients. "There's no right to call witnesses, no right to cross-examine. There's no recourse to a judge to try to block or get limits. There's nothing on a protective order or anything under seal."

It wasn't that Paoletta advocated rolling over, but he knew that if you provoked a congressional committee to get aggressive, there wasn't going to be a judge around to save a client from having his or her dirty laundry aired before the cameras. Waxman's committee (like the one Paoletta had worked on) didn't need to go to a judge, and if they were provoked to issue subpoenas, they might not be as nice.

Ultimately, Barnett didn't need to get Waxman to issue a subpoena. Just informing counsel for Clemens that they were considering "stronger options" than a courteous request did the trick, and finally, on Monday, February 11, the committee received the coveted document: a July 31, 1998, MRI report concluding that while there was no evidence of a "well-defined abscess" in Clemens's right buttocks, there was a pocket of fluid deep within the subcutaneous fat that was "likely related to the patient's prior attempted intramuscular injections."

The committee almost immediately turned the MRI report over to Mark Murphey, one of the top MRI experts in the country, who worked at the Armed Forces Institute of Pathology. The committee redacted Clemens's name from the document, and asked Murphey for his expert assessment. On Tuesday, February 12, Murphey responded with a report that the injury was consistent with a Winstrol injection.

Murphey was giving the committee only what knowledgeable sports doctors considered the likely explanation. Back in New York, Dr. Lewis Maharam, the medical director for the New York Road Runners and the chairman of the Board of Governors of the International Marathon Medical Directors Association, basically scoffed at the idea that a B_{12} shot could cause an abscess. "When sports doctors see butt abscesses in professional athletes, we know it is most likely due to an oil-based injection," Dr. Maharam said. "Anabolic steroids are oil-based. The oil does not allow 'bug fighters' to get to germs from a dirty injection. The infection gets walled off. Therefore, an MRI showing abscesses is a very likely result of steroid injections. An old saying in medicine is: when you hear hoofbeats, you think of horses first before zebras."

It was February 12, a day before the hearing, and Brian McNamee's lawyers turned on him in a way that left him angry, confused, and deeply insulted. While the investigators for the Committee on Oversight and Government Reform were trying to talk to the elusive nanny, McNamee was taking abuse while sitting in a leather swivel chair at a massive rectangular table in a 12th-floor conference room at the D.C. law offices of Dickstein Shapiro. His lawyers were simulating the hearing. Pretending to be hostile members of Congress, they sprayed McNamee with accusations, sanctimony, and derision. McNamee was getting angrier by the moment. So this was supposed to be pro bono?

McNamee had come down to the capital that Tuesday morning with his New York lawyers and camped out in the 12th-floor conference room at Dickstein Shapiro to prepare for the next day's hearings. If McNamee thought Novitzky and Parrella had been unrelenting, and the deposition somewhat grueling, the simulated hearing was a whole different thing — some kind of legal boot camp.

"We went through what a typical hearing would be. We had some questions that we had typed up and came up with," Paoletta said. "We tried to play the part. That's called a murder board. To prepare your client, you want to be much tougher on him than what he will face in the hearing. You want him to understand what is going to happen in this hearing, to know what he is going to say in response to every conceivable question."

Earl Ward, Richard Emery, and Debbie Greenberger sat across the table from their client and scowled contemptuously. Paoletta and one of his Dickstein colleagues, Andrew Snowdon, sat across from McNamee too, making for a Murderers' Row on the murder board.

"What the fuck are you talking about!" yelled one of them when McNamee spoke.

"That doesn't make sense!" hollered another.

It was murder, all right. Paoletta channeled all his years of experience with congressional hearings. He had spent a decade setting up inquisitions of CEOs, and felt he was pretty good at it. "It's easy to slip into my old role, ask questions, and say sort of snide things," he said. "Even snider than the members might say. You want to make comments, or say, 'I don't believe you.' Or, 'You keep saying . . . !' Or bring up unrelated things. Bring up a newspaper story. You just want to keep trying to get under their skin, so that they actually do react, and then they've gone through it," said Paoletta.

"It was a really grueling exercise, and we really gave it to him," added Ward. McNamee's deposition performance had left Ward and Emery worried, wondering if their client would wilt under the brutal glare of an agitated committee.

"We were pricks beyond belief to him," Emery said later. "We really beat Brian up. And he got very angry. And we said, 'You're going to be more angry tomorrow.' It was a disdainful and nasty cross-examination. He could see for himself how bad he looked. And he took that and ran with it."

The lawyers coached McNamee on the importance of brevity. His rambling in the deposition had already made him vulnerable to attacks; the committee members could eviscerate him for inconsistencies in his testimony.

One issue that kept rearing its head was the nanny, and here Paoletta's stature and background paid dividends. While the committee lawyers didn't share any information with Paoletta, they repeatedly called him and asked if McNamee was certain his testimony about Jose Canseco's party was correct. Their fixation alerted McNamee's team that there was an issue, although at this point they had no inkling of Clemens's secret communication with Strain two days earlier. "The nanny issue took on a life of its own," Paoletta said later. "Brian mentioned this in passing, but the Clemens team tried to make it a do or die issue. It became extremely critical that Brian was telling the truth on this point. Whenever Brian talked about being at Canseco's home, he mentioned this nanny. The Clemens team had seized on it and had produced information to make it appear that Brian was lying—and that made the committee very nervous. Senior committee staffers called me to ask, 'Mark, are you sure about the nanny story? We have to know if there's a problem with that story.' I said, 'Look, I know what you're talking about, I understand your concerns. I have gone over and over this story with Brian. Every time he says the same thing about the nanny. He is locked on this. He's not lying.' "

Paoletta believed McNamee unequivocally on the nanny issue. With pressure building in the few days before the hearing, Paoletta started to figure that the nanny could be their trump card—or the 3,000-pound anvil that sank McNamee's case.

As Tuesday afternoon turned to evening, the hearing a mere 12 hours away, McNamee's attorneys gained confidence. Brian was good. He knew what he knew, and he could tell it with ease no matter which way they came after him. They explained that this would be nothing like the civil meetings with Matt Parrella and George Mitchell: This was a televised congressional hearing. He couldn't allow himself to become bait for the hostile faction of the committee. And Paoletta's D.C. radar was picking up signs that there was some hostility indeed. Paoletta told Emery and Ward what he'd been learning: that the hearing would break down along partisan lines, and that it could get ugly. Emery was amazed at Paoletta's reconnaissance. "God knows who his sources were," he said. When the group broke for dinner, McNamee went off with family, and Ward and Emery visited a Greek restaurant. Over baklava, they felt lucky to have added Paoletta to the team.

"He was Brian's supereffective advocate," Emery said later of Paoletta. "Without Mark, we would have been bumbling fools. There's no doubt about it. We could have done it, but we were out of our league and Mark was right there.

"He got all the parking passes, knew where all the elevators were, all the guards. But it was more than that. It was a whole sense of how to treat people. When to be tough. When to be cooperative. His advice was flawless. I would go to him on any congressional issue."

The prep session gave McNamee confidence and a sense of peace. When he joined his father, John; his brother-in-law; and his niece for dinner at the Capital Grille later that night, the trainer was relaxed and ready for the next day's events. The lawyers had drilled into him the need to stay calm under what they knew would be an all-out assault from some members of the committee. Pretend you're "Sammy the Bull" Gravano and you're answering questions from Congress about how many people you've killed, they told him.

"So you killed 50 people?"

"Yeah, yeah," would be the matter-of-fact answer.

Gravano, who testified before a congressional committee investigating mob infiltration in boxing in 1993, is generally believed to have killed only 19 people, but McNamee got the point.

Almost three years after Mark McGwire emerged from room 2154 of the Rayburn House Office Building with his baseball legacy in ruins, Roger Clemens and Brian McNamee were due to appear in the same room for their own moment of accountability. About 9 A.M., an hour before the two men were supposed to arrive, a member of the staff of the House Committee on Oversight and Government Reform approached the witness table and left simple white placards bearing the names of the witnesses in black capital letters.

Photographers gathered around to capture the spare and ominous image. In between the two placards was a third, where George Mitchell's lieutenant, Charlie Scheeler, would be seated. Scheeler would speak for the 409-page report.

Exactly two months had passed since the report had sparked the blood feud between Clemens and McNamee, and now the two former accomplices were finally due to testify publicly in what Ben McGrath of *The New Yorker* would later call "a game of perjurers' chicken that seemed to promise judicial action rather than mere reprimand."

Long before the hearing was scheduled to begin, the hearing room and adjacent halls had been buzzing with the activity of television crews, print reporters, congressional staffers, and baseball fans. A nervous energy saturated everything. An unattended backpack had led to a security lockdown earlier that morning, but the threat had passed, and the diverse crowd milled about the ornate, wood-paneled room, chatting, sipping coffee, and checking BlackBerrys. Then a murmur went through the crowd, and in walked the Captain Ahab of steroids in sports, easy to spot with his shaved head and lanky 6-7 frame.

In the four years since Jeff Novitzky had raided the Bay Area Laboratory Co-Operative, the IRS agent had succeeded, for the most part, in keeping a low profile; only a few pictures of the nation's top steroid cop seemed to exist. But as Novitzky entered the hearing room there was an army of photographers waiting. From this day on, photos of the striking agent would be everywhere. Novitzky's body language suggested that he wasn't worried about anyone, particularly Roger Clemens, eating his lunch.

Accompanying Novitzky were IRS investigator Erwin Rogers and FBI agent Heather Young. The agents took their seats near the front of the room. Novitzky brushed a string of reporters aside, politely but firmly saying, "I can't comment today."

Novitzky may have been unwilling to give anyone a quote, but in the minutes before the hearing, a few hundred miles away in Pittsburgh, Andy Pettitte's lawyers Tom Farrell and Jay Reisinger hit send on an e-mail that contained an acknowledgment that their client had not come clean when he confirmed McNamee's drug allegations in the days after the Mitchell Report was released.

Just a few weeks earlier, Reisinger had informed his client that the Kelly Blair secret was in the hands of the New York *Daily News*—possibly it had also been revealed to Congress—and Pettitte had decided he had no choice but to confess to it in sworn testimony. Taken aback by Pettitte's apparent candor, the committee had granted his plea to spare him the indignity of having to testify about his father's HGH use. Now, just minutes before the hearing was to begin, Reisinger sent a statement to the reporters who had discovered Kelly Blair, confirming that Andy Pettitte had not only received HGH from Tom Pettitte in 2004, but that he had shared that information with the committee's lawyers during his February 4 deposition.

"Andy had not previously mentioned this usage because he acquired the substance from his father, who had obtained it without Andy's knowledge in an effort to overcome his very serious health problems, which have included serious cardiac conditions," the e-mail from Farrell and Reisinger said. "Andy did not want his father whom he deeply respects and loves to be brought into this matter and sought to shield him from publicity."

Pettitte's lawyers were the anti-Hardin; they had gotten out in front of the story instead of reacting to it. While Clemens and Hardin had gotten trapped repeatedly by breaking news that contradicted their public statements (Debbie's HGH use, the bloody needles, corroborating testimony from Clemens's former teammates), Pettitte and his lawyers had turned an inconvenient revelation to their advantage. They used the deposition to bolster their client's credibility and his reputation as a straight-talking, God-fearing good guy. Even though Pettitte had not been completely forthcoming about his PED use until his hand was forced, he looked genuinely forthcoming.

In short, the ball had taken a bad hop, and Pettitte played it well. Even releasing the statement was a tactical move; the news of Tom Pettitte's use was bound to come out eventually, they knew, so it was best to make sure it broke at exactly the moment when it was most likely to get drowned out by even more spectacular events.

The 2005 hearing with McGwire was noteworthy for a reason other than the testimony of the ballplayers: It was also a genuinely bipartisan effort. Republicans and Democrats couldn't agree on Iraq or taxes but they could join together to verbally slap around Bud Selig and Donald Fehr. But by February 13, 2008, even steroid bipartisanship was ancient history, and the hearing—entitled "The Mitchell Report: The Illegal Use of Steroids in Major League Baseball, Day 2"—was as polarized as everything else in Washington. By the end of the day, Roger Clemens, evolution, and gay marriage had at least one thing in common: They were all issues in America's Blue State–Red State culture wars.

The ranking Republican on the House Committee on Oversight and Government Reform was Tom Davis, and unlike the hyperpartisan, ultraconservative Dan Burton, the Virginia Republican was known as a business-oriented moderate skilled at building consensus. Unfortunately for Davis, House Majority Leader Tom DeLay, the Texas Republican who resigned from Congress in 2006 after he was indicted on corruption allegations, did not value bipartisan politics, preferring a more confrontational approach. Democrats complained that under Davis's leadership, the committee did nothing at a time when there were so many issues—the Iraq War, the federal response to Hurricane Katrina, to name just two—screamed for investigation. When Davis did jump into a subject, his actions often had DeLay's fingerprints all over them, such as when he issued a subpoena to keep the brain-damaged Terri Schiavo alive by a feeding tube against her husband's wishes. Davis had been considered a strong candidate for a Virginia Senate seat, but in 2008, frustrated with the incompetence of the Bush administration and disillusioned by Washington's paralyzing partisanship, he announced that he would not run for the Senate or for reelection to the House.

Ten minutes before the hearing was supposed to start, Davis huddled with Roger Clemens and his attorneys in a private Rayburn Building office. It wasn't too late, Davis told Clemens, to back out. He didn't have to face the committee, Davis said. He didn't have to go through the tough, humiliating questioning that was sure to come up. He didn't have to expose his Hall of Fame legacy to challenges and questioning.

"You can call it off," Davis told Clemens. "Waxman is all for calling it off. You can stop it now. Once the ball gets rolling there is no stopping it. Once you go out there, you can't come back. But you can call it off now."

Clemens waved Davis off like a catcher calling for an ill-advised pitch. Clemens wanted to make his case publicly. He wanted to tell the elected officials and the millions of people watching on television that he never used steroids, that his Hall of Fame–worthy career was built on sweat and hard work and nothing more. And so Clemens, wearing a dark suit, red tie, and light blue shirt, walked through a hallway filled with no shortage of fans and entered room 2154 at 10:04 A.M. At his side were his wife, Debbie, along with Rusty Hardin and Lanny Breuer. Clemens carried a black three-ring binder and his wife held a single flower—the yellow rose of Texas. As the group moved through the room and sat down at the witness table, every move Clemens made inspired a chorus of shutter clicks. Hardin, Breuer, and Debbie took the three seats directly behind Clemens. Several other lawyers from Hardin's firm in Houston sat another row back. Members of the committee were filing in slowly.

Brian McNamee, wearing a gray suit and silver tie, walked in a minute later with Richard Emery and Earl Ward. Compared with Clemens, who appeared somber and focused, McNamee seemed loose, almost eager to bring this chapter to a close. "You better bring your popcorn," he told reporters as he entered the room.

McNamee squeezed through the crowd to the witness table where Clemens and now Charlie Scheeler were already waiting. Emery, Paoletta, and Ward took their seats behind him and tried to look unfazed by the intensity of the scene. Off to their side, sitting near Emery's colleague Debra Greenberger, were McNamee's father and brother-in-law, there to show support. "Can you get me a ticket?" McNamee's brother-in-law had asked him. "I don't want to have to watch it on TV." As it happened, McNamee's father, the former NYPD inspector and FBI agent, sat almost directly in front of Novitzky, Young, and Rogers—within arm's reach of the federal law enforcement agents who had compelled his son to cooperate.

For the first time in months, McNamee and Clemens were sitting just a few feet from each other. They didn't say hello, didn't nod to each other, didn't even acknowledge each other's presence. The tension was suffocating. During a break later in the day's action, Scheeler would describe what it was like to sit between the two star witnesses.

"Like the worst middle seat on a plane you've ever had," Scheeler said.

The hearing room was packed. On the dais sat Waxman and Davis. Standing against the walls were the various committee staff lawyers and investigators who had conducted the probe over the previous weeks and months. They listened carefully, ready to run forward with notes for any member of Congress who might need the fruits of their research. So many reporters were present that an entire separate room had been reserved for them, with a live feed of the action in the hearing room aired live on C-SPAN and ESPN.

Waxman gaveled the meeting to order and asked for a moment of silence to honor Tom Lantos, the Holocaust survivor and California Democrat who had died of cancer a few days earlier. Then Waxman explained why the committee was so interested in the report that George Mitchell had compiled and Roger Clemens had attacked. During the 2005 McGwire hearing, when Republicans controlled Congress, the committee had urged Commissioner Bud Selig to investigate the game's steroid history, and the result, Waxman said, was "impressive and credible." The committee had planned to hold a general hearing on the report as a wrap-up to its previous work, Waxman added, but Clemens's very public and provocative challenges prompted the committee to shift direction and explore the information McNamee provided in the report about the pitcher's drug use. Waxman quoted Hardin, who during Clemens's deposition had called it a "horrible, disgraceful report."

"If the Mitchell Report is to be the last word on baseball's past, we believe we have a responsibility to investigate a serious claim of inaccuracy," Waxman said in his opening statement. Unlike Mitchell and his staff, Waxman noted, the committee had teeth; it could pressure witnesses to talk, subpoena documents, and refer the matter to the Department of

Justice if necessary. "As the chief investigative committee in the House of Representatives, we have greater authority and have been able to consider evidence that was not available to Senator Mitchell," Waxman said.

Next it was Davis's turn to speak. Looking rather tired, the ranking Republican who had just offered Clemens an out now acknowledged that many Americans thought Congress should focus on the war in Iraq or the economy, not baseball. But in one of the hearing's few moments of bipartisan consensus, Davis agreed with Waxman: "In the end, we decided we had a duty to probe the challenge, that we needed to help determine whether the Mitchell Report, with its 409-page sordid picture of backroom drug deals and players injecting each other with illegal substances right in their locker rooms, whether that report could and should still stand proof positive that baseball's efforts to combat illegal drug use needs a fresh look."

Waxman laid out what the committee lawyers had learned during its preliminary investigation in the weeks before the hearing. He thanked Chuck Knoblauch for his honesty and candor during his deposition, and noted that the retired Yankee second baseman had acknowledged incidents of HGH use not reported by Mitchell. "In a moving part of his deposition, Mr. Knoblauch said, 'My son was here today, and I am trying not to get emotional about this, but I am trying to teach him a lesson that you need to do things in life that you are going to be willing to talk about openly and to tell the truth,' " Waxman said. "On behalf of the committee, I want to thank Mr. Knoblauch for his cooperation and for his candor in accepting responsibility for his actions."

Waxman gave an even more enthusiastic endorsement of Andy Pettitte, building up Pettitte as the gold standard for credibility. He praised Pettitte for his cooperation, and referred to Pettitte's disclosure of additional use in 2004, but didn't mention Pettitte's father. "Mr. Pettitte's consistent honesty makes him a role model on and off the field," Waxman gushed.

While Waxman established Pettitte as a man of conscience, he portrayed Clemens and McNamee as far more complicated witnesses. Law enforcement officials had already vetted McNamee, and threatened to prosecute him if he didn't tell the truth. Mitchell, a Democratic Party patriarch who was still revered by many on Capitol Hill, also found him credible. But McNamee had lied to police about the 2001 incident in the St. Petersburg pool, and he had withheld the dirty needles and the bloody gauze from Justice Department investigators. Waxman wanted the record to reflect those facts.

Clemens, Waxman continued, was a credible and convincing person who had generously contributed his time and money to charitable causes. But in the two months since the Mitchell Report had been released, Waxman said, Clemens had contradicted himself numerous times. During his interview on *60 Minutes*, for example, Clemens said McNamee never told him about his role in the Mitchell investigation. Waxman pointed out that McNamee had tipped off Jim Murray eight days before the report was released; Rusty Hardin's investigators had even appeared on McNamee's doorstep a day before its release to interview the trainer about his cooperation with Mitchell, presenting McNamee with a form signed by both Clemens and Pettitte authorizing them to ask questions on behalf of the players. (Waxman didn't mention the December calls to Cabo because he didn't know about them.)

And, of course, there was Andy Pettitte, whose affidavit claimed Clemens had admitted using growth hormone during a conversation they had in 1999 or 2000. Waxman said Clemens and McNamee both agreed that the trainer had injected Debbie Clemens with HGH in 2003. "That makes it impossible that Mr. Clemens, when he spoke to Mr. Pettitte in 1999 or 2000, could have been referring to these injections of Mrs. Clemens."

Waxman told Clemens and McNamee that their dispute could not be waved off as a misunderstanding or different interpretations of the facts. "Someone isn't telling the truth," Waxman said. "If Mr. McNamee is lying, then he has acted inexcusably and he has made Mr. Clemens an innocent victim. If Mr. Clemens isn't telling the truth, then he has acted shamefully and has smeared Mr. McNamee. I don't think there is anything in between."

This showdown, Waxman added, had been unnecessary. He had intended to cancel the hearing after the depositions and issue a bipartisan report instead. But Clemens's attorneys, Hardin and Breuer, argued that it would be unfair to issue a report without giving the pitcher the opportunity to testify in public.

"So I decided to proceed with this hearing," Waxman said, "which I expect will be the last hearing this committee will have on baseball's past or the Mitchell Report."

As a ballplayer, there weren't many problems Clemens couldn't solve with his 98 mile-per-hour fastball, but since the release of the Mitchell Report, he had been thrust into an unfamiliar world of lawyers and lawmakers. In his opening statement, Clemens talked about the pressures he had faced over the past two months.

"I have chosen to live my life with a positive attitude, yet I am accused of being a criminal, and I am not supposed to be angry about that," Clemens said. "If I keep my emotions in check, then I am accused of not caring. When I did speak out, I was accused of protesting too much, so I am guilty. When I kept quiet at the advice of my attorney, until he could find out why in the world I was being accused of these things, I must have had something to hide, so I am guilty."

Clemens talked about the outpouring of support he had received from fans and friends since the release of the Mitchell Report, including from the 41st president of the United States. "I have had thousands of calls, e-mails from friends, working partners, teammates, fans, and men that have held the highest office in our country telling me to stand strong," Clemens said.

Later in the hearing, Clemens would explain this reference, claiming that while Senator Mitchell and his staff had never contacted him about McNamee's allegations when he was playing at Yankee Stadium—just a few miles north of Mitchell's Manhattan law office—former President George H. W. Bush had managed to reach him while he was in the middle of nowhere on a hunting trip. "When all this happened, the former president of the United States found me in a deer blind in south Texas and expressed his concerns, that this was unbelievable, and to stay strong and keep your—hold your head up high," Clemens said.

It was an attempt to remind the committee of his links to one of the most prominent families in the long history of the Republican Party—Clemens and Bush were practically neighbors—and it would not be the only appeal Clemens made to the Republican brand of patriotism. He told the panel that he pushed his aging body hard after Bud Selig asked him to represent the United States in the 2006 World Baseball Classic. "I told them, I could shake hands and wave flags and sell tickets for you if you want me to do that but it is going to take longer to get this body going. And I did, and I went out there and I did the best I very—I could probably do. And I was proud to have the USA on my chest."

In the written version of the statement submitted to the committee, Clemens went even further, coloring himself as an All-American success story who pulled himself up by his bootstraps, a loving husband and father, a troop-supporting patriot. Clemens wrote that he was one of six kids raised by a single mom who instilled the importance of hard work, commitment, and sacrifice in her children. "Anyone who has spent time around me knows that my family is and has always been my top priority. My wife, Debbie, and my sons—Koby, Kory, Kacy, and Kody—mean more to me than anything in this world," Clemens said, before adding that he'd "had the privilege and honor to visit our troops in Kuwait, Qatar and Afghanistan and salute them as our nation's true role models."

Despite his good deeds and commitment to excellence, Clemens told Congress that Brian McNamee, a man he once treated like a member of his family, had stabbed him in the back. "If I am guilty of anything," Clemens said, "it is of being too trusting of everyone, wanting to see the best in everyone, being too nice to everyone."

In concluding his statement, Clemens expressed frustration that his reputation would forever be stained because of the Mitchell Report. "No matter what we discuss here today, I am never going to have my name restored, but I have got to try and set the record straight," Clemens said. "However, by doing so, I am putting myself out there to all of you, knowing that because I said that I didn't take steroids that this is looked as an attack on Senator Mitchell's report. Where am I to go with that? I am not saying Senator Mitchell's report is entirely wrong. I am saying Brian McNamee's statements about me are wrong. Let me be clear. I have never taken steroids or HGH. Thank you."

Just before McNamee read his opening statement, Ward leaned over and whispered, "It's the bottom of the ninth and the bases are loaded." McNamee took out a pad and began doodling.

"What are you doing?" Ward whispered.

"Playing Hangman," McNamee responded.

Ward kicked him under the table and looked at the word McNamee was writing: "Liar."

McNamee introduced himself to the committee as "once the personal trainer for one of the greatest pitchers in the history of baseball, Roger William Clemens," transposing his first and second names. He read from a prepared statement in which every word was printed in capital letters. He said that he had helped taint the national pastime, and hoped that his testimony might help with a solution. McNamee's voice seemed to crack ever so slightly when he spoke of his father instilling in him the belief that people make mistakes and should acknowledge them no matter the consequences.

McNamee told the committee he regretted his role in Major League Baseball's steroid scandal and he regretted he had to testify "against a man

I once admired." He regretted having to give federal investigators and Senator Mitchell information that would tarnish Clemens's reputation. He regretted that while Pettitte and Knoblauch admitted McNamee had injected them with performance-enhancing drugs, Clemens had declared war on his onetime friend and trainer. He regretted having to revisit the 2001 incident in the St. Petersburg pool, and he regretted lying to the Florida cops who investigated the case.

"When I told Senator Mitchell that I injected Roger Clemens with performance-enhancing drugs, I told the truth," McNamee said. "I told the truth about steroids and human growth hormone. I injected those drugs into the body of Roger Clemens at his direction. Unfortunately, Roger has denied this and has led a full-court attack on my credibility. And let me be clear, despite Roger Clemens' statements to the contrary, I never injected Roger Clemens or anyone else with lidocaine or B_{12}. I have no reason to lie and every reason not to. If I do lie, I will be prosecuted."

McNamee told the committee that in his conversations with Justice Department investigators and Mitchell's staff, he had underestimated the number of times he injected Knoblauch and Clemens with performance-enhancing drugs, an admission committee Republicans later repeated to bruise his credibility. "I guess maybe I wanted to downplay the extent of their use because I felt I was betraying the players I had trained," he said. "In the following weeks and months, I have had the opportunity to think about these events and consider the specific drug regimens we used. As a result, I now believe that the numbers of times I injected Roger Clemens and Chuck Knoblauch was actually greater than I initially stated."

McNamee said he kept the syringes and bloody gauze pads he had provided to Novitzky and Parrella the previous month because while he liked and admired Clemens, he never really trusted him. "I just had the sense if this ever blew up and things got messy, Roger would be looking out for number one," the former cop said. "I viewed the syringes as evidence that would prevent me from being the only fall guy."

Elijah Cummings, the no-nonsense Democrat who had represented Baltimore in Congress for a dozen years, was the first member of the committee to question Clemens and McNamee. He reminded Clemens he was under oath, and then asked why Andy Pettitte would tell Congress that his good friend and longtime teammate was taking an illegal performance-enhancing drug if there were any doubts in his mind.

"I think he misremembers," said Clemens.

Like Mark McGwire's "I'm not here to talk about the past" three years earlier, it became the catchphrase that stuck with baseball fans long after the hearing, becoming a sort of shorthand for just how far one of sports' biggest stars had fallen from grace. It also exemplified how uncomfortable Clemens looked at the witness table, as if he'd rather be in a Siberian gulag than face this interrogation from Cummings. That's the way it was for much of the hearing. Clemens stuttered and stumbled, even when responding to questions from sympathetic lawmakers. The collar of his light blue shirt looked a size too tight and his face turned pink whenever he appeared to get frustrated. Right from the beginning, and throughout the hearing, Clemens compulsively licked his lips at nearly every pause in his testimony. After turning down Davis's last-minute offer to cancel the hearing, Clemens looked like he wished he had taken him up on it.

McNamee, in contrast, was calm and focused through most of his testimony. Where Clemens rambled, McNamee managed to keep most of his answers as short as a single sentence—a tip Paoletta had given him that had stuck. Although friends knew McNamee to have a hair-trigger temper, he never raised his voice or lost his composure. At times, McNamee looked like a boxer who had taken his opponents' best punches and realized they didn't hurt as much as he thought they would. It wasn't just the previous day's prep session; in the weeks leading up to the hearing, Clemens and Hardin had already taken some powerful shots at McNamee and he'd held his own. He was a former cop who had faced down real dirtbags in the streets of New York City. Compared with all that, the ranting of a few blowhard politicians and lawyers was nothing.

At times, McNamee even looked like he might be enjoying the chance to answer some of the questions. When Davis asked him why, during the phone conversation that was played at the Houston press conference in January, McNamee didn't simply say to his former employer, "Roger, I had to tell the truth," McNamee replied calmly and directly, his arms crossed on the witness table. "I realized it was being taped," McNamee said of the conversation, "and I also didn't know if anyone else was listening, so—I also was trying not to hurt him if it wasn't just him taping me. But if you listen to my jargon, I did say that. 'It is what it is.' "

"How in your jargon did you say that?" Davis asked.

"I said, 'It is what it is,' meaning that I did tell the truth," McNamee replied, a Cheshire cat grin on his face.

Later in the hearing, one of the members of the committee asked Waxman if this foreign term could be defined officially and the definition placed in the Congressional Record. "It's a very pivotal phrase that has been nationally debated," the congressman said.

"We'll hold the record open if you want to submit some documentation," Waxman said dryly, "and whatever it is, it is, we'll put it in the record."

Over the next few hours, the world heard for the first time about many of the wild discrepancies and sordid images revealed in the investigation conducted over the previous two weeks. There was talk of Clemens's golf receipt on the day of the Canseco party, an account of Debbie Clemens's HGH use, and the colorful anecdote of the Band-Aids that McNamee said Clemens carried after an injection had caused him to bleed through his designer pants. Clemens spoke about his belief in the healing power of B_{12}.

"Did you inject yourself with B_{12} or would Mr. McNamee ever inject you or do you remember?" Davis asked.

"I have never injected myself," Clemens said "Mr. McNamee's given me three shots when we were in Toronto, three shots of B_{12}, two in New York."

"OK," Davis said. "Mr. McNamee, do you concur with that?"

"The first time I heard of Roger taking B_{12} was on '60 Minutes,' " McNamee said. "I've never given Roger Clemens B_{12} and had never heard of B_{12} really before."

It was another line of questions about B_{12}, later in the hearings, that inspired the biggest laughs of the day. Democrat Bruce Braley of Iowa pointed out that B_{12} was only indicated for patients with anemia, senile dementia, Alzheimer's, or a dietary condition that gave them a deficiency. One by one, Braley asked Clemens if he had those conditions, and Clemens dutifully answered he had never been diagnosed with them.

"Have you ever been a vegetarian?" asked Braley.

"I am not a vegetarian," Clemens said.

"Have you ever been a vegan?" Braley asked.

"A what? I'm sorry," Clemens asked.

"A vegan."

"I don't know what that is," Clemens said, as the room cracked up. Not every moment of the proceedings would be grim.

· · ·

During his lobbying tour, Clemens clearly found a friend in Republican committee member Virginia Foxx, who represented a swath of North Carolina not far from the birthplace of Rusty Hardin. The grandmotherly Foxx, whom reporters nicknamed "Aunt Bee" after the character on *The Andy Griffith Show,* was as smitten with the whole Clemens team as she was hostile to Waxman. Having missed much of the hearing for other congressional business, she arrived in time to get a few minutes for questions, during which she invited Clemens to read a statement from his wife, Debbie, into the Congressional Record.

"This is from Debbie Clemens, my wife, who is in the room with me. 'I'm not sure of the dates but I read a news article about the benefits of growth hormone,'" Clemens began, quoting his wife, reading from the folder in front of him.

> "During that same week talking about the subject openly Brian McNamee, who was at our house in Houston training people, approached me to tell me about the article. He said it was not illegal and used for youthfulness. The next mid-morning he said he had—he had some and would be able to give me a test shot. He gave me one shot. He later left the house on his way to the airport. During that time Roger was not at home and I didn't have the opportunity to tell him about it later that evening when he arrived home. In telling Roger about that, that evening, I was also having circulation problems with itching. It happened the following night, just not as bad. I was very comfortable in trying it but it was a harmless act on my part. Also since McNamee had a Ph.D. he was a trusted good trainer. Roger said let's back off this. We need to know more about it."

Concluding the statement, Clemens said his wife had been "broken up" over the episode for a long time and that she now felt manipulated by McNamee—that she was "a pawn amongst his game." Foxx nodded sympathetically.

"I would have never instructed Brian McNamee to give my wife these shots," Clemens said. "Once again, I don't know enough about growth hormone. I would suggest that young kids, kids of all ages, athletics, I don't know enough about it. It doesn't help you. But I also have heard—again, different news articles where people for quality of life have used this product. I have learned more about growth hormone in the last month than I ever have known. I'm offended again that I—that I was instructed and I think he said earlier it was his instruction earlier in the day that I instructed him to give my wife growth hormone."

It took a series of questions from John Tierney, a Democrat representing the passionate Red Sox fans on the North Shore of Massachusetts, to show the world what a train wreck Clemens's deposition the week before had been. Quoting from the week-old transcript, Tierney pointed out an outrageous self-contradiction—that Clemens repeatedly swore he never discussed HGH with McNamee, but then later in the interview claimed he had confronted McNamee by telephone after learning McNamee had injected Debbie with the drug.

"But your own statements now showed that you had two specific and memorable conversations with him about HGH," Tierney asked. "So when you were asked on three specific occasions, why didn't you tell the committee about those conversations when you were asked, 'did you ever speak with Mr. McNamee about human growth hormone.' "

Clemens sat upright at the witness table, again licking his lips, his hands resting on the open binder in front of him with yellow tabs for parts to quickly flip to. Clemens held a pen in one hand and a yellow highlighter in the other. Behind him, Hardin scowled sourly into space. Clemens tried to explain that he had never discussed HGH "prior to" that conversation, and tried to move the conversation back to Andy Pettitte, but Tierney interrupted, pointing out that the questions were unambiguous; Clemens had been asked if he "ever" had discussed HGH.

"How do you reconcile three times saying you didn't, and then later, when somebody specifically finally asks you about your wife, you have a recollection of two very distinct and memorable conversations?" Tierney asked.

"Mr. Congressman, again, I never had any detailed discussions with Brian McNamee about HGH," Clemens said.

"Well, didn't you call him on the phone after your wife had told you that she had taken HGH?" Tierney asked.

"That very much is detailed conversation," Clemens said.

There were a few nervous coughs in the jam-packed room, but otherwise nothing but silence and the voices of the two men with the microphones, accents of Boston and Houston. Tierney insisted again that Clemens reconcile the conflicting statements. Clemens admitted that the call to McNamee following Debbie's injection was a "very heated conversation," but prior to that he and McNamee had never spoken about HGH before. Clemens licked his lips vigorously as Tierney pointed out that this raised "credibility issues."

Here Breuer leaned forward for the first time and whispered in Clemens's ear. As another flurry of camera shutters went off, Breuer advised Clemens on how to proceed.

"Again, prior to, Mr. Congressman, we had no detailed discussion about HGH," Clemens said.

"Prior to what?" Tierney asked.

Clemens then suggested—perhaps at Breuer's prompting—that the questions had been somewhat confusing, that the question about family members' use had come in a confusing form. But Tierney wouldn't have it; he pointed out that the question about discussing HGH with McNamee had been perfectly clear.

Next Tierney asked a series of questions about the shots that Debbie Clemens took, and why Clemens never called a doctor about her side effects. Clemens said that Debbie had felt "wigged out," and they had discussed calling a doctor. Licking his lips, Clemens then apparently decided it wouldn't hurt to cast aspersions on McNamee.

"And not only did the reason I searched his luggage for the fact that he would always leave his luggage behind and have us mail out his luggage and leave without his luggage at my house, no differently than when I spoke to him about bringing alcohol onto my property," Clemens said. "I had young kids. That is the conversation that was about. I was comfortable with my wife's reaction."

Tierney was unimpressed.

"If you want us to believe that Mr. McNamee injected your wife without your knowledge, that she started suffering serious side effects of the drug, that you were upset enough to call Mr. McNamee and then search his luggage," Tierney said. "But despite all that you never made inquiry of a doctor and you never even looked up to see what the effects might be, is that right?"

"Mr. Congressman, I don't believe I ever said serious effects," Clemens said. "She said she was having itching and she had some type of circulation problem that she was feeling."

Without ever abandoning his calm demeanor, Tierney had thrown Clemens against the ropes. But his time had expired, and now it was McNamee's turn to take some punches.

. . .

Perhaps McNamee's most aggressive interrogator was Dan Burton, the attack dog, who ripped the trainer with the same kamikaze zeal he displayed a decade earlier with his over-the-top attacks on the Clinton White House. He jumped into the holes in McNamee's testimony, drenching his questions in contempt: Why did McNamee wait for months after he was first interviewed by federal investigators to hand over the needles, gauze pads, and steroid bottles he claimed link Clemens to performance-enhancing drug use? Why did he produce this physical evidence long after the Mitchell Report was released?

"This is really disgusting," Burton seethed. "You lie when it is convenient for you. I don't know what to believe, but I know one thing I don't believe, and that's you."

Their exchange also exposed the hypocrisy and partisanship Americans dislike about their elected officials. Burton was fortunate that McNamee didn't haul out the cheat sheet his lawyers had prepared for him on Burton, just in case things got unbearably nasty. Among the points: Burton had attacked President Clinton about campaign fundraising, but his own fund-raising tactics had raised questions in Washington and in Indiana . . . Burton is a champion of family values who receives 100 percent ratings from the Christian Coalition for his votes on key issues, yet he also fathered an illegitimate son with a woman with whom he had an extramarital affair in the early 1980s . . . Burton was one of Clinton's most aggressive persecutors during the Monica Lewinsky scandal but he had been repeatedly accused of sexual harassment, as well as numerous sexual relationships with women on his congressional and campaign staffs . . . Burton introduced legislation in 1990 requiring the death penalty for drug dealers but stopped calling for penalties that severe when his son was arrested twice in 1994 on marijuana-related charges.

But the most relevant piece of Burton's background was perhaps the Indiana lawmaker's alliance with the dietary supplement industry. Burton had supported the Dietary Supplement Health and Education Act of 1994, a piece of legislation that dramatically changed the culture of sports, turning athletes—from high school kids to gold medal Olympians—into pill poppers.

The congressman, wearing a white monogrammed shirt that highlighted his pink face, looked positively apoplectic as he confronted McNamee, his hand on his cheek, his stiff hair an unnatural shade of orange. "Roger Clemens is a baseball—he's a titan in baseball," Burton said. "And you and with all these lies, if they're not true, are destroying him and his reputation. Now how does he get his reputation back if this is not true? And how can we believe you because you've lied and lied and lied and lied?"

McNamee sat with his arms folded and endured it all, just as his lawyers had advised. This gave Burton more time to vent, at times looking uninformed about the committee's research, mixing up dates and citations. At one point, Burton paused while Jennifer Safavian, the Republicans' chief investigator, whispered in his ear to inform him he was mistaken about the contents of a piece of paper he was referencing.

Throughout the whole beating, McNamee never took the bait. He smirked, knowing that he'd gotten the best of the frustrated congressman. He didn't need his cheat sheet.

Burton might have been right: McNamee might have dealt drugs and lied. But it was Clemens and his lawyers who had made a mistake that Mark Paoletta would never have permitted McNamee, Emery, and Ward to make: being slow and uncooperative with a congressional committee's investigation.

The Clemens legal team had been strategically sluggish in sharing two pieces of information the committee had wanted: the phone number of Lily Strain, and the results of the MRI conducted on the "palpable mass" on Clemens's backside in 1998. The committee staff had been angry, and now so was Stephen Lynch, a Democrat from towns south and west of Boston.

Taking over after Burton, Lynch coolly laid out a few facts uncovered in the previous week, letting the world hear for the first time the words "palpable mass" in relation to Clemens's buttocks. Lynch explained the strange explanations Clemens had for the injury, and the distance the committee had gone to get to the bottom of the mystery.

"This MRI was not provided in the original set of documents that the committee received," Lynch said. "In fact, it was not easy for the committee to receive — to obtain the MRI from counsel for Mr. Clemens."

Lynch described how the committee had spent a week requesting the document from Clemens's attorneys before finally receiving it two days before the hearing and discovering that Clemens's buttocks injury was "likely related to the patient's prior attempted intramuscular injections."

Lynch then revealed that the committee had taken the MRI results to Mark Murphey, the chief of musculoskeletal radiology at the Armed Forces Institute of Pathology, who Lynch said was "one of the country's leading experts on MRI." Lynch said that Dr. Murphey's opinion (delivered just the day earlier) was that the injury was "compatible with the Winstrol injection as the inflammatory component." Swiftly, Lynch requested and Waxman agreed that the Murphey opinion be inserted into the Congressional Record. Breuer stood up and asked to address Lynch, but Waxman refused to let him. Clemens was all alone.

"From what I understand, we provided everything that we could possibly provide to the staff," Clemens said. "We've fully cooperated with everything that was asked of us. I know obviously by looking at the medical records, I got a B_{12} shot and it obviously gave me some discomfort. I hate to get on Dr. Taylor who gave the shot, but if he gave me a bad shot."

Lynch's time ran out, and Davis stepped in. He entered a different physician's report into the record—this one provided by a Baylor University doctor whom Hardin had asked to review Clemens's medical records—and said it was unfair to ambush Clemens with Murphey's report.

"I don't really think this tells anybody—none of these doctors physically looked at you," Davis said, addressing Clemens. "They're looking at an MRI and taking a different view. And I'm just saying the doctor who looked at this originally came to a much different conclusion. People can judge whatever they want. But I think what's fair is fair on this." Davis declared that Lynch's questioning represented "literally a new definition of lynching."

Although Charlie Scheeler's role in the hearing mostly seemed to be making a brawl between Clemens and McNamee less convenient by six or seven feet, a few members of the committee did engage him with direct questions. In the course of his testimony, Scheeler did not dispute the suggestion that he was the actual first-draft author of the report, but said that Mitchell had reviewed every sentence, comma, and semicolon of it.

Scheeler disputed the assertions Hardin had put forth in the defamation suit, which suggested that after being browbeaten by the feds, McNamee had sat idly through his interviews with Mitchell while Novitzky read a bullet-point summary of McNamee's allegations and asked for confirmation.

Paul Kanjorski (D-Penn.) decided to engage him. Kanjorski, noting that he was a great admirer of George Mitchell's, turned to Scheeler with a series of questions about Jose Canseco's party. Scheeler defended the report's accuracy, and pointed out that the report never said drugs had been exchanged at the party. John Mica, a Republican from Florida, used up his five minutes with a rambling series of questions about the color of the drugs. McNamee said the Winstrol he gave Clemens was milky and white, and the testosterones were oily and honey-colored. Clemens said the B_{12} McNamee gave him was pink and red. "I do not know the color of lidocaine," he said. "Brian McNamee has never given me growth hormone or steroids."

Next came Carolyn Maloney, a Democrat representing parts of New York City that included Clemens's former home on the Upper East Side, where the injections were said to have occurred. Maloney pointed out that Clemens had told 60 Minutes that he didn't talk to Mitchell because his lawyers advised him not to. Then Maloney pointed out the six times in his deposition when Clemens told the committee under oath that he had no idea Mitchell wanted to talk to him.

"Congresswoman, the fact of the matter was I was never told by my baseball agent/attorney that we were asked to come down and see Senator Mitchell," Clemens said. "Like you said in that statement, if I knew the lies that Brian McNamee were telling about me I would have been down there to see Senator Mitchell in a heartbeat, in a New York minute, if you will. I was never told about that."

Maloney asked if Clemens thought the Hendricks brothers had done him a "terrible disservice." Clemens said, "I would say so." Maloney asked if Clemens had fired his agents for this "breach of trust." Clemens said he hadn't.

Indiana's Third Congressional District representative, Mark Souder, came next. He used much of his five allotted minutes to rant against the "wall of silence" coming out of baseball, pointing out that it took BALCO and Jose Canseco's book to spur action.

"When you testify in front of this committee it is better not to talk about the past than to lie about the past," he said. "Somebody is not telling the truth today."

Much would be written about how the hearing unfolded after Elijah Cummings's initial questions; the conventional wisdom was that the Democrats sided with McNamee while the Republicans sided with Clemens. That was a rather simplistic analysis of what transpired. Democrats didn't coddle McNamee the way some Republicans coddled Clemens. Democrats asked Clemens tough questions and confronted him with damaging evidence but they treated him with respect, never displaying the bile and rage Republicans exhibited when they teed off on McNamee. The attacks were so bad that Waxman felt obligated to issue an apology at the end of the hearing.

There were exceptions to the partisanship. Congressman Souder, for instance, was a Republican, but his sympathies seemed to lie with McNamee. Regarding McNamee's turning over of the medical waste, Souder said it was a familiar pattern in drug enforcement. "We often see witnesses who are caught, who go to the federal government and initially give us just enough so they think they are not going to go to jail, but they don't really turn over their major clients," Souder said. "And then something ticks them off, and they go a step further."

One Democratic lawmaker even lobbed the softball question that turned into one of the few highlights of the hearing for Clemens. "Can I look at my two children with a straight face and tell them that you, Roger Clemens, have always played the game with honesty and integrity," William Lacy Clay of Missouri asked in a "say it ain't so, Joe" moment. (This was almost word for word the same question Clay had asked Mark McGwire in 2005, prompting the slugger to issue his famous line about not wanting to discuss the past.) Clemens drove that one out of the park, painting himself as a working-class hero who transcended tough times to become a seven-time Cy Young Award winner. Clemens told Clay that his stepfather had died when Clemens was a kid, that his mother—who worked three jobs to support the family—gave him a strong work ethic and helped him land a scholarship at the University of Texas. He talked about how drugs had damaged his family—his sister-in-law was brutally murdered because of drugs, he said, and his mother pulled his brother out of college because of an incident involving marijuana.

Despite all his accomplishments, Clemens added, challenges remained: "Somebody's tried to break my spirit in this room. They are not going to break my spirit. I am going to continue to go out and do the things that I love and try to be honest and genuine to every person I can be. It is the way I was brought up. It is what I know. But you can tell your boys that I did it the right way, and I worked my butt off to do it."

Even Clemens wasn't ready for the butt kissing that would follow:

Clay: "Thank you for that response. You have a very compelling and telling story about your life and career. A colleague of mine, Mr. [Michael] Capuano of Massachusetts, wants to know what uniform you will wear to the Hall of Fame."

Clay was a lot tougher on McNamee, insinuating that the trainer dropped a dime on Clemens to save his own skin, but drawing on inaccurate information.

Mr. Clay. "I recognize how intense the pressure can be when testifying for a Federal prosecutor. Did their intimidation tactics influence you to give conflicting testimony?"

Mr. McNamee. "No, sir."

Mr. Clay. "You are sure about that?"

Mr. McNamee. "Yeah, I am pretty sure."

Mr. Clay. "Were you granted five years' probation in exchange for your testimony?"

Mr. McNamee. "No, sir."

Mr. Clay. "You don't have a deal sitting on the table with the Federal prosecutors . . ."

Mr. McNamee. "No, sir."

Mr. Clay. ". . . to come before this committee and to say what you have said? You don't have a deal at all?"

Mr. McNamee. "No deal, sir."

Mr. Clay. "Were you simply telling the prosecutors what they wanted to hear in order to secure a deal for yourself?"

Mr. McNamee. "No, sir."

Mr. Clay. "You have answered truthfully to all my questions?"

Mr. McNamee. "Yes, sir."

The lowest point in the hearing for Clemens and his lawyers came next, as Waxman took the microphone from his less informed colleagues and all but accused Clemens of witness tampering. When he asked Clemens whose idea it was to contact former nanny Lily Strain, gasps could be heard throughout the courtroom. Sitting behind McNamee, Mark Paoletta tried to cover his astonishment. "I was stunned that the Waxman staff had been able to run all this down so quickly and so below the radar," Paoletta later recalled. "I had no idea this was coming. The issue that they tried to use to destroy Brian's credibility—the nanny issue—had just destroyed Clemens right before my very eyes. I was six feet away watching his credibility and the Hall of Fame go 'poof.' The Waxman team left no stone unturned. Justice was served that day, at that moment."

Waxman began by outlining the difficulty his committee had getting a number for Strain from Clemens's attorneys, despite their promises and the simplicity of the request; despite asking on the previous Friday, and again on Sunday evening, it wasn't until Monday afternoon that the Clemens team provided the name and number—after Clemens had spoken with her.

"Well, what the nanny said to us when we finally contacted her yesterday was important in several respects," Waxman said. "First, she said that she was at Mr. Canseco's home during the relevant time period. In fact, she said that she and Mrs. Clemens and the children stayed overnight at the Cansecos.

"Secondly, she told us she did not remember any team party as described in the Mitchell Report. And third, she said that she did not— she did remember that you were at that home during the relevant time period, although she didn't know how long you stayed or whether you spent the night with your family."

Sitting right behind Waxman was Phil Barnett, the staff director of Waxman's committee staff, feeding Waxman pieces of paper and following along with every word as Waxman brought out the heavy artillery:

"The third point directly contradicted your deposition testimony, where you said you were not at Mr. Canseco's home at any point June 8th to June 10, 1998. But it is entirely understandable to me. It was 10 years ago.

"Here is what puzzles me about your actions: We have a transcript of the interview with the nanny, whose name I am not going to release to protect her privacy; but in this transcript she says that on Sunday, this last Sunday, you called her and asked her to come to your Houston home. She had not seen you in person since 2001. But after you called, she went to your home on Sunday afternoon. And I would like to read a portion of the transcript of the committee interview.

"Question: 'When you said you didn't remember a party, what did he say?'

"Answer: 'He says, you know, the reason you don't remember that party is because I wasn't there. He said because I know that he was playing with Jose.'

"Question: 'So did he ask you, do you remember a party, and then you said you did not remember a party?'

"Answer: 'That's right.'

"She also told the committee staff that you told her that she should tell the committee the truth. And after your meeting, an investigator working for you called her and asked her a series of additional questions.

"Your meeting took place two days after the committee staff made a simple request for your former nanny's name. And then it took 24 hours after your meeting for your attorneys to provide her name to the Republican and Democratic staffs."

Waxman paused, and shook his head. He said again that he was "puzzled" by all of it. "Was it your idea to meet with her before forwarding her name to us, or did someone suggest that to you?" Waxman said.

Clemens sat at the witness table, licking his lips. Rusty Hardin looked distraught.

"I was doing y'all a favor by finding a nanny that was—supposedly came in question," Clemens stuttered.

"You might have been trying to do us a favor, but who told you you should invite her to your house, that you haven't seen her in all those years."

Hardin and Breuer leapt to their feet. Waxman looked startled. "Mr. Chairman, this is unfair," Hardin said. "What his lawyers tell him is unfair for you to ask. And I will tell you in any case—"

"Okay," Waxman responded, banging his gavel to restore order. "Well, I accept that. I accept that. Would the gentlemen please be seated?

"Was it your idea? That is the question," Waxman asked, turning his attention back to Clemens. "Was it your idea?"

"It was my idea," Hardin interjected angrily, still on his feet, a mocking edge in his voice. "It was my idea to investigate what witnesses know, just like any other lawyer in the free world does."

Clemens hemmed and hawed through the rest of the exchange as Hardin sat behind him, looking like he'd just chewed up a mouthful of bitter pills. Breuer wrung his hands and shook his head as if he was contemplating something dreadful. This reflected poorly on them even more than on their client, and it was happening on live television.

"I don't know if there is anything improper in this but I do know it sure raises an appearance of impropriety," Waxman said. "The impression it leaves is terrible."

"Mr. Chairman, with all due respect, this is nothing but innuendo," Breuer said, standing now with Hardin, his left hand on Clemens's broad shoulder. "Your committee asked on Friday evening for this information. We have done everything to give you that information in a fast and thorough manner.

"And I spoke to your own staff member, who is speaking to you now," Breuer continued, pointing an accusatory finger at Barnett. "And your statement—and I have the highest respect for the chairman—is calculated to do nothing but to have innuendo against this man."

Paoletta watched from behind, thanking his lucky stars that he had joined the McNamee team. "Lanny Breuer is one of the best lawyers in D.C., particularly for this type of project, but I knew he had gotten himself into a bad situation," Paoletta would say later. "From the courtesy calls tour, to the belligerent press conferences, to the testimony Clemens gave, I knew Lanny was not driving that train. Lanny has never told me that, and he would never talk out of school, but Lanny is too good to make those mistakes. The strategy was all wrong from day one. It had the feel of someone who did not know this town, did not appreciate how to proceed in this setting. I am not sure any lawyer could have changed the course of Clemens driving off a cliff, but I am glad that I was not on that team. When Lanny and Hardin jumped up during the hearing to spar with the chairman, I actually felt bad for Lanny. He's a great lawyer, with a great reputation. But that was not a great day for him."

Throughout the exchange, Charlie Scheeler turned in his chair to face the spectacle that Breuer and Hardin presented. Clemens too looked vulnerable and powerless as he tried to fend off the hints of tampering from Waxman. He sat like a child while his lawyers stood behind him. Waxman let them talk, his gavel hanging in the air.

"Mr. Chairman, Mr. Chairman, I was doing y'all a favor; and as far as I was concerned, I haven't seen this lady in a long time," Clemens finally blurted, looking scared, cornered, and not particularly convincing. "She is a sweet lady, and I wanted to get her to you as quick as possible, if you had any questions for her."

Despite Clemens's protestations, he looked guilty. Waxman said that there would always be a question about whether Clemens "tried to influence her testimony." Clemens said he was "hurt" by that comment. And he was. A relatively innocent subplot of the Mitchell Report had exploded into something that made Clemens look deceptive, and Clemens had no one to thank for that but his attorneys.

Committee Democrats said they were stunned at the hearing's virulently partisan turn. The GOP members had been cordial at the first Mitchell Report hearing, the January session with the former senator, Selig, and Fehr. An educational session on HGH the previous day too had been free of confrontation. There was no indication that the hearing would turn nasty. They assumed the Republicans would play by the same rules that applied during the 2005 hearing.

A lot, however, had changed in three years. In 2005, the Republican Party controlled the White House, Congress, and was stacking the judiciary with conservative judges; House Majority Leader Tom DeLay and Bush political adviser Karl Rove had been building what they predicted would be a permanent majority. But by February 2008, the Republican Party was imploding. President Bush's approval ratings hit historic lows. Osama bin Laden had not been killed or captured. Most Americans were still bitterly opposed to the war in Iraq, despite whatever successes the Bush administration claimed the military surge had delivered. GOP leaders, most notably DeLay and Alaska senator Ted Stevens, faced corruption charges. Sex scandals—especially Senator Larry Craig's lewd conduct arrest in a Minneapolis airport bathroom—had made the GOP a late-night punch line.

The Republicans had suffered a terrible defeat in the 2006 midterm election, losing control of Congress, and in February 2008 the future didn't look any better. None of the party's presidential candidates appealed to all of its disparate constituencies. The economy was souring, the first indication of a global financial meltdown. In other words, the Republican Party had its back up against the wall, and as a long list of Democrats— Michael Dukakis, Max Cleland, and John Kerry, to name just a few—can testify, the GOP is a dangerous foe when it is cornered.

Some Republicans attacked McNamee with fury and abject disgust. "Mr. McNamee, you are a drug dealer," Christopher Shays said, contempt and anger dripping off his words.

"That's your opinion," McNamee responded.

"No, it's not my opinion," Shays fired back. "You were dealing with drugs."

When Shays yielded, Waxman pointed out that by Shays's logic, the players were drug dealers too. "That's a good point," Shays said. "If you had 89 players here, I'd feel a lot better about this hearing."

The exchange elucidated the tensions on the committee; Shays called it a "Roman circus," and his Republican colleague Lynn Westmoreland of Georgia called it a "show trial." North Carolina's Virginia Foxx, another Republican, used a portion of her allotted time to argue that in the previous year Waxman had been playing "gotcha games."

The Republicans later said they didn't come to the hearing bristling for a fight, but they felt they had to rush to Clemens's defense because of the early tone set by Waxman and Cummings. They privately griped about the canonization of Andy Pettitte—why was he put on a pedestal? Why was his testimony treated as if it were delivered from a burning bush?

Republican Darrell Issa of California, the only member of Congress to have attended one of the depositions, was just as harsh. "Shame on you," he said to McNamee. He said that McNamee's so-called Ph.D. degree—which McNamee had admitted came from a diploma mill—must stand for "pile it higher and deeper."

"I do what they ask," Issa said. "You know, that's what every drug pusher says, is we wouldn't be selling them if they weren't asking for them."

In one off-the-record conversation, a committee Republican challenged Pettitte's credibility by repeating an unsubstantiated rumor: After nine years in the Yankees' starting rotation, Pettitte signed a three-year, $31.5 million deal with the Houston Astros not because of the money or the chance to play closer to home, but because his wife, Laura, had learned that Pettitte had a New York girlfriend. The Republican could not produce any hard evidence that Pettitte had cheated on his wife—and he couldn't explain why Pettitte returned to the Bronx in 2007. But he also couldn't accept Pettitte as the final word in the McNamee-Clemens feud. If there was a chance Pettitte had lied about his own fidelity, he may have lied about Clemens and performance-enhancing drugs.

It didn't hurt that Clemens was a friend of the Bush family, and while Clemens had never been overtly political, it also didn't hurt that his personal mythology—a Texas gunslinger who embodied hard work and sacrifice—echoed values Republicans liked to trumpet. But Republican claims that they were simply responding to Democratic attacks on Clemens seemed strained, at best, when Foxx attacked the entire hearing as a waste of taxpayer money, ignoring the fact that the committee's ranking Republican, Tom Davis, had chaired the McGwire hearing three years earlier. And it was Foxx who pulled out a large poster featuring four pictures of Clemens at various stages of his career, and placed it on an easel. Foxx then opined that since Clemens hadn't become a musclebound caricature, McNamee's steroid allegations couldn't possibly be true. Dragging out a full-color poster was hardly a spontaneous move sparked by unfair Democratic attacks.

In many ways, Foxx's performance was straight out of *Reefer Madness*. Foxx wrongly assumed that everybody who ever experimented with performance-enhancing drugs became as ripped as the Incredible Hulk, just as earlier anti-drug crusaders assumed a toke off a joint left young people climbing the walls.

Much of the hearing had been downright weird. In an aside about B_{12}, Representative Issa had spoken about his mother's being premenopausal. John Duncan of Tennessee said he was dismayed to hear McNamee's testimony, because Duncan had been a batboy for the Knoxville Smokies, and "there was a bond between the batboys and the trainers."

Mercifully, Waxman was ready to end the hearing, but before he could, he would need to bang his gavel once more for silence—this time insisting that Clemens be silent. The interruption had come as Waxman read a concluding statement, summarizing the findings of the congressional probe, and mentioned Andy Pettitte's testimony being adverse to that of Clemens.

"Even though Mr. Clemens says his relationship with Mr. Pettitte was so close that they would know and share information with each other, evidently Mr. Pettitte didn't believe what Mr. Clemens said in that 2005 conversation."

"Doesn't mean he was not mistaken, sir," Clemens suddenly shouted. "It does not mean that he was not mistaken, sir."

"Excuse me," Waxman shouted, banging his gavel loudly. "But this is not your time to argue with me."

Waxman resumed, as Debbie Clemens reached out and placed a hand on the right arm of her husband, who sat looking as erect and pugnacious as he had for most of the long hearing.

"Mr. McNamee, you've taken a lot of hits today," Waxman said. "In my view, some were fair and some were really unwarranted . . . I want you to know though that as Chair of this committee I appreciate all your cooperation with our investigation. And I want to apologize to you for some of these comments that were made."

As Waxman spoke, Rusty Hardin and Lanny Breuer shook their heads in derision.

"But let me end by saying that we started this investigation in baseball to try to break that link of professional sports and the use of these drugs," Waxman said. "And we don't want to look at the past any longer in baseball and we didn't even want this hearing today, as I indicated in my opening. We want in the future to look at making sure that we don't have steroids, human growth hormone, and other dangerous drugs used by professional sports who are role models to our kids, because we're seeing the culture of the clubhouse become the culture of the high school gym."

With that, Waxman adjourned the meeting, banging his gavel one last time and, almost in the same move, switching off his microphone. This last action was something Clemens did not do, and as a roomful of people jumped up—cameras rushing forward, staffers moving to the dais, Clemens could be heard on his open microphone, speaking to no one in particular, still defiant, ready for a fight.

"I want to go talk to him about . . ." Clemens said. "I want to reaffirm . . . I don't appreciate . . ." His lawyers came forward and shook his hand, and Debbie leaned in close to talk to him. Clemens stood up, cast one quick look over the heads of the photographers to see Waxman already moving away, and then started to leave the room. At that moment Virginia Foxx came running over to the Clemens team. She wanted to meet Debbie and give her a hug. Foxx then went straight to Rusty Hardin, her fellow North Carolinan, and took his hand in hers. "Rusty, it was a treat to meet you guys," she gushed. Hardin leaned in to turn on his charm. "I'm delighted to meet you," he said. Foxx giggled girlishly.

In the end, though, Burton and Foxx and their outlandish attacks had helped accomplish what many had thought impossible: They turned Brian McNamee into a sympathetic figure. A poll conducted on *Sports Illustrated*'s Web site on the day of the hearing found that 84 percent of the 24,574 voters found McNamee to be the more convincing witness, while 16 percent said the seven-time Cy Young Award winner was more believable. By that point, McNamee didn't care. He'd won this round simply by not losing his cool. He'd beaten Clemens and his expensive lawyers by staying out of the way and letting them beat themselves.

In the pandemonium in the hallways after the hearing, Hardin spun like a top, saying the partisan divide had emerged because Waxman was not interested in dissenting opinions on the Mitchell Report.

"I'm sorry he feels that way," said Schiliro, Waxman's chief of staff. "We bent over backwards for both Mr. Clemens and Mr. Hardin, but we followed the facts. Mr. Hardin may not like the facts, but they are what they are."

Ward and Emery gave their own victorious press conference in the hallways, before returning to the underground parking garage where Paoletta and McNamee were waiting for them in the SUV Paoletta had brought. The small group had a little victory celebration. "It is what it is," they shouted, repeating McNamee's signature phrase, and giving each other high fives. Paoletta believed that the SUV parked next to theirs belonged to the Clemens team, so they hightailed it out of there.

The one-on-one between Clemens and McNamee might have been finished but Emery and Hardin sure weren't. Emery was certain he had just watched Clemens commit a host of crimes—not just perjury, but perhaps witness tampering as well. But having seen the surprising partisan breakdown, Emery was convinced orders had come from the White

House to protect Clemens, and Emery voiced his concerns that the president would bestow a pardon upon Clemens.

"The hint came from the contact from George Bush Sr.," Emery told the New York *Daily News.* "From that reference, you could ask if the representatives got direction from above. Maybe it's just presidential politics."

Hardin was outraged to hear about Emery's comments, which contained what he thought was more than just an implication that Clemens had committed a felony. "Richard Emery just has to quit smoking his own dope," Hardin said.

But Clemens didn't need to be convicted of or even indicted on a felony to become the recipient of a presidential pardon. President Gerald Ford had given a "prospective" pardon in 1974, when he granted a reprieve to Richard Nixon. And President George W. Bush had, not long before the hearing, granted clemency to Vice President Dick Cheney's former chief of staff, sparing Scooter Libby 30 months in jail for a perjury conviction.

But it quickly became apparent that Clemens would be radioactive for politicians. New York's Rev. Al Sharpton wondered aloud if the federal government, which had aggressively prosecuted Barry Bonds, Marion Jones, Trevor Graham, and other people of color caught lying about steroid use, would apply different standards for white athletes. "I think it was chilling to watch," Sharpton told the New York *Daily News.* "Do you have to be a different complexion to get protection? We will definitely be monitoring this."

An African-American member of the committee agreed. "What's fair for the goose has got to be fair for the gander," said Danny Davis (D-Ill.). "How do you investigate one group of players based on the same allegations and not investigate another?"

Davis himself seemed to have elicited a potential false statement out of Clemens during the hearing. Davis had come to the hearing with questions about Billy Belk and Jim Yarbrough, and the interview they had secretly recorded with McNamee the day before the release of the Mitchell Report. Clemens had told Davis he had "no idea the investigators were doing that with the lawyers."

It was disingenuous at best. Clemens had signed an authorization for the interview, and he and Hardin had listened to the phone call the evening after the interview as Belk and Yarbrough debriefed them about the call.

. . .

From that day forward, it was clear that Clemens had fallen harder than Mark McGwire ever had. The enduring images of the hearing were devastating to his image: Clemens sitting nervously while his lawyers stood behind him and argued with Waxman, Clemens licking his lips nervously while John Tierney explained the contradictions in the pitcher's statements, Clemens gulping, red in the face, while describing his wife's use of HGH.

But one of the defining statements of the hearing came not from Roger Clemens, nor even from Brian McNamee or Henry Waxman. One of the most memorable comments would come from Congressman Elijah Cummings, the Maryland Democrat who had extracted the "misremember" quote from Clemens. Cummings had been one of the first and last members of the committee to speak, and he seemed particularly well informed in his questions, and eager to be fair.

In a final exchange before adjournment, Waxman gave Cummings a moment to address Clemens. Cummings allowed Clemens to talk, but politely interrupted before time could run out. Then Cummings pointed out that Clemens, his attorneys, and pretty much everyone else involved with the saga had unambiguously endorsed the credibility of Andy Pettitte, who had been the great absent presence of the hearing.

"And your word is that Andy Pettitte is an honest man and his credibility pretty much impeccable," Cummings said. "Your lawyer says the same thing. But suddenly—and the committee gave him time after time after time to clear up his testimony and he consistently said the same thing under oath. Not only that, his wife, he goes and tells his wife everything and she says the same thing. But suddenly he misunderstood you."

Cummings then gave Clemens a look that said he genuinely wanted to give the seven-time Cy Young Award winner the benefit of the doubt, but could not. Then Cummings delivered the sound bite that probably gave voice to the feelings of millions of Americans who had watched the hearing.

"All I'm saying is it's hard to believe," Cummings said. "It's hard to believe you, sir. I hate to say that as—you're one of my heroes. But it's hard to believe."

CHAPTER FIFTEEN

February 17, 2008–Today

Pastor Tim Dunn, a brother-in-law to not just Andy Pettitte but also Kelly Blair of 1-on-1 Elite, stood at the pulpit at Central Baptist Church in Deer Park, Texas. It was February 17, four days after the congressional hearing, and he gave a sermon that included some conspicuous remarks about confession and forgiveness.

"I don't care what you've got going on in your life, you say, 'Well, I've messed up,' " Dunn said. "Whatever it is, you may think it's unforgivable. God doesn't think that. He made you. He wants to have a relationship with you, and all you have to do is confess it. He is faithful. Folks, I mess up, you mess up. God doesn't mess up."

Dunn's little sister, Laura, and her husband were not in the pews that Sunday. The pitcher was on his way to Tampa, Florida, to resume his baseball career with the Yankees.

In anticipation of the interest the sermon might hold, two uniformed members of the Deer Park Police Department guarded the lobby of the church as parishioners arrived, and one warned a photographer to stay away. Dunn declined to give an interview, but he and his flock were warm and welcoming to a notebook-carrying stranger attending the services. Dunn echoed the words Pettitte had used when he told the committee two weeks earlier that one day he would "have to give an account to God and not to nobody else."

"Jesus knows, and He'll forgive it," Dunn said. "If you confess it, the scripture says He is faithful and He will forgive us."

From the pews, the members seconded the preacher's words.

"That's right!" they called out. "Amen!"

Back in New York, that Sunday's edition of the *Daily News* named Kelly Blair's gym as the source of the growth hormone Tom Pettitte had given his son in 2004. The story described the shipments of Dianabol,

Winstrol-V, Deca-Durabolin, and HGH that Sammy Woodrow had seen moving through the gym, as well as the link to Craig Titus.

"I knew that Andy was hurt," Woodrow said, referring to Pettitte's elbow injury. "So I just figured, to avoid any bullshit, he [Tom Pettitte] was just getting it to help his son, you know?"

The story described 1-on-1 Elite as a junior-varsity version of BALCO, and noted that Brian McNamee had told the feds in recent weeks about Tom Pettitte's use and procurement. In Pasadena, trainers at the gym declined to be interviewed. One of the former trainers was a woman named Melody Manlove, whose father, John Manlove, was still seeking the Republican nomination for the congressional seat vacated by Tom DeLay. (He was running on a strong law-and-order platform.) When a reporter reached out to Melody Manlove through her MySpace profile, she said she had no knowledge of the trafficking of performance-enhancing drugs at her former workplace. She then cranked up the privacy settings on her MySpace page and posted a message in a box across the top of the page: "Loose lips sink ships and don't you forget it!"

Andy Pettitte didn't exactly sink ships when he kicked off spring training with his unprecedented press conference in Tampa the next day, but he did attract a massive crowd of reporters and an ESPN television audience who listened to him answer, as his lawyer, Jay Reisinger, put it, the questions that weren't "legal in nature." Pettitte sat at a table under a tent, flanked by Yankee GM Brian Cashman and new manager Joe Girardi, with Reisinger and Tom Farrell in the wings in case anything too horrifying came up. Derek Jeter, Jorge Posada, and Mariano Rivera sat a few feet away.

Pettitte disarmed the group of about 150 reporters by telling everyone that he'd wanted to get up and talk without having to read anything but that he wasn't smart enough to memorize everything that his wife, Laura, had jotted down while they were driving to Tampa. He then apologized to the Yankees and to his teammates and fans for having taken human growth hormone.

"And to anyone who is an Andy Pettitte fan," he said, "I'm sorry. I never want a young person to do what I did."

He then said he'd been put in a situation no one should have to be put in—right between two friends, McNamee and Clemens—and of having to tell Congress he'd gotten the HGH from his dad. He then began answering questions, beginning with whether he had been in contact with Clemens in recent weeks.

"No, we have not talked," he said, adding later that the two had last spoken about a month earlier.

He was asked about Clemens's claim that Pettitte had "misremembered" their conversation about HGH. "I'm not going to go there," he said. "I've had to testify under oath and so did Roger. Nobody tried to pressure me to do anything. . . . When you get put under oath—I've had to testify under oath and it's an intimidating process. . . . Man, I'm hoping and praying that I don't have to do anything else. One good thing is I've already testified. I'm gonna do everything possible to move forward."

Pettitte went to say he loved Clemens "like a brother," and that McNamee too was an "extremely good friend. Mac told the truth against me."

Unlike Clemens, Pettitte admitted that he'd known about the contents of the Mitchell Report several days before its release. "Brian had given me a call and told me."

Pettitte talked a little about his dad and said he had "prayed awfully hard" that he wouldn't have to testify at the hearing and answer questions about Tom Pettitte's HGH use. He'd relied on Romans 13:1–5, Bible verses that deal with submitting oneself to the authorities, in his decision to admit his HGH use and testify before the committee's investigators. "The authorities that exist have been established by God," the verses say. "Consequently, he who rebels against the authority is rebelling against what God has instituted, and those who do so will bring judgment on themselves."

Pettitte said he had apologized to George Steinbrenner—"face-to-face. I'm sorry"—and was at peace with the way he had handled things. "The easy way would have been not to have to face anybody anymore," he said. "That would have been the coward's way out."

With that, Pettitte left the tent and resumed his workouts and, basically, his career. It had been enough for most to simply hear him apologize and answer a few questions in person. He had come across as sincere and humble, his words believable. He'd been "stupid" and "desperate." No one seemed to need any more admissions from Andy Pettitte.

Three months later, ESPN reporter Mike Fish visited Pasadena and Deer Park and followed up on the revelations of February. Kelly Blair would admit using and dealing performance-enhancing drugs but deny that he was the one providing them to Tom Pettitte.

Tom Pettitte himself opened the door of his home momentarily to

Fish, said he didn't believe his son had cheated—"I don't think he is a cheater, 'cause I know his heart," Pettitte said—and described his own medical conditions.

"I know why I did HGH: for my own personal reasons, for my own personal health," the elder Pettitte would tell Fish before cutting the interview off. "I don't think as if I did anything illegal. True enough, I didn't get it . . . 'cause my doctor didn't give it to me. I asked him for it, and he wouldn't give it to me. When you're sick and tired of being sick and tired, you'll do what you can to help yourself. I would not ever come out and say that I think anybody should be doing it, 'cause I wouldn't want the kids to get the wrong impression. But it helped me. And that is the bottom line."

A week after the congressional hearing, Clemens's denials were still blowing up in his face, this time in the form of photographic evidence that seemed to place Clemens at the infamous 1998 barbecue at Jose Canseco's palatial South Florida home.

Clemens and his lawyers had turned the Canseco luncheon into a central pillar of the pitcher's defense. They came up with a mountain of evidence to counter McNamee's claim that Clemens had been there and had retired to a closed-door meeting with a mysterious muscle-head. There were the receipts that showed Clemens had played golf that day. There was the affidavit from Canseco expressing disappointment that Clemens wasn't there. There was the testimony from Lily Strain, the former nanny for Clemens's children.

Hardin was a lawyer in the mold of Johnnie Cochran, who had saved O. J. Simpson from a murder charge by pinning the whole case to a bloody glove that didn't seem to fit on Simpson's hand ("If it doesn't fit, you must acquit," Cochran had told the jury, memorably and convincingly). In Canseco's party, Hardin thought he'd found the analog to the bloody glove; if McNamee was wrong—or lying—about the party, what else was he wrong about? During Clemens's deposition, Hardin had made it explicit: "The whole house of cards falls," he said.

Clemens had followed Hardin's lead faithfully, going so far as to meet with Strain before the committee could reach her ("We are all trying to remember some kind of party at Canseco's house," Clemens claimed to have told her). In doing so, he had provoked the wrath of the committee, and in the face of Waxman's anger at the hearing, Clemens had finally admitted that he may have stopped by Canseco's to drop off his wife and brother-in-law. By that point, Clemens had already testified at least seven times that he wasn't at the party.

One person at the party, apparently, was an 11-year-old boy who lived in Canseco's South Florida neighborhood, invited by a contractor who had done some work at the home. The boy, a big baseball fan, had brought along a camera to capture the event. He had another guest take a picture of him posing with Clemens; another photo showed the boy with Canseco. The Clemens photo was framed and hung on the wall of the boy's bedroom, displayed for nearly a decade as a souvenir of a glorious afternoon spent lounging poolside with baseball heroes. Ten years later, the young man was a college baseball player and a prospect in Major League Baseball's upcoming amateur draft. He had followed Clemens's battle with McNamee with great interest, and on February 12, the day before the hearing, the young man's father contacted Rusty Hardin to offer him the pictures. Perhaps this explained why, during the hearing, Clemens seemed to back off his claim that he was nowhere near the party.

"On February 12th, a former neighbor of Jose Canseco's contacted me. He said he had a photograph of his son with Roger in a pool at a party at Canseco's house," Hardin said in a February 22 statement.

"He said that friends who had seen the photograph were suggesting to him that he sell it. I expressed no interest in buying it, but urged him to let our investigator visit with him, view the photograph, and interview him. He said he wanted to talk to his son first and would call me back that day. I gave him all of my phone numbers and urged him to call. Unfortunately, I never heard back from him."

Hardin failed to mention the photograph or the man's offer to the committee members who grilled McNamee and Clemens about the barbecue. Waxman and Davis didn't say anything publicly about the photos—but Richard Emery was glad to point out that Hardin had withheld evidence that could be damaging to Clemens's steroid denials.

"I find it interesting that it was offered to Hardin on February 12—and he walked away from it, probably because he didn't want any contradictory evidence that showed Clemens was at the party," Emery said.

The college ballplayer and his father may have been impressed by Clemens's career on the mound, but they were underwhelmed by his performance on the Hill. They were also appalled by the way Republicans, especially Indiana's Dan Burton, had treated McNamee during the congressional hearing. They contacted Emery and Earl Ward and told them about their photographs. They also had a friend contact several media outlets, including the New York *Daily News*, about buying the pictures. Emery notified congressional aides and federal agent Jeff Novitzky about his conversation with the college ballplayer's father. The photos were eventually turned over to federal investigators and never appeared in the newspaper accounts about their existence.

After months of claiming that Clemens was never near the party at Canseco's home—and making it a key argument in his defense of his client—Hardin was forced to backtrack.

"It is impossible for us to comment on the photograph itself because we haven't seen it," Hardin said. "We know that baseball announcers broadcasting the games at the time said Roger was not at the party. Jose Canseco has said Roger was not at the party, as has Canseco's former wife. Roger was playing golf at the time of the party, and has stated that he may have stopped by the Canseco house after playing golf before heading to the ballpark for the game."

Waxman and his congressional colleagues were still wrestling with the results of their two-month investigation into Clemens's attacks on the Mitchell Report when the photos emerged, raising fresh questions about the pitcher's credibility—and giving the lawmakers yet another reason to refer the entire matter to the Justice Department.

There was at least one other person in Canseco's inner circle who remembered quite clearly that Clemens was very much a part of the June 9, 1998, barbecue. Among the bustle of players, coaches, and Jose and Jessica Canseco's friends, the person recalled seeing two young kids running around the home with Strain. "Who the hell are these kids?" the person wondered. The answer came a short time later, when Canseco waltzed through one of the doors with Clemens in tow, well before the barbecue ended. The person remembered that various guests made a point to greet the young boys throughout the afternoon, one guest even taking time to read a few children's books to them.

A mobile mosh pit at the Astros' spring training facility in Kissimmee, Florida, of reporters and autograph seekers stepped over each other as they followed in Roger Clemens's wake on Wednesday, February 27. The pitching legend scribbled his name on a baseball for a fan, barely acknowledging the barrage of media questions. (Clemens had derisively dismissed the reporters when he'd arrived earlier in the day, telling them, "You guys need to get a life," he said. "There's a big-league team to the left, I think.") It was chilly in Kissimmee for late February, and Clemens was bundled up in a red Astros warm-up jacket and black sweatpants, a black Astros cap snug atop his head as he made the short walk between an enclosed pitching facility and the Astros' minor league clubhouse. In years past, this patch of real estate had been a safe haven for Clemens: He'd helped take the franchise to new heights, and in return the Astros had awarded him with a 10-year, $3 million personal services contract that would kick in once he retired. Until that day came, the legend still had a carte blanche invitation to roam Osceola County Stadium. Clemens would have probably engaged the media on any other afternoon, like he had so many times over the years, preaching about hard work and the dedication to his craft. Only twenty-four hours earlier, Clemens had inexplicably gabbed with reporters about whether he would actually try to play again. "At this point, I don't plan on playing, but, guys, I've said that for three years and the next thing you know I'm tying my cleats for real," Clemens said, seemingly oblivious to what was going on in the rest of his life.

But this Wednesday, the questions were different. Just a few hours earlier, Henry Waxman and Tom Davis made public the letter they had sent to Attorney General Michael Mukasey.

"We are writing to ask the Justice Department to investigate whether former professional baseball player Roger Clemens committed perjury and made knowingly false statements during the Oversight and Government Reform Committee's investigation of the use of steroids and performance-enhancing drugs in professional baseball," read the opening of the February 27 letter to Mukasey.

"We believe that his testimony in a sworn deposition on February 5, 2008, and at a hearing on February 13, 2008, that he never used anabolic steroids or human growth hormone, warrants further investigation. That testimony is directly contradicted by the sworn testimony of Brian McNamee, who testified that he personally injected Mr. Clemens with anabolic steroids and human growth hormone. Mr. Clemens's testimony is also contradicted by the sworn deposition testimony and affidavit submitted to the Committee by Andrew Pettitte, a former teammate of Mr. Clemens, whose testimony and affidavit reported that Mr. Clemens had admitted to him in 1999 or 2000 that he had taken human growth hormone."

So everything had culminated with this: Congress perceived Clemens to be a liar and now federal agents would begin to canvass the country in an effort to prove that. Stones would be overturned. Every segment of Clemens's private life would become fair game. Skeletons could emerge. It had the potential to get ugly.

If Clemens was cracking under the weight of those realizations, he barely showed it during the three-and-a-half-hour workout at the complex that February 27. The news of the criminal referral broke while he was tossing batting practice to the farmhands, including his son Koby. As Clemens barked out his customary trash talk to players in the batter's box, encouraging the young hitters at the same time, his focus never shifted.

When he left the complex later that afternoon, Clemens arranged for an Astros clubbie to back his black Hummer up to the base of the clubhouse's front wall—a driving distance of roughly 200 feet. That way, Clemens would avoid having to come within even arm's reach of the reporters. An Astros employee ordered the group to stand on the sidewalk on either side of the pathway in front of the massive vehicle.

"See y'all tomorrow," Clemens said when he emerged, flashing the peace sign and slipping into his sleek tank. Now he was safe in his car, tinted windows shielding his face. The Hummer rolled past the media before Clemens braked at the exit. Fans swarmed the driver's side window, one yelling, "You're a legend." The Rocket scribbled a few more autographs and then he was gone.

The criminal referral was the main news coming out of Capitol Hill that week but there was another little dustup as well. A year after Democratic senator Chuck Schumer introduced a bill that would classify human growth hormone as a controlled substance—and thereby make it illegal to obtain without a medical prescription—two Republican senators (Mike Enzi of Wyoming and Richard Burr of North Carolina) helped stymie the bill's passage. Schumer was floored.

"It is hard to grasp what possible objections anyone could have to making sure a substance as dangerous as HGH stays out of the wrong hands," said Schumer, who had hoped to hot-line—or expedite—the bill's passage by avoiding laborious debate over the bill's objectives.

The HGH debate had raged for three years after Major League Baseball banned its use prior to the 2005 season. Urine samples were the sole means by which players were tested—in accordance with baseball's collective bargaining agreement—and a new, blood sample–based HGH test was unreliable, in the eyes of the union and Don Fehr. While Schumer's bill was getting blocked that week, Fehr was making the rounds at spring training sites, talking about the collective bargaining agreement and the fallout of the Mitchell Report. He was more often than not fielding questions about HGH, which might as well have been a four-letter word. During a stop at Tradition Field in Port St. Lucie, where the Mets trained, that Friday, February 29, Fehr scoffed at questions about HGH testing. He was asked about the upcoming Beijing Olympics, where officials would implement HGH testing to determine its efficacy. Fehr was unimpressed.

"What we've said repeatedly and I'll repeat today—we've been waiting for the blood test to be available for [HGH] for a very long time. It still isn't," said Fehr. "When and if one is [available], the first thing we'll do is take a look at it. We'll see if it can be scientifically validated by people other than those trying to sell it to you."

While Fehr was grousing in Port St. Lucie that Friday, further north Clemens was conspicuously absent from Astros camp. After three straight days of working with the club's minor-leaguers, he was a no-show on February 29. The previous day, team owner Drayton McLane had made it clear that Clemens—even with his long-standing status as a Houston icon—was causing a distraction at spring training. McLane told reporters that Clemens's presence amid the legal firestorm "makes it more complex, it sure does. That brings a lot of media here. And the only regrettable part, it takes the focus off baseball."

The frustration of dealing with the Clemens circus was rubbing off on the players too. Astros catcher Brad Ausmus, who caught Clemens from 2004 through 2006, rolled his eyes when reporters approached his locker to ask about the criminal referral.

"I don't know if it's shocking or sad. I wish it wasn't happening," said Ausmus. "It's become boring, really, almost like following the Britney Spears saga. I think the government's involvement in baseball's steroid problems is a little bit extreme. However, I don't know if the government's involvement in a perjury investigation is extreme. If being under oath is going to carry any weight, you need to have the threat of perjury."

Even ESPN was turning Clemens away as the federal investigation loomed. That weekend—February 29 through March 2—Clemens was to have attended an ESPN fan fest event at Disney World in Orlando called "ESPN: The Weekend." But the network had contacted Clemens to advise him not to come, telling the pitcher it was in his best interest to stay away. That snub would be the first of several ugly divorces Clemens would weather over the course of the year.

A couple of hours after McLane's and Ausmus's remarks, Clemens again trudged up the ramp to the minor league clubhouse. "Have a nice day, man. You guys are wasting your time," he told the reporters. Forty-five minutes later, he was atop a mound on Field 4, morphing into a drill instructor, hiding whatever frustrations he felt behind the muscle of his fastball. He fired heat. He wiped his brow. He dug into the dirt. After a couple of minutes, Koby Clemens walked onto the field and spotted his father on the hill.

"How's the old man looking? Throwing strikes?" asked Koby. All the son had to do was watch his father at work to know the answer to his questions.

"You guys think you're seeing the baseball, but you're not," said Clemens, just after outfield prospect Jordan Parraz whiffed at a Rocket offering. Parraz finished his at-bats and slumped on the dugout bench, grumbling, "I fucking missed like every one of them. I'm not used to that."

After Clemens finished his session, his Hummer was driven up to the clubhouse wall again. He still wielded some measure of power, even if there were early signs that the empire around him was starting to crumble.

But those bruises to his psyche would come much later. As he pulled out of the Astros' spring training parking lot that Thursday, February 28, Clemens was, in a way, taking a hiatus from his craft. He was about to learn what Barry Bonds knew—that there was a limit to what the baseball establishment would tolerate when it came to the taint of criminality. Bonds was a game-changing free agent, but he was unable to find a job in baseball once his indictment landed, and as his agents bellyached about "collusion," their client, one of the best hitters in the game, remained on the sidelines.

Now, Clemens too was going offstage and more or less becoming a ghost haunting America's pastime.

The defamation suit Clemens had brought against Brian McNamee took a back seat in the weeks following the hearing and the criminal referral. Everyone but Richard Emery had been caught up in the latest developments of the Clemens saga. Just five days after Clemens left the Astros' Florida spring training site, Emery took the necessary steps to try to get the case tossed. Emery filed court papers that Tuesday, March 4, arguing that the claim should be dismissed on jurisdictional issues and that McNamee's statements to both federal authorities and to George Mitchell should be privileged.

"Brian did not speak to the press, only to Novitzky, Parrella, and George Mitchell's commission," Emery said. "And he was forced to speak to the Mitchell commission by Parrella and Novitzky. So there is a privilege for speaking to the government and those the government compels you to speak to."

Emery also argued in the papers that Hardin should be disqualified from the case since he had represented Andy Pettitte in the week before the Mitchell Report's release. Earl Ward had already said that Pettitte was the McNamee team's "star witness" in the defamation case and Pettitte would hold that title for any criminal proceeding that involved Clemens. Following arguments during a hearing in Houston on April 9, U.S. District Court Judge Keith Ellison allowed Hardin to stay on as Clemens's counsel, saying Pettitte was the party with standing on the issue, not McNamee; if Pettitte believed his rights were being violated, the judge said, then he or his lawyers would have appeared at the hearing. "Instead, he's sitting it out," Ellison said. The privilege issue would not be resolved for months, with Ellison holding a hearing later that fall in Houston to hear both sides argue that point. Ellison would call the privilege issue "the lynchpin" of the case when he made his remarks on November 3, though he would not rule on the motion to dismiss until February 2009.

Six weeks after the Clemens hearing, and a month after the committee's leaders asked the Justice Department to investigate whether Clemens had committed perjury, the panel's Republicans issued a 109-page report on March 25 that questioned McNamee's credibility and seemed to give credence to Clemens's drug denials. Finally, Clemens's legal team had something to be happy about. The report—entitled "Weighing the Committee Record: A Balanced Review of the Evidence Regarding Performance-Enhancing Drugs in Baseball"—didn't attempt to exonerate the pitcher, but it did seek to raise questions about many of the conclusions Democrats, and baseball fans, had reached during the hearing.

The main purpose of the report was to attack the Democrats and the eighteen-page memo prepared by the majority staff that had analyzed the credibility of seven statements Clemens made during his deposition and his hearing testimony. The Democrats, the Republicans suggested, had it in for Clemens.

"The Democratic memorandum," the GOP report said, "reads like an advocate's brief or a prosecutorial indictment of Roger Clemens."

Ranking Republican Tom Davis, of course, had signed on for the criminal referral. But now he seemed to be waffling a little bit.

"Did Roger Clemens lie to us?" Davis asked in a statement released on March 25 that accompanied the report. "Some of the evidence seems to say he did; other information suggests he told the truth. It's a far more complicated picture than some may want to believe. Memories fade and recollections differ. At this point, the Justice Department is best equipped to investigate that central question and reach a fair conclusion."

The report claimed that when Republicans presided over the 2005 steroid hearing, they focused on national drug policy, not the persecution of baseball players or executives. (Mark McGwire, Donald Fehr, and Bud Selig would undoubtedly disagree.) The 2008 hearing, the Republicans claimed, had turned into a show trial: a shift away from the generalized problem to McNamee vs. Clemens, a war between individuals.

The minority report regurgitated much of the evidence gathered in the feud between Clemens and McNamee, casting it in the best possible light for the Bush family friend. It addressed differing accounts of the 1998 party at Jose Canseco's home and Clemens's denials of drug use. It emphasized the refusal of the Blue Jays team physician, Ron Taylor, to say what had caused the injury to Clemens's backside. It attacked Democrats for consulting with MRI expert Mark Murphey about that injury—without mentioning what a rushed job that consult had been, thanks to the foot-dragging of Clemens's attorneys in sharing the MRI results.

"In the midst of a so-called bipartisan investigation, the Democratic staff found their own expert," the GOP report continued. "The Democratic staff failed to disclose this expert until 63 minutes before the Committee hearing. Read carefully, Murphey's report reveals the unusual request made by the Democratic staff. According to his report, identified as a 'Congressional Consult,' the Democratic staff asked him to evaluate the theoretical possibility that Clemens's MRI showed the presence of Winstrol. Such theoretical possibilities are no substitute for actual evidence."

It also highlighted contradictions in testimony between McNamee and Andy Pettitte. McNamee, for example, said he first discussed human growth hormone with Pettitte during the winter of 2001–2002 while working out in Clemens's gym. Pettitte, in his deposition, said he could not remember the first conversation he had with the trainer about the drug.

McNamee's lawyers dismissed the report as unnecessary posturing, further proof that committee Republicans had been ordered to attack the trainer and shield Clemens during their February 13 hearing.

"This case has already been referred to the Department of Justice," Earl Ward said. "Congress should just let the Justice Department do its job."

On Monday, March 31, Jose Canseco was the picture of happiness, his 6-4 frame immersed in a plush oversized leather chair in Manhattan's Omni Berkshire hotel lobby. Fresh off a late-afternoon taping with David

Letterman to promote his second book, *Vindicated*, Canseco stretched his legs out and sipped a rum drink through a red straw, settling into an interview with two New York *Daily News* reporters—another chance to throw bricks at Alex Rodriguez.

Vindicated was technically a sequel to *Juiced*, but really it was Canseco's big "Fuck you" to Major League Baseball and to Rodriguez. "So A-Rod," he wrote, "if you're reading this book, and if I'm not getting through to you, let's get clear on one thing: I hate your fucking guts."

While Canseco was pitching his book in December, he'd expressed shock that Rodriguez was absent from the Mitchell Report and hinted that his new book would address that oversight. Canseco was clearly aiming to take down A-Rod, even if he lacked the same ammunition—firsthand accounts of injecting other players with steroids—that he had packed into *Juiced*.

Now the book was out, and Canseco didn't seem nervous about the allegations he'd thrown out. His gray suit jacket was splayed open, his sunglasses perched atop his thick black hair, day-old stubble dotting his cheeks. Robert Saunooke, who had played football at Brigham Young, and Canseco's petite girlfriend, Heidi Northcott, had accompanied Canseco to New York for the launch of the book tour. It was Saunooke who had kept the project alive after Penguin dropped out in January, with reports that the publishing house had concerns that Canseco's sequel would not deliver any explosive news. Don Yaeger, a former *Sports Illustrated* associate editor, had been tapped as the ghostwriter in December 2007 when Penguin was still on board. Yaeger, whose previous collaboration on the Duke lacrosse scandal had been a best-seller, initially said that Canseco already had "a lot of stuff put together," but four days into 2008, having reviewed Canseco's material, Yaeger bowed out of the *Vindicated* project.

"I don't think there's a book there," Yaeger said. "I don't know what they're going to do. I don't think he's got what he claims to have, certainly doesn't have what he claims to have on A-Rod. There's no meat on the bones."

Yaeger's frank opinion had set the tone for sportswriters and Canseco critics, who echoed the refrain about *Vindicated* prior to its publication: If Canseco had damaging information on Rodriguez or other players using steroids or growth hormone, why hadn't he included the material in the first book? Canseco would claim in *Vindicated* that he had wanted to include Rodriguez in *Juiced*, but that his publisher, HarperCollins, had not allowed it. Canseco was vague on the reason the publisher was opposed to including Rodriguez, although it was assumed the lack of first-hand knowledge of his use was a good one.

Undaunted by Yaeger's pass, Saunooke pushed the project along and, within weeks, Simon & Schuster entered the fray. A deal was set and the book's publication date was originally planned for April 1, to coincide with the start of the baseball season. But copies of *Vindicated* were unwrapped early. The book's Valentine-red cover, featuring a baseball pierced by a syringe, was a visual flare on book racks and shelves. Copies popped up in Massachusetts and New York bookstores, and an obscure blogger named Joe Lavin, who found a copy of *Vindicated* in a Cambridge, Massachusetts, store, wrote about some of the more salacious parts.

"It's a roughly 250-page book that deals with many things, but, of course, all you want to know about are the Big Names," Lavin wrote on his Tuesday, March 25, blog.

"In here, Canseco accuses three more players of using steroids, and they are:

"(Spoiler Alert: Don't read any further if you don't want to know how the book ends!)

"Magglio Ordonez

"Roger Clemens

"Alex Rodriguez"

E-mails burned up the Internet. The dirt on A-Rod, although vague and written with a tone of obvious disdain, caused a seismic jolt in the last week of spring training. Canseco wrote that he had worked out with Rodriguez in "the latter half of the 1990s" when Rodriguez was a star shortstop with Seattle. Rodriguez was "skinny" at the time, but Canseco described how the two men had used the "five-thousand-square-foot gym" in Canseco's Florida home to train. Before long, Rodriguez was inquiring about steroids and Canseco was introducing him to a steroids dealer whom Canseco anonymously labeled "Max."

"So," Rodriguez says to Canseco in the book, "the 'roids: Do they fuck you up?"

"Do I look like I'm fucked up?" Canseco replied.

"The next day, Max called to thank me," Canseco wrote. "He said A-Rod has signed on. I didn't ask for specifics. I didn't ask if A-Rod had signed on to get trained, or to get shit from this guy. That wasn't my business."

The Yankees were on a road trip the day portions of *Vindicated* appeared in news reports, but Rodriguez stayed behind at Legends Field in Tampa. Most of the beat writers were traveling with the team, but a small group of reporters confronted Rodriguez outside the spring training complex. "I really have absolutely no reaction," Rodriguez said. The nonanswer did nothing to prevent a cascade of damaging headlines for the Yankee star the following morning: "A-Roid?" blared the *Daily News's* back page.

As Canseco chatted in the Omni hotel bar lobby that Monday, *Vindicated: Big Names, Big Liars, and the Battle to Save Baseball* had been on book stands for a few days. He was clearly relishing the way the book was causing the reigning American League Most Valuable Player to squirm. Rodriguez's "no comment" only validated Canseco's claims, at least in Canseco's mind.

"I've got the ace in the hole. And he knows it," Canseco said when asked if he would identify Max. "There's no way that [Rodriguez is] going to fight me. He's just trying to make it go away." Canseco added that Max's name would become public if Rodriguez pulled a Roger Clemens, and went on *60 Minutes* or filed a lawsuit.

Clemens's appearance in *Vindicated* was an altogether different animal. It had been a month and a half since the February hearing and two months since Canseco had signed the affidavit, yet Canseco again painted Clemens as someone who needed performance enhancers to prolong his pitching career.

"All those Cy Young Awards. The way he was throwing, hard and fast and steady without seeming to break a sweat. What else could it be?" Canseco wrote in the opening pages of his book. In the comfort of the Omni Berkshire, though, Canseco was in backtrack mode, steering clear of exposing Clemens as anything other than a talented pitcher he was happy to assist during the buildup to the February hearing.

"I signed [the affidavit] from what I knew to be the truth. Now, whether he did steroids beyond my knowledge, that's something totally different. But I signed an affidavit accurately to exactly what happened. Now the rest, I don't know," Canseco said. "He asked me, and Roger and I were friends. He asked me to tell the truth and that's what I did."

Canseco dismissed the notion that he should be worried about testifying at any trial for Clemens, outlining a hypothetical conversation between him and a questioner.

"I'll testify again. Same identical thing," said Canseco.

"Did you ever inject Roger?"

"No."

"Did you ever supply him?"

"No."

"Did you guys talk about steroids?"

"I talked about steroids with hundreds of players and hundreds of people outside of baseball. It doesn't mean they were using steroids."

"Did you joke about it?"

"Absolutely."

"Did you ever see him with a needle?"

"No."

"That's exactly what happened," Canseco said. "I can't perjure myself because I'm telling the absolute truth. There's no way."

It was a curiously talkative Canseco, who was known to eschew media interviews unless there was some monetary value attached. Late in the interview, before Saunooke and Northcott returned from the hotel bar, Canseco even suggested that the steroids era that he helped expose would eventually fade in the minds of baseball writers and fans, and that players tainted from steroid suspicions—like McGwire or Palmeiro—would get their due in Cooperstown.

"You know what, a couple of years down the line, people are going to forget the steroid era and these individuals will be inducted into the Hall of Fame. You cannot neglect those stats," Canseco mused. "Because, what're you going to have for the next 20 years? No Hall of Fame inductees? Think about it logically. You've got these handful of guys who you found used steroids. What about the guys who slipped through the cracks who used steroids? Either we're all guilty or we're all innocent. 'Fine, I'm guilty,' whatever. But you can't just hold a certain [number] of individuals guilty for using steroids, because 80 percent used them."

On April 22, less than a month after the *Vindicated* book tour launched, Canseco was sitting across from Jeff Novitzky and two FBI agents in a Los Angeles federal building answering questions as part of the ongoing Clemens perjury probe. Instead of Saunooke, L.A.-based attorney Gregory Emerson was by Canseco's side during the interview. Saunooke, who had helped Canseco weather an assault charge, the 2005 congressional hearing, and had handled his various and sometimes serious legal affairs over five years, was suddenly out. Canseco had fired him a week after the start of the book tour.

"I don't represent him anymore. I terminated my relationship with him," Saunooke said on April 10. "Just moving on. It's a number of things.

Irreconcilable differences, disagreement on some issues. I just don't need the hassle anymore." Saunooke later agreed that he'd been fired, and that Emerson had sent him a letter that said as much.

Canseco's April 22 meeting with federal agents lasted over three hours, with the discussion veering from details of the 1998 party to the two photographs that seemed to place Clemens at Canseco's home that day. Emerson said there were few surprises during the meeting, that his client was not considered a "target nor the subject of an investigation," adding that the FBI and Novitzky had already interviewed other teammates, trainers, and staff from the 1998 Blue Jays team.

Max's identity had been exposed by SI.com before the feds met with Canseco. Joseph Dion was a Canadian-born trainer who had moved to Miami in the late 1990s and who had trained Rodriguez—just as Canseco had written. Dion, however, said he had never introduced Rodriguez to steroids, much less supplied or injected him.

"That's really, really funny, because I am the one person that hates steroids," Dion told SI.com. "I'm against it 100 percent. And, A-Rod, at the time that I trained him—and this I swear to God—was 100 percent against steroids. He was one of the hardest-working guys, and most natural guy, that I've met in my life. He hated steroids. We talked about it."

(A year later, after *SI* reported that Rodriguez had tested positive in baseball's 2003 survey testing season, Dion stuck to much the same story.)

Emerson said that Dion's name was discussed during the interview with federal agents, and that Canseco had repeated what he had written in *Vindicated*.

"His name came up," said Emerson. "Jose simply confirmed his account in his book. There was not a whole lot on that. It kind of surprised me."

The whispers had been around for years. Roger Clemens, father of four, husband to Debbie, had plenty of women on the side in the years since his marriage in 1984. But it wasn't until Clemens unleashed his full-scale legal attack on Brian McNamee—beginning with the January 6 defamation suit in which he said McNamee's false allegations had injured his reputation and exposed him to "public hatred, contempt, ridicule and financial injury"—that the skeletons began to creep out of the Rocket's closet, revealing a secret, second life of affairs and flings. The first bomb hit on April 28 when the New York *Daily News* reported on Clemens's long affair with country singer Mindy McCready, a relationship that began when the singer was 15 and the pitcher was a 28-year-old married father of two. The story came just over two months after Clemens's wobbly performance at the hearing, where he had opened his testimony with the defiant depiction of his "family man" image: "Anyone who has spent time around me knows that my family is and has always been my top priority," he said. "My wife, Debbie, and my sons—Koby, Kory, Kacy, and Kody—mean more to me than anything in the world. Having said that, baseball has definitely provided me with significant opportunities off the field."

McNamee's lawyers had tried to warn Clemens that this kind of thing could happen if they persisted with the suit: Character would absolutely become an issue. Emery threatened to depose McCready and any of the other women that might emerge—and several more did. "The issue in Roger's suit against McNamee is Roger's reputation and how it has been damaged," said Emery. "If it's proved that he's a philanderer, his reputation is already damaged. When you sue for defamation, you put your whole reputation in the community at issue. Anything is fair game, including his claim of sanctimonious purity. We would cross-examine him and other witnesses who might impact on his alleged behavior. We would probably subpoena [McCready] and witnesses who knew [of the relationship]. He's a 'family man'—he implies that. It's about what his damages are. All is fair game."

Hardin wasn't about to do McCready any favors. When contacted by the *Daily News* before the story ran, Hardin said that Clemens considered McCready nothing more than a "family friend" and that Debbie Clemens knew the singer well. Hardin even confirmed most of the details of the report after initially scoffing at an interview request. "I won't be calling you back," Hardin sneered when he was first contacted by the paper. Less than an hour later, Hardin was back on the phone, saying he'd changed his mind—he'd talked with Clemens directly. Not only did the Clemens family know McCready, but Hardin confirmed that the singer had used Roger's plane and that Clemens had done several "favors" for her over the years. Hardin was adamant about one point: Clemens had never had sex with McCready. "He has never had a sexual relationship with her," Hardin said. "That's what I take you to mean by an affair. I'd be careful, guys." With that admonition, Hardin ended the call: "I've pretty much exhausted anything I know about it in this conversation."

Brian McNamee burst out laughing when told of Hardin's remarks and McCready was equally amused, confiding to family and friends that she'd never even been in the same room as Debbie Clemens, much less met the Rocket's wife: It was like saying Hillary Clinton shared beauty tips with Monica Lewinsky. But McCready's tone changed when she considered the legal predicament Clemens had forced her into by denying the affair happened. Her young son, Zander, was living in Fort Myers with McCready's mother, Gayle Inge, and Mindy was trying to regain custody of him. The custody struggle stretched back to the previous year when the singer had been sent to jail in Williamson County, Tennessee, following an altercation with her mother. The young boy, whose father was McCready's abusive ex-boyfriend, singer Billy McKnight, had spent most of his two years living with Inge.

"It doesn't make me look good to perjure myself, because I can't afford to be put in this position with my son. That's why it angers me very much," McCready said. "I think it is selfish of Roger to put me under scrutiny. I could lose my son. He doesn't have to worry about losing his kids."

The classic Clemens strategy was in full effect—deny, deny, deny— and attack anyone who contradicted those denials. A week after the *Daily News* report, Clemens apologized to his fans for "mistakes in my personal life," although there was no mention of McCready or what those mistakes were. Certainly, there was no acknowledgment of the "love at first sight, no doubt about it" bond detailed in the *Daily News* article. The denials would become a familiar refrain from the Clemens camp throughout 2008, with Clemens's crisis manager, Patrick Dorton, warning reporters on a regular basis not to write that Clemens had had sex with a 15-year-old. That would have been statutory rape.

McCready, who was trying to resurrect her music career after a slew of personal setbacks, confirmed the *Daily News* story and all its details later on the afternoon of the 28th, with a simple statement: "I cannot refute anything in the story." She had carried on a lengthy relationship with Clemens beginning in 1991 when she was 15, and the relationship had endured numerous breaks until it ended sometime in 2006. The two had met at a Fort Myers bar called the Hired Hand, where the teenage McCready was singing karaoke and drawing rave reviews from Clemens and some Red Sox teammates. Oblivious to how famous the man was whom she was introduced to later that night, after Clemens had fired a T-shirt onstage with his and his teammates' signatures, McCready was told Clemens was a baseball player who played for the Red Sox.

McCready made a call to her younger brother T.J.

"Yeah, I know who the Red Sox are," he said.

"Do you know a person named Roger Clemens?" asked Mindy.

"You are so stupid, of course I know who he is," said T.J.

"Well, he's standing in front of me and wants to know if you guys want to go to a baseball game," said Mindy.

There was no need for T.J. McCready to talk up the Sox pitcher to his sister. Clemens was working his Texas charm that evening, and soon enough McCready wound up in Clemens's hotel room, where they watched a movie before the teenager fell asleep on Clemens's chest. When McCready set off to make it as a singer in Nashville several years later, she and Clemens still maintained communication, even if the visits had become more infrequent. But by the time Clemens was winning back-to-back Cy Young Awards in 1997 and 1998, there was plenty of off-the-field heat with McCready. She was riding a wave of music fame with the hit "Guys Do It All the Time," the music video featuring the sexy blonde wearing sunglasses and boxing gloves, flashing a toned, bare midriff as she belted out lyrics with a Southern drawl: "Though I left my clothes all over the place and I took your 20 bucks/Though I didn't get the front yard cut 'cause I had to wash my truck."

It was during his Toronto years that Clemens was accused by McNamee of first dabbling with performance-enhancing drugs. If Clemens was injecting human growth hormone or any steroids, McCready was unaware of it or of any distinct changes in Clemens's body. One of the damning testimonials against Barry Bonds came from long-time mistress Kimberly Bell, who told a California grand jury about the home run king's transformation from an average-size player to a circus freak with bodybuilder's muscles due to steroid use. McCready said she never saw the small abscess on Clemens's buttocks, the one McNamee claimed in his congressional deposition that the Rocket developed.

"He's a freakin' health freak," McCready said. "All natural stuff, all the time. All natural. He's all about, 'Get your ass up and work.' "

As McCready's fame swelled and Clemens's career was in its rebirth, they indulged in lavish getaways. Whether they were at the Soho Grand Hotel in Manhattan or on junkets to Vegas or touching down in Palm Springs, McCready enjoyed the luxury of Clemens's private jet, as did her siblings. Extramarital affairs by athletes were certainly nothing new by the time Clemens and McCready became an item, but over the 15 years of his relationship with McCready, Clemens had been able to keep his private business mostly private, prompting several of their confidants to remark that it was a "damn miracle" no paparazzi photographs had surfaced. In the age of YouTube—where superstars and average Joes alike are subject to having their most mundane and intimate details broadcast on the Internet—it was indeed a damn miracle. Clemens and McCready drew the line when it came to exclusivity—in addition to McCready's other men, Clemens's romantic dalliances included golfer John Daly's ex-wife, Paulette Dean Daly; a Manhattan bartender named Angela Moyer; and the beautiful Jennifer.

"He had chicks stashed in every city—like every athlete, you play golf, you go get drunk, and [have sex]," said one Clemens friend. "In some ways, it's a lonely life."

Moyer tended bar at an Upper East Side watering hole called Sutton Place from 2000 to 2004, roughly the same time Clemens played for the Yankees, and he was regularly spotted in nightspots with her. There was also a liaison with Dean Daly, who had met Clemens when she was a "Classic Girl," one of the women who help in ceremonial duties at the Bob Hope Chrysler Classic, the annual Palm Springs golf tournament that Clemens and his buddies, including Kenny Jowdy and a Manhattan hedge fund manager named Jeff Altman, regularly attended. An Orange County friend of Daly's told the New York *Daily News* he had seen Clemens and the golfer's ex partying on Newport Beach's restaurant row on one occasion. "They were not an obvious item," the friend said. "They were never hanging all over each other. I never saw them walking arm-in-arm or kissy-kissy. But they weren't hiding anything, either." McCready had seen that firsthand when Clemens took McCready to the Bob Hope golf event and they ran into Dean Daly. The Classic Girl "threw herself" at the Rocket right in front of McCready, according to witnesses. "What the fuck? What do you think you're doing?" an incredulous McCready asked Clemens. "That girl knows you." A sheepish Clemens admitted only that he had met Dean Daly at some other function and that they were nothing more than friends.

Despite the gaps in their affair, Clemens and McCready seemed to care deeply for each other, even when their relationship was in an off-again phase. She had a serious relationship with Dean Cain of *Lois & Clark* fame and with former NHL player Drake Berehowsky. But none of those relationships matched her affair with Clemens, and she continued to refer to Clemens as "precious" after the two split for good. Clemens pined for McCready throughout her other relationships, dispensing advice to his "Mee Mee"—the affectionate nickname he gave her—or sending cash bundles via FedEx. As recently as 2007, when McCready landed in jail after a probation violation—following the argument with her mother—Clemens was sending her good luck messages through a third party.

It was Debbie Clemens's turn to fume when she found out about McCready's engagement to Cain back in 1997. Spotting the announcement in *People* magazine, Debbie Clemens launched a copy of the magazine at her husband's head in anger and disgust. "I guess you lost your girl," Debbie Clemens said as Clemens ducked. Even at that early stage, Clemens's marriage to "Day-ub"—McCready's impersonation of how Roger pronounced his wife's name—had shown some wear. Debbie was the dutiful wife compared with the extroverted party girl. Clemens would go days without talking to Debbie, which prompted McCready to unload an idle threat on the Rocket. "I wouldn't put up with that shit," she told him. "You go one day without calling me, don't ever call me again. You better never treat me like that."

Clemens was leveled by the news of McCready's pregnancy, initially cutting off communication. Within weeks, though, he was calling her again, telling her to "put a golf ball in his left hand," so that the toddler would develop into a southpaw. Clemens jokingly told her younger brothers Josh and T.J.—who stand 6'3" and 6'4½"—that he should "have some kids with your sister." None of the K boys came close to the towering 6'4" frame of their father.

McCready never anticipated that Clemens's legal entanglements would draw her into the morass. By early May 2008, the Justice Department's perjury investigation churning, Jeff Novitzky (who had switched agencies from the Internal Revenue Service to the Food and Drug Administration) and other law enforcement authorities interviewed some key figures tied to Clemens, including Canseco, in late April. Just over a month later, it was McCready's turn. McCready was grilled for several hours in Nashville by two FBI agents, with her attorney, Lee Ofman, present. The FBI meeting coupled with yet another string of legal stumbles—a court appearance for falsifying her community service records and the ongoing custody battle for her son—backed up McCready's work schedule. The documentary about her life, *Fallen Angel*, had a tentative July release according to the film's executive producer, Blake Freeman, but that deadline came and went. As for the new album she was working on, aside from a single she released to her fans for free in May—an emotional ballad entitled "I'm Still Here," which she wrote during her 2007 jail stint—her record company, Iconic, issued no update on when the singer's work might appear. By mid-July, she suffered what a family member said was a nervous breakdown. "She's at the end of her rope," the person said. The Clemens affair, the FBI, the media deluge, the multiple projects, and her probation violation had been too much. Lee Ofman, McCready's attorney, had been in contact with Rusty Hardin.

A week after her breakdown, McCready checked herself into a treatment center in Hunt, Texas, called La Hacienda, a facility known primarily as a drug and alcohol rehab center. Her New York–based publicist, Susan Blond Inc., issued a standard statement, asking for the media to respect McCready's privacy. While at La Hacienda, McCready immersed herself in daily classes, talking about her own personality strengths and faults. She wrote journal entries about her battles with the media. She mulled over her tie to Clemens, what it spelled for her personal and professional future. It was unclear if Clemens reached out to McCready at La Hacienda, as he had done while she was in jail. Upon release on September 3, McCready made a beeline to North Fort Myers and Zander. It was a chance to reconnect with her mother; her half-brother, Sky; stepfather, Michael; and father, Tim. McCready seemed to be recharged in her old roots, jokingly renaming the city "Fort Miserable." While bouncing up and down on a trampoline under a sprawling oak tree outside her mother's home one evening, she performed a couple of backflips for a reporter before tumbling onto the ground. Giggling, McCready brushed off her 7 For All Mankind jeans, but when she was shown a photograph of Clemens from a June minor league All-Star Game in Myrtle Beach, South Carolina, that Koby had played in for the Carolina League, she looked sad. In the image, Clemens is scowling, hands at his side, while Debbie Clemens sits in front of him, her digital camera trained on the field below. Clemens's mother-in-law, Jan Wilde, is standing to his right, while another Clemens son is off to his father's left.

"God, he looks so miserable," McCready said. "He doesn't even know where he came from anymore."

Maybe McCready didn't know where she'd come from either. Her release from La Hacienda paved the way for a final stint in a Tennessee jail, one that she welcomed so that she could satisfy the terms of her probation violation from earlier in the year. She was sentenced to a 60-day term, but ended up serving only half of the time.

"After this jail term, then I'm done and I'm free to be a country music star again. I'm very thankful she gave me this opportunity," McCready said, referring to Williamson County district attorney Kim Helper.

But the past soon caught up with McCready. In mid-November, she apologized to Debbie Clemens during a taped interview with *Inside Edition*, in which the piece claimed that the affair ended because Clemens refused to leave his wife for McCready. In an interview with the New York

Daily News, McCready refuted that, saying, "I never wanted to marry Roger Clemens. I wanted him to do right by his family."

A month later, with the Christmas holiday a week away, McCready was rushed to Nashville's Centennial Medical Center after police were called to her brother T.J.'s home the morning of December 17. In a police report, T. J. McCready said he answered the door of the home around 3:30 A.M. and found an "intoxicated" Mindy McCready outside. She had been at a bar with friends and they had been told by the bartender that "investigators" had been in asking about her. When T. J. McCready later checked on his sister in a bedroom, he discovered she had cut her wrists and that there was blood on the sheets, according to the report. McCready was released after a few days and returned to Fort Myers to be with her family over the holidays.

Following his "apology" on May 4, Clemens didn't offer any more public comments about the "mistakes" he'd made in his personal life, although they continued to emerge, some more embarrassing than others, and all involving women. Some called media outlets to talk about their flings with the Rocket. Some of the accounts were credible, some weren't. A Detroit stripper, who called a radio station with some racy allegations, and a budding porn star who went by the name of Abby Rode would emerge with their accounts of encounters with Clemens. But Rode had some e-mails and documentation to bolster her story. She described a rendezvous with Clemens in 2007 at the house he'd rented in Palm Springs during the Hope Classic, had the ring of authenticity to it. According to Rode, a friend of hers arranged for her to meet with Clemens and his friends for dinner at a steak house and a trip back to the house. "I had a friend, a social acquaintance who was a good friend of his," she said. "You gotta meet Rocket. I thought he was talking about his dog. 'It's my friend, he plays baseball.' I did not know who he was . . . My friend thought I would like him."

Rode said she was in Clemens's company for only one evening and it didn't go particularly well. "The evening devolved," she said. "His friends were going to have some other girls over. There were some nasty suggestions." She was under the impression that Clemens wanted to make sure she didn't tell anyone about the encounter, and one of the friends paid her $5,000 to keep it quiet. "I accepted it," she said. "Who wouldn't? He didn't make me sign anything or anything. His friend paid me with a credit card."

The group had been disappointed on all fronts, according to Rode. "I guess I wasn't impressed enough. They all seemed a little dejected that I wasn't impressed."

Rode launched her porn career right after her evening with Clemens and his friends. At the time of the meeting she was a model, "mostly fetish, lingerie, bondage, domination, all the fun stuff like that," but went to work for Brazzers, the makers of porn videos, shortly after the encounter. "They're wonderful, great to shoot for," she said of her employer. "You show up at 8, sit in a stylist's chair, get your wardrobe, rehearse your lines, do the sex for about 45 minutes, then about 6 you head home. It's a lot of work—you have to work out every day, only eat about three times a week. I have to stay under 120 pounds."

Abby Rode's name, of course, isn't really Abby Rode. She has a real name, which she rarely discloses to anyone, a scripted real name (Darlene Buchanan) that she uses in business and in some social circumstances, and her stage name. She may love her work but it can be dangerous. When your film credits include *Big Tits at School*, *Mommy's Got Boobs*, and *MILF Chronicles 2*, you aren't always sure who your fans are. "In my profession," Rode said, "there are stalkers. People can come after you. So I have a fake life and a fake name."

Rode said she wasn't looking for publicity, she has enough of that; she just wanted to let people know a little about how athletes really live their lives. Besides, she doesn't like cheaters. "I've dated a lot of athletes and been involved with them over the years," she said. "It's always kind of a rip-off when you meet them. I think people should know. Sports are supposed to be the best team wins—not by cheating."

By the time Judge Ellison denied Emery's motion to disqualify Hardin on May 6, Clemens's personal life was pretty much an open book. The secret affairs were no longer secret. The plane rides and the expensive gifts and the house parties in Palm Springs were known to all. New York defense attorney Ernest Nargi summed it up pretty well in the *Daily News*, saying that if he were Hardin, he would sit down and ask his client if he might want to consider dropping the defamation suit.

"If Roger was my client, I'd say, 'Look, let's sit down and find out what's out there,' " Nargi said. " 'How many women are there? A girl a day? Every 15 minutes is one going to materialize from a bar or a trailer?' Hardin needs to find out what's out there."

. . .

Following the congressional hearing in February and just before the flurry of motions in the Clemens-McNamee defamation suit in the spring of 2008, the BALCO prosecutors began wrapping up their long-running probe. With Marion Jones already in prison, Matt Parrella secured indictments against the relatively obscure track cyclist Tammy Thomas, Jamaican-born sprint coach Trevor Graham, and home run king Barry Bonds for lying under oath before the grand jury and giving false statements to Jeff Novitzky while he pursued steroid distributors. The first two indictments seemed like practice for the third; same judge, same prosecutors, similar charges. When Thomas's trial began in March, lawyers for Graham and Bonds watched from the gallery. They listened as Parrella argued that the dishonesty of the defendant had impeded the government in its effort to jail the drug distributors responsible for the corruption of American sports.

Thomas was a law student at the University of Oklahoma and was watching her second attempt at a career go down in flames. She had been banned for life from her sport in 2002 for testing positive for a designer steroid made by BALCO's rogue chemist Patrick Arnold. Now she almost surely would not be admitted to the bar. The trial was humiliating. The jury heard accounts of her steroid use and its side effects, including tales of facial hair, an Adam's apple, and male-pattern baldness. The jury heard about the time she answered the door of her home with shaving cream on her face. The cyclist sat stoic and silent through most of her trial, but once the guilty verdict was read she exploded, aiming one chilling outburst at the jury and another at the prosecutors. "I've already had one career taken from me," she yelled at jurors as they filed out. "Look me in the eye! You can't do it!" After the jury was excused, Thomas turned her wrath upon the prosecutors, confronting Parrella and Jeff Nedrow in the courtroom. "You're out to destroy lives, you like to destroy people's lives," Thomas shouted at them. Later, it was revealed that she also had an altercation with a law clerk.

Graham's trial followed in May of 2008. He was convicted of one count of lying to federal investigators after he had inexplicably violated the proffer agreement Novitzky had made with him in 2004. Graham was essential to the BALCO probe; he actually was responsible for starting the whole BALCO investigation. Back in 2003, he sent a syringe filled with the undetectable steroid THG to anti-doping authorities, implicating Victor Conte. But in June of 2004, Novitzky had sought to ask Graham about a Texas steroid dealer named Angel Heredia. Like McNamee, Graham signed a proffer agreement, expecting that he would receive immunity for crimes he confessed to as long as he was truthful with Novitzky and IRS agent Erwin Rogers. But in his interview, Graham distanced himself from the former Mexican discus champion, claiming Heredia had never supplied drugs to the world-class athletes Graham trained, that he'd never met Heredia in person, and hadn't talked to him since 1997. From the start, Novitzky and Rogers thought he was lying. As with so many involved with doping, Graham would do anything to prevent being branded a cheater—even risking prison.

In his trial, jurors saw a photo of Graham and Heredia together, listened to their taped phone calls, and heard testimony from a long string of runners who said Graham urged them to get drugs from Heredia, who testified he sent the drugs directly and indirectly through Graham to athletes, including Marion Jones, Tim Montgomery, Jerome Young, Antonio Pettigrew, and sprinter Dennis Mitchell. Pettigrew, who had never tested positive in a career that included a 2000 Olympic 4 × 400 gold medal, confessed to doping while on the witness stand during the Graham trial—he would later have to give up his medal.

"I had access to different labs and had access to different drugs," Heredia told the jury, describing trips he took with Graham's athletes to laboratories across the Mexican border, where the runners underwent blood tests to determine how much chemical enhancement they could undergo while still falling within parameters set out by Olympic drug-testing laboratories. Prosecutors played tapes of covertly recorded conversations between Heredia and Graham at a track meet in Oregon in 2006, when Heredia had become a government informant in exchange for favorable immigration status.

"I told them nothing," Graham said to Heredia on the tape, apparently trying to assure Heredia that their conspiracy was undetected.

In the end, the jury returned a guilty verdict, but could not agree on the two counts in which Graham was accused of providing his clients with performance-enhancing drugs, and the jury foreman later blasted the government for what he called a "lust for blood." The foreman questioned the credibility of almost all the government's witnesses, but mostly that of Heredia. The foreman said he thought the government was willing "to do a deal with a true devil" to secure a conviction.

The jurors convicted Graham on the charge relating to the phone calls, a hollow victory for Novitzky and Parrella but a warning to any witness who might be considering not telling the truth to a federal agent.

Earl Ward, for one, heard the message loud and clear: Trevor Graham happened to be Ward's cousin.

With the exception of a few motions in the defamation suit (Hardin amended the suit to complain that McNamee had committed the intentional infliction of emotional distress against Clemens, who had never been known for his vulnerability), the summer of 2008 was for the most part quiet on the Houston and New York front. But on June 5 in the Dallas suburb of Plano, Texas, a convicted steroid dealer named David Jacobs killed himself and his on-again, off-again girlfriend, 30-year-old fitness model Amanda Jo Earhart-Savell.

Jacobs was found dead in the Plano home where he'd mixed raw materials imported from China into potent steroids he claimed to have sold to NFL players. Earhart-Savell's body was nearby. The muscle-bound Jacobs committed suicide by firing a .40-caliber Glock into his abdomen and head after having turned the gun on Earhart-Savell. He reportedly met with NFL security officials two weeks before the murder-suicide and provided them with e-mails, canceled checks, and other documented evidence from players he had dealings with. On May 1, Jacobs had been sentenced to three years' probation and fined $25,000 after pleading guilty to conspiring to possess anabolic steroids with intent to distribute. Authorities said Jacobs oversaw a massive distribution ring but was spared a tougher sentence when he agreed to cooperate. After his death, police recovered 146 vials of steroids, 10 syringes, scales, bags with steroids and marijuana, several computers, a .22-caliber semiautomatic, and ammunition from Jacobs's home. David Jacobs lived down the road from the home of Don Hooton, the father who had spoken so passionately at the 2005 hearing about the refusal of baseball players like Mark McGwire to take responsibility for their actions.

For the Clemens PR team, the court cases in San Francisco and the dire news out of Dallas must have seemed a world away; they had another embarrassing mini-crisis on their hands. Researchers at the University of Miami, Tufts University, and Marywood University in Scranton, Pennsylvania, were conducting studies to determine if Viagra—the impotence cure officially known as sildenafil citrate—aided training and improved performance by delivering oxygen, nutrients, and performance-enhancing drugs to muscles. The World Anti-Doping Agency also entered the fray, funding a new study to determine if Viagra could be used to enhance performance, particularly in cycling and high-altitude sports. In May at the Giro d'Italia, Italy's biggest bike race, pro cyclist Andrea Moletta was suspended after the national police searched his father's car and found 82 Viagra pills and a syringe. Barry Bonds had used Viagra to counteract sexual dysfunction, a side effect of steroid use, his then girlfriend, Kimberly Bell, told *Playboy*. And in March, NFL draft prospect Heath Benedict had been found dead at his Jacksonville, Florida, home. A local medical examiner's report described the suspicious circumstances of the death, including a syringe and needle found nearby and bottles that were labeled "L-Dex" and "L-Via"—which the report interpreted as anabolic steroids and liquid Viagra.

When the New York *Daily News* reported on June 10 that baseball players had also discovered the benefits of Viagra and that Clemens had stashed clearly marked, diamond-shaped Viagra pills in a GNC vitamin bottle in his locker at Yankee Stadium, the wisecracks about his girlfriends could be heard in ballparks from New York to L.A. Outed as a philanderer and under investigation by the FBI, teased as a user of Viagra, Clemens was virtually in hiding by the summer of 2008. The seven-time Cy Young winner with 354 big league wins on his résumé shied from the spotlight, shuffling from one minor league park to the next in support of his son Koby. He seemed a forgotten soldier from a defeated army, stuck behind enemy lines, moving from safe house to safe house.

In June, Clemens was spotted in Myrtle Beach, South Carolina, bringing the whole family along to celebrate his eldest son's first All-Star Game at a pro level. That Koby was playing for the Carolina All-Star squad was an impressive feat in itself. The 21-year-old catcher's apprenticeship behind the plate had begun only six months earlier, when he converted to that position from third base.

Despite the dramatic change in his father's life over the previous year, Koby Clemens said he was able to keep his focus, that his dad's legal troubles had not distracted him from baseball. "I've grown up with it my entire life, so I'm just used to it," Koby said. "I mean, you're not going to get much out of me where it's gonna faze me, because I've seen or heard it all. Especially this year there's been a lot of things going on with the news and everything. Once I'm on the field, it makes everything better, makes everything easier."

Three security guards stationed themselves outside the Clemens ballpark suite during the game. Koby's three brothers—Kory, Kacy, and

Kody—were there, along with Debbie and her mother, Jan Wilde, all watching from the corner suite on the first base side. Clemens wore a red Adidas shirt, off-white baseball cap, and jeans, his game credential slung through his belt and dangling over his left thigh. His wedding ring was a conspicuous accessory on his left ring finger. Debbie was dressed in all white, her eyes hidden behind sunglasses for most of the early evening. The McCready headlines had blared across newspapers two months earlier, yet Debbie and Roger were still together, making it a point to be seen in public, albeit at a 5,200-seat minor league park.

As the game wore on, Clemens appeared in the outdoor seats only a handful of times, his facial expression a mix of stoicism and detachment. In the top of the eighth inning, with two outs and the score knotted at 1–1, Winston-Salem righthander Kanekoa Texeira uncorked a wild pitch. Catcher Carlos Santana, who had singled, scampered around second and tried to advance to third. Koby whipped off his catcher's mask, streaked to retrieve the ball, and fired to third baseman Niuman Romero. As Romero tagged out Santana to end the inning, Roger Clemens pumped his fist and Debbie jumped wildly up and down. Music blared over the speakers as Koby ran off the field.

In the celebration with his teammates near home plate, Koby glanced up toward the suite, spotted his father and grinned. The elder Clemens, ever the military sergeant, gestured firmly toward the home clubhouse, where Team Clemens would convene after the game. The Rocket then turned and signed a few autographs, looking around quickly to make sure there were no reporters around. This was no time for a face-to-face meeting with the press. Better to keep moving, keep out of sight, a minor league nomad with a major league résumé, now reduced to furtive anonymity.

If his six-figure deal with Simon & Schuster had provided any monetary relief earlier in the year, Jose Canseco was now the picture of financial ruin. He had lost his Encino, California, mansion to foreclosure in April. A Broward County judge had awarded $342,000 in unpaid legal fees to his former attorney Robert Saunooke, and according to publishing sources, *Vindicated* had sold only 20,000 of the 145,000 books that had been shipped. It was under these circumstances that Canseco flew across the country to Atlantic City to appear on July 13 in "The War at the Shore," a celebrity boxing match against Philadelphia cult hero Vai Sikahema. A former return man with the Eagles—he made headlines when he boxed a goalpost at Giants Stadium with a flurry of punches after scoring an Eagles touchdown—Sikahema was a former amateur boxer with 80 bouts under his belt.

Canseco certainly didn't appear destitute at the weigh-in, his face tanned, a thick necklace draped around his neck. He swept into the room to hushed whispers, but without an entourage or any semblance of fanfare. His diminutive girlfriend, Heidi Northcott, shadowed the former millionaire slugger, her blond hair contrasting with Canseco's black tank top and black jeans. The couple was whisked to one corner of the room, where brawny security guards behind velvet ropes kept the sparse crowd at arm's length. Canseco boasted of his "incredible knock-out power" and said Sikahema had no chance in the scheduled fight. "I can knock out any man with my left-hand jab," Canseco said.

Sikahema, who entered with a sizable group of Tongan relatives, was offended that Canseco was even attempting to enter a boxing ring. "You better pack your lunch 'cause I'm going to kick your ass," said Sikahema, who is seven inches shorter and 43 pounds lighter than the 6'4", 248-pound Canseco.

The following evening, the summer air still thick with humidity, a crowd of 1,300 plunked down $50 and $30 per ticket to watch amateur boxing in the confines of Bernie Robbins minor league baseball stadium, home of the A.C. Surf. Wearing 14-ounce boxing gloves, Canseco trudged out of right field around 9:30 and took his place in one corner. He had to endure a 10-minute *haka*, a Polynesian war dance, by Sikahema's relatives, 15 men of varying ages, dressed in grass skirts, wearing face paint and carrying flaming torches. The men hissed and screamed in Canseco's direction while Northcott nervously massaged her boyfriend's shoulders.

The bout, a scheduled three-round event with each round lasting two minutes, never got past the one-minute, thirty-seven-second mark. Sikahema leveled Canseco with a left hook within the first 30 seconds. The lumbering Canseco dropped to his knees, rose to his feet, and withstood another flurry of punches before falling for good. Sikahema roared as Canseco slinked out of the ring to a deafening mix of cheers and steroid chants, the taunts following him as he made the long walk back to the exit under the right field stands. Canseco earned a mere $35,000 to get flattened by Sikahema.

"My suspicions were proven out—that he was not tough," Sikahema said a week after the fight. "I was surprised how easy it was. I thought he would put up some resistance, but he had nothing inside. Two things saved him: the 14-ounce gloves and the head gear. If we had used 10-

ounce gloves, I would have shattered his jaw. What a punk. I have no respect for somebody like that. . . . He's a very impressive-looking guy, but the guy is a walking corpse, because he's rotted inside out. He's a pathetic figure."

Yankee Stadium was the most famous athletic facility in the world for 85 years, a sports mecca that had hosted some of the most thrilling sports moments in history. Babe Ruth and Reggie Jackson swatted moon shots over its fence; Mickey Mantle and Joe DiMaggio patrolled its center field. The NFL's Giants battled the Baltimore Colts in "The Greatest Game Ever Played," and Joe Louis needed just one round to whip both Max Schmeling and Adolf Hitler's claims of Aryan supremacy in their historic 1938 fight. Yankee Stadium was more than just a sports facility, it was a national cathedral. Popes had celebrated Mass on the Stadium's lush field, and when Nelson Mandela was freed after nearly a lifetime in a South African prison for resisting apartheid, New York welcomed him with a massive rally at the old ballpark. Stunned New Yorkers turned to Yankee Stadium in the weeks after the September 11 terrorist attacks; a September 24, 2001, interfaith prayer service at the Stadium paid tribute to the victims of that awful day and helped a battered city pick itself back up.

The Stadium's historic run was scheduled to end in 2008; the Yankees were moving across 161st Street for the 2009 season, to a new ballpark built on parkland commandeered by public officials for the richest team in baseball. The last regular season game at the Stadium, September 21 against the Baltimore Orioles, would be a milestone even if the club had already clinched its expected playoff berth. But by summer's end, with the team mired in third place behind the Tampa Bay Rays and the Boston Red Sox, it became apparent that the Stadium would lie fallow in October for the first time in 13 years. The end had come.

The evening of September 21 was perfect for a baseball game—the sky was clear, the temperature was mild, and a big, yellow moon hung over the Bronx. The Yankees opened the gates seven hours before the game's start, and thousands of fans arrived early to walk around the warning track, scoop up dirt, and reflect on the role Yankee Stadium had played in their lives.

"If an icon like this can go away, then it makes you question your own significance," John Graziadei, a lifelong Yankee fan from Westfield, New Jersey, said of the Stadium.

The pregame ceremony celebrated the Yankees' long and rich history.

The team's living legends—including Reggie Jackson, Yogi Berra, Don Larsen, Whitey Ford, Goose Gossage—took their positions on the field. Willie Randolph, who had been dumped earlier that year as the manager of the crosstown Mets, slid into second base like it was 1977 all over again. Kay Murcer, Randy Maris, Michael Munson, David Mantle, and other relatives stood in for deceased Yankee greats. Julia Ruth Stevens, the 91-year-old daughter of the Babe, threw out the ceremonial first pitch of the game.

The steroids scandal that had hung over Major League Baseball for a decade was put aside, if just for the night. The ceremony commemorating Yankee Stadium's last game would be about baseball, not about Winstrol, human growth hormone, amphetamines, or any of the other drugs that had gotten as much attention as ERAs and batting averages in recent years. Even players who had been associated with steroids were honored. Chuck Knoblauch, like other players who could not make it to New York for the farewell ceremony, was celebrated on the outfield video board. BALCO customer Jason Giambi started at first base for the Yanks. Andy Pettitte was the winning pitcher in the 7–3 New York victory.

But there was no mention of perhaps the greatest pitcher to ever don a Yankee uniform. It was as if Roger Clemens was an old Soviet leader who had fallen out of favor and was scrubbed from the history books. The Yankees, confronted with Clemens's serial adultery, his misguided defamation lawsuit, and the perjury investigation that threatened to land him in prison, found it easier to rewrite recent history than to deal with Clemens's recent chapters. Joe Torre, who led the team to four championships, wasn't mentioned either; he had just gone through a bitter split with the Yankees the year before when he turned down their one-year contract offer that called for a pay cut. But at least Torre was featured on the scoreboard programming. The Yankees acted as if Clemens had never worn pinstripes, never led them to two of their World Series championships. One of the people who helped coordinate the celebration later told the *Daily News* that the Yankees didn't mention Clemens because they didn't know how fans would respond.

"They didn't want boos to be the last memory of Roger at the Stadium," the person said.

A few days later, the *New York Post* reported that Clemens was "heartbroken" by the snub. The Rocket's mother-in-law, Jan Wilde, told the paper that Clemens watched the game at his Piney Point home on a battery-operated TV, because electric service had not been restored after Hurricane Ike ripped through East Texas earlier that month. According to the story, Clemens held hands with Wilde and Debbie Clemens and turned to mush when he realized he had been exiled from Yankee history. "Debbie and I held his hand while we watched the game, and he was heartbroken," the *Post* quoted Wilde as saying. "Not mad. He still loves baseball and the Yankees, but it was sad what they did to him."

The story seemed implausible to anyone who knew Clemens: Did anyone really believe that hard-nosed Roger Clemens, one of the toughest competitors in baseball history, cried in front of his television while his wife and mother-in-law held his hand? Clemens denied the *Post* account a month later in an interview with Houston's KRIV-TV before teeing off at a golf tournament. He said that he had been in Florida watching his son Koby play in an Instructional League game and was flying back to Houston when the Yankees commemorated their final game at the Stadium. Some suspected that the story had been planted by Clemens's agents, Alan and Randy Hendricks. The whole episode underscored one thing about Clemens: He had become radioactive.

When Clemens had returned to Houston in 2004 to join the Astros, he asked sportscaster Giff Nielsen if he could become involved with the former Oiler quarterback's charity golf tournament. The event was rechristened the "Roger Clemens–Giff Nielsen Day of Golf for Kids," and it raised millions of dollars for children's charities. One of the prizes was the opportunity to play golf with Clemens in Cabo (Clemens had been playing with charity supporters when he got the call from his agents telling him he was in the Mitchell Report). In the fall of 2008, Nielsen told Clemens he could no longer be affiliated with what had become an important event for Houston's business and social elite.

"We decided we would go our separate ways until his off-field stuff is settled," Nielsen said. "I approached him, and as we talked, we reached a mutual agreement that we would put our relationship on hold."

Another blow came in December 2008, when Houston's Memorial Hermann Medical Center announced that it was removing Clemens's name from its three-year-old Roger Clemens Institute for Sports Medicine. The hospital issued a statement that said the new name better reflected the broad range of programs offered by the health care network. It didn't need to state the obvious: An endorsement from Roger Clemens was now toxic.

For three months following the debacle in Atlantic City, it seemed as if Canseco would fade into oblivion, his immediate legacy the image of a sweaty, disheveled former baseball star on all fours in an Atlantic City out-door boxing ring.

But a trip across the border to Mexico turned nightmarish for Canseco. On October 9, border agents stopped Heidi Northcott's black 2004 BMW at the San Ysidro checkpoint in the early afternoon. Upon inspection, the agents found six vials of the fertility drug human chorionic gonadotropin and 10 syringes in the center armrest console. The drug, banned by the World Anti-Doping Agency for males and which requires a prescription in the United States, is used by hard-core steroid users who want to stimulate testosterone and sperm production. Northcott's daughter was also in the car.

Immigration and Customs Enforcement agents detained Canseco for nine and a half hours, according to Gregory Emerson, Canseco's lawyer, before Canseco signed a waiver that allowed ICE agents to search his L.A. home. A bleary-eyed Emerson oversaw the ICE home search around 12:30 Friday morning as Canseco was driving back from San Diego. No steroids or other contraband were uncovered.

"I think that ICE had to try and legitimize 9½ hours of detention, so they said, 'If we don't try to stick something to this guy, it's going to look really bad.' The ICE agents found nothing in Jose's home. Really, in the big scheme of things, this has nothing to do with baseball or steroid use," said Emerson. He added that he didn't think the setback would in any way affect Canseco and his role in the Clemens perjury probe.

On October 20, the A&E network aired *The Last Shot*, a stark look at Canseco's current life that had been filmed in 2008 between June and Labor Day. The producers would not say whether Canseco was paid for his cooperation, but the footage depicts a different man than the one the public saw during the *Vindicated* book tour or even during the Atlantic City debacle. Canseco admitted to being scared for his health after years of steroid abuse and said that his biggest regret was writing *Juiced*.

"If I could meet with Mark McGwire and these players, I definitely would apologize to them," Canseco said. "They were my friends. I admired them. I respected them."

The A&E documentary made no mention of *Vindicated*, the Atlantic City bout, or Saunooke's judgment against Canseco. There was a small disclaimer added to the end of the program that briefly explained the border incident.

As Barack Obama was rolling to a historic victory on November 4, Canseco appeared before U.S. Magistrate Ruben Brooks in the Edward J. Schwartz United States Courthouse in San Diego. He pleaded guilty to

misbranding of a drug, a misdemeanor, and received a slap on the wrist—
12 months unsupervised probation and a $25 fine. Emerson said he was
grateful that authorities had used "constraint" with his client. Canseco's
life, in Emerson's opinion, was complicated enough.

"For Jose, it's a day-by-day thing. He wakes up trying to figure out what
kind of job he can find."

Federal grand juries convene in secrecy, enjoy the power to subpoena witnesses and other evidence, and can spend more than a year considering
charging someone with a felony offense. On January 15, 2009, such a
grand jury summoned Kirk Radomski to the E. Barrett Prettyman Federal
Courthouse in Washington, D.C., for testimony. The courthouse sat in
plain sight of the Capitol building, less than a mile from the offices of the
House Committee on Oversight and Government Reform, where committee members had been persuaded, in the hearing they'd held back in
February, that a crime had been committed.

Exactly one year had passed since former senator George Mitchell
came to Congress to say he stood by his report, despite the vehement
objections of Roger Clemens. Now, Washington was preparing for the
inauguration of a new president, but the executive branch had some
unfinished business to attend to: George W. Bush had apparently decided
not to issue a preemptive pardon for his family friend Clemens. In this
case, lying to Congress was something that could not be tolerated. And so
Radomski spent two hours in front of a grand jury, telling his story once
again, answering questions primarily about Miguel Tejada, who exactly
one year earlier had been referred to the Justice Department on suspicion
he had lied to Congress.

Radomski was told to save his Tuesdays and Thursdays for the coming
months for questions about Roger Clemens. It was hard to believe that
just over two years earlier it had seemed that the only people with the
power to determine Clemens's fate were the roughly 500 baseball writers
who elected new members to the baseball Hall of Fame each year. Now,
the two people with the most control over the pitcher's future were a pair
of assistant U.S. attorneys named Daniel P. Butler and Steven Durham,
each based in the District of Columbia's office. Butler, a former champion Paralympics swimmer, and Durham, the chief of the fraud and public corruption section for the district, were charged with handling the
Clemens case, and they were tight-lipped about their work. At their
fingertips was a wealth of information gathered during the previous year

by Jeff Novitzky, Heather Young, and FBI agent John Longmire, who had been searching for additional sources of Clemens's drugs.

In that period, the feds had interviewed at least eight individuals, including Kelly Blair, Kevin Schexnider, Kenny Jowdy, and Mindy McCready. Schexnider told the *Daily News* that the grilling had been like a scene out of the film *Men in Black*, with Young asking most of the questions and Longmire just glaring at him. The same agents also interviewed Michael Scally, a former bodybuilder and doctor in Houston who saw patients referred to him by Blair.

Young and Longmire talked to Shaun Kelley, a former bodybuilder and owner of a Houston weight-loss center where Clemens's stepsister Bonnie Owens had once worked. Kelley told the *Daily News* he had met Clemens through various social circles in Houston, but vociferously denied ever having talked to Clemens about drugs. Kelley was outraged the feds interviewed his former clients, including Pasadena doctor Stephen Fein.

One of Kelley's problems was that he regularly made referrals to a doctor named Lisa Routh, who regularly prescribed testosterone and human growth hormone to patients in the name of quality of life. Routh, whose daughter and son-in-law worked for Kelley prior to a bitter falling out, told the *Daily News* that she regularly prescribed hormone treatments to menopausal women, professional wrestlers, and a large number of Boston policemen (they "get on a frickin' plane and come down here twice a year," she said, "for frickin' growth hormone and testosterone").

Kelley cut ties with Routh and convinced the FBI to let him take a lie-detector test, during which he denied any knowledge of Clemens' using steroids. As of March 24, 2009, Kelley had not been called to appear before the grand jury, and didn't expect to.

In July of 2008, Radomski was moving a massive television in his house when he found an envelope containing a stack of shipping receipts underneath it, allegedly showing that he shipped two kits of human growth hormone directly to the Texas home of Clemens. The Clemens package was addressed to William Roger Clemens, in care of Brian McNamee. The timing of the shipment to Clemens's home coincided roughly with the dates when Debbie Clemens had her injection.

"I said from day one, the government has known I sent packages to Roger Clemens's house," Radomski said. "But I couldn't find any receipts to prove that until now."

On September 11, federal agents came to New York to collect cheek swabs from Brian McNamee and his attorneys. They collected cells from anyone who had handled the medical waste, suggesting that the feds had found DNA on the syringes and/or the gauze and were ruling out those whom it couldn't belong to.

Other witnesses may have appeared before the jury prior to Radomski (he later said the jurors seemed pretty well educated about the issues) but the burly Long Islander's appearance was the first to be brought to the attention of the public. Radomski — now partly through his probationary sentence — had raised his public profile by writing and promoting a book called *Bases Loaded: The Inside Story of the Steroid Era in Baseball by the Central Figure in the Mitchell Report.* As he came and went from the grand jury rooms on January 15, the author was hard to miss; with the bulky torso of a bodybuilder, he loomed over the U.S. marshals that escorted him through the courthouse.

Butler and Durham had bundled the Clemens matter together with the case of Tejada of the Houston Astros, who had told congressional investigators in 2005 he had no knowledge about performance-enhancing substances. The Mitchell Report, however, included checks that Tejada had written, purportedly for testosterone and HGH. It was apparently a fairly easy case for Butler and Durham to prove; Tejada had denied even talking about such drugs. It wasn't uncommon for prosecutors to combine investigations the way they did with Clemens and Tejada. The legal subject matter surrounding both alleged crimes was similar — the dealing of performance-enhancing drugs, false statements made under oath. Once a grand jury was educated about such matters, it was more efficient for prosecutors to get several indictments out of the mix.

On February 10, the grand jury charged Tejada for making misrepresentations to Congress. The next day, he appeared in the E. Barrett Prettyman Courthouse to plead guilty. He later gave a tearful apology to his fans, and was embraced by his teammates at spring training. He maintained that he never used the drugs that he bought, and most everyone associated with the Astros star bought that story. Even the owner of the team, Drayton McLane, said he believed that Tejada had never used performance-enhancing drugs.

The day after Radomski's appearance before the grand jury, it was Brian McNamee's turn to meet with prosecutors. On the morning of January 16, 2009, McNamee, Richard Emery, and Earl Ward took the train to Washington to meet with Butler and Durham in preparation for more sworn testimony before the actual grand jury. Several weeks later, on February 10, Andy Pettitte snuck in to Washington to speak with the prosecutors too.

The wheelchair-bound Butler was the lead prosecutor in the case. A lawyer since 1981 and a prosecutor since 1984, he had prosecuted every kind of crime, from homicides to civil rights violations. In 2005 he won guilty verdicts against a group of men who committed a string of armed bank robberies in the D.C. area. In 2008, Butler and a colleague won guilty verdicts on four counts against Deborah Jeane Palfrey, the so-called D.C. Madam, who for more than a decade had run a prostitution ring that catered to a client list that included U.S. Senator David Vitter (R-La.). Clemens had reason to fear Butler; during the Palfrey trial, the relentless Butler and another prosecutor called prostitutes and their clients to the witness stand, and relied on financial records gathered by an agent from the Internal Revenue Service. Butler was persistent in asking the women who worked for Palfrey about the exact nature of their work, in order to establish beyond a reasonable doubt what the "escort service" did. Two weeks after the jury found Palfrey guilty of racketeering, money laundering, and mail fraud, she committed suicide, hanging herself to avoid a jail sentence.

If Clemens wanted any help, he wouldn't get it from his former lawyer Lanny Breuer. On January 22, two days after he was sworn in as president, Barack Obama nominated Breuer to lead the Criminal Division of the Department of Justice. It just wouldn't do to have the man who had accused Brian McNamee of manufacturing the medical waste in a position to influence the outcome of a case where that material would become a crucial piece of evidence, so Breuer was expected to recuse himself of any role in the Clemens investigation. "He should, and I'm sure he will, recuse himself on anything having to do with Clemens," Senator Chuck Schumer (D.-NY) said on March 10, the day that Breuer faced Schumer and the rest of the Senate Judiciary Committee in a confirmation hearing. Obama's pick for Attorney General, Eric Holder, had by then already recused himself from the Clemens matter because Holder had been a partner at Breuer's firm, Covington and Burling.

Breuer wasn't the only character from the Mitchell Report saga who ended up working for Obama. At the end of 2008, Obama tapped Phil Schiliro, the longtime congressional aide who persuaded Henry Waxman to tackle the whole issue of steroids in sports in the first place, as the incoming president's assistant for legislative affairs, making Schiliro the president's chief lobbyist on Capitol Hill. Schiliro soon found himself with a far tougher job than locating Chuck Knoblauch and the Clemens family nanny: His first assignment was to persuade recalcitrant Republicans to support President Obama's economic stimulus bill.

Clemens wouldn't find much support from the Republicans who'd squired him around the Capitol and asked him for autographs almost a year before, either. Tom Davis, the ranking Republican at the time of the hearing and the man who had offered to call off the proceeding 10 minutes before it began, told *USA Today* after Tejada was charged with lying to representatives of the committee he once chaired that Clemens should cut his losses. Christopher Shays, a Connecticut Republican who lost his seat in the last election and who had called McNamee a drug dealer during the hearing, was even harsher, saying Clemens should be indicted for lying to Congress. "I mean, the guy lied," said Shays. "He used drugs and he lied about it. And he was incredibly arrogant about it."

On Saturday, February 7, the biggest star in baseball was outed as a user of steroids: Alex Rodriguez of the New York Yankees was reported by *Sports Illustrated* to have tested positive for two muscle-building substances—the hard-core steroids Primobolan and testosterone—in 2003, when baseball began its supposedly anonymous survey testing.

The news was a devastating blow for Major League Baseball. The most visible player in the game, Rodriguez was the youngest player in the sport's history to hit 500 home runs, but perhaps more important, he was supposed to signify redemption for baseball, a squeaky-clean challenge to the tainted home run records held by Barry Bonds. Instead, Rodriguez would now have to fight for his own redemption. There were still nine years on his monster contract with the Yankees, who were counting on him as the primary draw to their expensive new stadium, and there were still unanswered questions about how long he had used steroids, who supplied him, who knew about his use.

In the days after the report, Rodriguez tried his hardest to take the Andy Pettitte route, perhaps seeing how destructive denial had been for Bonds and Clemens. Rodriguez first went to ESPN for an exclusive interview with Peter Gammons that was quickly derided as insufficient (Gammons allowed A-Rod to be evasive about the origins of the drugs, and allowed Rodriguez to smear one of the writers of the *SI* story, Selena Roberts).

Pettitte was perceived to have faced the truth even when it was so painful as to include stories about his father's illegal procurement of human growth hormone. Whether Rodriguez could do the same was unclear; being honest might require making his own family members vulnerable to criminal prosecution. While Pettitte had been trapped between loyalty to two friends—his teammate and his trainer—Rodriguez was trapped between earning back the trust of his fans and possibly selling out people who had committed crimes to help him cheat.

The following week, on February 17, a more chastened Rodriguez appeared at spring training for a 33-minute press conference. There, Rodriguez said his "cousin" had injected him twice a month during three six-month stretches in 2001, 2002, and 2003, with a substance they called "boli" that had been acquired over-the-counter in the Dominican Republic. Rodriguez never said anything about testosterone, the other drug he reportedly tested positive for (stacking the two substances together, mixing them in the same syringe, is a common bodybuilding regimen).

Rodriguez tried to dismiss his use as "amateur hour" and said it was the result of being "young and stupid." He wouldn't say that he had cheated or that he had gained an advantage from his usage. He claimed not to have known for certain that what he was injecting was a steroid, but it appeared he knew that it was illicit given that he and his cousin, who would eventually be identified as Yuri Sucart, of Miami, had kept the injections a secret.

"I didn't think they were steroids," Rodriguez claimed. "It was over-the-counter. It was pretty basic. It was really amateur hour. It was two guys doing a very amateur and immature thing. We probably didn't even take it right. All these years I never thought I did anything that was wrong."

When pressed by the mostly accommodating press corps, Rodriguez finally admitted that he knew what the score was. "I knew we weren't taking Tic-Tacs," said A-Rod. "I knew it could be potentially something that was wrong. I wouldn't imagine taking something like that today, obviously. It's a different world. A different culture."

Rodriguez's attempt to write off his drug use as a youthful indiscretion didn't explain his relationship with the controversial trainer Angel Presinal. Presinal, who had worked with some of baseball's biggest stars and the Dominican Republic's 2006 World Baseball Classic team, had traveled to Toronto with the Cleveland Indians as Juan Gonzalez's personal trainer in 2001 when Canadian authorities found a bag at the airport containing steroids and hypodermic needles. Officials shipped the bag to the Indians' hotel to see who would claim it, and the bag was picked up by Presinal, who said it belonged to Gonzalez, then an outfielder for the Indians. Presinal was banned by MLB from clubhouses and private areas of ballparks after the incident, but A-Rod worked with him for several years beginning in 2003. The superstar and the scandal-stained trainer traveled together extensively in 2007, and they were spotted together in New York and Miami as recently as the fall of 2008.

The embattled Rodriguez hired Washington attorney James E. Sharp and Pittsburgh lawyer Jay Reisinger, who had guided Andy Pettitte and Sammy Sosa through their own drug scandals, to represent him. Reisinger and his longtime partner Tom Farrell were still untangling themselves from Marc Dreier; their alliance with Dreier was a misstep by otherwise cautious attorneys. Dreier would be arrested in December, accused of cheating hedge funds out of more than $400 million. To his victims, Dreier was cut from the same cloth as Bernie Madoff. Dreier pleaded not guilty. Reisinger and Farrell cut ties with him as fast as they could.

Just a few days before, on February 12, the judge overseeing the defamation case in Houston made news of his own: Judge Keith Ellison threw what Earl Ward gleefully called a "knockout punch" to Clemens's case against McNamee. Ellison dismissed most of the suit on jurisdictional grounds, but also agreed in his 24-page ruling that McNamee's statements about Clemens in the Mitchell Report were part of an ongoing investigation, and therefore could not be the basis of Clemens's defamation suit, the argument on which Richard Emery had hinged his defense. The ruling was an almost complete victory for McNamee in the costly and bruising yearlong battle.

The decision came right around the same time that political consultant Josh Isay, who had run Manhattan District Attorney Robert Morgenthau's reelection campaign four years earlier, contacted Ward about an opportunity: Would Ward consider running on the Democratic ticket as the replacement for the retiring Morgenthau? The approach was careful, quiet, and very attractive: The race to replace the legendary DA had become fractured, with Morgenthau backing one candidate and party members backing two others. "The stars were perfectly aligned for someone of my background," Ward said. "Because the race was so fractured, the thinking was that an African-American candidate could win a significant proportion of the minority vote and the progressive white vote."

Ward wrestled with the decision, talked about it with Tom Harvey, and finally decided it wasn't a fit. How could a dedicated defense attorney with Ward's convictions make the transition to prosecutor? "I decided that wasn't what I had been fighting for all these years," Ward said. "I'm a defense attorney, not a prosecutor. I hate to see people go to jail—even Roger Clemens. I decided it was something that didn't truly reflect my principles."

Ward felt enormous relief when he made his decision, along with some sadness for the missed opportunity. "I felt good that I said no," Ward said, "but then I thought, 'Holy shit! I could be THE MAN!' " Harvey was sad too. "Geez," he said, "we coulda had the DA in our hip pocket."

McNamee found it hard to believe that the fight was almost over. "I guess the truth will set you free," he said.

Emery was ecstatic, if still hesitant to celebrate too early. There was still one issue standing: whether statements McNamee had made to Pettitte about Clemens's alleged steroid use could constitute defamation, although Ellison wrote in his opinion that Clemens would have to amend his complaint to provide the exact statements Clemens considered defamatory, as well as details and context about those conversations. McNamee's team felt that Hardin wouldn't be able to prove damages; the guts of the case had been ripped from the lawsuit.

"The Mitchell Report was damaging to Clemens — Pettitte's statements damaged no one," Emery said. "It's much ado about nothing. If Rusty Hardin is so foolish as to go forward, we'll have the wonderful opportunity to depose Clemens and Pettitte. The part we lost, I'm happy to lose.

"Any normal person would withdraw," Emery added. "But they are not normal."

It was hard to tell if Clemens viewed the lawsuit as a failure — shortly after the ruling he was off on another vacation with his family, even though he was telling friends he fully expected an indictment. Hardin said simply that he was pleased the judge ruled that he has jurisdiction on the Pettitte front. "We are reviewing other parts of the decision that we disagree with to determine how we should best proceed," he said, certainly aware that McNamee's lawyers would consider filing an action that might include an abuse of process claim asking for attorneys' fees and damages once the case was resolved; back in December they had reserved the right to make a defamation claim against Clemens. Emery might also find a way to depose all those women Clemens had affairs with after all.

Set to begin with jury selection on March 2, 2009, *USA v. Barry Lamar Bonds* was the last and greatest chapter in the BALCO probe. In the early months of 2009, assistant U.S. Attorney Matthew Parrella and the two other prosecutors who had overseen the BALCO probe over the previous five and a half years — Jeff Nedrow and Jeffrey Finigan — were dead set on nailing Bonds for perjury and obstruction of justice.

The latter charge seemed gratuitous. By the time Bonds's trial began, the BALCO distributors were no longer relevant; Victor Conte and his accomplices had done their prison time and been released. Still, the fact that Tammy Thomas had lied under oath and Trevor Graham had made false statements in an interview seemed to anger Parrella, who argued in court that such violations undermined the entire justice system and slowed down investigations.

With Bonds, the U.S. Attorney's Office was trying to land the biggest fish in the BALCO probe. The prosecution had dumped an enormous amount of time and resources into making a felon out of the home run champion. The perjury and obstruction of justice charges against him potentially carried long jail sentences, but the previous year had seen two BALCO figures—Tammy Thomas and Trevor Graham—get off with probationary sentences. Still, they made felons out of Thomas and Graham, and gave the government some practice for the Bonds trial.

The Bonds case looked like it would be a bruiser too. The government's witness list, filed on February 13, included Bonds's former teammates, entourage members, and his girlfriend Kimberly Bell, who the government said would give personal observations regarding the changes in the defendant's body, including bloating, acne, testicle shrinkage, and other side effects of steroid use. The government was counting on less cooperation from Bonds's personal trainer Greg Anderson, who was said to be the link between Bonds and BALCO. Anderson was still refusing to testify, despite pressure placed on him by the government that included a raid on the house of his mother-in-law for a probe involving her finances. As the March trial date neared, Anderson was preparing to go back to jail for the third time for refusing to talk about Bonds.

If Roger Clemens had known in 1998 how much attention the issue of steroids in sports would be getting a decade later, it is possible he might never have approached Brian McNamee in the Toronto clubhouse and asked for help with an injection of Winstrol. Back then, Clemens and McNamee were just two men trying to hold on to a game that each of them had loved since they were boys. For each, their place in the game was precarious. Clemens was a 35-year-old fireballer showing the first signs of weakness in a sport increasingly dominated by sluggers, and McNamee was a lowly strength coach eager to appease the players he had been hired to look after. In Canada, they became accomplices in an effort to steal a few extra moments in America's pastime. For a long time it seemed as if there was no greater consequence than a palpable mass on the buttocks—a small price to pay for proving wrong the Dan Duquettes of the world.

As a boy, Clemens used baseball as an escape from the loneliness that seemed to be his destiny. Not long after his stepfather died—the nine-year-old Clemens's sisters rushed him to the basement when Woody Booher had his heart attack, and Clemens was said to have watched from the window as the ambulance took his stepfather away to die—Clemens channeled all his energy and angst into the game. Years later, that game brought him riches, adulation, and acceptance, all of which meant so much to him. His tenacity was what set him apart from the other players. His refusal to lose was what made him compelling, and what ultimately caused his downfall. The net closed slowly on Clemens over the years. By the time he finally realized it had snared him, he lashed out, hiding behind the union and agents and his myriad lawyers and the delusions that had always helped him survive and triumph. But those delusions were an insufficient defense against a criminal justice system provoked into action. Clemens's downfall was swift after that point: Only ten weeks passed between the release of the Mitchell Report and the criminal referral.

Eleven years after that first injection, Clemens has put himself on the verge of a federal indictment, and McNamee is trying to pick up the pieces of a broken life, searching for shreds of income and honor. He too has aided in his own destruction. His misplaced sense of loyalty gave Clemens and his crackpot team of advisers an opening to launch a legal and PR attack that sprayed a Texas oilfield's worth of gasoline on the embers of the Mitchell Report.

If Clemens is indicted, a jury will decide his fate. As for baseball, public opinion is still whipping back and forth. Many observers of baseball's steroid wars complain that the government has taken it upon itself to police sports. They point to the massive expenditure of taxpayer dollars required for a congressional committee to investigate the Mitchell Report. And legitimate questions have been raised—by no less authorities than federal appellate judges such as Sidney Thomas of the Ninth Circuit Court—about Jeff Novitzky's bare-knuckle tactics. But the players whose privacy has been compromised gave their support to a union that fought against a drug-testing program every step of the way, even after the Mitchell Report was made public. The reality is that baseball is not just a game, it is also a multibillion-dollar industry that has perpetually proved unable to police itself; those are the conditions necessary for government intervention, and, in fact, it has taken only a handful of law enforcement officials to bring the sport to account. Fans of track and field and cycling can attest that this is a very small price to pay for saving a sport from losing credibility.

By the time the Mitchell Report appeared, sports fans desperately needed their ball fields to provide refuge from the corruption infusing every level of the country. With two wars and a seemingly bottomless financial catastrophe darkening the horizon, people looked to the sports pages for an escape from disappointment. At the exact moment that baseball's purity was becoming most important to fans, the sport's corruption became most obvious. Roger Clemens had spectacularly bad timing.

Clemens is certainly not the only baseball player to get rich using steroids. But when he dipped into his many millions in earnings to hand a significant chunk over to a flashy lawyer and set out to silence his accuser, he perpetuated the original sin of cheating. In suing McNamee, Clemens demonstrated that he thought he was above the demands of fair play, insulated from the rebuke of an underling. The drug use doesn't bother half as many people as the lying does. Clemens insulted the intelligence of his fans, raising the stakes on himself way beyond the original gamble of steroid use; the deeper he goes, the more attention he brings to the reality of his crime—not drug use, cheating.

In a national culture that celebrates testosterone, particularly as it marches on parade through the arenas of professional sports leagues, it is ironic that so much legal and moral blood gets spilled over synthetic anabolic steroids, which are designed to mimic the structure of the primary male sex hormone. Every day, doctors prescribe anabolic steroids for a narrow range of therapeutic purposes. Tiny doses can assist tissue repair, albeit with the risk of liver damage, sexual side effects, or depression. That risk may be small but for the vast majority of patients, such treatment isn't worth such a risk.

Doctors weigh quality of life in every risk assessment choice they made. For players like Clemens—whose arm was worth as much as $15,000 per pitch—the decision was strictly mathematical. Anabolic steroids are banned in baseball but baseball spent a long time not enforcing its own rules. Major-leaguers got mixed messages. Long before 2007 a doping culture was in place. Home runs saved baseball, but they also helped ruin it. Batters weren't the only players turning to muscle-building performance enhancers: Pitchers needed to level the playing field. Ballooning salaries and guaranteed contracts put pressure on everyone to produce, no matter the cost. For the sport, the root problem was money, not drugs. The game had made performance-enhancing drugs worth the risk and the physical cost. If you needed a reason why doping had taken hold, you simply had to look at the rising salaries, something George Mitchell never mentioned in his report.

As spring training 2009 opened and the new baseball season approached, Clemens remained mostly out of the public eye while his agents and lawyers awaited word from the government. Even as revelations broke daily about A-Rod, Bonds, and the personal trainers who were their secretive fitness gurus, the sounds of the game filtered through the American ballparks. Baseball was here again. There would always be another flame-thrower knocking back hitters, snarling at his doubters, scrawling his name across a boy's baseball mitt, his trainer waiting silently in the shadows.

Sources

The following is a chapter-by-chapter accounting of some of the journalism that has illuminated this book. We also relied on a mountain of documentary evidence including sworn depositions, medical records, courtroom transcripts, photographs, e-mails, text messages, and records from criminal investigations such as Kirk Radomski's plea agreement, for example, or Jeff Novitzky's application for a search warrant on Jason Grimsley's home.

While this book relies heavily on documentary evidence, the primary sources for *American Icon* were the people who generously submitted to hundreds of interviews with us. The number of people who spoke to us—validating and explaining the testimony and artifacts and stories we brought to them—are too many to list here. Most spoke to us on the record, but others could not do so because in sharing information with us they were taking various degrees of personal risk—professional, legal, and even physical.

Chapter One: June 1998

Assael, Shaun, Luke Cyphers, and Amy K. Nelson. "McNamee Takes Center Stage." *ESPN The Magazine*, December 13, 2007.

Bird, Heather. "Jose: 'Bash' but No Longer Brash." *Toronto Sun*, June 14, 1998.

Bryant, Howard. *Juicing the Game*. New York: Viking, 2005.

Golden, Ed. Untitled account of Fenway Park fans shouting "steroids, steroids" at Canseco during 1988 playoffs. Associated Press, October 6, 1988.

Graziano, Dan. "Late-Night Special; After 5:05, Marlins Beat Blue Jays in 17th." *Palm Beach Post*, June 9, 1998.

Hagan, Joe. "Roger and Him." *New York*, February 11, 2008.

Heyman, Jon. "The Sixth Man." SportsIllustrated.com, November 14, 2006.

Hoch, Bryan. "Clemens, Pettitte Prominent in Report." MLB.com, December 13, 2007.

Ishoy, Ron. "Slugger Selling Gem of a Home." *Miami Herald*, October 13, 1997.

Madden, Bill. "Roger Thanks Boss for Helping Contract to Sky-Rocket." New York *Daily News*, February 18, 1997.

Marantz, Steve. "The Great Lakes Gang." *Sporting News*, September 19, 1994.

Maske, Mark. "After the Strike, Baseball's Disgusted Fans Decide to Strike Back." *Washington Post*, April 30, 1995.

O'Keeffe, Michael, and Teri Thompson. *The Card*. New York: William Morrow, 2007.

Silverman, Michael. "End of an Era; No Return Fire from Sox; Brass Tried to Keep Ace." *Boston Herald*, December 14, 1996.

U.S. Census Bureau American FactFinder Quick Tables, Breezy Point (ZIP Code 11697).

Chapter Two: 1999

Botte, Peter. "Rocket Fizzles vs. A's; Walks 5, Cuffed for 9 Hits, 5 Runs." New York *Daily News*, August 11, 1999.

——. "Rocket Waiting to Take Off." New York *Daily News*, August 7, 1999.

Botte, Peter, and Dave Goldiner. "Bye, Boomer—And Hi, Rocket; Yankees Give Up Wells for Clemens." New York *Daily News*, February 19, 1999.

Bryant, Howard. *Juicing the Game*. New York: Viking, 2005.

Heyman, Jon. "Round Trippers." *Newsday* (New York), August 15, 1999.

Jordan, Pat. "Late Innings: Roger Clemens Refuses to Grow Up." *New York Times Magazine*, March 4, 2001.

Kriegel, Mark. "Clemens Hurls Gem for Ring." New York *Daily News*, October 28, 1999.

Olney, Buster. "Clemens Must Wait Another Day." *New York Times*, September 11, 2001.

Chapter Three: 2000

Connolly, Dan. "Ex-Oriole Segui: I Used Steroids; He's Expecting to be in Report." *Baltimore Sun*. December 11, 2007.

Graziano, Dan. "An Exercise in Durability." *Star-Ledger* (New Jersey), April 21, 2000.

Heyman, Jon. "Inside Dish Rumblings and Locker Room Whispers." *Sporting News*, March 27, 2000.

——. "Rocket Science: No Clues." *Newsday* (New York), April 6, 2000.

Mitchell, Steve. "HGH Illegal as Anti-Aging Treatment." United Press International, October 25, 2005.

Olney, Buster. "Baseball: Subway Series; for Yankees, It's a Workout in Progress." *New York Times*, October 21, 2000.

——. "Clemens Throws a Bat, then Dominates the Mets." *New York Times*, October 23, 2000.

Perls, Thomas. "The Growth Hormone Craze: Prepared Testimony for the Oversight Committee." Boston University School of Medicine, February 12, 2008.

Rocca, Lawrence. "Pals in Pinstripes; Clemens, Canseco Glad to Be Together and Yankees." *Newsday* (New York), August 30, 2000.

Verducci, Tom. "Rocket Science." *Sports Illustrated*, September 10, 2001.

Chapter Four: 2001

Davidoff, Ken. "Rangers Ponder Pudge on the Block." *Newsday* (New York), May 16, 2001.

Grann, David. "Baseball Without Metaphor." *New York Times Magazine*, September 1, 2002.

Justice, Richard. "At 38, Clemens Showing No Signs of Slowing Down." *Houston Chronicle*, July 11, 2001.

McCarron, Anthony. "Creating a More Robust Andy." New York *Daily News*, February 25, 2001.

Nichols, Rachel Alexander. "Clemens Throws Age a Curve; At 39, Yankees Ace Is on His Way to 300 Wins and a Sixth Cy Young Award." *Washington Post*, August 4, 2001.

Shaughnessy, Dan. "Riled Sox Fans Await High-Flying Clemens; Ex-Hub Ace Starts for N.Y. Tonight." *Boston Globe*, August 31, 2001.

Verducci, Tom. "Rocket Science." *Sports Illustrated*, September 10, 2001.

Chapter Five: 2002

Chass, Murray. "Last-Minute Deal in Baseball Talks Prevents a Strike." *New York Times*, August 31, 2002.

Feldman, Claudia. "Pettitte Joins Home Team." *Houston Chronicle*, December 12, 2003.

Giannone, John. "Andy Is Just Dandy as Fielder, Fielders Pitch In for 1–0 Gem." New York *Daily News*, October 28, 1996.

Horswell, Cindy. "Hometown Pride Follows Every Pitch by Astros." *Houston Chronicle*, October 21, 2005.

Lupica, Mike. "Yankee Doodle Andy Kid Lays Down the Lore." New York *Daily News*, October 25, 1996.

Madden, Bill, and Michael O'Keeffe. "Baseball Home Safe with Deal." New York *Daily News*, August 31, 2002.

Olney, Buster. "Clemens Must Wait Another Day." *New York Times*, September 11, 2001.

Pettitte, Andy, and Bob Reccord with Mark Tabb. *Strike Zone: Targeting a Life of Integrity and Purity*. Nashville: Broadman and Holman, 2005.

Russell, Sabin. "HGH: Aging Baby Boomers Turn to Hormone." *San Francisco Chronicle*, November 17, 2003.

Verducci, Tom. "The Home Team; Returning to Their Houston Roots, Inseparable Pals Roger Clemens and Andy Pettitte Want to Share the Fun of Pitching the Astros to a Title." *Sports Illustrated*, February 24, 2004.

Chapter Six: 2003

Brennan, Sean. "Clemens Enshrined as Yank? Hall, Yes!" New York *Daily News*, June 15, 2003.

Kepner, Tyler. "For Clemens, It's Time for Life After 300." *New York Times*, June 15, 2003.

McCarron, Anthony. "Bullpen Fuels Rocket Fizzle; Acevedo Coughs Up Roger's 3rd 300 Bid." New York *Daily News*, June 8, 2003.

——. "Roger Wins 300th Game; Mister Milestone Adds 4,000th K." New York *Daily News*, June 14, 2003.

——. "Roger, Yanks Look All Wet; Bid for 300 Fizzles as Clouds Remain." New York *Daily News*, May 27, 2003.

Quinn, T. J. "Mrs. C, Fans Miss Out." New York *Daily News*, June 8, 2003.

Red, Christian. "Wife Is There for Hits and Mrs." New York *Daily News*, June 14, 2003.

Red, Christian, with Anthony McCarron. "Fans, Family Boost Rocket." New York *Daily News*, May 27, 2003.

Chapter Seven: 2004

American Heart Association. "Questions and Answers About Chelation Therapy." www.AmericanHeart.org.

Associated Press. "Pettitte Has Torn Flexor Tendon." August 18, 2004.

Barron, David. "18 Million Reasons to Play." *Houston Chronicle*, January 22, 2005.

Borden, Sam. "In the Broken Heart of Texas; Homecoming Bittersweet for Andy and Roger." New York *Daily News*, August 29, 2004.

Botte, Peter. "Andy Welcomed 'Home.' " New York *Daily News*, December 22, 2006.

Giannone, John. "Andy Is Just Dandy as Fielder." New York *Daily News*, October 28, 1996.

Green, Saul. "Chelation Therapy: Unproven Claims and Unsound Theories." www .QuackWatch.com.

Lupica, Mike. "Yankee Doodle Andy Kid Lays Down the Lore." New York *Daily News*, October 25, 1996.

McTaggart, Brian. "Pettitte's Surgery Deemed Success." *Houston Chronicle*, August 25, 2004.

Quinn, T. J. "D.C. Beanball Hits Baseball," New York *Daily News*, March 18, 2006.

Rubin, Roger. "Andy Heads for DL." New York *Daily News*, April 22, 2002.

Verducci, Tom. "The Home Team." *Sports Illustrated*, February 24, 2004.

Weisman, Jonathan. "White House Feels Waxman's Oversight Gaze." *Washington Post*, October 25, 2007.

Chapter Eight: 2005

Baker, Russ. "Portrait of a Political 'Pit Bull.' " *Salon*, December 22, 1998.

Fleeman, Michael. *Killer Bodies.* New York: St. Martin's, 2007.

Lindsey, Daryl. "Dan Burton's Class House." *Salon*, February 28, 2001.

Mower, Lawrence. "Bodybuilder Admits Killing." *Las Vegas Review-Journal*, May 31, 2008.

Chapter Nine: 2006

CNN Transcripts. Major League Baseball News Conference on Steroids Investigation, March 30, 2006

de Jesus Ortiz, Jose. "Errors Sting Astros." *Houston Chronicle*, June 29, 2006.

Duncan, Chris. "Clemens Outdueled by Rookie in Season Debut." *Associated Press*, June 23, 2006.

Freeman, Sholnn. "Union Membership up Slightly in 2007." *Washington Post*, January 26, 2008.

Hagan, Joe. "Roger and Him." *New York*, February 4, 2008.

Heyman, Jon. "MLB Investigation Upsets Union." *Newsday* (New York), May 6, 2006.

Kepner, Tyler, and Jack Curry. "Back to Start, Pettitte Is a Yankee Again." *New York Times*, December 9, 2006.

Madden, Bill, and T. J. Quinn with Michael O'Keeffe. "Barry Won't Cooperate." New York *Daily News*, March 30, 2006.

McTaggart, Brian. "Clemens Willing to Bide His Time." *Houston Chronicle*, March 26, 2006.

Olney, Buster. "An Outside-the-Park Investigation." *New York Times*, April 1, 2006.

———. "Yankee Ends Real Corker of a Mystery." *New York Times*, April 11, 1999.

Pugmire, Lance. "Clemens Is Named in Drug Affidavit." *Los Angeles Times*, October 1, 2006.

Red, Christian, Michael O'Keeffe, and Nathaniel Vinton. "Mindy Moves Past Roger." New York *Daily News*, September 14, 2008.

Sherman, Joel. "Union Has 'Roid Rage." *New York Post*, May 6, 2006.

Sherman, William, and T. J. Quinn. "Andy Totes Baggage to the Bronx." New York *Daily News*, December 10, 2006.

Thompson, Teri, T. J. Quinn, Peter Botte, and Kristie Ackert. "Roger in 'Roid Storm." New York *Daily News*, October 2, 2006.

Thompson, Teri, Nathaniel Vinton, Michael O'Keeffe, and Christian Red. "You Mean Nice-Guy Roger Is Married?" New York *Daily News*, May 4, 2008.

Chapter Ten: April 25–May 8, 2007

Brennan, Sean. "Yankees Like the New Guy." New York *Daily News*, May 7, 2007.

Heyman, Jon. "MLB Investigation Upsets Union." *Newsday* (New York), May 6, 2006.

Quinn, T. J., and Amelia Hansen. "A New Drug Stink Hits Baseball." New York *Daily News*, April 28, 2007.

Red, Christian. "Rocket Zeroes in on Relaunch." New York *Daily News*, May 29, 2007.

Red, Christian, with T. J. Quinn. "Roger Seeks Workout Buddy as Old Trainer Receives the Splitter." New York *Daily News*, May 16, 2007.

Chapter Eleven: May 15–December 12, 2007

Atwood, Margaret. "A Matter of Life and Debt." *New York Times*, October 21, 2008.

Bradlow, Eric, Shane Jensen, Justin Wolfers, and Adi Wyner. "Report Backing Clemens Chooses Its Facts Carefully." *New York Times*, February 10, 2008.

Cronan, Carl. "Clemens to Spin Legends Field Turnstiles." *Business Journal* (Tampa Bay, Florida), May 16, 2007.

Feinsand, Mark. "Karstens Breaks Leg." New York *Daily News*, April 29, 2007.

Jaccarino, Mike, Michael O'Keeffe, and Alison Gendar. "Cop Link in 'Roid Raid." New York *Daily News*, October 17, 2007.

Lapointe, Joe. "Clemens Works on Arm as Others Pick His Brain." *New York Times*, May 16, 2007.

Leusner, Jim, Pedro Ruz Gutierrez, and Sarah Lundy. "Steroid Raids Net Four in Orlando." *Orlando Sentinel*, February 28, 2007.

Llosa, Fernando, L. Jon. Wertheim, and David Epstein. "Rx for Trouble: Inside the Steroid Ring." *Sports Illustrated*, March 12, 2007.

Lyons, Brendan J. "Steroids Beyond Sports." *Times Union* (Albany, New York), January 13, 2008.

——. "A Web of Easy Steroids." *Times Union* (Albany, New York), February 28, 2007.

Nightengale, Bob. "Giambi: Baseball's Apology Needed over Steroid Issue." *USA Today*, May 23, 2007.

——. "The Playing Fields Offered an Escape." *USA Today*, February 8, 2001.

O'Keeffe, Michael. "Judge 86s Signature 'Roid Case." New York *Daily News*, September 12, 2008.

——. "Legal Muscle for Pharmacy, Sues Albany DA and Probers." New York *Daily News*, October 9, 2008.

O'Keeffe, Michael, and T. J. Quinn. "Ready to Spill Baseball Juice." New York *Daily News*, July 17, 2007.

——. "200G Worth of Steroids Found; Mother Lode Seized from Brooklyn Pharmacy." New York *Daily News*, May 10, 2007.

O'Keeffe, Michael, and Teri Thompson. "Baseball's Privy to Juicy Details." New York *Daily News*, December 12, 2007.

Perls, Thomas H., Neal R. Reisman, and S. Jay Olshansky. "Provision or Distribution of Growth Hormone for Antiaging." *Journal of the American Medical Association*, October 26 2005.

Quinn, T. J. "Inside a Steroid Bust." New York *Daily News*, May 13, 2007.

——. "MLB, Albany DA Meet." New York *Daily News*, September 11, 2007.

——. "MLB, Albany DA Near Cooperation." New York *Daily News*, September 14, 2007.

Quinn, T. J., and Amelia Hansen. "A New Drug Stink Hits Baseball." New York *Daily News*, April 28, 2007.

Quinn, T. J., Michael O'Keeffe, Christian Red, and Joe Mahoney. "Dozens Tied to 'Roid Sting." New York *Daily News,* February 28, 2007.

Quinn, T. J. Christian Red, Michael O'Keeffe, and Bill Madden. "Red Faces for Ankiel, Cards." New York *Daily News,* September 7, 2007.

Red, Christian. "All Systems Go for Rocket." New York *Daily News,* May 16, 2007.

———. "Rocket Not Rockin.' " New York *Daily News,* May 24, 2007.

———. "Rocket Strong in Single-A." New York *Daily News,* May 19, 2007.

———. "Rocket Zeroes in on Relaunch." New York *Daily News,* May 29, 2007.

———. "Soares Score Ruffles Feathers in Upstate N.Y." New York *Daily News,* March 4, 2007.

Red, Christian, and T. J. Quinn. "Roger Seeks Workout Buddy as Old Trainer Receives the Splitter." New York *Daily News,* May 16, 2007.

Thompson, Teri. "Anti-Doping Head Wants Gov't Help." New York *Daily News,* May 14, 2007.

Williams, Lance, and Mark Fainaru-Wada. "Drug Scandal Hits Playoffs." *San Francisco Chronicle,* October 21, 2007.

Wise, Lindsay. "Eighteen Years Later, A Break in 'Lover's Lane' Case." *Houston Chronicle,* May 19, 2008

Chapter Twelve: December 13, 2007–January 7, 2008

Assael, Shaun, Luke Cyphers, and Amy K. Nelson. "McNamee Takes Center Stage." *ESPN The Magazine,* December 13, 2007.

Azzara, Mike. "Of Baseball, Steroids and Island Secession." *Staten Island Advance,* May 4, 2008.

Barron, David, and Mary Flood. "Fighting Back; Clemens Winds Up, Lets Denials Fly; Interviews: Begins Effort to Clear His Name on '60 Minutes' and in Print." *Houston Chronicle,* January 7, 2008.

Botte, Peter. "Andy Welcomed 'Home.' " New York *Daily News,* December 22, 2006.

Bryant, Howard. *Juicing the Game.* New York: Viking, 2005.

Clemens, Roger. "The Rocket; Roger Clemens' Reputation as a Baseball Pitcher and His Life Away from the Game." CBS, *60 Minutes,* April 8, 2001.

Canseco, Jose. Interview. FoxNews.com, December 13, 2007.

Chass, Murray. "Lawyer for Clemens Explains Strategy." *New York Times,* January 1, 2008.

Colloff, Pamela. "The Trick Is Not to Act like a Lawyer." *Texas Monthly,* September 2002.

Driscoll, John. "Willie." Wesleyan.edu, June 28, 2006.

Dwyer, Jim. "One Protest, 52 Arrests, and a $2 Million Payout." *New York Times,* August 20, 2007.

Feinsand, Mark. "Jose: A-Rod Got off Hook." New York *Daily News,* December 14, 2007.

Feldman, Claudia. "Pettitte Joins Home Team." *Houston Chronicle,* December 12, 2003.

Giannone, John. "Andy Is Just Dandy as Fielder, Fielders Pitch In for 1–0 Gem." New York *Daily News,* October 28, 1996.

Greenhouse, Linda. "Justices Void New York City's Government; Demand Voter Equality in All Boroughs." *New York Times,* March 23, 1989.

Hagan, Joe. "Roger and Him." *New York,* February 4, 2008.

Hardin, Rusty. Opening remarks and post–press conference remarks. Houston press conference, January 7, 2008.

Heyman, Jon. "Exclusive: McNamee Stands by Story; Clemens' Ex-Trainer Reacts to *60 Minutes* interview." SI.Com, January 8, 2008.

Hoch, Bryan. "Clemens, Pettitte Prominent in Report." MLB.com, December 13, 2007.

Horswell, Cindy. "Hometown Pride Follows Every Pitch by Astros." *Houston Chronicle*, October 21, 2005.

Kepner, Tyler. "Justice Attempts to Clear His Name." *New York Times*, December 14, 2007.

Lupica, Mike. "Whole Truth Is Only Way He's Going to Get Himself out of This Mess—and Prison Term." New York *Daily News*, January 7, 2008.

———. "Yankee Doodle Andy Kid Lays Down the Lore." New York *Daily News*, October 25, 1996.

Mahoney, Joe, and Helen Peterson. "Primary Ordered Open; US Judges Tosses 2 GOP Ballot Rule." New York *Daily News*, February 5, 2000.

McCall, George S. "Jury Bias and the Corporate Client: How to Personalize the Impersonal." *Federation of Defense and Corporate Counsel Quarterly*, Winter 2008.

Mitchell, George, profile, http://www.dlapiper.com/george_mitchell; and http://library .bowdoin.edu/arch/mitchell.

Mitchell, George, and DLA Piper. "Report to the Commissioner of Baseball of an Independent Investigation into the Illegal Use of Steroids and Other Performance Enhancing Substances by Players in Major League Baseball." December 13, 2007.

Nightengale, Bob. "The Playing Fields Offered an Escape." *USA Today*, February 8, 2001.

O'Keeffe, Michael, Christian Red, and Teri Thompson. "Clemens Now a Jolly Roger." New York *Daily News*, December 21, 2007.

———. "Congress Calls on Rocket to Testify." New York *Daily News*, January 5, 2008.

———. "Jason Grimsley Affidavit Unsealed; Clemens and Pettitte Not Named." New York *Daily News*, December 21, 2007.

O'Keeffe, Michael, and Teri Thompson. *The Card.* New York: William Morrow, 2007.

O'Keeffe, Michael, and Teri Thompson. "Baseball's Privy to Juicy Details," New York *Daily News*, December 12, 2007

———. "Q&A with George Mitchell." New York *Daily News*, December 15, 2007.

———. "Roger's Steroid Heater: Prove It! Tells '60 Mins.' Charge Is a Lie, Dares Trainer to Come Forward." New York *Daily News*, January 7, 2008.

Passan, Jeff. "Depositions Paint Complex McNamee Portrait." *Yahoo! Sports*, February 14, 2008.

Perls, Thomas H., Neal R. Reisman, and S. Jay Olshansky. "Provision or Distribution of Growth Hormone for Antiaging." *Journal of the American Medical Association*, October, 26 2005.

Pettitte, Andy, and Bob Reccord, with Mark Tabb. *Strike Zone: Targeting a Life of Integrity and Purity.* Nashville: Broadman and Holman, 2005.

Red, Christian, and Teri Thompson. "Setting the Record Straight on Roger. McNamee Lawyers Talk Openly About Clemens, Pettitte, Mitchell and Client." New York *Daily News*, January 6, 2008.

"Report to the Commissioner of Baseball of an Independent Investigation Into the Illegal Use of Steroids and Other Performance Enhancing Substances by Players in Major League Baseball," George J. Mitchell and DLA Piper U.S. LLP, December 13, 2007.

Rubin, Roger. "Andy Heads for DL; Elbow Discomfort Disarms Yank Lefty." New York *Daily News*, April 22, 2002.

Schmidt, Michael S. "Wallace, Fan of Clemens, Becomes His Questioner." *New York Times*, December 25, 2007.

Thompson, Teri, and Michael O'Keeffe. " 'Roids Report Bombs Bronx. New York *Daily News*, December 14, 2007.

Tilghman, Andrew. "Murphy Found Innocent of Sex Abuse Charges." *Houston Chronicle*, December 7, 2004.

Tolson, Mike. "One Lawyer's 'Money Pitch.'" *Houston Chronicle*, June 5, 2005.

Verducci, Tom. "The Home Team; Returning to Their Houston Roots, Inseparable Pals Roger Clemens and Andy Pettitte Want to Share the Fun of Pitching the Astros to a Title." *Sports Illustrated*, February 24, 2004.

Wallace, Mike. "Clemens Vehemently Denies Steroid Use." *60 Minutes*, CBS News, January 6, 2008.

Wilson, Duff. "Entertainer and Fighter Is Clemens's Lead Lawyer." *New York Times*, December 28, 2007.

Wise, Lindsay. "Eighteen Years Later, a Break in 'Lover's Lane' Case." *Houston Chronicle*, May 19, 2008.

Chapter Thirteen: January 8–February 4, 2008

Barker, Jeff. "Clemens Evidence Shown; House Committee Sees Photos from Ace's Former Trainer." *Baltimore Sun*, February 8, 2008.

Callahan, Tom. "A Trying Time for Rookies; Making Their Pitch, Hoping to Be a Hit," *Time*, April 2, 1984.

de Jesus Ortiz, Jose. "Clemens Drops in to Tutor the Elite; House Hearing Not Addressed at Astros' Minicamp." *Houston Chronicle*, January 31, 2008.

Duncan, Chris. "Roger Clemens Shows Up at Houston Astros Training Camp." Associated Press, January 31, 2008.

Eisler, Kim Isaac, "Big Guns." *Washingtonian*, December 2007.

Fleeman, Michael. *Killer Bodies*. New York: St. Martin's, 2007.

Hays, Kristen. "Andersen's Top Lawyer a Veteran Litigator." Associated Press, May 2, 2002.

Jennings, Randy. "Clemens Talks, but Not About Steroids." *Dallas Morning News*, January 13, 2008.

Johnson, Carrie. "Auditor Tells of Lawsuit Fears; Andersen's Duncan Anticipated SEC Probe." *Washington Post*, May 15, 2002.

Kornblut, Anne E. "Two Parties Are at Odds Only Against Witnesses." *Washington Post*, March 18, 2005.

Kosterlitz, Julie. "Watch Out for Waxman." *National Journal*, March 11, 1989.

Longstreth, Andrew. "Covington's Decision to Represent Clemens Irks Major League Baseball." *American Lawyer*, February 11, 2008.

McCarron, Anthony. "Where Are They Now? Mets' Ron Taylor Has Lifetime of Saves as Physician." New York *Daily News*, November 8, 2008.

McTaggart, Brian. "There's a Clemens in Camp, but It's Not Roger." *Houston Chronicle*, January 29, 2008.

Mower, Lawrence. "Bodybuilder Admits Killing." *Las Vegas Review-Journal*, May 31, 2008.

Myerson, Harold. "The Liberal Lion in Winter." *Los Angeles Times*, December 4, 1994.

O'Donnell, Jayne. "Rep. Tauzin Turns Business Scandals into Must-See TV." *USA Today*, July 26, 2002.

Quinn, T. J. "D.C. Beanball Hits Baseball." New York *Daily News*, March 18, 2006.

Thompson, Teri, Michael O'Keeffe, Christian Red, and Nathaniel Vinton. "News Probes Gym That was Tom Pettitte's HGH Source." New York *Daily News*, February 14, 2008.

Thompson, Teri, Nathaniel Vinton, Michael O'Keeffe, and Christian Red. "Andy Pettitte

May Sing About Steroids Chat, Brian McNamee's Lawyer Says." New York *Daily News*, January 29, 2008.

Wilson, Duff. "Clemens Hires Top Washington Lawyer." *New York Times*, January 18, 2008.

Chapter Fourteen: February 5–13, 2008

Baker, Peter. "Tom Davis Gives Up." *New York Times Magazine*, October 3, 2008.

Baker, Russ. "Portrait of a Political 'Pit Bull.' " *Salon*, December 22, 1998.

Blum, Ronald, and Howard Fendrich. "McNamee Says He Injected Clemens' Wife." Associated Press Online, February 9, 2008.

DuBose, Ben. "Clemens Gets His Close-up; While Pitcher Meets with Committee Members, Former Trainer Releases Photos He Says Are Evidence Steroids Were Used." *Los Angeles Times*, February 8, 2008.

Fairbanks, Doug. "This Circus Is a Drag," *Daily Press*, Newport News, Virginia, February 26, 2008.

Lupica, Mike. "Hardin Puts up His Dukes with Outlandish Ramblings." New York *Daily News*, February 8, 2008.

———. "It Is Hard to Believe You, Sir." New York *Daily News*, February 14, 2008.

O'Keeffe, Michael, Teri Thompson, Christian Red, and Nathaniel Vinton. "Justice Should Relieve Congress, Rep. Says Clemens Case Needs to Move to a 'Criminal Referral.' " New York *Daily News*, February 10, 2008.

O'Keeffe, Michael, Teri Thompson, and Nathaniel Vinton. "Hardin: Probe in Roger Future." New York *Daily News*, February 11, 2008.

"Political Radar: Elder Bush Makes an Endorsement: Roger Clemens," ABC News, Blogs .abcnews.com/political radar/2008/02/elder-bush-make.html, February 14, 2008.

Red, Christian. "Roger Signs for House Staffers." New York *Daily News*, February 9, 2008.

Red, Christian, Michael O'Keeffe, Teri Thompson, and Nathaniel Vinton. "Rocket Faces Bloody Mess, McNamee People Demand Roger's DNA." New York *Daily News*, February 8, 2008.

Schlosser, Eric. "The Politics of Pot: A Government in Denial." *Rolling Stone*, March 4, 1999.

———. *Reefer Madness*. New York: Houghton Mifflin, 2003.

Sheinin, Dave, and Barry Svrluga. "Clemens and McNamee Have Their Say on the Hill." *Washington Post*, February 8, 2008.

Thompson, Teri, Michael O'Keeffe, Christian Red, and Nathaniel Vinton. "News Probes Gym That Was Tom Pettitte's HGH Source." New York *Daily News*, February 14, 2008.

Vinton, Nathaniel, Christian Red, and Michael O'Keeffe. "Andy Affidavit Downs Rocket." New York *Daily News*, February 13, 2008.

Weisman, Jonathan. "White House Feels Waxman's Oversight Gaze." *Washington Post*, October 25, 2007.

Wilson, Duff. "Autographs May Have Violated Ethics Law." *New York Times*, February 13, 2008.

Wilson, Duff, and Michael Schmidt. "As Trainer Is Questioned, Clemens Meets and Greets." *New York Times*, February 8, 2008.

———. "Clemens Campaigns as His Wife Is Named." *New York Times*, February 9, 2008.

———. "Hearing Is of Special Interest to an IRS Special Agent." *New York Times*, February 10, 2008.

Chapter Fifteen: February 17, 2008–Today

Canseco, Jose. *Juiced: Wild Times, Rampant 'Roids, Smash Hits and How Baseball Got Big*. New York: HarperCollins, 2005.

Jordan, Pat. "Late Innings: Roger Clemens Refuses to Grow Up." *New York Times*, March 4, 2001.

McCarron, Anthony. "Rocket Avoids Answering About Possible Probe." New York *Daily News*, February 28, 2008.

———. "Rocket Makes Astro of Self." New York *Daily News*, February 27, 2008.

Red, Christian. "Astros May Rethink Deal with Roger." New York *Daily News*, February 29, 2008.

———. "To Fehr, Progress on HGH Is a Testy Issue." New York *Daily News*, March 1, 2008.

Red, Christian, Michael O'Keeffe, and Teri Thompson. "Rocket Case in Limbo as Judge Mulls." New York *Daily News*, November 4, 2008.

Red, Christian, Teri Thompson, Nathaniel Vinton, and Michael O'Keeffe. "Republicans Block HGH Bill, Unknown GOP Pair Foils Schumer." New York *Daily News*, February 27, 2008.

Thompson, Teri, and Michael O'Keeffe. "McNamee's Lawyers Seek Dismissal of Rocket's Suit." New York *Daily News*, March 4, 2008.

Thompson, Teri, Michael O'Keeffe, Christian Red, and Nathaniel Vinton. "New Photographic Evidence Could Prove Damaging to Roger Clemens." New York *Daily News*, February 22, 2008.

Thompson, Teri, Michael O'Keeffe, Nathaniel Vinton, and Christian Red. "Roger Clemens' Attorney: Maybe Rocket Was at Jose Canseco Party." New York *Daily News*, February 23, 2008.

Thompson, Teri, Christian Red, Nathaniel Vinton, and Michael O'Keeffe. "Augmented Tale of Rocket Party." New York *Daily News*, February 26, 2008.

Acknowledgments

This book reflects the reporting that appeared in the pages of the New York *Daily News* over the last year and a half especially, and we'd like to thank our Chairman and Publisher, Mort Zuckerman, for creating the Sports I-Team and allowing us to pursue the stories that led to this book. This kind of team is unprecedented in American newspapers, and we are grateful for the support. Special acknowledgment goes to the Deputy Publisher and Editor-in-Chief of the *Daily News*, Martin Dunn, who always recognizes the value of enterprise reporting and gave us the green light on this project, and to Chief Executive Officer Marc Kramer, Vice-President/Director of Editorial Operations Ed Fay, and Sports Editor Leon Carter for their support and encouragement. We relied on the reporting and the counsel of Mike Lupica and Bill Madden, who are generous in both time and spirit whenever we have questions or need help. To Jim Rich, Eric Barrow, and everyone in the sports department: It is an honor to work with all of you. You put out the best sports section in America. Thanks to Anne Carroll for her terrific legal help.

Our agent, Esther Newberg, the world's biggest Red Sox fan, saw the potential in this project (with an assist from Mike Lupica) and enlisted the help of Peter Gethers, an extraordinary editor at Knopf and Random House, to guide us through the maze of reporting and writing what we hope resulted in a complete account of the fall of an American icon. Thank you, Peter, for everything. And thanks to everyone else at Knopf, particularly Christina Malach, who kept things from falling through the cracks and even came through with a scoop in the clutch.

In some ways this work is a tale of legal intrigue, and we'd like to express our gratitude to the lawyers who represented the principals in this book. Brian McNamee's attorneys Earl Ward and Richard Emery took our calls and answered our questions at all hours of the day or night. Rusty Hardin, Roger Clemens's lawyer, responded promptly to most of our queries, often with humor and wit. Mark Paoletta and Lanny Breuer helped us understand the mechanics of Capitol Hill proceedings. Thanks also to Clemens's public relations specialists, Patrick Dorton and Joe Householder. Tom Harvey, you're our first phone call from jail.

We received help from a long list of others, including Mindy McCready; her mother, Gayle Inge; her father, Tim McCready, and her brothers, Josh and T.J. It's never dull with the McCready clan, so the laughs and help are appreciated.

Thanks to the crew in the greater Houston area, including Sammy Woodrow and Shaun Kelley, and the folks in Washington, especially Karen Lightfoot. Our reporting was also illuminated by Rob Saunooke and Paula Canny. Special thanks to Victor Conte and Kirk Radomski.

We would also like to thank our families and friends for their unwavering support and encouragement, especially all our parents—Jess and Nettie Thompson, Michael and Patricia O'Keeffe, Don and Jill Red, and John and Mary Ann Vinton. They are the best cheerleaders on earth. Thanks also to Sally Otos, Nancy Thompson, Cheryl Thompson, David Heim, Jeff Sears, Lorna Clark, Liz Steffey, Zoë Pagnamenta, and Andrew Vinton for their patience and advice. Franklin Burroughs, Peter Coviello, Sig Gissler, and Craig Wolff are terrific teachers. Thanks to Beth O'Neil, who endured numerous deadlines, late-night phone calls, and early-morning departures and never wavered in her encouragement and support. Aunt Frannie's hospitality made the Houston reporting so much more pleasant. Peggy Smith, thank you for all you do.

We offer our love and encouragement to all the future writers in our families—John Sears, Erin Heim, Aidan O'Keeffe, and the Red kids.

Index